C++ Keywords

C++ reserves and gives predefined meanings to the following keywords.
You may not redefine keywords or use them for other purposes.

asm	else	new	this
auto	enum	operator	throw
bool	explicit	private	true
break	export	protected	try
case	extern	public	typedef
catch	false	register	typeid
char	float	reinterpret_cast	typename
class	for	return	union
const	friend	short	unsigned
const_cast	goto	signed	using
continue	if	sizeof	virtual
default	inline	static	void
delete	int	static_cast	volatile
do	long	struct	wchar_t
double	mutable	switch	while
dynamic_cast	namespace	template	

Data Abstraction
and Problem Solving
with C++

WALLS AND MIRRORS

Fourth Edition

Data Abstraction and Problem Solving with C++

WALLS AND MIRRORS

Fourth Edition

Frank M. Carrano
University of Rhode Island

Addison
Wesley

Boston San Francisco New York
London Toronto Sydney Tokyo Singapore Madrid
Mexico City Munich Paris Cape Town Hong Kong Montreal

Executive Editor: Susan Hartman Sullivan
Senior Acquisitions Editor: Michael Hirsch
Project Editor: Katherine Harutunian
Marketing Manager: Nathan Schultz
Senior Marketing Coordinator: Lesly Hershman
Senior Production Supervisor: Jeffrey Holcomb
Project Management: Kevin Sullivan, Argosy Publishing
Copyeditor: Carol Noble
Proofreaders: Ginjer Clarke, Sherri Dietrich
Indexer: Ellen Troutman
Cover Design Manager: Joyce Cosentino Wells
Cover Designer: Leslie Haimes
Cover Image: ©2004 Corbis
Interior Design: Delgado and Company, Inc.
Prepress and Manufacturing: Caroline Fell

Access the latest information about Addison-Wesley titles from our World Wide Web site:
http://www.aw-bc.com/computing

Library of Congress Cataloging-in-Publication Data

Carrano, Frank M.
    Data abstraction and problem solving with C++ : walls and mirrors / Frank M.
    Carrano.—4th ed.
      p. cm.
    ISBN 0-321-24725-6
      1. C++ (Computer program language) 2. Abstract data types (Computer science) 3.
    Problem solving—Data processing. I. Title

QA76.73.C153C38 2004
005.13'3—dc22

                                                                2003064778

ISBN 0-321-24725-6
12345678910-HP-08070605

P R E F A C E

Welcome to the fourth edition of *Data Abstraction and Problem Solving with C++: Walls and Mirrors*. Since the publication of the third edition, we all have gained experience with teaching data abstraction in an object-oriented way using C++. This edition reflects that experience and the evolution that C++ has taken.

This book is based on the original *Intermediate Problem Solving and Data Structures: Walls and Mirrors* by Paul Helman and Robert Veroff (© 1986 by The Benjamin/Cummings Publishing Company, Inc.). This work builds on their organizational framework and overall perspective and includes technical and textual content, examples, figures, and exercises derived from the original work. Professors Helman and Veroff introduced two powerful analogies, walls and mirrors, that have made it easier for us to teach—and to learn—computer science.

With its focus on data abstraction and other problem-solving tools, this book is designed for a second course in computer science. In recognition of the dynamic nature of the discipline and the great diversity in undergraduate computer science curricula, this book includes comprehensive coverage of enough topics to make it appropriate for other courses as well. For example, you can use this book in courses such as introductory data structures or advanced programming and problem solving. The goal remains to give students a superior foundation in data abstraction, object-oriented programming, and other modern problem-solving techniques.

To the Student

Thousands of students before you have read and learned from *Walls and Mirrors*. The walls and mirrors in the title represent two fundamental problem-solving techniques that appear throughout the presentation. Data abstraction isolates and hides the implementation details of a module from the rest of the program, much as a wall can isolate and hide you from your neighbor. Recursion is a repetitive technique that solves a problem by solving smaller problems of exactly the same type, much as mirror images grow smaller with each reflection.

This book was written with you in mind. As former college students, and as educators who are constantly learning, we appreciate the importance of a clear presentation. Our goal is to make this book as understandable as possible. To help you learn and to review for exams, we have included such learning aids as margin notes, chapter summaries, self-test exercises with answers, and a glossary. As a help during programming, you will find C++ reference material in the appendixes and inside the covers. You should review the list of this book's features given later in this preface in the section "Pedagogical Features."

The presentation makes some basic assumptions about your knowledge of C++. Some of you may need to review this language or learn it for the first time by consulting Appendix A of this book. You will need to know about the selection statements *if* and *switch*; the iteration statements *for*, *while*, and *do*; functions and argument passing; arrays; strings; structures; and files. This book covers C++ classes in Chapters 1, 3, and 8 and does not assume that you already know this topic. We assume no experience with recursive functions, which are included in Chapters 2 and 5.

All of the C++ source code that appears in this book is available for your use. Later in this preface, the description of supplementary materials tells you how to obtain these files. Note, however, that your instructor may already have obtained them for you.

To the Instructor

This edition of *Walls and Mirrors* uses C++ to enhance its emphasis on data abstraction and data structures. The book carefully accounts for the strengths and weaknesses of the C++ language and remains committed to a pedagogical approach that makes the material accessible to students at the introductory level.

Prerequisites

We assume that readers either know the fundamentals of C++ or know another language and have an instructor who will help them make the transition to C++ by using the provided appendix. The book formally introduces C++ classes, and so does not assume prior knowledge of them. Included are the basic concepts of object-oriented programming, inheritance, virtual functions, and class templates, all in C++. Although the book provides an introduction to these topics in connection with the implementations of abstract data types (ADTs) as classes, the emphasis remains on the ADTs, not on C++. The material is presented in the context of object-based programming, but it assumes that future courses will cover object-oriented design and software engineering in detail, so that the focus can remain on data abstraction. We do, however, introduce the Unified Modeling Language (UML) as a design tool.

Flexibility

The extensive coverage of this book should provide you with the material that you want for your course. You can select the topics you desire and present them in an order that fits your course. The chapter dependency chart shows which chapters should be covered before a given chapter can be taught.

In Part I, you can choose among topics according to your students' background. Three of the chapters in this part provide an extensive introduction to data abstraction and recursion. Both topics are important, and there are various opinions about which should be taught first.

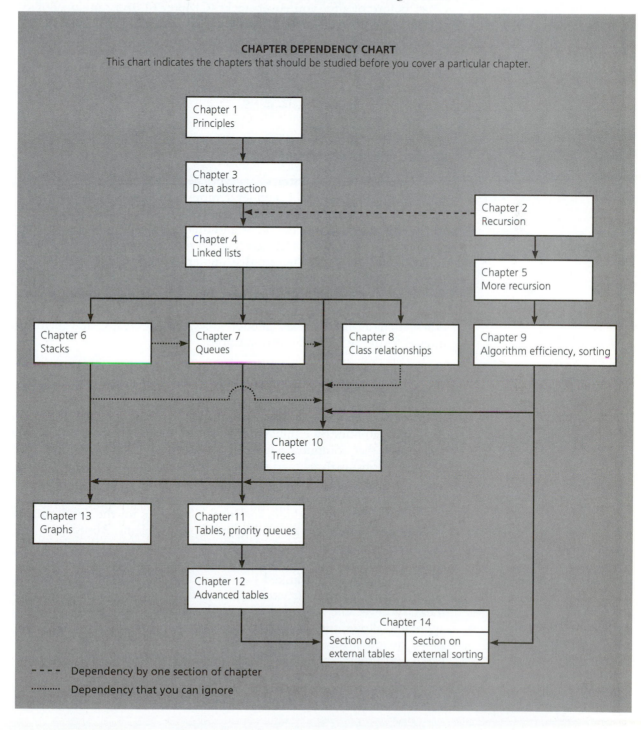

CHAPTER DEPENDENCY CHART
This chart indicates the chapters that should be studied before you cover a particular chapter.

Chapter 1
Principles

Chapter 3
Data abstraction

Chapter 2
Recursion

Chapter 4
Linked lists

Chapter 5
More recursion

Chapter 6
Stacks

Chapter 7
Queues

Chapter 8
Class relationships

Chapter 9
Algorithm efficiency, sorting

Chapter 10
Trees

Chapter 13
Graphs

Chapter 11
Tables, priority queues

Chapter 12
Advanced tables

Chapter 14

| Section on external tables | Section on external sorting |

- - - - Dependency by one section of chapter
.... Dependency that you can ignore

Although in this book a chapter on recursion both precedes and follows the chapter on data abstraction, you can simply rearrange this order.

Part II treats topics that you can also cover in a flexible order. For example, you can cover all or parts of Chapter 8 on advanced C++ either before or after you cover stacks (Chapter 6). You can cover algorithm efficiency and sorting (Chapter 9) any time after Chapter 5. You can introduce trees before queues or graphs before tables, or cover hashing, balanced search trees, or priority queues any time after tables and in any order. You also can cover external methods (Chapter 14) earlier in the course. For example, you can cover external sorting after you cover mergesort in Chapter 9.

Data Abstraction

The design and use of abstract data types permeate this book's problem-solving approach. Several examples demonstrate how to design an ADT as part of the overall design of a solution. All ADTs are first specified—in both English and pseudocode—and then used in simple applications before implementation issues are considered. The distinction between an ADT and the data structure that implements it remains in the fore-front throughout the discussion. The book explains both encapsulation and C++ classes early. Students see how C++ classes hide an implementation's data structure from the client of the ADT. Abstract data types such as lists, stacks, queues, trees, tables, heaps, and priority queues form the basis of our discussions.

Problem Solving

This book helps students learn to integrate problem-solving and programming abilities by emphasizing both the thought processes and the techniques that computer scientists use. Learning how a computer scientist develops, analyzes, and implements a solution is just as important as learning the mechanics of the algorithm; a cookbook approach to the material is insufficient.

The presentation includes analytical techniques for the development of solutions within the context of example problems. Abstraction, the successive refinement of both algorithms and data structures, and recursion are used to design solutions to problems throughout the book.

C++ pointers and linked list processing are introduced early and used in building data structures. The book also introduces at an elementary level the order-of-magnitude analysis of algorithms. This approach allows the consideration—first at an informal level, then more quantitatively—of the advantages and disadvantages of array-based and pointer-based data structures. An emphasis on the trade-offs among potential solutions and implementations is a central problem-solving theme.

Finally, programming style, documentation including preconditions and postconditions, debugging aids, and loop invariants are important parts of the problem-solving methodology used to implement and verify solutions. These topics are covered throughout the book.

Applications

Classic application areas arise in the context of the major topics of this book. For example, the binary search, quicksort, and mergesort algorithms provide important applications of recursion and introduce order-of-magnitude analysis. Such topics as balanced search trees, hashing, and file indexing continue the discussion of searching. Searching and sorting are considered again in the context of external files.

Algorithms for recognizing and evaluating algebraic expressions are first introduced in the context of recursion and are considered again later as an application of stacks. Other applications include, for example, the Eight Queens problem as an example of backtracking, event-driven simulation as an application of queues, and graph searching and traversals as other important applications of stacks and queues.

New and Revised Material

This edition retains the underlying approach and philosophy of the third edition. We present data abstraction and programming both as general concepts and in the context of C++. Many changes, additions, and deletions to the text, figures, and margin notes were made to update and clarify the presentation.

The following is a list of major changes to the book.

- All C++ programs have been tested and revised to ensure compliance with the latest ANSI standards for the language.

- Additional examples of using the Standard Template Library are presented.

- New exercises have been added to each chapter.

- Additional programming problems have been included throughout the book.

- The book's overall design has been enhanced to improve the text's readability.

Overview

The pedagogical features and organization of this book were carefully designed to facilitate learning and to allow instructors to tailor the material easily to a particular course.

Pedagogical Features

This book contains the following features that help students not only during their first reading of the material, but also during subsequent review:

- Chapter outlines and previews.

- Boxes listing key concepts in the material.

- Margin notes.

- Chapter summaries.

- Cautionary warnings about common errors and misconceptions.

- Self-test exercises with answers.

- Chapter exercises and programming problems. The most challenging exercises are labeled with asterisks. Answers to the exercises appear in the *Instructor's Resource Manual*.

- Specifications for all major ADTs in both English and pseudocode, as well as in UML notation.

- C++ class definitions for all major ADTs.

- Examples that illustrate the role of classes and ADTs in the problem-solving process.

- Appendixes, including a review of C++.

- Glossary of terms.

Organization

The chapters in this book are organized into two parts. In most cases, Chapters 1 through 11 will form the core of a one-semester course. Chapters 1 or 2 might be review material for your students. The coverage given to Chapters 11 through 14 will depend on the role the course plays in your curriculum. More detailed suggestions for using this book with different courses appear in the *Instructor's Resource Manual*.

Part I: Problem-Solving Techniques. The first chapter in Part I emphasizes the major issues in programming and software engineering. A new introduction to the Unified Modeling Language (UML) is given here. The next chapter discusses recursion for those students who have had little exposure to this important topic. The ability to think recursively is one of the most useful skills a computer scientist can possess and is often of great value in helping one to better understand the nature of a problem. Recursion is discussed extensively in this chapter and again in Chapter 5 and is used throughout the book. Included examples range from simple recursive definitions to recursive algorithms for language recognition, searching, and sorting.

Chapter 3 covers data abstraction and abstract data types (ADTs) in detail. After a discussion of the specification and use of an ADT, the chapter presents C++ classes and uses them to implement ADTs. This chapter includes a brief introduction to inheritance, the C++ namespace, and exceptions. Chapter 4 presents additional implementation tools in its discussion of C++ pointer variables and linked lists. This chapter also introduces class templates, the C++ Standard Template Library (STL), containers, and iterators.

You can choose among the topics in Part I according to the background of your students and cover these topics in several orders.

Part II: Problem Solving with Abstract Data Types. Part II continues to explore data abstraction as a problem-solving technique. Basic abstract data types such as the stack, queue, binary tree, binary search tree, table, heap, and priority queue are first specified and then implemented as classes. The ADTs are used in examples and their implementations are compared.

Chapter 8 extends the coverage of C++ classes by further developing inheritance, class templates, and iterators. The chapter then introduces virtual functions and friends. Chapter 9 formalizes the earlier discussions of an algorithm's efficiency by introducing order-of-magnitude analysis and Big O notation. The chapter examines the efficiency of several searching and sorting algorithms, including the recursive mergesort and quicksort.

Part II also includes advanced topics—such as balanced search trees (2-3, 2-3-4, red-black, and AVL trees) and hashing—that are examined as table implementations. These implementations are analyzed to determine the table operations that each supports best.

Finally, data storage in external direct access files is considered. Mergesort is modified to sort such data, and external hashing and B-tree indexes are used to search it. These searching algorithms are generalizations of the internal hashing schemes and 2-3 trees already developed.

Supplementary Materials

The following supplemental materials for this text are available to all readers at www.aw-bc.com/support:

- Source code. All of the C++ classes, functions, and programs that appear in the book are available to readers.

- Errata. We have tried not to make mistakes, but mistakes are inevitable. A list of detected errors is available and updated as necessary. You are invited to contribute your finds.

In addition, the following supplements are available to qualified instructors. Please contact your Addison-Wesley sales representative, or send email to aw.cse@aw.com, for information on how to access them:

- Instructor's Resource Manual

- PowerPoint slides

- Test Bank

Talk to Us

Walls and Mirrors continues to evolve. Your comments, suggestions, and corrections will be greatly appreciated. You can contact us directly by e-mail at

carrano@acm.org

or through the publisher:

Computer Science Editorial Office
Addison-Wesley
75 Arlington Street
Boston, MA 02116

Acknowledgements

Paul Nagin contributed extensively to this fourth edition. From 1986 to 2001, he was at Hofstra University in Long Island, where he was Professor of Computer Science, department chair, and assistant dean. He has a long-standing commitment to computer science education and distance learning. He is currently CEO of Chimborazzo, LLC, a company that specializes in the production of textbooks and supplements. Rita Mitra, also of Chimborazzo, assisted in this project. The author and the editorial and production team for *Data Abstraction and Problem Solving with C++*, Fourth Edition, is indebted to Paul for his thoroughness, timeliness, and attention to detail.

Janet Prichard was a valuable partner on the third edition of this book. Her contributions are still felt throughout this fourth edition.

Additionally, we would like to thank the following reviewers for many valuable insights, feedback, and suggestions for this new edition. In alphabetical order, they are: Brian Bershad, University of Washington; Karsten Henckell, New College of Florida; Larry M. Holt, Rollins College; Waleed Meleis, Northeastern University; James R. Miller, University of Kansas; Mateen Rizki, Wright State University; and Daniel Rosenkrantz, State University of New York, Albany.

We especially thank the people who produced this book. Our editors at Addison-Wesley, Michael Hirsch and Katherine Harutunian, along with our longtime editor, Susan Hartman Sullivan, provided invaluable guidance and assistance. This book would not have been printed on time without our project manager at Argosy Publishing, Kevin Sullivan. Thank you, Kevin, for keeping us on schedule.

Many thanks to Jeff Holcomb, Joyce Wells, Lesly Hershman, and Caroline Fell for their expertise and care throughout the production of this book.

Many other wonderful people have contributed in various ways. They are Doug McCreadie, Michael Hayden, Sarah Hayden, Andrew

Hayden, Albert Prichard, Ted Emmott, Maybeth Conway, Lorraine Berube, Marge White, James Kowalski, Gerard Baudet, Joan Peckham, Ed Lamagna, Victor Fay-Wolfe, Bala Ravikumar, Lisa DiPippo, Jean-Yves Hervé, Hal Records, Wally Wood, Elaine Lavallee, Ken Sousa, Sally Lawrence, Lianne Dunn, Gail Armstrong, Tom Manning, Jim Labonte, Jim Abreu, and Bill Harding.

Numerous other people provided input for the previous editions of *Walls and Mirrors* at various stages of its development. All of their comments were useful and greatly appreciated. In alphabetical order, they are Karl Abrahamson, Stephen Alberg, Ronald Alferez, Vicki Allan, Jihad Almahayni, James Ames, Claude W. Anderson, Andrew Azzinaro, Tony Baiching, Don Bailey, N. Dwight Barnette, Jack Beidler, Wolfgang W. Bein, Sto Bell, David Berard, John Black, Richard Botting, Wolfin Brumley, Daryl Carr, Philip Carrigan, Stephen Clamage, Michael Clancy, David Clayton, Michael Cleron, Chris Constantino, Shaun Cooper, Charles Denault, Vincent J. DiPippo, Suzanne Dorney, Colleen Dunn, Carl Eckberg, Sebastian Elbaum, Matthew Evett, Karla Steinbrugge Fant, Jean Foltz, Mike Fulford, Susan Gauch, Martin Granier, Sr., Marguerite Hafen, Randy Hale, George Hamer, Judy Hankins, Jean Harnett, Lisa Hellerstein, Lasse Hellvig, Mary Lou Hines, Jack Hodges, Stephanie Horoschak, Lily Hou, John Hubbard, Tom Irdy, Kris Jensen, Thomas Judson, Edwin J. Kay, Laura Kenney, Roger King, Ladislav Kohout, Jim LaBonte, Jean Lake, Janusz Laski, Cathie LeBlanc, Greg Lee, Urban LeJeune, Matt Licklider, Adam Lindstrom, John M. Linebarger, Ken Lord, Paul Luker, Ethan Mallove, Manisha Mande, Pierre-Arnoul de Marneffe, John Marsaglia, Tim Martin, Jane Wallace Mayo, Mark McCormick, Dan McCracken, Vivian McDougal, Shirley McGuire, Sue Medeiros, James R. Miller, Jim Miller, Guy Mills, Rameen Mohammadi, Cleve Moler, Narayan Murthy, David Naff, Paul Nagin, Rayno Niemi, Debbie Noonan, John O'Donnell, Andrew Oldroyd, Larry Olsen, Raymond L. Paden, Roy Pargas, Brenda C. Parker, Thaddeus F. Pawlicki, Keith Pierce, Lucasz Pruski, George B. Purdy, David Radford, Bina Ramamanthy, Steve Ratering, Stuart Regis, J. D. Robertson, Robert A. Rossi, Jerry Roth, John Rowe, Michael E. Rupp, Sharon Salveter, Charles Saxon, Chandra Sekharan, Linda Shapiro, Yujian Sheng, Mary Shields, Ren-Ben Shiu, Dmitri Slobodin, Ronnie Smith, Carl Spicola, Richard Snodgrass, Neil Snyder, Chris Spannabel, Paul Spirakis, Clinton Staley, Matt Stallman, Mark Stehlick, Benjamin T. Schomp, Harriet Taylor, David Teague, Virginia Teller, David Tetreault, Hans-Joerg Tiede, Dwight Tuinista, John Turner, Karen Van Houten, Robert Vincent, Susan Wallace, James E. Warren, Xiaoqiao Wei, Jerry Weltman, Nancy Wiegand, Howard Williams, Brad Wilson, James Wirth, Kathy Yerian, Salih Yurttas, Rick Zaccone, and Alan Zaring.

Thank you all.

F. M. C.

BRIEF CONTENTS

CONTENTS

CHAPTER 5   Recursion as a Problem-Solving Technique 242

PART II Problem Solving with Abstract Data Types 279

Problem-Solving Techniques

The primary concern of the five chapters in Part I of this book is to develop a repertoire of problem-solving techniques that form the basis of the rest of the book. Chapter 1 begins by describing the characteristics of a good solution and the ways to achieve one. These techniques emphasize abstraction, modularity, and information hiding. The remainder of Part I discusses data abstraction for solution design, C++ pointers and classes for use in implementations, and recursion as a problem-solving strategy.

Principles of Programming and Software Engineering

PREVIEW

This chapter summarizes several fundamental principles that serve as the basis for dealing with the complexities of large programs. The discussion both reinforces the basic principles of programming and demonstrates that writing well-designed and well-documented programs is cost-effective. The chapter also presents a brief discussion of algorithms and data abstraction and indicates how these topics relate to the book's main theme of developing problem-solving and programming skills. In subsequent chapters, the focus shifts from programming principles to ways of organizing and using data. Even when the focus of discussion is on these new techniques, you should note how all solutions adhere to the basic principles discussed in this chapter.

1.1 Problem Solving and Software Engineering

Where did you begin when you wrote your last program? After reading the problem specifications and after the requisite amount of procrastination, most novice programmers simply begin to write code. Obviously, their goal is to get their programs to execute, preferably with correct results. Therefore, they run their programs, examine error messages, insert semicolons, change the logic, delete semicolons, pray, and otherwise torture their programs until they work. Most of their time is probably spent checking both syntax and program logic. Certainly, your programming skills are better now than when you wrote your first program, but will you be able to write a really large program by using the approach just described? Maybe, but there are better ways.

Coding without a solution design increases debugging time

Realize that an extremely large software development project generally requires a team of programmers rather than a single individual. Teamwork requires an overall plan, organization, and communication. A haphazard approach to programming will not serve a team programmer well and will not be cost-effective. Fortunately, a branch of computer science—**software engineering**—provides techniques to facilitate the development of computer programs.

Software engineering facilitates development of programs

Whereas a first course in computer science typically emphasizes programming issues, the focus in this book will be on the broader issues of problem solving. This chapter begins with an overview of the problem-solving process and the various ways of approaching a problem.

What Is Problem Solving?

Here the term **problem solving** refers to the entire process of taking the statement of a problem and developing a computer program that solves that problem. This process requires you to pass through many phases, from gaining an understanding of the problem to be solved, through designing a conceptual solution, to implementing the solution with a computer program.

Exactly what is a solution? Typically, a **solution** consists of two components: algorithms and ways to store data. An **algorithm** is a step-by-step specification of a method to solve a problem within a finite amount of time. One action that an algorithm often performs is to operate on a collection of data. For example, an algorithm may have to put new data into a collection, remove data from a collection, or ask questions about a collection of data.

A solution specifies algorithms and ways to store data

Perhaps this description of a solution leaves the impression that all the cleverness in problem solving goes into developing the algorithm and that how you store your data plays only a supporting role. This impression is far from the truth. You need to do much more than simply store your data. When constructing a solution, you must organize your data collection so that you can operate on the data easily in the manner that the algorithm requires. In fact, most of this book describes ways of organizing data.

When you design a solution to a given problem, you can utilize several techniques that will make your task easier. This chapter introduces those techniques, and subsequent chapters provide more detail.

The Life Cycle of Software

The development of good software involves a lengthy and continuing process known as the **software life cycle**. This process begins with an initial idea, includes the writing and debugging of programs, and continues for years to involve corrections and enhancements to the original software. Figure 1-1 pictures the nine phases of the software life cycle as segments on a waterwheel.[1] This arrangement suggests that the phases are part of a cycle and are not simply a linear list. Although you start by specifying a problem, typically you move from any phase to any other phase. For example, testing a program can suggest changes to either the problem specifications or the solution design. Also notice that the nine phases surround a documentation core in the figure. Documentation is

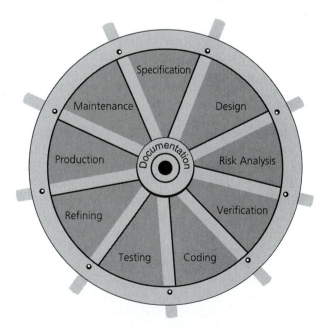

FIGURE 1-1   The life cycle of software as a waterwheel that can rotate from one phase to any other phase

---

[1] Thanks to Raymond L. Paden for suggesting that "wheel" be "waterwheel."

not a separate phase, as you might expect. Rather, it is integrated into all phases of the software life cycle.

Here, then, are the phases in the life cycle of typical software. Although all phases are important, only those that are most relevant to this book are discussed in detail.

Phase 1: Specification. Given an initial statement of the software's purpose, you must clearly specify all aspects of the problem. Often the people who describe the problem are not programmers, so the initial problem statement might be imprecise. The specification phase, then, requires that you bring precision and detail to the original problem statement and that you communicate with both programmers and non-programmers.

Here are some questions that you must answer as you write the specifications for the software: What is the input data? What data is valid and what data is invalid? Who will use the software, and what user interface should be used? What error detection and error messages are desirable? What assumptions are possible? Are there special cases? What is the form of the output? What documentation is necessary? What enhancements to the program are likely in the future?

One way to improve communication among people and to clarify the software specifications is to write a prototype program that simulates the behavior of portions of the desired software product. For example, a simple—even inefficient—program could demonstrate the proposed user interface for analysis. It is better to discover any difficulties or to change your mind now than after programming is underway or even complete.

Your previous programming assignments probably stated the program specifications for you. Perhaps aspects of these specifications were unclear and you had to seek clarification, but most likely you have had little practice in writing your own program specifications.

Phase 2: Design. Once you have completed the specification phase, you must design a solution to the problem. Most people who design solutions of moderate size and complexity find it difficult to cope with the entire program at once. The best way to simplify the problem-solving process is to divide a large problem into small, manageable parts. The resulting program will contain **modules,** which are self-contained units of code. A module could be a single function, or several functions and other blocks of code. You should design modules that are as independent, or **loosely coupled,** as possible, except, of course, for their **interfaces,** which are the communication mechanisms among modules. You can develop such modules in virtual isolation from the other modules. Each module should perform one well-defined task; that is, it should be **highly cohesive.** Thus, modularity describes a program that is organized into loosely coupled, highly cohesive modules.

During the design phase, it is also important that you clearly specify not only the purpose of each module but also the **data flow** among

Make the problem statement precise and detailed

Prototype programs can clarify the problem

Loosely coupled modules are independent

Highly cohesive modules perform one well-defined task

Specify each module's purpose, assumptions, input, and
output

modules. For example, you should provide answers to these questions for each module: What data is available to the module before its execution? What does the module assume? What actions have taken place, and what does the data look like after the module executes? Thus, you should specify in detail the assumptions, input, and output for each module.

For example, if you as program designer needed to sort an array of integers, you might write the following specifications for a sort function:

The function will receive an array of *num* integers, where *num* > 0.

The function will return the array with the integers sorted.

Specifications as a contract

You can view these specifications as the terms of a contract between your function and the module that calls it.

If you alone write the entire program, this contract helps you systematically decompose the problem into smaller tasks. If the program is a team project, the contract helps delineate responsibilities. Whoever writes the sort function must live up to this contract. After the sort function has been written and tested, the contract tells the rest of the program how to call the sort function properly and the result of doing so.

A module's specification
should not describe a method
of solution

Notice, however, that a module's contract does not commit the module to a particular method of performing its task. If another part of the program assumes anything about the method, it does so at its own risk. Thus, for example, if at some later date you rewrite your function to use a different sorting algorithm, you should not need to change the rest of the program at all. As long as the new function honors the terms of the original contract, the rest of the program should be oblivious to the change.

This should not be news to you. Although you might not have explicitly used the term "contract" before, the concept should be familiar. You write a contract when you write a function's **precondition**, which is a statement of the conditions that must exist at the beginning of a function, as well as when you write its **postcondition**, which is a statement of the conditions at the end of a function. For example, the sort function that adheres to the previous contract could appear in pseudocode[2] as

Function specifications
include precise preconditions
and postconditions

First-draft specifications

```
sort(anArray, num)
// Sorts an array.
// Precondition: anArray is an array of num
// integers; num > 0.
// Postcondition: The integers in anArray are sorted.
```

These particular pre- and postconditions actually are deficient, as may be the case in a first-draft contract. For example, does "sorted"

---

[2] Pseudocode in this book appears in italics.

mean ascending order or descending order? How large can *num* be? While implementing this function, you might assume that "sorted" means "ascending order" and that *num* will not exceed 100. Imagine the difficulties that can arise when another person tries to use *sort* to sort an array of 500 integers into descending order. This user does not know your assumptions unless you documented them by revising the pre- and postconditions, as follows:

```
sort(anArray, num)
// Sorts an array into ascending order.
// Precondition: anArray is an array of num integers
// and 1 <= num <= MAX_ARRAY, where MAX_ARRAY is a
// global constant that specifies the maximum size
// of anArray.
// Postcondition: anArray[0] <= anArray[1] <= ... <=
// anArray[num-1], num is unchanged.
```

Revised specifications

When you write a precondition, begin by describing the function's input arguments, mention any global named constants that the function uses, and finally list any assumptions that the function makes. Similarly, when you write a postcondition, begin by describing the function's output arguments—or in the case of a valued function, the value it returns—and then describe any other action that has occurred.

Novice programmers tend to dismiss the importance of precise documentation, particularly when they are simultaneously designer, programmer, and user of a small program. If you design *sort* but do not write down the terms of the contract, will you remember them when you later implement the function? Will you remember how to use *sort* weeks after you have written it? To refresh your memory, would you rather examine your C++ code or read a simple set of pre- and postconditions? As the size of a program increases, good documentation becomes even more important, regardless of whether you are sole author or part of a team.

Precise documentation is essential

You should not ignore the possibility that you or someone else has already implemented some of the required modules. C++ facilitates the reuse of software components, which are typically organized into libraries that have been compiled. That is, you will not always have access to a function's C++ code. The C++ standard provides a library that is an example of such a collection of preexisting software. For example, you know how to use the standard function *sqrt* contained in the C++ math library (*cmath*), yet you do not have access to its source statements, because it is precompiled. You know, however, that if you pass *sqrt* a floating-point expression, it will return the floating-point square root of the value of that expression. You can use *sqrt* even though you do not know its implementation. Furthermore, it may be that *sqrt* was written in a language other than C++! There is so much

Incorporate existing software components into your design

about *sqrt* that you do not know, yet you can use it in your program without concern, *as long as you know its specifications*.

If, in the past, you have spent little or no time in the design phase for your programs, you must change this habit! The end result of the design phase should be a modular solution that is easy to translate into the constructs of a particular programming language. By spending adequate time in the design phase, you will spend less time when you write and debug your program.

This chapter will resume this discussion of modular design later.

Phase 3: Risk analysis. Building software entails risks. Some risks are the same for all software projects and some are peculiar to a particular project. You can predict some risks, while others are unknown. Risks can affect a project's timetable or cost, the success of a business, or the health and lives of people. You can eliminate or reduce some risks, but others you cannot. Techniques exist to identify, assess, and manage the risks of creating a software product. You will learn these techniques if you study software engineering in a subsequent course. The outcome of risk analysis will affect the other phases of the life cycle.

You can predict and manage some, but not all, risks

Phase 4: Verification. Formal, theoretical methods are available for proving that an algorithm is correct. Although research in this area is incomplete, it is useful to mention some aspects of the verification process.

An **assertion** is a statement about a particular condition at a certain point in an algorithm. Preconditions and postconditions are simply assertions about conditions at the beginning and end of functions. An **invariant** is a condition that is always true at a particular point in an algorithm. A **loop invariant** is a condition that is true before and after each execution of an algorithm's loop. As you will see, loop invariants can help you write correct loops. By using invariants, you can detect errors before you begin coding and thereby reduce your debugging and testing time. Overall, invariants can save you time.

You can prove the correctness of some algorithms

Proving that an algorithm is correct is like proving a theorem in geometry. For example, to prove that a function is correct, you would start with its preconditions—which are analogous to the axioms and assumptions in geometry—and demonstrate that the steps of the algorithm lead to the postconditions. To do so, you would consider each step in the algorithm and show that an assertion before the step leads to a particular assertion after the step.

By proving the validity of individual statements, you can prove that sequences of statements, and then functions, and finally the program are correct. For example, suppose you show that if assertion A_1 is true and statement S_1 executes, assertion A_2 is true. Also, suppose you have shown that assertion A_2 and statement S_2 lead to assertion A_3. You can then conclude that if assertion A_1 is true, executing the sequence of statements S_1 and S_2 will lead to assertion A_3. By continuing in this manner, you eventually will be able to show that the program is correct.

Clearly, if you discovered an error during the verification process, you would correct your algorithm and possibly modify the problem specifications. Thus, by using invariants, it is likely that your algorithm will contain fewer errors *before* you begin coding. As a result, you will spend less time debugging your program.

You can formally prove that particular constructs such as *if* statements, loops, and assignments are correct. An important technique uses loop invariants to demonstrate the correctness of iterative algorithms. For example, we will prove that the following simple loop computes the sum of the first *n* elements in the array *item*:

```
// computes the sum of item[0], item[1], . . .,
// item[n-1] for any n >= 1
int sum = 0;
int j = 0;
while (j < n)
{   sum += item[j];
    ++j;
}   // end while
```

Before this loop begins execution, *sum* is 0 and *j* is 0. After the loop executes once, *sum* is *item[0]* and *j* is 1. In general,

> *sum* is the sum of the elements *item[0]* through *item[j-1]*   **Loop invariant**

This statement is the invariant for this loop.

The invariant for a correct loop is true at the following points:

- Initially, after any initialization steps, but before the loop begins execution

- Before every iteration of the loop

- After every iteration of the loop

- After the loop terminates

For the previous loop example, these points are as follows:

```
int sum = 0;
int j = 0;
                          ←  The invariant is true here

while (j < n)
{                         ←  The invariant is true here
    sum += item[j];
    ++j;
                          ←  The invariant is true here
}   // end while
                          ←  The invariant is true here
```

You can use these observations to prove the correctness of an iterative algorithm. For the previous example, you must show that each of the following four points is true:

Steps to establish the
correctness of an algorithm

1. **The invariant must be true initially**, before the loop begins execution for the first time. In the previous example, *sum* is 0 and *j* is 0 initially. In this case, the invariant states that *sum* contains the sum of the elements *item[0]* through *item[-1]*; the invariant is true because there are no elements in this range.

2. **An execution of the loop must preserve the invariant**. That is, if the invariant is true before any given iteration of the loop, you must show that it is true after the iteration. In the example, the loop adds *item[j]* to *sum* and then increments *j* by 1. Thus, after an execution of the loop, the most recent element added to *sum* is *item[j-1]*; that is, the invariant is true after the iteration.

3. **The invariant must capture the correctness of the algorithm**. That is, you must show that if the invariant is true when the loop terminates, the algorithm is correct. When the loop in the previous example terminates, *j* contains *n*, and the invariant is true: *sum* contains the sum of the elements *item[0]* through *item[n-1]*, which is the sum that you intended to compute.

4. **The loop must terminate**. That is, you must show that the loop will terminate after a finite number of iterations. In the example, *j* begins at 0 and then increases by 1 at each execution of the loop. Thus, *j* eventually will equal *n* for any $n \geq 1$. This fact and the nature of the *while* statement guarantee that the loop will terminate.

Not only can you use invariants to show that your loop is correct, but you can also use them to show that your loop is wrong. For example, suppose that the expression in the previous *while* statement was *j <= n* instead of *j < n*. Steps 1 and 2 of the previous demonstration would be the same, but Step 3 would differ: When the loop terminated, *j* would contain *n* + 1 and, because the invariant would be true, *sum* would contain the sum of the elements *item[0]* through *item[n]*. Because this is not the desired sum, you know that something is wrong with your loop.

Notice the clear connection between Steps 1 through 4 and **mathematical induction**.[3] Showing the invariant to be true initially, which establishes the **base case**, is analogous to establishing that a property of the natural numbers is true for 0. Showing that each iteration of the loop preserves the invariant is the **inductive step**. This step is analogous

---

[3] A review of mathematical induction appears in Appendix D.

to showing that if a property is true for an arbitrary natural number k, then the property is true for the natural number $k + 1$. After performing the four steps just described, you can conclude that the invariant is true after every iteration of the loop—just as mathematical induction allows you to conclude that a property is true for every natural number.

Identifying loop invariants will help you write correct loops. You should state the invariant as a comment that either precedes or begins each loop, as appropriate. For example, in the previous example, you might write the following:

```
// Invariant: 0 <= j <= n and
// sum = item[0] +...+ item[j-1]
while (j < n)
    . . .
```

State loop invariants in your programs

You should confirm that the invariants for the following unrelated loops are correct. Remember that each invariant must be true both before the loop begins and after each iteration of the loop, including the final one. Also, you might find it easier to understand the invariant for a *for* loop if you temporarily convert it to an equivalent *while* loop.

```
// Computes n! for an integer n >= 0
int f = 1;
// Invariant: f == (j-1)!
for (int j = 1; j <= n; ++j)
    f *= j;

// Computes an approximation to ex for a real x
double t = 1.0;
double s = 1.0;
int    k = 1;
// Invariant: t == xk-1/(k-1)! and
// s == 1+x+x2/2!+...+xk-1/(k-1)!
while (k <= n)
{   t *= x/k;
    s += t;
    ++k;
}   // end while
```

Examples of loop invariants

Phase 5: Coding. The coding phase involves translating the algorithms into a particular programming language and removing the syntax errors. Although this phase is probably your concept of what programming is all about, it is important to realize that the coding phase is not the major part of the life cycle for most software—actually, it is a relatively minor part.

Coding is a relatively minor phase in the software life cycle

Phase 6: Testing. During the testing phase, you need to remove as many logical errors as you can. One approach is to test the individual

Design a set of test data to test your program

functions of the objects first, using valid data that leads to a known result. If certain data must lie within a range, include values at the endpoints of the range. For example, if the input value for *n* can range from 1 to 10, be sure to include test cases in which *n* is 1 and 10. Also include invalid data to test the error-detection capability of the program. Try some random data, and finally try some actual data. Testing is both a science and an art. You will learn more about testing in subsequent courses.

Phase 7: Refining the solution.   The result of Phases 1 through 6 of the solution process is a working program, which you have tested extensively and debugged as necessary. If you have a program that solves your original problem, you might wonder about the significance of this phase of the solution process.

Often the best approach to solving a problem is first to make some simplifying assumptions during the design of the solution—for example, you could assume that the input will be in a certain format and will be correct—and next to develop a complete working program under these assumptions. You can then add more sophisticated input and output routines, additional features, and more error checks to the working program.

Thus, the approach of simplifying the problem initially makes a refinement step necessary in the solution process. Of course, you must take care to ensure that the final refinements do not require a complete redesign of the solution. You can usually make these additions cleanly, however, particularly when you have used a modular design. In fact, the ability to proceed in this manner is one of the key advantages of having a modular design! Also, realize that any time you modify a program—no matter how trivial the changes might seem—you must thoroughly test it again.

This discussion illustrates that the phases within the life cycle of software are not completely isolated from one another and are not linear. To make realistic simplifying assumptions early in the design process, you should have some idea of how you will account for those assumptions later on. Testing a program can suggest changes to its design, but changes to a program require that you test the program again.

Phase 8: Production.   When the software product is complete, it is distributed to its intended users, installed on their computers, and used.

Phase 9: Maintenance.   Maintaining a program is not like maintaining a car. Software does not wear out if you neglect it. However, users of your software invariably will detect errors that you did not discover during the testing phase. Correcting these errors is part of maintaining the software. Another aspect of the maintenance phase involves enhancing the software by adding more features or by modifying existing portions to suit the users better. Rarely will the people who design and implement the original program perform this maintenance step. Good documentation then becomes even more important.

Develop a working program under simplifying assumptions; then add refining sophistication

Changes to a program require that you test it again

Correcting user-detected errors and adding features are aspects of software maintenance

Is a program's life cycle relevant to your life? It definitely should be! You should view Phases 1 through 7 as the steps in a problem-solving process. Using this strategy, you first design and implement a solution (Phases 1 through 6) based on some initial simplifying assumptions. The outcome is a well-structured program that solves a somewhat simplified problem. The last step of the solution process (Phase 7) refines your work into a sophisticated program that meets the original problem specifications.

What Is a Good Solution?

Before you devote your time and energy to the study of problem-solving techniques, it seems only fair that you see at the outset why mastery of these techniques will help make you a good problem solver. An obvious statement is that the use of these techniques will produce good solutions. This statement, however, leads to the more fundamental question, what *is* a good solution? A brief attempt at answering this question concludes this section.

Because a computer program is the final form your solutions will take, consider what constitutes a good computer program. Presumably, you write a program to perform some task. In the course of performing that task, there is a real and tangible **cost of a program**. This cost includes such factors as the computer resources (computing time and memory) that the program consumes, the difficulties encountered by those who use the program, and the consequences of a program that does not behave correctly.

However, the costs just mentioned do not give the whole picture. They pertain to only one phase of the life cycle of a solution—the phase in which it is an operational program. In assessing whether or not a solution is good, you also must consider the phases during which you developed the solution and the phases after you wrote the initial program that implemented the solution. Each of these phases incurs costs, too. The total cost of a solution must take into account the value of the time of the people who developed, refined, coded, debugged, and tested it. A solution's cost must also include the cost of maintaining, modifying, and expanding it.

Thus, when calculating the overall cost of a solution, you must include a diverse set of factors. If you adopt such a multidimensional view of cost, it is reasonable to evaluate a solution against the following criterion:

> *A solution is good if the total cost it incurs over all phases of its life cycle is minimal.*

A multidimensional view of a solution's cost

It is interesting to consider how the relative importance of the various components of this cost has changed since the early days of computing. In the beginning, the cost of computer time relative to human time was extremely high. In addition, people tended to write programs to perform very specific, narrowly defined tasks. If the task changed somewhat, a new program was written. Program maintenance was probably not much of an issue, so there was little concern if a program was hard to read. A program typically had only one user, its author. As a consequence, programmers tended not to worry about misuse or ease of use of their programs; a program's interface generally was not considered important.

In this type of environment, one cost clearly overshadowed all others: computer resources. If two programs performed the same task, the one that required less time and memory was better. How things have changed! Since the early days of computers, computing costs have dropped dramatically, thus making the value of the problem solver's and programmer's time a much more significant factor in the cost of a solution. Another consequence of the drop in computing costs is that computers now are used to perform tasks in a wide variety of areas, many of them nonscientific. People who interact with computers often have no technical expertise and no knowledge of the workings of programs. People want their software to be easy to use.

Today, programs are larger and more complex than ever before. They are often so large that many people are involved in their design, use, and maintenance. Good structure and documentation are thus of the utmost importance. As programs perform more highly critical tasks, the prices for malfunctions will soar. Thus, society needs both well-structured programs and techniques for formally verifying their correctness. People will not and should not entrust their livelihoods—or their lives—to a program that only its authors can understand and maintain.

Programs must be well structured and documented

These developments have made obsolete the notion that the most efficient solution is always the best. If two programs perform the same task, it is no longer true that the faster one is necessarily better. Programmers who use every trick in the book to save a few microseconds of computing time at the expense of clarity are not in tune with the cost structure of today's world. You must write programs with people as well as computers in mind.

At the same time, do not get the impression that the efficiency of a solution is no longer important. To the contrary, many situations occur for which efficiency is the prime determinant of whether a solution is even usable. The point is that a solution's efficiency is only one of many factors that you must consider. If two solutions have approximately the same efficiency, other factors should dominate the comparison. However, when the efficiencies of solutions differ *significantly*, this difference can be the overriding concern. The stages of the problem-solving process at which you should be most concerned about efficiency are those during which you develop the underlying methods of solution. The choice of a solution's components—the algorithms and ways to store data—rather than the code you write, leads to significant differences in efficiency.

Efficiency is only one aspect of a solution's cost

This book advocates a problem-solving philosophy that views the cost of a solution as multidimensional. This philosophy is reasonable in today's world, and it likely will be reasonable in the years to come.

1.2 Achieving a Modular Design

You have seen the importance of specifying each module during the design of a solution by writing precise pre- and postconditions, but how do you determine the modules in the first place? The techniques that help you choose modules for a particular solution are the subject of entire texts and future courses and quickly go beyond this book's scope. This section will provide, however, an overview of two important design techniques. Both techniques use abstraction, so we begin with this essential concept.

Abstraction and Information Hiding

When you design a modular solution to a problem, each module begins as a box that states what it does but not how it does it. No one box may "know" how any other box performs its task—it may know only what that task is. For example, if one part of a solution is to sort some data, one of the boxes will be a sorting algorithm, as Figure 1-2 illustrates. The other boxes will know that the sorting box sorts, but they will not know how it sorts. In this way the various components of a solution are kept isolated from one another.

Specify what to do, not how to do it

    Abstraction separates the purpose of a module from its implementation. Modularity and abstraction complement each other. Modularity breaks a solution into modules; abstraction specifies each module clearly *before* you implement it in a programming language. For example, what does the module assume and what action does it take? Such specifications will clarify the design of your solution because you will be able to focus on the high-level functionality of your solution without the distraction of implementation details. In addition, these

Write specifications for each module before implementing it

Specifications do not indicate how to implement a module

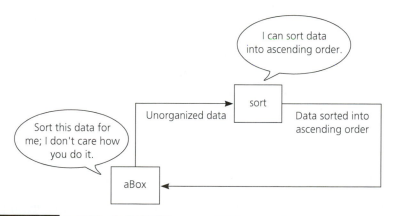

FIGURE 1-2   The details of the sorting algorithm are hidden from other parts of the solution

principles allow you to modify one part of a solution without significantly affecting the other parts. For example, you should be able to change the sorting algorithm in the previous example without affecting the rest of the solution.

As the problem-solving process proceeds, you gradually refine the boxes until eventually you implement their actions by writing C++ code—typically, functions. You should separate the purpose of a function from its implementation. This process is known as **functional** (or **procedural**) **abstraction**. Once a function is written, you can use it without knowing the particulars of its algorithm as long as you have a statement of its purpose and a description of its arguments. Assuming that the function is documented properly, you will be able to use it knowing only its declaration and its initial descriptive comments; you will not need to look at its implementation.

Functional abstraction is essential to team projects. After all, in a team situation, you will have to use functions written by others, frequently without knowledge of their algorithms. Will you actually be able to use such a function without studying its code? In fact, you do each time you use a C++ Standard Library function, such as *sqrt*, as was noted earlier.

Consider now a collection of data and a set of operations on the data. The operations might include ones that add new data to the collection, remove data from the collection, or search for some data. **Data abstraction** focuses on what the operations do instead of on how you will implement them. The other modules of the solution will "know" *what* operations they can perform, but they will not know *how* the data is stored or *how* the operations are performed.

For example, you have used an array, but have you ever stopped to think about what an array actually is? You will see many pictures of arrays throughout this book. This artist's conception of an array might resemble the way a C++ array is implemented on a computer, and then again it might not. The point is that you are able to use an array without knowing what it "looks like"—that is, how it is implemented. Although different systems may implement arrays in different ways, the differences are transparent to the programmer. For instance, regardless of how the array *years* is implemented, you can always store the value 1492 in location *index* of the array by using the statement

```
years[index] = 1492;
```

and later write out that value by using the statement

```
cout << years[index] << endl;
```

Thus, you can use an array without knowing the details of its implementation, just as you can use the function *sqrt* without knowing the details of its implementation.

<aside>
Specify what a function does, not how to do it

Specify what you will do to data, not how to do it
</aside>

Most of this book is about data abstraction. To enable you to think abstractly about data—that is, to focus on what operations you will perform on the data instead of how you will perform them—you should define an **abstract data type**, or **ADT**. An ADT is a collection of data *and* a set of operations on the data. You can use an ADT's operations, if you know their specifications, without knowing how the operations are implemented or how the data is stored.

Ultimately, someone—perhaps you—will implement the ADT by using a **data structure,** which is a construct that you can define within a programming language to store a collection of data. For example, you might store some data in a C++ array of integers or in an array of objects or in an array of arrays.

An ADT is not a fancy name for a data structure

Within problem solving, ADTs support algorithms, and algorithms are part of what constitutes an ADT. As you design a solution, you should develop algorithms and ADTs in tandem. The global algorithm that solves a problem suggests operations that you need to perform on the data, which in turn suggest ADTs and algorithms for performing the operations on the data. However, the development of the solution may proceed in the opposite direction as well. The kinds of ADTs that you are able to design can influence the strategy of your global algorithm for solving a problem. That is, your knowledge of which data operations are easy to perform and which are difficult can have a large effect on how you approach a problem.

Develop algorithms and ADTs in tandem

As you probably have surmised from this discussion, you often cannot sharply distinguish between an "algorithms problem" and a "data structures problem." Frequently, you can look at a program from one perspective and feel that the data structures support a clever algorithm and then look at the same program from another perspective and feel that the algorithms support a clever data structure.

Information hiding. As you have seen, abstraction tells you to write functional specifications for each module that describe its outside, or public, view. However, abstraction also helps you identify details that you should hide from public view—details that should not be in the specifications but should be private. The principle of **information hiding** tells you not only to hide such details within a module, but also to ensure that no other module can tamper with these hidden details.

All modules and ADTs should hide something

Information hiding limits the ways in which you need to deal with functions and data. As a user of a module, you do not worry about the details of its implementation. As an implementer of a module, you do not worry about its uses.

Object-Oriented Design

One way to achieve a modular solution is by identifying within a problem components—called **objects**—that combine data and operations

Objects encapsulate data and operations

on the data. Such an object-oriented approach to modularity produces a collection of objects that have behaviors.

Although you may have been unaware of them, you have seen objects before. The alarm clock that awoke you this morning encapsulates both time and operations such as "set the alarm." To *encapsulate* means to encase or enclose; thus, **encapsulation** is a technique that hides inner details. Whereas functions encapsulate actions, objects encapsulate data as well as actions. Even though you request the clock to perform certain operations, you cannot see how it works. You see only the results of those operations.

Encapsulation hides inner details

FIGURE 1-3   A digital clock

Suppose that you want to write a program to display a clock on your computer screen. To simplify the example, consider a digital clock without an alarm, as Figure 1-3 illustrates. You would begin the task of designing a modular solution by identifying the objects in the problem.

Several methods are available for identifying objects, but no single one is always the best approach. One simple method[4] considers the nouns and verbs in the problem specifications. The nouns will suggest objects whose actions are indicated by the verbs. For example, you could specify the clock problem as follows:

Specifications for a program that displays a digital clock

> The program will maintain a digital clock that displays the time in hours and minutes. The hour indicator and minute indicator are both digital devices that display values from 1 to 12 and 0 to 59, respectively. You should be able to set the time by setting the hour and minute indicators, and the clock should maintain the time by updating these indicators.

Even without a detailed problem specification, you know that one of the objects is the clock itself. The clock performs operations such as

```
Set the time
Advance the time
Display the time
```

The hour indicator and minute indicator are also objects and are quite similar to each other. Each indicator performs operations such as

```
Set its value
Advance its value
Display its value
```

In fact, both indicators can be the same type of object. A set of objects that has the same type is called a **class**. Thus, what you need to specify is not a particular object, but a class of objects. In fact, you need a class of clocks and a class of indicators. A clock object, which is an **instance**

An object is an instance of a class

---

[4] The method is not foolproof. The problem specification must use nouns and verbs consistently. If, for example, "display" is sometimes a verb and sometimes a noun, identifying objects and their operations can be unclear.

of the clock class, will then contain two indicator objects, which are instances of the indicator class.

Classes also specify the data and operations for the objects. The individual data items specified in a class are called **data members**, **data fields**, or **attributes**. The operations specified in the class are often referred to as **methods** or functions.

Chapter 3 discusses encapsulation further and, in particular, introduces C++ classes. In subsequent chapters, you will study various ADTs and their implementations as C++ classes. The focus will be on data abstraction and encapsulation. This approach to programming is object based.

Object-oriented programming, or **OOP**, adds two more principles to encapsulation:

KEY CONCEPTS

Three Principles of Object-Oriented Programming

1. Encapsulation: Objects combine data and operations.

2. Inheritance: Classes can inherit properties from other classes.

3. Polymorphism: Objects can determine appropriate operations at execution time.

Classes can inherit properties from other classes. For example, once you have defined a class of clocks, you can design a class of alarm clocks that inherits the properties of a clock but adds operations to provide an alarm. You will be able to produce an alarm clock quickly because the clock portion is done. Thus, **inheritance** allows you to reuse classes that you defined earlier—perhaps for different but related purposes—with appropriate modification.

Inheritance may make it impossible for the compiler to determine which operation you require in a particular situation. However, **polymorphism**—which literally means *many forms*—enables this determination to be made at execution time. That is, the outcome of a particular operation depends upon the objects on which the operation acts. For example, if you use the + operator with numeric operands in C++, addition occurs, but when you use the **overloaded operator** + with strings, concatenation occurs. Although in this simple example the compiler can determine the correct meaning of +, polymorphism allows situations in which the meaning of an operation is unknown until execution time.

An overloaded operator has multiple meanings

Chapter 8 discusses inheritance and polymorphism further.

Top-Down Design

Generally, an object-oriented approach produces modular solutions for problems that primarily involve data. When you need to design an algorithm for a particular function, or sometimes when the emphasis of your problem is on algorithms and not data, a **top-down design** will lead to a modular solution. Whereas object-oriented design identifies objects by focusing on the nouns in the problem statement, top-down design identifies actions by focusing on the verbs.

A structure chart shows the relationship among modules

The philosophy of a top-down design is that you should address a task at successively lower levels of detail. Consider a simple example: Suppose that you wanted to find the median among a collection of test scores. Figure 1-4 uses a **structure chart** to illustrate the hierarchy of, and interaction among, the modules that solve this problem. At first, each module is little more than a statement of *what* it needs to solve and is devoid of detail. You refine each module by partitioning it into additional smaller modules. The result is a hierarchy of modules; each module is refined by its successors, which solve smaller problems and contain more detail about *how* to solve the problem than their predecessors. The refinement process continues until the modules at the bottom of the hierarchy are simple enough for you to translate directly into C++ functions and isolated blocks of code that solve very small, independent problems.

Notice in Figure 1-4 that you can break the solution down into three independent tasks:

A solution consisting of independent tasks

```
Read the test scores
Sort the scores
Get the "middle" score
```

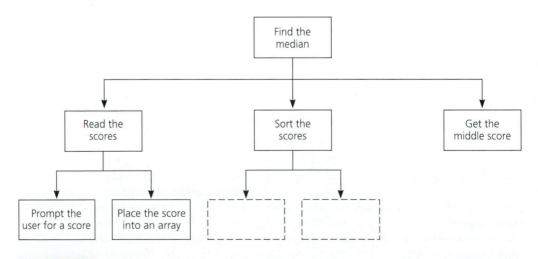

FIGURE 1-4   A structure chart showing the hierarchy of modules

If the three modules in this example perform their tasks, then by calling them in order you will correctly find the median, regardless of *how* each module performs its task.

You begin to develop each module by dividing it into subtasks. For example, you can refine the task of reading the test scores by dividing it into the following two modules:

```
Prompt the user for a score
Place the score into an array
```

Subtasks

You continue the solution process by developing, in a similar manner, modules for each of these two tasks. Finally, you can use pseudocode to specify the details of the algorithms.

General Design Guidelines

Typically, you use object-oriented design (OOD), top-down design (TDD), abstraction, and information hiding when you design a solution to a problem. The following design guidelines summarize an approach that leads to modular solutions.

KEY CONCEPTS

Design Guidelines

1. Use OOD and TDD together to produce modular solutions. That is, develop abstract data types and algorithms in tandem.

2. Use OOD for problems that primarily involve data.

3. Use TDD to design algorithms for an object's operations.

4. Consider TDD to design solutions to problems that emphasize algorithms over data.

5. Focus on *what*, not *how*, when designing both ADTs and algorithms.

6. Consider incorporating previously written software components into your design.

Modeling Object-Oriented Designs Using UML

The **Unified Modeling Language (UML)** is a modeling language used to express object-oriented designs. UML provides specifications for both diagrams and text-based descriptions. The diagrams are particularly useful in showing the overall design of a solution, including class specifications and the various ways that the classes interact with each

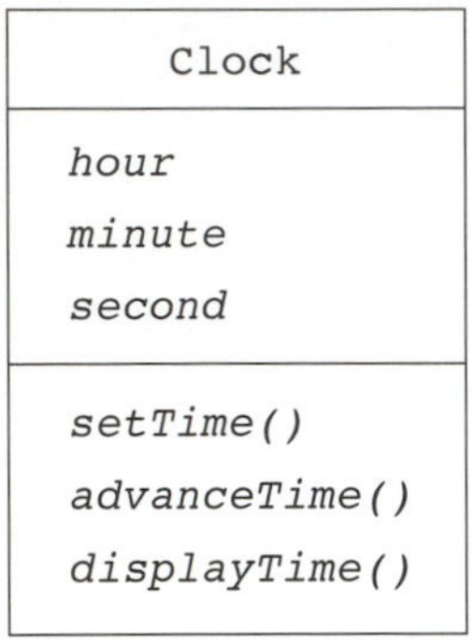

Clock
hour
minute
second
setTime()
advanceTime()
displayTime()

FIGURE 1-5   UML diagram for the class *Clock*

other. It is fairly common to have a number of classes involved in a solution, and thus the ability to show the interaction among classes is one of the strengths of UML.

This text focuses on the design of the classes themselves, and therefore only the class diagrams and associated syntax are presented here. Class diagrams specify the name of the class, the data members of the class, and the operations. Figure 1-5 shows a class diagram for the class *Clock* discussed earlier. The top section contains the class name. The middle section contains the data members that represent the data in the class, and the bottom section contains the operations. Note that the diagram is quite general; it does not really dictate how the class is actually implemented. It typically represents a conceptual model of the class that is language independent.

In conjuction with the class diagrams, UML also provides a text-based notation to represent the data members and operations for classes. This notation can be incorporated into the class diagrams, but usually not to the fullest extent because it tends to clutter the diagrams. This text-based representation is used to describe the classes in this text, because it provides a more complete specification than the diagrams.

The UML syntax for data members is

$$\textit{visibility name: type} = \textit{defaultValue}$$

where

- *visibility* is + (*public*) or − (*private*). A third possibility is # (*protected*), which is discussed in Chapter 8.

- *name* is the name of the data member.

- *type* is the data type of the data member.

- *defaultValue* is an initial value for the data member.

As seen in the class diagrams, at a minimum the name should be provided. The *defaultValue* is used only in situations where a default value is appropriate. In some cases you may also want to omit the *type* of the data member and leave it to the implementation to provide that detail. This text will use the following names for common argument types: *integer* for integer values, *float* for floating-point values, *boolean* for boolean values, and *string* for string values. Note that these names do not match the corresponding C++ data types because this notation is meant to be language independent.

Here is the text-based notation for the data members in the class *Clock* shown in Figure 1-5:

```
-hour: integer
-minute: integer
-second: integer
```

The data members *hour*, *minute*, and *second* are declared private, as suggested by the concept of information hiding.

The UML syntax for operations is more involved:

$$\textit{visibility name(parameter-list): return-type } \{\textit{property-string}\}$$

where

- *visibility* is the same as specified for data members.
- *name* is the name of the operation.
- *parameter-list* contains comma-separated parameters whose syntax is as follows:

$$\textit{direction name: type} = \textit{defaultValue}$$

where

- *direction* is used to show whether the parameter is used for input (`in`), output (`out`), or both (`inout`).
- *name* is the parameter.
- *type* is the data type of the parameter.
- *defaultValue* is a value that should be used for the parameter if no argument is provided.
- *return-type* is the data type of the result of the operation. If the operation does not return a value, this is left blank.
- *property-string* indicates property values that apply to the operation.

Like the class diagrams for data members, the class diagrams for operations at a minimum provide the *name* of the operation. Sometimes the *parameter-list* is included if it clarifies the understanding of the class functionality.

The *property-string* has a variety of possible values, but of interest in this text is the property `query`. It is a way to indicate that the operation does not modify any data in the class.

Here is the text-based notation for the operations in the class *Clock*:

```
+setTime(in hr: integer, in min: integer, in sec: integer)
-advanceTime()
+displayTime() {query}
```

Here we specified the operations *setTime* and *displayTime* as public, and *advanceTime* as private. The function *displayTime* also has the property *query* specified, as an indication that it does not change any of the data; the function is used only to display the data.

UML class diagrams provide additional notation to illustrate relationships between classes. Suppose that you are asked to model a banking system application. The specification is as follows:

Design a banking system that assigns checking and savings accounts to customers. The bank information includes a name and routing number. Both types of accounts allow balance retrieval, deposits, and withdrawals. A customer may have multiple accounts. Each customer's name and address are stored in the system, and each account has a number assigned to it. Savings accounts earn interest and checking accounts charge for each check when the balance falls below a minimum amount. These adjustments are reflected when the customer requests the current account balance.

Several classes might be designed to represent the various aspects of a bank, as illustrated in Figure 1-6. These classes include a *Bank* class, an *Account* class, and a *Customer* class. Associations between classes are shown with a line, with the option to specify the **cardinality** between the associations. For example, a customer can have one or more accounts, which is illustrated with the notation "1...*" (one to many). Classes may also have different types of relationships with each other. For example, the *Savings* and *Checking* account classes are both derived from the *Account* class, and they inherit the *Account* class's data members and operations. Inheritance is represented with an open triangle pointing to the parent class. Note that the *Checking* and *Savings* classes have their own *getBalance* functions, which **override**, or replace, the

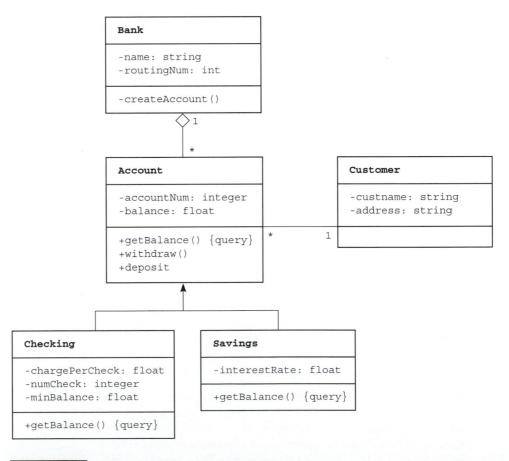

FIGURE 1-6   UML diagram for a banking system

getBalance function of the parent class, in order to make the necessary calculations for charges and interest. A class may also have a relationship with another class by containing an instance of that class as part of its definition. In the banking example, a bank contains one or more accounts. This type of relationship is called **containment** and is represented by positioning a diamond next to the containing class. Inheritance and containment are discussed in more detail in Chapter 8.

Advantages of an Object-Oriented Approach

The time that you expend on program design can increase when you use object-oriented programming (OOP). In addition, the solution that OOP techniques produce will typically be more general than is absolutely necessary to solve the problem at hand. The extra effort that OOP requires, however, is usually worth it.

When using object-oriented design in the solution to a problem, you need to identify the classes that are involved. You identify the purpose of each class and how it interacts with other classes. This leads to a specification for each class that identifies the operations and data. You then focus on the implementation details for each of the classes, including the use of top-down design to facilitate the development of the operations. It is easier to do the implementation when you focus on one class at a time.

Once you have implemented a class, you must test it at two different levels. First, you must test the class operations. This is usually done by writing a small program that calls the various operations and tests the results against the specifications provided for the operation. Once you have tested each individual class in this way, you should test scenarios in which the classes are expected to work together to solve the larger problem.

When you identify the classes involved in your solution, you will often find that you want a family of related classes. This stage of the design process is time-consuming, particularly if you have no existing classes upon which to build. Once you have implemented a class (called the **ancestor class**), the implementation of each new class (the **descendant class**) proceeds more rapidly, because you can reuse the properties and operations of the ancestor class. For example, as was mentioned earlier, once you have defined a class of clocks, you can design a class of alarm clocks that inherits the properties of a clock but adds operations to provide an alarm. The implementation of the class of alarm clocks would have been much more time-consuming if you did not have a class of clocks on which to base it. Looking ahead, you can reuse previously implemented classes in future programs, either as is or with modifications that can include new classes derived from your existing ones. This reuse of classes can actually reduce the time requirements of an object-oriented design.

OOP also has a positive effect on other phases of the software life cycle, such as program maintenance and verification. You can make

A family of related classes

Reuse existing classes

Program maintenance and verification are easier when you use inheritance

one modification to an ancestor class and affect all of its descendants. Without inheritance, you would need to make the same change to many modules. In addition, you can add new features to a program by adding descendant classes that do not affect their ancestors and, therefore, do not introduce errors into the rest of the program. You can also add a descendant class that modifies its ancestor's original behavior, even though that ancestor was written and compiled long ago.

1.3 A Summary of Key Issues in Programming

Given that a good solution is one that, in the course of its life cycle, incurs a small cost, the next questions to ask are, what are the specific characteristics of good solutions, and how can you construct good solutions? This section summarizes the answers to these very difficult questions.

The programming issues that this section discusses should be familiar to you. However, the novice programmer usually does not truly appreciate their importance. After the first course in programming, many students still simply want to "get the thing to run." The discussion that follows should help you realize just how important these issues really are.

One of the most widespread misconceptions held by novice programmers is that a computer program is "read" only by a computer. As a consequence, they tend to consider only whether the computer will be able to "understand" the program—that is, will the program compile, execute, and produce the correct output? The truth is, of course,

People read programs, too

that other people often must read and modify programs. In a typical programming environment, many individuals share a program. One person may write a program, which other people use in conjunction with other programs written by other people, and a year later, a different person may modify the program. It is therefore essential that you take great care to design a program that is easy to read and understand.

You should always keep in mind the following six issues of program structure and design:

KEY CONCEPTS

Six Key Programming Issues

1. Modularity
2. Modifiability
3. Ease of use
4. Fail-safe programming
5. Style
6. Debugging

Modularity

As this book will continually emphasize, you should strive for modularity in all phases of the problem-solving process, beginning with the initial design of a solution. You know from the earlier discussion of modular design that many programming tasks become more difficult as the size and complexity of a program grows. Modularity slows the rate at which the level of difficulty grows. More specifically, modularity has a favorable impact on the following aspects of programming:

- **Constructing the program.** The primary difference between a small modular program and a large modular program is simply the number of modules each contains. Because the modules are independent, writing one large modular program is not very different from writing many small, independent programs, although the interrelationships among modules make the design much more complicated. On the other hand, working on a large non-modular program is more like working on many interrelated programs simultaneously. Modularity also permits team programming, where several programmers work independently on their own modules before combining them into one program.

  Modularity facilitates programming

- **Debugging the program.** Debugging a large program can be a monstrous task. Imagine that you type a 10,000-line program and eventually get it to compile. Neither of these tasks would be much fun. Now imagine that you execute your program and, after a few hundred lines of output, you notice an incorrect number. You should anticipate spending the next day or so tracing through the intricacies of your program before discovering a problem such as an array index that is too large.

  Modularity isolates errors

  A great advantage of modularity is that the task of debugging a large program is reduced to one of debugging many small programs. When you begin to code a module, you should be almost certain that all other modules coded so far are correct. That is, before you consider a module finished, you should test it extensively, both separately and in context with the other modules, by calling it with actual arguments carefully chosen to induce all possible behaviors of the modules. If this testing is done thoroughly, you can feel fairly sure that any problem is a result of an error in the last module added. *Modularity isolates errors.*

  More theoretically, as was mentioned before, you can use formal methods to establish the correctness of a program. Modular programs are amenable to this verification process.

- **Reading the program.** A person reading a large program may have trouble seeing the forest for the trees. Just as a modular design helps the programmer cope with the complexities of solving a problem, so too will a modular program help its reader understand how the program works. A modular program is easy to follow because the reader can get a good idea of what

  Modular programs are easy to read

is going on without reading any of the code. A well-written function can be understood fairly well from only its name, initial comments, and the names of the other functions that it calls. Readers of a program need to study actual code only if they require a detailed understanding of how the program operates. Program readability is discussed further in the section on style later in this chapter.

Modularity isolates modifications

- **Modifying the program.** Modifiability is the topic of the next section, but as the modularity of a program has a direct bearing on its modifiability, a brief mention is appropriate here. A small change in the requirements of a program should require only a small change in the code. If this is not the case, it is likely that the program is poorly written and, in particular, that it is not modular. To accommodate a small change in the requirements, a modular program usually requires a change in only a few of its modules, particularly when the modules are independent (that is, loosely coupled) and each module performs a single well-defined task (that is, is highly cohesive).

  When making changes to a program, it is best to make a few at a time. By maintaining a modular design, you can reduce a fairly large modification to a set of small and relatively simple modifications to isolated parts of the program. *Modularity isolates modifications.*

Modularity eliminates redundancies

- **Eliminating redundant code.** Another advantage of modular design is that you can identify a computation that occurs in many different parts of the program and implement it as a function. Thus, the code for the computation will appear only once, resulting in an increase in both readability and modifiability. The example in the next section demonstrates this point.

Modifiability

Imagine that the specification for a program changes after some period of time. Frequently, people require that a program do something differently than they specified originally, or they ask that it do more than they requested originally. This section offers three examples of how you can make a program easy to modify: the use of functions, named *constants*, and *typedef* statements.

Functions. Suppose that a library uses a large program to catalog its books. At several points the program displays the information about a requested book. At each of these points, the program could include a *cout* statement to display the book's call number, author, and title. Alternatively, you could replace each occurrence of this statement with a call to a function *displayBook* that displays the same information about the book.

Not only does the use of the function have the obvious advantage of eliminating redundant code, it also makes the resulting program easier to modify. For example, to change the format of the output, you need to change only the implementation of *displayBook* instead of numerous occurrences of the *cout* statement. If you had not used a function, the modification would have required you to make changes at each point where the program displays the information. Merely finding each of these points could be difficult, and you probably would overlook a few. In this simple example, the advantages of using functions should be clear.

For another illustration, recall the earlier example of a solution that, as one of its tasks, sorted some data. Developing the sorting algorithm as an independent module and eventually implementing it as a function would make the program easier to modify. For instance, if you found that the sorting algorithm was too slow, you could replace the sort function without even looking at the rest of the program. You simply could "cut out" the old function and "paste in" the new one. If instead the sort was integrated into the program, the required surgery might be quite intricate.

In general, be concerned if you need to rewrite a program to accommodate small modifications. Usually, it is easy to modify a well-structured program slightly: Because each module solves only a small part of the overall problem, a small change in problem specifications usually affects only a few of the modules.

Named constants. The use of named constants is another way to enhance the modifiability of a program. For example, the restriction that an array must be of a predefined, fixed size causes a bit of difficulty. Suppose that a program uses an array to process the SAT scores of the computer science majors at your university. When the program was written, there were 202 computer science majors, so the array was declared by

```
int scores[202];
```

The program processes the array in several ways. For example, it reads the scores, writes the scores, and averages the scores. The pseudocode for each of these tasks contains a construct such as

```
for (index = 0 through 201)
    Process the score
```

If the number of majors should change, not only do you need to revise the declaration of *scores*, but you also must change each loop that processes the array to reflect the new array size. In addition, other statements in the program might depend on the size of the array. A 202 here, a 201 there—which to change?

On the other hand, if you use a named constant such as

```
const int NUMBER_OF_MAJORS = 202;
```

Functions make a program easier to modify

Named constants make a program easier to modify

you can declare the array by using

```
int scores[NUMBER_OF_MAJORS];
```

and write the pseudocode for the processing loops in this form:

```
for (index = 0 through NUMBER_OF_MAJORS - 1)
    Process the score
```

If you write expressions that depend on the size of the array in terms of the constant *NUMBER_OF_MAJORS* (such as *NUMBER_OF_MAJORS - 1*), you can change the array size simply by changing the definition of the constant and compiling the program again.

typedef statements make a program easier to modify

The *typedef* statement.   Suppose that your program performs floating-point computations of type *float*, but you discover that you need greater precision than *float* variables provide. To change the relevant *float* declarations to *long double*, for example, you would have to locate all such declarations and decide whether to make the change.

You can simplify this change by using a *typedef* statement, which gives another name to an existing data type. For example, the statement

```
typedef float RealType;
```

declares *RealType* as a synonym for *float* and allows you to use *RealType* and *float* interchangeably. If you declare all the relevant items in the previous program as *RealType* instead of *float*, you can make your program easier to modify and to read. To revise the precision of the computations, you would simply change the *typedef* statement to

```
typedef long double RealType;
```

Ease of Use

Another area in which you need to keep people in mind is the design of the user interface. Humans often process a program's input and output. Here are a few obvious points:

Prompt the user for input

- In an interactive environment, the program should always prompt the user for input in a manner that makes it quite clear what it expects. For example, the prompt "?" is not nearly as enlightening as the prompt "Please enter account number for deposit." You should never assume that the users of your program will know what response the program requires.

Echo the input

- A program should always echo its input. Whenever a program reads data, either from a user or from a file, the program should include the values it reads in its output. This inclusion serves two purposes: First, it gives the user a check on the data entered—a guard against typos and errors in data transmission. This check is particularly useful in the case of interactive input. Second, the output is more meaningful and self-explanatory when it contains a record of what input generated the output.

- The output should be well labeled and easy to read. An output of

Label the output

```
1800  6  1
Jones, Q.  223 2234.00 1088.19  N, J  Smith, T. 111
110.23 I,  Harris, V.  44  44000.00 22222.22
```

is more prone to misinterpretation than

```
CUSTOMER ACCOUNTS AS OF 1800 HOURS ON JUNE 1

Account status codes: N=new, J=joint, I=inactive

NAME          ACC#    CHECKING     SAVINGS      STATUS

Jones, Q.     223     $ 2234.00    $ 1088.19    N, J
Smith, T.     111     $  110.23    ---------    I
Harris, V.     44     $44000.00    $22222.22    ------
```

These characteristics of a good user interface are only the basics. Several more subtle points separate a program that is merely usable from one that is user friendly. Students tend to ignore a good user interface, but by investing a little extra time here, you can make a big difference: the difference between a good program and one that only solves the problem. For example, consider a program that requires a user to enter a line of data in some fixed format, with exactly one blank between the items. A free-form input that allows any number of blanks between the items would be much more convenient for the user. It takes so little time to add a loop that skips blanks, so why require the user to follow an exact format? Once you have made this small additional effort, it is a permanent part of both your program and your library of techniques. The user of your program never has to think about input format.

A good user interface is important

Fail-Safe Programming

A fail-safe program is one that will perform reasonably no matter how anyone uses it. Unfortunately, this goal is usually unattainable. A more realistic goal is to anticipate the ways that people might misuse the program and to guard carefully against these abuses.

This discussion considers two types of errors. The first type is an *error in input data*. For example, suppose that a program expects a non-negative integer but reads −12. When a program encounters this type of problem, it should not produce incorrect results or abort with a vague error message. Instead, a fail-safe program provides a message such as

Check for errors in input

```
-12 is not a valid number of children.
Please enter this number again.
```

The second type of error is an *error in the program logic*. Although a discussion of this type of error belongs in the debugging section at the end of this chapter, detecting errors in program logic is also an issue of fail-safe programming. A program that appears to have been running correctly may at some point behave unexpectedly, even if the data that it reads are valid. For example, the program may not have accounted for the particular data that elicited the surprise behavior, even though you tried your best to test the program's logic. Or perhaps you modified the program and that modification invalidated an assumption that you made in some other part of the program. Whatever the difficulty, a program should have built-in safeguards against these kinds of errors. It should monitor itself and be able to indicate that *something is wrong and you should not trust the results*.

Guarding against errors in input data.   Suppose that you are computing statistics about the people in income brackets between $10,000 and $100,000. The brackets are rounded to the nearest thousand dollars: $10,000, $11,000, and so on to $100,000. The raw data is a file of one or more lines of the form

G   N

where *N* is the number of people with an income that falls into the *G*-thousand-dollar group. If several people have compiled the data, several entries for the same value of *G* might occur. As the user enters data, the program must add up and record the number of people for each value of *G*. From the problem's context, it is clear that *G* is an integer in the range 10 to 100 inclusive, and *N* is a nonnegative integer.

As an example of how to guard against errors in input, consider an input function for this problem. The first attempt at writing this function will illustrate several common ways in which a program can fall short of the fail-safe ideal. Eventually you will see an input function that is much closer to the fail-safe ideal than the original solution.

A first attempt at the function might be

```cpp
const int LOW_END=10;   // low end of incomes
const int HIGH_END=100; // high end of incomes
const int TABLE_SIZE = HIGH_END - LOW_END + 1;
typedef int TableType[TABLE_SIZE];

int index(int group)
// Returns the array index that corresponds to group number.
{
    return group - LOW_END;
}  // end index
```

```
void readData(TableType incomeData)
// ----------------------------------------------------------
// Reads and organizes income statistics.
// Precondition: The calling module gives directions and
// prompts user. Input data is error-free and each input
// line is in the form G N, where N is the number of
// people with an income in the G-thousand-dollar group
// and LOW_END <= G <= HIGH_END. An input line with values
// of zero for both G and N terminates the input.
// Postcondition: incomeData[G-LOW_END] = total number of
// people with an income in the G-thousand-dollar group for
// each G read. The values read are displayed.
// ----------------------------------------------------------
{
   int group, number;                           // input values

   // clear array
   for (group = LOW_END; group <= HIGH_END; ++group)
      incomeData[index(group)] = 0;

   for (cin >> group >> number;
        (group != 0) || (number != 0);
        cin >> group >> number)
   {  // Invariant: group and number are not both 0
      cout << "Income group " << group << " contains "
           << number << " people.\n";
      incomeData[index(group)] += number;
   }  // end for
}  // end readData
```

This function is not fail-safe

This function has some problems. If an input line contains unexpected data, the program will not behave reasonably. Consider two specific possibilities:

- The first integer on the input line, which the function assigns to *group*, is not in the range *LOW_END* to *HIGH_END*. The reference *incomeData[index(group)]* will then be incorrect.

- The second number on the input line, which the function assigns to *number*, is negative. Although a negative value for *number* is invalid because you cannot have a negative number of people in an income group, the function will add *number* to the group's array entry. Thus, the array *incomeData* will be incorrect.

After the function reads values for *group* and *number*, it must check to see whether *group* is in the range *LOW_END* to *HIGH_END* and whether *number* is positive. If either value is not in that range, you must handle the input error.

Instead of checking *number*, you might think to check the value of *incomeData[index(group)]*, after adding *number*, to see whether it

Test for invalid input data

is positive. This approach is insufficient, however. First, notice that it is possible to add a negative value to an entry of *incomeData* without that entry becoming negative. For example, if *number* is $-4,000$ and the corresponding entry in *incomeData* is 10,000, the sum is 6,000. Thus, a negative value for *number* could remain undetected and invalidate the results of the rest of the program.

One possible course of action for the function to take when it detects invalid data is to set an error flag and terminate. Another possibility is for it to set an error flag, ignore the bad input line, and continue. Which action is correct really depends on how the program uses the data once it is read.

The following *readData* function attempts to be as universally applicable as possible and to make the program that uses it as modifiable as possible. When the function encounters an error in input, it sets a flag, ignores the data line, and continues. By setting a flag, the function leaves it to the calling module to determine the appropriate action— such as abort or continue—when an input error occurs. Thus, you can use the same input function in many contexts and can easily modify the action taken upon encountering an error.

A function that includes
fail-safe programming

```cpp
bool readData(TableType incomeData)
// ------------------------------------------------------------
// Reads and organizes income statistics.
// Precondition: The calling program gives directions and
// prompts the user. Each input line contains exactly two
// integers in the form G N, where N is the number of
// people with an income in the G-thousand-dollar group and
// LOW_END <= G <= HIGH_END. An input line with values of
// zero for both G and N terminates the input.
// Postcondition: incomeData[G-LOW_END] = total number of
// people with an income in the G-thousand-dollar group.
// The values read are displayed. If either G or N is
// erroneous (G and N are not both 0, and either G < LOW_END,
// G > HIGH_END, or N < 0), the function ignores the data
// line, sets the return value to false, and continues.
// In this case, the calling program should take action. The
// return value is true if the data is error free.
// ------------------------------------------------------------
{
   int group, number;  // input values
   bool dataCorrect = true;  // no data error found as yet

   for (group = LOW_END; group <= HIGH_END; ++group)
      incomeData[index(group)] = 0;

   for (cin >> group >> number;
        (group != 0) || (number != 0);
        cin >> group >> number)
```

```
{   // Invariant: group and number are not both 0
    cout << "Input line specifies that income group "
         << group << "\ncontains " << number
         << " people.\n";

    if ((group >= LOW_END) && (group <= HIGH_END) &&
        (number >= 0))
        // input data is valid -- add it to tally
        incomeData[index(group)] += number;

    else
        // error in input data: set error flag and
        // ignore input line
        dataCorrect = false;
}   // end for
return dataCorrect;
}   // end readData
```

Although this input function will behave gracefully in the face of most common input errors, it is not completely fail-safe. What happens if an input line contains only one integer? What happens if an input line contains a noninteger? The function would be more fail-safe if it read its input character by character, converted the characters to an integer, and checked for end of line. In most contexts, this processing would be a bit extreme. However, if the people who enter the data frequently err by typing nonintegers, you could alter the input function easily because the function is an isolated module. In any case, the function's initial comments should include any assumptions it makes about the data and an indication of what might make the program abort abnormally.

Guarding against errors in program logic. Now consider the second type of error that a program should guard against: errors in its own logic. These are errors that you may not have caught when you debugged the program or that you may have introduced through program modification.

Unfortunately, a program cannot reliably let you know when something is wrong with it. (Could you rely on a program to tell you that something is wrong with its mechanism for telling you that something is wrong?) You can, however, build into a program checks that ensure that certain conditions always hold when the program is correctly implementing its algorithm. As was mentioned earlier, such conditions are called invariants.

As a simple example of an invariant, consider again the previous example. *All integers in the array* `incomeData` *must be greater than or equal to zero.* Although the previous discussion argued that the function `readData` should not check the validity of the entries of `incomeData` instead of checking `number`, it could do so *in addition to* checking `number`. For example, if the function finds that an element in the array

Functions should check their invariants

incomeData is outside some range of believability, it can signal a potential problem to its users.

Another general way in which you should make a program fail-safe is to make each function check its precondition. For example, consider the following function, *factorial*, which returns the factorial of an integer:

```
int factorial(int n)
// --------------------------------------------------
// Computes the factorial of an integer.
// Precondition: n >= 0.
// Postcondition: Returns n * (n–1)*...*1, if n > 0;
// returns 1 if n = 0.
// --------------------------------------------------
{
   int fact = 1;

   for (int i = n; i > 1; --i)
      fact *= i;

   return fact;
}  // end factorial
```

The initial comments in this function contain a precondition— information about what assumptions are made—*as should always be the case.* The value that this function returns is valid only if the precondition is met. If *n* is less than zero, the function will return the incorrect value of 1.

In the context of the program for which this function was written, it may be reasonable to make the assumption that *n* will never be negative. That is, if the rest of the program is working correctly, it will call *factorial* only with correct values of *n*. Ironically, this last observation gives you a good reason for *factorial* to check the value of *n*: If *n* is less than zero, the warning that results from the check indicates that something may be wrong elsewhere in the program.

Another reason the function *factorial* should check whether *n* is less than zero is that the function should be correct outside the context of its program. That is, if you borrow the function for use in another program, the function should warn you if you use it incorrectly by passing it an *n* that is negative. A stronger check than simply the statement of the precondition in a comment is desirable. Thus, *a function should state its assumptions and, when possible, check that its arguments conform to these assumptions.*

In this example, *factorial* could check the value of *n* and, if it is negative, return zero, because factorials are never zero. The program that uses *factorial* could then check for this unusual value.

Alternatively, *factorial* could abort execution if its argument was negative. Many programming languages, including C++, support a mechanism for error handling called an **exception**. A module indicates that an error has occurred by **throwing** an exception. A module reacts to an exception that another module throws by **catching** the exception and executing code to deal with the error condition. Chapter 3 provides more information about exceptions.

C++ also provides a convenient macro `assert(expr)` that both displays an informative message and aborts a program if the expression `expr` is zero. You can use `assert` to check for both error conditions and the validity of preconditions within your program. Appendix C provides more information about `assert`.

Error handling is discussed further in the next section about programming style.

Style

This section considers the following eight issues of personal style in programming:

KEY CONCEPTS

Eight Issues of Style

1. Extensive use of functions

2. Use of private data members

3. Avoidance of global variables in functions

4. Proper use of reference arguments

5. Proper use of functions

6. Error handling

7. Readability

8. Documentation

Admittedly, much of the following discussion reflects the personal taste of the authors; certainly other good programming styles are possible.

Extensive use of functions. It is difficult to overuse functions. If a set of statements performs an identifiable, recurring task, it should be a function. However, a task need not be recurrent to justify the use of a function.

It is difficult to overuse functions

Although a program with all its code in-line runs faster than one that calls functions, programs without functions are not cheaper to use. The use of functions is cost-effective if you consider human time as a significant component of the program's cost. You have already seen the advantages of a modular program. In addition, compilers can reduce the time penalties for certain function calls by replacing them with in-line statements that perform the same tasks as the functions.

Use of private data members. Each object has a set of functions that represents the operations that can be performed on the object. The object also contains data members for storing information within the object. You should hide the exact representation of these data members from modules that use the object by making all of the data members private. Doing so supports the principle of information hiding. The details of the object's implementation are hidden from view, with functions providing the only mechanism for getting information to and from the object. Even when the only operations involved with a particular data member are retrieve and modify, the object should provide a simple function—called an **accessor**—that returns the value of the data member and another function—called a **mutator**—that sets the value of the data member. For example, a *Person* object could provide access to the data member *theName* through the functions *getName* to return the person's name and *setName* to change the person's name.

Avoidance of global variables in functions. One of the main advantages of functions is that they can implement the concept of an isolated module. This isolation is sacrificed when a function accesses a global variable, because the effects of a function's action are no longer self-contained or limited to output arguments. That is, such a function has a **side effect**. Hence, the isolation of both errors and modifications is greatly compromised when global variables appear in functions.

Do not use global variables

Proper use of reference arguments. A function does interact, in a controlled fashion, with the rest of the program via its arguments. **Value arguments**, which are the default when you do not write **&** after the formal argument's data type, pass values into the function, but any change that the function makes to these formal arguments is not reflected in the actual arguments back in the calling program. The communication between the calling program and the function is one-way. Because the restriction to one-way communication supports the notion of an isolated module, you should use value arguments when possible.

Value arguments pass values into a function

    When is it appropriate to use **reference arguments**? The obvious situation is when a function needs to return several values to the calling program. Another situation involves efficiency. Suppose that a function has an argument x whose value it does not alter. The natural choice is for x to be a value argument. However, invoking a function with a value argument x causes the function to copy the value of the actual argument that corresponds to x into temporary storage that is local to the function. This copying incurs very little overhead if x is a simple variable, but the computing time and storage required to copy a large object might be significant. However, if x were a reference argument, no copy of it would be made, and thus computer resources would be saved.

Reference arguments return values from a function

The problem with making x a reference argument is that it conveys misinformation about the function's relation to the rest of the program. By convention, you use a reference argument to communicate a value from the function back to the calling program. Reference arguments whose values remain unchanged, however, make the program more difficult to read and more prone to errors if modifications are required. The situation is analogous to using a variable whose value never changes when you really should use a constant. The solution is to precede the formal argument declaration with *const*, which prevents the function from changing the corresponding actual argument.

When copying the argument is expensive, use a *const* reference argument instead of a value argument

Proper use of functions. As you know, a **valued function** returns a value by using a *return* statement, whereas a ***void* function** does not. A valued function enables a programmer to write new *expressions*. Any time you need to calculate a value, you can call a user-defined valued function as if it were part of the language. This use corresponds to the mathematical notion of a function. Thus, *a valued function should never do anything but return a single result*. Imagine evaluating the expression $2 * x$ and having the values of five other variables change! That is, a valued function should not have a side effect.

In general, a valued function should not

- Use reference arguments. If you need reference arguments, use a *void* function.

- Perform input or output.

Generally, valued functions should not have side effects

Admittedly, certain situations encourage a relaxation of these restrictions, especially in C++. One such situation involves error handling, which is discussed next. In fact, many C++ standard functions return a value in addition to altering arguments. Often this value reflects the success or failure of the function.

Error handling. A fail-safe program checks for errors in both its input and its logic and attempts to behave gracefully when it encounters them. A function should check for certain types of errors, such as invalid input or argument values. What action should a function take when it encounters an error? Depending on context, the appropriate action in the face of an error can range from ignoring erroneous data and continuing execution to terminating the program. The function *readData* in the income statistics program earlier in this chapter returned a boolean value to the calling module to indicate that it had encountered an invalid line of data. Thus, the function left it to the calling module to decide on the appropriate action. In general, functions should either return a value or throw an exception instead of displaying a message when an error occurs.

In case of an error, functions should return a value or throw an exception, but not display a message

Readability. For a program to be easy to follow, it should have a good structure and design, a good choice of identifiers, good indentation and use of blank lines, and good documentation. You should avoid clever programming tricks that save a little computer time at the expense of much human time. You will see examples of these points in programs throughout the book.

Choose identifiers that describe their purpose, that is, are self-documenting. Distinguish between keywords, such as *int*, and user-defined identifiers. This book uses the following conventions:

Identifier style

- Keywords are lowercase and appear in boldface.

- Names of standard functions are lowercase.

- User-defined identifiers use both upper- and lowercase letters, as follows:

  □ Class names are nouns, with each word in the identifier capitalized.

  □ Function names within a class are verbs, with the first letter lowercase and subsequent internal words capitalized.

  □ Variables begin with a lowercase letter, with subsequent words in the identifier capitalized.

  □ Data types declared in a *typedef* statement and names of structures and enumerations each begin with an uppercase letter.

  □ Named constants and enumerators are entirely uppercase and use underscores to separate words.

- Two other naming conventions are followed as a learning aid:

Two learning aids

  □ Data types declared in a *typedef* statement end in *Type*.

  □ Exception names end in *Exception*.

Use a good indentation style to enhance the readability of a program. The layout of a program should make it easy for a reader to identify the program's modules. Use blank lines to offset each function. Also, within both functions and the main program, you should offset with blank lines and indent individual blocks of code visibly. These blocks are generally—but are not limited to—the actions performed within a control structure, such as a *while* loop or an *if* statement.

You can choose from among several good indentation styles. The four most important general requirements of an indentation style are that

Guidelines for indentation style

- Blocks should be indented sufficiently so that they stand out clearly.

- Indentation should be consistent: Always indent the same type of construct in the same manner.

- The indentation style should provide a reasonable way to handle the problem of **rightward drift**, the problem of nested blocks bumping against the right-hand margin of the page.

- In a compound statement, the open and closed braces should line up:

```
{   <statement1>
    <statement2>
         .
         .
         .
    <statementn>
}
```

Although it is preferable to place the open brace on its own line, space restrictions in this book prevent doing so except at the beginning of a function's body.

Within these guidelines there is room for personal taste. Here is a summary of the style you will see in this book:

- A *for* or *while* statement is written for a simple action as

Indentation style in this book

```
while (expression)
    statement
```

and for a compound action as

```
while (expression)
{   statements
}  // end while
```

- A *do* statement is written for a simple action as

```
do
    statement
while (expression);
```

and for a compound action as

```
do
{   statements
}  while (expression);
```

- An *if* statement is written for simple actions as

```
if (expression)
    statement1
else
    statement2
```

and for compound actions as

```
if (expression)
{   statements
}

else
{   statements
}   // end if
```

One special use of the *if* statement warrants another style. Nested *if* statements that choose among three or more different courses of action, such as

```
if (condition₁)
    action₁
else if (condition₂)
        action₂
        else if (condition₃)
            action₃
```

are written as

```
if (condition₁)
    action₁
else if (condition₂)
    action₂
else if (condition₃)
    action₃
```

This indentation style better reflects the nature of the construct, which is like a generalized *switch* statement:

```
case condition₁ : action₁; break;
case condition₂ : action₂; break;
case condition₃ : action₃; break;
```

- Braces are used to increase readability, even when they are not a syntactic necessity. For example, in the construct

```
while (expression)
{   if (condition₁)
        statement₁
    else
        statement₂
}   // end while
```

the braces are syntactically unnecessary because an *if* is a single statement. However, the braces highlight the scope of the *while* loop.

Documentation. A program should be well documented so that others can read, use, and modify it easily. Many acceptable styles for documentation are in use today, and exactly what you should include often depends on the particular program or your individual circumstances. The following are the essential features of any program's documentation:

Essential Features of Program Documentation

1. An initial comment for the program that includes

   a. Statement of purpose

   b. Author and date

   c. Description of the program's input and output

   d. Description of how to use the program

   e. Assumptions such as the type of data expected

   f. Statement of exceptions; that is, what could go wrong

   g. Brief description of the major classes

2. Initial comments in each class that state its purpose and describe the data contained in the class (constants and variables)

3. Initial comments in each function that state its purpose, preconditions, postconditions, and functions called

4. Comments in the body of each function to explain important features or subtle logic

Beginning programmers tend to downplay the importance of documentation because the computer does not read comments. By now, you should realize that people also read programs. Your comments must be clear enough for someone else to either use your function in a program or modify it. Thus, some of your comments are for people who want to use your function, while others are for people who will revise its implementation. You should distinguish between different kinds of comments.

Consider who will read your comments when you write them

Beginners have a tendency to document programs as a last step. You should, however, write documentation as you develop the program. Since the task of writing a large program might extend over a period of several weeks, you may find that the function that seemed so obvious when you wrote it last week will seem confusing when you try to revise it next week. Why not benefit from your own documentation by writing it now rather than later?

You benefit from your own documentation by writing it now instead of later

Debugging

No matter how much care you take in writing a program, it will contain errors that you need to track down. Fortunately, programs that are modular, clear, and well documented are generally amenable to debugging. Fail-safe techniques, which guard against certain errors and report them when they are encountered, are also a great aid in debugging.

Many students seem to be totally baffled by errors in their programs and have no idea how to proceed. These students simply have not learned to track down errors systematically. Without a systematic approach, finding a small mistake in a large program can indeed be a difficult task.

The difficulty that many people have in debugging a program is perhaps due in part to a desire to believe that their program is really doing what it is supposed to do. For example, on receiving an execution-time error message at line 1098, a student might say, "That's impossible. The statement at line 1098 was not even executed, because it is in the `else` clause, and I am positive that it was not executed." This student must do more than simply protest. The proper approach is either to trace the program's execution by using available debugging facilities or to add `cout` statements that show which part of the `if` statement was executed. By doing so, you verify the value of the expression in the `if` statement. If the expression is 0 when you expect it to be 1, the next step is to determine how it became 0.

How can you find the point in a program where something becomes other than what it should be? Typically, a programming environment allows you to trace a program's execution either by single-stepping through the statements in the program or by setting breakpoints at which execution will halt. You also can examine the contents of particular variables by either establishing watches or inserting temporary `cout` statements. The key to debugging is simply to use these techniques to tell you what is going on. This may sound pretty mundane, but the real trick is to use these debugging aids in an effective manner. After all, you do not simply put breakpoints, watches, and `cout` statements at random points in the program and have them report random information.

Use either watches or temporary `cout` statements to find logic errors

The main idea is systematically to locate the points of the program that cause the problem. A program's logic implies that certain conditions should be true at various points in the program. (Recall that these conditions are called invariants.) If the program's results differ from your expectations as stated in the invariants (you *did* write invariants, didn't you?), an error occurs. To correct the error, you must find the first point in the program at which this difference is evident. By inserting either breakpoints and watches or `cout` statements at strategic locations of a program—such as at the entry and departure points of loops and functions—you can systematically isolate the error.

Systematically check a program's logic to determine where an error occurs

These diagnostic techniques should inform you whether things start going wrong before or after a given point in the program. Thus, after you run the program with an initial set of diagnostics, you should be able to trap the error between two points. For example, suppose that things are fine before you call function F_1, but something is wrong by the time you call F_2. This kind of information allows you to focus your attention between these two points. You continue the process until eventually the search is limited to only a few statements. There is really no place in a program for an error to hide.

The ability to place breakpoints, watches, and *cout* statements in appropriate locations and to have them report appropriate information comes in part from thinking logically about the problem and in part from experience. Here are a few general guidelines.

Debugging functions. You should examine the values of a function's arguments at its beginning and end by using either watches or *cout* statements. Ideally, you should debug each major function separately before using it in your program.

Debugging loops. You should examine the values of key variables at the beginnings and ends of loops, as the comments in this example indicate:

```
// check values of start and stop before entering loop
for (index = start; index <= stop; ++index)
{   // check values of index and key variables
    // at the beginning of iteration

        .
        .
        .


    // check values of index and key variables
    // at the end of iteration
}   // end for
// check values of start and stop after exiting loop
```

Debugging *if* statements. Just before an *if* statement, you should examine the values of the variables within its expression. You can use either breakpoints or *cout* statements to determine which branch the *if* statement takes, as this example indicates:

```
// check variables within expression before executing if
if (expression)
{   cout << "Condition is true (value of expression is 1).";
    . . .
}

else
{   cout << "Condition is false (value of expression is 0).";
    . . .
}   // end if
```

Using *cout* statements. Sometimes *cout* statements can be more convenient than watches. Such *cout* statements should report both the values of key variables and the location in the program at which the variables have those values. You can use a comment to label the location, as follows:

```
// This is point A
cout << "At point A in the function computeResults:\n"
     << "x=" << x << ", y=" << y << endl;
```

Remember to either disable or remove these statements when your program finally works.

Using special dump functions. Often the variables whose values you wish to examine are arrays or other, more complex data structures. If so, you should write dump functions to display the data structures in a highly readable manner. You can easily move the single statement that calls each dump function from one point in the program to another as you track down an error. The time you spend on these functions often proves to be worthwhile, as you can call them repeatedly while debugging different parts of the program.

Hopefully, this discussion has conveyed the importance of the *effective use of diagnostic aids in debugging*. Even the best programmers have to spend some time debugging. Thus, to be a truly good programmer, you must be a good debugger.

Summary

1. Software engineering is a branch of computer science that studies ways to facilitate the development of computer programs.

2. The life cycle of software consists of several phases: specifying the problem, designing the algorithm, analyzing the risks, verifying the algorithm, coding the programs, testing the programs, refining the solution, using the software, and maintaining the software.

3. A loop invariant is a property of an algorithm that is true before and after each iteration of a loop. Loop invariants are useful in developing iterative algorithms and establishing their correctness.

4. When evaluating the quality of a solution, you must consider a diverse set of factors: the solution's correctness, its efficiency, the time that went into its development, its ease of use, and the cost of modifying and expanding it.

5. A combination of object-oriented and top-down design techniques will lead to a modular solution. For problems that primarily involve data management, encapsulate data with operations on that data by designing classes. The nouns in the problem statement can help you identify appropriate classes. Break algorithmic tasks into independent subtasks that you gradually refine. In all cases, practice abstraction; that is, focus on what a module does instead of how it does it.

6. UML is a modeling language used to express object-oriented designs. It provides a notation to specify the data and operations and uses diagrams to show relationships among classes.

7. Take great care to ensure that your final solution is as easy to modify as possible. Generally, a modular program is easy to modify because changes in the program's requirements frequently affect only a handful of the modules. Programs should not depend on the particular implementations of its modules.

8. A function should be as independent as possible and perform one well-defined task.

9. A function should always include an initial comment that states its purpose, its precondition—that is, the conditions that must exist at the beginning of a module—and its postcondition—the conditions at the end of a module.

10. A program should be as fail-safe as possible. For example, a program should guard against errors in input and errors in its own logic. By checking invariants—which are conditions that are true at certain points in a program—you can monitor correct program execution.

11. The effective use of available diagnostic aids is one of the keys to debugging. You should use watches or *cout* statements to report the values of key variables at key locations. These locations include the beginnings and ends of functions and loops, and the branches of selection statements.

12. To make it easier to examine the contents of arrays and other, more complex data structures while debugging, you should write dump functions that display the contents of the data structures. You can easily move calls to such functions as you track down an error.

Cautions

1. Your programs should guard against errors. A fail-safe program checks that an input value is within some acceptable range and reports if it is not. An error in input should not cause a program to terminate before it clearly reports what the error was. A fail-safe program also attempts to detect errors in its own logic. For example, in many situations functions should check that their arguments have valid values.

2. You can write better, correct programs in less time if you pay attention to the following guidelines: Write precise specifications for the program. Use a modular design. Write pre- and postconditions for each function before you implement them. Use meaningful identifiers and consistent indentation. Write comments, including assertions and invariants.

Self-Test Exercises

The answers to all Self-Test Exercises are at the back of this book.

1. What is the loop invariant for the following?

```
int index = 0;
int sum = item[0];

while (index < n)
{   ++index;
    sum += item[index];
}   //end while
```

2. Write specifications using UML notation for a function that computes the sum of the first five positive integers in an array of *n* arbitrary integers.

Exercises

1. The price of an item you want to buy is given in dollars and cents. You pay for it in cash by giving the clerk *d* dollars and *c* cents. Write specifications for a function that computes the change, if any, that you should receive. Include a statement of purpose, the pre- and postconditions, and a description of the arguments.

2. A date consists of a month, day, and year. Frequently, we represent each of these items as integers. For example, July 4, 1776, is month 7, day 4, and year 1776.

   a. Write specifications for a function that advances any given date by one day. Include a statement of purpose, the pre- and postconditions, and a description of the arguments.

   b. Write a C++ implementation of this function. Design and specify any other functions that you need. Include comments that will be helpful to someone who will maintain your implementation in the future.

3. Consider the following program, which interactively reads and writes the identification number, age, salary (in thousands of dollars), and name of each individual in a group of employees. How can you improve the program? Some of the issues are obvious, others are more subtle. Try to keep in mind all of the topics discussed in this chapter.

```
int main()
{
    int x1, x2, x3, i;
    char name[8];
```

```
for (cin >> x1 >> x2 >> x3; x1 != 0;
     cin >> x1 >> x2 >> x3)
{  for (i = 0; i < 8; ++i)
       cin >> name[i];

   cout << x1 << x2 << x3 << endl;

   for (i = 0; i < 8; ++i)
       cout << name[i];
   cout << endl;
}  // end for
   return 0;
}  // end main
```

4. What is the problem with the following code fragment?

```
num = 50;
while (num >= 0)
{
    cout << num << endl;
    num = num + 1;
}
```

5. This chapter stressed the importance of adding fail-safe checks to a program wherever possible. What can go wrong with the following function? How can you protect yourself?

```
double compute(double x)
{
    return sqrt(x)/cos(x);
}  // end compute
```

6. Write the loop invariants for the function *factorial*, which appears in the section "Fail-Safe Programming."

7. Write the loop invariant for the following:

```
int i = 20;
while (i > 1)
    i--;
```

8. Using a *for* loop, write a program that displays the squares of all integers greater than 0 and less than or equal to a given number *n*.

9. Write the function that Self-Test Exercise 2 describes, and state the loop invariants.

10. By using loop invariants, demonstrate that the algorithm in Self-Test Exercise 1 correctly computes *item[0]* + *item[1]* + · · · + *item[n]*.

11. The following program is supposed to compute the **floor** of the square root of its input value *x*. (The floor of a number *n* is the largest integer less than or equal to *n*.)

```
// Computes and writes floor(sqrt(x)) for
// an input value x >= 0.
int main()
{
   int x;   // input value

   // initialize
   int result = 0;  // will equal floor of sqrt(x)
   int temp1 = 1;
   int temp2 = 1;

   cin >> x;           // read input

   // compute floor
   while (temp1 < x)
   {   ++result;
       temp2 += 2;
       temp1 += temp2;
   }   // end while

   cout << "The floor of the square root of "
        << x << " is " << result << endl;
   return 0;
}   // end main
```

This program contains an error.

a. What output does the program produce when *x* = 64?

b. Run the program and remove the error. Describe the steps you took to find the error.

c. How can you make the program more user friendly and fail-safe?

12. Suppose that, due to some severe error, you must abort a program from a location deep inside nested function calls, *while* loops, and *if* statements. Write a diagnostic function that you can call from anywhere in a program. This function should take an error code as an argument (some mnemonic enumeration), display an appropriate error message, and terminate program execution.

Programming Problems

1. Add a *Transaction* class to the banking example in the section "Modeling Object-Oriented Design Using UML." This class keeps track of the date, time, amount, and type of transaction (checking or savings).

2. Consider a program that will read employee information into an array of structures, sort the array by employee identification number, write out the sorted array, and compute various statistics on the data, such as the average age of an employee. Write complete specifications using UML notation for this problem and design a modular solution. What functions did you identify during the design of your solution? Write specifications, including preconditions and postconditions, for each function.

3. Revise the UML diagram in Programming Problem 2 to reflect an object-oriented design. For example, instead of using an array of structures, you might design *Employee* and *EmployeeStats* classes with the appropriate functions.

4. Write a program that sorts and evaluates bridge hands. The input is a stream of character pairs that represent playing cards. For example,

```
2C  QD  TC  AD  6C  3D  TD  3H  5H  7H  AS  JH  KH
```

represents the 2 of clubs, queen of diamonds, 10 of clubs, ace of diamonds, and so on. Each pair consists of a rank followed by a suit, where rank is A, 2, . . . , 9, T, J, Q, or K, and suit is C, D, H, or S. You can assume each input line represents exactly 13 cards and is error-free. Input is terminated by an end of file.

For each line of input, form a hand of 13 cards. Display each hand in a readable form arranged both by suits and by rank within suit (aces are high). Then evaluate the hand by using the following standard bridge values:

Aces count 4

Kings count 3

Queens count 2

Jacks count 1

Voids (no cards in a suit) count 3

Singletons (one card in a suit) count 2

Doubletons (two cards in a suit) count 1

Long suits with more than 5 cards in the suit
  count 1 for each card over 5 in number

For example, for the previous sample input line, the program should produce the output

```
CLUBS         10    6    2
DIAMONDS      A     Q    10   3
HEARTS        K     J    7    5    3
SPADES        A
Points = 16
```

because there are two aces, one king, one queen, one jack, one singleton, no doubletons, and no long suits. (The singleton ace of spades counts as both an ace and a singleton.)

Optional: See how much more flexible and fail-safe you can make your program. That is, try to remove as many of the previous assumptions in input as you can.

5. Write a program that will act as an interactive calculator capable of handling very large (larger than the largest *long* integer) nonnegative integers. This calculator need perform only the operations of addition and multiplication.

In this program, each input line is of the form

num_1 *op* num_2

and should produce output such as

```
      num₁
op    num₂
--------
      num₃
```

where num_1 and num_2 are (possibly very large) nonnegative integers, *op* is the single character + or *, and num_3 is the integer that results from the desired calculation.

Design your program carefully. You will need the following:

- A data structure to represent large numbers: for example, an array of digits in a number.

- A function to read in numbers. Skip leading zeros. Do not forget that zero is a valid number.

- A function to write numbers. Do not write leading zeros, but if the number consists of all zeros, write a single zero.

- A function to add two numbers.

- A function to multiply two numbers.

In addition, you should

- Check for overflow (numbers with more than `MAX_SIZE` digits) when reading, adding, and multiplying numbers.

- Have a good user interface.

Optional: Allow signed integers (negative as well as positive integers) and write a function for subtraction.

CHAPTER 2

Recursion: The Mirrors

PREVIEW

The goal of this chapter is to ensure that you have a basic understanding of recursion, which is one of the most powerful methods of solution available to the computer scientist. This chapter assumes that you have had little or no previous introduction to recursion. If, however, you have already studied recursion, you can review this chapter as necessary.

By presenting several relatively simple problems, the chapter demonstrates the thought processes that lead to recursive solutions. These problems are diverse and include examples of counting, searching, and organizing data. In addition to presenting recursion from a conceptual viewpoint, this chapter discusses methods that will help you understand the mechanics of recursion. These methods are particularly useful for tracing and debugging recursive functions.

Some recursive solutions are far more elegant and concise than the best of their nonrecursive counterparts. For example, the classic Towers of Hanoi problem appears to be quite difficult, yet it has an extremely simple recursive solution. On the other hand, some recursive solutions are terribly inefficient, as you will see, and should not be used.

Chapter 5 continues the formal discussion of recursion by examining more difficult problems. Recursion will play a major role in many of the solutions that appear throughout the remainder of this book.

2.1 Recursive Solutions

Recursion is an extremely powerful problem-solving technique. Problems that at first appear to be quite difficult often have simple recursive solutions. Like top-down design, recursion breaks a problem into several smaller problems. What is striking about recursion is that these smaller problems are of *exactly the same type* as the original problem—mirror images, so to speak.

Recursion breaks a problem into smaller identical problems

Did you ever hold a mirror in front of another mirror so that the two mirrors face each other? You will see many images of yourself, each behind and slightly smaller than the other. Recursion is like these mirror images. That is, a recursive solution solves a problem by solving a smaller instance of the same problem! It solves this new problem by solving an even smaller instance of the same problem. Eventually, the new problem will be so small that its solution will be either obvious or known. This solution will lead to the solution of the original problem.

For example, suppose that you could solve problem P_1 if you had the solution to problem P_2, which is a smaller instance of P_1. Suppose further that you could solve problem P_2 if you had the solution to problem P_3, which is a smaller instance of P_2. If you knew the solution to P_3 because it was small enough to be trivial, you would be able to solve P_2. You could then use the solution to P_2 to solve the original problem P_1.

Some recursion solutions are inefficient and impractical

Complex problems can have simple recursive solutions

Recursion can seem like magic, especially at first, but as you will see, recursion is a very real and important problem-solving approach that is an alternative to **iteration**. An iterative solution involves loops. You should know at the outset that not all recursive solutions are better than iterative solutions. In fact, some recursive solutions are impractical because they are so inefficient. Recursion, however, can provide elegantly simple solutions to problems of great complexity.

As an illustration of the elements in a recursive solution, consider the problem of looking up a word in a dictionary. Suppose you wanted to look up the word "vademecum." Imagine starting at the beginning of the dictionary and looking at every word in order until you found "vademecum." That is precisely what a **sequential search** does, and, for obvious reasons, you want a faster way to perform the search.

One such method is the **binary search**, which in spirit is similar to the way in which you actually use a dictionary. You open the dictionary—probably to a point near its middle—and by glancing at the page, determine which "half" of the dictionary contains the desired word. The following pseudocode is a first attempt to formalize this process:

A binary search of a dictionary

```
// Search a dictionary for a word by using a recursive
// binary search

if (the dictionary contains only one page)
```

```
      Scan the page for the word
  else
  {  Open the dictionary to a point near the middle
     Determine which half of the dictionary contains the word
     if (the word is in the first half of the dictionary)
        Search the first half of the dictionary for the word
     else
        Search the second half of the dictionary for the word
  }
```

Parts of this solution are intentionally vague: How do you scan a single page? How do you find the middle of the dictionary? Once the middle is found, how do you determine which half contains the word? The answers to these questions are not difficult, but they will only obscure the solution strategy right now.

The previous search strategy reduces the problem of searching the dictionary for a word to a problem of searching half of the dictionary for the word, as Figure 2-1 illustrates. Notice two important points. First, once you have divided the dictionary in half, you already know how to search the appropriate half: You can use exactly the same strategy that you employed to search the original dictionary. Second, note that there is a special case that is different from all the other cases: After you have divided the dictionary so many times that you are left with only a single page, the halving ceases. At this point, the problem is sufficiently small that you can solve it directly by scanning the single page that remains for the word. This special case is called the base case (or **basis** or **degenerate case**).

This strategy is one of **divide and conquer**. You solve the dictionary search problem by first *dividing* the dictionary into two halves and then *conquering* the appropriate half. You solve the smaller problem by using the same divide-and-conquer strategy. The dividing continues until you reach the base case. As you will see, this strategy is inherent in many recursive solutions.

To further explore the nature of the solution to the dictionary problem, consider a slightly more rigorous formulation.

A base case is a special case whose solution you know

A binary search uses a divide-and-conquer strategy

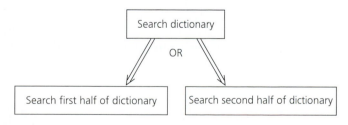

FIGURE 2-1   A recursive solution

```
search(in aDictionary:Dictionary, in word: string)

    if (aDictionary is one page in size)
       Scan the page for word
    else
    {  Open aDictionary to a point near the middle
       Determine which half of aDictionary contains word

       if (word is in the first half of aDictionary)
          search(first half of aDictionary, word)
       else
          search(second half of aDictionary, word)
    }
```

Writing the solution as a function allows several important observations:

A recursive function calls itself

1. One of the actions of the function is to call itself; that is, the function *search* calls the function *search*. This action is what makes the solution recursive. The solution strategy is to split *aDictionary* in half, determine which half contains *word*, and apply the same strategy to the appropriate half.

Each recursive call solves an identical, but smaller, problem

2. Each call to the function *search* made from within the function *search* passes a dictionary that is one-half the size of the previous dictionary. That is, at each successive call to *search(aDictionary, word)*, the size of *aDictionary* is cut in half. The function solves the search problem by solving another search problem that is identical in nature but smaller in size.

A test for the base case enables the recursive calls to stop

3. There is one search problem that you handle differently from all of the others. When *aDictionary* contains only a single page, you use another method: You scan the page directly. Searching a one-page dictionary is the base case of the search problem. When you reach the base case, the recursive calls stop and you solve the problem directly.

Eventually, one of the smaller problems must be the base case

4. The manner in which the size of the problem diminishes ensures that you will eventually reach the base case.

These facts describe the general form of a recursive solution. Though not all recursive solutions fit these criteria as nicely as this solution does, the similarities are far greater than the differences. As you attempt to construct a new recursive solution, you should keep in mind the following four questions:

KEY CONCEPTS

Four Questions for Constructing Recursive Solutions

1. How can you define the problem in terms of a smaller problem of the same type?

2. How does each recursive call diminish the size of the problem?

3. What instance of the problem can serve as the base case?

4. As the problem size diminishes, will you reach this base case?

Now consider two relatively simple problems: computing the factorial of a number and writing a string backward. Their recursive solutions further illustrate the points raised by the solution to the dictionary search problem. These examples also illustrate the difference between a recursive valued function and a recursive *void* function.

A Recursive Valued Function: The Factorial of *n*

Consider a recursive solution to the problem of computing the factorial of an integer *n*. This problem is a good first example because its recursive solution is easy to understand and neatly fits the mold described earlier. However, because the problem has a simple and efficient iterative solution, you should not use the recursive solution in practice.

To begin, consider the familiar iterative definition of *factorial*(*n*) (more commonly written *n*!):

$$factorial(n) = n * (n - 1) * (n - 2) * \cdots * 1 \text{ for any integer } n > 0$$

$$factorial(0) = 1$$

The factorial of a negative integer is undefined. You should have no trouble writing an iterative factorial function based on this definition.

To define *factorial*(*n*) recursively, you first need to define *factorial*(*n*) in terms of the factorial of a smaller number. To do so, simply observe that the factorial of *n* is equal to the factorial of (*n* − 1) multiplied by *n;* that is,

$$factorial(n) = n * [(n - 1) * (n - 2) * \cdots * 1]$$
$$= n * factorial(n - 1)$$

Do not use recursion if a problem has a simple, efficient iterative solution

An iterative definition of factorial

A recurrence relation

The definition of *factorial*(*n*) in terms of *factorial*(*n* − 1), which is an example of a **recurrence relation**, implies that you can also define *factorial*(*n* − 1) in terms of *factorial*(*n* − 2), and so on. This process is analogous to the dictionary search solution, in which you search a dictionary by searching a smaller dictionary in exactly the same way.

The definition of *factorial*(*n*) lacks one key element: the base case. As was done in the dictionary search solution, here you must define one case differently from all the others, or else the recursion will never stop. The base case for the factorial function is *factorial*(0), which you know is 1. Because *n* originally is greater than or equal to zero and each call to *factorial* decrements *n* by 1, you will always reach the base case. With the addition of the base case, the complete recursive definition of the factorial function is

$$factorial(n) = \begin{cases} 1 & \text{if } n = 0 \\ n * factorial(n-1) & \text{if } n > 0 \end{cases}$$

A recursive definition of factorial

To be sure that you understand this recursive definition, apply it to the computation of *factorial*(4). Since 4 > 0, the recursive definition states that

factorial(4) = 4 * *factorial*(3)

Similarly,

factorial(3) = 3 * *factorial*(2)

factorial(2) = 2 * *factorial*(1)

factorial(1) = 1 * *factorial*(0)

You have reached the base case, and the definition directly states that

factorial(0) = 1

At this point, the application of the recursive definition stops and you still do not know the answer to the original question: What is *factorial*(4)? However, the information to answer this question is now available:

Since *factorial*(0) = 1, then *factorial*(1) = 1 * 1 = 1

Since *factorial*(1) = 1, then *factorial*(2) = 2 * 1 = 2

Since *factorial*(2) = 2, then *factorial*(3) = 3 * 2 = 6

Since *factorial*(3) = 6, then *factorial*(4) = 4 * 6 = 24

You can think of recursion as a process that divides a problem into a task that you can do and a task that a friend can do for you. For example, if I ask you to compute *factorial*(4), you could first determine whether you know the answer immediately. You know immediately that *factorial*(0) is 1—that is, you know the base case—but you do not know the value of *factorial*(4) immediately. However, if your friend computes *factorial*(3) for you, you could compute *factorial*(4) by multiplying *factorial*(3) and 4. Thus, your task will be to do this multiplication, and your friend's task will be to compute *factorial*(3).

Your friend now uses the same process to compute *factorial*(3) as you are using to compute *factorial*(4). Thus, your friend determines that *factorial*(3) is not the base case, and so asks another friend to compute *factorial*(2). Knowing *factorial*(2) enables your friend to compute *factorial*(3), and when you learn the value of *factorial*(3) from your friend, you can compute *factorial*(4).

Notice that the recursive definition of *factorial*(4) yields the same result as the iterative definition, which gives 4 * 3 * 2 * 1 = 24. To prove that the two definitions of *factorial* are equivalent for all nonnegative integers, you would use mathematical induction. (See Appendix D.) Chapter 5 discusses the close tie between recursion and mathematical induction.

The recursive definition of the factorial function has illustrated two points: (1) *Intuitively*, you can define *factorial*(n) in terms of *factorial*(n − 1), and (2) *mechanically*, you can apply the definition to determine the value of a given factorial. Even in this simple example, applying the recursive definition required quite a bit of work. That, of course, is where the computer comes in.

Once you have a recursive definition of *factorial*(n), it is easy to construct a C++ function that implements the definition:

```cpp
int fact(int n)
// ----------------------------------------------------
// Computes the factorial of a nonnegative integer.
// Precondition: n must be greater than or equal to 0.
// Postcondition: Returns the factorial of n; n is
// unchanged.
// ----------------------------------------------------
{
   if (n == 0)
      return 1;
   else
      return n * fact(n-1);
}  // end fact
```

Suppose that you use the statement

```cpp
cout << fact(3);
```

to call the function. Figure 2-2 depicts the sequence of computations that this call would require.

This function fits the model of a recursive solution given earlier in this chapter as follows:

1. One action of *fact* is to *call itself*.

2. At each recursive call to *fact*, the integer whose factorial you need to compute is *diminished by 1*.

fact satisfies the four criteria of a recursive solution

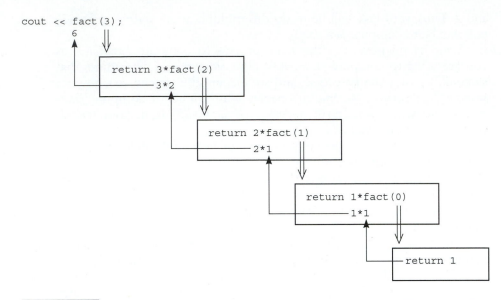

FIGURE 2-2   *fact(3)*

3. The function handles the factorial of 0 differently from all the other factorials: It does not generate a recursive call. Rather, you know that *fact(0)* is 1. Thus, the *base case* occurs when *n* is 0.

4. Given that *n* is nonnegative, item 2 of this list assures you that you will always *reach the base case*.

At an intuitive level, it should be clear that the function *fact* implements the recursive definition of *factorial*. Now consider the mechanics of executing this recursive function. The logic is straightforward except perhaps for the expression in the *else* clause. This expression has the following effect:

1. Each operand of the product *n * fact(n-1)* is evaluated.

2. The second operand—*fact(n-1)*—is a call to the function *fact*. Although this is a recursive call (the function *fact* calls the function *fact*), there really is nothing special about it. Imagine substituting a call to another function—the standard function *abs*, for example—for the recursive call to *fact*. The principle is the same: Simply evaluate the function.

In theory, evaluating a recursive function is no more difficult than evaluating a nonrecursive function. In practice, however, the bookkeeping can quickly get out of hand. The **box method** is a systematic way to trace the actions of a recursive function. You can use the box method both to help you understand recursion and to debug recursive functions. However, such a mechanical device is no substitute for an intuitive understanding of recursion. The box method illustrates how compilers frequently implement recursion. As you read the following description of the method, realize that each box roughly corresponds to an **activation record**, which a compiler typically uses in its implementation of a function call. Chapter 6 will discuss this implementation further.

The box method. The box method is illustrated here for the recursive function *fact*. As you will see in the next section, this method is somewhat simpler for a *void* function, as no value needs to be returned.

1. Label each recursive call in the body of the recursive function. Several recursive calls might occur within a function, and it will be important to distinguish among them. These labels help you keep track of the correct place to which you must return after a function call completes. For example, mark the expression *fact(n-1)* within the body of the function with the letter A:

   ```
   if (n == 0)
       return 1;
   else
       return n * fact(n-1);
                     Ⓐ
   ```

   You return to point A after each recursive call, substitute the computed value for *fact(n-1)*, and continue execution by evaluating the expression *n * fact(n-1)*.

2. Represent each call to the function during the course of execution by a new box in which you note the **local environment of the function**. More specifically, each box will contain

   a. The value arguments of the formal argument list.

   b. The function's local variables.

   c. A placeholder for the value returned by each recursive call from the current box. Label this placeholder to correspond to the labeling in Step 1.

   d. The value of the function itself.

   When you first create a box, you will know only the values of the input arguments. You fill in the values of the other items as you determine them from the function's execution. For example, you would create the box in Figure 2-3 for the call *fact(3)*. (You will see in later examples that you must handle reference arguments somewhat differently from value arguments and local variables.)

   ```
   n = 3
   A: fact(n-1) = ?
   return ?
   ```

   FIGURE 2-3 A box

3. Draw an arrow from the statement that initiates the recursive process to the first box. Then, when you create a new box after a recursive call, as described in Step 2, you draw an arrow from the box that makes the call to the newly created box. Label each arrow to correspond to the label (from Step 1) of the recursive call; this label indicates exactly where to return after the call

completes. For example, Figure 2-4 shows the first two boxes generated by the call to *fact* in the statement *cout << fact(3)*.

4. After you create the new box and arrow as described in Steps 2 and 3, start executing the body of the function. Each reference to an item in the function's local environment references the corresponding value in the current box, regardless of how you generated the current box.

5. On exiting the function, cross off the current box and follow its arrow back to the box that called the function. This box now becomes the current box, and the label on the arrow specifies the exact location at which execution of the function should continue. Substitute the value returned by the just-terminated function call into the appropriate item in the current box.

Figure 2-5 is a complete box trace for the call *fact(3)*. In the sequence of diagrams in this figure, the current box is the deepest along the path of arrows and is shaded, whereas crossed-off boxes are dashed.

Invariants. Writing invariants for recursive functions is as important as writing them for iterative functions, and often is simpler. For example, consider the recursive function *fact*:

```
int fact(int n)
// Precondition: n must be greater than or equal to 0.
// Postcondition: Returns the factorial of n.
{
    if (n == 0)
        return 1;
    else   // Invariant: n > 0, so n-1 >= 0.
            // Thus, fact(n-1) returns (n-1)!
        return n * fact(n-1);   // n * (n-1)! is n!
}  // end fact
```

The function requires as its precondition a nonnegative value of *n*. At the time of the recursive call *fact(n-1)*, *n* is positive, so $n - 1$ is nonnegative. Because the recursive call satisfies *fact*'s precondition, you can expect from the postcondition that *fact(n-1)* will return the factorial of $n - 1$. Therefore, *n * fact(n-1)* is the factorial of *n*. Chapter 5

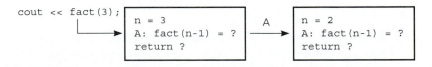

FIGURE 2-4   The beginning of the box method

uses mathematical induction to prove formally that `fact(n)` returns the factorial of *n*.

If you ever violated `fact`'s precondition, the function would not behave correctly. That is, if the calling program ever passed a negative value to `fact`, an infinite sequence of recursive calls, terminated only by a system-defined limit, would occur because the function would never reach the base case. For example, `fact(-4)` would call `fact(-5)`, which would call `fact(-6)`, and so on.

The function ideally should protect itself by testing for a negative *n*. If *n* < 0, the function could, for example, either return 0 or set an error flag. Chapter 1 discussed error checking in the two sections "Fail-Safe Programming" and "Style"; you might want to review that discussion at this time.

Violating `fact`'s precondition causes "infinite" recursion

A Recursive *void* Function: Writing a String Backward

Now consider a problem that is slightly more difficult: Given a string of characters, write it in reverse order. For example, write the string "cat" as "tac". To construct a recursive solution, you should ask the four questions in the Key Concepts box on page 57.

The initial call is made, and method `fact` begins execution:

```
n = 3
A: fact(n-1)=?
return ?
```

At point A a recursive call is made, and the new invocation of the method `fact` begins execution:

```
n = 3          A    n = 2
A: fact(n-1)=?  ──►  A: fact(n-1)=?
return ?             return ?
```

At point A a recursive call is made, and the new invocation of the method `fact` begins execution:

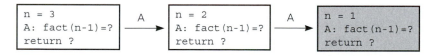

At point A a recursive call is made, and the new invocation of the method `fact` begins execution:

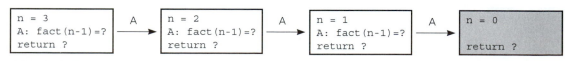

FIGURE 2-5   Box trace of `fact(3)`

(continues)

This is the base case, so this invocation of `fact` completes:

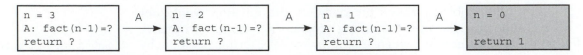

The method value is returned to the calling box, which continues execution:

```
n = 3             A   n = 2             A   n= 1               n = 0
A: fact(n-1)=?        A: fact(n-1)=?        A: fact(n-1)=1     
return ?              return ?              return ?           return 1
```

The current invocation of `fact` completes:

```
n = 3             A   n = 2             A   n = 1              n = 0
A: fact(n-1)=?        A: fact(n-1)=?        A: fact(n-1)=1     
return ?              return ?              return 1           return 1
```

The method value is returned to the calling box, which continues execution:

```
n = 3             A   n = 2                 n = 1              n = 0
A: fact(n-1)=?        A: fact(n-1)=1        A: fact(n-1)=1     
return ?              return ?              return 1           return 1
```

The current invocation of `fact` completes:

```
n = 3             A   n = 2                 n = 1              n = 0
A: fact(n-1)=?        A: fact(n-1)=1        A: fact(n-1)=1     
return ?              return 2              return 1           return 1
```

The method value is returned to the calling box, which continues execution:

```
n = 3                 n = 2                 n = 1              n = 0
A: fact(n-1)=2        A: fact(n-1)=1        A: fact(n-1)=1     
return ?              return 2              return 1           return 1
```

The current invocation of `fact` completes:

```
n = 3                 n = 2                 n = 1              n = 0
A: fact(n-1)=2        A: fact(n-1)=1        A: fact(n-1)=1     
return 6              return 2              return 1           return 1
```

The value 6 is returned to the initial call.

FIGURE 2-5

(continued)

You can construct a solution to the problem of writing a string of length n backward in terms of the problem of writing a string of length $n - 1$ backward. That is, each recursive step of the solution diminishes by 1 the length of the string to be written backward. The fact that the strings get shorter and shorter suggests that the problem of writing some very short strings backward can serve as the base case. One very short string is the empty string, the string of length zero. Thus, you can choose for the base case the problem

`Write the empty string backward`   The base case

The solution to this problem is to do nothing at all—a very straightforward solution indeed! (Alternatively, you could use the string of length 1 as the base case.)

Exactly how can you use the solution to the problem of writing a string of length $n - 1$ backward to solve the problem of writing a string of length n backward? This approach is analogous to the one used to construct the solution to the factorial problem, where you specified how to use *factorial*($n - 1$) in the computation of *factorial*(n). Unlike the factorial problem, however, the string problem does not suggest an immediately clear way to proceed. Obviously, not any string of length $n - 1$ will do. For example, there is no relation between writing "apple" (a string of length 5) backward and writing "pear" (a string of length 4) backward. You must choose the smaller problem carefully so that you can use its solution in the solution to the original problem.

The string of length $n - 1$ that you choose must be a substring (part) of the original string. Suppose that you strip away one character from the original string, leaving a substring of length $n - 1$. For the recursive solution to be valid, the ability to write the substring backward, combined with the ability to perform some minor task, must result in the ability to write the original string backward. Compare this approach with the way you computed *factorial* recursively: The ability to compute *factorial*($n - 1$), combined with the ability to multiply this value by n, resulted in the ability to compute *factorial*(n).

You need to decide which character to strip away and which minor task to perform. Consider the minor task first. Because you are writing characters, a likely candidate for the minor task is writing a single character. As for the character that you should strip away from the string, there are several possible alternatives. Two of the more intuitive alternatives are

`Strip away the last character`

or

`Strip away the first character`

How can you write an *n*-character string backward, if you can write an (*n* – 1)-character string backward?

Consider the first of these alternatives, stripping away the last character, as Figure 2-6 illustrates.

For the solution to be valid, you must write the last character in the string first. Therefore, you must write the last character before you write the remainder of the string backward. A high-level recursive solution, given the string *s*, is

writeBackward writes a string backward

```
writeBackward(in s:string)

    if (the string is empty)
        Do nothing -- this is the base case
    else
    {   Write the last character of s
        writeBackward(s minus its last character)
    }
```

This solution to the problem is conceptual. To obtain a C++ function, you must resolve a few implementation issues. Suppose that the function will receive two arguments: a string *s* to be written backward and an integer *size* that specifies the length of the string. To simplify matters, you can assume that the string begins at position 0 and ends at position *size* − 1. That is, all characters, including blanks, in that range are part of the string. The C++ function *writeBackward* appears as follows:

```
void writeBackward(string s, int size)
// -------------------------------------------------
// Writes a character string backward.
// Precondition: The string s contains size
// characters, where size >= 0.
// Postcondition: s is written backward, but remains
// unchanged.
// -------------------------------------------------
{
    if (size > 0)
    {   // write the last character
        cout << s.substr(size-1, 1);
```

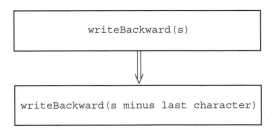

FIGURE 2-6 A recursive solution

```
     // write the rest of the string backward
     writeBackward(s, size-1);  // Point A
  }  // end if

  // size == 0 is the base case - do nothing
}  // end writeBackward
```

Notice that the recursive calls to *writeBackward* use successively smaller values of *size*. This decrease in *size* has the effect of stripping away the last character of the string and ensures that the base case will be reached.

You can trace the execution of *writeBackward* by using the box method. As was true for the function *fact*, each box contains the local environment of the recursive call—in this case, the input arguments *s* and *size*. The trace will differ somewhat from the trace of *fact* shown in Figure 2-5 because, as a *void* function, *writeBackward* does not use a *return* statement to return a computed value. Figure 2-7 traces the call to the function *writeBackward* with the string "cat".

writeBackward does not return a computed value

Now consider a slightly different approach to the problem. Recall the two alternatives for the character that you could strip away from the string: the last character or the first character. The solution just given strips away the last character of the string. It will now be interesting to construct a solution based on the second alternative:

Strip away the first character

To begin, consider a simple modification of the previous pseudocode solution that replaces each occurrence of "last" with "first." Thus, the function writes the first character rather than the last and then recursively writes the remainder of the string backward.

```
writeBackward1(in s:string)

  if (the string s is empty)
     Do nothing -- this is the base case
  else
  {  Write the first character of s
     writeBackward1(s minus its first character)
  }
```

Does this solution do what you want it to? If you think about this function, you will realize that it writes the string in its normal left-to-right direction instead of backward. After all, the steps in the pseudocode are

```
Write the first character of s
Write the rest of s
```

The initial call is made, and the function begins execution:

Output line: **t**

Point A (`writeBackward(s, size-1)`) is reached, and the recursive call is made.

The new invocation begins execution:

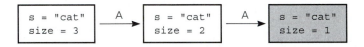

Output line: **ta**

Point A is reached, and the recursive call is made.

The new invocation begins execution:

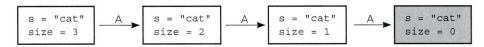

Output line: **tac**

Point A is reached, and the recursive call is made.

The new invocation begins execution:

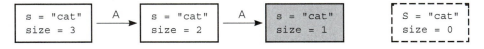

This is the base case, so this invocation completes.

Control returns to the calling box, which continues execution:

This invocation completes. Control returns to the calling box, which continues execution:

This invocation completes. Control returns to the calling box, which continues execution:

This invocation completes. Control returns to the statement following the initial call.

FIGURE 2-7   Box trace of `writeBackward("cat", 3)`

These steps simply write the string *s*. Naming the function *writeBackward* does not guarantee that it will actually write the string backward—recursion really is not magic!

You can write *s* backward correctly by using the following recursive formulation:

```
Write s minus its first character backward
Write the first character of s
```

In other words, you write the first character of *s* only *after* you have written the rest of *s* backward. This approach leads to the following pseudocode solution:

```
writeBackward2(in s:string)

   if (the string s is empty)
      Do nothing -- this is the base case
   else
   {  writeBackward2(s minus its first character)
      Write the first character of s
   }
```

The translation of *writeBackward2* into C++ is similar to that of the original *writeBackward* function and is left as an exercise.

It is instructive to carefully trace the actions of the two pseudocode functions *writeBackward* and *writeBackward2*. First, add statements to each function to provide output that is useful to the trace, as follows:

```
writeBackward(in s:string)

   cout << "Enter writeBackward with string: " << s << endl;
   if (the string is empty)
      Do nothing -- this is the base case
   else
   {  cout << "About to write last character of string: "
           << s << endl;
      Write the last character of s
      writeBackward(s minus its last character)  // Point A
   }
   cout << "Leave writeBackward with string: " << s << endl;
```

cout statements can help you trace the logic of a recursive function

```
writeBackward2(in s:string)

   cout << "Enter writeBackward2 with string: "
        << s << endl;
   if (the string is empty)
      Do nothing -- this is the base case
```

```
    else
    {  writeBackward2(s minus its first character) // Point A
       cout << "About to write first character of string: "
            << s << endl;
       Write the first character of s
    }
    cout << "Leave writeBackward2 with string: "
         << s << endl;
```

Figures 2-8 and 2-9 show the output of the revised pseudocode functions *writeBackward* and *writeBackward2*, when initially given the string "cat".

You need to be comfortable with the differences between these two functions. The recursive calls that the two functions make generate a different sequence of values for the argument *s*. Despite this fact, both functions correctly write the string argument backward. They compensate for the difference in the sequence of values for *s* by writing different characters in the string at different times relative to the recursive calls. In terms of the box traces in Figures 2-8 and 2-9, *writeBackward* writes a character just before generating a new box (just before a new recursive call), whereas *writeBackward2* writes a character just after crossing off a box (just after returning from a recursive call). When these differences are put together, the result is two functions that employ different strategies to accomplish the same task.

This example also illustrates the value of the box method, combined with well-placed *cout* statements, in debugging recursive functions. The *cout* statements at the beginning, interior, and end of the recursive functions report the value of the argument *s*. In general, when debugging a recursive function, you should also report both the values of local variables and the point in the function where each recursive call occurred, as in this example:

Well-placed but temporary *cout* statements can help you debug a recursive function

```
abc(...)

    cout << "Calling function abc from point .\n";
    abc(...)  // this is point

    cout << "Calling function abc from point B.\n";
    abc(... )  // this is point B
```

Remove *cout* statements after you have debugged the function

Realize that the *cout* statements do not belong in the final version of the function.

The initial call is made, and the function begins execution:

Output stream:

> **Enter writeBackward, string: cat**
> **About to write last character of string: cat**
> **t**

Point A is reached, and the recursive call is made. The new invocation begins execution:

```
s = "cat"   ──A──▶   s = "ca"
```

Output stream:

> Enter writeBackward, string: cat
> About to write last character of string: cat
> t
> **Enter writeBackward, string: ca**
> **About to write last character of string: ca**
> **a**

Point A is reached, and the recursive call is made. The new invocation begins execution:

```
s = "cat"   ──A──▶   s = "ca"   ──A──▶   s = "c"
```

Output stream:

> Enter writeBackward, string: cat
> About to write last character of string: cat
> t
> Enter writeBackward, string: ca
> About to write last character of string: ca
> a
> **Enter writeBackward, string: c**
> **About to write last character of string: c**
> **c**

Point A is reached, and the recursive call is made. The new invocation begins execution:

This invocation completes execution, and a return is made

FIGURE 2-8   Box trace of *writeBackward("cat", 3)* in pseudocode

(continues)

Output stream:

```
Enter writeBackward, string: cat
About to write last character of string: cat
t
Enter writeBackward, string: ca
About to write last character of string: ca
a
Enter writeBackward, string: c
About to write last character of string: c
c
Enter writeBackward, string:
Leave writeBackward, string:
```

This invocation completes execution, and a return is made.

Output stream:

```
Enter writeBackward, string: cat
About to write last character of string: cat
t
Enter writeBackward, string: ca
About to write last character of string: ca
a
Enter writeBackward, string: c
About to write last character of string: c
c
Enter writeBackward, string:
Leave writeBackward, string:
Leave writeBackward, string: c
```

This invocation completes execution, and a return is made.

Output stream:

```
Enter writeBackward, string: cat
About to write last character of string: cat
t
Enter writeBackward, string: ca
About to write last character of string: ca
a
Enter writeBackward, string: c
About to write last character of string: c
c
Enter writeBackward, string:
Leave writeBackward, string:
Leave writeBackward, string: c
Leave writeBackward, string: ca
```

This invocation completes execution, and a return is made.

FIGURE 2-8

(continues)

Output stream:

```
Enter writeBackward, string: cat
About to write last character of string: cat
t
Enter writeBackward, string: ca
About to write last character of string: ca
a
Enter writeBackward, string: c
About to write last character of string: c
c
Enter writeBackward, string:
Leave writeBackward, string:
Leave writeBackward, string: c
Leave writeBackward, string: ca
Leave writeBackward, string: cat
```

FIGURE 2-8

(continued)

The initial call is made, and the function begins execution:

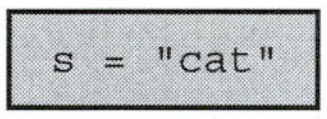

```
s = "cat"
```

Output stream:

Enter writeBackward2, string: cat

Point A is reached, and the recursive call is made. The new invocation begins execution:

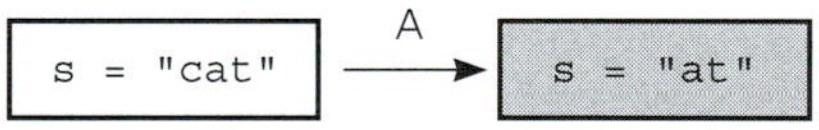

Output stream:

```
Enter writeBackward2, string: cat
Enter writeBackward2, string: at
```

Point A is reached, and the recursive call is made. The new invocation begins execution:

Output stream:

```
Enter writeBackward2, string: cat
Enter writeBackward2, string: at
Enter writeBackward2, string: t
```

Point A is reached, and the recursive call is made. The new invocation begins execution:

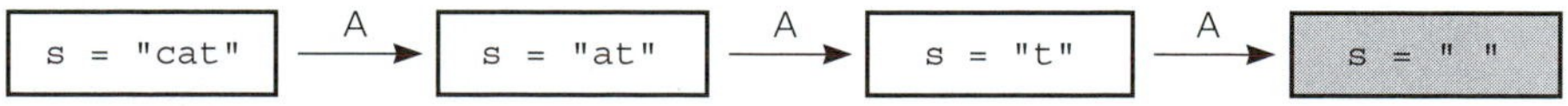

This invocation completes execution, and a return is made.

FIGURE 2-9

(continues)

Output stream:

```
Enter writeBackward2, string: cat
Enter writeBackward2, string: at
Enter writeBackward2, string: t
Enter writeBackward2, string:
Leave writeBackward2, string:
About to write first character of string: t
t
Leave writeBackward2, string: t
```

This invocation completes execution, and a return is made.

Output stream:

```
Enter writeBackward2, string: cat
Enter writeBackward2, string: at
Enter writeBackward2, string: t
Enter writeBackward2, string:
Leave writeBackward2, string:
About to write first character of string: t
t
Leave writeBackward2, string: t
About to write first character of string: at
a
Leave writeBackward2, string: at
```

| s = "cat" | s = "at" | s = "t" | s = " " |

This invocation completes execution, and a return is made.

Output stream:

```
Enter writeBackward2, string: cat
Enter writeBackward2, string: at
Enter writeBackward2, string: t
Enter writeBackward2, string:
Leave writeBackward2, string:
About to write first character of string: t
t
Leave writeBackward2, string: t
About to write first character of string: at
a
Leave writeBackward2, string: at
About to write first character of string: cat
c
Leave writeBackward2, string: cat
```

FIGURE 2-9

(continued)

2.2 Counting Things

The next three problems require you to count certain events or combinations of events or things. They are good examples of problems with more than one base case. They also provide good examples of tremendously inefficient recursive solutions. Do not let this inefficiency discourage you. Your goal right now is to understand recursion by examining simple problems. Soon you will see useful and efficient recursive solutions.

Multiplying Rabbits (The Fibonacci Sequence)

Rabbits are very prolific breeders. If rabbits did not die, their population would quickly get out of hand. Suppose we assume the following "facts," which were obtained in a recent survey of randomly selected rabbits:

- Rabbits never die.

- A rabbit reaches sexual maturity exactly two months after birth, that is, at the beginning of its third month of life.

- Rabbits are always born in male–female pairs. At the beginning of every month, each sexually mature male–female pair gives birth to exactly one male–female pair.

Suppose you started with a single newborn male–female pair. How many pairs would there be in month 6, counting the births that took place at the beginning of month 6? Since 6 is a relatively small number, you can figure out the solution easily:

Month 1: 1 pair, the original rabbits.

Month 2: 1 pair still, since the rabbits are not yet sexually mature.

Month 3: 2 pairs; the original pair has reached sexual maturity and has given birth to a second pair.

Month 4: 3 pairs; the original pair has given birth again, but the pair born at the beginning of month 3 are not yet sexually mature.

Month 5: 5 pairs; all rabbits alive in month 3 (2 pairs) are now sexually mature. Add their offspring to those pairs alive in month 4 (3 pairs) to yield 5 pairs.

Month 6: 8 pairs; 3 newborn pairs from the pairs alive in month 4 plus 5 pairs alive in month 5.

You can now construct a recursive solution for computing *rabbit(n)*, the number of pairs alive in month *n*. You must determine how you can use *rabbit(n − 1)* to compute *rabbit(n)*. Observe that *rabbit(n)* is the sum of the number of pairs alive just prior to the start of month *n* and the number of pairs born at the start of month *n*. Just prior to the start of month *n*, there are *rabbit*(*n* − 1) pairs of rabbits. Not all of these rabbits are sexually mature at the start of month *n*. Only those that were alive in month *n* − 2 are ready to reproduce at the start of month *n*. That is, the number of pairs born at the start of month *n* is *rabbit*(*n* − 2). Therefore, you have the recurrence relation

The number of pairs in month *n*

$$rabbit(n) = rabbit(n − 1) + rabbit(n − 2)$$

Figure 2-10 illustrates this relationship.

This recurrence relation introduces a new point. In some cases, you solve a problem by solving more than one smaller problem of the same type. This change does not add much conceptual difficulty, but you must be very careful when selecting the base case. The temptation is simply to say that *rabbit*(1) should be the base case because its value is 1 according to the problem's statement. But what about *rabbit*(2)? Applying the recursive definition to *rabbit*(2) would yield

$$rabbit(2) = rabbit(1) + rabbit(0)$$

Thus, the recursive definition would need to specify the number of pairs alive in month 0—an undefined quantity.

One possible solution is to define *rabbit*(0) to be 0, but this approach seems artificial. A slightly more attractive alternative is to treat *rabbit*(2) itself as a special case with the value of 1. Thus, the recursive definition has two base cases, *rabbit*(2) and *rabbit*(1). The recursive definition becomes

Two base cases are necessary because there are two smaller problems

$$rabbit(n) = \begin{cases} 1 & \text{if } n \text{ is 1 or 2} \\ rabbit(n − 1) + rabbit(n − 2) & \text{if } n > 2 \end{cases}$$

Incidentally, the series of numbers *rabbit*(1), *rabbit*(2), *rabbit*(3), and so on is known as the **Fibonacci sequence**, which models many naturally occurring phenomena.

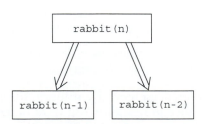

FIGURE 2-10   Recursive solution to the rabbit problem

A C++ function to compute *rabbit(n)* is easy to write from the previous definition:

```cpp
int rabbit(int n)
// ------------------------------------------------------
// Computes a term in the Fibonacci sequence.
// Precondition: n is a positive integer.
// Postcondition: Returns the nth Fibonacci number.
// ------------------------------------------------------
{
   if (n <= 2)
      return 1;

   else  // n > 2, so n-1 > 0 and n-2 > 0
      return rabbit(n-1) + rabbit(n-2);
}  // end rabbit
```

rabbit computes the Fibonacci sequence but does so inefficiently

Should you actually use this function? Figure 2-11 illustrates the recursive calls that *rabbit(7)* generates. Think about the number of recursive calls that *rabbit(10)* generates. At best, the function *rabbit* is inefficient. Thus, its use is not feasible for large values of *n*. This problem is discussed in more detail at the end of this chapter, at which time you will see some techniques for generating a more efficient solution from this same recursive relationship.

Organizing a Parade

You have been asked to organize the Fourth of July parade, which will consist of bands and floats in a single line. Last year, adjacent bands tried to outplay each other. To avoid this problem, the sponsors have asked you never to place one band immediately after another. In how many ways can you organize a parade of length *n*?

Assume you have at least *n* marching bands and *n* floats from which to choose. When counting the number of ways to organize the parade, assume that the parades *band-float* and *float-band*, for example, are different parades and count as two ways.

The parade can end with either a float or a band. The number of ways to organize the parade is simply the sum of the number of parades of each type. That is, let

$P(n)$ be the number of ways to organize a parade of length *n*

$F(n)$ be the number of parades of length *n* that end with a float

$B(n)$ be the number of parades of length *n* that end with a band

Then

$$P(n) = F(n) + B(n)$$

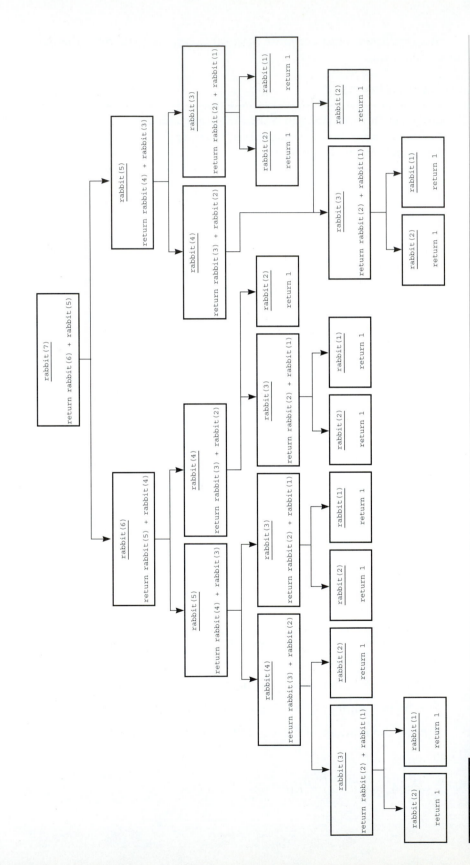

FIGURE 2-11 The recursive calls that *rabbit(7)* generates

First, consider $F(n)$. You will have a parade of length n that ends with a float simply by placing a float at the end of *any* acceptable parade of length $n - 1$. Hence, the number of acceptable parades of length n that end with a float is precisely equal to the total number of acceptable parades of length $n - 1$; that is

The number of acceptable parades of length n that end with a float

$$F(n) = P(n - 1)$$

Next, consider $B(n)$. The only way a parade can end with a band is if the unit just before the end is a float. (If it is a band, you will have two adjacent bands.) Thus, the only way to organize an acceptable parade of length n that ends with a band is first to organize a parade of length $n - 1$ that ends with a float and then add a band to the end. Therefore, the number of acceptable parades of length n that end with a band is precisely equal to the number of acceptable parades of length $n - 1$ that end with a float:

$$B(n) = F(n - 1)$$

You use the earlier fact that $F(n) = P(n - 1)$ to obtain

The number of acceptable parades of length n that end with a band

$$B(n) = P(n - 2)$$

Thus, you have solved $F(n)$ and $B(n)$ in terms of the smaller problems $P(n - 1)$ and $P(n - 2)$, respectively. You then use

$$P(n) = F(n) + B(n)$$

to obtain

$$P(n) = P(n - 1) + P(n - 2)$$

The number of acceptable parades of length n

The form of this recurrence relation is identical to the solution for the multiplying rabbits problem.

As you saw in the rabbit problem, two base cases are necessary because the recurrence relation defines a problem in terms of two smaller problems. As you did for the rabbit problem, you can choose $n = 1$ and $n = 2$ for the base cases. Although both problems use the same n's for their base cases, there is no reason to expect that they use the same values for these base cases. That is, there is no reason to expect that *rabbit*(1) is equal to $P(1)$ and that *rabbit*(2) is equal to $P(2)$.

A little thought reveals that for the parade problem,

$$P(1) = 2 \quad \text{(The parades of length 1 are *float* and *band*.)}$$

$$P(2) = 3 \quad \text{(The parades of length 2 are *float-float*, *band-float*, and *float-band*.)}$$

Two base cases are necessary because there are two smaller problems

In summary, the solution to this problem is

$$P(1) = 2$$

$$P(2) = 3$$

$$P(n) = P(n - 1) + P(n - 2) \quad \text{for } n > 2$$

A recursive solution

This example demonstrates the following points about recursion:

- Sometimes you can solve a problem by breaking it up into cases—for example, parades that end with a float and parades that end with a band.

- The values that you use for the base cases are extremely important. Although the recurrence relations for P and *rabbit* are the same, the different values for their base cases ($n = 1$ or 2) cause different values for larger n. For example, *rabbit*(20) = 6,765, while $P(20) = 17,711$. The larger the value of n, the larger the discrepancy. You should think about why this is so.

Mr. Spock's Dilemma (Choosing *k* Out of *n* Things)

The five-year mission of the *U.S.S. Enterprise* is to explore new worlds. The five years are almost up, but the *Enterprise* has just entered an unexplored solar system that contains n planets. Unfortunately, time will allow for visits to only k planets. Mr. Spock begins to ponder how many different choices are possible for exploring k planets out of the n planets in the solar system. Because time is short, he does not care about the order in which he visits the same k planets.

Mr. Spock is especially fascinated by one particular planet, Planet X. He begins to think—in terms of Planet X—about how to pick k planets out of the n. "There are two possibilities: Either we visit Planet X, or we do not visit Planet X. If we do visit Planet X, I will have to choose $k - 1$ other planets to visit from the $n - 1$ remaining planets. On the other hand, if we do not visit Planet X, I will have to choose k planets to visit from the remaining $n - 1$ planets."

Mr. Spock is on his way to a recursive method of counting how many groups of k planets he can possibly choose out of n. Let $c(n, k)$ be the number of groups of k planets chosen from n. Then, in terms of Planet X, Mr. Spock deduces that

$c(n, k) =$ (the number of groups of k planets that include Planet X)

$+$

(the number of groups of k planets that do not include Planet X)

The number of ways to choose k out of n things is the sum of the number of ways to choose k − 1 out of n − 1 things and the number of ways to choose k out of n − 1 things

But Mr. Spock has already reasoned that the number of groups that include Planet X is $c(n - 1, k - 1)$, and the number of groups that do not include Planet X is $c(n - 1, k)$. Mr. Spock has figured out a way to solve his counting problem in terms of two smaller counting problems of the same type:

$$c(n, k) = c(n - 1, k - 1) + c(n - 1, k)$$

Mr. Spock now has to worry about the base case(s). He also needs to demonstrate that each of the two smaller problems eventually reaches a base case. First, what selection problem does he immediately know the answer to? If the *Enterprise* had time to visit all the planets (that is, if $k = n$), no decision would be necessary; there is only one group of all the planets. Thus, the first base case is

$$c(k, k) = 1$$

If $k < n$, it is easy to see that the second term in the recursive definition $c(n - 1, k)$ is "closer" to the base case $c(k, k)$ than is $c(n, k)$. However, the first term, $c(n - 1, k - 1)$, is not closer to $c(k, k)$ than is $c(n, k)$—they are the same "distance" apart. *When you solve a problem by solving two (or more) smaller problems, each of the smaller problems must be closer to a base case than the original problem.*

Mr. Spock realizes that the first term does, in fact, approach another trivial selection problem. This problem is the counterpart of his first base case, $c(k, k)$. Just as there is only one group of all the planets ($k = n$), there is also only one group of zero planets ($k = 0$). When there is no time to visit any of the planets, the *Enterprise* must head home without any exploration. Thus, the second base case is

$$c(n, 0) = 1$$

This base case does indeed have the property that $c(n - 1, k - 1)$ is closer to it than is $c(n, k)$. (Alternatively, you could define the second base case to be $c(n, 1) = n$.)

Mr. Spock adds one final part to his solution:

$$c(n, k) = 0 \quad \text{if } k > n$$

Although k could not be greater than n in the context of this problem, the addition of this case makes the recursive solution more generally applicable.

To summarize, the following recursive solution solves the problem of choosing k out of n things:

$$c(n, k) = \begin{cases} 1 & \text{if } k = 0 \\ 1 & \text{if } k = n \\ 0 & \text{if } k > n \\ c(n - 1, k - 1) + c(n - 1, k) & \text{if } 0 < k < n \end{cases}$$

The number of groups of k things recursively chosen out of n things

You can easily derive the following function from this recursive definition:

```
int c(int n, int k)
// --------------------------------------------------
// Computes the number of groups of k out of n things.
// Precondition: n and k are nonnegative integers.
// Postcondition: Returns c(n, k).
// --------------------------------------------------
{
   if ( (k == 0) || (k == n) )
      return 1;
   else if (k > n)
      return 0;
   else
      return c(n-1, k-1) + c(n-1, k);
}  // end c
```

Like the *rabbit* function, this function is inefficient and not practical to use. Figure 2-12 shows the number of recursive calls that the computation of *c(4, 2)* requires.

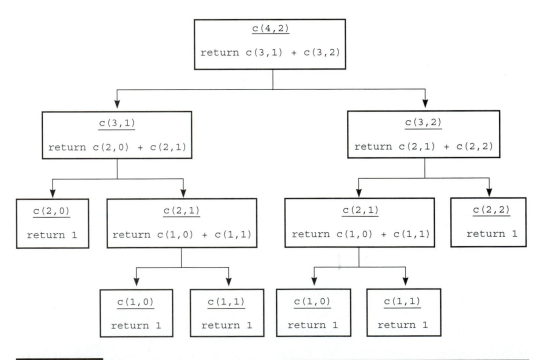

FIGURE 2-12   The recursive calls that *c(4, 2)* generates

2.3 Searching an Array

Searching is an important task that occurs frequently. This chapter began with an intuitive approach to a binary search algorithm. This section develops the binary search and examines other searching problems that have recursive solutions. The goal is to develop further your notion of recursion.

Finding the Largest Item in an Array

Suppose that you have an array *anArray* of integers and you want to find the largest one. You could construct an iterative solution without too much difficulty, but instead consider a recursive formulation:

```
if (anArray has only one item)
   maxArray(anArray) is the item in anArray
else if (anArray has more than one item)
   maxArray(anArray) is the maximum of
      maxArray(left half of anArray) and
      maxArray(right half of anArray)
```

Notice that this strategy fits the divide-and-conquer model that the binary search algorithm used at the beginning of this chapter. That is, the algorithm proceeds by dividing the problem and conquering the subproblems, as Figure 2-13 illustrates. However, there is a difference between this algorithm and the binary search algorithm. While the binary search algorithm conquers only one of its subproblems at each step, *maxArray* conquers both. In addition, after *maxArray* conquers the subproblems, it must reconcile the two solutions—that is, it must find the maximum of the two maximums. Figure 2-14 illustrates the computations that are necessary to find the largest integer in the array that contains 1, 6, 8, and 3 (denoted here by <1, 6, 8, 3>).

maxArray conquers both of its subproblems at each step

You should develop a recursive solution based on this strategy. In so doing, you may stumble on several subtle programming issues. The

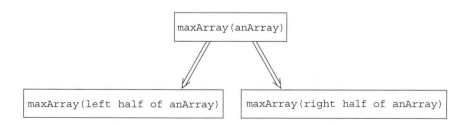

FIGURE 2-13   Recursive solution to the largest-item problem

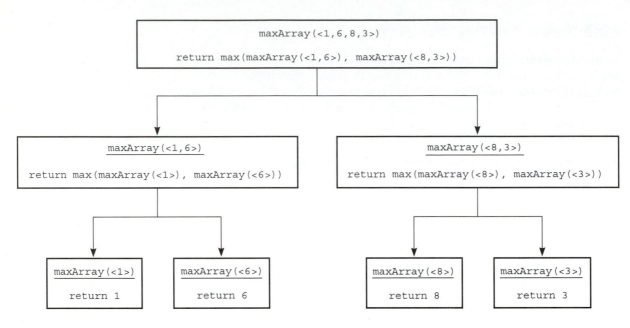

FIGURE 2-14   The recursive calls that *maxArray(<1,6,8,3>)* generates

binary search problem that follows raises virtually all of these issues, but this is a good opportunity for you to get some practice implementing a recursive solution.

Binary Search

The beginning of this chapter presented—at a high level—a recursive binary search algorithm for finding a word in a dictionary. We now develop this algorithm fully and illustrate some important programming issues.

Recall the earlier solution to the dictionary problem:

A binary search conquers one of its subproblems at each step

```
search(in aDictionary:Dictionary, in word:string)

    if (aDictionary is one page in size)
        Scan the page for word
    else
    {   Open aDictionary to a point near the middle
        Determine which half of aDictionary contains word

        if (word is in the first half of aDictionary)
            search(first half of aDictionary, word)
        else
            search(second half of aDictionary, word)
    }
```

Now alter the problem slightly by searching an array *anArray* of integers for a given value. The array, like the dictionary, must be sorted, or else a binary search is not applicable. Hence, assume that

```
anArray[0] ≤ anArray[1] ≤ anArray[2] ≤ · · · ≤ anArray[size-1]
```

where *size* is the size of the array. A high-level binary search for the array problem is

```
binarySearch(in anArray:ArrayType, in value:ItemType)

    if (anArray is of size 1)
        Determine if anArray's item is equal to
            value
    else
    {  Find the midpoint of anArray
        Determine which half of anArray contains value
        if (value is in the first half of anArray)
            binarySearch(first half of anArray, value)
        else
            binarySearch(second half of anArray, value)
    }
```

Although the solution is conceptually sound, you must consider several details before you can implement the algorithm:

1. **How will you pass "half of *anArray*" to the recursive calls to *binarySearch*?** You can pass the entire array at each call but have *binarySearch* search only *anArray[first..last]*,[1] that is, the portion *anArray[first]* through *anArray[last]*. Thus, you would also pass the integers *first* and *last* to *binarySearch*:

   ```
   binarySearch(anArray, first, last, value)
   ```

   With this convention, the new midpoint is given by

   ```
   mid = (first + last)/2
   ```

   Then *binarySearch(first half of anArray, value)* becomes

   ```
   binarySearch(anArray, first, mid-1, value)
   ```

   and *binarySearch(second half of anArray, value)* becomes

   ```
   binarySearch(anArray, mid+1, last, value)
   ```

   The array halves are
   anArray[first..mid-1]
   and
   anArray[mid+1..last];
   neither half contains
   anArray[mid]

---

[1] You will see this notation in the rest of the book to represent a portion of an array.

2. **How do you determine which half of the array contains value?** One possible implementation of

```
if (value is in the first half of anArray)
```

is

```
if (value < anArray[mid])
```

However, there is no test for equality between *value* and *anArray[mid]*. This omission can cause the algorithm to miss *value*. After the previous halving algorithm splits *anArray* into halves, *anArray[mid]* is not in either half of the array. (In this case, two halves do not make a whole!) Therefore, you must determine whether *anArray[mid]* is the value you seek *now* because later it will not be in the remaining half of the array. The interaction between the halving criterion and the termination condition (the base case) is subtle and is often a source of error. We need to rethink the base case.

Determine whether
anArray[mid] is the value
you seek

3. **What should the base case(s) be?** As it is written, *binarySearch* terminates only when an array of size 1 occurs; this is the only base case. By changing the halving process so that *anArray[mid] remains in one of the halves,* it is possible to implement the binary search correctly so that it has only this single base case. However, it can be clearer to have two distinct base cases as follows:

   a. *first > last.* You will reach this base case when *value* is not in the original array.

   b. *value == anArray[mid].* You will reach this base case when *value* is in the original array.

   These base cases are a bit different from any you have encountered previously. In a sense, the algorithm determines the answer to the problem from the base case it reaches. Many search problems have this flavor.

4. **How will *binarySearch* indicate the result of the search?** If *binarySearch* successfully locates *value* in the array, it could return the index of the array item that is equal to *value*. Since this index would never be negative, *binarySearch* could return a negative value if it does not find *value* in the array.

The C++ function *binarySearch* that follows implements these ideas. The two recursive calls to *binarySearch* are labeled as *X* and *Y* for use in a later box trace of this function.

```
int binarySearch(const int anArray[], int first,
                 int last, int value)
// -------------------------------------------------------
// Searches the array items anArray[first] through
// anArray[last] for value by using a binary search.
// Precondition: 0 <= first, last <= SIZE-1, where
// SIZE is the maximum size of the array, and
// anArray[first] <= anArray[first+1] <= ... <=
// anArray[last].
// Postcondition: If value is in the array, the function
// returns the index of the array item that equals value;
// otherwise the function returns -1.
// -------------------------------------------------------
{
   int index;
   if (first > last)
      index = -1;       // value not in original array


   else
   {  // Invariant: If value is in anArray,
      //            anArray[first] <= value <= anArray[last]
      int mid = (first + last)/2;
      if (value == anArray[mid])
         index = mid;   // value found at anArray[mid]


      else if (value < anArray[mid])
         // point X
         index = binarySearch(anArray, first, mid-1, value);


      else
         // point Y
         index = binarySearch(anArray, mid+1, last, value);
   }  // end else
   return index;
}  // end binarySearch
```

Notice that *binarySearch* has the following invariant: If *value* occurs
in the array, then *anArray[first]* ≤ *value* ≤ *anArray[last]*.

Figure 2-15 shows box traces of *binarySearch* when it searches
the array containing 1, 5, 9, 12, 15, 21, 29, and 31. Notice how the
labels *X* and *Y* of the two recursive calls to *binarySearch* appear in the
diagram. Exercise 13 at the end of this chapter asks you to perform
other box traces with this function.

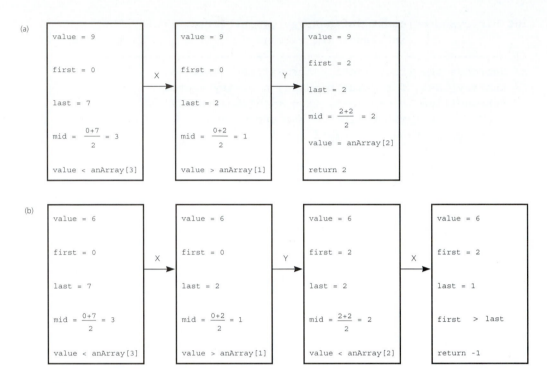

FIGURE 2-15 Box traces of *binarySearch* with *anArray* = <1, 5, 9, 12, 15, 21, 29, 31>: (a) a successful search for 9; (b) an unsuccessful search for 6

There is another implementation issue—one that deals specifically with C++—to consider. Recall that an array is never passed to a function by value and is therefore not copied. This aspect of C++ is particularly useful in a recursive function such as *binarySearch*. If the array *anArray* is large, many recursive calls to *binarySearch* may be necessary. If each call copied *anArray*, much memory and time would be wasted. On the other hand, because *anArray* is not copied, the function can alter the array's items unless you specify *anArray* as *const*, as was done for *binarySearch*.

A box trace of a recursive function that has an array argument requires a new consideration. Because the array *anArray* is neither a value argument nor a local variable, it is not a part of the function's local environment, and so the entire array *anArray* should not appear within each box. Therefore, as Figure 2-16 shows, you represent *anArray* outside the boxes, and all references to *anArray* affect this single representation.

Because an array argument is always passed by reference, a function can alter it unless you specify the array as *const*

Represent reference arguments outside of the boxes in a box trace

Finding the *k*th Smallest Item of an Array

Our discussion of searching concludes with a more difficult problem. Although you could skip this example now, Chapter 9 uses aspects of it in a sorting algorithm.

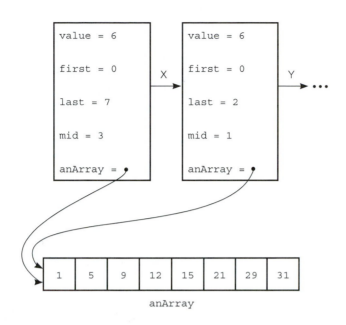

FIGURE 2-16 Box method with a reference argument

The previous two examples presented recursive methods for finding the largest item in an arbitrary array and for finding an arbitrary item in a sorted array. This example describes a recursive solution for finding the kth smallest item in an arbitrary array *anArray*. Would you ever be interested in such an item? Statisticians often want the median value in a collection of data. The median value in an ordered collection of data occurs in the middle of the collection. In an unordered collection of data, there are about the same number of values smaller than the median value as there are larger values. Thus, if you have 49 items, the 25th smallest item is the median value.

Obviously, you could solve this problem by sorting the array. Then the kth smallest item would be *anArray[k-1]*. Although this approach is a legitimate solution, it does more than the problem requires; a more efficient solution is possible. The solution outlined here finds the kth smallest item without completely sorting the array.

By now, you know that you solve a problem recursively by writing its solution in terms of one or more smaller problems of the same type in such a way that this notion of *smaller* ensures that you will always reach a base case. For all of the earlier recursive solutions, the reduction in problem size between recursive calls is *predictable*. For example, the factorial function always decreases the problem size by 1; the binary search always halves the problem size. In addition, the base cases for all the previous problems except the binary search have a static, predefined size. Thus, by knowing only the size of the original problem, you can determine the number of recursive calls that are necessary before you reach the base case.

For all previous examples, you know the amount of reduction made in the problem size by each recursive call

The solution that you are about to see for finding the kth smallest item departs from these traditions. Although you solve the problem in terms of a smaller problem, just how much smaller this problem is depends on the items in the array and cannot be predicted in advance. Also, the size of the base case depends on the items in the array, as it did for the binary search. (Recall that you reach a base case for a binary search when the middle item is the one sought.)

> **You cannot predict in advance the size of either the smaller problems or the base case in the recursive solution to the kth smallest-item problem**

This "unpredictable" type of solution is caused by the nature of the problem: The relationship between the rankings of the items in any predetermined parts of the array and the ranking of the items in the entire array is not strong enough to determine the kth smallest item. For example, suppose that *anArray* contains the items shown in Figure 2-17. Notice that 6, which is in *anArray[3]*, is the third smallest item in the first half of *anArray* and that 8, which is in *anArray[4]*, is the third smallest item in the second half of *anArray*. Can you conclude from these observations anything about the location of the third smallest item in all of *anArray*? The answer is no; these facts about parts of the array do not allow you to draw any useful conclusions about the entire array. You should experiment with other fixed splitting schemes as well.

The recursive solution proceeds by

1. Selecting a **pivot item** in the array

2. Cleverly arranging, or **partitioning**, the items in the array about this pivot item

3. Recursively applying the strategy to *one* of the partitions

> **Partition *anArray* into three parts: items $< p$, p, and items $\geq p$**

Suppose that you want to find the kth smallest item in the array segment *anArray[first..last]*. Let the pivot p be any item of the array segment. (For now, ignore how to choose p.) You can partition the items of *anArray[first..last]* into three regions: S_1, which contains the items less than p; the pivot p itself; and S_2, which contains the items greater than or equal to p. This partition implies that all the items in S_1 are smaller than all the items in S_2. Figure 2-18 illustrates this partition.

All items in *anArray[first..pivotIndex-1]* are less than p, and all items in *anArray[pivotIndex+1..last]* are greater than or equal to p. Notice that the sizes of the regions S_1 and S_2 depend on both p and the other items of *anArray[first..last]*.

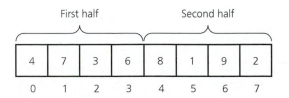

FIGURE 2-17   A sample array

This partition induces three "smaller problems," such that the solution to one of the problems will solve the original problem:

1. If S_1 contains k or more items, S_1 contains the k smallest items of the array segment `anArray[first..last]`. In this case, the kth smallest item must be in S_1. Since S_1 is the array segment `anArray[first..pivotIndex-1]`, this case occurs if $k < pivotIndex - first + 1$.

2. If S_1 contains $k - 1$ items, the kth smallest item must be the pivot p. This is the base case; it occurs if $k = pivotIndex - first + 1$.

3. If S_1 contains fewer than $k - 1$ items, the kth smallest item in `anArray[first..last]` must be in S_2. Because S_1 contains $pivotIndex - first$ items, the kth smallest item in `anArray[first..last]` is the $(k - (pivotIndex - first + 1))^{\text{st}}$ smallest item in S_2. This case occurs if $k > pivotIndex - first + 1$.

A recursive definition can summarize this discussion. Let

> `kSmall(k, anArray, first, last)` = k^{th} smallest item in `anArray[first..last]`

After you select the pivot item p and partition `anArray[first..last]` into S_1 and S_2, you have that

`kSmall(k, anArray, first, last)`

$$
= \begin{cases}
\texttt{kSmall(k, anArray, first, pivotIndex - 1)} & \\
\qquad\qquad \texttt{if k < pivotIndex - first + 1} & \\
\texttt{p} \qquad\qquad \texttt{if k = pivotIndex - first + 1} & \\
\texttt{kSmall(k - (pivotIndex - first + 1),anArray,} & \\
\qquad \texttt{pivotIndex + 1, L)} & \\
\qquad\qquad \texttt{if k > pivotIndex - first + 1} &
\end{cases}
$$

The kth smallest item in `anArray[first..last]`

There is always a pivot, and because it is not part of either S_1 or S_2, the size of the array segment to be searched decreases by at least 1 at

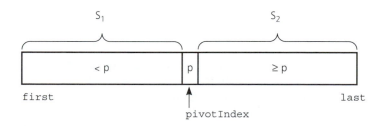

FIGURE 2-18 A partition about a pivot

each step. Thus, you will eventually reach the base case: The desired item is a pivot. A high-level pseudocode solution is as follows:

```
kSmall(in k:integer, in anArray:ArrayType,
       in first:integer, in last:integer):ItemType
// Returns the kth smallest value in anArray[first..last].

   Choose a pivot item p from anArray[first..last]
   Partition the items of anArray[first..last] about p

   if (k < pivotIndex - first + 1)
      return kSmall(k, anArray, first, pivotIndex - 1)

   else if (k == pivotIndex - first + 1)
      return p

   else
      return kSmall(k - (pivotIndex - first + 1), anArray,
                    pivotIndex + 1, last)
```

This pseudocode is not far from a C++ function. The only questions that remain are how to choose the pivot item p and how to partition the array about the chosen p. The choice of p is arbitrary. Any p in the array will work, although the sequence of choices will affect how soon you reach the base case. Chapter 9 gives an algorithm for partitioning the items about p. There you will see how to turn the function *kSmall* into a sorting algorithm.

2.4 Organizing Data

Given some data organized in one way, you might need to organize the data in another way. Thus, you will actually change some aspect of the data and not, for example, simply search it. The problem in this section is called the Towers of Hanoi. Although this classic problem probably has no direct real-world application, we consider it because its solution so well illustrates the use of recursion.

The Towers of Hanoi

Many, many years ago, in a distant part of the Orient—in the Vietnamese city of Hanoi—the emperor's wiseperson passed on to join his ancestors. The emperor needed a replacement wiseperson. Being a rather wise person himself, the emperor devised a puzzle, declaring that its solver could have the job of wiseperson.

The emperor's puzzle consisted of n disks (he didn't say exactly how many) and three poles: A (the source), B (the destination), and C (the spare). The disks were of different sizes and had holes in the middle so that they could fit on the poles. Because of their great weight, the disks could be placed only on top of disks larger than themselves. Initially, all the disks were on pole *A,* as shown in Figure 2-19a. The puzzle was to move the disks, one by one, from pole *A* to pole *B.* A person could also use pole *C* in the course of the transfer, but again a disk could be placed only on top of a disk larger than itself.

As the position of wiseperson was generally known to be a soft job, there were many applicants. Scholars and peasants alike brought the emperor their solutions. Many solutions were thousands of steps long, and many contained deeply nested loops and control structures. "I can't understand these solutions," bellowed the emperor. "There must be an easy way to solve this puzzle."

And indeed there was. A great Buddhist monk came out of the mountains to see the emperor. "My son," he said, "the puzzle is so easy,

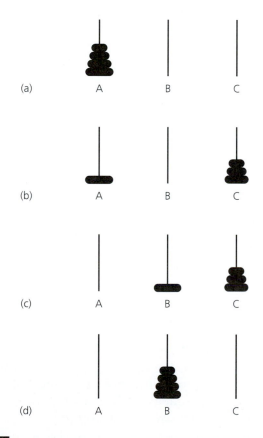

FIGURE 2-19   (a) The initial state;
(b) move *n* − 1 disks from A to C;
(c) move one disk from A to B;
(d) move *n* − 1 disks from C to B

it almost solves itself." The emperor's security chief wanted to throw this strange person out, but the emperor let him continue.

"If you have only one disk (that is, $n = 1$), move it from pole A to pole B." So far, so good, but even the village idiot got that part right. "If you have more than one disk (that is, $n > 1$), simply

1. Ignore the bottom disk and solve the problem for $n - 1$ disks, with the small modification that pole C is the destination and pole B is the spare. (See Figure 2-19b.)

2. After you have done this, $n - 1$ disks will be on pole C, and the largest disk will remain on pole A. So solve the problem for $n = 1$ (recall that even the village idiot could do this) by moving the large disk from A to B. (See Figure 2-19c.)

3. Now all you have to do is move the $n - 1$ disks from pole C to pole B; that is, solve the problem with pole C as the source, pole B as the destination, and pole A as the spare." (See Figure 2-19d.)

There was silence for a few moments, and finally the emperor said impatiently, "Well, are you going to tell us your solution or not?" The monk simply gave an all-knowing smile and vanished.

The emperor obviously was not a recursive thinker, but you should realize that the monk's solution is perfectly correct. The key to the solution is the observation that you can solve the Towers problem of n disks by solving three smaller—in the sense of number of disks—Towers problems. Let *towers(count, source, destination, spare)* denote the problem of moving *count* disks from pole *source* to pole *destination*, using pole *spare* as a spare. Notice that this definition makes sense even if there are more than *count* disks on pole *source*; in this case, you concern yourself with only the top *count* disks and ignore the others. Similarly, the poles *destination* and *spare* might have disks on them before you begin; you ignore these, too, except that you may place only smaller disks on top of them.

The problem statement

You can restate the emperor's problem as follows: Beginning with n disks on pole A and 0 disks on poles B and C, solve *towers(n, A, B, C)*. You can state the monk's solution as follows:

The solution

Step 1. Starting in the initial state—with all the disks on pole A—solve the problem

towers(n-1, A, C, B)

That is, ignore the bottom (largest) disk and move the top $n - 1$ disks from pole A to pole C, using pole B as a spare. When you are finished, the largest disk will remain on pole A, and all the other disks will be on pole C.

Step 2. Now, with the largest disk on pole A and all others on pole C, solve the problem

towers(1, A, B, C)

That is, move the largest disk from pole *A* to pole *B*. Because this disk is larger than the disks already on the spare pole *C,* you really could not use the spare. However, fortunately— and obviously—you do not need to use the spare in this base case. When you are done, the largest disk will be on pole *B* and all other disks will remain on pole *C.*

Step 3. Finally, with the largest disk on pole *B* and all the other disks on pole *C,* solve the problem

```
towers(n-1, C, B, A)
```

That is, move the *n* − 1 disks from pole *C* to pole *B,* using *A* as a spare. Notice that the destination pole *B* already has the largest disk, which you ignore. When you are done, you will have solved the original problem: All the disks will be on pole *B.*

The problem `towers(count, source, destination, spare)` has the following pseudocode solution:

```
solveTowers(count, source, destination, spare)

   if (count is 1)
      Move a disk directly from source to destination

   else
   {  solveTowers(count-1, source, spare, destination)
      solveTowers(1, source, destination, spare)
      solveTowers(count-1, spare, destination, source)
   }  // end if
```

This recursive solution follows the same basic pattern as the recursive solutions you saw earlier in this chapter:

   1. You solve a Towers problem by solving other Towers problems.

   2. These other Towers problems are smaller than the original problem; they have fewer disks to move. In particular, the number of disks decreases by 1 at each recursive call.

   3. When a problem has only one disk—the base case—the solution is easy to solve directly.

   4. The way that the problems become smaller ensures that you will reach a base case.

The solution to the Towers problem satisfies the four criteria of a recursive solution

Solving the Towers problem requires you to solve many smaller Towers problems recursively. Figure 2-20 illustrates the resulting recursive calls and their order when you solve the problem for three disks.

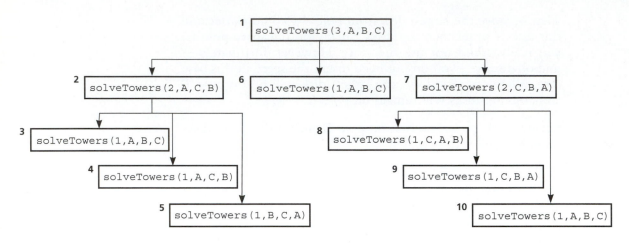

FIGURE 2-20   The order of recursive calls that results from *solveTowers(3, A, B, C)*

Now consider a C++ implementation of this algorithm. Notice that since most computers do not have arms (at the time of this writing), the function moves a disk by giving directions to a human. Thus, the formal arguments that represent the poles are of type *char*, and the corresponding actual arguments could be *'A'*, *'B'*, and *'C'*. The call *solveTowers(3, 'A', 'B', 'C')* produces this output:

The solution for three disks

```
Move top disk from pole A to pole B
Move top disk from pole A to pole C
Move top disk from pole B to pole C
Move top disk from pole A to pole B
Move top disk from pole C to pole A
Move top disk from pole C to pole B
Move top disk from pole A to pole B
```

The C++ function follows:

```
void solveTowers(int count, char source, char destination,
                 char spare)
{
   if (count == 1)
   {  cout << "Move top disk from pole " << source
           << " to pole " << destination << endl;
   }
   else
   {  solveTowers(count-1, source, spare, destination); // X
      solveTowers(1, source, destination, spare);       // Y
      solveTowers(count-1, spare, destination, source); // Z
   }  // end if
}  // end solveTowers
```

The three recursive calls in the function are labeled *X*, *Y*, and *Z*. These labels appear in the box trace of *solveTowers(3, 'A', 'B', 'C')* in Figure 2-21. The recursive calls are also numbered to correspond to the numbers used in Figure 2-20. (Figure 2-21 abbreviates *destination* as *dest* to save space.)

2.5 Recursion and Efficiency

Recursion is a powerful problem-solving technique that often produces very clean solutions to even the most complex problems. Recursive solutions can be easier to understand and to describe than iterative solutions. By using recursion, you can often write simple, short implementations of your solution.

The overriding concern of this chapter has been to give you a solid understanding of recursion so that you will be able to construct recursive solutions on your own. Most of our examples, therefore, have been simple. Unfortunately, many of the recursive solutions in this chapter are so inefficient that you should not use them. The recursive functions *binarySearch* and *solveTowers* are the notable exceptions, as they are quite efficient.[2]

Two factors contribute to the inefficiency of some recursive solutions:

- The overhead associated with function calls

- The inherent inefficiency of some recursive algorithms

Factors that contribute to the inefficiency of some recursive solutions

The first of these factors does not pertain specifically to recursive functions but is true of functions in general. In most implementations of C++ and other high-level programming languages, a function call incurs a bookkeeping overhead. As was mentioned earlier, each function call produces an activation record, which is analogous to a box in the box method. Recursive functions magnify this overhead because a single initial call to the function can generate a large number of recursive calls. For example, the call *factorial(n)* generates *n* recursive calls. On the other hand, the use of recursion, as is true with modularity in general, can greatly clarify complex programs. This clarification frequently more than compensates for the additional overhead. Thus, the use of recursion is often consistent with the multidimensional view of the cost of a computer program, as Chapter 1 describes.

Recursion can clarify complex solutions

However, you should not use recursion just for the sake of using recursion. For example, you probably should not use the recursive *factorial* function in practice. You can easily write an iterative *factorial* function given the iterative definition that was stated earlier in this chapter. The iterative function is almost as clear as the recursive one and is more efficient. There is no reason to incur the overhead of recursion when its use does not gain anything. *Recursion is truly valuable when a problem has no simple iterative solutions.*

Do not use a recursive solution if it is inefficient and you have a clear, efficient iterative solution

---

[2] Chapters 5 and 9 present other practical, efficient applications of recursion.

The initial call 1 is made, and `solveTowers` begins execution:

```
count   = 3
source  = A
dest    = B
spare   = C
```

At point X, recursive call 2 is made, and the new invocation of the function begins execution:

```
count   = 3          count   = 2
source  = A     X    source  = A
dest    = B          dest    = C
spare   = C          spare   = B
```

At point X, recursive call 3 is made, and the new invocation of the function begins execution:

```
count   = 3          count   = 2          count    = 1
source  = A     X    source  = A     X    source  = A
dest    = B          dest    = C          dest     = B
spare   = C          spare   = B          spare    = C
```

This is the base case, so a disk is moved, the return is made, and the function continues execution.

```
count   = 3          count   = 2          count   = 1
source  = A     X    source  = A          source  = A
dest    = B          dest    = C          dest    = B
spare   = C          spare   = B          spare   = C
```

At point Y, recursive call 4 is made, and the new invocation of the function begins execution:

```
count   = 3          count   = 2          count    = 1
source  = A     X    source  = A     Y    source  = A
dest    = B          dest    = C          dest     = C
spare   = C          spare   = B          spare    = B
```

This is the base case, so a disk is moved, the return is made, and the function continues execution.

```
count   = 3          count   = 2          count   = 1
source  = A     X    source  = A          source  = A
dest    = B          dest    = C          dest    = C
spare   = C          spare   = B          spare   = B
```

At point Z, recursive call 5 is made, and the new invocation of the function begins execution:

```
count   = 3          count   = 2          count    = 1
source  = A     X    source  = A     Z    source  = B
dest    = B          dest    = C          dest     = C
spare   = C          spare   = B          spare    = A
```

This is the base case, so a disk is moved, the return is made, and the function continues execution.

```
count   = 3          count   = 2          count   = 1
source  = A     X    source  = A          source  = B
dest    = B          dest    = C          dest    = C
spare   = C          spare   = B          spare   = A
```

FIGURE 2-21   Box trace of `solveTowers(3, 'A', 'B', 'C')`

(continues)

This invocation completes, the return is made, and the function continues execution.

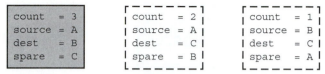

At point Y, recursive call 6 is made, and the new invocation of the function begins execution:

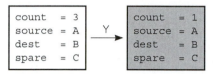

This is the base case, so a disk is moved, the return is made, and the function continues execution.

```
count   = 3          count   = 1
source  = A          source  = A
dest    = B          dest    = B
spare   = C          spare   = C
```

At point Z, recursive call 7 is made, and the new invocation of the function begins execution:

```
count   = 3     Z    count   = 2
source  = A  ------>  source  = C
dest    = B          dest    = B
spare   = C          spare   = A
```

At point X, recursive call 8 is made, and the new invocation of the function begins execution:

```
count   = 3    Z     count   = 2    X     count   = 1
source  = A  ----->  source  = C  ----->  source  = C
dest    = B          dest    = B          dest    = A
spare   = C          spare   = A          spare   = B
```

This is the base case, so a disk is moved, the return is made, and the function continues execution.

```
count   = 3    Z     count   = 2          count   = 1
source  = A  ----->  source  = C          source  = C
dest    = B          dest    = B          dest    = A
spare   = C          spare   = A          spare   = B
```

At point Y, recursive call 9 is made, and the new invocation of the function begins execution:

```
count   = 3    Z     count   = 2    Y     count   = 1
source  = A  ----->  source  = C  ----->  source  = C
dest    = B          dest    = B          dest    = B
spare   = C          spare   = A          spare   = A
```

This is the base case, so a disk is moved, the return is made, and the function continues execution.

FIGURE 2-21

(continues)

At point Z, recursive call 10 is made, and the new invocation of the function begins execution:

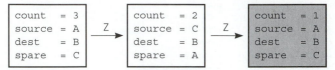

This is the base case, so a disk is moved, the return is made, and the function continues execution.

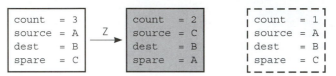

This invocation completes, the return is made, and the function continues execution.

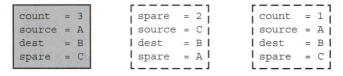

FIGURE 2-21

(continued)

The second point about recursion and efficiency is that some recursive algorithms are inherently inefficient. This inefficiency is a very different issue than that of overhead. It has nothing to do with how a compiler happens to implement a recursive function but rather is related to the method of solution that the algorithm employs.

As an example, recall the recursive solution for the multiplying rabbits problem that you saw earlier in this chapter:

The recursive version of `rabbit` is inherently inefficient

$$rabbit(n) = \begin{cases} 1 & \text{if } n \text{ is 1 or 2} \\ rabbit(n-1) + rabbit(n-2) & \text{if } n > 2 \end{cases}$$

The diagram in Figure 2-11 illustrated the computation of *rabbit*(7). Earlier, you were asked to think about what the diagram would look like for *rabbit*(10). If you thought about this question, you may have come to the conclusion that such a diagram would fill up most of this chapter. The diagram for *rabbit*(100) would fill up most of this universe!

The fundamental problem with *rabbit* is that it computes the same values over and over again. For example, in the diagram for *rabbit*(7), you can see that *rabbit*(3) is computed five times. When *n* is moderately large, many of the values are recomputed literally trillions of times. This enormous number of computations makes the solution infeasible, even if each computation required only a trivial amount of work (for example, if you could perform a million of these computations per second).

You can use `rabbit`'s recurrence relation to construct an efficient iterative solution

However, do not conclude that the recurrence relation is of no use. One way to solve the rabbit problem is to construct an iterative solution based on this same recurrence relation. The iterative solution goes forward instead of backward and computes each value only once. You can use the following iterative function to compute *rabbit*(*n*) even for very large values of *n*.

```
int iterativeRabbit(int n)
// Iterative solution to the rabbit problem.
{
    // initialize base cases:
    int previous = 1;       // initially rabbit(1)
    int current = 1;        // initially rabbit(2)
    int next = 1;           // result when n is 1 or 2

    // compute next rabbit values when n >= 3
    for (int i = 3; i <= n; ++i)
    { // current is rabbit(i-1), previous is rabbit(i-2)
        next = current + previous;  // rabbit(i)
        previous = current;         // get ready for
        current = next;             // next iteration
    }  // end for

    return next;
}  // end iterativeRabbit
```

Thus, an iterative solution can be more efficient than a recursive solution. In certain cases, however, it may be easier to discover a recursive solution than an iterative solution. Therefore, you may need to convert a recursive solution to an iterative solution. This conversion process is easier if your recursive function calls itself once, instead of several times. Be careful when deciding whether your function calls itself more than once. Although the function *rabbit* calls itself twice, the function *binarySearch* calls itself once, even though you see two calls in the C++ code. Those two calls appear within an *if* statement; only one of them will be executed.

Convert from recursion to iteration if it is easier to discover a recursive solution but more efficient to use an iterative solution

Converting a recursive solution to an iterative solution is even easier when the solitary recursive call is the last *action* that the function takes. This situation is called **tail recursion**. For example, the function *writeBackward* exhibits tail recursion because its recursive call is the last action that the function takes. Before you conclude that this is obvious, consider the function *fact*. Although its recursive call appears last in the function definition, *fact*'s last action is the multiplication. Thus, *fact* is not tail recursive.

A tail-recursive function

Recall the definition of *writeBackward*:

```
void writeBackward(string s, int size)
{
    if (size > 0)
    { // write last character
```

```
        cout << s.substr(size-1, 1);
        writeBackward(s, size - 1);  // write rest
    }  // end if
}  // end writeBackward
```

Because this function is tail recursive, its last recursive call simply repeats the function's action with altered arguments. You can perform this repetitive action by using an iteration that will be straightforward and often more efficient. For example, the following definition of *writeBackward* is iterative:

Removing tail recursion is often straightforward

```
void writeBackward(string s, int size)
// Iterative version.
{
   while (size > 0)
   {  cout << s.substr(size-1, 1);
      --size;
   }  // end while
}  // end writeBackward
```

Because tail-recursive functions are often less efficient than their iterative counterparts and because the conversion of a tail-recursive function to an equivalent iterative function is rather mechanical, some compilers automatically replace tail recursion with iteration. Eliminating other forms of recursion is usually more complex, as you will see in Chapter 6, and is a task that *you* would need to undertake, if necessary.

Some recursive algorithms, such as *rabbit*, are inherently inefficient, while other recursive algorithms, such as the binary search,[3] are extremely efficient. You will learn how to determine the relative efficiency of a recursive algorithm in more advanced courses concerned with the analysis of algorithms. Chapter 9 introduces some of these techniques briefly.

Chapter 5 continues the discussion of recursion by examining several difficult problems that have straightforward recursive solutions. Other chapters in this book use recursion as a matter of course.

Summary

1. Recursion is a technique that solves a problem by solving a smaller problem of the same type.

2. When constructing a recursive solution, keep the following four questions in mind:

   a. How can you define the problem in terms of a smaller problem of the same type?

---

[3] The binary search algorithm also has an iterative formulation.

b. How does each recursive call diminish the size of the problem?

c. What instance of the problem can serve as the base case?

d. As the problem size diminishes, will you reach this base case?

3. When constructing a recursive solution, you should assume that a recursive call's postcondition is true if its precondition is true.

4. You can use the box method to trace the actions of a recursive function. These boxes resemble activation records, which many compilers use to implement recursion. (Chapter 6 discusses implementing recursion further.) Although the box method is useful, it cannot replace an intuitive understanding of recursion.

5. Recursion allows you to solve problems—such as the Towers of Hanoi—whose iterative solutions are difficult to conceptualize. Even the most complex problems often have straightforward recursive solutions. Such solutions can be easier to understand, describe, and implement than iterative solutions.

6. Some recursive solutions are much less efficient than a corresponding iterative solution due to their inherently inefficient algorithms and the overhead of function calls. In such cases, the iterative solution can be preferable. You can use the recursive solution, however, to derive the iterative solution.

7. If you can easily, clearly, and efficiently solve a problem by using iteration, you should do so.

Cautions

1. A recursive algorithm must have a base case, whose solution you know directly without making any recursive calls. Without a base case, a recursive function will generate an infinite sequence of calls. When a recursive function contains more than one recursive call, you often will need more than one base case.

2. A recursive solution must involve one or more smaller problems that are each closer to a base case than is the original problem. You must be sure that these smaller problems eventually reach the base case. Failure to do so could result in an algorithm that does not terminate.

3. When developing a recursive solution, you must be sure that the solutions to the smaller problems really do give you a solution to the original problem. For example, *binarySearch* works because each smaller array is sorted and the value sought is between its first and last items.

4. The box method, in conjunction with well-placed *cout* statements, can be a good aid in debugging recursive functions. Such statements should report the point in the program from which each recursive call occurs as well as the values of input arguments and local variables at both entry to and exit from the function. Be sure to remove these *cout* statements from the final version of the function.

5. A recursive solution that recomputes certain values frequently can be quite inefficient. In such cases, iteration may be preferable to recursion.

Self-Test Exercises

1. The following function computes the product of the first $n \geq 1$ real numbers in an array. Show how this function satisfies the properties of a recursive function.

```
double product(const double anArray[], int n)
// Precondition: 1 <= n <= max size of anArray.
// Postcondition: Returns the product of the first n
// items in anArray; anArray is unchanged.
{
   if (n == 1)
      return anArray[0];
   else
      return anArray[n-1] * product(anArray, n-1);
}  // end product
```

2. Rewrite the function in Self-Test Exercise 1 as a *void* function.

3. Given an integer $n > 0$, write a recursive function *countDown* that writes the integers $n, n - 1, \ldots, 1$. *Hint:* What task can you do and what task can you ask a friend to do for you?

4. Write a recursive function that computes the product of the items in the array *anArray[first..last]*.

5. Of the following recursive functions that you saw in this chapter, identify those that exhibit tail recursion: *fact*, *writeBackward*, *writeBackward2*, *rabbit, c* in the Spock problem, *P* in the parade problem, *maxArray*, *binarySearch*, and *kSmall*. Are the functions in Self-Test Exercises 1 through 4 tail recursive?

6. Compute *c(4, 2)* in the Spock problem.

7. Trace the execution of the function *solveTowers* to solve the Towers of Hanoi problem for two disks.

Exercises

1. The following recursive function *getNumberEqual* searches the array *x* of *n* integers for occurrences of the integer *desiredValue*.

It returns the number of integers in *x* that are equal to *desired-Value*. For example, if *x* contains the 10 integers 1, 2, 4, 4, 5, 6, 7, 8, 9, and 12, then *getNumberEqual(x, 10, 4)* returns the value 2 because 4 occurs twice in *x*.

```
int getNumberEqual(const int x[], int n, int desiredValue)
{
    int count;

    if (n <= 0)
        return 0;
    else
    {   if (x[n-1] == desiredValue)
            count = 1;
        else
            count = 0;

        return getNumberEqual(x, n-1, desiredValue) + count;
    }  // end else
}  // end getNumberEqual
```

Demonstrate that this function is recursive by listing the criteria of a recursive solution and stating how the function meets each criterion.

2. Perform a box trace of the following calls to recursive functions that appear in this chapter. Clearly indicate each subsequent recursive call.

a. *rabbit(5)*

b. *countDown(5)* (You wrote *countDown* in Self-Test Exercise 3.)

3. Write a recursive function that will compute the sum of the first *n* integers in an array of at least *n* integers. *Hint:* Begin with the nth integer.

4. Given two integers, *start* and *end*, where *end* is greater than *start*, write a recursive C++ function that returns the sum of the integers from *start* through *end*, inclusive.

5. Revise the function *writeBackward*, discussed in the section "A Recursive *void* Function: Writing a String Backward," so that its base case is a string of length 1.

6. Describe the problem with the following recursive function:

```
public void printNum (int n)
{
    cout << n << endl;
    printNum (n - 1);
}
```

7. Given an integer $n > 0$, write a recursive C++ function that writes the integers $1, 2, \ldots, n$.

8. Given an integer $n > 0$, write a recursive C++ function that returns the sum of 1 through n.

9. Write a recursive C++ function that writes the digits of a positive decimal integer in reverse order.

10. **a.** Write a recursive C++ function *writeLine* that writes a character repeatedly to form a line of n characters. For example, *writeLine('*', 5)* produces the line *****.

    b. Now write a recursive function *writeBlock* that uses *writeLine* to write m lines of n characters each. For example, *writeBlock('*', 5, 3)* produces the output

    ```
    *****
    *****
    *****
    ```

11. What output does the following program produce?

    ```cpp
    int getValue(int a, int b, int n);

    int main()
    {
       cout << getValue(1, 7, 7) << endl;
       return 0;
    }  // end main

    int getValue(int a, int b, int n)
    {
       int returnValue;

       cout << "Enter: a = " << a << " b = " << b << endl;

       int c = (a + b)/2;
       if (c * c <= n)
          returnValue = c;
       else
          returnValue = getValue(a, c-1, n);

       cout << "Leave: a = " << a << " b = " << b << endl;
       return returnValue;
    }  // end getValue
    ```

12. What output does the following program produce?

```
int search(int first, int last, int n);
int mystery(int n);

int main()
{
   cout << mystery(30) << endl;
   return 0;
}  // end main

int search(int first, int last, int n)
{
   int returnValue;

   cout << "Enter: first = " << first << " last = "
        << last << endl;

   int mid = (first + last)/2;
   if ( (mid * mid <= n) && (n < (mid+1) * (mid+1)) )
      returnValue = mid;
   else if (mid * mid > n)
      returnValue = search(first, mid-1, n);
   else
      returnValue = search(mid+1, last, n);

   cout << "Leave: first = " << first << " last = "
        << last << endl;
   return returnValue;
}  // end search

int mystery(int n)
{
   return search(1, n, n);
}  // end mystery
```

13. Consider the following function that converts a positive decimal number to base 8 and displays the result.

```
void displayOctal(int n)
{
   if (n > 0)
   {  if (n/8 > 0)
         displayOctal(n/8);
      cout << n % 8;
```

```
   }  // end if
}  // end displayOctal
```

Describe how the algorithm works. Trace the function with $n = 100$.

14. Consider the following program:

```cpp
int f(int n);

int main()
{
   cout << "The value of f(8) is " << f(8) << endl;
   return 0;
}  // end main

int f(int n)
// Precondition: n >= 0.
{
   cout << "Function entered with n = " << n << endl;
   switch (n)
   {  case 0: case 1: case 2:
         return n + 1;
      default:
         return f(n-2) * f(n-4);
   }  // end switch
}  // end f
```

Show the exact output of the program. What argument values, if any, could you pass to the function f to cause the program to run forever?

15. Consider the following function:

```cpp
void recurse(int x, int y)
{
   if (y > 0)
   {  ++x;
      --y;
      cout << x << " " << y << endl;
      recurse(x, y);
      cout << x << " " << y << endl;
   }  // end if
}  // end recurse
```

Execute the function with $x = 5$ and $y = 3$. How is the output affected if x is a reference argument instead of a value argument?

16. Perform a box trace of the recursive function `binarySearch`, which appears in the section "Binary Search," with the array 1, 5, 9, 12, 15, 21, 29, 31 for each of the following search values:

    a. 5   **b.** 13   **c.** 16

17. Imagine that you have 101 dalmatians; no two dalmatians have the same number of spots. Suppose that you create an array of 101 integers: The first integer is the number of spots on the first dalmatian, the second integer is the number of spots on the second dalmatian, and so on.

    Your friend wants to know whether you have a dalmatian with 99 spots. Thus, you need to determine whether the array contains the integer 99.

a. If you plan to use a binary search to look for the 99, what, if anything, would you do to the array before searching it?

b. What is the index of the integer in the array that a binary search would examine first?

c. If all of your dalmatians have more than 99 spots, exactly how many comparisons will a binary search require to determine that 99 is not in the array?

18. This problem considers several ways to compute x^n for some $n \geq 0$.

a. Write an iterative function *power1* to compute x^n for $n \geq 0$.

b. Write a recursive function *power2* to compute x^n by using the following recursive formulation:

$x^0 = 1$
$x^n = x * x^{n-1}$ if $n > 0$

c. Write a recursive function *power3* to compute x^n by using the following recursive formulation:

$x^0 = 1$
$x^n = (x^{n/2})^2$ if $n > 0$ and n is even
$x^n = x * (x^{n/2})^2$ if $n > 0$ and n is odd

d. How many multiplications will each of the functions *power1*, *power2*, and *power3* perform when computing 3^{32}? 3^{19}?

e. How many recursive calls will *power2* and *power3* make when computing 3^{32}? 3^{19}?

19. Modify the recursive *rabbit* function so that it is visually easy to follow the flow of execution. Instead of just adding "Enter" and "Leave" messages, indent the trace messages according to how "deep" the current recursive call is. For example, the call *rabbit(4)* should produce the output

```
Enter rabbit:    n = 4
   Enter rabbit:    n = 3
      Enter rabbit:    n = 2
      Leave rabbit:    n = 2    value = 1
      Enter rabbit:    n = 1
      Leave rabbit:    n = 1    value = 1
   Leave rabbit:    n = 3    value = 2
   Enter rabbit:    n = 2
   Leave rabbit:    n = 2    value = 1
Leave rabbit:    n = 4    value = 3
```

Note how this output corresponds to Figure 2-11.

20. Consider the following recurrence relation:

$f(1) = 1; f(2) = 1; f(3) = 1; f(4) = 3; f(5) = 5;$

$f(n) = f(n - 1) + 3 * f(n - 5)$ for all $n > 5$.

a. Compute $f(n)$ for the following values of n: 6, 7, 12, 15.

b. If you were careful, rather than computing $f(15)$ from scratch (the way a recursive C++ function would compute it), you would have computed $f(6)$, then $f(7)$, then $f(8)$, and so on up to $f(15)$, recording the values as you computed them. This ordering would have saved you the effort of ever computing the same value more than once. (Recall the nonrecursive version of the *rabbit* program discussed at the end of this chapter.)

Note that during the computation, you never need to remember all of the previously computed values—only the last five. Taking advantage of these observations, write a C++ function that computes $f(n)$ for arbitrary values of n.

21. Write iterative versions of the following recursive functions: *fact*, *writeBackward*, *binarySearch*, *kSmall*.

22. Prove that the function *iterativeRabbit*, which appears in the section "Recursion and Efficiency," is correct by using invariants.

23. Consider the problem of finding the greatest common divisor (gcd) of two positive integers a and b. The algorithm presented here is a variation of Euclid's algorithm, which is based on the following theorem:[4]

THEOREM. If a and b are positive integers with $a > b$ such that b is not a divisor of a, then $gcd(a, b) = gcd(b, a \bmod b)$.

---

[4] This book uses mod as an abbreviation for the mathematical operation modulo. In C++, the modulo operator is %.

This relationship between $gcd(a, b)$ and $gcd(b, a \bmod b)$ is the heart of the recursive solution. It specifies how you can solve the problem of computing $gcd(a, b)$ in terms of another problem of the same type. Also, if b does divide a, then $b = gcd(a, b)$, so an appropriate choice for the base case is $(a \bmod b) = 0$.

This theorem leads to the following recursive definition:

$$gcd(a, b) = \begin{cases} b & \text{if } (a \bmod b) = 0 \\ gcd(b, a \bmod b) & \text{otherwise} \end{cases}$$

The following function implements this recursive algorithm:

```cpp
int gcd(int a, int b)
{
   if (a % b == 0)   // base case
      return a;
   else
      return gcd(b, a % b);
}  // end gcd
```

a. Prove the theorem.

b. What happens if $b > a$?

c. How is the problem getting smaller? (That is, do you always approach a base case?) Why is the base case appropriate?

24. Let $c(n)$ be the number of different groups of integers that can be chosen from the integers 1 through $n - 1$ so that the integers in each group add up to n (for example, $4 = 1 + 1 + 1 + 1 = 1 + 1 + 2 = 2 + 2 \cdots$). Write recursive definitions for $c(n)$ under the following variations:

a. You count permutations. For example, 1, 2, 1 and 1, 1, 2 are two groups that each add up to 4.

b. You ignore permutations.

25. Consider the following recursive definition:

$$Acker(m, n) = \begin{cases} n + 1 & \text{if } m = 0 \\ Acker(m - 1, 1) & \text{if } n = 0 \\ Acker(m - 1, Acker(m, n - 1)) & \text{otherwise} \end{cases}$$

This function, called *Ackermann's function*, is of interest because it grows rapidly with respect to the sizes of m and n. What is $Acker(1, 2)$? Implement the function in C++ and do a box trace of $Acker(1, 2)$. (*Caution:* Even for modest values of m and n, Ackermann's function requires *many* recursive calls.)

Programming Problems

1. Implement a recursive function that computes a^n, where a is a real number and n is a nonnegative integer.

2. Implement *maxArray*, discussed in the section "Finding the Largest Item in an Array," as a C++ function. What other recursive definitions of *maxArray* can you describe?

3. Implement the *binarySearch* algorithm presented in this chapter for an array of strings.

4. Implement *kSmall*, discussed in the section "Finding the kth Smallest Item in an Array," as a C++ function. Use the first item of the array as the pivot.

CHAPTER 3

Data Abstraction: The Walls

PREVIEW

This chapter elaborates on data abstraction, which was introduced in Chapter 1 as a technique for increasing the modularity of a program—for building "walls" between a program and its data structures. During the design of a solution, you will discover that you need to support several operations on the data and therefore need to define abstract data types (ADTs). This chapter will introduce some simple ADTs and use them to demonstrate the advantages of ADTs in general. In Part II of this book, you will see several other important ADTs.

Only after you have clearly specified the operations of an ADT should you consider data structures for implementing it. This chapter explores implementation issues and introduces C++ classes as a way to hide the implementation of an ADT from its users.

3.1 Abstract Data Types

Modularity is a technique that keeps the complexity of a large program manageable by systematically controlling the interaction of its components. You can focus on one task at a time in a modular program without other distractions. Thus, a modular program is easier to write, read, and modify. Modularity also isolates errors and eliminates redundancies.

A modular program is easier to write, read, and modify

You can develop modular programs by piecing together existing software components with functions that have yet to be written. In doing so, you should focus on *what* a module does and not on *how* it does it. To use existing software, you need a clear set of specifications that details how the modules behave. To write new functions, you need to decide what you would like them to do and proceed under the assumption that they exist and work. In this way you can write the functions in relative isolation from one another, knowing what each one will do but not necessarily *how* each will eventually do it. That is, you should practice functional abstraction.

Write specifications for each module before implementing it

While writing a module's specifications, you must identify details that you can hide within the module. The principle of information hiding involves not only hiding these details, but also making them *inaccessible* from outside a module. One way to understand information hiding is to imagine walls around the various tasks a program performs. These walls prevent the tasks from becoming entangled. The wall around each task *T* prevents the other tasks from "seeing" how *T* is performed. Thus, if task *Q* uses task *T*, and if the method for performing task *T* changes, task *Q* will not be affected. As Figure 3-1 illustrates, the wall prevents task *Q*'s method of solution from depending on task *T*'s method of solution.

Isolate the implementation details of a module from other modules

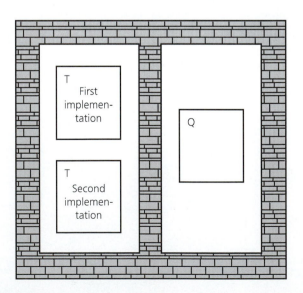

FIGURE 3-1   Isolated tasks: The implementation of task *T* does not affect task *Q*

The isolation of the modules cannot be total, however. Although task *Q* does not know *how* task *T* is performed, it must know *what* task *T* is and how to initiate it. For example, suppose that a program needs to operate on a sorted array of names. The program may, for instance, need to search the array for a given name or display the names in alphabetical order. The program thus needs a function *S* that sorts an array of names. Although the rest of the program knows that function *S* will sort an array, it should not care how *S* accomplishes its task. Thus, imagine a tiny slit in each wall, as Figure 3-2 illustrates. The slit is not large enough to allow the outside world to see the function's inner workings, but things can pass through the slit into and out of the function. For example, you can pass the array into the sort function, and the function can pass the sorted array out to you. What goes in and comes out is governed by the terms of the function's specifications, or contract: *If you use the function in this way, this is exactly what it will do for you.*

Often the solution to a problem requires operations on data. Such operations are broadly described in one of three ways:

- **Add** data to a data collection.

- **Remove** data from a data collection.

- **Ask questions** about the data in a data collection.

Typical operations on data

The details of the operations, of course, vary from application to application, but the overall theme is the management of data. Realize, however, that not all problems use or require these operations.

Data abstraction asks that you think in terms of *what* you can do to a collection of data independently of *how* you do it. Data abstraction is a technique that allows you to develop each data structure in relative isolation from the rest of the solution. The other modules of the solution will "know" what operations they can perform on the data, but they should not depend on how the data is stored or how the operations are performed. Again, the terms of the contract are *what* and not *how*. Thus, data abstraction is a natural extension of functional abstraction.

Both functional and data abstraction ask you to think "what," not "how"

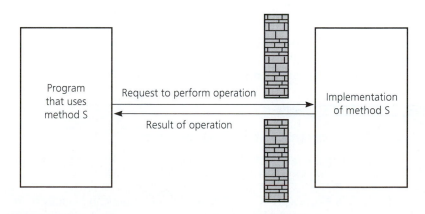

FIGURE 3-2 A slit in the wall

An ADT is a collection of
data and a set of operations
on that data

A collection of data together with a set of operations on that data are called an abstract data type, or ADT. For example, suppose that you need to store a collection of names in a manner that allows you to search rapidly for a given name. The binary search algorithm described in Chapter 2 enables you to search an array efficiently, if the array is sorted. Thus, one solution to this problem is to store the names sorted in an array and to use a binary search algorithm to search the array for a specified name. You can view the *sorted array together with the binary search algorithm* as an ADT that solves this problem.

Specifications indicate what
ADT operations do, but not
how to implement them

Data structures are part of an
ADT's implementation

The description of an ADT's operations must be rigorous enough to specify completely their effect on the data, yet it must not specify how to store the data nor how to carry out the operations. For example, the ADT operations should not specify whether to store the data in consecutive memory locations or in disjoint memory locations. You choose a particular data structure when you **implement** an ADT.

Recall that a data structure is a construct that you can define within a programming language to store a collection of data. For example, arrays and structures, which are built into C++, are data structures. However, you can invent other data structures. For example, suppose that you wanted a data structure to store both the names and salaries of a group of employees. You could use the following C++ statements:

```
const int MAX_NUMBER = 500;
string names[MAX_NUMBER];
double salaries[MAX_NUMBER];
```

Here the employee *names[i]* has a salary of *salaries[i]*. The two arrays *names* and *salaries* together form a data structure, yet C++ has no single data type to describe it.

Carefully specify an ADT's
operations before you
implement them

When a program must perform data operations that are not directly supported by the language, you should first design an abstract data type and carefully specify what the ADT operations are to do (the contract). Then—*and only then*—should you implement the operations with a data structure. If you implement the operations properly, the rest of the program will be able to assume that the operations perform as specified—that is, that the terms of the contract are honored. However, the program must not depend on a particular method for supporting the operations.

An abstract data type is not another name for a data structure.

KEY CONCEPTS

ADTs versus Data Structures

1. An abstract data type is a collection of data and a set of operations on that data.

2. A data structure is a construct within a programming language that stores a collection of data.

ADTs and data structures are not the same

To give you a better idea of the conceptual difference between an ADT and a data structure, consider a refrigerator's ice dispenser, as Figure 3-3 illustrates. It has water as input and produces as output either chilled water, crushed ice, or ice cubes according to which one of three buttons you push. It also has an indicator that lights when no ice is presently available. The dispenser is analogous to an ADT. The water is analogous to data; the operations are *chill*, *crush*, *cube*, and *isEmpty*. At this level of design, you are not concerned with how the dispenser will perform its operations, only that it performs them. If you want crushed ice, do you really care how the dispenser accomplishes its task as long as it does so correctly? Thus, after you have specified the dispenser's functions, you can design many uses for crushed ice without knowing how the dispenser accomplishes its tasks and without the distraction of engineering details.

Eventually, however, someone must build the dispenser. Exactly how will this machine produce crushed ice, for example? It could first make ice cubes and then either crush them between two steel rollers or smash them into small pieces by using hammers. Many other techniques are possible. The internal structure of the dispenser corresponds to the implementation of the ADT in a programming language, that is, to a data structure.

Although the owner of the dispenser does not care about its inner workings, he or she does want a design that is as efficient in its operation as possible. Similarly, the dispenser's manufacturer wants a design that is as easy and cheap to build as possible. You should have these same concerns when you choose a data structure to implement an ADT in C++. Even if you do not implement the ADT yourself, but instead use an already implemented ADT, you—like the person who buys a refrigerator—should care about at least the ADT's efficiency.

Notice that the dispenser is surrounded by steel walls. The only breaks in the walls accommodate the input (water) to the machine and its output (chilled water, crushed ice, or ice cubes). Thus, the machine's interior mechanisms are not only hidden from the user but also are inaccessible. In addition, the mechanism of one operation is hidden from and inaccessible to another operation.

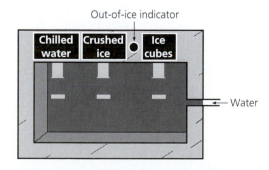

FIGURE 3-3   A dispenser of chilled water, crushed ice, and ice cubes

This modular design has benefits. For example, you can improve the operation *crush* by modifying its module without affecting the other modules. You could also add an operation by adding another module to the machine without affecting the original three operations. Thus, both abstraction and information hiding are at work here.

To summarize, data abstraction results in a wall of ADT operations between data structures and the program that accesses the data within these data structures, as Figure 3-4 illustrates. If you are on the program's side of the wall, you will see an interface that enables you to communicate with the data structure. That is, you request the ADT operations to manipulate the data in the data structure, and they pass the results of these manipulations back to you.

This process is analogous to using a vending machine. You press buttons to communicate with the machine and obtain something in return. The machine's external design dictates how you use it, much as an ADT's specifications govern what its operations are and what they do. As long as you use a vending machine according to its design, you can ignore its inner technology. As long as you agree to access data only by using ADT operations, your program can be oblivious to any change in the data structures that implement the ADT.

The following pages describe how to use an abstract data type to realize data abstraction's goal of separating the operations on data from the implementation of these operations. In doing so, we will look at several examples of ADTs.

A program should not depend on the details of an ADT's implementation

Using an ADT is like using a vending machine

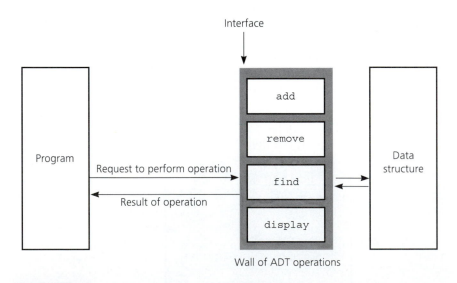

FIGURE 3-4   A wall of ADT operations isolates a data structure from the program that uses it

3.2 Specifying ADTs

To elaborate on the notion of an ADT, consider a list that you might encounter, such as a list of chores, a list of important dates, a list of addresses, or the grocery list pictured in Figure 3-5. As you write a grocery list, where do you put new items? Assuming that you write a neat one-column list, you probably add new items to the end of the list. You could just as well add items to the beginning of the list or add them so that your list is sorted alphabetically. Regardless, the items on a list appear in a sequence. The list has one first item and one last item. Except for the first and last items, each item has a unique **predecessor** and a unique **successor.** The first item—the **head** or **front** of the list—does not have a predecessor, and the last item—the **tail** or end of the list—does not have a successor.

Lists contain items of the same type: You can have a list of grocery items or a list of phone numbers. What can you do to the items on a list? You might count the items to determine the length of the list, add an item to the list, remove an item from the list, or look at (retrieve) an item. The items on a list, together with operations that you can perform on the items, form an ADT. You must specify the behavior of the ADT's operations on its data, that is, the list items. It is important that you focus only on specifying the operations and not on how you will implement them. That is, do not bring to this discussion any preconceived notion of a data structure that the term "list" might suggest.

Where do you add a new item and which item do you want to look at? The various answers to these questions lead to several kinds of lists. You might decide to add, delete, and retrieve items only at the end of the list or only at the front of the list or at both the front and end of the list. The specifications of these lists are left as an exercise; next we will discuss a more general list.

The ADT List

Once again, consider the grocery list pictured in Figure 3-5. The previously described lists, which manipulate items at one or both ends of the list, are not really adequate for an actual grocery list. You would probably want to access items anywhere on the list. That is, you might look at the item at position i, delete the item at position i, or insert an item at position i on the list. Such operations are part of the ADT **list**.

Note that it is customary to include an initialization operation that creates an empty list and an operation that destroys a list. Other operations that determine whether the list is empty or the length of the list are also useful.

Although the six items on the list in Figure 3-5 have a sequential order, they are not necessarily sorted by name. Perhaps the items appear in the order in which they occur on the grocer's shelves, but more likely they appear in the order in which they occurred to you as you wrote the list. The ADT list is simply an ordered collection of items that you reference by position number.

milk
eggs
butter
apples
bread
chicken

FIGURE 3-5   A grocery list

You reference list items by their position within the list

KEY CONCEPTS

ADT List Operations

1. Create an empty list.

2. Destroy a list.

3. Determine whether a list is empty.

4. Determine the number of items on a list.

5. Insert an item at a given position in the list.

6. Delete the item at a given position in the list.

7. Look at (retrieve) the item at a given position in the list.

The following pseudocode specifies the operations for the ADT list in more detail. Figure 3-6 shows the UML diagram for this ADT.

To get a more precise idea of how the operations work, apply them to the grocery list

milk, eggs, butter, apples, bread, chicken

where milk is the first item on the list and chicken is the last item. To begin, consider how you can construct this list by using the ADT list operations. One way is first to create an empty list *aList* and then use a series of insertion operations to append successively the items to the list as follows:

```
aList.createList()
aList.insert(1, milk, success)
aList.insert(2, eggs, success)
aList.insert(3, butter, success)
aList.insert(4, apples, success)
aList.insert(5, bread, success)
aList.insert(6, chicken, success)
```

List
items
createList() *destroyList()* *isEmpty()* *getLength()* *insert()* *remove()* *retrieve()*

FIGURE 3-6   UML diagram for ADT *List*

The notation[1] *aList.O* indicates that an operation *O* applies to the list *aList*.

Notice that the list's insertion operation can insert new items into any position of the list, not just at its front or end. According to *insert*'s specification, if a new item is inserted into position *i*, the position of each item that was at a position of *i* or greater is increased by 1. Thus, for example, if you start with the previous grocery list and you perform the operation

```
aList.insert(4, nuts, success)
```

---

[1] This notation is compatible with the planned C++ implementation of the ADT.

Pseudocode for the ADT List Operations

```
// ListItemType is the type of the items stored in the list.

+createList()
// Creates an empty list.

+destroyList()
// Destroys a list.

+isEmpty():boolean {query}
// Determines whether a list is empty.

+getLength():integer {query}
// Returns the number of items that are in a list.

+insert(in index:integer, in newItem:ListItemType,
        out success:boolean)
// Inserts newItem at position index of a list, if
// 1 <= index <= getLength()+1.
// If index <= getLength(), items are renumbered as
// follows: The item at index becomes the item at
// index+1, the item at index+1 becomes the
// item at index+2, and so on. The success flag indicates
// whether the insertion was successful.

+remove(in index:integer, out success:boolean)
// Removes the item at position index of a list, if
// 1 <= index <= getLength(). If index < getLength(), items
// are renumbered as follows: The item at index+1 becomes
// the item at index, the item at index+2 becomes the item
// at index+1, and so on. The success flag indicates whether
// the deletion was successful.

+retrieve(in index:integer, out dataItem:ListItemType,
        out success:boolean) {query}
// Copies the item at position index of a list into
// dataItem, if 1 <= index <= getLength(). The list is left
// unchanged by this operation. The success flag indicates
// whether the retrieval was successful.
```

the list *aList* becomes

> *milk, eggs, butter, nuts, apples, bread, chicken*

All items that had position numbers greater than or equal to 4 before the insertion now have their position numbers increased by 1 after the insertion.

Similarly, the deletion operation specifies that if an item is deleted from position *i*, the position of each item that was at a position greater than *i* is decreased by 1. Thus, for example, if `aList` is the list

milk, eggs, butter, nuts, apples, bread, chicken

and you perform the operation

`aList.remove(5, success)`

the list becomes

milk, eggs, butter, nuts, bread, chicken

All items that had position numbers greater than 5 before the deletion now have their position numbers decreased by 1 after the deletion.

These examples illustrate that an ADT can specify the effects of its operations without having to indicate how to store the data. The specifications of the seven operations are the sole terms of the contract for the ADT list: *If you request that these operations be performed, this is what will happen.* The specifications contain no mention of how to store the list or how to perform the operations; they tell you only what you can do to the list. It is of fundamental importance that the specification of an ADT *not* include implementation issues. This restriction on the specification of an ADT is what allows you to build a wall between an implementation of an ADT and the program that uses it. (Such a program is called a **client**.) The behavior of the operations is the only thing on which a program should depend.

An ADT specification should not include implementation issues

A program should depend only on the behavior of the ADT

Note that the insertion, deletion, and retrieval operations specify the argument *success*, which provides the ADT with a simple mechanism to communicate operation failure to its client. For example, if you try to delete the tenth item from a five-item list, *remove* can set *success* to *false*. Likewise, *insert* can set *success* to *false* if, for example, the list is full or *index* is out of range. In this way, *success* enables the client to handle error situations in an implementation-independent way.

What does the specification of the ADT list tell you about its behavior? It is apparent that the list operations fall into the three broad categories presented earlier in this chapter:

- The operation *insert* adds data to a data collection.

- The operation *remove* removes data from a data collection.

- The operations *isEmpty*, *getLength*, and *retrieve* ask questions about the data in a data collection.

Once you have satisfactorily specified the behavior of an ADT, you can design applications that access and manipulate the ADT's data solely in terms of its operations and without regard for its implementation. As a simple example, suppose that you want to display the items on a list. Even though the wall between the implementation of the ADT list and the rest of the program prevents you from knowing how the list is stored, you can write a function *displayList* in terms of the operations that define the ADT list. The pseudocode for such a function follows:[2]

```
displayList(in aList:List)
// Displays the items on the list aList.

    for (position = 1 through aList.getLength())
    {  aList.retrieve(position, dataItem, success)
       Display dataItem
    }  // end for
```

Notice that as long as the ADT list is implemented correctly, the *displayList* function will perform its task. In this case, *retrieve* successfully retrieves each list item, because *position*'s value is always valid, so *success* can be ignored.

The function *displayList* does not depend on *how* you implement the list. That is, the function will work regardless of whether you use an array or some other data structure to store the list's data. This feature is a definite advantage of abstract data types. In addition, by thinking in terms of the available ADT operations, you will not be distracted by implementation details. Figure 3-7 illustrates the wall between *displayList* and the implementation of the ADT list.

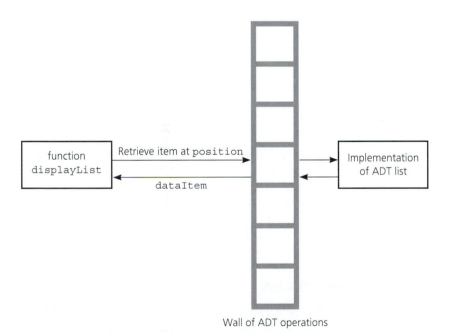

Wall of ADT operations

FIGURE 3-7   The wall between *displayList* and the implementation of the ADT list

---

[2] In this example, *displayList* is not an ADT operation, so a functional notation that specifies *aList* as an argument is used.

As another application of the ADT operations, suppose that you want a function *replace* that replaces the item in position *i* with a new item. If the *i*th item exists, *replace* deletes the item and inserts the new item at position *i*, as follows:

```
replace(in aList:List, in i:integer,
        in newItem:ListItemType, out success:boolean)
// Replaces the i^th item on the list aList with newItem.
// The success flag indicates whether the replacement
// was successful.

    aList.remove(i, success)
    if (success)
        aList.insert(i, newItem, success)
```

If *remove* is successful, it sets *success* to *true*. By testing *success*, *replace* will attempt the insertion only if the deletion actually occurred. Then *insert* sets *success*, which *replace* returns to the function that called it. If *remove* is unsuccessful for any reason, including an incorrect value of *i*, it sets *success* to *false*. The *replace* function then ignores the insertion and returns *success*.

You can use ADT operations in an application without the distraction of implementation details

In both of the preceding examples, notice how you can focus on the task at hand without the distraction of implementation details such as arrays. With less to worry about, you are less likely to make an error in your logic when you use the ADT operations in applications such as *displayList* and *replace*. Likewise, when you finally implement the ADT operations in C++, you will not be distracted by these applications. In addition, because *displayList* and *replace* do not depend on any implementation decisions that you make, they are not altered by your decisions. These assertions assume that you do not change the specifications of the ADT operations when you implement them. However, as Chapter 1 pointed out, developing software is not a linear process. You may realize during implementation that you need to refine your specifications. Clearly, changes to the specification of any module affect any already-designed uses of that module.

To summarize, you can specify the behavior of an ADT independently of its implementation. Given such a specification, and without any knowledge of how the ADT will be implemented, you can design applications that utilize the ADT's operations to access its data.

The ADT Sorted List

One of the most frequently performed computing tasks is the maintenance, in some *specified* order, of a collection of data. Many examples immediately come to mind: students placed in order by their names, baseball players listed in order by their batting averages, and corporations listed in order by their assets. This is called **sorted order**. In contrast, the items on a grocery list might be ordered—the order in which they appear on the grocer's shelves, for example—but they are probably not sorted by name.

The problem of *maintaining* sorted data requires more than simply sorting the data. Often you need to insert some new data item into its proper, sorted place. Similarly, you often need to delete some data item. For example, suppose your university maintains an alphabetical list of the students who are currently enrolled. The registrar must insert names into and delete names from this list because students constantly enroll in and leave school. These operations should preserve the sorted order of the data.

The following specifications define the operations for the ADT **sorted list**.

The ADT sorted list maintains items in sorted order

KEY CONCEPTS

Pseudocode for the ADT Sorted List Operations

```
// ListItemType is the type of the items stored in the list.


+createSortedList()
// Creates an empty sorted list.


+destroySortedList()
// Destroys a sorted list.


+sortedIsEmpty():boolean {query}
// Determines whether a sorted list is empty.


+sortedGetLength():integer {query}
// Returns the number of items that are in a sorted list.


+sortedInsert(in newItem:ListItemType, out success:boolean)
// Inserts newItem into its proper sorted position in a
// sorted list. The success flag indicates whether the
// insertion was successful.


+sortedRemove(in anItem:ListItemType, out success:boolean)
// Deletes anItem from a sorted list. The success flag
// indicates whether the deletion was successful.


+sortedRetrieve(in index:integer, out dataItem:ListItemType,
                out success:boolean) {query}
// Sets dataItem to the item at position index of a sorted
// list, if 1 <= index <= sortedGetLength(). The list is left
// unchanged by this operation. The success flag indicates
// whether the retrieval was successful.


+locatePosition(in anItem:ListItemType,
                out isPresent:boolean):integer {query}
// Returns the position where the item belongs or exists
// in a sorted list. The isPresent flag indicates whether
// anItem is currently in the list. The item anItem and the
// list are unchanged.
```

The ADT sorted list differs from the ADT list in that a sorted list inserts and deletes items by their values and not by their positions. For example, *sortedInsert* determines the proper position for *newItem* according to its value. Also, *locatePosition*—which determines the position of any item, given its value—is a sorted list operation but not a list operation. However, *sortedRetrieve* is like list's *retrieve*: Both operations retrieve an item, given its position. The function *sortedRetrieve* enables you, for example, to write another function to retrieve and then display each item in a sorted list.

Designing an ADT

The design of an abstract data type should evolve naturally during the problem-solving process. As an example of how this process might occur, suppose that you want to determine the dates of all the holidays in a given year. One way to do this is to examine a calendar. That is, you could consider each day in the year and ascertain whether that day is a holiday. The following pseudocode is thus a possible solution to this problem:

```
listHolidays(in year:integer)
// Displays the dates of all holidays in a given year.

   date = date of first day of year
   while (date is before the first day of year+1)
   {  if (date is a holiday)
        write (date," is a holiday")

      date = date of next day
   }  // end while
```

What data does a problem require?

What data are involved here? Clearly, this problem operates on dates, where a date consists of a month, day, and year. What operations will you need to solve the holiday problem? Your ADT must specify and restrict the legal operations on the dates just as the fundamental data type *int* restricts you to operations such as addition and comparison. You can see from the previous pseudocode that you must

What operations does a problem require?

- Determine the date of the first day of a given year.

- Determine whether a date is before another date.

- Determine whether a date is a holiday.

- Determine the date of the day that follows a given date.

Thus, you could define the following operations for your ADT:

```
+firstDay(in year:integer):Date {query}
// Returns the date of the first day of a given year.

+isBefore(in date1:Date,
         in date2:Date) : boolean {query}
// Returns true if date1 is before date2,
// otherwise returns false.

+isHoliday(in aDate:Date) : boolean {query}
// Returns true if date is a holiday,
// otherwise returns false.

+nextDay(in aDate:Date) : Date {query}
// Returns the date of the day after a given date.
```

The `listHolidays` pseudocode now appears as follows:

```
listHolidays(in year:integer)
// Displays the dates of all holidays in a given year.

    date = firstDay(year)
    while (isBefore(date, firstDay(year+1)))
    {  if (isHoliday(date))
          write (date," is a holiday ")
       date = nextDay(date)
    }  // end while
```

Thus, you can design an ADT by identifying data and choosing operations that are suitable to your problem. After specifying the operations, you use them to solve your problem independently of the implementation details of the ADT.

An appointment book. As another example of an ADT design, imagine that you want to create a computerized appointment book that spans a one-year period. Suppose that you make appointments only on the hour and half hour between 8 a.m. and 5 p.m. You want your system to store a brief notation about the nature of each appointment along with the date and time.

To solve this problem, you can define an ADT appointment book. The data items in this ADT are the appointments, where an appointment consists of a date, time, and purpose. What are the operations? Two obvious operations are

- Make an appointment for a certain date, time, and purpose. (You will want to be careful that you do not make an appointment at an already occupied time.)

- Cancel the appointment for a certain date and time.

In addition to these operations, it is likely that you will want to

- Ask whether you have an appointment at a given time.

- Determine the nature of your appointment at a given time.

Finally, ADTs typically have initialization and destruction operations. Thus, the ADT appointment book can have the following operations:

```
+createAppointmentBook()
// Creates an empty appointment book.

+isAppointment(in apptDate:Date,
               in apptTime:Time) : boolean {query}
// Returns true if an appointment exists for the date
// and time specified; otherwise returns false.

+makeAppointment(in apptDate:Date, in apptTime:Time,
                 in purpose:string) : boolean
// Inserts the appointment for the apptDate, apptTime, and
// purpose specified as long as it does not conflict with
// an existing appointment.
// Returns true if successful, false otherwise.

+cancelAppointment(in apptDate:Date,
                   in apptTime:Time) : boolean
// Deletes the appointment for the apptDate and apptTime
// specified.
// Returns true if successful, false otherwise

+checkAppointment(in apptDate:Date, in apptTime:Time,
                  out purpose:string) {query}
// Retrieves the purpose of the appointment at the given
// apptDate/apptTime, if one exists. Otherwise, purpose
// is set equal to a null string
```

You can use these ADT operations to design other operations on the appointments. For example, suppose that you want to change the date or time of a particular appointment within the existing appointment book *apptBook*. The following pseudocode indicates how to accomplish this task by using the previous ADT operations:

```
// change the date or time of an appointment

read (oldDate, oldTime, newDate, newTime)
// get purpose of appointment
apptBook.checkAppointment(oldDate, oldTime, oldPurpose)
if (oldPurpose not null)
{  // see if new date/time is available
```

```
if (apptBook.isAppointment(newDate, newTime))
    // new date/time is booked
    write ("You already have an appointment at ", newTime,
            " on ", newDate)

else  // new date/time is available
{   apptBook.cancelAppointment(oldDate, oldTime)
    if (apptBook.makeAppointment(newDate, newTime, oldPurpose))
        write ("Your appointment has been rescheduled to ",
                newTime, " on ", newDate)
}  // end if
}  // end if
else
    write ("You do not have an appointment at ", oldTime,
            " on ", oldDate)
```

Again notice that you can design applications of ADT operations without knowing how the ADT is implemented. The exercises at the end of this chapter provide examples of other tasks that you can perform with this ADT.

You can use an ADT without knowledge of its implementation

ADTs that suggest other ADTs.   Both of the previous examples require you to represent a date; the appointment book example also requires you to represent the time. C++ has a date-time *struct* specified in *time.h* that you can use to represent the date and the time. You can also design ADTs to represent these items in a more object-oriented way. It is not unusual for the design of one ADT to suggest other ADTs. In fact, you can use one ADT to implement another ADT. The programming problems at the end of this chapter ask you to design and implement the simple ADTs date and time.

   This final example also describes an ADT that suggests other ADTs for its implementation. Suppose that you want to design a database of recipes. You could think of this database as an ADT: The recipes are the data items, and some typical operations on the recipes could include the following:

You can use an ADT to implement another ADT

```
+insertRecipe(in aRecipe:Recipe, out success:boolean)
// Inserts recipe into the database.

+deleteRecipe(in aRecipe:Recipe, out success:boolean)
// Deletes recipe from the database.

+retrieveRecipe(in name:string, out aRecipe:Recipe,
                out success:boolean) {query}
// Retrieves the named recipe from the database.
```

This level of the design does not indicate such details as where *insertRecipe* will place a recipe into the database.

Now imagine that you want to write a function that scales a recipe retrieved from the database: If the recipe is for *n* people, you want to revise it so that it will serve *m* people. Suppose that the recipe contains measurements such as 2½ cups, 1 tablespoon, and ¼ teaspoon. That is, the quantities are given as mixed numbers—integers and fractions—in units of cups, tablespoons, and teaspoons.

This problem suggests another ADT—measurement—with the following operations:

```
+getMeasure() : Measurement {query}
// Returns the measure.


+setMeasure(in m: Measurement)
// Sets a measure.


+scaleMeasure(out newMeasure:Measurement,
              in scaleFactor:float)
// Multiplies measure by a fractional scaleFactor, which
// has no units, to obtain newMeasure.


+convertMeasure(in oldUnits:MeasureUnit,
                out newMeasure:Measurement,
                in newUnits:MeasureUnit) {query}
// Converts measure from its old units to newMeasure in
// new units.
```

Suppose that you want the ADT measurement to perform exact fractional arithmetic. Because our planned implementation language C++ does not have a data type for fractions and floating-point arithmetic is not exact, another ADT called fraction is in order. Its operations could include addition, subtraction, multiplication, and division of fractions. For example, you could specify addition as

```
+addFractions(in first:Fraction,
              in second:Fraction) : Fraction
// Adds two fractions and returns the sum reduced to lowest
// terms.
```

Moreover, you could include operations to convert a mixed number to a fraction and vice versa when feasible.

When you finally implement the ADT measurement, you can use the ADT fraction. That is, you can use one ADT to implement another ADT.

Axioms (Optional)

The previous specifications for ADT operations have been stated rather informally. For example, they rely on your knowing the meaning of "an item is at position i" in an ADT list. This notion is simple, and most people will understand its intentions. However, some ADTs are much more complex and less intuitive than a list. For such ADTs, you should use a more rigorous method of defining the behavior of their operations: You must supply a set of mathematical rules—called **axioms**—that precisely specify the behavior of each ADT operation.

An axiom is a
mathematical rule

An axiom is actually an invariant—a true statement—for an ADT operation. For example, you are familiar with axioms for algebraic operations; in particular, you know the following rules for multiplication:

$$(a \times b) \times c = a \times (b \times c)$$

Axioms for multiplication

$$a \times b = b \times a$$

$$a \times 1 = a$$

$$a \times 0 = 0$$

These rules, or axioms, are true for any numeric values of a, b, and c, and describe the behavior of the multiplication operator $\times$.

In a similar fashion, you can write a set of axioms that completely describes the behavior of the operations for the ADT list. For example,

Axioms specify the behavior
of an ADT

> *A newly created list is empty*

is an axiom because it is true for all newly created lists. You can state this axiom succinctly in terms of the ADT list operations as follows:

        `(aList.createList()).isEmpty()` is true

That is, the list `aList` is empty.

The statement

> *If you insert an item x into the ith position of an ADT list, retrieving the ith item will result in x*

is true for all lists, and so it is an axiom. You can state this axiom in terms of the ADT list operations, as follows:[3]

        `(aList.insert(i, x)).retrieve(x) = x`

That is, `retrieve` retrieves from position i of list `aList` the item x that `insert` has put there. To simplify the notation, the `success` arguments are omitted and `retrieve` is treated as if it were a valued function.

The following axioms formally define the ADT list:

---

[3] The = notation within these axioms denotes algebraic equality.

KEY CONCEPTS

Axioms for the ADT List

1. `(aList.createList()).getLength() = 0`

2. `(aList.insert(i, x)).getLength() =`
   `aList.getLength() + 1`

3. `(aList.remove(i)).getLength() =`
   `aList.getLength() - 1`

4. `(aList.createList()).isEmpty() = true`

5. `(aList.insert(i, item)).isEmpty() = false`

6. `(aList.createList()).remove(i) = error`

7. `(aList.insert(i, x)).remove(i) = aList`

8. `(aList.createList()).retrieve(i) = error`

9. `(aList.insert(i, x)).retrieve(i) = x`

10. `aList.retrieve(i) =`
    `(aList.insert(i, x)).retrieve(i+1)`

11. `aList.retrieve(i+1) =`
    `(aList.remove(i)).retrieve(i)`

A set of axioms does not make the pre- and postconditions for an ADT's operations unnecessary. For example, the previous axioms do not describe *insert*'s behavior when you try to insert an item into position 50 of a list of two items. One way to handle this situation is to include the restriction

`1 <= index <= getLength()+1`

in *insert*'s precondition. Another way—which you will see when we implement the ADT list later in this chapter—does not restrict *index*, but rather sets an argument *success* to *false* if *index* is outside the previous range. Thus, you need both a set of axioms and a set of pre- and postconditions to define the behavior of an ADT's operations completely.

Use axioms to determine the effect of a sequence of ADT operations

You can use axioms to determine the outcome of a sequence of ADT operations. For example, if *aList* is a list of characters, how does the sequence of operations

`aList.insert(1, b)`
`aList.insert(1, a)`

affect *aList*? We will show that *a* is the first item in this list and that *b* is the second item by using *retrieve* to retrieve these items.

You can write the previous sequence of operations in another way as

`(aList.insert(1, b)).insert(1, a)`

or

`tempList.insert(1, a)`

where `tempList` represents `aList.insert(1, b)`. Now retrieve the first and second items in the list `tempList.insert(1, a)`, as follows:

`(tempList.insert(1, a)).retrieve(1) = a`   by axiom 9

and

```
(tempList.insert(1, a)).retrieve(2)
  = tempList.retrieve(1)              by axiom 10
  = (aList.insert(1, b)).retrieve(1)  by definition of tempList
  = b                                 by axiom 9
```

Thus, *a* is the first item in the list and *b* is the second item.

Axioms are treated further in exercises in the rest of the book.

3.3 Implementing ADTs

The previous sections emphasized the specification of an abstract data type. When you design an ADT, you concentrate on what its operations do, but you ignore how you will implement them. The result should be a set of clearly specified ADT operations.

How do you implement an ADT once its operations are clearly specified? That is, how do you store the ADT's data and carry out its operations? Earlier in this chapter you learned that when implementing an ADT, you choose data structures to represent the ADT's data. Thus, your first reaction to the implementation question might be to choose a data structure and then to write functions that access it in accordance with the ADT operations. Although this point of view is not incorrect, hopefully you have learned not to jump right into code. In general, you should refine an ADT through successive levels of abstraction. That is, you should use a top-down approach to designing an algorithm for each of the ADT operations. You can view each of the successively more concrete descriptions of the ADT as implementing its more abstract predecessors. The refinement process stops when you reach data structures that are available in your programming language. The more primitive your language, the more levels of implementation you will require.

The choices that you make at each level of the implementation can affect its efficiency. For now, our analyses will be intuitive, but Chapter 9 will introduce you to quantitative techniques that you can use to weigh the trade-offs involved.

Recall that the program that uses the ADT should see only a wall of available operations that act on data. Figure 3-8 illustrates this wall once again. Both the data structure that you choose to contain the data and the implementations of the ADT operations are hidden behind the wall. By now, you should realize the advantage of this wall.

In a non-object-oriented implementation, both the data structure and the ADT operations are distinct pieces. The client agrees to honor the wall by using only the ADT operations to access the data structure. Unfortunately, the data structure is hidden only if the client does not look over the wall! Thus, the client can violate the wall—either intentionally or accidentally—by accessing the data structure directly, as Figure 3-9 illustrates. Why is such an action undesirable? Later, this chapter will use an array *items* to store an ADT list's items. In a program that uses such a list, you might, for example, accidentally access the first item in the list by writing

```
firstItem = items[0];
```

instead of by invoking *retrieve*. If you changed to another implementation of the list, your program would be incorrect. To correct your program, you would need to locate and change all occurrences of *items[0]*—but first you would have to realize that *items[0]* is in error!

Object-oriented languages such as C++ provide a way for you to enforce the wall of an ADT, thereby preventing access of the data structure in any way other than by using the ADT operations. We will spend some time now exploring this aspect of C++ by discussing classes, namespaces, and exceptions.

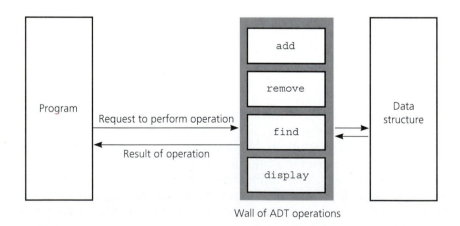

Wall of ADT operations

FIGURE 3-8   ADT operations provide access to a data structure

C++ Classes

Recall from Chapter 1 that object-oriented programming, or OOP, views a program not as a sequence of actions but as a collection of components called objects. Encapsulation—one of OOP's three fundamental principles[4]—enables you to enforce the walls of an ADT. It is, therefore, essential to an ADT's implementation and our main focus here.

Encapsulation combines an ADT's data with its operations—called methods—to form an object. Rather than thinking of the many components of the ADT in Figure 3-8, you can think at a higher level of abstraction when you consider the object in Figure 3-10 because it is a single entity. The object hides its inner detail from the programmer who uses it. Thus, an ADT's operations become an object's behaviors.

Encapsulation hides implementation details

We could use a ball as an example of an object. Because thinking of a basketball, volleyball, tennis ball, or soccer ball probably suggests images of the game rather than the object itself, let's abstract the notion of a ball by picturing a sphere. A sphere of a given radius has attributes such as volume and surface area. A sphere as an object should be able to report its radius, volume, surface area, and so on. That is, the sphere object has methods that return such values. This section will develop the notion of a sphere as an object. Later, in Chapter 8, you will see how to derive a ball from a sphere.

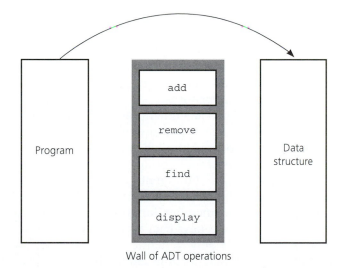

Wall of ADT operations

FIGURE 3-9   Violating the wall of ADT operations

---

[4] The other principles are inheritance and polymorphism, discussed in Chapter 8.

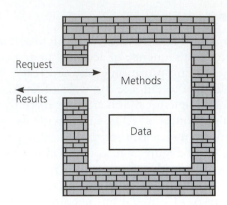

FIGURE 3-10   An object's data and methods are encapsulated

A C++ class defines a new
data type

How do you actually define an object in C++? Recall that Chapter 1 introduced the class as a set of objects of the same kind. In C++, a class is actually a new data type whose instances are objects. The syntax for a class is like that for a C++ structure. Like a structure, a class can contain data members. You reference these data members in the same way that you reference the data members in a structure: You qualify a data member's name with an instance of the class. A class can also contain **member functions**, collectively known as class members, which typically act on the data members. You invoke a member function by qualifying its name with the instance of the class in the same way that you reference data members.

An object is an instance of
a class

By default, all members in a class are private—they are not directly accessible by your program—unless you designate them as public. The implementations of a class's member functions, however, can use any private members. In contrast, all members of a structure are public unless you designate them as private.

Because a C++ structure can contain member functions, a class and a structure have the same effect, if you explicitly designate both their public and private members. Although you could use *struct* and *class* interchangeably, you should not do so. A structure is appropriate when you want to group data of different types, but you do not want to create a new data type. The structures in this book contain only data members and possibly one member function to initialize them. You should use a class to define a new data type when you implement an ADT. This book uses *class* only to define object types and will always indicate the public and private portions explicitly.

A constructor creates and
initializes an object

A destructor destroys
an object

The ADTs that you saw earlier had operations for their creation and destruction. Classes have such methods, called **constructors** and **destructors**. A constructor creates and initializes new instances of a class. A destructor destroys an instance of a class, when the object's lifetime ends. A typical class has several constructors but only one destructor. For many classes, you can omit the destructor. In such cases, the compiler will generate a destructor for you. For the classes in this chapter, the compiler-generated destructor is sufficient. Chapter 4 discusses how and why you would write your own destructor.

In C++, a constructor has the same name as the class. Constructors have no return type—not even *void*—and cannot use *return* to return a value. Constructors can have arguments. We discuss constructors in more detail shortly, after we look at an example of a class definition.

The header file. You should place each class definition in its own **header file** or **specification file**—whose name by convention ends in *.h*.[5] The following header file, *Sphere.h*, contains a class definition for sphere objects:

```cpp
// ****************************************************
// Header file Sphere.h for the class Sphere.
// ****************************************************
const double PI = 3.14159;
class Sphere
{
public:
   Sphere();
   // Default constructor: Creates a sphere and
   // initializes its radius to a default value.
   // Precondition: None.
   // Postcondition: A sphere of radius 1 exists.

   Sphere(double initialRadius);
   // Constructor: Creates a sphere and initializes
   // its radius.
   // Precondition: initialRadius is the desired
   // radius.
   // Postcondition: A sphere of radius initialRadius
   // exists.

   void setRadius(double newRadius);
   // Sets (alters) the radius of an existing sphere.
   // Precondition: newRadius is the desired radius.
   // Postcondition: The sphere's radius is newRadius.

   double getRadius() const;
   // Determines a sphere's radius.
   // Precondition: None.
   // Postcondition: Returns the radius.

   double getDiameter() const;
   // Determines a sphere's diameter.
```

---

[5] Other conventions, such as *.hpp* or *.hxx*, exist.

```
// Precondition: None.
// Postcondition: Returns the diameter.


double getCircumference() const;
// Determines a sphere's circumference.
// Precondition: PI is a named constant.
// Postcondition: Returns the circumference.


double getArea() const;
// Determines a sphere's surface area.
// Precondition: PI is a named constant.
// Postcondition: Returns the surface area.


double getVolume() const;
// Determines a sphere's volume.
// Precondition: PI is a named constant.
// Postcondition: Returns the volume.


void displayStatistics() const;
// Displays statistics of a sphere.
// Precondition: None.
// Postcondition: Displays the radius, diameter,
// circumference, area, and volume.


private:
   double theRadius;  // the sphere's radius
};  // end class
// End of header file.
```

A class's data members should be private

You should almost always place a class's data members within its private section. Typically, you provide methods—such as *setRadius* and *getRadius*—to access the data members. In this way, you control how and if the rest of the program can access the data members. This design principle should lead to programs that not only are easier to debug, but also have fewer logical errors from the beginning.

Some function declarations, such as

```
double getRadius() const;
```

***const* functions cannot change a class's data members**

are tagged with *const*. Such functions cannot alter the data members of the class. Making *getRadius* a *const* function is a fail-safe technique that ensures that it will only return the current value of the sphere's radius, without changing it.

Comments in the header file specify the member functions

A programmer who uses your class in a program usually sees only the header file, as you will soon learn. For this reason, your author prefers to place the documentation for the member functions in the header file and to place the class's public section before its private section.

Let's begin implementing the class *Sphere* by examining its constructors.

Constructors.   A constructor allocates memory for an object and can initialize the object's data to particular values. A class can have more than one constructor, as is the case for the class *Sphere*.

The first constructor in *Sphere* is the **default constructor**

```
Sphere();
```

A default constructor by definition has no arguments. Typically, a default constructor initializes data members to values that the class implementation chooses. For example, the implementation

```
Sphere::Sphere(): theRadius(1.0)
{
}  // end default constructor
```

sets *theRadius* to 1.0.

Notice the qualifier *Sphere::* that precedes the constructor's name. When you implement any member function, you qualify its name with its class type followed by the **scope resolution operator** *::* to distinguish it from other functions that might have the same name.

Although you could simply use an assignment statement to assign a value to *theRadius*, it is preferable to use an **initializer**—*theRadius(1.0)* in this case. Each initializer uses a functional notation that consists of a data member name followed by its initial value enclosed in parentheses. If you write more than one initializer,[6] you separate them with commas. A colon precedes the first (or only) initializer. Often the implementation of a constructor consists only of initializers, so its body is empty, as is the case here. Note that you can use these initializers with constructors but not with other member functions.

When you declare an instance of the class, a constructor is invoked implicitly. For example, the statement

```
Sphere unitSphere;
```

invokes the default constructor, which creates the object *unitSphere* and sets its radius to 1.0. Notice that you do not include parentheses after *unitSphere*.

The next constructor in *Sphere* is

```
Sphere(double initialRadius);
```

A default constructor has no arguments

Use initializers within a constructor's implementation to set data members to initial values

Use initializers only within constructors

---

[6] When a class has several data members, the constructor initializes them in the order in which they appear in the class definition instead of the order in which the initializers appear in the constructor definition. You should use the same order in both cases to avoid confusion, even if the initialization order does not make a difference.

It creates a sphere object of radius *initialRadius*. This constructor needs only to initialize the private data member *theRadius* to *initialRadius*. Its implementation[7] is

```
Sphere::Sphere(double initialRadius):
                              theRadius(initialRadius)
{
}  // end constructor
```

You implicitly invoke this constructor by writing a declaration such as

```
Sphere mySphere(5.1);
```

In this case, the object *mySphere* has a radius of 5.1.

If you omit all constructors from your class, the compiler will generate a default constructor—that is, one with no arguments—for you. A compiler-generated default constructor, however, might not initialize data members to values that you will find suitable.

If you define a constructor that has arguments, but you omit the default constructor, the compiler will not generate one for you. Thus, you will not be able to write statements such as

```
Sphere defaultSphere;
```

The implementation file. Typically, you place the implementation of a class's member functions in an **implementation file** whose name ends in *.cpp*.[8] An implementation file for *Sphere* follows. Notice that within the definition of a member function, you can reference the class's data member or invoke its other member functions without preceding the member names with *Sphere::*

The implementation file contains the definitions of the class's member functions

```
// *********************************************************
// Implementation file Sphere.cpp for the class Sphere.
// *********************************************************
#include "Sphere.h"    // header file
#include <iostream.h>

Sphere::Sphere(): theRadius(1.0)
{
}  // end default constructor

Sphere::Sphere(double initialRadius)
{
   if (initialRadius > 0)
```

---

[7] This implementation will be improved shortly to guard against a negative radius.
[8] Other conventions, such as *.c*, *.cpp*, and *.cxx*, exist.

```
      theRadius = initialRadius;
   else
      theRadius = 1.0;
}  // end constructor

void Sphere::setRadius(double newRadius)
{
   if (newRadius > 0)
      theRadius = newRadius;
   else
      theRadius = 1.0;
}  // end setRadius

double Sphere::getRadius() const
{
   return theRadius;
}  // end getRadius

double Sphere::getDiameter() const
{
   return 2.0 * theRadius;
}  // end getDiameter

double Sphere::getCircumference() const
{
   return PI * getDiameter();
}  // end getCircumference

double Sphere::getArea() const
{
   return 4.0 * PI * theRadius * theRadius;
}  // end getArea

double Sphere::getVolume() const
{
   double radiusCubed = theRadius * theRadius * theRadius;
   return (4.0 * PI * radiusCubed)/3.0;
}  // end getVolume
```

A local variable such as *radiusCubed* should not be a data member

```
void Sphere::displayStatistics() const
{
   cout << "\nRadius = " << getRadius()
        << "\nDiameter = " << getDiameter()
        << "\nCircumference = " << getCircumference()
        << "\nArea = " << getArea()
        << "\nVolume = " << getVolume() << endl;
}  // end displayStatistics
// End of implementation file.
```

From within *displayStatistics*, you can invoke the member function *getRadius* or access the private data member *theRadius*

You should distinguish between a class's data members and any local variables that the implementation of a member function requires. It is inappropriate for such local variables to be data members of the class.

Using the Class *Sphere*.   The following simple program demonstrates the use of the class *Sphere*:

```
#include <iostream.h>
#include "Sphere.h"

int main()
{
   Sphere unitSphere;          // radius is 1.0
   Sphere mySphere(5.1);       // radius is 5.1

   unitSphere.displayStatistics();
   mySphere.setRadius(4.2);    // resets radius to 4.2
   cout << mySphere.getDiameter() << endl;

   return 0;
}  // end main
```

An object such as *mySphere* can, on request, reset the value of its radius; return its radius; compute its diameter, surface area, circumference, and volume; and display these statistics. These requests to an object are called **messages** and are simply calls to functions. Thus, an object responds to a message by acting on its data. To invoke an object's member function, you qualify the function's name—such as *setRadius*—with the object variable—such as *mySphere*.

Notice that the previous program included the header file *Sphere.h*, but did not include the implementation file *Sphere.cpp*.[9] You compile a class's implementation file separately from the program that uses the class. The way in which you tell the operating system where to locate the compiled implementation depends on the particular system.

The previous program is an example of a client of a class. A client of a particular class is simply a program or module that uses the class. We will reserve the term **user** for the person who uses a program.

Inheritance.   A brief discussion of inheritance is provided here, because it is a common way to create new classes in C++. A more complete discussion of inheritance appears in Chapter 8.

---

[9] Appendix A provides more information about header and implementation files in the section "Libraries."

Suppose we want to create a class for colored spheres, knowing that we have already developed the class *Sphere*. We could write an entirely new class for the colored spheres, but if colored spheres are actually like spheres in the class *Sphere*, we can reuse the *Sphere* implementation and add color operations and characteristics by using inheritance. Here is a specification of the class *ColoredSphere* that uses inheritance:

```
#include "Sphere.h"
enum Color {RED, BLUE, GREEN, YELLOW};
class ColoredSphere: public Sphere
{
public:
   ColoredSphere(Color initialColor);
   ColoredSphere(Color initialColor,
                 double initialRadius);
   void setColor(Color newColor);
   Color getColor() const;
private:
   Color c;
};   //end ColoredSphere class
```

A class derived from the class Sphere

The class *Sphere* is called the **base class** or **superclass,** and *Colored-Sphere* is called the **derived class** or **subclass** of the class *Sphere*.

Any instance of the derived class is also considered to be an instance of the base class and can be used in a program anywhere that an instance of the base class can be used. Also, when the clause *public* is used with the base class, any of the publicly defined functions or data members that can be used with instances of the base class can be used with instances of the derived class. The derived class instances also have the functions and data members that are publicly defined in the derived class definition.

The implementation of the functions for the class *ColoredSphere* is as follows:

```
ColoredSphere::ColoredSphere(Color initialColor)
                          :Sphere()
{
   c = initialColor;
}  // end constructor

ColoredSphere::ColoredSphere(Color initialColor,
                          double initialRadius)
                          :Sphere(initialRadius)
{
   c = initialColor;
}  // end constructor
```

```
void ColoredSphere::setColor(Color newColor)
{
   c = newColor;
}  // end setColor

Color ColoredSphere::getColor() const
{
   return c;
}  // end getColor
```

In the constructors for the *ColoredSphere* class, notice the use of the constructors *Sphere()* and *Sphere(initialRadius)*. Often, the derived class implementation will use the base class constructor in this manner and then add initializations that are specific to the derived class.

Here is a function that uses the *ColoredSphere* class:

```
void useColoredSphere()
{
   ColoredSphere ball(RED);
   ball.setRadius(5.0);
   cout << "The ball diameter is " << ball.getDiameter();
   ball.setColor(BLUE);
   ...
}  // end useColoredSphere
```

An instance of a derived class can invoke public methods of the base class

This function uses the constructor and the method *setColor* from the derived class *ColoredSphere*. It also uses the methods *setRadius* and *getDiameter* that are defined in the base class *Sphere*.

C++ Namespaces

Often, a solution to a problem will have groups of related classes and other declarations, such as functions, variables, types, and constants. C++ provides a mechanism for logically grouping these declarations and definitions into a common declarative region known as a **namespace**. You declare a namespace as follows:

```
namespace namespaceName
{
  // Place declarations here
}
```

The contents of the namespace can be accessed by code inside or outside the namespace. Inside the namespace, code can access elements directly. But accessing the same elements from outside the namespace requires special syntax. For example, suppose you have the following namespace, called *smallNamespace*:

```
namespace smallNamespace
{
   int count = 0;
   void abc();
} // end smallNamespace
```

A function declared in the namespace can be implemented directly in the namespace or can have its implementation appear elsewhere with the scope resolution operator specified. For example, here is the implementation of the function *abc*:

```
void smallNamespace::abc()
{
   // implementation
   . . .
} // end abc
```

You can access elements from outside the namespace *small-Namespace* by using the scope resolution operator. For example,

```
smallNamespace::count += 1;
smallNamespace::abc();
```

Because this syntax can become cumbersome when you're using many elements of the namespace, C++ also provides the *using* declaration. The *using* declaration allows the names of the elements to be used directly, without the scope resolution operator. For example, the previous code becomes:

```
using namespace smallNamespace;
count += 1;
abc();
```

A second form of the *using* declaration allows you to target specific elements in the namespace for the shortened notation. For example,

```
using smallNamespace::abc;
smallNamespace::count += 1;
abc();
```

This *using* declaration specifies that only the function *abc* can be accessed using the shortened notation. Access to the *count* variable still requires the scope resolution operator.

Items declared in the C++ Standard Library are declared in the namespace called *std*. When you wish to use elements in the Standard Library with the shortened notation, you must include the following *using* declaration in your code:

```
using namespace std;
```

Most of the C++ *include* files have been updated in the latest version of the standard. Usually, the newer version has the same name as the older version, but without the *.h* extension. For example, to include the older specification in a program that contains many of the C++ input and output functions, you would use the following *include* statement:

```
#include <iostream.h>
```

To use the newer version of this file, you would write

```
#include <iostream>
using namespace std;
```

The *using namespace* statement indicates that you want to use the shortened notation.

When declarations are made outside of a namespace, they are said to exist in the **global namespace**. Most of the classes created in this text are declared in the global namespace for simplicity.

An Array-Based Implementation of the ADT List

We will now implement the ADT list as a class. Recall that the ADT list operations are

```
+createList()
+destroyList()
+isEmpty():boolean
+getLength():integer
+insert(in index:integer, in newItem:ListItemType,
        out success:boolean)
+remove(in index:integer, out success:boolean)
+retrieve(in index:integer,
        out dataItem:ListItemType,
        out success:boolean)
```

You need to represent the items in the ADT list and its length. Your first thought is probably to store the list's items in an array *items*. In fact, you might believe that the list is simply a fancy name for an array. This belief is not quite true, however. An **array-based implementation** is a natural choice because both an array and a list identify their items by number. However, the ADT list has operations such as *getLength* that an array does not. In the next chapter, you will also see another implementation of the ADT list that does not use an array.

In any case, you can store a list's k^{th} item in *items[k-1]*. How much of the array will the list occupy? Possibly all of the array, but probably not. That is, you need to keep track of the array elements that you have assigned to the list and those that are available for use in the future. The maximum length of the array—its physical size—is a known, fixed value such as *MAX_LIST*. You can keep track of the current number of items on the list—that is, the list's length or logical size—in a variable *size*. An obvious benefit of this approach is that implementing the operation *getLength* will be easy. Thus, we could use the following statements for the implementation:

```
const int MAX_LIST = 100;        // max length of list
typedef int ListItemType;        // data type of list items
ListItemType items[MAX_LIST];    // array of list items
int size;                        // length of list
```

Figure 3-11 illustrates the data members for an array-based implementation of an ADT list of integers. To insert a new item at a given position in the array of list items, you must shift to the right the items from this position on, and insert the new item in the newly created opening. Figure 3-12 depicts this insertion.

Shift array elements to insert an item

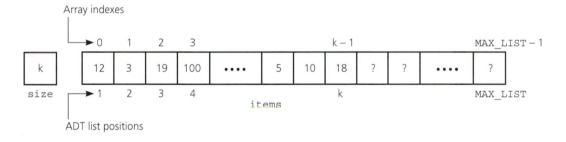

FIGURE 3-11 An array-based implementation of the ADT list

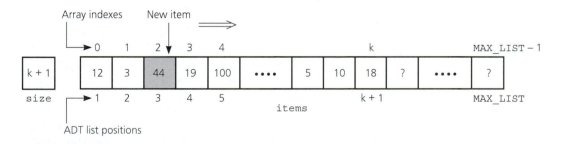

FIGURE 3-12 Shifting items for insertion at position 3

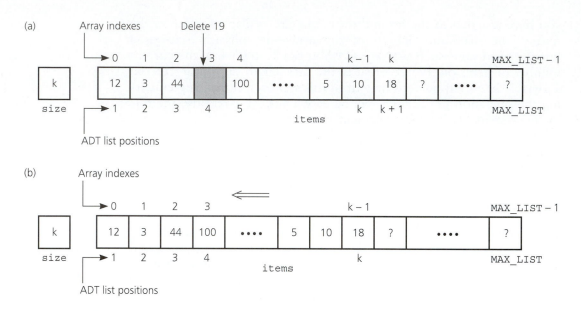

FIGURE 3-13   (a) Deletion causes a gap; (b) fill gap by shifting

Now consider how to delete an item from the list. You could blank it out, but this strategy can lead to gaps in the array, as Figure 3-13a illustrates. An array that is full of gaps has three significant problems:

- $size - 1$ is no longer the index of the last item in the array. You need another variable, *lastPosition*, to contain this index.

- Because the items are spread out, the function *retrieve* might have to look at every cell of the array even when only a few items are present.

- When *items[MAX_LIST - 1]* is occupied, the list could appear full, even when fewer than *MAX_LIST* items are present.

Shift array elements to delete an item

Thus, what you really need to do is shift the elements of the array to fill the gap left by the deleted item, as shown in Figure 3-13b.

Implement the ADT list as a class

You should implement each ADT operation as a function of a class. Each operation will require access to both the array *items* and the list's length *size*, so make *items* and *size* data members of the class. To

items and *size* are private data members

hide *items* and *size* from the clients of the class, make these data members private. Although it is not obvious why at this point, it will be convenient to define the function *translate(position)*, which returns the index of the array element that contains the list item at position *position*. That is, *translate(position)* returns the index value *position* − 1. Such a function is not one of the ADT operations and should not be available to the client. It simply makes the imple-

translate is a private member function

menter's task easier. Thus, you should hide *translate* from the client by defining it within the class's private section.

In the following header file *ListA.h* for the class of lists, the constructor corresponds to the ADT operation *createList*. A compiler-generated destructor—which corresponds to the ADT operation *destroyList*—is sufficient for this class, so we did not write one of our own.

```
// **********************************************************
// Header file ListA.h for the ADT list
// Array-based implementation
// **********************************************************
const int MAX_LIST = maximum-size-of-list;
typedef desired-type-of-list-item ListItemType;

class List
{
public:
   List();   // default constructor
             // destructor is supplied by compiler

// list operations:
   bool isEmpty() const;
   // Determines whether a list is empty.
   // Precondition: None.
   // Postcondition: Returns true if the list is empty;
   // otherwise returns false.

   int getLength() const;
   // Determines the length of a list.
   // Precondition: None.
   // Postcondition: Returns the number of items
   // that are currently in the list.

   void insert(int index, ListItemType newItem,
               bool& success);
   // Inserts an item into the list at position index.
   // Precondition: index indicates the position at which
   // the item should be inserted in the list.
   // Postcondition: If insertion is successful, newItem is
   // at position index in the list, and other items are
   // renumbered accordingly, and success is true;
   // otherwise success is false.
   // Note: Insertion will not be successful if
   // index < 1 or index > getLength()+1.

   void remove(int index, bool& success);
   // Deletes an item from the list at a given position.
   // Precondition: index indicates where the deletion
   // should occur.
```

```
// Postcondition: If 1 <= index <= getLength(),
// the item at position index in the list is
// deleted, other items are renumbered accordingly,
// and success is true; otherwise success is false.

void retrieve(int index, ListItemType& dataItem,
              bool& success) const;
// Retrieves a list item by position.
// Precondition: index is the number of the item to
// be retrieved.
// Postcondition: If 1 <= index <= getLength(),
// dataItem is the value of the desired item and
// success is true; otherwise success is false.

private:
    ListItemType items[MAX_LIST];  // array of list items
    int          size;             // number of items in list

    int translate(int index) const;
    // Converts the position of an item in a list to the
    // correct index within its array representation.
};  // end List class
// End of header file.
```

The implementations of the functions that the previous header file declares appear in the following file *ListA.cpp*:

```
// ***********************************************************
// Implementation file ListA.cpp for the ADT list
// Array-based implementation
// ***********************************************************
#include "ListA.h"  //header file
List::List() : size(0)
{
}   // end default constructor

bool List::isEmpty() const
{
    return size == 0;
} // end isEmpty

int List::getLength() const
{
    return size;
} // end getLength

void List::insert(int index, ListItemType newItem,
                  bool& success)
```

```
{
    success =  (index >= 1) &&
               (index <= size+1) &&
               (size < MAX_LIST);

    if (success)
    {  // make room for new item by shifting all items at
       // positions >= index toward the end of the
       // list (no shift if index == size+1)
       for (int pos = size; pos >= index; --pos)
          items[translate(pos+1)] = items[translate(pos)];

       // insert new item
       items[translate(index)] = newItem;
       ++size;  // increase the size of the list by one
    }  // end if
} // end insert

void List::remove(int index, bool& success)
{
    success = (index >= 1) && (index <= size);

    if (success)
    {  // delete item by shifting all items at positions >
       // index toward the beginning of the list
       // (no shift if index == size)
       for (int fromPosition = index+1;
               fromPosition <= size; ++fromPosition)
          items[translate(fromPosition-1)] =
                             items[translate(fromPosition)];
       --size;  // decrease the size of the list by one
    }  // end if

}  // end remove

void List::retrieve(int index, ListItemType& dataItem,
                    bool& success) const
{
    success = (index >= 1) &&
              (index <= size) ;

    if (success)
       dataItem = items[translate(index)];
} // end retrieve

int List::translate(int index) const
{
    return index-1;
} // end translate
//  End of implementation file.
```

The following program segment demonstrates the use of the class *List*:

```cpp
#include "ListA.h"    // ADT list operations
int main()
{
   List          aList;
   ListItemType  dataItem;
   bool          success;

   aList.insert(1, 20, success);
   . . .
   aList.retrieve(1, dataItem, success);
   . . .
```

A client of the class cannot access the class's private members directly

Note that references within this program, such as *aList.size*, *aList.items[4]*, and *aList.translate(6)*, would be illegal because *size*, *items*, and *translate* are within the private portion of the class.

In summary, to implement an ADT, given implementation-independent specifications of the ADT operations, you first must choose a data structure to contain the data. Next, you define and implement a class within a header file. The ADT operations are public member functions within the class, and the ADT data are class members that are typically private. You then implement the class's member functions within an implementation file. The program that uses the class will be able to access the data only by using the ADT operations.

C++ Exceptions

An exception is a mechanism for handling an error during execution

Many programming languages, including C++, support exceptions, which are a mechanism for handling errors. If you detect an error during execution, you can throw an exception. The code that deals with the exception is said to catch or handle it.

Catching exceptions.   To catch an exception, C++ provides **try-catch blocks**. You place a statement that might cause an exception within a *try* block. The *try* block must be followed by one or more *catch* blocks. Each *catch* block indicates a type of exception you want to handle. A *try* block can have many *catch* blocks associated with it, because even a single statement might cause more than one type of exception. In addition, the *try* block can contain many statements, any of which might cause an exception. Here is the general syntax for a *try* block:

Use a *try* block for statements that can throw an exception

```cpp
try
{
   statement(s);
}
```

and here is the syntax for a *catch* block:

```
catch (ExceptionClass identifier)
{
    statement(s);
}
```

Use a *catch* block for each type of exception that you handle

When a statement in a *try* block causes an exception, the remainder of the *try* block is abandoned, and control passes to the statements in the *catch* block that correspond to the type of exception thrown. The statements in the *catch* block are then executed and, upon completion of the *catch* block, execution resumes at the point following the last *catch* block. If there is no applicable *catch* block for an exception, abnormal program termination usually occurs.

Note that if an exception occurs in the middle of a *try* block, the destructors of all objects local to that block are called. This ensures that all resources allocated in that block are released, even if the block is not completely executed.

Throwing exceptions. When you detect an error within a function, you can throw an exception by executing a statement with the following form:

```
throw ExceptionClass(stringArgument);
```

Use a *throw* statement to throw an exception

Here *ExceptionClass* is the type of exception you want to throw, and *stringArgument* is an argument to the *ExceptionClass* constructor that provides a more detailed description of what may have caused the exception. When a *throw* statement executes, the remaining code in the function does not execute, and the exception is propagated back to the point where the function was called. See Appendix A for a more complete description.

You may find that the C++ Standard Library has an exception class already defined that suits the exception needs of your program. You may also want to define your own exception class. Usually, the C++ exception class *exception*, or one of its derived classes, is used as the base class for the exception. This provides a standardized interface for working with exceptions. In particular, all of the exceptions in the C++ Standard Library have a member function *what* that returns a message describing the exception. You will need to use the *std* namespace if you base your class on the C++ exception class *exception*.

You can define your own exception class

To indicate the exceptions that will be thrown by a function, you include a *throw* clause in the function's header as follows:

```
void myMethod(int x) throw(BadArgException, MyException)
{
  if (x == MAX)
      throw BadArgException("BadArgException: reason");
```

A function whose code can throw an exception

```
    // some code here
...
   throw MyException("MyException: reason");
}  // end myMethod
```

Including a *throw* statement in the function specification ensures that the function can throw only those exceptions. An attempt to throw any other exception will result in a runtime error.

An Implementation of the ADT List Using Exceptions

We will now implement the ADT list using exceptions. In the original implementation, the *success* flag was used to indicate whether or not the operation had succeeded. This implementation will use exceptions to indicate when an operation is unsuccessful.

The *List* class has two types of error scenarios that we will respond to by throwing an exception: an out-of-bounds list index and an attempt to insert into a full list. Attempting to delete or retrieve from an empty list will be treated as an out-of-bounds list index error.

The following defines the exception *ListIndexOutOfRangeException*, which will be used for the out-of-bounds list index error. It is based on the more general *out_of_range* exception from the C++ Standard Library.

```
#include <stdexcept>
#include <string>
using namespace std;
class ListIndexOutOfRangeException: public out_of_range
{
public:
   ListIndexOutOfRangeException(const string & message = "")
                     : out_of_range(message.c_str())
   { }
};  // end ListIndexOutOfRangeException
```

The following defines the exception *ListException*, which will be used when the array storing the list becomes full:

```
#include <stdexcept>
#include <string>

using namespace std;

class ListException: public logic_error
{
public:
```

```
    ListException(const string & message = "")
                        : logic_error(message.c_str())
    { }
};  // end ListException
```

We can now specify the *List* class presented earlier in the chapter with these exceptions as follows:

```
// ************************************************************
// Header file ListAexcept.h for the ADT list
// Array-based implementation with exceptions
// ************************************************************
#include "ListException.h"
#include "ListIndexOutOfRangeException.h"
const int MAX_LIST = maximum-size-of-list;
typedef desired-type-of-list-item ListItemType;

class List
{
public:
    List();  // default constructor
             // destructor is supplied by compiler

// list operations:
    bool isEmpty() const;
    // Exception: None.

    int getLength() const;
    // Exception: None.

    void insert(int index, ListItemType newItem)
        throw(ListIndexOutOfRangeException, ListException);
    // Exception: Throws ListIndexOutOfRangeException if
    // index < 1 or index > getLength()+1.
    // Exception: Throws ListException if newItem cannot be
    // placed in the list because the array is full.

    void remove(int index)
        throw(ListIndexOutOfRangeException);
    // Exception: Throws ListIndexOutOfRangeException if
    // index < 1 or index > getLength().

    void retrieve(int index, ListItemType& dataItem) const
        throw(ListIndexOutOfRangeException);
    // Exception: ListIndexOutOfRangeException if
    // index < 1 or index > getLength().
private:
    ListItemType items[MAX_LIST];  // array of list items
    int          size;             // number of items in list
```

```
    int translate(int index) const;
}; // end List class
// End of header file.
```

The implementation of *insert* is shown below. The implementation (with exceptions) of the *List* functions *remove* and *retrieve* is left as an exercise.

```
void List::insert(int index, ListItemType newItem)
            throw(ListIndexOutOfRangeException, ListException)
{
   if (size >= MAX_LIST)
      throw ListException(
         "ListException: List full on insert");

   if (index >= 1 && index <= size+1)
   {
      for (int pos = size; pos >= index; --pos)
         items[translate(pos+1)] = items[translate(pos)];
      // insert new item
      items[translate(index)] = newItem;
      ++size;   // increase the size of the list by one
   }
   else  // index out of range
      throw ListIndexOutOfRangeException(
        "ListIndexOutOfRangeException: Bad index on insert");
   // end if
} // end insert
```

Summary

1. Data abstraction is a technique for controlling the interaction between a program and its data structures. It builds walls around a program's data structures, just as other aspects of modularity build walls around a program's algorithms. Such walls make programs easier to design, implement, read, and modify.

2. The specification of a set of data-management operations together with the data values on which they operate define an abstract data type (ADT).

3. The formal mathematical study of ADTs uses systems of axioms to specify the behavior of ADT operations.

4. Only after you have fully defined an ADT should you think about how to implement it. The proper choice of a data structure to implement an ADT depends both on the details of the ADT operations and on the context in which you will use the operations.

5. Even after you have selected a data structure as an implementation for an ADT, the remainder of the program should not depend on your particular choice. That is, you should access the data structure by using only the ADT operations. Thus, you hide the implementation behind a wall of ADT operations. To enforce the wall within C++, you define the ADT as a class, thus hiding the ADT's implementation from the program that uses the ADT.

6. An object encapsulates both data and operations on that data. In C++, objects are instances of a class, which is a programmer-defined data type.

7. A C++ class contains at least one constructor, which is an initialization method, and a destructor, which is a cleanup method that destroys an object when its lifetime ends.

8. If you do not define a constructor for a class, the compiler will generate a default constructor—that is, one without arguments—for you. If you do not define a destructor, the compiler will generate one for you. A compiler-generated destructor is sufficient for the classes in this chapter; Chapter 4 describes when you need to write your own.

9. Members of a class are private unless you designate them as public. The client of the class, that is, the program that uses the class, cannot use members that are private. However, the implementations of functions can use them. Typically, you should make the data members of a class private and provide public functions to access some or all of the data members.

10. Because certain classes have applications in many programs, you should take steps to facilitate their use. You can define and implement a class within header and implementation files, which a program can include when it needs to use the class.

11. A namespace provides a mechanism for logically grouping related classes, functions, variables, types, and constants.

12. If you detect an error during execution, you can throw an exception. The code that deals with the exception is said to catch or handle it.

Cautions

1. After you design a class, try writing some code that uses your class before you commit to your design. Not only will you see whether your design works for the problem at hand, but also you will test your understanding of your own design and check the comments that document your specifications.

2. When you implement a class, you might discover problems with either your class design or your specifications. If these problems occur, change your design and specifications, try using the class again, and continue implementing. These comments are consistent with the discussion of the software life cycle in Chapter 1.

3. A program should not depend on the particular implementations of its ADTs. By using a class to implement an ADT, you encapsulate the ADT's data and operations. In this way, you can hide implementation details from the program that uses the ADT. In particular, by making the class's data members private, you can change the class's implementation without affecting the client.

4. By making a class's data members private, you make it easier to locate errors in a program's logic. An ADT—and hence a class—is responsible for maintaining its data. If an error occurs, you look at the class's implementation for the source of the error. If the client could manipulate this data directly because the data was public, you would not know where to look for errors.

5. When a member function does not alter the class's data members, make it a *const* function as a safeguard against an implementation error.

6. Variables that are local to a function's implementation should not be data members of the class.

7. If you define a constructor for a class but do not also define a default constructor, the compiler will not generate one for you. In this case, a statement such as

```
List myList;
```

is illegal.

8. An array-based implementation of an ADT restricts the number of items that you can store. Thus, the implementation should check whether the data structure has space available before inserting a new item, and the client should take appropriate action if the insertion is impossible.

9. An exception that is not handled by using a *try-catch* block may cause abnormal program termination.

Self-Test Exercises

1. What is the significance of "wall" and "contract"? Why do these notions help you become a better problem solver?

2. Write a pseudocode function *swap(aList, i, j)* that interchanges the items currently in positions *i* and *j* of a list. Define the

function in terms of the ADT list operations, so that it is independent of any particular implementation of the list. Assume that the list, in fact, has items at positions *i* and *j*. What impact does this assumption have on your solution? (See Exercise 2.)

3. What grocery list results from the following sequence of ADT list operations?

```
aList.createList()
aList.insert(1, butter, success)
aList.insert(1, eggs, success)
aList.insert(1, milk, success)
```

4. Write specifications for a list whose insertion, deletion, and retrieval operations are at the end of the list.

5. Write preconditions and postconditions for each of the ADT sorted list operations.

6. Write a pseudocode function that creates a sorted list *sortedList* from the list *aList* by using the operations of the ADTs list and sorted list.

7. The specifications of the ADTs list and sorted list do not mention the case in which two or more items have the same value. Are these specifications sufficient to cover this case, or must they be revised?

Exercises

1. Consider an ADT list of integers. Write a function that computes the sum of the integers in the list *aList*. The definition of your function should be independent of the list's implementation.

2. Implement the function *swap*, as described in Self–Test Exercise 2, but remove the assumption that the *i*th and *j*th items on the list exist. Add an argument *success* that indicates whether the swap was successful.

3. Use the function *swap* that you wrote in Exercise 2 to write a function that reverses the order of the items in a list *aList*.

4. The section "The ADT List" describes the functions *displayList* and *replace*. As given in this chapter, these operations exist outside of the ADT, that is, they are not ADT list operations. Instead, their implementations are written in terms of the ADT list operations.

   a. What is an advantage and a disadvantage of the way that *displayList* and *replace* are implemented?

   b. What is an advantage and a disadvantage of adding the operations *displayList* and *replace* to the ADT list?

5. In mathematics, a set is a group of distinct items. Specify operations such as equality, subset, union, and intersection as a part of the ADT set.

6. Design and implement an ADT that represents a bank account. The data of the ADT should include the customer name, the account number, and the account balance. The initialization operation should set the data to client-supplied values. Include operations for a deposit and a withdrawal, the addition of interest to the balance, and the display of the statistics of the account.

7. Specify operations that are a part of the ADT character string. Include typical operations such as length computation and concatenation (appending one string to another).

8. Write pseudocode implementations of the operations of an ADT that represents a rectangle. Include typical operations, such as setting and retrieving the dimensions of the rectangle, finding the area and the perimeter of the rectangle, and displaying the statistics of the rectangle.

9. Implement in C++ the pseudocode for the ADT rectangle that you created in Exercise 8.

10. Write a pseudocode function in terms of the ADT appointment book, described in the section "Designing an ADT," for each of the following tasks. Do you need to add operations to the ADT to perform these tasks?

   a. Change the purpose of the appointment at a given date and time.

   b. Display all the appointments for a given date.

11. Consider the ADT polynomial—in a single variable x—whose operations include the following:

```
degree()
// Returns the degree of a polynomial.
coefficient(power)
// Returns the coefficient of the x^power term.
changeCoefficient(newCoefficient, power)
// Replaces the coefficient of the x^power term
// with newCoefficient.
```

For this problem, consider only polynomials whose exponents are nonnegative integers. For example,

$$p = 4x^5 + 7x^3 - x^2 + 9$$

The following examples demonstrate the ADT operations on this polynomial.

$p.degree()$ is 5 (the highest power of a term with a nonzero coefficient) *p.coefficient(3)* is 7 (the coefficient of the x^3 term)

p.coefficient(4) is 0 (the coefficient of a missing term is implicitly 0)

p.changeCoefficient(-3, 7) produces the polynomial

$$p = -3x^7 + 4x^5 + 7x^3 - x^2 + 9$$

Using these ADT operations, write statements to perform the following tasks:

a. Display the coefficient of the term that has the highest power.

b. Increase the coefficient of the x^3 term by 8.

c. Compute the sum of two polynomials.

12. Write pseudocode implementations of the ADT polynomial operations, as defined in Exercise 11, in terms of the ADT list operations.

13. Imagine an unknown implementation of an ADT sorted list of integers. This ADT organizes its items into ascending order. Suppose that you have just read *n* integers into a one-dimensional array of integers called *data*. Write some C++ statements that use the ADT sorted list operations to sort the array into ascending order.

14. Use the axioms for the ADT list, as given in this chapter in the section "Axioms," to prove that the sequence of operations

```
Insert A into position 2
Insert B into position 2
Insert C into position 2
```

has the same effect on a nonempty list of characters as the sequence

```
Insert C into position 2
Insert B into position 3
Insert A into position 4
```

15. Define a set of axioms for the ADT sorted list and use them to prove that the sorted list of characters, which is defined by the sequence of operations

```
Create an empty sorted list
Insert S
Insert T
Insert R
Delete T
```

is exactly the same as the sorted list defined by the sequence

```
Create an empty sorted list
Insert T
Insert R
Delete T
Insert S
```

16. Repeat Exercise 20 in Chapter 2, using a variation of the ADT list to implement the function $f(n)$.

17. Write pseudocode that merges two sorted lists into a new third sorted list by using only ADT sorted list operations.

18. Implement the `List` functions `retrieve` and `remove` to use exceptions.

Programming Problems

1. Design and implement an ADT that represents a triangle. The data for the ADT should include the three sides of the triangle but could also include the triangle's three angles. This data should be in the private section of the class that implements the ADT.

   Include at least two initialization operations: one that provides default values for the ADT's data, and another that sets this data to client-supplied values. These operations are the class's constructors.

   The ADT also should include operations that look at the values of the ADT's data; change the values of the ADT's data; compute the triangle's area; and determine whether the triangle is a right triangle, an equilateral triangle, or an isosceles triangle.

2. Design and implement an ADT that represents the time of day. Represent the time as hours and minutes on a 24-hour clock. The hours and minutes are the private data members of the class that implements the ADT.

   Include at least two initialization operations: one that provides a default value for the time, and another that sets the time to a client-supplied value. These operations are the class's constructors.

   Include operations that set the time, increase the present time by a number of minutes, and display the time in 12-hour and 24-hour notations.

3. Design and implement an ADT that represents a calendar date. You can represent a date's month, day, and year as integers (for example, 4/1/2004). Include operations that advance the date by one day and display the date by using either numbers or words for the months. As an enhancement, include the name of the day.

4. Design and implement an ADT that represents a price in U.S. currency as dollars and cents. After you complete the implementation, write a client function that computes the change due a customer who pays x for an item whose price is y.

5. Define a class for an array-based implementation of the ADT sorted list. Consider a recursive implementation for `locatePosition`. Should `sortedInsert` and `sortedRemove` call `locatePosition`?

6. Write recursive array-based implementations of the insertion, deletion, and retrieval operations for the ADTs list and sorted list.

7. Implement the ADT set that you specified in Exercise 5 by using only arrays and simple variables.

8. Implement the ADT character string that you specified in Exercise 7.

9. Implement the ADT polynomial that Exercise 11 describes.

10. Implement the ADT appointment book, described in the section "Designing an ADT." Add operations as necessary. For example, you should add operations to read and write appointments.

11. a. Specify and implement an ADT for rational numbers. Provide operations that read, write, add, subtract, multiply, and divide fractions. The results of all arithmetic operations should be in lowest terms, so include a private function `reduceToLowestTerms`. Exercise 23 in Chapter 2 will help you with the details of this function. (Should your read and write operations call `reduceToLowestTerms`?) To simplify the determination of a fraction's sign, you can assume that the denominator of the fraction is positive.

b. Specify and implement an ADT for mixed numbers, each of which contains an integer portion and a fractional portion in lowest terms. Assume the existence of the ADT fraction (see part a). Provide operations that read, write, add, subtract, multiply, and divide mixed numbers. The results of all arithmetic operations should have fractional portions that are in lowest terms. Also include an operation that converts a fraction to a mixed number.

c. Implement the ADT recipe book as described in the section "Designing an ADT" and, in doing so, implement the ADT measurement. Add operations as necessary. For example, you should add operations to the recipe book to read, write, and scale recipes.

12. Add exception handling to Programming Problem 2 for the operations that set or increase the time.

13. Implement a program based on the UML specification in Programming Problem 3 of Chapter 1.

14. Repeat Programming Problem 4 of Chapter 1 in light of your knowledge of ADTs and classes.

15. Repeat Programming Problem 5 of Chapter 1 in light of your knowledge of ADTs and classes.

CHAPTER 4

Linked Lists

PREVIEW

This chapter introduces you to C++ pointers and the data structure linked list. You will see algorithms for fundamental linked list operations such as insertion and deletion. The chapter also describes several variations of the basic linked list. As you will see, you can use a linked list and its variations when implementing many of the ADTs that appear throughout the remainder of this book. The material in this chapter is thus essential to much of the presentation in the following chapters.

4.1 Preliminaries

The ADT list, as described in the previous chapter, has operations to insert, delete, and retrieve items, given their positions within the list. A close examination of the array-based implementation of the ADT list reveals that an array is not always the best data structure to use to maintain a collection of data. An array has a **fixed size**—at least in most commonly used programming languages—but the ADT list can have an arbitrary length. Thus, in the strict sense, you cannot use an array to implement a list because it is certainly possible for the number of items in the list to exceed the fixed size of the array. When developing implementations for ADTs, you often are confronted with this fixed-size problem. In many contexts, you must reject an implementation that has a fixed size in favor of one that can grow dynamically.

In addition, although the most intuitive means of imposing an order on data is to order it physically, this approach has its disadvantages. In a physical ordering, the successor of an item x is the next data item in sequence after x, that is, the item "to the right" of x. An array orders its items physically and, as you saw in the previous chapter, when you use an array to implement a list, you must shift data when you insert or delete an item at a specified position. Shifting data can be a time-consuming process that you should avoid, if possible. What alternatives to shifting data are available?

To get a conceptual notion of a list implementation that would not involve shifting, consider Figure 4-1. This figure should help free you from the notion that the only way to maintain a given order of data is to store the data in that order. In these diagrams, each item of the list actually *points to* the next item. Thus, if you know where an item is,

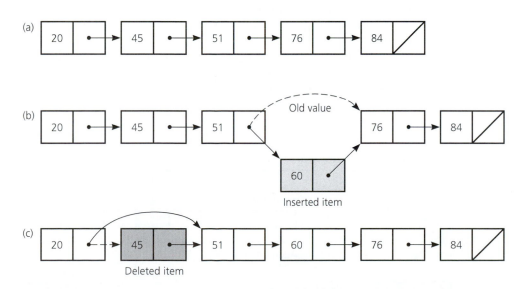

FIGURE 4-1 (a) A linked list of integers; (b) insertion; (c) deletion

you can determine its successor, which can be anywhere physically. This flexibility not only allows you to insert and delete data items without shifting data, it also allows you to increase the size of the list easily. If you need to insert a new item, you simply find its place in the list and set two **pointers**. Similarly, to delete an item, you find the item and change a pointer to bypass the item.

An item in a linked list points to its successor

Because the items in this data structure are *linked* to one another, it is called a **linked list**. As you will see shortly, *a linked list is able to grow as needed*, whereas an array can hold only a fixed number of data items. In many applications, this flexibility gives a linked list a significant advantage.

Before we examine linked lists and their use in the implementation of an ADT, we need to know more about pointers. Like many programming languages, C++ has pointers that you can use to build a linked list. The next section discusses the mechanics of these pointers.

Pointers

When you declare an ordinary variable x to be `int`, the C++ compiler allocates a memory cell that can hold an integer. You use the identifier x to refer to this cell. To put the value 5 in the cell, you could write

```
x = 5;
```

To display the value that is in the cell, you could write

```
cout << "The value of x is " << x << endl;
```

A **pointer variable,** or simply a **pointer**, contains the location, or **address** in memory, of a memory cell. By using a pointer to point to a particular memory cell, you can locate the cell and, for example, determine its content.

Figure 4-2 illustrates a pointer p that points to a memory cell containing an integer.

The notion of one memory cell that refers to another memory cell is a bit tricky. In Figure 4-2, keep in mind that the content of p is not a

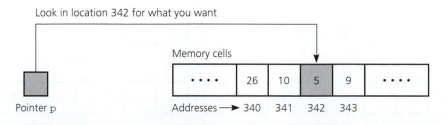

FIGURE 4-2   A pointer to an integer

typical value. The content of p is of interest only because it tells you where in memory to look for the integer value 5. That is, you can get to the integer value *indirectly* by using the address that p contains.

Now for two big questions:

- How do you get a pointer variable p to point to a memory cell?
- How do you use p to get to the content of the memory cell to which p points?

Before we answer either question, we need to declare p as a pointer variable. For example, the declaration

```
int *p;
```
p is a pointer variable

declares p to be an integer pointer variable; that is, p can point only to memory cells that contain integers. You can declare pointers to any type except files.

You need to be careful when declaring more than one pointer variable. The declaration

```
int *p, q;
```
q is not a pointer variable

declares p to be a pointer to an integer, but declares q to be an integer. That is, the statement is equivalent to

```
int *p;
int  q;
```

To declare both p and q correctly as integer pointer variables, write

```
int *p
int *q;
```

or[1]

```
int *p, *q;
```

Memory for the pointer variables p and q, and for the integer variable x in

```
int x;
```

is allocated at compilation time, that is, before the program executes. Such memory allocation is called **static allocation** and the variables

---

[1] In the context of pointers, the `*` operator is unary (like the `!` operator) and right associative. Whether you write `int *p` or `int* p`, `*` applies to the variable `p` and not the data type `int`.

are called statically allocated variables. Execution of the program does not affect the memory requirements of statically allocated variables.

Initially, the contents of *p*, *q*, and *x* are undetermined, as Figure 4-3a illustrates. However, you can place the address of *x* into *p* and therefore have *p* point to *x* by using the C++ address–of operator &, as follows:

```
p = &x;
```

Figure 4-3b illustrates the result of this assignment. Notice that the assignment statement

```
p = x;   // THIS STATEMENT IS ILLEGAL
```

is illegal because there is a type clash: *x* is an integer variable, while *p* is a pointer variable, which can contain only an address of a memory cell that contains an integer.

Pointer *p* now points to a memory cell. The notation **p* represents *the memory cell to which p points.* You can store a value in the memory cell to which *p* points by writing the assignment statement

*p is the memory cell to which *p* points

```
*p = 6;
```

as Figure 4-3c illustrates. (You could, of course, write *x = 6* to make the same assignment.) After this assignment, the expression **p* has the value 6, because 6 is now the value in the memory cell to which *p* points. Thus, you could, for example, use *cout* << **p* to display 6.

Memory allocation can also occur at execution time and is called **dynamic allocation**. A variable allocated then is called a dynamically allocated variable. C++ enables dynamic allocation of memory by providing the operator *new*, which acts on a data type, as in

new allocates memory dynamically

```
p = new int;
```

The expression *new int* allocates a new memory cell that can contain an integer and returns a pointer to this new cell, as Figure 4-3d illustrates. The initial content of this new cell is undetermined. Note that *new char* would allocate a new memory cell that can contain a character, and so on.

Observe that this newly created memory cell has no programmer-defined name. The only way to access its content or to put a value in it is indirectly via the pointer that *new* creates, that is, by using **p* in the previous example. As Figure 4-3e shows, the statement **p = 7* assigns 7 to the newly created memory cell.

Suppose that you now assign to the pointer *q* the value in *p* by writing the statement

Copying a pointer

```
q = p;
```

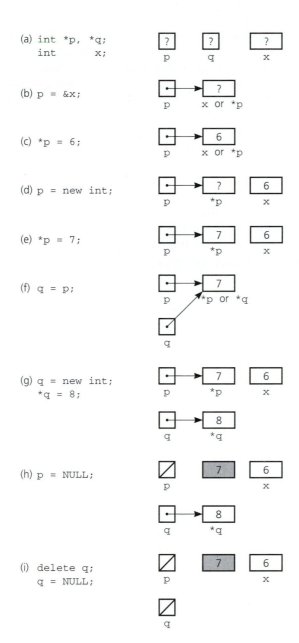

FIGURE 4-3 (a) Declaring pointer variables; (b) pointing to statically allocated memory; (c) assigning a value; (d) allocating memory dynamically; (e) assigning a value; (f) copying a pointer; (g) allocating memory dynamically and assigning a value; (h) assigning *NULL* to a pointer variable; (i) deallocating memory

Pointer *q* now points to the same memory cell that *p* points to, as Figure 4-3f illustrates. Alternatively, you could let *q* point to a new memory cell, as Figure 4-3g shows, and assign a value to this new cell. These steps are like the ones pictured in parts d and e of this figure.

Suppose that you no longer need the value in a pointer variable. That is, you do not want the pointer to point to any particular memory cell. C++ environments provide the constant *NULL*,[2] which you can assign to a pointer of any type. By convention, a *NULL* pointer value means that the pointer does not point to anything. Do not confuse a pointer variable whose value is *NULL* with one whose value is not initialized. Until you explicitly assign a value to a newly declared pointer variable, its value—like that of any other variable—is undefined. You should not assume that its value is *NULL*. In Figure 4-3a, *p* and *q* are examples of pointer variables whose values are undefined.

Now suppose that you no longer need a dynamically allocated memory cell. Simply changing all pointers to the cell wastes memory, because the cell remains allocated to the program, even though it is no longer accessible. For example, Figure 4-3h shows the result of assigning *NULL* to *p*. (In the figures, a diagonal line represents a *NULL* value.) The cell to which *p* originally pointed—it still contains 7—is in limbo. To avoid this situation—which is called a **memory leak**—C++ provides the operator *delete* as a counterpart to *new*. Conceptually, the expression

delete q

returns to the system the memory cell to which *q* points. That is, *delete* in effect deallocates memory from a program, thus freeing the memory for future use by the program. Because *delete* does not deallocate *q* itself and leaves the content of *q* undefined, a reference to **q* at this point can be disastrous. Thus, you should assign *NULL* to *q* after applying the *delete* operator as a precaution against following *q* to a deallocated memory cell. Figure 4-3i shows the results of these actions.

However, consider the situation

```
p = new int;
q = p;
delete p;
p = NULL;
```

as illustrated in Figure 4-4. Even though *p* is *NULL*, *q* still points to the deallocated node. Later the system might reallocate this node—via the *new* operator—and *q* might still point to it. You can imagine some of the errors that might ensue if a program mistakenly followed the pointer *q* and reached a node within an entirely unexpected data

A pointer whose value is NULL does not point to anything

delete returns memory to the system for reuse

delete q does not deallocate q; it leaves q undefined

A pointer to a deallocated memory cell is possible and dangerous

---

[2] Several header files, such as *cstdlib* and often *cstddef*, define *NULL*. Its value is 0. Many C++ programmers prefer to use 0 instead of *NULL*. However, for clarity, this book uses *NULL*.

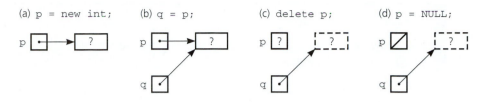

FIGURE 4-4   An incorrect pointer to a deallocated node

structure! It would be useful if the *delete* operator could eliminate the potential for this type of program error by setting to *NULL* all pointers to a deallocated node. Unfortunately, this task is very difficult. Because *delete* cannot determine which variables—in addition to *p*—point to the node to be freed, it will have to remain the programmer's responsibility not to follow a pointer to a freed node.

The sequence of statements in Figure 4-5 should serve to illustrate pointers further. Note that ADT implementations and data structures that use C++ pointers are called **pointer-based**.

KEY CONCEPTS

C++ Pointer Variables

1. The declaration

```
int *p;
```

statically allocates a pointer variable *p* whose value is undefined but is not *NULL*. The pointer variable *p* can point to a memory cell that contains an integer in this example.

2. The statement

```
p = new int;
```

dynamically allocates a new memory cell that can contain an integer. The pointer variable *p* points to this new cell. (However, see item 5 on this list.)

3. The expression *∗p* represents the memory cell to which the pointer variable *p* points.

4. If the pointer variable *p* contains *NULL*, it does not point to anything.

5. If, for some reason, *new* cannot allocate memory, it returns *NULL*. Thus, following a statement such as

```
p = new int;
```

continued on next page

continued from previous page

6. you can compare *p* with *NULL* to test whether memory was successfully allocated.

7. The statement

```
delete p;
```

8. returns to the system the memory cell to which *p* points. It does not delete *p* itself. Remember that *p* is a variable, and as such, its lifetime is not affected by *delete*.

Dynamic Allocation of Arrays

When you declare an array in C++ by using statements such as

An ordinary C++ array is statically allocated

```
const int MAX_SIZE = 50;
double anArray[MAX_SIZE];
```

the compiler reserves a specific number—*MAX_SIZE*, in this case—of memory cells for the array. This memory allocation occurs before your program executes, so it is not possible to wait until execution to give *MAX_SIZE* a value. We have already discussed the problem this fixed-size data structure causes when your program has more than *MAX_SIZE* items to place into the array.

You just learned how to use the *new* operator to allocate memory dynamically, that is, during program execution. Although the previous section showed you how to allocate a single memory cell, you actually can allocate many cells at one time. If you write

Use the *new* operator to allocate an array dynamically

```
int arraySize = 50;
double *anArray = new double[arraySize];
```

The pointer variable *anArray* will point to the first item in an array of 50 items. Unlike *MAX_SIZE*, *arraySize* can change during program execution. You can assign *arraySize* a value and, thus, determine how large your array will be at execution time. Good, but how do you use this array?

Regardless of how you allocate an array—statically, as in the first example, or dynamically, as in the second—you can use an index and the familiar array notation to access its elements. For example, *anArray[0]* and *anArray[1]* are the first two items in the array *anArray*.

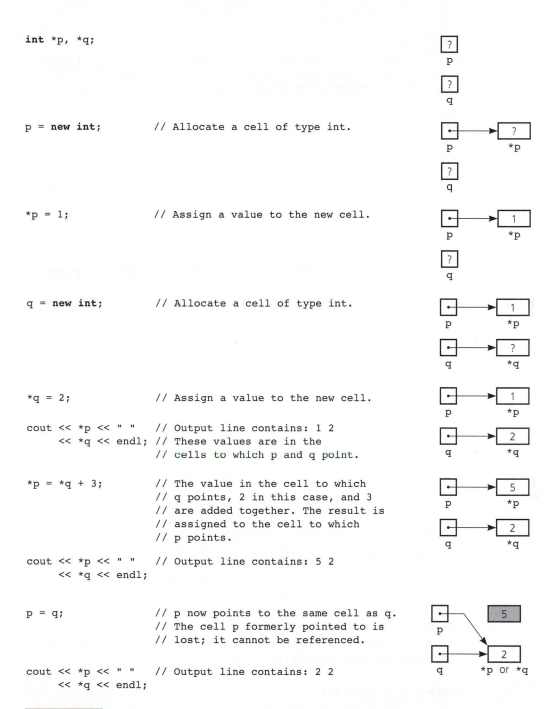

```
int *p, *q;


p = new int;           // Allocate a cell of type int.




*p = 1;                // Assign a value to the new cell.




q = new int;           // Allocate a cell of type int.




*q = 2;                // Assign a value to the new cell.

cout << *p << " "      // Output line contains: 1 2
     << *q << endl;    // These values are in the
                       // cells to which p and q point.

*p = *q + 3;           // The value in the cell to which
                       // q points, 2 in this case, and 3
                       // are added together. The result is
                       // assigned to the cell to which
                       // p points.

cout << *p << " "      // Output line contains: 5 2
     << *q << endl;


p = q;                 // p now points to the same cell as q.
                       // The cell p formerly pointed to is
                       // lost; it cannot be referenced.


cout << *p << " "      // Output line contains: 2 2
     << *q << endl;
```

FIGURE 4-5 Programming with pointer variables and dynamically allocated memory

(continues)

```
*p = 7;             // The cell to which p points (which
                    // is also the cell to which q points)
                    // now contains the value 7.

cout << *p << " "   // Output line contains: 7 7
     << *q << endl;

p = new int;        // This changes what p points to,
                    // but not what q points to.




delete p ;          // Return to the system the cell to
                    // which p points.

p = NULL;           // Set p to NULL, a good practice
                    // following delete.

q = NULL;           // The cell to which q previously
                    // pointed is now lost. You cannot
                    // reference it.
```

FIGURE 4-5

(continued)

You also can use a pointer notation to reference any array element. C++ treats the name of an array as a pointer to its first element. For example,

An array name is a pointer to the array's first element

> *anArray* is equivalent to *anArray[0]*
>
> *(anArray+1)* is equivalent to *anArray[1]*

and so on. (This notation is called pointer arithmetic.) We are not suggesting that you use this notation, however.

When you allocate an array dynamically, you need to return its memory cells to the system when you no longer need them. As in the previous section, you use the *delete* operator to perform this task. To deallocate the array *anArray*, you write

delete returns a dynamically allocated array to the system for reuse

```
delete [ ] anArray;
```

You write brackets when you apply *delete* to an array.

Now suppose that your program uses all of the array *anArray*, despite having determined its size during execution. You can allocate a new and larger array, copy the old array into the new array, and finally deallocate the old array. The following statements double the size of *anArray*:

You can increase the size of a dynamically allocated array

```
double* oldArray = anArray;          // copy pointer to array
anArray = new double[2*arraySize];   // double array size
for (int index = 0; index < arraySize; ++index)
   anArray[index] = oldArray[index]; // copy old array
delete [ ] oldArray;                 // deallocate old array
```

Subsequent discussions in this book will refer to both statically and dynamically allocated arrays. Our array-based ADT implementations will use statically allocated arrays for simplicity. The programming problems will ask you to create array-based implementations that use dynamically allocated arrays.

Pointer-Based Linked Lists

A linked list, such as the one in Figure 4-1a, contains components that are linked to one another. Each component—usually called a **node**—contains both a data item—an integer, for example—and a "pointer" to the next item. Typically, such pointers are C++ pointer variables; however, another possibility is mentioned at the end of this section. Although you have seen most of the mechanics of pointers, using pointers to implement a linked list is probably not yet completely clear to you. Consider now how you can set up such a linked list.

Because each node in the linked list must contain two pieces of information—the data item and a pointer to the next node in the list—it is natural to conclude that each node in the list should be a C++ structure. One member of the structure is the data item and the other is a pointer, as Figure 4-6 illustrates.

item   next

FIGURE 4-6 A node

Suppose that the data portion of each node contains an integer. What type of pointer should you use within a node, and to what will it point? You might guess that the pointer should point to an integer, but actually it must point to a structure because the nodes of the linked list are indeed structures and not integers. Because pointers can point to any data type except files, pointers can, in fact, point to structures. Thus, a structure of type *Node*, for example, will have as one of its members a pointer to another structure of type *Node*.

The C++ definitions are thus

```
struct Node
{ int    item;
  Node *next;
};  // end struct
```

A node in a linked list is usually a struct

Now the statement

```
Node *p;
```

Defining a pointer to a node

defines a pointer variable *p* that can point to a node of type *Node*.

The nodes of a linked list should be dynamically allocated. For example,

Dynamically allocating a node

```
p = new Node;
```

allocates a node to which *p* points. As with any other structure, you need to access the members of a node. You will need a new notation to do so, however, because the node does not have a user-defined name. To reference the member *item*, for example, of the node to which *p* points, you write[3]

Referencing a node member

```
p->item
```

To complete our general description of the linked list, we must consider two other issues. First, what is the value of the member *next* in the last node on the list? By setting this member to *NULL*, you easily can detect when you are at the end of the linked list.

Second, nothing so far points to the beginning of the linked list. If you cannot get to the beginning of the list, you cannot get to the second node on the list, and if you cannot get to the second node on the list, you cannot get to the third node on the list, and so on. The solution is to have an additional pointer whose sole purpose is to point to the first node on the linked list. Such a node is called the **head pointer** or simply the head of the linked list.

The head pointer points to the first node in a linked list

Figure 4-7 illustrates a linked list with a head pointer. Remember that each pointer in the linked list is a pointer to a *struct*, that is, an entire node; it is not a pointer to only the data portion of the node.

Observe in Figure 4-7 that the pointer variable *head* is different from the other pointers in the diagram in that it is not within one of the nodes. Rather, it is a simple pointer variable that is external to the linked list, whereas the *next* members are internal pointers within the nodes of the list. The variable *head* simply enables you to access the list's

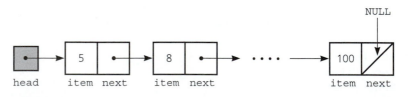

FIGURE 4-7   A head pointer to a list

---

[3] An alternative notation, *(*p).item*, is possible, but this book will not use it. Although this notation is analogous to the use of the dot operator to reference the members of a named structure, the -> operator is more suggestive of pointers.

beginning. Also, note that *head* always exists, even at times when there are no nodes on the linked list. The statement

```
Node *head;
```

creates the variable *head*, whose value, like that of other uninitialized variables, is undefined. To what value should you initialize *head* and to what value should you change it if a list ever becomes empty? In both cases, assigning *head* the value *NULL* is a logical choice, as this indicates that *head* does not point to anything.

If *head* is *NULL*, the linked list is empty

It is a common mistake to think that before you can assign *head* a value, you must execute the statement *head = new Node*. This misconception is rooted in the belief that the variable *head* does not exist before the call. This is not at all true; *head* is a pointer variable waiting to be assigned a value. Thus, for example, you can assign *NULL* to *head* without first using *new*. In fact, the sequence

```
head = new Node;   // An incorrect use of new
head = NULL;
```

A common misconception

destroys the content of the only pointer—*head*—to the newly created node, as Figure 4-8 illustrates. Thus, you have needlessly created a new node and then made it inaccessible. Remember that any time you allocate memory by using *new*, you must eventually deallocate it by using *delete*.

As was mentioned earlier, you do not need pointers to implement a linked list. Programming Problem 11 at the end of this chapter discusses an implementation that uses an array to represent the items on a linked list. Although sometimes useful, such implementations are unusual.

4.2 Programming with Linked Lists

The previous section illustrated how you can use pointer variables to implement a linked list. This section begins by developing algorithms for displaying the data portions of such a linked list and for inserting items into and deleting items from a linked list. These linked list operations are the basis of many of the data structures that appear throughout the remainder of the book. Thus, the material in this section is essential to much of the discussion in the following chapters.

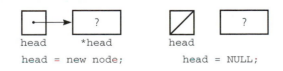

| head | *head |
| head = new node; |

| head |
| head = NULL; |

FIGURE 4-8   A lost cell

Displaying the Contents of a Linked List

Suppose now that you have a linked list, as was pictured in Figure 4-7, and that you want to display the data in the list. A high-level pseudocode solution is

```
Let a current pointer point to the first node in
   the linked list
while (the current pointer is not NULL)
{  Display the data portion of the current node
   Set the current pointer to the next pointer of the
      current node
}  // end while
```

This solution requires that you keep track of the current position within the linked list. Thus, you need a pointer variable *cur* that points to the current node. Initially, *cur* must point to the first node. Since *head* points to the first node, simply copy *head* into *cur* by writing

```
Node *cur = head;
```

To display the data portion of the current node, you can use the statement

```
cout << cur->item << endl;
```

Finally, to advance the current position to the next node, you write

```
cur = cur->next;
```

Figure 4-9 illustrates this action. If the previous assignment statement is not clear, consider

```
temp = cur->next;
cur = temp;
```

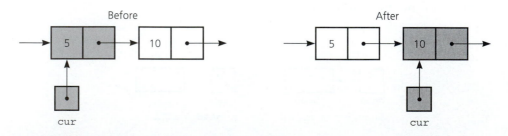

FIGURE 4-9   The effect of the assignment *cur = cur->next*

and then convince yourself that the intermediate variable `temp` is not necessary.

These ideas lead to the following loop in C++:

```
// Display the data in a linked list to which head points.
// Loop invariant: cur points to the next node to be
// displayed
for (Node *cur = head; cur != NULL; cur = cur->next)
   cout << cur->item << endl;
```

Here *cur* points to each node in a nonempty linked list during the course of the *for* loop's execution, and so the data portion of each node is displayed. After the last node is displayed, *cur* becomes *NULL* and the *for* loop terminates. When the list is empty—that is, when *head* is *NULL*—the *for* loop is correctly skipped.

A common error in the *for* statement is to compare *cur->next* instead of *cur* with *NULL*. When *cur* points to the last node of a nonempty linked list, *cur->next* is *NULL*, and so the *for* loop would terminate before displaying the data in the last node. In addition, when the list is empty—that is, when *head* and, therefore, *cur* are *NULL*—*cur->next* is undefined. Such references are incorrect and should be avoided.

Displaying a linked list is an example of a common operation, list traversal. A traversal sequentially **visits** each node in the list until it reaches the end of the list. Our example displays the data portion of each node when it visits the node. Later in this book, you will see that you can do other useful things to a node during a visit.

A traverse operation visits each node in the linked list

Displaying a linked list does not alter it; you will now see operations that modify a linked list by deleting and inserting nodes. These operations assume that the linked list has already been created. Ultimately, you will see how to build a linked list by inserting nodes into an initially empty list.

Deleting a Specified Node from a Linked List

So that you can focus on how to delete a particular node from a linked list, assume that the linked list shown in Figure 4-10 already exists. Notice that, in addition to *head*, the diagram includes two external pointer variables, *cur* and *prev*, whose data type is **Node*. The task is to delete the node to which *cur* points. As you soon will see, you also need *prev* to complete the deletion. For the moment, do not worry about how to establish *cur* and *prev*.

As Figure 4-10 indicates, you can delete a node *N*, to which *cur* points, by altering the value of the pointer *next* in the node that precedes *N*. You need to set this pointer so that it points to the node that follows *N*, thus bypassing *N* on the chain. (The dashed line indicates the old pointer value.) Notice that this pointer change does not directly affect node *N*. Node *N* remains in existence, and it points to the same

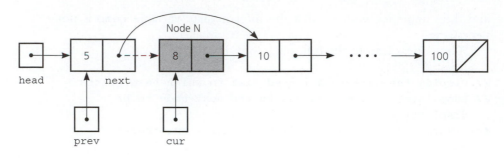

FIGURE 4-10   Deleting a node from a linked list

node that it pointed to before the deletion. However, the node has effectively been deleted from the linked list. For example, the `for` statement in the previous section would not display the contents of node *N*.

To accomplish this pointer change, notice first that if you had only the pointer `cur` pointing to *N*, you would have no direct way to access the node that precedes *N*. After all, you cannot follow the links on the list backward. However, notice the pointer variable `prev` in Figure 4-10. It points to the node that precedes *N* and makes it possible for you to alter that node's `next` pointer, thereby deleting node *N* from the linked list. The following assignment statement is all that you need to delete the node to which `cur` points:

Deleting an interior node

```
prev->next = cur->next;
```

A question comes to mind at this point:

- Does the previous method work for any node *N*, regardless of where in the linked list it appears?

No, the method does not work if the node to be deleted is the *first* node in the list, because it certainly does not make sense to assert that *prev* points to the node that precedes this node! Thus, *deletion of the first node in a linked list is a special case*, as Figure 4-11 depicts. In this case, *cur* points to the first node and *prev* is *NULL*.

When you delete the first node of the list, you must change the value of *head* to reflect the fact that, after the deletion, the list has a new first node. That is, the node that was second prior to the deletion is now first. You make this change to *head* by using the assignment statement

Deleting the first node is a special case

```
head = head->next;
```

As was the case for the deletion of an interior node, the pointers bypass the old first node, although it still exists. Notice also that if the node to be deleted is the *only* node in the list—and thus it is both the first node and the last node—the previous assignment statement assigns the value

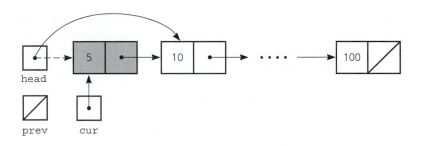

FIGURE 4-11   Deleting the first node

NULL to the variable *head*. Recall that the value *NULL* in *head* indicates an empty list, and so this assignment statement handles the deletion of the only node in a list correctly.

It is really a bit wasteful that node *N* still exists after its deletion from the linked list. Regardless of where in the list node *N* was, *cur* still points to it. If you change the value of *cur* so that it no longer points to *N*, then *N* will be in a state of limbo—it still requires storage space, even though the program can no longer access it. (You would have a memory leak.) If a program were to accumulate many nodes in this limbo state, its storage requirements might become unreasonably high.

Therefore, before you change the value of *cur*, you should use the statements

```
cur->next = NULL;
delete cur;
cur = NULL;
```

Return deleted nodes to the system by using *delete*

to return node *N* to the system. The system can now use this returned memory and possibly even reallocate it to your program as a result of the *new* operator. Suppose that this reallocation actually occurs when you ask for a new node for your linked list. You can be sure that your new node, which is really node *N*, does not still point to your linked list, because you executed the statement *cur->next = NULL* before you deallocated node *N*. Setting both *cur->next* and *cur* to *NULL* is an example of defensive programming that can avoid devastating, subtle errors later in the program.

So far, we have deleted the node *N* to which *cur* points, given a pointer *prev* to the node that precedes *N*. However, another question remains:

- How did the variables *cur* and *prev* come to point to the appropriate nodes?

To answer this question, consider the context in which you might expect to delete a node. In one common situation, you need to delete a node that you specify by position. Such is the case if you use a linked list to implement an ADT list. In another situation, you need to delete a node that contains a particular data value. Such is the case if you use a linked list to implement an ADT sorted list. In both of these situations, you do not pass the values of *cur* and *prev* to the deletion function, but instead the function establishes these values as its first step by searching the linked list for the node *N* that either is at a specified position or contains the data value to be deleted. Once the function finds the node *N*—and the node that precedes *N*—the deletion of *N* proceeds as described previously. The details of determining *cur* and *prev* for deletion are actually the same as for insertion, and they appear in the next section.

To summarize, the deletion process has three high-level steps:

Three steps to delete a node from a linked list

1. Locate the node that you want to delete.

2. Disconnect this node from the linked list by changing pointers.

3. Return the node to the system.

Later in this chapter, we shall incorporate this deletion process into the implementation of the ADT list.

Inserting a Node into a Specified Position of a Linked List

Figure 4-12 illustrates the technique of inserting a new node into a specified position of a linked list. You insert the new node, to which the pointer variable *newPtr* points, between the two nodes that *prev* and *cur* point to. As the diagram suggests, you can accomplish the insertion by using the pair of assignment statements

Inserting a node between nodes

```
newPtr->next = cur;
prev->next = newPtr;
```

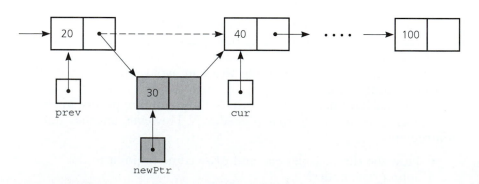

FIGURE 4-12   Inserting a new node into a linked list

The following two questions are analogous to those previously asked about the deletion of a node:

- How did the variables *newPtr*, *cur*, and *prev* come to point to the appropriate nodes?

- Does the method work for inserting a node into any position of a linked list?

The answer to the first question, like the answer to the analogous question for deletion, is found by considering the context in which you will use the insertion operation. You establish the values of *cur* and *prev* by traversing the linked list until you find the proper position for the new item. You then create a new node, to which *newPtr* points, by using the *new* operator, as follows:

```
newPtr = new Node;
```

After you initialize the data portion of this new node, you insert the node into the list, as was just described.

The answer to the second question is that *insertion, like deletion, must account for special cases*. First, consider the insertion of a node at the beginning of the linked list, as shown in Figure 4-13. You must make *head* point to the new node, and the new node must point to the node that had been at the beginning of the list. You accomplish this by using these statements:

```
newPtr->next = head;
head = newPtr;
```

Inserting a node at the beginning of a linked list

Observe that if the list is empty before the insertion, *head* is *NULL*, so the *next* pointer of the new item is set to *NULL*. This step is correct because the new item is the last item—as well as the first item—on the list.

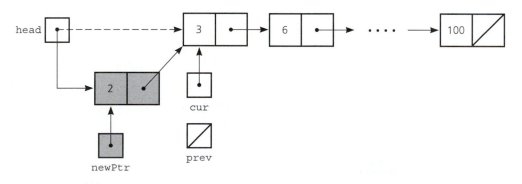

FIGURE 4-13 Inserting at the beginning of a linked list

Figure 4-14 shows the insertion of a new node at the end of a linked list. This insertion is potentially a special case because the intention of the pair of assignment statements

```
newPtr->next = cur;
prev->next = newPtr;
```

is to insert the new node *between* the node that *cur* points to and the node that *prev* points to. If you are to insert the new node at the end of the list, to what node should *cur* point? In this situation it makes sense to view the value of *cur* as *NULL* because, as you traverse the list, *cur* becomes *NULL* as it moves past the end of the list. Observe that if *cur* has the value *NULL* and *prev* points to the last node on the list, the previous pair of assignment statements will indeed insert the new node at the end of the list. Thus, insertion at the end of a linked list is not a special case.

To summarize, the insertion process requires three high-level steps:

1. Determine the point of insertion.

2. Create a new node and store the new data in it.

3. Connect the new node to the linked list by changing pointers.

Determining *cur* and *prev*. Let us now examine in more detail how to determine the pointers *cur* and *prev* for the insertion operation just described. As was mentioned, this determination depends on the context in which you will insert a node. As an example, consider a linked list of integers that are sorted into ascending order. To simplify the discussion, assume that the integers are distinct; that is, no duplicates are present in the list.

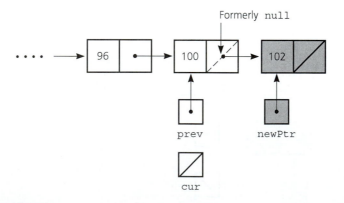

FIGURE 4-14   Inserting at the end of a linked list

To determine the point at which the value *newValue* should be inserted into a sorted linked list, you must traverse the list from its beginning until you find the appropriate place for *newValue*. This appropriate place is just before the node that contains the first data item greater than *newValue*. You know that you will need a pointer *cur* to the node that is to follow the new node; that is, *cur* points to the node that contains the first data item greater than *newValue*. You also need a pointer *prev* to the node that is to precede the new node; that is, *prev* points to the node that contains the last data item smaller than *newValue*. Thus, as you traverse the linked list, you keep both a current pointer *cur* and a *trailing* pointer *prev*. When you reach the node that contains the first value larger than *newValue*, the trailing pointer points to the previous node. At this time, you can insert the new node between the two nodes to which *prev* and *cur* point, as was described earlier.

A first attempt at some pseudocode follows:

```
// determine the point of insertion into a sorted
// linked list

// initialize prev and cur to start the traversal
// from the beginning of the list
prev = NULL
cur = head

// advance prev and cur as long as newValue > the
// current data item
// Loop invariant: newValue > data items in all
// nodes at and before node to which prev points
while (newValue > cur->item)   // causes a problem!
{  prev = cur
   cur = cur->next
}  // end while
```

A first attempt at a solution

Unfortunately, the *while* loop causes a problem when the new value is greater than all the values in the list, that is, when the insertion will be at the end of the linked list (or when the linked list is empty). Eventually, the *while* statement compares *newValue* to the value in the last node. During that execution of the loop, *cur* is assigned the value *NULL*. After this iteration, *newValue* is again compared to *cur->item*, which, when *cur* is *NULL*, is incorrect.

To solve this problem, you need another test in the termination condition of the *while* statement so that the loop exits when *cur* becomes *NULL*. Thus, you replace the *while* statement with

```
while (cur ≠ NULL and newValue > cur->item)
```

The revised pseudocode is

The correct solution

```
// determine the point of insertion into a sorted
// linked list

// initialize prev and cur to start the traversal
// from the beginning of the list
prev = NULL
cur = head

// advance prev and cur as long as newValue > the
// current data item
// Loop invariant: newValue > data items in all
// nodes at and before node to which prev points
while (cur ≠ NULL and newValue > cur->item)
{  prev = cur
   cur = cur->next
}  // end while
```

Notice how the `while` statement also solves the problem of inserting a node at the end of the linked list. In the case where `newValue` is greater than all the values in the list, `prev` points to the last node in the list and `cur` becomes `NULL`, thus terminating the `while` loop. (See Figure 4-15.) Therefore, as you saw earlier, you can insert the new node at the end of the list by using the standard pair of assignment statements

Insertion at the end of a linked list is not a special case

```
newPtr->next = cur;
prev->next = newPtr;
```

Now consider the insertion of a node at the beginning of the linked list. This situation arises when the value to be inserted is *smaller* than all the values currently in the list. In this case, the `while` loop in the previous pseudocode is never entered, so `prev` and `cur` maintain their original values, as Figure 4-16 illustrates. In particular, `prev` maintains its original value of `NULL`. This is the only situation in which

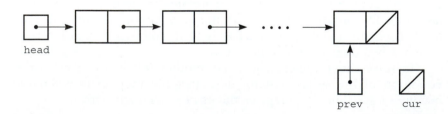

FIGURE 4-15   When *prev* points to the last node and *cur* is *NULL*, insertion will be at the end of the linked list

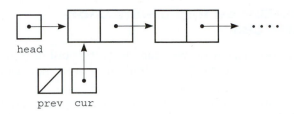

head

prev cur

FIGURE 4-16 When *prev* is *NULL* and *cur* points to the first node, insertion or deletion will be at the beginning of the linked list

the value of *prev* is equal to *NULL* after execution of the *while* loop ends. Thus, you can detect an insertion at the beginning of the list by comparing *prev* to *NULL*.

> When *prev* is *NULL*, insertion will be at the beginning of the linked list

Observe that the solution also correctly handles insertion into an empty linked list as an insertion at the beginning of the list. When the list is empty, the statement *cur = head* assigns *cur* an initial value of *NULL*, and thus the *while* loop is never entered. Therefore, *prev* maintains its original value of *NULL*, indicating an insertion at the beginning of the list.

> Insertion into an empty linked list is really an insertion at the beginning of the list

A little thought should convince you that the solution that determines the point of insertion also works for deletion. If you want to delete a given integer from a linked list of sorted integers, you obviously want to traverse the list until you find the node that contains the value sought. The previous pseudocode will do just that: *cur* will point to the desired node and *prev* either will point to the preceding node or, if the desired node is first on the list, will be *NULL*, as in Figure 4-16.

The following C++ statements implement the previous pseudocode:

```
// determine the point of insertion or deletion
// for a sorted linked list
// Loop invariant: newValue > data items in all
// nodes at and before node to which prev points
for (prev = NULL, cur = head;
     (cur != NULL) && (newValue > cur->item);
     prev = cur, cur = cur->next);
```

> A C++ solution for the point of insertion or deletion

Recall that the *&&* (*and*) operator in C++ does not evaluate its second operand if its first operand is 0 (false). Thus, when *cur* becomes *NULL*, the loop exits without attempting to evaluate *cur->item*. It is, therefore, essential that *cur != NULL* be first in the logical expression.

Determining the values of *cur* and *prev* is simpler when you insert or delete a node by position instead of by its value. This determination is necessary when you use a linked list to implement the ADT list, as you will see next.

A Pointer-Based Implementation of the ADT List

This section considers how you can use C++ pointers instead of an array to implement the ADT list. Unlike the array-based implementation, a pointer-based implementation does not shift items during insertion and deletion operations. It also does not impose a fixed maximum length on the list—except, of course, as imposed by the storage limits of the system.

As in Chapter 3, and as we will do in the rest of the book, we will implement this ADT as a C++ class. For the array-based implementation, we wrote declarations for public member functions corresponding to the ADT list operations. These declarations will appear unchanged in the pointer-based implementation.

You need to represent the items in the ADT list and its length. Figure 4-17 indicates one possible way to represent this data by using pointers. Here *head* points to a linked list of the items in the ADT list, where the first node in the linked list contains the first item in the ADT list, and so on. The integer *size* is the current number of items in the list. Both *head* and *size* will be private data members of our class.

As you saw previously, you use two pointers—*cur* and *prev*—to manipulate a linked list. These pointer variables will be local to the member functions that need them; they are not appropriate data members of the class.

cur and *prev* should not be data members of the class

Recall that the ADT list operations for insertion, deletion, and retrieval specify the position number *I* of the relevant item. In an attempt to obtain values for *cur* and *prev* from *I*, suppose that you define a function *find(I)* that returns a pointer to the Ith node in the linked list. If *find* provides a pointer *cur* to the Ith node, how will you get a pointer *prev* to the previous node, that is, to the $(I - 1)^{st}$ node? You can get the value of *prev* by invoking *find(I-1)*. Instead of calling *find* twice, however, note that once you have *prev*, *cur* is simply *prev->next*. The only exception to using *find* in this way is for the first node, but you know immediately from *I* whether the operation involves the first node. If it does, you know the pointer to the first node, namely *head*, without invoking *find*.

find is a private member function

The function *find* is not an ADT operation. Because *find* returns a pointer, you would not want any client to call it. Such clients should be able to use the ADT without knowledge of the pointers that the implementation uses. It is perfectly reasonable for the implementation

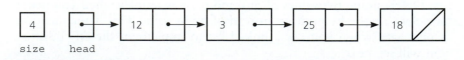

size   head

FIGURE 4-17   A pointer-based implementation of the ADT list

of an ADT to define variables and functions that the rest of the program should not access. Therefore, *find* is a private member function that only the implementations of the ADT operations call.

The following header file for the pointer-based implementation of the ADT list summarizes our discussion so far. Note that you define the node for the linked list in the private section of the class. Also, you must provide a destructor and another constructor called a copy constructor, as you will soon see. The pre- and postconditions for the ADT list operations are the same as for the array-based implementation that you saw in Chapter 3; they are omitted here to save space. Also, the exception classes defined for lists in Chapter 3 are assumed to be the same in this implementation.

```cpp
// ******************************************************
// Header file ListP.h for the ADT list.
// Pointer-based implementation.
// ******************************************************
#include "ListException.h"
#include "ListIndexOutOfRangeException.h"
typedef desired-type-of-list-item ListItemType;

class List
{
public:
// constructors and destructor:
   List();                        // default constructor
   List(const List& aList);       // copy constructor
   ~List();                       // destructor

// list operations:
   bool isEmpty() const;
   int getLength() const;
   void insert(int index, ListItemType newItem)
       throw(ListIndexOutOfRangeException, ListException);
   void remove(int index)
       throw(ListIndexOutOfRangeException);
   void retrieve(int index, ListItemType& dataItem) const
       throw(ListIndexOutOfRangeException);

private:
   struct ListNode            // a node on the list
   {
      ListItemType    item;   // a data item on the list
      ListNode        *next;  // pointer to next node
   };  // end struct

   int        size;  // number of items in list
   ListNode *head;   // pointer to linked list of items
```

A copy constructor and a destructor are necessary for a pointer-based implementation

```
    ListNode *find(int index) const;
    // Returns a pointer to the index-th node
    // in the linked list.
}; // end class
// End of header file.
```

The implementation file begins as follows:

```
// ************************************************************
// Implementation file ListP.cpp for the ADT list.
// Pointer-based implementation.
// ************************************************************
#include "ListP.h"      // header file
#include <cstddef>      // for NULL
#include <cassert>      // for assert()

// definitions of member functions follow:
    . . .
```

You include the implementations of the class's member functions at this point in the implementation file. We now examine each of these implementations.

Default constructor. The default constructor simply initializes the data members *size* and *head*:

```
List::List(): size(0), head(NULL)
{
}  // end default constructor
```

Since the compiler-generated default constructor would not necessarily initialize *size* and *head* to appropriate values, you must provide your own.

Copy constructor. The second constructor in *List* is the copy constructor

```
List(const List& aList);
```

Situations that invoke the copy constructor

The copy constructor makes a copy of an object. It is invoked implicitly when you either pass an object to a function by value, return an object from a valued function, or define and initialize an object, as in

```
List yourList(myList);
```

where *myList* exists already.

A compiler-generated copy constructor performs a shallow copy

When copying an object involves only copying the values of its data members, the copy is called a **shallow copy**. If a shallow copy is sufficient, you can omit the copy constructor, in which case the compiler generates a copy constructor that performs a shallow copy. Such was the case for the classes you saw in Chapter 3. For example, the array-based implementation of the ADT list used a compiler-generated copy constructor to copy both the array of list items and the number of items.

For our new pointer-based implementation, a compiler-generated copy constructor would copy only the data members *size* and *head*. Figure 4-18a shows the result of this shallow copy for the linked list in Figure 4-17. Both the original pointer *head* and its copy point to the same linked list. In other words, the nodes of the linked list are not copied. If you need to create a copy of the list, you must write your own copy constructor. That is, a **deep copy** is needed, as Figure 4-18b illustrates. Thus, the copy constructor appears as follows:

```
List::List(const List& aList): size(aList.size)
{
   if (aList.head == NULL)
      head = NULL;  // original list is empty

   else
   {  // copy first node
      head = new ListNode;
      assert(head != NULL);  // check allocation
      head->item = aList.head->item;
```

(a)

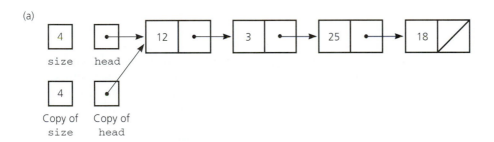

(b)

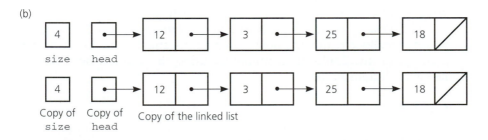

FIGURE 4-18 Copies of the linked list in Figure 4-17: (a) a shallow copy; (b) a deep copy

```
      // copy rest of list
      ListNode *newPtr = head;  // new list pointer
      // newPtr points to last node in new list
      // origPtr points to nodes in original list
      for (ListNode *origPtr = aList.head->next;
                    origPtr != NULL;
                    origPtr = origPtr->next)
      {  newPtr->next = new ListNode;
         assert(newPtr->next != NULL);
         newPtr = newPtr->next;
         newPtr->item = origPtr->item;
      }  // end for

      newPtr->next = NULL;
   }  // end if
}  // end copy constructor
```

As you can see, the copy constructor is an expensive operation. It requires that the original list be traversed, and for each element of the original list, a duplicate is made in the new list.

Also note that the copy constructor uses the *assert* method to verify that the node was allocated properly. An alternative would be to throw an exception. But throwing exceptions from constructors requires great care; you must be sure to properly deallocate any memory allocated in the constructor before throwing the exception.

Destructor. Each class has only one destructor. The destructor destroys an instance of the class, that is, an object, when the object's lifetime ends. Typically, the destructor is invoked implicitly when the block or function in which the object was created (defined) exits.

Classes that use only statically allocated memory can depend on the compiler-generated destructor, as was the case for the classes in Chapter 3. However, when a class uses dynamically allocated memory, as in the present pointer-based implementation, you need to write a destructor that deallocates this memory.

You must write a destructor if your class allocates memory dynamically

A destructor's name is given by ~ followed by the class name. A destructor cannot have arguments, has no return type—not even *void*—and cannot use *return* to return a value.

The destructor for our present implementation of *List* requires you to deallocate the memory assigned to the linked list. You can accomplish this deallocation simply by using the *remove* operation to delete each item in the list.

```
List::~List()
{
   while (!isEmpty())
      remove(1);
} // end destructor
```

Notice that after you delete the first item in the list, the remaining items are renumbered. Thus, to delete all items, you can repeatedly delete the first item.

Destructors for objects that contain dynamically allocated memory—such as the destructor just given—should use *delete* to deallocate the memory associated with the object. As you will soon see, *remove* uses *delete* and so performs the deallocation for this destructor.

List operations. The list operations *isEmpty* and *getLength* have straightforward implementations:

```cpp
bool List::isEmpty() const
{
   return size == 0;
}  // end isEmpty


int List::getLength() const
{
   return size;
}  // end getLength
```

Because a linked list does not provide direct access to a specified position, the retrieval, insertion, and deletion operations must all traverse the list from its beginning until the specified point is reached. The function *find* performs this traversal and has the following implementation:

```cpp
List::ListNode *List::find(int index) const
// ------------------------------------------------
// Locates a specified node in a linked list.
// Precondition: index is the number of the
// desired node.
// Postcondition: Returns a pointer to the desired
// node. If index < 1 or index > the number of
// nodes in the list, returns NULL.
// ------------------------------------------------
{
   if ( (index < 1) || (index > getLength()) )
      return NULL;

   else  // count from the beginning of the list
   { ListNode *cur = head;
      for (int skip = 1; skip < index; ++skip)
         cur = cur->next;
      return cur;
   }  // end if
}  // end find
```

The function *find* returns *NULL* as a way of signaling an illegal value of *index*.

The retrieval operation calls *find* to locate the desired node:

```
void List::retrieve(int index,
                    ListItemType& dataItem) const
{
   if ((index < 1) || (index > getLength()))
      throw ListIndexOutOfRangeException(
      "ListOutOfRangeException: retrieve index out of range");
   else
   {  // get pointer to node, then data in node
      ListNode *cur = find(index);
      dataItem = cur->item;
   }  // end if
} // end retrieve
```

The pointer-based implementations of the insertion and deletion operations use the linked list processing techniques developed earlier in this chapter. To insert an item after the first item of a list, you must first obtain a pointer to the preceding item. Insertion into the first position of a list is a special case.

```
void List::insert(int index, ListItemType newItem)
{
   int newLength = getLength() + 1;

   if ((index < 1) || (index > newLength))
      throw ListIndexOutOfRangeException(
      "ListOutOfRangeException: insert index out of range");
   else
   {  // create new node and place newItem in it
      ListNode *newPtr = new ListNode;
      if (newPtr == NULL)
         throw ListException(
         "ListException: insert cannot allocate memory");
      else
      {  size = newLength;
         newPtr->item = newItem;

         // attach new node to list
         if (index == 1)
         {  // insert new node at beginning of list
            newPtr->next = head;
            head = newPtr;
         }
```

```
     else
     {  ListNode *prev = find(index-1);
        // insert new node after node
        // to which prev points
        newPtr->next = prev->next;
        prev->next = newPtr;
     }  // end if
   } // end if
} // end if
} // end insert
```

The deletion operation is analogous to insertion. To delete an item that occurs after the first item of a list, you must first obtain a pointer to the item that precedes it. Deletion from the first position of a list is a special case.

```
void List::remove(int index)
{
   ListNode *cur;

   if ((index < 1) || (index > getLength()))
      throw ListIndexOutOfRangeException(
"ListOutOfRangeException: remove index out of range");
   else
   {  --size;
      if (index == 1)
      {  // delete the first node from the list
         cur = head;  // save pointer to node
         head = head->next;
      }

      else
      {  ListNode *prev = find(index-1);
         // delete the node after the
         // node to which prev points
         cur = prev->next;  // save pointer to node
         prev->next = cur->next;
      }  // end if

      // return node to system
      cur->next = NULL;
      delete cur;
      cur = NULL;
   } // end if
}  // end remove
```

Comparing Array-Based and Pointer-Based Implementations

Typically, the various implementations that a programmer contemplates for a particular ADT have advantages and disadvantages. When you must select an implementation, you should weigh these advantages and disadvantages before you make your choice. As you will see, the decision among possible implementations of an ADT is one that you must make time and time again. This section compares the two implementations of the ADT list that you have seen as an example of how you should proceed in general.

Arrays are easy to use, but they have a fixed size

The array-based implementation that you saw in Chapter 3 appears to be a reasonable approach. An array behaves like a list, and arrays are easy to use. However, as was already mentioned, an array has a fixed size; it is possible for the number of items in the list to exceed this fixed size. In practice, when choosing among implementations of an ADT, you must ask the question, does the fixed-size restriction of an array-based implementation present a problem in the context of a particular application? The answer to this question depends on two factors. The obvious factor is whether or not, for a given application, you can predict in advance the maximum number of items in the ADT at any one time. If you cannot, it is quite possible that an operation—and hence the entire program—will fail because the ADT in the context of a particular application requires more storage than the array can provide.

Can you predict the maximum number of items in the ADT?

Will an array waste storage?

On the other hand, if, for a given application, you can predict in advance the maximum number of items in the ADT list at any one time, you must explore a more subtle factor: Would you waste storage by declaring an array to be large enough to accommodate this maximum number of items? Consider a case in which the maximum number of items is large, but you suspect that this number rarely will be reached. For example, suppose that your list could contain as many as 10,000 items, but the actual number of items in the list rarely exceeds 50. If you declare 10,000 array locations at compilation time, at least 9,950 array locations will be wasted most of the time. In both of the previous cases, the array-based implementation given in Chapter 3 is not desirable.

Increasing the size of a dynamically allocated array can waste storage and time

What if you use a dynamically allocated array? Because you would use the *new* operator to allocate storage dynamically, you will be able to provide as much storage as the list needs (within the bounds of the particular computer, of course). Thus, you do not have to predict the maximum size of the list. However, if you double the size of the array each time you reach the end of the array—which is a reasonable approach to enlarging the array—you still might have many unused array locations. In the example just given, you could allocate an array of 50 locations initially. If you actually have 10,000 items in your list, array doubling will eventually give you an array of 12,800 locations, 2,800 more than you need. Remember also that you waste time by copying the array and then deallocating it each time you need more space.

Now suppose that your list will never contain more than 25 items. You could allocate enough storage in the array for the list and know that you would waste little storage when the list contained only a few items. With respect to its size, an array-based implementation is perfectly acceptable in this case.

A pointer-based implementation can solve any difficulties related to the fixed size of an array-based implementation. You use the *new* operator to allocate storage dynamically, so you do not need to predict the maximum size of the list. Because you allocate memory one item at a time, the list will be allocated only as much storage as it needs. Thus, you will not waste storage.

There are other differences between the array-based and pointer-based implementations. These differences affect both the time and memory requirements of the implementations. Any time you store a collection of data in an array or a linked list, the data items become ordered; that is, there is a first item, a second item, and so on. This order implies that a typical item has a predecessor and a successor. In an array *anArray*, the location of the next item after the item in *anArray[i]* is *implicit*—it is in *anArray[i+1]*. In a linked list, however, you *explicitly* determine the location of the next item by using the pointer in the current node. This notion of an implicit versus explicit next item is one of the primary differences between an array and a linked list. Therefore, an advantage of an array-based implementation is that it does not have to store explicit information about where to find the next data item, thus requiring less memory than a pointer-based implementation.

Another, more important advantage of an array-based implementation is that it can provide **direct access** to a specified item. For example, if you use the array *items* to implement the ADT list, you know that the item associated with list position *i* is stored in *items[i-1]*. Accessing either *items[0]* or *items[49]* takes the same amount of time. That is, the **access time** is constant for an array.

On the other hand, if you use a linked list to implement the ADT list, you have no way of immediately accessing the node that contains the ith item. To get to the appropriate node, you use the *next* pointers to traverse the linked list from its beginning until you reach the ith node. That is, you access the first node and get the pointer to the second node, access the second node and get the pointer to the third node, and so on until you finally access the ith node. Clearly, the time it takes you to access the first node is less than the time it takes to access the 50th node. The access time for the ith node depends on *i*.

The type of implementation chosen will affect the efficiency of the ADT list operations. An array-based *retrieve* is almost instantaneous, regardless of which list item you access. A pointer-based *retrieve*, however, requires *i* steps to access the ith item in the list.

You already know that the array-based implementation of the ADT list requires you to shift the data when you insert items into or delete items from the list. For example, if you delete the first item of a 20-item list, you must shift 19 items. In general, deleting the ith item of a list of

An array-based implementation is a good choice for a small list

Linked lists do not have a fixed size

The item after an array item is implied; in a linked list, an item points explicitly to the next item

An array-based implementation requires less memory than a pointer-based implementation

You can access array items directly with equal access time

You must traverse a linked list to access its ith node

The time to access the ith node in a linked list depends on i

size items requires *size-i* shifts. Thus, *remove* requires *size-1* shifts to delete the first item, but zero shifts to delete the last item. The function *insert* has similar requirements.

Insertion into and deletion from a linked list do not require you to shift data

In contrast, you do not need to shift the data when you insert items into or delete items from the linked list of a pointer-based implementation. The functions *insert* and *remove* require essentially the same effort, regardless of the length of the list or the position of the operation within the list, once you know the point of insertion or deletion. Finding this point, however, requires a list traversal, the time for which will vary depending on where in the list the operation will occur. Recall that the private member function *find* performs this traversal. If you examine the definition of *find*, you will see that *find(i)* requires *i* assignment operations. Thus, *find*'s effort increases with *i*.

Insertion into and deletion from a linked list require a list traversal

We will continue to compare various solutions to a problem throughout this book. Chapter 9 introduces a more formal way to discuss the efficiency of algorithms. Until then, our discussions will be informal.

Saving and Restoring a Linked List by Using a File

You can save and restore a linked list by using an external file so that you can preserve the list between runs of a program. To demonstrate the technique, we will save and restore a linked list of integers like the lists that were used earlier in this chapter. The algorithm that restores a linked list also demonstrates how you can build a linked list from scratch.

Recall the following statements:

```
struct Node
{  int    item;
   Node *next;
};  // end struct
```

```
Node *head;
```

Do not write the pointers to the file

If your program needs to write a linked list of integers to a file in a way that will allow you to restore the list later, what should you write to the file? You might be tempted to write each node in its entirety—that is, to write each node's data and pointer portions. However, writing the pointers serves no useful purpose because, once the program has terminated, the pointer values saved from the nodes are meaningless. Although these values are addresses of memory locations that were part of the linked list before you wrote it to the file, the addresses are not useful after program execution terminates. That is, when you execute the program again, the saved addresses may reference memory locations of some completely different data structure within the program or even within another program altogether. Thus, the solution of writing out the entire node to a file is not a good one.

You want to be able to create a linked list that contains the same data as a linked list that existed earlier. Whether the new list uses the same memory locations as the old list is not important. Thus, all you really need to save in the file is the data portion of each node.

Save a linked list by writing only its data to a file

Figure 4-19 illustrates saving a linked list in a file. (To save space, the figure does not illustrate end-of-line symbols.) The following C++ statements perform this task by writing the data—integers in this case—to a text file.

```cpp
// Saves a linked list's data in a text file of
// integers; head points to the linked list.

// fileName is a string that names an external text
// file to be created
ofstream outFile(fileName);

// traverse the list to the end, writing each item
for (Node *cur = head; cur != NULL; cur = cur->next)
   outFile << cur->item << endl;

outFile.close();
// Assertion: The text file contains the linked
// list's data in its original order.
```

Once you have saved the linked list's data in the file, the data endures in the file after the program that originally created the list has terminated. Thus, you can create a linked list from this data any time you wish. Notice that the previous statements write the integers to the file in the order that they appear in the list. Thus, to re-create the linked list, you must read the file and place each newly read integer at the end of the list, as Figure 4-20 illustrates.

A pseudocode solution for restoring the linked list is

```
while (not end of file)
{  Read the next integer
   Append the integer to the end of the linked list
}  // end while
```

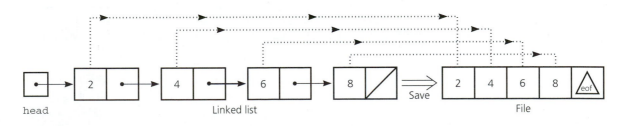

head   Linked list   File

FIGURE 4-19   Saving a linked list in a file

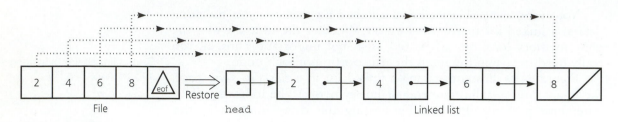

FIGURE 4-20   Restoring a linked list from a file

To add a new integer to the end of the linked list, you must perform these four steps:

Four steps to add a node to the end of a linked list

1. Allocate a new node for the linked list.

2. Set the pointer in the last node in the list to point to the new node.

3. Put the new integer in the new node.

4. Set the pointer in the new node to *NULL*.

Each time you read a new integer, you must get to the last node in the linked list. One way to accomplish this is to traverse the list each time you read a new integer. A much more efficient method uses a **tail pointer** *tail* to remember where the end of the linked list is—just as *head* remembers where the beginning of the list is. Like *head*, *tail* is external to the list. Figure 4-21 illustrates a linked list that has both head and tail pointers.

Use a tail pointer to facilitate adding nodes to the end of a linked list

With *tail* pointing to the end of the linked list, you can perform both Step 1 and Step 2 by using the single statement

```
tail->next = new Node;
```

This statement sets the *next* pointer in the last node in the list to point to a newly allocated node. You thus have an easy method for adding a new integer to the end of the list. Initially, however, when you insert the first integer into an empty linked list, *tail*—like *head*—is *NULL*. If you treat the first insertion as a special case, you get the following C++

Treat the first insertion as a special case

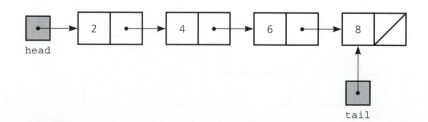

FIGURE 4-21   A linked list with head and tail pointers

statements. For simplicity, we assume that the *new* operator is always successful, and we leave the details of a refined solution as an exercise.

```
// Creates a linked list from the data in a text
// file. The pointer variables head and tail are
// initially NULL. fileName is a string that names
// an existing external text file.

ifstream inFile(fileName);
int      nextItem;

if (inFile >> nextItem)                 // is file empty?
{  // file not empty:
   head = new Node;
   // add the first integer to the list
   head->item = nextItem;
   head->next = NULL;
   tail = head;

   // add remaining integers to linked list
   while (inFile >> nextItem)
   {  tail->next = new Node;
      tail = tail->next;
      tail->item = nextItem;
      tail->next = NULL;
   }  // end while
}  // end if

inFile.close();

// Assertion: head points to the first node of the
// created linked list; tail points to the last
// node. If the file is empty, head and tail are
// NULL (list is empty).
```

Creating a linked list from data in a file

Note that *tail* could either be a local variable that ceases to exist after the statements complete execution, or exist as long as *head* exists. That is, your linked list could always have both a head and a tail pointer.

Now suppose that a file *inFile* contains integers that are not in the order you want. For example, suppose that you want the integers to appear in ascending order in your linked list, but in the file they are in no particular order at all. If you have a function *linkedListInsert* that inserts new items into their proper sorted order, the following pseudocode solves the problem:

```
head = NULL
while (inFile >> nextItem)
   linkedListInsert(head, nextItem)
```

Creating a sorted linked list from arbitrary data in a file

This algorithm is known as an **insertion sort** and is among the sorting algorithms that Chapter 9 considers.

You can add the operations *save* and *restore* to the ADT list by using the previous discussion as the basis for their implementations.

Passing a Linked List to a Function

A function with access to a linked list's head pointer has access to the entire list

How can a function access a linked list? It is sufficient for the function to have access to the list's head pointer. From this variable alone, the function can access the entire linked list. In the pointer-based implementation of the ADT list that you saw earlier in this chapter, the head pointer *head* to the linked list that contains the ADT's items is a private data member of the class *List*. The member functions of this class use *head* directly to manipulate the linked list.

Would you ever want *head* to be an argument of a function? Certainly not for functions outside of the class, because such functions should not have access to the class's underlying data structure. Although on the surface it would seem that you would never need to pass the head pointer to a member function, that is not the case. Recursive functions, for example, might need the head pointer as an argument. You will see examples of such functions in the next section. Realize that these functions must not be public members of their class. If they were, clients could access the linked list directly, thereby violating the ADT's wall.

Pass the head pointer to a function as a reference argument

If you need to pass a linked list's head pointer to a function, should the head pointer be a value argument or a reference argument? If you plan to alter the list, it must be a reference argument, but the reason for this is not immediately clear. If your first instinct is that the formal argument *headPtr* must be a reference argument because the function will alter the nodes on the list to which *headPtr* points, you have reached the right conclusion but for the wrong reason.

Consider what would happen if you passed the head pointer as a value argument. Figure 4-22 illustrates that although the function copies the actual argument *head* into the formal argument *headPtr*, the list nodes themselves are *not* copied. Thus, if the function makes any changes to the nodes on the list, the changes are made to the actual

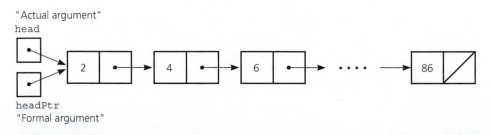

FIGURE 4-22   A head pointer as a value argument

nodes, not to local copies of the nodes; that is, *any changes the function makes to the list are not localized to the function.*

Therefore, passing the head pointer of a list to a function as a value argument allows the function to modify the nodes on the list and even to insert and delete nodes. It would seem, then, that the head pointer could be a value argument in the function. This would be correct if not for the possibility that the function will change the value of the head pointer itself. If, for example, the function inserts a new node at the beginning of the list, it changes the value of `headPtr`, and this change must be reflected in the actual argument `head` that corresponds to `headPtr`. This required change in `head` is the only reason that `headPtr` needs to be a reference argument!

A linked list passed as an argument to a function is not copied, even if its head pointer is a value argument

Processing Linked Lists Recursively

It is possible, and sometimes desirable, to process linked lists recursively. This section examines recursive traversal and insertion operations on a linked list. If the recursive functions in this section are members of a class, they should not be public because they require the linked list's head pointer as an argument.

Traversal. As a first example, consider a linked list of characters that form a string. That is, assume you have the following:

```
struct Node

{ char  item;
   Node *next;
};  // end struct
Node *stringPtr;
```

A linked list of characters that form a string

The pointer variable *stringPtr* points to the head of the linked list that contains the string.

Suppose that you want to display the string. That is, you want to write the characters in the string in the order in which they appear in the linked list. The recursive strategy is simply

Write the first character of the string
Write the string minus its first character

The following C++ function implements this strategy:

```
void writeString(Node *stringPtr)
// ----------------------------------------------------------
// Writes a string.
// Precondition: The string is represented as a linked list
// to which the pointer stringPtr points.
// Postcondition: The string is displayed. The linked list
// and stringPtr are unchanged.
// ----------------------------------------------------------
```

```
{
   if (stringPtr != NULL)
   {  // write the first character
      cout << stringPtr->item;

      // write the string minus its first character
      writeString(stringPtr->next);
   }  // end if
}  // end writeString
```

This function is uncomplicated. It requires that you have direct access only to the first character of the string. The linked list provides this direct access because the list's first node, to which the list's head *stringPtr* points, contains the string's first character. Furthermore, you can easily pass the string minus its first character to *writeString*: If *stringPtr* points to the beginning of the string, *stringPtr->next* points to the string minus its first character. You should compare *writeString* to the iterative technique that we used earlier in this chapter to display a linked list.

Compare the recursive *writeString* **to the iterative technique**

Now suppose that you want to display the string backward. Chapter 2 already developed two recursive strategies for writing a string backward. Recall that the strategy of the function *writeBackward* is

writeBackward **strategy**

Write the last character of the string
Write the string minus its last character backward

The strategy of the function *writeBackward2* is

writeBackward2 **strategy**

Write the string minus its first character backward
Write the first character of the string

You saw that these two strategies work equally well when the string is an array. However, when a linked list represents the string, the first strategy is very difficult to implement: If *stringPtr* points to the node that contains the first character of the string, how do you get to the last character? Even if you had some way to get to the last node in the list quickly—such as by having a tail pointer, as described earlier in this chapter—it would be very difficult for you to move toward the front of the string at each recursive call. That is, it would be difficult for you to access the ends of the successively shorter strings that the recursive calls generate. (Later you will see a doubly linked list, which would solve this problem.)

This discussion illustrates one of the primary disadvantages of linked lists: Whereas an array provides direct access to any of its items, a linked list does not. Fortunately, however, the strategy of function *writeBackward2* requires that you have direct access only to the first character of the string. This access is the same that *writeString* requires: The list's head pointer *stringPtr* points to the first

When the string is in a linked list, *writeBackward2* **is much easier to implement recursively than** *writeBackward*

character of the string, and *stringPtr->next* points to the string minus its first character.

The following C++ function implements the *writeBackward2* strategy when the string is stored in a linked list:

```
void writeBackward2(Node *stringPtr)
// -----------------------------------------------------------
// Writes a string backward.
// Precondition: The string is represented as a linked list
// to which the pointer stringPtr points.
// Postcondition: The string is displayed backward. The
// linked list and stringPtr are unchanged.
// -----------------------------------------------------------
{
   if (stringPtr != NULL)
   {  // write the string minus its first character backward
      writeBackward2(stringPtr->next);

      // write the first character
      cout << stringPtr->item;
   }  // end if
}  // end writeBackward2
```

Self-Test Exercise 8 asks you to trace this function. This trace will be similar to the box trace in Figure 2-9. Exercise 5 asks you to write an iterative version of this function. Which version is more efficient?

Insertion. Now view the insertion of a node into a sorted linked list from a new perspective, that is, recursively. Later in this book you will need a recursive algorithm to perform an insertion into a linked structure. Interestingly, recursive insertion eliminates the need for both a trailing pointer and a special case for inserting into the beginning of the list.

Consider the following recursive view of a sorted linked list: A linked list is sorted if its first data item is less than its second data item and the list that begins with the second data item is sorted. More formally, you can state this definition as follows:

The linked list to which *head* points is a sorted linked list if

head is *NULL* (the empty list is a sorted linked list)

or

head->next is *NULL* (a list with a single node is a sorted linked list)

or

head->item < head->next->item, and *head->next* points to a sorted linked list

A recursive definition of a sorted linked list

You can base a recursive insertion algorithm on this definition. Notice that the following function inserts the node at one of the base cases—either when the list is empty or when the new data item is smaller than all the data items in the list. In both cases, you need to insert the new data item at the beginning of the list.

```
void linkedListInsert(Node *& headPtr,
                      ListItemType newItem)

{
   if ((headPtr == NULL) || (newItem < headPtr->item))
   { // base case: insert newItem at beginning
     // of the linked list to which headPtr points
     Node *newPtr = new Node;
     if (newPtr == NULL)
         throw ListException(
           "ListException: insert cannot allocate memory");
     else
     { newPtr->item = newItem;
       newPtr->next = headPtr;
       headPtr = newPtr;
     } // end if
   }
   else
       linkedListInsert(headPtr->next, newItem);
}  // end linkedListInsert
```

Insertion occurs at the base case

Although *linkedListInsert* does not maintain a trailing pointer, inserting the new node is easy when the base case is reached. The conceptually difficult part of this algorithm is the statement

```
headPtr = newPtr;
```

This assignment is all that is necessary to make the *next* pointer of the appropriate node point to the new node. Note that *headPtr* points to the beginning of a sorted linked list. Recall that to insert the node to which *newPtr* points at the beginning of this list, you need to make *headPtr* point to that node. But does this action really change the appropriate pointer in the actual argument list (the original list to which the external pointer *head* points)? Yes it does, assuming that *headPtr* is a *reference argument*.

headPtr must be a reference argument

To understand the previous remarks, first consider the case in which the new item is to be inserted at the beginning of the original list to which the external pointer *head* points. In this case, no recursive calls are made, and thus when the base case is reached—that is, when *newItem == headPtr->item*—the actual argument that corresponds to *headPtr* is *head*, as Figure 4-23a illustrates. Hence, assuming that *headPtr* is a reference argument, the assignment *headPtr = newPtr* sets the value of *head* to *newPtr*—that is, *head* now points to the new node, as Figure 4-23b shows.

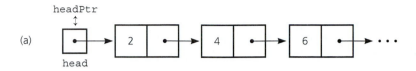

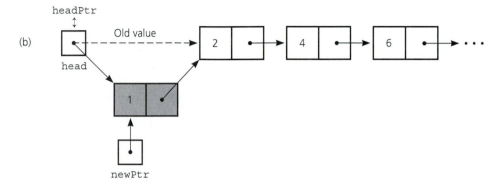

FIGURE 4-23 (a) A sorted linked list; (b) the assignment made for insertion at the beginning of the list

The general case in which the new item is inserted into the interior of the list to which *head* points is very similar. When the base case is reached, what is the actual argument that corresponds to *headPtr*? It is the *next* pointer of the node that should precede the new node; that is, it is the *next* pointer of the last node whose data item is less than *newItem*. Therefore, since *headPtr* is a reference argument, the assignment *headPtr = newPtr* sets the *next* pointer of the appropriate node to point to the new node. Figure 4-24 traces the recursive calls for an insertion into the interior of a linked list.

Finally, consider a context for *linkedListInsert*. Recall from Chapter 3 the ADT sorted list, which maintains its data in sorted order. The ADT operation *sortedInsert(newItem)* inserts *newItem* into its proper order in the sorted list. If you write a pointer-based implementation for the sorted list, *sortedInsert* would be a public member function of your class. This function could call *linkedListInsert* to do the insertion recursively. However, *linkedListInsert* requires the linked list's head pointer as an argument. Since the head pointer is private and hidden from the client, you would not want *linkedListInsert* to be an ADT operation. Thus, you would make it private. The details of this scenario are left as an exercise. (See Programming Problem 2.)

Though it could be argued that you should perform the operations on a sorted linked list recursively (after all, recursion does eliminate special cases and the need for a trailing pointer), the primary purpose in

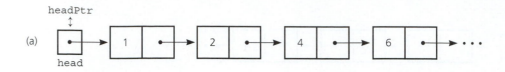

(a)

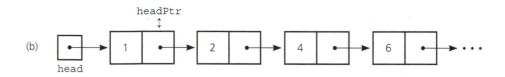

(b)

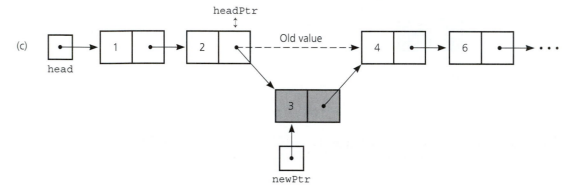

(c)

FIGURE 4-24   (a) The initial call *linkedListInsert(head, 3)*; (b) the first recursive call; (c) the second recursive call inserts at the beginning of the list to which *headPtr* points

presenting the recursive *linkedListInsert* is to prepare you for the binary search tree algorithms presented in Chapter 10.

Objects as Linked List Data

Although for simplicity the previous linked lists contained integer data, you need not restrict yourself to simple data types. In fact, the advantages of a linked list are more dramatic when its data are instances of a class. For example, suppose that you want a linked list of people. You could define the class *Person* that contains data such as name and address, as well as operations on that data. The following statements describe such a linked list:

```
typedef Person ItemType;

struct Node
{  ItemType item;
```

Data in a linked list node can be an instance of a class

```
    Node    *next;
};  // end struct

Node *head;
```

The use of *typedef* to declare *ItemType* makes changes to the type of data in the linked list simple to make.

4.3 Variations of the Linked List

This section briefly introduces several variations of the linked list that you have just seen. These variations are often useful, and you will encounter them later in this text. Many of the implementation details are left as exercises. Note that in addition to the data structures discussed in this section, it is possible to have other data structures such as arrays of pointers to linked lists and linked lists of linked lists. These data structures are also left as exercises.

Circular Linked Lists

When you use a computer that is part of a network, you share the services of another computer—called a *server*—with many other users. A similar sharing of resources occurs when you access a central computer by using a remote terminal. The system must organize the users so that only one user at a time has access to the shared computer. By ordering the users, the system can give each user a turn. Because users regularly enter and exit the system (by logging on or logging off), a linked list of user names allows the system to maintain order without shifting names when it makes insertions to and deletions from the list. Thus, the system can traverse the linked list from the beginning and give each user on the list a turn on the shared computer. What must the system do when it reaches the end of the list? It must return to the beginning of the list. However, the fact that the last node of a linked list does not point to another node can be an inconvenience.

If you want to access the first node of a linked list after accessing the last node, you must resort to the head pointer. Suppose that you change the *next* portion of the list's last node so that, instead of containing *NULL*, it points to the first node. The result is a **circular linked list**, as illustrated in Figure 4-25. In contrast, the linked list you saw earlier is said to be a **linear linked list**.

Every node in a circular linked list points to a successor, so you can start at any node and traverse the entire list. Although you could think of a circular list as not having either a beginning or an end, you still would have an external pointer to one of the nodes in the list. Thus, it remains natural to think of both a first and a last node in a circular list. If the external pointer points to the "first" node, you still would have to

Every node in a circular linked list has a successor

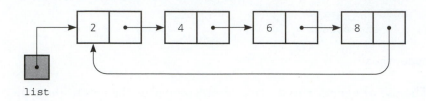

FIGURE 4-25   A circular linked list

traverse the list to get to the last node. However, if the external pointer—call it *list*—points to the "last" node, as it does in Figure 4-26, you can access both the first and last nodes without a traversal, because *list->next* points to the first node.

No node in a circular linked list contains *NULL*

A *NULL* value in the external pointer indicates an empty list, as it did for a linear list. However, no node in a circular list contains *NULL* in its *next* pointer. Thus, you must alter the algorithm for detecting when you have traversed an entire list. By simply comparing the current pointer *cur* to the external pointer *list*, you can determine when you have traversed the entire circular list. For example, the following C++ statements display the data portions of every node in a circular list, assuming that *list* points to the "last" node and *display* is a function that displays a node's data in an appropriate format:

Write the data that are in a circular linked list

```
// display the data in a circular linked list;
// list points to its last node
if (list != NULL)
{  // list is not empty
   Node *first = list->next; // point to first node

   Node *cur = first;        // start at first node
   // Loop invariant: cur points to next node to
   // display
```

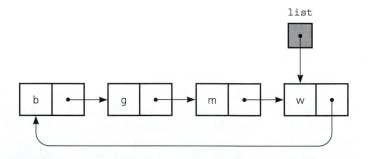

FIGURE 4-26   A circular linked list with an external pointer to the last node

```
   do
   {  display(cur->item);      // write data portion
      cur = cur->next;         // point to next node
   } while (cur != first);     // list traversed?
}  // end if
```

Operations such as insertion into and deletion from a circular linked list are left as exercises.

Dummy Head Nodes

Both the insertion and deletion algorithms presented earlier for linear linked lists require a special case to handle action at the first position of a list. Many people prefer a method that eliminates the need for the special case. One such method is to add a **dummy head node**—as Figure 4-27 depicts—that is always present, even when the linked list is empty. In this way, the item at the first position of the list is actually in the second node. Also, the insertion and deletion algorithms initialize *prev* to point to the dummy head node rather than to *NULL*. Thus, for example, in the deletion algorithm, the statement

prev->next = cur->next;

deletes from the list the node to which *cur* points, regardless of whether or not this node is the first element in the list.

Despite the fact that a dummy head node eliminates the need for a special case, in general handling the first list position separately can be less distracting than altering the list's structure by adding a dummy head node. However, dummy head nodes are useful with doubly linked lists, as you will see in the next section.

Doubly Linked Lists

Suppose that you wanted to delete a particular node from a linked list. If you were able to locate the node directly without a traversal, you would not have established a trailing pointer to the node that precedes it in the list. Without a trailing pointer, you would be unable to delete the node. You could overcome this problem if you had a way to back up from the node that you wished to delete to the node that precedes it. A **doubly linked list** solves this problem because each of its nodes has pointers to both the next node and the previous node.

Each node in a doubly linked list points to both its predecessor and its successor

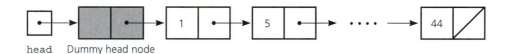

head   Dummy head node

FIGURE 4-27   A dummy head node

Consider a sorted linked list of customer names such that each node contains, in addition to its data member, two pointer members, *precede* and *next*. As usual, the *next* pointer of node N points to the node that follows N in the list. The *precede* pointer points to the node that precedes N in the list. The form of this sorted linked list of customers is as shown in Figure 4-28.

Notice that if **cur** points to a node N, you can get a pointer to the node that precedes N in the list by using the assignment statement

```
prev = cur->precede;
```

A doubly linked list thus allows you to delete a node without traversing the list to establish a trailing pointer.

Because there are more pointers to set, the mechanics of inserting into and deleting from a doubly linked list are a bit more involved than for a singly linked list. In addition, the special cases at the beginning or the end of the list are more complicated. It is common to eliminate the special cases by using a dummy head node. Although dummy head nodes may not be worthwhile for singly linked lists, the more complicated special cases for doubly linked lists make them very attractive.

As Figure 4-29a shows, the external pointer *listHead* always points to the dummy head node. Notice that the dummy head node has the same data type as the other nodes in the list; thus it also contains *precede* and *next* pointers. You can link the list so that it becomes a **circular doubly linked list**. The *next* pointer of the dummy head node then points to the first "real node"—for example, the first customer name—in the list, and the *precede* pointer of the first real node points back to the dummy head node. Similarly, the *precede* pointer of the dummy head node points to the last node in the list, and the *next* pointer of the last node points to the dummy head node. Note that the dummy head node is present even when the list is empty. In this case, both pointer members of the dummy head node point to the head node itself, as Figure 4-29b illustrates.

Dummy head nodes are useful in doubly linked lists

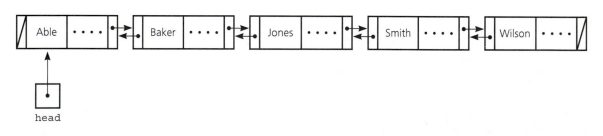

FIGURE 4-28   A doubly linked list

(a) `listHead`

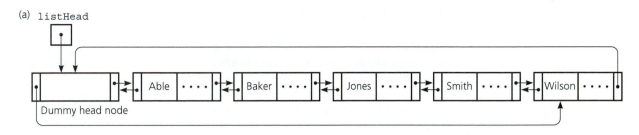

Dummy head node

(b) `listHead`

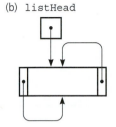

FIGURE 4-29   (a) A circular doubly linked list with a dummy head node; (b) an empty list with a dummy head node

By using a circular doubly linked list, you can perform insertions and deletions without special cases: Inserting into and deleting from the first or last position is the same as for any other position. Consider, for example, how to delete the node N that `cur` points to. As Figure 4-30 illustrates, you need to

A circular doubly linked list eliminates special cases for insertion and deletion

1. Change the `next` pointer of the node that precedes N so that it points to the node that follows N.

2. Change the `precede` pointer of the node that follows N so that it points to the node that precedes N.

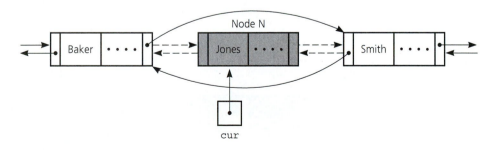

FIGURE 4-30   Pointer changes for deletion

The following C++ assignment statements accomplish these two steps:

Deleting a node

```
// delete the node to which cur points
(cur->precede)->next = cur->next;
(cur->next)->precede = cur->precede;
```

You should convince yourself that these statements work even when the node to be deleted is the first, last, or only data (nonhead) node in the list. Note that the parentheses are unnecessary because -> is left-associative.

Now consider how to insert a node into a circular doubly linked list. In general, the fact that the list is doubly linked does not mean that you avoid traversing the list to find the proper place for the new item. For example, if you insert a new customer name, you must find the proper place within the sorted linked list for the new node. The following pseudocode sets *cur* to point to the node that contains the first name greater than *newName*. Thus, *cur* will point to the node that is to follow the new node on the list:

Traverse the list to locate the insertion point

```
// find the insertion point
cur = listHead->next   // point to first node, if any
while (cur ≠ listHead and newName > cur->item)
   cur = cur->next
```

Notice that if you want to insert the new node either at the end of the list or into an empty list, the loop will set *cur* to point to the dummy head node.

As Figure 4-31 illustrates, once *cur* points to the node that is to follow the new node, you need to

1. Set the *next* pointer in the new node to point to the node that is to follow it.

2. Set the *precede* pointer in the new node to point to the node that is to precede it.

3. Set the *precede* pointer in the node that is to follow the new node so that it points to the new node.

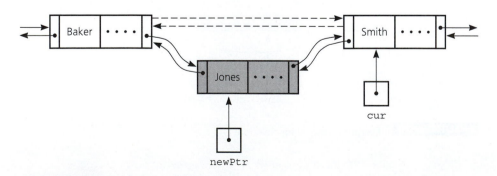

FIGURE 4-31   Pointer changes for insertion

4. Set the *next* pointer in the node that is to precede the new
node so that it points to the new node.

The following C++ statements accomplish these four steps, assuming
that *newPtr* points to the new node:

```
// insert the new node pointed to by newPtr before
// the node pointed to by cur
newPtr->next = cur;
newPtr->precede = cur->precede;
cur->precede = newPtr;
newPtr->precede->next = newPtr;
```

Inserting a node

You should convince yourself that these statements work even when
you insert the node into the beginning of a list; at the end of a list, in
which case *cur* points to the head node; or into an empty list, in which
case *cur* also points to the head node.

4.4 Application: Maintaining an Inventory

Imagine that you have a part-time job at the local DVD store. Realiz-
ing that you know a good deal about computers, the store owner asks
you to write an interactive program that will maintain the store's inventory of DVDs that are for sale. The inventory consists of a list of movie
titles and the following information associated with each title:

- **Have value:** number of DVDs currently in stock.

- **Want value:** number of DVDs that should be in stock. (When the
  have value is less than the want value, more DVDs are ordered.)

- **Wait list:** list of names of people waiting for the title if it is
  sold out.

Because the owner plans to turn off the power to the computer when the
store is closed, your inventory program will not be running at all times.
Therefore, the program must save the inventory in a file before execution
terminates and later restore the inventory when it is run again.

Program input and output are as follows:

Input

- A file that contains a previously saved inventory.

- A file that contains information on an incoming shipment of
  DVDs. (See command D.)

- Single-letter commands—with arguments where necessary—
  that inquire about or modify the inventory and that the user will
  enter interactively.

Output

- A file that contains the updated inventory. (Note that you remove from the inventory all items whose have values and want values are zero and whose wait lists are empty. Thus, such items do not appear in the file.)

- Output as specified by the individual commands.

The program should be able to execute the following commands:

Program commands

H	(help)	Provide a summary of the available commands.
I *\<title\>*	(inquire)	Display the inventory information for a specified title.
L	(list)	List the entire inventory (in alphabetical order by title).
A *\<title\>*	(add)	Add a new title to the inventory. Prompt for initial want value.
M *\<title\>*	(modify)	Modify the want value for a specified title.
D	(delivery)	Take delivery of a shipment of DVDs, assuming that the clerk has entered the shipment information (titles and counts) into a file. Read the file, reserve DVDs for the people on the wait list, and update the have values in the inventory accordingly. Note that the program must add an item to the inventory if a delivered title is not present in the current inventory.
O	(order)	Write a purchase order for additional DVDs based on a comparison of the have and want values in the inventory, so that the have value is brought up to the want value.
R	(return)	Write a return order based on a comparison of the have and want values in the inventory and decrease the have values accordingly (make the return). The purpose is to reduce the have value to the want value.

| S *<title>* | (sell) | Decrease the count for the specified title by 1. If the title is sold out, put a name on the wait list for the title. |
| Q | (quit) | Save the inventory and wait lists in a file and terminate execution. |

The problem-solving process that starts with a statement of the problem and ends with a program that effectively solves the problem—that is, a program that meets its specification—has three main stages:

1. The design of a solution

2. The implementation of the solution

3. The final set of refinements to the program

Realize, however, that you cannot complete one stage in total isolation from the others. Also realize that at many steps in the development of a solution, you must make choices. Although the following discussion may give the impression that the choices are clear-cut, such is not always the case. In reality, both the trade-offs between choices and the false starts (wrong choices considered) are often numerous.

This problem primarily involves data management and requires certain program commands. These commands suggest the following operations on the inventory:

- List the inventory in alphabetical order by title (L command).

Operations on the inventory

- Find the inventory item associated with a title (I, M, D, O, and S commands).

- Replace the inventory item associated with a title (M, D, R, and S commands).

- Insert new inventory items (A and D commands).

Recall that each title might have an associated wait list of people who are waiting for that title. You must be able to

- Add new people to the end of the wait list when they want a DVD that is sold out (S command).

- Delete people from the beginning of the wait list when new DVDs are delivered (D command).

- Display the names on a wait list for a particular title (I and L commands).

In addition, you must be able to

- Save the current inventory and associated wait lists when program execution terminates (Q command).

- Restore the current inventory and associated wait lists when program execution begins again.

You could think of these operations as part of an ADT inventory. Your next step should be to specify each of the operations fully. Because this chapter is about linked lists and implementation issues, the completion of the specifications will be left as an exercise. We will turn our attention to a data structure that could implement the inventory.

Each data item in the ADT inventory represents a movie and contains a title, the number of DVDs in stock (a have value), the number desired (a want value), and a wait list. How will you represent the wait list? If the wait list is an array of names, not only will you limit the length of each wait list, but also each inventory item will be large. If you implement the wait list as a linked list, however, the inventory item can simply contain the linked list's head pointer. Because you must be able to add new names to the end of an item's wait list, a tail pointer for the wait list will enable more-efficient insertions. Thus, each item will also contain a pointer to the last name in its wait list, as Figure 4-32a illustrates.

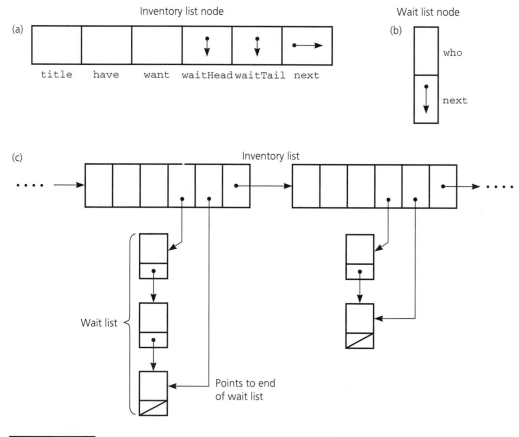

FIGURE 4-32 (a) Inventory-list node; (b) wait-list node; (c) orthogonal structure for the inventory

Maintaining the inventory in alphabetical order by title will facilitate searching for a particular title. If you use an array to contain the inventory items, you can use a binary search. Inserting and deleting items, however, requires you to shift array elements, which can be expensive given that the items are relatively large. Using a linked list for the inventory avoids these data shifts but makes a binary search impractical. (How do you quickly locate the middle item in a linked list?) Weighing these trade-offs, we choose a linked list to represent the inventory.

To summarize, we have made the following choices:

- The inventory is a linked list of data items, sorted by the title that each item represents.

A linked list represents the inventory

- Each inventory item contains a title, a have value, a want value, a pointer to the beginning of a linked list of people's names (the wait list), and a pointer to the last name in the wait list.

Figure 4-32 and the following C++ statements summarize these choices:

```
// wait list - people waiting for certain titles
struct WaitNode
{  string    who;
   WaitNode *next;
};  // end struct

// inventory list - list of stock items
struct StockNode
{  string    title;
   int       have, want;
   WaitNode  *waitHead, *waitTail;
   StockNode *next;
};  // end struct
```

An initial data structure

Before you can proceed with the implementation, you must consider how you will save the inventory in a file. Recall that you save a linked list in a file by saving only the data portion of the list items. However, there is one slight complication here: Each inventory item contains pointers and has an associated sublist—the wait list. Thus,

- You can redefine the inventory structure, as Figure 4-33 shows, so that the title, the have value, and the want value are in a new structure that you can write to a file.

- You can use a second file for the names in the wait lists.

- To restore the wait lists, you must know their lengths. In particular, if you store the names in all the wait lists together in a single file, you must be able to determine where one list ends and the next begins.

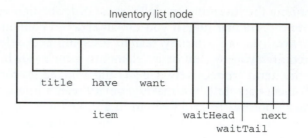

Inventory list node

title   have   want

item   waitHead   next
                                                   waitTail

FIGURE 4-33 Modified node structure

The need for a second file is not a difficulty, but you must modify the original statement of the inventory problem to accommodate this change because it specifies "a file." This change is not at all unreasonable, given the spirit of the problem.

To address the third observation, recall that the have value of a stock item is the number of items currently in stock. It is reasonable to adopt the convention that a negative have value is the number of DVDs that you are short—the size of the wait list!

The following is a revision of the previous definitions and reflects this discussion:

A refined data structure

```
// wait list - people waiting for certain titles
struct WaitNode
{  string    who;
   WaitNode *next;
};  // end struct

// stock item
class StockItem
{
public:
   . . .
private:
   string title;
   int     have, want;
};  // end class

// inventory list - list of stock items
struct StockNode
{  StockItem    item;
   WaitNode *waitHead, *waitTail;
   StockNode *next;
};  // end struct
```

Notice that no operation explicitly deletes an inventory item. You remove items whose have values and want values are zero and whose wait lists are empty from the inventory simply by not saving them in the file when the Q command executes. Because this removal occurs just before the program terminates—and all memory is returned to the system—nothing is gained by explicitly deleting these particular nodes.

The completion of this solution is left as an exercise.

4.5 The C++ Standard Template Library

Many modern programming languages, such as C++, provide classes that implement many of the more commonly used ADTs. In C++, many of these classes are defined in the **Standard Template Library**, or **STL**. The STL contains a number of template classes that can be applied to nearly any type of data.

The STL contains template classes for some common ADTs

Many of the ADTs that are presented in this text have a corresponding class in the STL. For example, a `list` class is defined in the STL that is similar to the `List` class presented earlier in this chapter. You might be wondering why we spend so much time on developing ADTs in this text if they are already provided in the STL. There are many reasons for doing so; here are just a few:

- Developing simple ADTs provides a foundation for learning to develop other ADTs.

Reasons to write your own implementations of ADTs

- You may find yourself working in a language that does not provide any predefined ADTs. You need to have the ability to develop ADTs on your own, and hence you must understand the process.

- If the ADTs defined by the language you are using are not sufficient, you may need to develop your own or enhance existing ones.

The STL provides support for predefined ADTs through the use of three basic items: containers, algorithms, and iterators. Containers are objects that hold other objects, such as a list. Algorithms, such as a sorting algorithm, act on containers. **Iterators** provide a way to cycle through the contents of a container. Of immediate interest here are the STL containers and iterators.

A container is an object that holds other objects

Containers

Containers rely heavily on the C++ **class template** construct. Class templates allow you to develop a class and defer certain data-type information until you are ready to use the class. For example, our list class was developed independently from the type of the list items. The implementation used a `typedef` statement to define the actual `ListItemType`.

With templates, this data type is left as a data-type parameter in the definition of the class. The class definition is preceded by `template <class T>`, where the data-type parameter T represents the data type that the client will specify. Here is an example of a simple class template:

```
template <class T> class MyClass
{
public:
   MyClass();
   MyClass(T initialData);

   void setData(T newData);
   T getData();
private:
   T theData;
};
```

Chapter 8 describes how to create your own class templates.

When you (the client) declare instances of the class, you specify the actual data type that the parameter T represents. For example, a simple program that uses this class template could begin as follows:

```
int main()
{
   MyClass<int> a;
   MyClass<double> b(5.4);

   a.setData(5);
   cout << b.getData() << endl;
```

Notice how the declarations of *a* and *b* specify the data type of *MyClass*'s data member *theData*.

STL containers actually use two data-type parameters. The first is usually the data type for the items in the container. The second is an **allocator**. Allocators manage memory allocation for a container. The default allocator is an object of class *allocator* and is sufficient for most uses. Since this default is commonly used, the STL definitions shown in this text will omit the allocator in the STL specifications.

Iterators

Iterators are a generalization of pointers. They give you the ability to cycle through the items in a container in much the same way that we used a pointer to traverse a linked list. If you have an iterator called *curr*, you can access the item in the container that *curr* references by using the notation **curr*.

The STL actually classifies iterators into five categories. These categories determine the operations available with the iterator. The STL container classes presented in this text support the **bidirectional itera-tor**, so we will describe that one here. A bidirectional iterator enables you to move to either the next or previous item in a container. The statement

```
++curr;
```

uses the ++ increment operator to move the iterator to the next item in the container. To move the iterator back to a previous element in the container, you use the -- decrement operator.

The container classes typically provide at least two functions that are useful for working with iterators. The first function,

```
iterator begin();
```

initializes an iterator to reference the first item in the container. The second function,

```
iterator end();
```

returns a value that indicates whether you have reached the end of the container. This value is also returned by the *begin* function if the list is empty. Note that this value is not *NULL*, though the call to the *end* method is used like the value *NULL*.

The following example shows how you can use an iterator with the standard template class *list*:

```
list<int> myList;
list<int>::iterator curr;

// right now, the list is empty;
// start the iterator at the beginning of myList
curr = myList.begin();
// test for empty list
if (curr == myList.end())
   cout << "The list is empty" << endl;

// insert five items into the list myList
for (int j = 0; j < 5; j++)
   // places item j at the front of the list
   curr = myList.insert(curr, j);

// now output each item in the list starting with the
// first item in the list; keep moving the iterator
// to the next item in the list until the end of
// the list is reached
for (curr = myList.begin(); curr != myList.end(); curr++)
   cout << *curr << " ";
cout << endl;
```

If you attempt to use an iterator before it is initialized, you may have unpredictable results or runtime errors.

Chapter 8 describes how to create your own iterator.

The Standard Template Library Class *list*

The STL class *list* is typically implemented using some form of a doubly linked list, such as the circular doubly linked list described on pages 211–215. It is optimized for insertion and deletion of elements, but does not provide subscripting, because element access would be inefficient. Bidirectional iterators are provided to access list elements. The function *begin* returns an iterator to the first item in the list, and the function *end* returns an iterator to the dummy header node in the list. Here is a partial listing of the methods of the STL class *list*:

```
template <class T> class std::list
{
public:
   list();
   // Default constructor; initializes an empty list.
   // Precondition: None.
   // Postcondition: An empty list exists.

   list(size_type num, const T& val = T());
   // Constructor; initializes list to have num elements
   // with the value val.
   // Precondition: None.
   // Postcondition: A list with num elements.

   list(const list<T> & anotherList);
   // Constructor; initializes list to have the same
   // elements as list anotherList.
   // Precondition: None.
   // Postcondition: A list with the same elements as
   // anotherList.

   bool empty() const;
   // Determines whether a list is empty.
   // Precondition: None.
   // Postcondition: Returns true if the list is empty;
   // otherwise returns false.

   size_type size() const;
   // Determines the length of the list. size_type is
   // an integral type.
   // Precondition: None.
   // Postcondition: Returns the number of items that
   // are currently in the list.
```

```
size_type max_size();
// Determines the maximum number of items the list
// can hold.
// Precondition: None.
// Postcondition: Returns the maximum number of items.

iterator insert(iterator i, const T& val = T());
// Inserts an item val into the list immediately
// before the element specified by the iterator i.
// Precondition: The iterator must be initialized, even
// if the list is empty.
// Postcondition: Item val is inserted into the list and
// an iterator to the newly inserted item is returned.

void remove(const T& val);
// Removes all items with value val from the list.
// Precondition: None.
// Postcondition: The list has no item with value val.

iterator erase(iterator i);
// Removes the item in the list pointed to by iterator i.
// Precondition: The iterator must be initialized to
// point to an element in the list.
// Postcondition: Returns an iterator to the item
// following the removed item. If the item removed is the
// last item in the list, the iterator value will be the
// same as the value returned by end().

iterator begin();
// Returns an iterator to the first item in the list.
// Precondition: None.
// Postcondition: If the list is empty, the iterator
// value will be the same as the value returned by end().

iterator end();
// Returns an iterator value that can be used to test
// whether the end of the list has been reached.
// Precondition: None.
// Postcondition: The iterator value for the end of the list
// is returned

void sort();
// Sorts elements according to the operator < and maintains the
// relative order of equal elements.
// Precondition: None.
// Postcondition: The list is sorted in ascending order.

} // end STL class list
```

The default sorting algorithm for this class sorts elements in ascending order. To use a different sorting algorithm, you can write a sort predicate that overrides the function operator (). A **function object**, which is an object that behaves like a function, uses the member function *operator* to define the desired behavior. For example, the following code will allow strings to be sorted in descending order by overriding the default *std::greater<int>* function object for *sort*.

```
template<> struct std::greater<string*>
{
    // override operator() to create a function object
    bool operator() (string* s1, string *s2)
    {
        return (*s1) > (*s2);
    }
};
```

Here is an example of how the STL class *list* is used to maintain a grocery list:

```
#include <list>
#include <iostream>
#include <string>
using namespace std;

int main()
{
   list<string> groceryList;  // create an empty list
   list<string>::iterator i = groceryList.begin();

   i = groceryList.insert(i, "apples");
   i = groceryList.insert(i, "bread");
   i = groceryList.insert(i, "juice");
   i = groceryList.insert(i, "carrots");

   cout << "Number of items on my grocery list: "
        << groceryList.size() << endl;

   cout << "Items are:" << endl;
   i = groceryList.begin();
   while (i != groceryList.end())
   {  cout << *i << endl;
      i++;
   } // end while
} // end main
```

The output of this program is

```
Number of items on my grocery list: 4
Items are:
carrots
juice
bread
apples
```

Here is a modified version, which stores pointers to strings instead of storing the strings themselves, and displays the grocery list after sorting with the predicate given previously.

```cpp
#include <list>
#include <iostream>
#include <string>
using namespace std;

// define a list of pointer strings
typedef list<string*, allocator<string*> > STRING_PTR;

// override the default behavior of sort
template<> struct std::greater<string*>
{
    // override operator() to create a function object
    bool operator() (string* s1, string *s2)
    {
        return (*s1) > (*s2);
    }
};

int main()
{
    // create a list of pointer strings and a list iterator
    STRING_PTR groceryList;
    STRING_PTR::iterator i;

    // create pointers to strings in a random order
    // insert the string pointers to the end of the list
    string* str = new string ("apples");
    groceryList.insert(groceryList.end(), str);
    str = new string ("bread");
    groceryList.insert(groceryList.end(), str);
    str = new string ("juice");
    groceryList.insert(groceryList.end(), str);
    str = new string ("carrots");
    groceryList.insert(groceryList.end(), str);

    cout << "Number of items on my grocery list: "
         << groceryList.size() << endl;
```

```
// sort with the overridden function object
groceryList.sort(greater<string*>());

// print out the list of strings
cout << "Items after the predicate sort are:" << endl;
i = groceryList.begin();
while (i != groceryList.end())
{   cout << (*(*i)).c_str() << endl;
    i++;
}
}
```

The output of this program is:

```
Number of items on my grocery list: 4
Items after the predicate sort are:
juice
carrots
bread
apples
```

Summary

1. The *new* operator enables you to dynamically allocate memory that you can use for either an array or a linked list. The *delete* operator allows you to recycle memory by returning it to the system for reallocation by the *new* operator.

2. Pointer variables are an extremely useful data type. You can use them to implement the data structure known as a linked list by using statements such as the following:

```
struct Node
{   desired-data-type item;
    Node           *next;
};  // end struct
```

Each pointer in a linked list is a pointer to a *struct*, that is, the entire node. For example, if *p* is a variable of type *Node* * that points to a node in this linked list,

- *p* is the node.

- *p->item* is the data portion of the node.

- *p->next* points to the next node.

3. Algorithms for inserting data into and deleting data from a linked list both involve these steps: Traverse the list from the beginning until you reach the appropriate position; perform pointer changes to alter the structure of the list. In addition, you use the *new* operator to dynamically allocate a new node for insertion, whereas you use the *delete* operator to deallocate the deleted node.

4. Inserting a new node at the beginning of a linked list or deleting the first node of a linked list are cases that you treat differently from insertions and deletions anywhere else in the list.

5. An array-based implementation uses an implicit ordering scheme—for example, the item that follows *anArray[i]* is stored in *anArray[i+1]*. A pointer-based implementation uses an explicit ordering scheme—for example, to find the item that follows the one in node *N*, you follow node *N*'s pointer. A pointer-based implementation, therefore, requires additional memory to represent the pointers.

6. You can access any element of an array directly, but you must traverse a linked list to access a particular node. Therefore, the access time for an array is constant, whereas the access time for a linked list depends on the location of the node within the list.

7. You can insert items into and delete items from a pointer-based linked list without shifting data. This characteristic is an important advantage of a linked list over an array.

8. A class that allocates memory dynamically needs an explicit copy constructor that copies an instance of the class. It is invoked implicitly when you pass an object to a function by value, return an object from a valued function, or define and initialize an object. If you do not define a copy constructor, the compiler will generate one for you. A compiler-generated copy constructor is sufficient only for classes that use statically allocated memory.

9. A class that allocates memory dynamically needs an explicit destructor. The destructor should use *delete* to deallocate the memory associated with the object. If you do not define a destructor, the compiler will generate one for you. A compiler-generated destructor is sufficient only for classes that use statically allocated memory.

10. Although you can use the *new* operator to allocate memory dynamically for either an array or a linked list, you can increase the size of a linked list one node at a time more efficiently than you can increase the size of an array. When you increase the size of a dynamically allocated array, you must copy the original array elements into the new array and then deallocate the original array.

11. A binary search of a linked list is impractical because you cannot quickly locate its middle item.

12. You can store a linked list in a file by writing the data portion of the nodes in the order in which they appear in the list. As a result, it is easy to restore the linked list directly from the file at a later time.

13. You can use recursion to perform operations on a linked list. Such use will eliminate special cases and the need for a trailing pointer.

14. The recursive insertion algorithm for a sorted linked list works because each smaller linked list is also sorted. When the algorithm makes an insertion at the beginning of one of these lists, the inserted node will be in the proper position in the original list. The algorithm is guaranteed to terminate because each smaller list contains one fewer node than the preceding list and because the empty list is a base case.

15. In a circular linked list, the last node points to the first node, so that every node has a successor. If the list's external pointer points to the last node instead of the first node, you can access both the last node and the first node without traversing the list.

16. Dummy head nodes provide a method for eliminating the special cases for insertion into and deletion from the beginning of a linked list. The use of dummy head nodes is a matter of personal taste for singly linked lists, but it is helpful for a doubly linked list.

17. A doubly linked list allows you to traverse the list in either direction. Each node points to its successor as well as to its predecessor. Because insertions and deletions with a doubly linked list are more involved than with a singly linked list, it is convenient to use both a dummy head node and a circular organization to eliminate complicated special cases for the beginning and end of the list.

18. A class template enables you to defer the choice of certain data-type information until you use the class.

19. The Standard Template Library contains template classes for some common ADTs.

20. A container is an object that holds other objects. An iterator cycles through the contents of a container.

Cautions

1. Because the value of a pointer variable is an address, displaying a pointer is not something you will do ordinarily.

2. Although you can declare several variables, all of which have the same fundamental data type, in one declaration that contains comma-separated names, do not use this notation when declaring pointer variables. Thus,

```
int a, b, c;
```

declares the integer variables *a*, *b*, and *c*, but

```
char *s, t;
```

means

```
char *s; char t;
```

instead of

```
char *s; char *t;
```

You should avoid such constructs.

3. An uninitialized pointer variable has an undefined value, not the value *NULL*.

4. If *p* is an uninitialized pointer variable, a reference to **p* can cause unpredictable, even catastrophic results.

5. An attempt to reference a pointer variable that has the value *NULL* is wrong, but it might not be illegal. For example, if p has the value *NULL*, you should avoid expressions such as *p->item* and *p->next* when processing a linked list. Failure to do so can cause a program to run incorrectly.

6. The sequence

```
p = new int;
p = NULL;
```

allocates a memory cell and then destroys the only means of accessing it. Do not use *new* when you simply want to assign a value to a pointer.

7. Remember that *delete p* deallocates the node to which *p* points; it does not deallocate *p*. The pointer *p* still exists, but contains an undefined value. You should not reference *p* or any other pointer variable that still points to the deallocated node. To help you avoid this kind of error, you should assign *NULL* to *p* after executing *delete p*. However, if variables other than *p* point to the deallocated node, the possibility of error still exists.

8. If you allocate memory by using *new*, deallocate it by using *delete*. If you allocate memory by using *new []*, deallocate it by using *delete []*.

9. Insertions into and deletions from the beginning of a linked list are special cases unless you use a dummy head node. Failure to

recognize this fact can result in a reference to a pointer whose value is *NULL*; such a reference is incorrect.

10. When traversing a linked list by using the pointer variable *cur*, you must be careful not to reference *cur* after it has "passed" the last node in the list, because it will have the value *NULL* at that point. For example, the loop

```
while (value > cur->item)
   cur = cur->next;
```

is incorrect if *value* is greater than all the data values in the linked list, because *cur* becomes *NULL*. Instead you should write

```
while ((cur != NULL) && (value > cur->item))
   cur = cur->next;
```

Because C++ uses short-circuit evaluation of logical expressions, if *cur* becomes *NULL*, the expression *cur->item* will not be evaluated.

11. A doubly linked list is a data structure that programmers tend to overuse. However, a doubly linked list is appropriate to use when you have direct access to a node. In such cases, you would not have traversed the list from its beginning. If the list were singly linked, you would not have a pointer to the preceding node. Because doubly linking the list provides an easy way to get to the node's predecessor as well as its successor, you can, for example, delete the node readily.

12. When you pass an array as an argument to a function, the function sees a pointer to the first element of the array and accesses other array elements by using this pointer. Any assignment to an array element, therefore, changes the actual argument, not a copy of it. For this reason, arrays cannot be value arguments.

Self-Test Exercises

1. Trace the execution of this program by hand.

```
#include <iostream>
using namespace std;

int main()
{
   int *p = new int;
   int *q = new int;
   cout << p << " " << q << endl;
```

```
    *p = 7;
    *q = 11;
    int *r = q;
    cout << *p << " " << *q << " " << *r << endl;

    *r = *q + *p;
    cout << *p << " " << *q << " " << *r << endl;

    q = new int;
    *q = 4;
    cout << *p << " " << *q << " " << *r << endl;

    delete r;
    r = NULL;

    return 0;
}  // end main
```

2. Consider the algorithm for deleting a node from a linked list that this chapter describes.

   a. Is deletion of the last node of a linked list a special case? Explain.

   b. Is deletion of the only node of a one-node linked list a special case? Explain.

   c. Does deleting the first node take more effort than deleting the last node? Explain.

3. a. Write C++ statements that create the linked list pictured in Figure 4-34, as follows. Beginning with an empty linked list, first create and attach a node for J, then create and attach a node for E, and finally create and attach a node for B.

   b. Repeat Part a, but instead create and attach nodes in the order B, E, J.

4. Consider the sorted linked list of single characters in Figure 4-34. Suppose that *prev* points to the first node in this list and *cur* points to the second node.

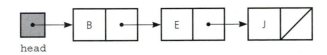

head

FIGURE 4-34 Linked list for Self-Test Exercises 3, 4, and 8

a. Write C++ statements that delete the second node and return it to the system. (*Hint:* First modify Figure 4-34.)

b. Now assume that *cur* points to the first node of the remaining two nodes of the original list. Write C++ statements that delete the first node and return it to the system.

c. Now *head* points to the only node that is left in the list. Write C++ statements that insert a new node that contains A into the list so that the list remains sorted.

d. Revise Figure 4-34 so that your new diagram reflects the results of the previous deletions and insertion.

5. Write a C++ function that displays only the ith integer in a linked list of integers. Assume that $i \geq 1$ and that the linked list contains at least i nodes.

6. How many assignment operations does the function that you wrote for Self-Test Exercise 5 require?

7. Write a recursive C++ function that retrieves the ith integer in a linked list of integers. Assume that $i \geq 1$ and that the linked list contains at least i nodes. (*Hint:* If $i = 1$, return the first integer in the list; otherwise, retrieve the $(i - 1)^{st}$ integer from the rest of the list.)

8. Trace the execution of `writeBackward2(head)`, where *head* points to the linked list of the characters pictured in Figure 4-34. (`writeBackward2` appears on page 205 of this chapter.)

9. The pointer-based implementation of the destructor in the class *List* contains the following loop:

```
while (!isEmpty())
   remove(1);
```

a. Why does this loop work?

b. Can you correctly replace the loop with

```
for (int position = getLength(); position >= 1;
     --position)
   remove(1);
```

c. Does your answer to Part b differ if you replace *remove(1)* with *remove(position)*?

d. Do your answers to Parts b and c differ if you replace the *for* statement with

```
for (int position = 1; position <= getLength();
                                   ++position)
```

10. Revise the destructor in the class *List* so that it directly deletes each node of the underlying linked list without using *remove*.

Exercises

1. This exercise assumes that you have completed Self-Test Exercise 4 and know the final status of the linked list. For each of the following, write the C++ statements that perform the requested operation on the list. Also draw a picture of the status of the list after each operation is complete. When you delete a node from the list, return it to the system. All insertions into the list should maintain the list's sorted order. Do not use any of the functions that were presented in this chapter.

   a. Assume that *prev* points to the first node and *cur* points to the second node. Insert F into the list.

   b. Assume that *prev* points to the second node and that *cur* points to the third node of the list after you revised it in Part a. Delete the last node of the list.

   c. Assume that *prev* points to the last node of the list after you revised it in Part b, and assume that *cur* is *NULL*. Insert G into the list.

2. Consider a linked list of items that are in no particular order.

   a. Write a function that inserts a node at the beginning of the linked list and a function that deletes the first node of the linked list.

   b. Repeat Part a, but this time perform the insertion and deletion at the end of the list instead of at the beginning.

   c. Repeat Part b, but this time assume that the list has a tail pointer as well as a head pointer.

3. Write a function to count the number of items in a linked list

   a. Iteratively

   b. Recursively

4. Write a function that will delete from a linked list of integers the node that contains the largest integer. Can you do this with a single traversal of the list?

5. The section "Processing Linked Lists Recursively" discussed a linked list of characters that represented a string.

   a. Write an iterative function that displays such a string. Compare the efficiencies of your function and the function *writeString*.

b. Write an iterative function that displays such a string backward. Compare the efficiencies of your function and the function `writeBackward2`.

6. Write a function to merge two linked lists of integers that are sorted into ascending order. The result should be a third linked list that is the sorted combination of the original lists. Do not destroy the original lists.

7. In the section "Saving and Restoring a Linked List by Using a File," the program segment that restores a linked list from a file requires that the head pointer be `NULL` initially. What happens if this assumption is not true? That is, suppose that the head pointer points to a nonempty linked list, and then you restore the linked list from a file.

8. Compare the number of operations required to display each node in a linked list of integers with the number of operations required to display each item in an array of integers. A loop that displays the items in a linked list is given in the section "Displaying the Contents of a Linked List."

9. Compare the array-based and pointer-based implementations of the ADT list operation `remove(index)`. Describe the work required for various values of `index` under each implementation. What are the implications for efficiency if the cost of shifting data is large compared to the cost of following a pointer? When would this situation occur? What if the costs are approximately the same?

10. Write the pseudocode for a function that inserts a new node at the end of a doubly linked list.

11. Write a function that inserts a new node at the start of a doubly linked list.

12. Using the class `Sphere` given on pages 137–138, write a program that instantiates four `Sphere` objects (assigning a radius to each instance) and adds them to a pointer-based linked list. Include a function to display the statistics of each `Sphere` in the list.

13. Assume that the pointer `list` points to the last node of a circular linked list like the one in Figure 4-26. Write a loop that displays the data portion of every node in the list.

14. Given a class that has a circular linked list as its only data member, write the implementation for its

   a. Destructor

   b. Copy constructor

15. Write a function that deletes the ith node from a circular linked list.

16. Imagine a circular linked list of integers that are sorted into ascending order, as Figure 4-35a illustrates. The external pointer *list* points to the last node, which contains the largest integer. Write a function that revises the list so that its data are sorted into descending order, as Figure 4-35b illustrates. Do not allocate or deallocate nodes.

17. Revise the implementations of the ADT list operations *insert* and *remove* under the assumption that the linked list has a dummy head node.

18. Add the operations *save* and *restore* to the pointer-based implementation of the ADT list. These operations use a file to save and restore the list items.

19. Consider the sorted doubly linked list shown in Figure 4-29a. This list is circular and has a dummy head node. Suppose that *newName* contains a name that you want to add to this list. Write some C++ code that inserts a new node containing *newName* into its proper sorted order within the list.

20. Consider the sorted doubly linked list shown in Figure 4-29a. This list is circular and has a dummy head node. Suppose that *newName* contains a name that you want to delete from the list. Write some C++ statements that delete the node containing *newName*.

21. Repeat Exercises 19 and 20 for the sorted doubly linked list shown in Figure 4-28. This list is not circular and does not have a dummy head node. Watch out for the special cases at the beginning and end of the list.

(a)

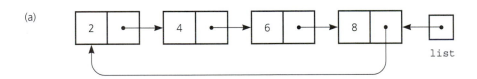

(b)

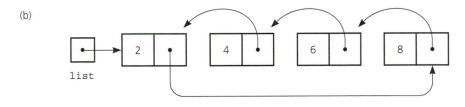

FIGURE 4-35   Two circular linked lists

22. If you have a collection of data about people, suppose that you represent each person as a C++ structure whose data members store a name, a Social Security number, an address, and so on. If you use an ADT list to maintain the structures, what changes, if any, do you need to make to the specification and implementation of the list? What if you used a class instead of a structure to represent a person?

23. You can have a linked list of linked lists, as Figure 4-32 indicates. Assume the C++ definitions on page 219. Suppose that *cur* points to a desired stock item (node) in the inventory list. Write some C++ statements that add a name to the end of the wait list associated with the node to which *cur* points.

Programming Problems

1. Chapter 3 introduced the ADT sorted list, which maintains its data in sorted order. For example, a sorted list of names would be maintained in alphabetical order, and a sorted list of numbers would be maintained either in increasing or decreasing order. The operations for a sorted list are summarized on page 125.

   Some operations—*sortedIsEmpty*, *sortedLength*, and *sortedRetrieve*, for example—are just like those for the ADT list. Insertion and deletion operations, however, are by value, not by position as they are for a list. For example, when you insert an item into a sorted list, you do not specify where in the list the item belongs. Instead, the insertion operation determines the correct position of the item by comparing its value with those of the existing items on the list. A new operation, *locatePosition*, determines from the value of an item its numerical position within the sorted list.

   Note that the specifications given in Chapter 3 do not say anything about duplicate entries in the sorted list. Depending on your application, you might allow duplicates, or you might want to prevent duplicates from entering the list. For example, a sorted list of Social Security numbers probably should disallow duplicate entries. In this example, an attempt to insert a Social Security number that already exists in the sorted list would fail.

   Write a nonrecursive, pointer-based implementation of the ADT sorted list of integers as a C++ class such that

   a. Duplicates are allowed

   b. Duplicates are not allowed, and operations must prevent duplicates from entering the list

2. Repeat Programming Problem 1, but write a recursive, pointer-based implementation instead. Recall from this chapter that the recursive functions must be in the private section of the class.

3. Write an implementation of the ADT list that uses a dynamically allocated array to represent the list items.

4. Write a pointer-based implementation of the ADT two-ended list, which has insertion and deletion operations at both ends of the list,

   a. Without a tail pointer

   b. With a tail pointer

5. Implement the node structure, constructor, and destructor for a circular doubly linked list with a dummy head node. Complete the insert and remove functions for this list, as described in the section "Doubly Linked Lists."

6. Implement the ADT character string, which you specified in Exercise 7 of Chapter 3, by using a linked list of characters. How can you implement the string so that you can obtain its length without traversing the linked list and counting?

7. Enhance the ADT character string (see Programming Problem 6) by adding more-sophisticated string operations. For example, find the index of the leftmost occurrence of a character in a string; determine whether one string is a substring of another.

8. Consider a sparse implementation of the ADT polynomial that stores only the terms with nonzero coefficients. For example, you can represent the polynomial p in Exercise 11 of Chapter 3 with the linked list in Figure 4-36.

   a. Complete the sparse implementation.

   b. Define a traverse operation for the ADT polynomial that will allow you to add two sparse polynomials without having to consider terms with zero coefficients explicitly.

9. When you play a board or card game or when you use a shared computing resource, you get a turn and then wait until everyone else has had a turn. Although the number of players in a game remains relatively static, the number of users of a shared computing service fluctuates. Let's assume that this fluctuation will occur.

   Design an ADT that keeps track of turns within a group of people. You should be able to add or delete people and determine whose turn occurs now.

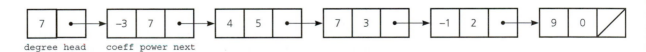

degree head   coeff power next

FIGURE 4-36   A sparse polynomial

Begin with a given group of people; assign these people an initial order. (This order can be random or specified by the user.) The first new person joining the group should get a turn after all others have had an equal number of turns. Each subsequent new person should get a turn after the person who joined the group most recently has a turn.

Also design an ADT to represent a person. (You can be conservative with the amount of data that this ADT contains.) The data that your first ADT stores are instances of the ADT person.

Implement your ADTs as C++ classes. Use a circular linked list as the data structure that keeps track of turns. Implement this linked list by using pointers and not by using any other class.

Write a program that uses and, therefore, tests your ADTs completely. Your program should process several insertion and deletion operations, and demonstrate that people are given turns correctly.

10. Repeat Programming Problem 9, using the ADT you created to represent a person and the STL class *list*.

11. Occasionally, a linked structure that does not use pointers is useful. One such structure uses an array whose items are "linked" by array indexes. Figure 4-37a illustrates an array of nodes that represents the linked list in Figure 4-34. Each node has two members, *item* and *next*. The *next* member is an integer index to the array element that contains the next node in the linked list. Note that the *next* member of the last node contains −1. The integer variable *head* contains the index of the first node in the list.

The array elements that currently are not a part of the linked list make up a **free list** of available nodes. These nodes form another linked list, with the integer variable *free* containing the index of the first free node. To insert an item into the original linked list, you take a free node from the beginning of the free list and insert it into the linked list (Figure 4-37b). When you delete an item from the linked list, you insert the node into the beginning of the free list (Figure 4-37c). In this way, you can avoid shifting data items.

Implement the ADT list by using this array-based linked list.

12. Write the program for the DVD inventory problem that this chapter describes.

13. Modify and expand the inventory program that you wrote for Programming Problem 12. Here are a few suggestions:

a. Add the ability to manipulate more than one inventory with the single program.

b. Add the ability to keep various statistics about each of the inventory items (such as the average number sold per week for the last 10 weeks).

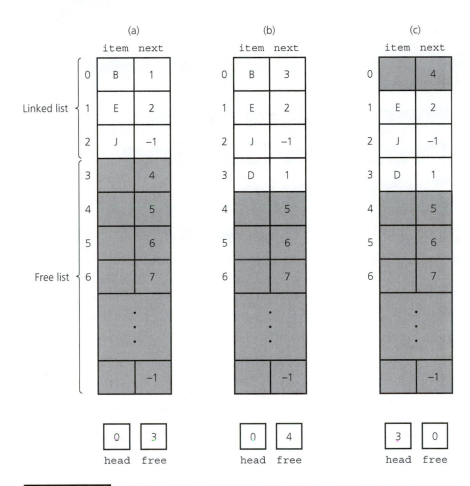

FIGURE 4-37 (a) An array-based implementation of the linked list in Figure 4-34; (b) after inserting D in sorted order; (c) after deleting B

c. Add the ability to modify the have value for an inventory item (for example, when a DVD is damaged or returned by a customer). Consider the implications for maintaining the relationship between a have value and the size of the corresponding wait list.

d. Make the wait lists more sophisticated. For example, keep names and addresses; mail letters automatically when a DVD comes in.

e. Make the ordering mechanism more sophisticated. For instance, do not order DVDs that have already been ordered but have not yet been delivered.

CHAPTER 5

Recursion as a Problem-Solving Technique

PREVIEW

Chapter 2 presented the basic concepts of recursion, and now this chapter moves on to some extremely useful and somewhat complex applications in computer science. The recursive solutions to the problems you will see are far more elegant and concise than the best of their nonrecursive counterparts.

This chapter introduces two new concepts: backtracking and formal grammars. Backtracking is a problem-solving technique that involves guesses at a solution. Formal grammars enable you to define, for example, syntactically correct algebraic expressions. The chapter concludes with a discussion of the close relationship between recursion and mathematical induction; you will learn how to use mathematical induction to study properties of algorithms.

More applications of recursion appear in subsequent chapters.

5.1 Backtracking

This section considers an organized way to make successive guesses at a solution. If a particular guess leads to a dead end, you back up to that guess and replace it with a different guess. This strategy of retracing steps in reverse order and then trying a new sequence of steps is called **backtracking**. You can combine recursion and backtracking to solve the following problem.

Backtracking is a strategy for guessing at a solution and backing up when an impasse is reached

The Eight Queens Problem

A chessboard contains 64 squares that form 8 rows and 8 columns. The most powerful piece in the game of chess is the queen because it can attack any other piece within its row, within its column, or along its diagonal. The Eight Queens problem asks you to place eight queens on the chessboard so that no queen can attack any other queen.

Place eight queens on the chessboard so that no queen can attack any other queen

One strategy is to guess at a solution. However, there are C(64, 8) = 4,426,165,368 ways to arrange 8 queens on a chessboard of 64 squares—so many ways that it would be exhausting to check all of them for a solution to this problem. Nevertheless, a simple observation eliminates many arrangements from consideration: No queen can reside in a row or a column that contains another queen. Alternatively, each row and column can contain exactly one queen. Thus, attacks along rows or columns are eliminated, leaving only 8! = 40,320 arrangements of queens to be checked for attacks along diagonals. A solution now appears more feasible.

Suppose that you provide some organization for the guessing strategy by placing one queen per column, beginning with the first square of column 1. When you consider column 2, you eliminate its first square because row 1 contains a queen, you eliminate its second square because of a diagonal attack, and you finally place a queen in the third square of column 2. Figure 5-1a shows the placement of five queens as

Place queens one column at a time

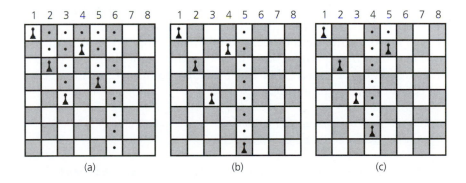

(a)   (b)   (c)

FIGURE 5-1   (a) Five queens that cannot attack each other, but that can attack all of column 6; (b) backtracking to column 5 to try another square for the queen; (c) backtracking to column 4 to try another square for the queen and then considering column 5 again

a result of this procedure. The dots in the figure indicate squares that are rejected because a queen in that square is subject to attack by another queen in an earlier column.

Notice that the five queens in Figure 5-1a can attack any square in column 6. Therefore, you cannot place a queen in column 6, so you must back up to column 5 and move its queen. As Figure 5-1b indicates, the next possible square in column 5 is in the last row. When you consider column 6 once again, there are still no choices for a queen in that column. As you have exhausted the possibilities in column 5, you must back up to column 4. The next possible square in column 4 is in row 7, as Figure 5-1c indicates. You then consider column 5 again and place a queen in row 2.

If you reach an impasse, backtrack to the previous column

How can you use recursion in the solution that was just described? Consider an algorithm that places a queen in a column, given that you have placed queens correctly in the preceding columns. First, if there are no more columns to consider, you are finished; this is the base case. Otherwise, after you successfully place a queen in the current column, you need to consider the next column. That is, you need to solve the same problem with one fewer column; this is the recursive step. Thus, you begin with eight columns, consider smaller problems that decrease in size by one column at each recursive step, and reach the base case when you have a problem with no columns.

This solution appears to satisfy the criteria for a recursive solution. However, you do not know whether you can successfully place a queen in the current column. If you can, you recursively consider the next column. If you cannot place a queen in the current column, you need to backtrack, as has already been described.

The Eight Queens problem can be solved in a variety of ways. The solution in this chapter uses two ADTs: a *Board* class to represent the chessboard, and a *Queen* class to represent a queen on the board. A *Queen* object keeps track of its row and column placement, and contains a static pointer to the *Board*. It also has operations to move to the next row and to determine whether it is subject to attack. A *Board* object keeps track of the *Queens* currently on the board and contains operations to perform the Eight Queens problem and display the solution.

The following pseudocode describes the algorithm for placing queens in columns, given that the previous columns contain queens that cannot attack one another:

The solution combines
recursion with backtracking

```
placeQueens (in queenPtr:Queen *)
// Places queens in eight columns

    if (queen's column is greater than the last column)
        The problem is solved

    else
    {   while (unconsidered squares exist in queen's column
                and the problem is unsolved)
```

```
    {   Determine the next square in queen's column that is
            not under attack by a queen in an earlier column
        if (such a square exists)
        {   Place a queen in the square
            // try next column
            placeQueens (create queen(firstRow, queen's column+ 1))
            if (no queen is possible in the next column)
            {   Delete the new queen
                Remove the last queen placed on the board and
                    consider the next square in that column
            } // end if
        } // end if
    } // end while
} // end if
```

The Eight Queens problem is initiated by the function *doEight-Queens*, which calls *placeQueens* with a new queen in the upper left corner of the board:

```
doEightQueens()
{   placeQueens(newQueen(firstRow, firstColumn))
}
```

After *doEightQueens* has completed, the board may display the solution, if one was found.

Implementing Eight Queens Using the STL Class *vector*

The *Board* ADT in the solution described thus far may be represented in a number of ways. The simplest representation would be a two-dimensional array; however, such an array wastes space because only 8 squares out of 64 are used. Another approach would be to use a one-dimensional array of only the squares that contain a queen. Because the algorithm uses backtracking, a dynamic array is the optimal choice. The *vector* container in the STL is often used in place of an array type, because it allows the number of elements to vary dynamically and provides several built-in functions. Indexing is provided with array-type subscripting or with the *at* function, which provides range checking as well. Some of the more common operations of *vector* are listed below:

```
template <class T> class std::vector
{
public:
    vector()
    // Default constructor
    // Precondition: None.
    // Postcondition: An empty vector exists.
```

```
vector(size_type n)
// Creates a vector with n elements
// Precondition: None.
// Postcondition: A vector of n elements exists.

bool empty() const;
// Determines whether the vector is empty.
// Precondition: None.
// Postcondition: Returns true if the vector is empty,
// otherwise returns false.

size_type size() const;
// Determines the length of the vector.
// The return type size_type is an integral type.
// Precondition: None.
// Postcondition: Returns the number of items that
// are currently in the vector.

void push_back(const T&);
// Inserts a new element at the end of the vector.
// Precondition: None.
// Postcondition: The new element is the last element
// in the vector.

void pop_back();
// Removes the last element of the vector.
// Precondition: There is at least one element in the vector.
// Postcondition: The last element of the vector is removed.

iterator insert(iterator i, const T& val);
// Inserts an item val into the vector
// before the element specified by the iterator i.
// Precondition: The iterator is initialized.
// Postcondition: Item val is inserted into the vector and
// an iterator to the newly inserted item is returned.

iterator erase(iterator i);
// Removes element at i.
// Precondition: The iterator must be initialized.
// Postcondition: Returns an iterator to the item
// following the removed item.

void clear();
// Erases all the elements in the vector.
// Precondition: None.
// Postcondition: The vector has no elements.

iterator begin();
```

```
// Returns an iterator to the first element in the
// vector.
// Precondition: None.
// Postcondition: If the vector is empty,
// the value returned by end() is returned.

iterator end();
// Returns an iterator to test for the end of the
// vector.
// Precondition: None.
// Postcondition: The value for the end of the vector was
// returned.

}   // end STL vector
```

The *Board* class contains a *vector* of pointers to *Queen* objects, as well as several functions to manipulate the *Queens* on the board. Note that private operations for the board use zero-indexing, but that in order to simulate a chessboard, *doEightQueens* can take column numbers 1 to 8 as an argument and then translate them to zero-indexing. The *Queen* and *Board* specifications are as follows:

```
// ****************************************************
// Header file Queen.h
// ****************************************************
#ifndef QUEEN_H
#define QUEEN_H

class Board;

class Queen
{
public:
    Queen();                // Puts queen in upper left corner of board.
    Queen(int inRow, int inCol);  // Places queen in supplied location.

    int getCol() const;         // Returns column number.
    int getRow() const;         // Returns row number.
    void nextRow();             // Moves queen to next row.

    bool isUnderAttack() const;
    // Determines whether the queen is under attack by another queen.
    // If there is a queen in the same row or the same diagonal,
    // returns true; otherwise, returns false.

    static void setBoard(const Board *bPtr);
    // Saves a pointer to the board for all queens.
private:
```

```
    // Row and column of queen if it is on the board.
    // Otherwise, prospective row and column of queen.
    int row;
    int col;

    static const Board *boardPtr; // All queens share the same board.

};

#endif

// ****************************************************
// Header file Board.h
// ****************************************************
#ifndef BOARD_H
#define BOARD_H

#include "Queen.h"
#include <vector>
#include <cassert>
#include <iostream>

using namespace std;

static const int BOARD_SIZE = 8;

class Board
{
public:
    Board();  // Supplies the Queen class with a pointer to the board.
    ~Board(); // Clears the board and removes pointer from queens.

    void clear();       // Clears board.
    void display() const; // Displays board.

    void doEightQueens();
    // Initiates the Eight Queens problem.

    int getNumQueens() const;
    // Returns the number of queens on the board.

    const Queen *getQueen(int index) const;
    // Returns a pointer to the queen at the designated index.

private:

    bool isQueen(int inRow, int inCol) const;
    // Determines whether there is a queen in position (inRow, inCol).
```

```
    bool placeQueens(Queen *queenPtr);
    // Attempts to place queens on board
    // starting with the designated queen.

    void removeQueen();
    // Removes the last queen on the board, but does not delete it.

    void setQueen(const Queen *queenPtr);
    // Places a queen on the board.

    vector<const Queen *> queens;  // array of queens on the board
};

#endif
```

An implementation of *placeQueens* follows:

```
bool Board::placeQueens(Queen *queenPtr)
{
    // Base case.  Trying to place Queen in
    // a non-existent column.
    if (queenPtr->getCol() >= BOARD_SIZE)
    {   delete queenPtr;
        return true;
    }

    bool isQueenPlaced = false;

    while (!isQueenPlaced && queenPtr->getRow() < BOARD_SIZE)
    {   // If the queen can be attacked, then
        // try moving it to the next row in the
        // current column.
        if (queenPtr->isUnderAttack())
            queenPtr->nextRow();
        // Else put this queen on the board and
        // try putting a new queen in the first row
        // of the next column.
        else
        {   setQueen(queenPtr);
            Queen *newQueenPtr = new Queen(0, queenPtr->getCol() + 1);
            isQueenPlaced = placeQueens(newQueenPtr);
            // If it wasn't possible to put the new
            // queen in the next column, backtrack
            // by deleting the new queen and
            // removing the last queen placed and
            // moving it down one row.
            if (!isQueenPlaced)
            {   delete newQueenPtr;
```

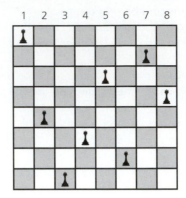

FIGURE 5-2   A solution to the Eight Queens problem

```
          removeQueen();
          queenPtr->nextRow();
        } // end if
      } // end if
    } // end while
    return isQueenPlaced;
} // end placeQueens
```

Figure 5-2 indicates the solution that the previous algorithm finds. By modifying the argument to *doEightQueens*, you can discover other solutions to the Eight Queens problem. The Programming Problems at the end of this chapter ask you to consider other solutions to this algorithm, as well as additional modifications.

5.2 Defining Languages

English and C++ are two languages with which you are familiar. A **language** is nothing more than a set of strings of symbols from a finite alphabet. For example, if you view a C++ program as one long string of characters, you can define the set of all syntactically correct C++ programs. This set is the language

$$C++Programs = \{\text{strings } w : w \text{ is a syntactically correct} \\ \text{C++ program}\}$$

Notice that whereas all programs are strings, not all strings are programs. A C++ compiler is a program that, among other things, determines whether a given string is a member of the language *C++Programs;* that is, the compiler determines whether the string is a syntactically correct C++ program. Of course, this definition of *C++Programs* is not descriptive enough to allow the construction of a compiler. The definition specifies a characteristic of the strings in the set *C++Programs:* The strings are syntactically correct C++ programs. However, this definition does not give the rules for determining whether a string is in the set or not; that is, the definition does not specify what is meant by a syntactically correct C++ program.

The word "language" does not necessarily mean a programming language or a communication language. For example, the set of algebraic expressions forms a language

> *AlgebraicExpressions* = {*w* : *w* is an algebraic expression}

The language *AlgebraicExpressions* is the set of strings that meets certain rules of syntax; however, the set's definition does not give these rules.

In both examples, the rules for forming a string within the language are missing. A **grammar** states the rules of a language. The grammars that you will see in this chapter are recursive in nature. One of the great benefits of using such a grammar to define a language is that you can often write a straightforward recursive algorithm, based on the grammar, that determines whether a given string is in the language. Such an algorithm is called a **recognition algorithm** for the language.

A grammar states the rules for forming the strings in a language

As it is a complex task to present a grammar for the set *C++Programs*, we instead will look at grammars for some simpler languages, including several common languages of algebraic expressions.

The Basics of Grammars

A grammar uses several special symbols:

- *x* | *y* means *x* or *y*.

Symbols that grammars use

- *x y* means *x* followed by *y*. (When the context requires clarification, the notation *x* · *y* will be used. The symbol · means concatenate, or append.)

- < *word* > means any instance of *word* that the definition defines.

A grammar for the language

> *C++Ids* = {*w* : *w* is a legal C++ identifier}

is simple, so we begin with it. As you know, a legal C++ identifier begins with a letter and is followed by zero or more letters and digits. In this context, the underscore (_) is a letter. One way to represent this definition of an identifier is with a syntax diagram, as shown in Figure 5-3.

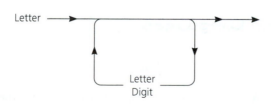

FIGURE 5-3   A syntax diagram for C++ identifiers

A syntax diagram is convenient for people to use, but a grammar is a better starting point if you want to write a function that will recognize an identifier. A grammar for the language *C++Ids* is

A grammar for the language of C++ identifiers

$< identifier > = < letter > \mid < identifier > < letter > \mid < identifier > < digit >$

$< letter > = a \mid b \mid \cdots \mid z \mid A \mid B \mid \cdots \mid Z \mid \_$

$< digit > = 0 \mid 1 \mid \cdots \mid 9$

The definition reads as follows:

> *An identifier is a letter, or an identifier followed by a letter, or an identifier followed by a digit.*

Many grammars are recursive

The most striking aspect of this definition is that *identifier* appears in its own definition: This grammar is recursive, as are many grammars.

Given a string *w*, you can determine whether it is in the language *C++Ids* by using the grammar to construct the following recognition algorithm: If *w* is of length 1, it is in the language if the character is a letter. (This statement is the base case, so to speak.) If *w* is of length greater than 1, it is in the language if the last character of *w* is either a letter or a digit, and *w* minus its last character is an identifier.

The pseudocode for a recursive valued function that determines whether a string is in *C++Ids* follows:

A recognition algorithm for C++ identifiers

```
isId(in w:string):boolean
// Returns true if w is a legal C++ identifier;
// otherwise returns false.

    if (w is of length 1)    // base case
        if (w is a letter)
            return true
        else
            return false
    else if (the last character of w is a letter or a digit)
        return isId(w minus its last character)   // Point X

    else
        return false
```

Figure 5-4 contains a trace of this function for the string *A2B*.

Two Simple Languages

Now consider two more simple examples of languages, their grammars, and resulting recognition algorithms.

Palindromes. A palindrome is a string that reads the same from left to right as it does from right to left. For example, "radar" and "deed" are both palindromes. You can define the language of palindromes as follows:

The initial call is made and the function begins execution.

```
w = "A2B"
```

At point X, a recursive call is made and the new invocation of isId begins execution:

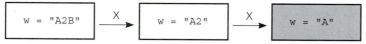

At point X, a recursive call is made and the new invocation of isId begins execution:

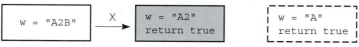

This is the base case, so this invocation of isId completes:

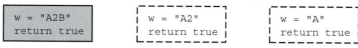

```
w = "A2B"    X    w = "A2"    X    w = "A"
                                   return true
```

The value is returned to the calling function, which completes execution:

```
w = "A2B"    X    w = "A2"         w = "A"
                  return true      return true
```

The value is returned to the calling function, which completes execution:

```
w = "A2B"         w = "A2"         w = "A"
return true       return true      return true
```

FIGURE 5-4   Trace of isId("A2B")

Palindromes = {*w* : *w* reads the same left to right as right to left}

How can you use a grammar to define the language *Palindromes*? You need to devise a rule that allows you to determine whether a given string *w* is a palindrome. In the spirit of recursive definitions, you should state this rule in terms of determining whether a *smaller string* is a palindrome. Your first instinct might be to choose *w* minus its last (or first) character for the smaller string. However, this does not work because there is no relationship between the statements

> *w* is a palindrome

and

> *w* minus its last character is a palindrome

That is, *w* might be a palindrome, although *w* minus its last character is not, as is the case for "deed." Similarly, *w* minus its last character might be a palindrome, although *w* is not, as is the case for "deeds."

A little thought reveals that you must consider characters in pairs: There *is* a relationship between the statements

> *w* is a palindrome

and

w minus its first and last characters is a palindrome

Specifically, w is a palindrome if and only if

A recursive description of a palindrome

- The first and last characters of w are the same

and

- w minus its first and last characters is a palindrome

You need a base case that you will reach after stripping away enough pairs of characters. If w has an even number of characters, you will eventually be left with two characters, and then, after you strip away another pair, you will be left with zero characters. A string of length zero is called the **empty string** and is a palindrome. If w has an odd number of characters, you will eventually be left with one character, after which you cannot strip away another pair. Hence, you must have a second base case: A string of length 1 is a palindrome.

Strings of length 0 or 1 are the base cases

This discussion leads to the following grammar for the language *Palindromes*:

$$< pal > = \text{empty string} \mid < ch > \mid \text{a} < pal > \text{a} \mid \text{b} < pal > \text{b} \mid \cdots \mid \text{Z} < pal > \text{Z}$$

$$< ch > = \text{a} \mid \text{b} \mid \cdots \mid \text{z} \mid \text{A} \mid \text{B} \mid \cdots \mid \text{Z}$$

A grammar for the language of palindromes

Based on this grammar, you can construct a recursive valued function for recognizing palindromes. The pseudocode for such a function follows:

A recognition algorithm for palindromes

```
isPal(in w:string):boolean
// Returns true if the string w of letters is a palindrome;
// otherwise returns false.

   if (w is the empty string or w is of length 1)
      return true

   else if (w's first and last characters are the same
            letter)
      return isPal(w minus its first and last characters)

   else
      return false
```

Strings of the form A^{n}B^n. The symbol A^{n}B^n is standard notation for the string that consists of n consecutive A's followed by n consecutive B's. Another simple language consists of such strings:

$$L = \{w : w \text{ is of the form A}^n\text{B}^n \text{ for some } n \geq 0\}$$

The grammar for this language is actually very similar to the grammar for palindromes. You must strip away both the first and last characters

and check to see that the first character is an A and the last character is
a B. Thus, the grammar is

$$< legal\text{-}word > = \text{empty string} \mid A < legal\text{-}word > B$$

A grammar for the language
of strings $A^n B^n$

The pseudocode for a recognition function for this language follows:

```
isAnBn(in w:string):boolean
// Returns true if w is of the form AⁿBⁿ;
// otherwise returns false.

    if (the length of w is zero)
        return true

    else if (w begins with the character A and ends with the
             character B)
        return isAnBn(w minus its first and last characters)

    else
        return false
```

A recognition algorithm for
strings $A^n B^n$

Algebraic Expressions

One of the tasks a compiler must perform is to recognize and evaluate algebraic expressions. For example, consider the C++ assignment statement

```
y = x + z * (w/k + z * (7 * 6));
```

A C++ compiler must determine whether the right side is a syntactically legal algebraic expression; if so, the compiler must then indicate
how to compute the expression's value.

There are several common definitions for a "syntactically legal"
algebraic expression. Some definitions force an expression to be *fully
parenthesized*, that is, to have parentheses around each pair of operands
together with their operator. Thus, you would have to write
`((a * b) * c)` rather than `a * b * c`. In general, the stricter a definition,
the easier it is to recognize a syntactically legal expression. On the other
hand, conforming to overly strict rules of syntax is an inconvenience
for programmers.

This section presents three different languages for algebraic expressions. The expressions in these languages are easy to recognize and evaluate but are generally inconvenient to use. However, these languages
provide us with good, nontrivial applications of grammars. We will see
other languages of algebraic expressions whose members are difficult to
recognize and evaluate but are convenient to use. To avoid unnecessary
complications, assume that you have only the binary operators +, −, *,
and / (no unary operators or exponentiation). Also, assume that all
operands in the expression are single-letter identifiers.

Infix, prefix, and postfix expressions.   The algebraic expressions you learned about in school are called **infix expressions**. The term "infix" indicates that every binary operator appears *between* its operands. For example, in the expression

$$a + b$$

the operator + is between its operands a and b. This convention necessitates associativity rules, precedence rules, and the use of parentheses to avoid ambiguity. For example, the expression

$$a + b * c$$

is ambiguous. What is the second operand of the +? Is it b or is it $(b * c)$? Similarly, the first operand of the * could be either b or $(a + b)$. The rule that * has higher precedence than + removes the ambiguity by specifying that b is the first operand of the * and that $(b * c)$ is the second operand of the +. If you want another interpretation, you must use parentheses:

$$(a + b) * c$$

Even with precedence rules, an expression like

$$a / b * c$$

is ambiguous. Typically, / and * have equal precedence, so you could interpret the expression either as $(a / b) * c$ or as $a / (b * c)$. The common practice is to *associate from left to right*, thus yielding the first interpretation.

Two alternatives to the traditional infix convention are **prefix** and **postfix expressions**. Under these conventions, an operator appears either before its operands (prefix) or after its operands (postfix). Thus, the infix expression

$$a + b$$

is written in prefix form as

$$+ \, a \, b$$

and in postfix form as

$$a \, b \, +$$

> In a prefix expression, an operator precedes its operands

> In a postfix expression, an operator follows its operands

To further illustrate the conventions, consider the two interpretations of the infix expression $a + b * c$ just considered. You write the expression

$$a + (b * c)$$

in prefix form as

$$+ \, a * b \, c$$

The + appears before its operands a and $(* \, b \, c)$, and the * appears before its operands b and c. The same expression is written in postfix form as

$$a \, b \, c * +$$

The $*$ appears after its operands b and c, and the $+$ appears after its operands a and $(b\ c\ *)$.

Similarly, you write the expression

$$(a + b) * c$$

in prefix form as

$$* + a\ b\ c$$

The $*$ appears before its operands $(+\ a\ b)$ and c, and the $+$ appears before its operands a and b. The same expression is written in postfix form as

$$a\ b + c\ *$$

The $+$ appears after its operands a and b, and the $*$ appears after its operands $(a\ b\ +)$ and c.

If the infix expression is fully parenthesized, converting it to either prefix or postfix form is straightforward. Because each operator then corresponds to a pair of parentheses, you simply move the operator to the position marked by either the "("—if you want to convert to prefix form—or the ")"—if you want to convert to postfix form. This position either precedes or follows the operands of the operator. All parentheses would then be removed.

For example, consider the fully parenthesized infix expression

$$((a + b) * c)$$

To convert this expression to prefix form, you first move each operator to the position marked by its corresponding open parenthesis:

$$(\ (\ a\ b\ )\ c\ )$$
$$*\ +$$

Converting to prefix form

Next, you remove the parentheses to get the desired prefix expression:

$$*\ +\ a\ b\ c$$

Similarly, to convert the infix expression to postfix form, you move each operator to the position marked by its corresponding closed parenthesis:

$$(\ (\ a\ b\ )\ c\ )$$
$$+\ \ \ *$$

Converting to postfix form

Then you remove the parentheses:

$$a\ b + c\ *$$

When an infix expression is not fully parenthesized, these conversions are more complex. Chapter 6 discusses the general case of converting an infix expression to postfix form.

Prefix and postfix expressions never need precedence rules, association rules, and parentheses

The advantage of prefix and postfix expressions is that they never need precedence rules, association rules, and parentheses. Therefore, the grammars for prefix and postfix expressions are quite simple. In addition, the algorithms that recognize and evaluate these expressions are relatively straightforward.

Prefix expressions.   A grammar that defines the language of all prefix expressions is

< *prefix* > = < *identifier* > | < *operator* > < *prefix* > < *prefix* >

< *operator* > = + | − | ∗ | /

< *identifier* > = a | b | · · · | z

From this grammar you can construct a recursive algorithm that recognizes whether a string is a prefix expression. If the string is of length 1, it is a prefix expression if and only if the string is a single lowercase letter. Strings of length 1 can be the base case. If the length of the string is greater than 1, then for it to be a legal prefix expression, it must be of the form

< *operator* > < *prefix* > < *prefix* >

Thus, the algorithm must check to see that

- The first character of the string is an operator.

and

- The remainder of the string consists of two consecutive prefix expressions.

If *E* is a prefix expression, *E Y* cannot be

The first task is trivial, but the second is a bit tricky. How can you determine whether you are looking at two consecutive prefix expressions? A key observation is that if you add *any* string of nonblank characters to the end of a prefix expression, you will no longer have a prefix expression. That is, if E is a prefix expression and Y is any nonempty string of nonblank characters, then $E Y$ cannot be a prefix expression. This is a subtle point; Exercise 17 at the end of this chapter asks you to prove it.

Given this observation, you can begin to determine whether you have two consecutive prefix expressions by identifying a first prefix expression. If you find one, the previous observation implies that only one end-point is possible for this first expression.

If you find that the first prefix expression ends at position *end1*, then you attempt to find a second prefix expression beginning at position *end1* + 1. If you find the second expression, you must check that you are at the end of the string in question.

By using these ideas, you can show, for example, that +/ab-cd is a prefix expression. For +/ab-cd to be a prefix expression, it must be of the form $+E_1E_2$, where E_1 and E_2 are prefix expressions. Now you can write

$$E_1 = /E_3E_4 \text{ where}$$

$$E_3 = a$$

$$E_4 = b$$

Since E_3 and E_4 are prefix expressions, E_1 is a prefix expression. Similarly, you can write

$$E_2 = -E_5E_6 \text{ where}$$

$$E_5 = c$$

$$E_6 = d$$

and see that E_2 is a prefix expression.

If you assume that the class for prefix expressions has a private data member `strExp` that is a string, you can write a function to determine whether an expression is a prefix expression. First, you construct a recursive valued function `endPre(first)` that returns the index of the end of the prefix expression that begins at position `first` of `strExp`. If no such prefix expression exists, `endPre` should return −1. The function appears in pseudocode as follows:

```
+endPre(in first: integer)
// Finds the end of a prefix expression, if one exists.
// Precondition: The substring of strExp from index first
// through the end of the string contains no blank characters.
// Postcondition: Returns the index of the last character
// in the prefix expression that begins at index first of
// strExp.
// If no such prefix expression exists, endPre should
// return -1.

   last = strExp.length - 1
   if (first < 0 or first > last)
      return -1

   ch = character at position first of strExp
   if (ch is an identifier)
      // index of last character in simple prefix
      // expression
      return first

   else if (ch is an operator)
   {  // find the end of the first prefix expression
      firstEnd = endPre(first+1)    // Point X

      // if the end of the first expression was found
      // find the end of the second prefix expression
      if (firstEnd > —1)
```

endPre determines the end of a prefix expression

```
        return endPre(firstEnd+1)  // Point Y
    else
        return -1
}  // end if

else
    return -1
```

Figure 5-5 contains a trace of *endPre* when the initial expression is *+/ab-cd*.

Now you can use the function *endPre* to determine whether the data member *strExp* is a prefix expression as follows:

A recognition algorithm for prefix expressions

```
isPre():boolean
// Determines whether an expression is a prefix expression.
// Precondition: The class has a data member strExp that
// contains a string with no blank characters.
// Postcondition: Returns true if the expression is in
// prefix form; otherwise returns false.

    lastChar = endPre(0)

    return (lastChar >= 0 and lastChar == strExp.length()-1)
```

Having determined that a string is a prefix expression, how can you evaluate it? Since each operator is followed by its two operands, you can look ahead in the expression for them. However, such operands can themselves be prefix expressions, which you must evaluate first. These prefix expressions are subexpressions of the original expression and must therefore be "smaller." A recursive solution to this problem seems natural.

The following function, which appears in pseudocode, evaluates a prefix expression. This algorithm is simpler than one that evaluates infix expressions.

An algorithm to evaluate a prefix expression

```
evaluatePrefix(inout strExp:string):float
// Evaluates a prefix expression strExp.
// Precondition: strExp is a string containing a valid
// prefix expression with no blanks.
// Postcondition: Returns the value of the prefix
// expression. The input string is destroyed.

    ch = first character of strExp
    Delete the first character from strExp
    if (ch is an identifier)
        // base case - single identifier
        return value of the identifier
    else if (ch is an operator named op)
```

The initial call is made and `endPre` begins execution:

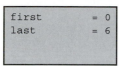

```
first        = 0
last         = 6
```

First character of `strExp` is +, so at point X, a recursive call is made and the new invocation of `endPre` begins execution:

```
first        = 0
last         = 6
X: endPre(1)
```
X →
```
first        = 1
last         = 6
```

Next character of `strExp` is /, so at point X, a recursive call is made and the new invocation of `endPre` begins execution:

```
first        = 0
last         = 6
X: endPre(1)
```
X →
```
first        = 1
last         = 6
X: endPre(2)
```
X →
```
first        = 2
last         = 6
```

Next character of `strExp` is a, which is a base case. The current invocation of `endPre` completes execution and returns its value:

```
first        = 0
last         = 6
X: endPre(1)
```
X →
```
first        = 1
last         = 6
firstEnd     = 2
```
```
first        = 2
last         = 6
return 2
```

Because `firstEnd > −1`, a recursive call is made from point Y and the new invocation of `endPre` begins execution:

```
first        = 0
last         = 6
X: endPre(1)
```
X →
```
first        = 1
last         = 6
firstEnd     = 2
Y: endPre(3)
```
Y →
```
first        = 3
last         = 6
```

Next character of `strExp` is b, which is a base case. The current invocation of `endPre` completes execution and returns its value:

```
first        = 0
last         = 6
X: endPre(1)
```
X →
```
first        = 1
last         = 6
firstEnd     = 2
return 3
```
```
first        = 3
last         = 6
return 3
```

The current invocation of `endPre` completes execution and returns its value:

```
first        = 0
last         = 6
firstEnd     = 3
```
```
first        = 1
last         = 6
firstEnd     = 2
return 3
```

Because `firstEnd > −1`, a recursive call is made from point Y and the new invocation of `endPre` begins execution:

```
first        = 0
last         = 6
firstEnd     = 3
Y: endPre(4)
```
Y →
```
first        = 4
last         = 6
```

FIGURE 5-5   Trace of `endPre(0)`, where `strExp` is +/ab-cd

(continues)

Next character of strExp is -, so at point X, a recursive call is made and the new invocation of endPre begins execution:

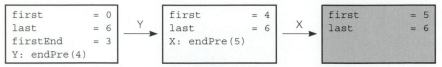

Next character of strExp is c, which is a base case. The current invocation of endPre completes execution and returns its value:

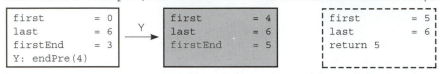

Because firstEnd > -1, a recursive call is made from point Y and the new invocation of endPre begins execution:

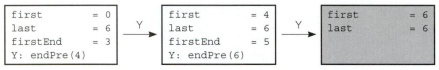

Next character of strExp is d, which is a base case. The current invocation of endPre completes execution and returns its value:

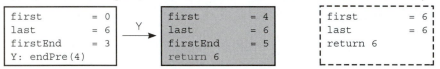

The current invocation of endPre completes execution and returns its value:

```
first       = 0        first       = 4
last        = 6        last        = 6
firstEnd    = 3        firstEnd    = 5
return 6               return 6
```

The current invocation of endPre completes execution and returns its value to the original call to endPre:

```
first       = 0
last        = 6
firstEnd    = 3
return 6
```

FIGURE 5-5

(continued)

```
{   operand1 = evaluatePrefix(strExp)
    operand2 = evaluatePrefix(strExp)
    return operand1 op operand2
} // end if
```

Notice that each recursive call to *evaluatePrefix* removes from *strExp* the most recently evaluated prefix expression. To implement this function in C++ requires that *strExp* be passed as a reference parameter so that changes in it are saved.

Postfix expressions. A grammar that defines the language of all postfix expressions is

$$< postfix > \ = \ < identifier > \ | \ < postfix > \ < postfix > \ < operator >$$

$$< operator > \ = + \ | \ - \ | \ * \ | \ /$$

$$< identifier > \ = \text{a} \ | \ \text{b} \ | \ \cdots \ | \ \text{z}$$

Some calculators require that you enter two numbers before you enter the operation that you want to perform. Such calculators, in fact, require you to enter postfix expressions.

Here we shall develop an algorithm for converting a prefix expression to a postfix expression. Chapter 6 presents a nonrecursive algorithm for evaluating postfix expressions. Together these two algorithms give you another method for evaluating a prefix expression. To simplify the conversion algorithm, assume that by using the prefix recognition algorithm you have a syntactically correct prefix expression.

If you think recursively, the conversion from prefix form to postfix form is straightforward. If the prefix expression *exp* is a single letter, then

$$postfix(exp) = exp$$

Otherwise *exp* must be of the form

$$< operator > \ < prefix1 > \ < prefix2 >$$

The corresponding postfix expression is then

$$< postfix1 > \ < postfix2 > \ < operator >$$

where $< prefix1 >$ converts to $< postfix1 >$ and $< prefix2 >$ converts to $< postfix2 >$. Therefore,

$$postfix(exp) = postfix(prefix1) + postfix(prefix2) + \ < operator >$$

Thus, at a high level, the conversion algorithm is

```
if (exp is a single letter)
    return exp
else
    return postfix(prefix1) + postfix(prefix2) + <operator>
```

An algorithm that converts a prefix expression to postfix form

The following pseudocode function *convert* refines this algorithm. The string *pre* contains the prefix expression, and the string *post* will contain the resulting postfix expression. Notice that each recursive call to *convert* reduces the size of *pre* by removing the first character and uses the resulting string in the next recursive call to *convert*. As in *evaluatePrefix*, *pre* should be a reference parameter. Initially, *post* must be empty.

```
convert(inout pre:string, out post:string)
// Converts a prefix expression pre to postfix form.
// Precondition: The string pre is a valid prefix
// expression.
// Postcondition: post is the equivalent postfix expression.
// The input string is destroyed.
```

A recursive algorithm that converts a prefix expression to postfix form

```
// check the first character of the given string
ch = first character in pre
Delete the first character of pre

if (ch is a lowercase letter)          // check character
   // base case - single identifier
   post = post + ch                    // concatenate to post

else  // ch is an operator
{  // do the conversion recursively
   convert(pre, post)                  // first prefix expr
   convert(pre, post)                  // second prefix expr
   post = post + ch                    // concatenate operator
}  // end if
```

Fully parenthesized expressions. Most programmers would object to using prefix or postfix notation for their algebraic expressions, so most programming languages use infix notation. However, infix notation requires precedence rules, rules for association, and parentheses to avoid ambiguity within the expressions.

You can make precedence and association rules unnecessary by placing parentheses around each pair of operands together with their operator, thereby avoiding any ambiguity. A grammar for the language of all fully parenthesized infix expressions is

A grammar for the language of fully parenthesized algebraic expressions

$$< infix > = < identifier > \ | \ (< infix > < operator > < infix >)$$

$$< operator > = + \ | \ - \ | \ * \ | \ /$$

$$< identifier > = a \ | \ b \ | \ \cdots \ | \ z$$

Although the grammar is simple, the language is rather inconvenient for programmers.

Therefore, most programming languages support a definition of algebraic expressions that includes both precedence rules for the operators and rules of association so that fully parenthesized expressions are not required. However, the grammars for defining such languages are more involved and the algorithms for recognizing and evaluating their expressions are more difficult than those you have seen in this section. Programming Problem 8 at the end of this chapter describes such a grammar without left-to-right association rules and asks you to write a recognition algorithm. Chapter 6 presents a nonrecursive evaluation algorithm for algebraic expressions that use both precedence and left-to-right association rules.

5.3 The Relationship Between Recursion and Mathematical Induction

A very strong relationship exists between recursion and mathematical induction. Recursion solves a problem by specifying a solution to one or more base cases and then demonstrating how to derive the solution to a problem of an arbitrary size from the solutions to smaller problems of the same type. Similarly, mathematical induction proves a property about the natural numbers by proving the property about a base case—usually 0 or 1—and then proving that the property must be true for an arbitrary natural number n if it is true for the natural numbers smaller than n.

Given the similarities between recursion and mathematical induction, it should not be surprising that induction is often employed to prove properties about recursive algorithms. What types of properties? You can, for example, prove that an algorithm actually performs the task that you intended. As an illustration, we will prove that the recursive factorial algorithm of Chapter 2 does indeed compute the factorial of its argument. Another use of mathematical induction is to prove that a recursive algorithm performs a certain amount of work. For example, we will prove that the solution to the Towers of Hanoi problem—also from Chapter 2—makes exactly $2^N - 1$ moves when it starts with N disks.

You can use induction to prove that a recursive algorithm either is correct or performs a certain amount of work

The Correctness of the Recursive Factorial Function

The following pseudocode describes a recursive function that computes the factorial of a nonnegative integer n:

```
fact(in n:integer):integer

    if (n is 0)
        return 1
    else
        return n * fact(n - 1)
```

You can prove that the function `fact` returns the values

$$fact(0) \; = 0! = 1$$

$$fact(n) \; = n! = n * (n-1) * (n-2) * \cdots * 1 \quad \text{if } n > 0$$

The proof is by induction on n.

Basis.   *Show that the property is true for n = 0.* That is, you must show that `fact(0)` returns 1. But this result is simply the base case of the function: `fact(0)` returns 1 by its definition.

You now must establish that

property is true for an arbitrary k $\Rightarrow$ property is true for k + 1

Inductive hypothesis.   *Assume that the property is true for n = k.* That is, assume that

$$fact(k) = k * (k - 1) * (k - 2) * \cdots * 2 * 1$$

Inductive conclusion.   *Show that the property is true for n = k + 1.* That is, you must show that `fact(k + 1)` returns the value

$$(k + 1) * k * (k - 1) * (k - 2) * \cdots * 2 * 1$$

By definition of the function `fact`, `fact(k + 1)` returns the value

$$(k + 1) * fact(k)$$

But by the inductive hypothesis, `fact(k)` returns the value

$$k * (k - 1) * (k - 2) * \cdots * 2 * 1$$

Thus, `fact(k + 1)` returns the value

$$(k + 1) * k * (k - 1) * (k - 2) * \cdots * 2 * 1$$

which is what you needed to show to establish that

property is true for an arbitrary k $\Rightarrow$ property is true for k + 1

The inductive proof is thus complete.

The Cost of Towers of Hanoi

In Chapter 2, you saw the following solution to the Towers of Hanoi problem:

```
solveTowers(count, source, destination, spare)

   if (count is 1)
      Move a disk directly from source to destination

   else
   {  solveTowers(count-1, source, spare, destination)
      solveTowers(1, source, destination, spare)
      solveTowers(count-1, spare, destination, source)
   }  // end if
```

We now pose the following question: If you begin with N disks, how many moves does `solveTowers` make to solve the problem?

Let *moves*(*N*) be the number of moves made starting with *N* disks. When *N* = 1, the answer is easy:

$$moves(1) = 1$$

When *N* > 1, the value of *moves*(*N*) is not so apparent. An inspection of the `solveTowers` algorithm, however, reveals three recursive calls. Therefore, if you knew how many moves `solveTowers` made starting with *N* − 1 disks, you could figure out how many moves it made starting with *N* disks; that is,

$$moves(N) = moves(N-1) + moves(1) + moves(N-1)$$

Thus, you have a recurrence relation for the number of moves required for *N* disks:

$$moves(1) \ \ = 1$$
$$moves(N) = 2 * moves(N-1) + 1 \qquad \text{if } N > 1$$

A recurrence relation for the number of moves that `solveTowers` requires for *N* disks

For example, you can determine *moves*(3) as follows:

$$moves(3) = 2 * moves(2) + 1$$
$$= 2 * (2 * moves(1) + 1) + 1$$
$$= 2 * (2 * 1 + 1) + 1$$
$$= 7$$

Although the recurrence relation gives you a way to compute *moves*(*N*), a **closed-form formula**—such as an algebraic expression—would be more satisfactory because you could substitute any given value for *N* and obtain the number of moves made. However, the recurrence relation is useful because there are techniques for obtaining a closed-form formula from it. Since these techniques are not relevant to us right now, we simply pull the formula out of the blue and use mathematical induction to prove that it is correct.

The solution to the previous recurrence relation is

$$moves(N) = 2^N - 1, \text{ for all } N \geq 1$$

A closed-form formula for the number of moves that `solveTowers` requires for *N* disks

Notice that $2^3 - 1$ agrees with the value 7 that was just computed for *moves*(3).

The proof that $moves(N) = 2^N - 1$ is by induction on *N*.

Basis. *Show that the property is true for N = 1.* Here, $2^1 - 1 = 1$, which is consistent with the recurrence relation's specification that *moves*(1) = 1.

You now must establish that

property is true for an arbitrary k $\Rightarrow$ *property is true for k + 1*

Inductive hypothesis.   *Assume that the property is true for N = k.* That is, assume

$$moves(k) = 2^k - 1$$

Inductive conclusion.   *Show that the property is true for N = k + 1.* That is, you must show that $moves(k + 1) = 2^{k+1} - 1$. Now

$$moves(k + 1) = 2 * moves(k) + 1 \quad \text{from the recurrence relation}$$
$$= 2 * (2^k - 1) + 1 \quad \text{by the inductive hypothesis}$$
$$= 2^{k+1} - 1$$

which is what you needed to show to establish that

property is true for an arbitrary k ⟹ property is true for k + 1

The inductive proof is thus complete.

Do not get the false impression that proving properties of programs is an easy matter. These two proofs are about as easy as any will be. However, well-structured programs are far more amenable to these techniques than are poorly structured programs.

Appendix D provides more information about mathematical induction.

Summary

1. Backtracking is a solution strategy that involves both recursion and a sequence of guesses that ultimately lead to a solution. If a particular guess leads to an impasse, you retrace your steps in reverse order, replace that guess, and try to complete the solution again.

2. A grammar is a device for defining a language, which is a set of strings of symbols. By using a grammar to define a language, you often can construct a recognition algorithm that is directly based on the grammar. Grammars are frequently recursive, thus allowing you to describe vast languages concisely.

3. To illustrate the use of grammars, we defined several different languages of algebraic expressions. These languages have their relative advantages and disadvantages. Prefix and postfix expressions, while difficult for people to use, have simple grammars and eliminate ambiguity. On the other hand, infix expressions are easier for people to use, but require parentheses, precedence rules, and rules of association to eliminate ambiguity. Therefore, the grammar for infix expressions is more involved.

4. A close relationship between mathematical induction and recursion exists. You can use induction to prove properties about a recursive algorithm. For example, you can prove that a recursive algorithm is correct, and you can derive the amount of work it requires.

Cautions

1. The subproblems that a recursive solution generates eventually must reach a base case. Failure to do so could result in an algorithm that does not terminate. Solutions that involve backtracking are particularly subject to this kind of error.

2. Grammars, like recursive algorithms, must have carefully chosen base cases. You must ensure that when a string is decomposed far enough, it will always reach the form of one of the grammar's base cases.

3. The subtleties of some of the algorithms you encountered in this chapter indicate the need for mathematical techniques to prove their correctness. The application of these techniques during the design of the various components of a solution can help to eliminate errors in logic before they appear in the program. One such technique is mathematical induction; another is the use of loop invariants, which we discussed in Chapter 1 and will discuss again in subsequent chapters.

Self-Test Exercises

1. Consider a Four Queens problem, which has the same rules as the Eight Queens problem but uses a 4 by 4 board. Find all solutions to this new problem by applying backtracking by hand.

2. Write the prefix expression that represents the following infix expression: $(a/b)*c-(d+e)*f$

3. Write the postfix expression that represents the following infix expression: $(a*b-c)/d+(e-f)$

4. Write the infix expression that represents the following prefix expression: $--a/b+c*def$

5. Is the following string a prefix expression? $+-/a\,bc*+def*gh$

6. Consider the language of these strings: $, cc$d, cccc$dd, ccccc$ddd, and so on. Write a recursive grammar for this language.

Exercises

1. Trace the following recursive functions:

   a. *isPal* with the string abcdeba

   b. *isAnBn* with the string AABB

   c. *endPre* with the expression $-*/abcd$

2. Consider the language that the following grammar defines:

   $<S> = \$ \mid <W> \mid \$<S>$

   $<W> = abb \mid a<W>bb$

   Write all strings that are in this language and that contain seven or fewer characters.

3. Write a recursive grammar for the language of strings of one or more letters. The first letter of each string must be uppercase and all other letters in the string must be lowercase.

4. Consider a language of character strings that contain only dots and dashes. All strings in this language contain at least four characters and begin with either two dots or two dashes. If the first two characters are dots, the last one must be a dash; if the first two characters are dashes, the last one must be a dot. Write a recursive grammar for this language.

5. Consider a language of strings that contains only X's, Y's and Z's. A string in this language must begin with an X. If a Y is present in a string, it must be the last character of the string.

   a. Write a recursive grammar for this language.

   b. Write all the possible two-character strings of this language.

6. Consider a language of words, where each word is a string of dots and dashes. The following grammar describes this language:

   $< word > = < dot > \mid < dash > < word > \mid < word > < dot >$

   $< dot > = \cdot$

   $< dash > = -$

   a. Write all three-character strings that are in this language.

   b. Is the string $\cdots - -$ in this language? Explain.

   c. Write a seven-character string that contains more dashes than dots and is in the language. Show how you know that your answer is correct.

   d. Write pseudocode for a recursive recognition function `isIn(str)` that returns *true* if the string `str` is in this language and returns *false* otherwise.

7. Consider the following grammar:

   $< word > = R \mid < D > \mid < D > < word > < S >$

   $< D > = Q \mid P$

   $< S > = 1$

   Write pseudocode for a recursive function that returns *true* if a string is in this language and returns *false* otherwise.

8. Consider the following grammar:

$<G>$ = empty string | $<E>$ | $<V> <E>$ | $<E> <G> <V>$

$<E>$ = & | #

$<V>$ = W | A

   a. Write pseudocode for a recursive function that returns *true* if a string is in this language and returns *false* otherwise.

   b. Is the string &W#W in this language?

9. Let L be the language

   $L = \{S : S$ is of the form A^nB^{2n}, for some $n > 0\}$

   Thus, a string is in L if and only if it starts with a sequence of A's and is followed by a sequence of twice as many B's. For example, AABBBB is in L, but ABBB, ABBABB, and the empty string are not.

   a. Give a grammar for the language L.

   b. Write a recursive function that determines whether the string *strExp* is in L.

10. Is $+*a-b/c++de-fg$ a prefix expression? Explain in terms of the grammar for prefix expressions.

11. Is $ab/c*efg*h/+d-+$ a postfix expression? Explain in terms of the grammar for postfix expressions.

12. Consider the language that the following grammar defines:

   $< S > = < L > | < D > < S > < S >$

   $< L > = A | B$

   $< D > = 1 | 2$

   a. Write all three-character strings that are in this language.

   b. Write one string in this language that contains more than three characters.

13. Consider a language of the following character strings: The letter A; the letter B; the letter C followed by a string that is in the language; the letter D followed by a string in the language. For example, these strings are in this language: A, CA, CCA, DCA, B, CB, CCB, DB, and DCCB.

   a. Write a grammar for this language.

   b. Is CAB in this language? Explain.

   c. Write a recursive recognition algorithm for this language.

14. Consider the language that the following grammar defines:

$$< word > = \$ \mid a< word >a \mid b< word >b \mid \cdots \mid y< word >y \mid z< word >z$$

Equivalently,

$$L = \{w\$\text{reverse}(w) : w \text{ is a string of letters of length} \geq 0\}$$

Note that this language is very similar to the language of palindromes, but there is a special middle character here.

The algorithm that this chapter gave for recognizing palindromes can be adapted easily to this language. The algorithm, which is recursive and processes the string `str` from both ends toward the middle, is based on the following facts:

- A string with no characters is not in the language.

- A string with exactly one character is in the language if the character is a $.

- A longer string is in the language if the ends are identical letters and the inner substring (from the second character to the next-to-last character of `str`) is in the language.

Describe a recursive recognition algorithm that processes the string from left to right, reading one character at a time and not explicitly saving the string for future reference. Write a C++ function that implements your algorithm.

15. Consider the following recursive function:

```
int p(int x)
{   if (x < 3)
        return x;
    else
        return p(x-1) * p(x-3);
} // end p
```

Let $m(x)$ be the number of multiplication operations that the execution of `p(x)` performs.

a. Write a recursive definition of $m(x)$.

b. Prove that your answer to Part *a* is correct by using mathematical induction.

16. Consider palindromes that consist only of lowercase letters, such as "level" and "deed," but not "RadaR," "ADA," or "101." Let $c(n)$ be the number of palindromes of length n.

a. Write a recursive definition of $c(n)$.

b. Prove that your answer to Part *a* is correct by using mathematical induction.

17. Prove the following for single-letter operands: If E is a prefix expression and Y is a nonempty string of nonblank characters, then EY cannot be a legal prefix expression. (*Hint*: Use a proof by induction on the length of E.)

18. Chapter 2 gave the following definition for $c(n, k)$, where n and k are assumed to be nonnegative integers:

$$c(n, k) = \begin{cases} 1 & \text{if } k = 0 \\ 1 & \text{if } k = n \\ 0 & \text{if } k > n \\ c(n-1, k-1) + c(n-1, k) & \text{if } 0 < k < n \end{cases}$$

Prove by induction on n that the following is a closed form for $c(n, k)$:

$$c(n, k) = \frac{n!}{(n-k)!k!}$$

Programming Problems

1. Complete the classes `Queen` and `Board` for the Eight Queens problem.

2. Revise the program that you just wrote for the Eight Queens problem so that it answers the following questions:

   a. How many backtracks occur? That is, how many times does the program remove a queen from the board?

   b. How many calls to `isUnderAttack` are there?

   c. How many recursive calls to `placeQueens` are there?

*3. You can begin the Eight Queens problem by placing a queen in the second square of the first column instead of in the first square. You can then call `placeQueens` to begin with the second column. This revision should lead you to a new solution. Write a program that finds all solutions to the Eight Queens problem.

4. Do you know how to find your way through a maze? After you write this program, you will never be lost again!

   Assume that a maze is a rectangular array of squares, some of which are blocked to represent walls. The maze has one entrance and one exit. For example, if x's represent the walls, a maze could appear as follows:

```
XXXXXXXXXXXXXXXXXX X
X      X          XXXX X
X XXXXX XXXXX     XX X
X XXXXX XXXXXXX XX X
X X               XX XX X
X XXXXXXXXXX XX      X
XXXXXXXXXXXXXOXXXXXXX
```

A creature, indicated in the previous diagram by o, sits just inside the maze at the entrance (bottom row). Assume that the creature can move in only four directions: north, south, east, and west. In the diagram, north is up, south is down, east is to the right, and west is to the left. The problem is to move the creature through the maze from the entrance to the exit (top row), if possible. As the creature moves, it should mark its path. At the conclusion of the trip through the maze, you should see both the correct path and incorrect attempts.

Squares in the maze have one of several states: CLEAR (the square is clear), WALL (the square is blocked and represents part of the wall), PATH (the square lies on the path to the exit), and VISITED (the square was visited, but going that way led to an impasse).

This problem uses two ADTs that must interact. The ADT creature represents the creature's current position and contains operations that move the creature. The creature should be able to move north, south, east, and west one square at a time. It should also be able to report its position and mark its trail.

The ADT maze represents the maze itself, which is a two-dimensional rectangular arrangement of squares. You could number the rows of squares from the top beginning with zero, and number the columns of squares from the left beginning with zero. You could then use a row number and a column number to uniquely identify any square within the maze. The ADT clearly needs a data structure to represent the maze. It also needs such data as the height and width of the maze, given in numbers of squares; the length of a side of a square; and the row and column coordinates of both the entrance to and the exit from the maze.

The ADT maze should also contain, for example, operations that create a specific maze, given a text file of data; display a maze; determine whether a particular square is part of the wall; determine whether a particular square is part of the path; and so on.

The search algorithm and its supporting functions are outside both of these ADTs. Thus, the maze and the creature will be arguments that you must pass to these functions.

The text file that you will use to represent a maze is simple. An example of how this can be done for the previously given maze follows:

```
20    7      ←width and height of maze in squares
0    18      ←row and column coordinate of maze exit
6    12      ←row and column coordinate of maze entrance

XXXXXXXXXXXXXXXXXX X
X        X       XXXX X
X XXXXX XXXXX    XX X
X XXXXX XXXXXXX XX X
X X             XX XX X
X XXXXXXXXXX XX      X
XXXXXXXXXXXX XXXXXX
```

Each line in the file corresponds to a row in the maze; each character in a line corresponds to a column in the maze. X's indicate blocked squares (the walls), and blanks indicate clear squares. This notation is convenient because you can see what the maze looks like as you design it.

If you are at the maze's entrance, you can systematically find your way out of the maze by using the following search algorithm. It involves backtracking, that is, retracing your steps when you reach an impasse.

1. First, check whether you are at the exit. If you are, you're done (a very simple maze); if you are not, go to Step 2.

2. Try to move to the square directly to the north by calling the function *goNorth* (Step 3).

3. If *goNorth* was successful, you are done. If it was unsuccessful, try to move to the square directly to the west by calling the function *goWest* (Step 4).

4. If *goWest* was successful, you are done. If it was unsuccessful, try to move to the square directly to the south by calling the function *goSouth* (Step 5).

5. If *goSouth* was successful, you are done. If it was unsuccessful, try to move to the square directly to the east by calling the function *goEast* (Step 6).

6. If *goEast* was successful, you are done. If it was unsuccessful, you are still done, because no path exists from the entrance to the exit.

The function *goNorth* will examine all the paths that start at the square to the north of the present square as follows. If the square directly to the north is clear, is inside the maze, and has not been visited before, move into this square and mark it as part of the path. (Note that you are moving from the south.) Check whether you are at the exit. If you are, you're done. Otherwise, try to find a path to the exit from here by trying all paths leaving this square except the one going south (going south would put you back in the square from which you just came) as follows. Call *goNorth*; if it is not successful, call *goWest* and, if it is not successful, call *goEast*. If *goEast* is not successful, mark this square as visited, move back into the square to the south, and return.

The following pseudocode describes the *goNorth* algorithm:

```
goNorth(maze, creature, success)

   if (the square to the north is clear,
        inside the maze, and unvisited)
   {  Move to the north
      Mark the square as part of the path
      if (at exit)
   success = true
```

```
              else
              {  goNorth(maze, creature, success)
                 if (!success)
                 {  goWest(maze, creature, success)
                    if (!success)
                    {  goEast(maze, creature, success)
                       if (!success)
                       {  Mark square visited
                          Backtrack south
                       } // end if
                    } // end if
                 } // end if
              } // end if
          }
       else
          success = false
```

The *goWest* function will examine all the paths that start at the square to the west of the present square as follows. If the square directly to the west is clear, is inside the maze, and has not been visited before, move into this square and mark it as part of the path. (Note that you are moving from the east.) Check whether you are at the exit. If you are, you're done. Otherwise, try to find a path to the exit from here by trying all paths leaving this square except the one going east (this would put you back in the square from which you just came) as follows. Call *goNorth*; if it is not successful, call *goWest* and, if it is not successful, call *goSouth*. If *goSouth* is not successful, mark this square as visited, move back into the square to the east, and return.

The functions *goEast* and *goSouth* are analogous to the functions just described.

5. Write a program that will recognize and evaluate prefix expressions. First design and implement a class of prefix expressions. This class should contain methods to recognize and evaluate prefix expressions. This chapter discusses the algorithms you will need to implement these methods.

6. Implement a recognition algorithm for the language in Exercise 5.

7. Implement the algorithm described in this chapter to convert a prefix expression to postfix form.

8. The following is a grammar that allows you to omit parentheses in infix algebraic expressions when the precedence rules remove ambiguity. For example, $a + b * c$ means $a + (b * c)$. However, the grammar requires parentheses when ambiguity would otherwise result. That is, the grammar does not permit left-to-right association when several operators have the same precedence. For example, $a / b * c$ is illegal. Notice that the definitions introduce factors and terms.

$< expression > \ = \ < term > \ | \ < term > + < term > \ | \ < term > - < term >$

$< term > \ = \ < factor > \ | \ < factor > * < factor > \ | \ < factor > / < factor >$

$< factor > \ = \ < letter > \ | \ (< expression >)$

$< letter > \ = \ \text{a} \ | \ \text{b} \ | \cdots | \ \text{z}$

The recognition algorithm is based on a recursive chain of sub-tasks: *find an expression* → *find a term* → *find a factor*. What makes this a recursive chain is that *find an expression* uses *find a term*, which in turn uses *find a factor*. *Find a factor* either detects a base case or uses *find an expression*, thus forming the recursive chain.

The pseudocode for the recognition algorithm follows:

```
FIND AN EXPRESSION
// The grammar specifies that an expression is either
// a single term or a term followed by a + or a -,
// which then must be followed by a second term.

   Find a term
   if (the next symbol is a + or a -)
      Find a term


FIND A TERM
// The grammar specifies that a term is either a
// single factor or a factor followed by a * or a /,
// which must then be followed by a second factor.

   Find a factor
   if (the next symbol is a * or a /)
      Find a factor


FIND A FACTOR
// The grammar specifies that a factor is either a
// single letter (the base case) or an
// expression enclosed in parentheses.

   if (the first symbol is a letter)
      Done
   else if (the first symbol is a '(')
   {  Find an expression starting at character after '('
      Check for ')'
   }
   else
      No factor exists
```

Design and implement a class of infix expressions, as described by the given grammar. Include a method to recognize a legal infix expression.

PART II

Problem Solving with Abstract Data Types

P art I of this book reviewed aspects of problem solving that are closely related to programming issues, presented data abstraction as a technique for solution design that permeates our approach to problem solving, introduced C++ classes as a way to hide a solution's implementation details and to increase its modularity, introduced the linked list as a data structure that you will see throughout this book, and developed recursion as a problem-solving technique that is useful in the construction of algorithms. The primary concerns of the remainder of this book are the aspects of problem solving that involve the *management of data*—that is, the identification and implementation of some of the more common data-management operations.

You saw in Part I that you can organize data either by position—as in the ADT list—or by value—as in the ADT sorted list. In general, these organizations are appropriate for applications of rather different natures. For example, if an application needs to ask a question about the first person in a line, you should organize the data by position. On the other hand, if an application needs to ask a question about the employee named Smith, you should organize the data by value. In Part II, you will see other ADTs that use these two data organizations.

Our study of data management has three goals. The first is to identify useful sets of operations—that is, to identify abstract data types. The second goal is to examine applications that use these abstract data types. The third goal is to construct implementations for the abstract data types—that is, to develop data structures and classes. As you will discover, the nature of the operations of an abstract data type, along with the application in which you will use it, greatly influences the choice of its implementation.

Stacks

PREVIEW

This chapter introduces a well-known ADT called a stack and presents both its applications and implementations. You will see how the operations on a stack give it a last-in, first-out behavior. Two of the several applications of a stack that the chapter considers are evaluating algebraic expressions and searching for a path between two points. Finally, the chapter discusses the important relationship between stacks and recursion.

6.1 The Abstract Data Type Stack

The specification of an abstract data type that you can use to solve a particular problem can emerge during the design of the problem's solution. The ADT developed in the following example happens to be an important one: the ADT stack.

Developing an ADT During the Design of a Solution

When you type a line of text on a keyboard, you are likely to make mistakes. If you use the backspace key to correct these mistakes, each backspace erases the previous character entered. Consecutive backspaces are applied in sequence and so erase several characters. For instance, if you type the line

```
abcc←ddde←←←ef←fg
```

where ← represents the backspace character, the corrected input would be

```
abcdefg
```

How can a program read the original line and get the correct input? In designing a solution to this problem, you eventually must decide how to store the input line. In accordance with the ADT approach, you should postpone this decision until you have a better idea of what operations you will need to perform on the data.

A first attempt at a solution leads to the following pseudocode:

```
// read the line, correcting mistakes along the way
while (not end of line)
{  Read a new character ch
   if (ch is not a '←')
      Add ch to the ADT
   else
      Remove from the ADT the item
        that was added most recently
}  // end while
```

Initial draft of a solution

This solution calls to attention two of the operations that the ADT will have to include:

- Add a new item to the ADT.

- Remove from the ADT the item that was added most recently.

Two ADT operations that are required

Notice that potential trouble lurks if you type a ← when the ADT is empty, that is, when the ADT contains no characters. If this situation should occur, you have two options: (1) have the program terminate and write an error message, or (2) have the program ignore the ← and continue. Either option is reasonable, so let's suppose that you decide to ignore the ← and continue. Therefore, the algorithm becomes

The "read and correct" algorithm

```
// read the line, correcting mistakes along the way
while (not end of line)
{  Read a new character ch
   if (ch is not a '←')
      Add ch to the ADT
   else if (the ADT is not empty)
      Remove from the ADT the item
         that was added most recently
   else
      Ignore the '←'
}  // end while
```

From this pseudocode you can identify a third operation required by the ADT:

Another required ADT operation

- Determine whether the ADT is empty.

This solution places the corrected input line in the ADT. Now suppose that you want to display the line. At first, it appears that you can accomplish this task by using the ADT operations already identified, as follows:

A false start at writing the line

```
// write the line
while (the ADT is not empty)
{  Remove from the ADT the item
      that was added most recently
   Write .....Uh-oh!
}
```

This pseudocode is incorrect for two reasons:

Reasons why the attempted solution is incorrect

1. When you remove an item from the ADT, the item is gone, so you cannot write it. What you should have done was to *retrieve* from the ADT the item that was added most recently. Recall that the retrieval operation in Chapter 3 meant to *look at, but leave unchanged*. Only after retrieving and writing the item should you remove it from the ADT.

2. The most recently added item is the last character of the input line. You certainly do not want to write it first. The resolution of this particular difficulty is left to you as an exercise.

If we address only the first difficulty, the following pseudocode writes the input line in reversed order:

The write-backward algorithm

```
// write the line in reversed order
while (the ADT is not empty)
```

```
{  Retrieve from the ADT the item that was
     added most recently and put it in ch
   Write ch
   Remove from the ADT the item
     that was added most recently
}  // end while
```

Thus, a fourth operation is required by the ADT:

■ Retrieve from the ADT the item that was added most recently.

Another required ADT operation

Although you have yet to think about an implementation of the ADT, you know that you must be able to perform four specific operations.[1] These operations define the required ADT, which happens to be well known: It is usually called a **stack**. As you saw in Chapter 3, it is customary to include initialization and destruction operations in an ADT. Thus, the following operations define the ADT stack.

KEY CONCEPTS

ADT Stack Operations

1. Create an empty stack.

2. Destroy a stack.

3. Determine whether a stack is empty.

4. Add a new item to the stack.

5. Remove from the stack the item that was added most recently.

6. Retrieve from the stack the item that was added most recently.

The term "stack" is intended to conjure up visions of things encountered in daily life, such as a stack of dishes in the school cafeteria, a stack of books on your desk, or a stack of assignments waiting for you to work on them. In common English usage, "stack of" and "pile of" are synonymous. To computer scientists, however, a stack is not just any old pile. A stack has the property that the last item placed on the stack will be the first item removed. This property is commonly referred to as **last in, first out**, or simply **LIFO**.

Last in, first out

A stack of dishes in a cafeteria makes a very good analogy of the abstract data type stack, as Figure 6-1 illustrates. As new dishes are

---

[1] As you will learn if you complete Exercise 7 at the end of this chapter, the final algorithm to write the line correctly instead of in reversed order does not require additional ADT operations.

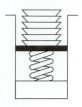

FIGURE 6-1   Stack of cafeteria dishes

added, the old dishes drop farther into the well beneath the surface. At any particular time, only the dish last placed on the stack is above the surface and visible. This dish is at the **top of the stack** and the one that must be removed next. In general, the dishes are removed in exactly the opposite order from that in which they were added.

The LIFO property of stacks seems inherently unfair. Think of the poor person who finally gets the last dish on the cafeteria's stack, a dish that may have been placed there six years ago. Or how would you like to be the first person to arrive on the stack for a movie—as opposed to the line for a movie. You would be the last person allowed in! These examples demonstrate the reason that stacks are not especially prevalent in everyday life. The property that we usually desire in our daily lives is **first in, first out**, or **FIFO**. A **queue**, which you will study in the next chapter, is the abstract data type with the FIFO property. Most people would much prefer to wait in a movie *queue*—as a line is called in Britain—rather than in a movie *stack*. However, while the LIFO property of stacks is not appropriate for very many day-to-day situations, it is precisely what is needed for a large number of problems that arise in computer science.

Notice how well the analogy holds between the abstract data type stack and the stack of cafeteria dishes. The operations that manipulate data in the ADT stack are the *only* such operations, and they correspond to the only things that you can do to a stack of dishes. You can determine whether the stack of dishes is empty but not how many dishes are on the stack; you can inspect the top dish but no other dish; you can place a dish on top of the stack but at no other position; and you can remove a dish from the top of the stack but from no other position. If you were not permitted to perform any of these operations, or if you were permitted to perform any other operations, the ADT would not be a stack.

Although the stack of cafeteria dishes suggests that, as you add or remove dishes, the other dishes move, do not have this expectation of the ADT stack. The stack operations involve only the top item and imply only that the other items in the stack remain in sequence. Implementations of the ADT stack operations might or might not move the stack's items. The implementations given in this chapter do not move data items.

Refining the definition of the ADT stack.   Before we specify the details of the stack operations, consider the removal and retrieval operations more carefully. The current definition enables you to remove the stack's top without inspecting it, or to inspect the stack's top without removing it. Both tasks are reasonable and occur in practice. However, if you wanted to inspect *and* remove the top item of a stack—a task that is not unusual—you would need the sequence of operations

- Retrieve from the stack the item that was added most recently.

- Remove from the stack the item that was added most recently.

An additional operation that retrieves and then removes the top of a stack would allow you to perform this common task in one operation.

The following pseudocode specifies the operations for the ADT stack in more detail, and includes a combined retrieval and removal operation. The names given here for the operations that add and remove items are conventional for stacks. Figure 6-2 shows a UML diagram for the class *Stack*.

KEY CONCEPTS

Pseudocode for the ADT Stack Operations

```
// StackItemType is the type of the items stored in the stack.

+createStack()
// Creates an empty stack.

+destroyStack()
// Destroys a stack.

+isEmpty():boolean {query}
// Determines whether a stack is empty.

+push(in newItem:StackItemType) throw StackException
// Adds newItem to the top of a stack. Throws StackException
// if the insertion is not successful.

+pop() throw StackException
// Removes the top of a stack; that is, removes the item
// that was added most recently. Throws StackException if
// the deletion is not successful.

+pop(out stackTop:StackItemType) throw StackException
// Retrieves into stackTop and then removes the top of a
// stack. That is, retrieves and removes the item that was
// added most recently. Throws StackException if the
// deletion is not successful.

+getTop(out stackTop:StackItemType) {query} throw StackException
// Retrieves into stackTop the top of a stack. That is,
// retrieves the item that was added most recently.
// Retrieval does not change the stack. Throws

// StackException if the retrieval is not successful.
```

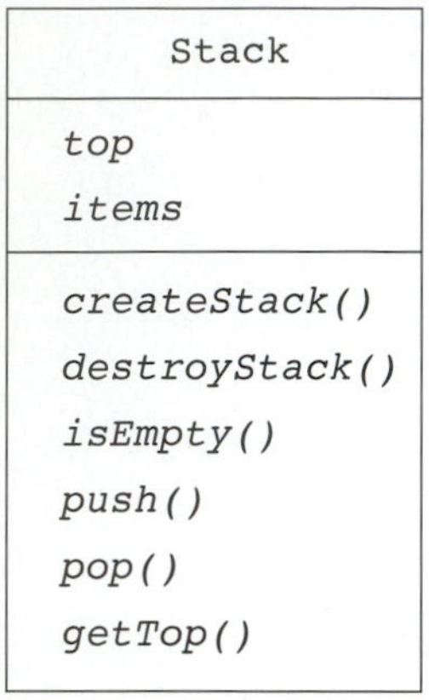

Recall that Chapter 1 urged you to focus on the specification of a module before you considered its implementation. After specifying an ADT's operations in pseudocode, you should try to use them as a check of your design. Such a test can highlight any deficiencies in your specifications or design. For example, you can use the previous stack operations to refine the algorithms developed earlier in this chapter.

Using the ADT stack in a solution. You now can refine the algorithms developed earlier in this chapter by using the stack operations:

```
+readAndCorrect(out aStack:Stack)
// Reads the input line. For each character read,
// either enters it into stack aStack or, if it is
// '←', corrects the contents of aStack.

    aStack.createStack²
    Read newChar
    while (newChar is not the end-of-line symbol)
    {  if (newChar is not '←')
          aStack.push(newChar)
       else if (!aStack.isEmpty())
          aStack.pop()

       Read newChar
    }  // end while


+displayBackward(in aStack:Stack)
// Displays the input line in reversed order by
// writing the contents of stack aStack.

    while (!aStack.isEmpty())
    {  aStack.pop(newChar)
       Write newChar
    }  // end while

    Advance to new line
```

We have used the stack operations without knowing their implementations or even what a stack looks like. Because the ADT approach builds a wall around the implementation of the stack, your program can use a stack independently of the stack's implementation. As long as the program correctly uses the ADT operations—that is, as long as it honors the contract—it will work regardless of how you implement the ADT.

---

² You implement the step *aStack.createStack()* in C++ by declaring *aStack* as an instance of the *Stack* class, since *createStack* is implemented as the class's constructor.

Stack
top
items
createStack()
destroyStack()
isEmpty()
push()
pop()
getTop()

FIGURE 6-2   UML diagram for the class *Stack*

The refined algorithms

The contract, therefore, must be written precisely. That is, before you implement any ADT operations, you should specify both their preconditions and their postconditions. Realize, however, that during program design, the first attempt at specification is often informal and is only later made precise by the writing of preconditions and postconditions. For example, the previous specifications of the ADT stack leave the following questions unanswered:

- How will *pop* and *getTop* affect an empty stack?

- What value will *pop* and *getTop* assign to *stackTop* when the stack is empty?

Questions that the informal specifications of the stack leave unanswered

The preconditions and postconditions, which appear later in this chapter as comments in the C++ implementation of the stack, provide one way to answer these questions.

Axioms (*optional*). As Chapter 3 noted, intuitive specifications, such as those given previously for the stack operations, are not really sufficient to define an ADT formally. For example, to capture formally the intuitive notion that the last item inserted into the stack *aStack* is the first item to be removed, you could write an axiom such as

```
(aStack.push(newItem)).pop() = aStack
```

An example of an axiom

That is, if you push *newItem* onto *aStack* and then pop it, you are left with the original stack *aStack*. Exercise 15 at the end of this chapter discusses the axioms for a stack further.

6.2 Simple Applications of the ADT Stack

This section presents two rather simple examples for which the LIFO property of stacks is appropriate. Note that we will be using the ADT stack operations, even though we have not discussed their implementations yet.

Checking for Balanced Braces

C++ uses curly braces, "{" and "}", to delimit groups of statements. For example, braces begin and end a function's body. If you treat a C++ program as a string of characters, you can use a stack to verify that a program contains balanced braces. For example, the braces in the string

abc{defg{ijk}{l{mn}}op}qr

are balanced, while the braces in the string

abc{def}}{ghij{kl}m

are not balanced. You can check whether a string contains balanced braces by traversing it from left to right. As you move from left to right, you match each successive close brace "}" with the most recently encountered unmatched open brace "{"; that is, the "{" must be to the left of the current "}". The braces are balanced if

Requirements for balanced braces

1. Each time you encounter a "}", it matches an already encountered "{"

2. When you reach the end of the string, you have matched each "{"

The solution requires that you keep track of each unmatched "{" and discard one each time you encounter a "}". One way to perform this task is to push each "{" encountered onto a stack and pop one off each time you encounter a "}". Thus, a first-draft pseudocode solution is

Initial draft of a solution

```
while (not at the end of the string)
{  if (the next character is a '{')
      aStack.push('{')
   else if (the character is a '}')
      aStack.pop()
}  // end while
```

Although this solution correctly keeps track of braces, missing from it are the checks that conditions 1 and 2 are met—that is, that the braces are indeed balanced. To verify condition 1 when a "}" is encountered, you must check to see whether the stack is empty before popping from it. If it is empty, you terminate the loop and report that the string is not balanced. To verify condition 2, you check that the stack is empty when the end of the string is reached.

Thus, the pseudocode solution to check for balanced braces in `aString` becomes

A detailed pseudocode solution to check a string for balanced braces

```
aStack.createStack()
balancedSoFar = true
i = 0

while (balancedSoFar and i < length of aString)
{  ch = character at position i in aString
   ++i

   // push an open brace
   if (ch is '{')
      aStack.push('{')

   // close brace
   else if (ch is '}')
      if (!aStack.isEmpty())
         aStack.pop()    // pop a matching open brace
```

```
    else                // no matching open brace
        balancedSoFar = false

    // ignore all characters other than braces
}   // end while

if (balancedSoFar and aStack.isEmpty())
    aString has balanced braces
else
    aString does not have balanced braces
```

Figure 6-3 shows the stacks that result when this algorithm is applied to several simple examples.

Note that the *push* operation can fail for implementation-dependent reasons. For example, *push* throws *StackException* if either the array in an array-based implementation is full or *new* is unable to allocate memory for a pointer-based implementation. In the spirit of fail-safe programming, a function that implements this balanced-braces algorithm could check for a thrown *StackException* after *push* by using *try-catch* blocks. Alternatively, the function could let its invoking function handle the exception.

It may have occurred to you that a simpler solution to this problem is possible. You need only keep a count of the current number of unmatched open braces.[3] You need not actually store the open braces in

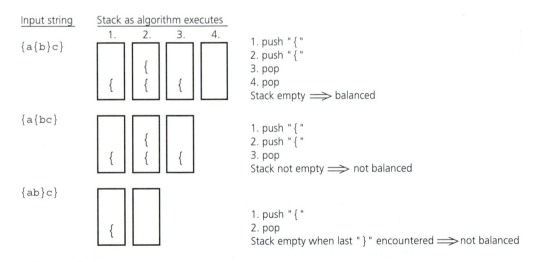

FIGURE 6-3 Traces of the algorithm that checks for balanced braces

---

[3] Each time you encounter an open brace, you increment the count; each time you encounter a close brace, you decrement the count. If this count ever falls below zero or if it is greater than zero when the end of the string is reached, the string is unbalanced.

a stack. However, the stack-based solution is conceptually useful as it previews more legitimate uses of stacks. For example, Exercise 6 at the end of this chapter asks you to extend the algorithm given here to check for balanced parentheses and square brackets in addition to braces.

Recognizing Strings in a Language

Consider the problem of recognizing whether a particular string is in the language

$$L = \{w\$w' : w \text{ is a possibly empty string of characters other than } \$,$$
$$w' = \text{reverse}(w) \}$$

For example, the strings AA, ABCCBA, and $ are in L, but AB$AB and ABC$CB are not. (Exercise 14 in Chapter 5 introduced a similar language.) This language is like the language of palindromes that you saw in Chapter 5, but strings in this language have a special middle character.

A stack is useful in determining whether a given string is in L. Suppose you traverse the first half of the string and push each character onto a stack. When you reach the $ you can undo the process: For each character in the second half of the string, you pop a character off the stack. However, you must match the popped character with the current character in the string to ensure that the second half of the string is the reverse of the first half. The stack must be empty when—and only when—you reach the end of the string; otherwise, one "half" of the string is longer than the other, and so the string is not in L.

The following algorithm uses this strategy. To avoid unnecessary complications, assume that *aString* contains exactly one $.

```
aStack.createStack()

// push the characters before $, that is, the
// characters in w, onto the stack
i = 0
ch = character at position i in aString
while (ch is not '$')
{   aStack.push(ch)
    ++i
    ch = character at position i in aString
}   // end while

// skip the $
++i

// match the reverse of w
inLanguage = true   // assume string is in language
while (inLanguage and i < length of aString)
    try
```

```
      {   aStack.pop(stackTop)
          ch = character at position i in aString
          if (stackTop equals ch)
              ++i   // characters match
          else
              // top of stack is not ch
              // (characters do not match)
              inLanguage = false   // reject string
      } // end try
      catch StackException
      {  // pop failed, stack is empty (first half of string
         // is shorter than second half)
             inLanguage = false
      }  // end catch

if (inLanguage and aStack.isEmpty())
   aString is in language
else
   aString is not in language
```

Notice that the two algorithms presented in this section depend only on the specifications of the stack operations and not on their implementations.

6.3 Implementations of the ADT Stack

This section develops three C++ implementations of the ADT stack. The first implementation uses an array to represent the stack, the second uses a linked list, and the third uses the ADT list. Figure 6-4 illustrates these three implementations.

Here is the class *StackException* that is used in the stack implementations:

```cpp
#include <stdexcept>
#include <string>
using namespace std;

class StackException: public logic_error
{
public:
   StackException(const string & message="")
         : logic_error(message.c_str())
   {}
};  // end StackException
```

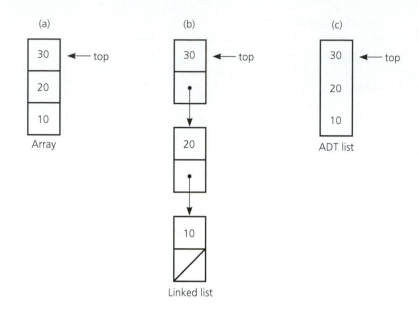

(a)

30 ← top
20
10

Array

(b)

30 ← top

20

10

Linked list

(c)

30 ← top
20
10

ADT list

FIGURE 6-4   Implementations of the ADT stack that use (a) an array; (b) a linked list; (c) an ADT list

An Array-Based Implementation of the ADT Stack

Figure 6-5 suggests that you use an array *items* to represent the items in a stack and an index *top* such that *items[top]* is the stack's top. We want to define a class whose instances are stacks and whose private data members are *items* and *top*.

The default constructor for this class corresponds to and replaces the ADT operation *createStack*; the destructor corresponds to and replaces the ADT operation *destroyStack*. Since the data will be stored in statically allocated memory, the compiler-generated destructor and copy constructor are sufficient.[4]

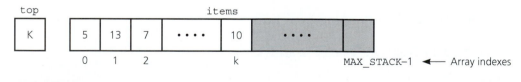

top

K

items

5 13 7 . . . . 10 . . . .

0   1   2   k   MAX_STACK−1 ← Array indexes

FIGURE 6-5   An array-based implementation

---

[4] If you use a dynamically allocated array, you must provide a destructor and copy constructor.

The following files contain an array-based implementation of the ADT stack:

```
// ***********************************************************
// Header file StackA.h for the ADT stack.
// Array-based implementation.
// ***********************************************************
#include "StackException.h"
const int MAX_STACK = maximum-size-of-stack;
typedef desired-type-of-stack-item StackItemType;

class Stack
{
public:
// constructors and destructor:
   Stack();  // default constructor
   // copy constructor and destructor are
   // supplied by the compiler

// stack operations:
   bool isEmpty() const;
   // Determines whether a stack is empty.
   // Precondition: None.
   // Postcondition: Returns true if the stack is empty;
   // otherwise returns false.

   void push(StackItemType newItem) throw(StackException);
   // Adds an item to the top of a stack.
   // Precondition: newItem is the item to be added.
   // Postcondition: If the insertion is successful, newItem
   // is on the top of the stack.
   // Exception: Throws StackException if the item cannot
   // be placed on the stack.

   void pop() throw(StackException);
   // Removes the top of a stack.
   // Precondition: None.
   // Postcondition: If the stack is not empty, the item
   // that was added most recently is removed. However, if
   // the stack is empty, deletion is impossible.
   // Exception: Throws StackException if the stack is empty.

   void pop(StackItemType& stackTop) throw(StackException);
   // Retrieves and removes the top of a stack.
   // Precondition: None.
   // Postcondition: If the stack is not empty, stackTop
   // contains the item that was added most recently and the
   // item is removed. However, if the stack is empty,
```

```
        // deletion is impossible and stackTop is unchanged.
        // Exception: Throws StackException if the stack is empty.

        void getTop(StackItemType& stackTop) const
                throw(StackException);
        // Retrieves the top of a stack.
        // Precondition: None.
        // Postcondition: If the stack is not empty, stackTop
        // contains the item that was added most recently.
        // However, if the stack is empty, the operation fails
        // and stackTop is unchanged. The stack is unchanged.
        // Exception: Throws StackException if the stack is empty.

private:
    StackItemType items[MAX_STACK];   // array of stack items
    int           top;                // index to top of stack
};  // end class
// End of header file.
```

The implementations of the functions that the previous header file declares are in the following file *StackA.cpp*:

```
// ********************************************************
// Implementation file StackA.cpp for the ADT stack.
// Array-based implementation.
// ********************************************************
#include "StackA.h"  // Stack class specification file

Stack::Stack(): top(-1)
{
}  // end default constructor

bool Stack::isEmpty() const
{
    return top < 0;
}  // end isEmpty

void Stack::push(StackItemType newItem) throw(StackException)
{
// if stack has no more room for another item
    if (top >= MAX_STACK-1)
        throw StackException(
                    "StackException: stack full on push");
    else
    {   ++top;
        items[top] = newItem;
    }  // end if
}  // end push
```

```cpp
void Stack::pop() throw(StackException)
{
   if (isEmpty())
      throw StackException(
                     "StackException: stack empty on pop");
   else
      --top;      // stack is not empty; pop top
} // end pop

void Stack::pop(StackItemType& stackTop) throw(StackException)
{
   if (isEmpty())
      throw StackException(
                     "StackException: stack empty on pop");
   else
   {  // stack is not empty; retrieve top
      stackTop = items[top];
      --top;      // pop top
   } // end if
} // end pop

void Stack::getTop(StackItemType& stackTop) const
                     throw(StackException)
{
   if (isEmpty())
      throw StackException(
                  "StackException: stack empty on getTop");
   else
      // stack is not empty; retrieve top
      stackTop = items[top];
} // end getTop
// End of implementation file.
```

A program that uses a stack could begin as follows:

```cpp
#include <iostream>
#include "StackA.h"
using namespace std;

int main()
{
   StackItemType anItem;
   Stack aStack;

   cin >> anItem;          // read an item
   aStack.push(anItem);    // push it onto stack
   . . .
```

By implementing the stack as a class, and by declaring *items* and *top* as private, you ensure that the client cannot violate the ADT's

Private data members are hidden from the client

StackException provides a simple way to indicate unusual events

walls. If you did not hide your implementation within a class, or if you made the array *items* public, the client could access the elements in *items* directly instead of by using the ADT stack operations. Thus, the client could access any elements in the stack, not just its top element. You might find this capability attractive, but in fact it violates the specifications of the ADT stack. If you truly need to access all the items of your ADT randomly, do not use a stack!

Again, note that *StackException* provides a simple way for the implementer to indicate to the stack's client unusual circumstances, such as an attempted insertion into a full stack or a deletion from an empty stack.

Finally, note that *push* receives *newItem* as a value argument. Therefore, *push* copies the value of *newItem* before using it. When the items on the stack are simply integers or characters, such copies are not expensive to make. However, if the items on the stack are instances of another class, copying them can be expensive. You can avoid making a copy of *newItem* by passing it as a constant reference argument.

A Pointer-Based Implementation of the ADT Stack

Many applications require a pointer-based implementation of a stack so that the stack can grow and shrink dynamically. Figure 6-6 illustrates a pointer-based implementation of a stack where *topPtr* is a pointer to the head of a linked list of items. Because memory is allocated dynamically for a linked list, you must write both a copy constructor and a destructor for the class of stacks.

As before, we organize the implementation into a header file and an implementation file. Note that the preconditions and postconditions given earlier for the array-based implementation apply here as well, and so are omitted to save space.

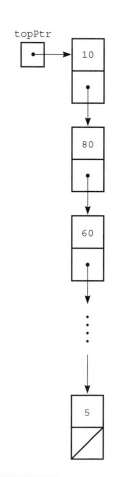

FIGURE 6-6   A pointer-based implementation

```
// ************************************************************
// Header file StackP.h for the ADT stack.
// Pointer-based implementation.
// ************************************************************
#include "StackException.h"
typedef desired-type-of-stack-item StackItemType;

class Stack
{
public:
// constructors and destructor:
   Stack();                           // default constructor
   Stack(const Stack& aStack);        // copy constructor
   ~Stack();                          // destructor

// stack operations:
```

```
   bool isEmpty() const;
   void push(StackItemType newItem) throw(StackException);
   void pop() throw(StackException);
   void pop(StackItemType& stackTop) throw(StackException);
   void getTop(StackItemType& stackTop) const
                                     throw(StackException);

private:
   struct StackNode                    // a node on the stack
   {
      StackItemType item;          // a data item on the stack
      StackNode     *next;         // pointer to next node
   };  // end struct

   StackNode *topPtr; // pointer to first node in the stack
};  // end Stack class
// End of header file.


// ***********************************************************
// Implementation file StackP.cpp for the ADT stack.
// Pointer-based implementation.
// ***********************************************************
#include "StackP.h"  // header file
#include <cstddef>    // for NULL
#include <cassert>    // for assert

Stack::Stack() : topPtr(NULL)
{
}  // end default constructor

Stack::Stack(const Stack& aStack)
{
   if (aStack.topPtr == NULL)
      topPtr = NULL;  // original list is empty

   else
   {  // copy first node
      topPtr = new StackNode;
      assert(topPtr != NULL);
      topPtr->item = aStack.topPtr->item;

      // copy rest of list
      StackNode *newPtr = topPtr;    // new list pointer
      for (StackNode *origPtr = aStack.topPtr->next;
                     origPtr != NULL;
                     origPtr = origPtr->next)
      {  newPtr->next = new StackNode;
         assert(newPtr->next != NULL);
```

```
            newPtr = newPtr->next;
            newPtr->item = origPtr->item;
        }  // end for

        newPtr->next = NULL;
    }  // end if
}  // end copy constructor

Stack::~Stack()
{
    // pop until stack is empty
    while (!isEmpty())
        pop();
    // Assertion: topPtr == NULL
}  // end destructor

bool Stack::isEmpty() const
{
    return topPtr == NULL;
}  // end isEmpty

void Stack::push(StackItemType newItem) throw(StackException)
{
    // create a new node
    StackNode *newPtr = new StackNode;

    if (newPtr == NULL)  // check allocation
        throw StackException(
        "StackException: stack push cannot allocate memory");
    else
    {  // allocation successful; set data portion of new node
        newPtr->item = newItem;
        // insert the new node
        newPtr->next = topPtr;
        topPtr = newPtr;
    }  // end if
}  // end push

void Stack::pop() throw(StackException)
{
    if (isEmpty())
        throw StackException(
                "StackException: stack empty on pop");
    else
    {  // stack is not empty; delete top
        StackNode *temp = topPtr;
        topPtr = topPtr->next;
        // return deleted node to system
```

```
         temp->next = NULL;   // safeguard
         delete temp;
    }  // end if
}  // end pop

void Stack::pop(StackItemType& stackTop) throw(StackException)
{
    if (isEmpty())
       throw StackException(
          "StackException: stack empty on pop");
    else
    {  // stack is not empty; retrieve and delete top
       stackTop = topPtr->item;
       StackNode *temp = topPtr;
       topPtr = topPtr->next;

       // return deleted node to system
       temp->next = NULL;   // safeguard
       delete temp;
    }  // end if
}  // end pop

void Stack::getTop(StackItemType& stackTop) const
                   throw(StackException)
{
    if (isEmpty())
       throw StackException(
              "StackException: stack empty on getTop");
    else
       // stack is not empty; retrieve top
       stackTop = topPtr->item;
}  // end getTop
// End of implementation file.
```

The class just given includes a copy constructor that performs a deep copy of the stack. If we did not write our own copy constructor, the compiler-generated copy constructor for this pointer-based implementation would copy only the pointer to the head of the linked list that represents the stack. Thus, both the original pointer and the copy of that pointer would point to the same linked list; the stack itself would not be copied. You must write a copy constructor that explicitly makes a copy of all the nodes in a pointer-based stack.

You need an explicit copy constructor

An Implementation That Uses the ADT List

You can use the ADT list to represent the items in a stack, as Figure 6-7 illustrates. If the item in position 1 of a list represents the top of the stack, you can implement the stack operation *push(newItem)* as the list operation *insert(1, newItem)*. Similarly, you can implement the stack

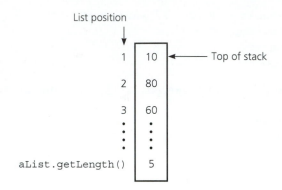

List position

1   10   ← Top of stack

2   80

3   60
·   ·
·   ·
·   ·

aList.getLength()   5

FIGURE 6-7   An implementation that uses the ADT list

operation *pop()* as the list operation *remove(1)* and the stack operation *getTop(stackTop)* as the list operation *retrieve(1, stackTop)*.

Recall that Chapters 3 and 4 presented the ADT list as the class *List*. (See, for example, page 189.) The following class for the ADT stack uses an instance of *List* to represent the stack. Preconditions and postconditions in the header file are omitted to save space but are the same as those given earlier in this chapter.

```
// ***********************************************************
// Header file StackL.h for the ADT stack.
// ADT list implementation.
// ***********************************************************
#include "StackException.h"
#include "ListP.h"      // list operations

typedef ListItemType StackItemType;

class Stack
{
public:
// constructors and destructor:
   Stack();                        // default constructor
   Stack(const Stack& aStack);     // copy constructor
   ~Stack();                       // destructor

// Stack operations:
   bool isEmpty() const;
   void push(StackItemType newItem) throw(StackException);
   void pop() throw(StackException);
   void pop(StackItemType& stackTop) throw(StackException);
   void getTop(StackItemType& stackTop) const throw(StackException);
```

```cpp
private:
   List aList;  // list of stack items
};  // end class
// End of header file.


// *********************************************************
// Implementation file StackL.cpp for the ADT stack.
// ADT list implementation.
// *********************************************************
#include "StackL.h"    // header file

Stack::Stack()
{
}  // end default constructor

Stack::Stack(const Stack& aStack): aList(aStack.aList)
{
}  // end copy constructor

Stack::~Stack()
{
}  // end destructor

bool Stack::isEmpty() const
{
   return aList.isEmpty();
}  // end isEmpty

void Stack::push(StackItemType newItem) throw(StackException)
{
   try
   {
      aList.insert(1, newItem);
   } // end try
   catch (ListException e)
   {
      throw StackException(
         "StackException: cannot push item");
   } // end catch
}  // end push

void Stack::pop() throw(StackException)
{
   try
   {
      aList.remove(1);
```

```
    } // end try
    catch (ListIndexOutOfRangeException e)
    {
        throw StackException(
            "StackException: stack empty on pop");
    } // end catch
} // end pop

void Stack::pop(StackItemType& stackTop)
                       throw(StackException)
{
    try
    {
        aList.retrieve(1, stackTop);
        aList.remove(1);
    } // end try
    catch (ListIndexOutOfRangeException e)
    {
        throw StackException(
            "StackException: stack empty on pop");
    } // end catch
}   // end pop

void Stack::getTop(StackItemType& stackTop) const
                        throw(StackException)
{
    try
    {
        aList.retrieve(1, stackTop);
    } // end try
    catch (ListIndexOutOfRangeException e)
    {
        throw StackException(
            "StackException: stack empty on getTop");
    } // end catch
}   // end getTop
// End of implementation file.
```

The data member *aList* is an instance of another class, *List*. A data member of a class can be an instance of any class other than the one currently being defined (*Stack*, in this example). Also, *List*'s constructor is called before *Stack*'s constructor. The copy constructor of *Stack* copies *aList* by invoking *List*'s copy constructor.

The body of the destructor is empty. If you declare an explicit destructor in the class definition, you must implement it, even if there is nothing explicit for you to do. However, in this case, you could omit the destructor and use the compiler-generated one. As long as *List* has a correct destructor, the destructor for *Stack* will execute correctly.

Comparing Implementations

You have seen implementations of the ADT stack that used an array, a linked list, and an ADT list to represent the items in a stack. We have treated the array and linked list as data structures, but the list is an ADT that we have implemented by using either an array or a linked list. Thus, all our implementations of the ADT stack are ultimately array-based or pointer-based.

Once again the reasons for making the choice between array-based and pointer-based implementations are the same as discussed in earlier chapters. The array-based implementation given in this chapter uses statically allocated memory. As such, it prevents the *push* operation from adding an item to the stack if the stack's size limit, which is the size of the array, has been reached. If this restriction is not acceptable, you must use either a dynamically allocated array or a pointer-based implementation. For the problem that reads and corrects an input line, for example, the fixed-size restriction might not present a difficulty: If the system allows a line length of only 80 characters, you reasonably could use a statically allocated array to represent the stack.

> **Fixed size versus dynamic size**

Suppose that you decide to use a pointer-based implementation. Should you choose the implementation that uses a linked list or the one that uses a pointer-based implementation of the ADT list? Because a linked list actually represents the items on the ADT list, you might feel that using an ADT list to represent a stack is not as efficient as using a linked list directly. You would be right, but notice that the ADT list approach is much simpler to write. If you have battled pointers to produce a correct pointer-based implementation of the ADT list, why do so again when you can *reuse* your work in the implementation of the stack? Which approach would you choose to produce a correct implementation of the stack in the least time? Chapter 8 discusses further the reuse of previously written classes.

> **Reuse of an already implemented class saves you time**

The Standard Template Library Class *stack*

Chapter 4 introduced the Standard Template Library (STL) and the container type *list*. The STL also contains the container *stack*, which is like the class *Stack* that you saw in this chapter. The STL *stack*, however, is a template class. It also provides one additional function, *size*, that determines the number of items in the stack. Finally, our stack functions *isEmpty* and *getTop* have different names in the STL class. Here is a slightly simplified specification for the STL *stack* container:

> **The STL class *stack* is a template class**

```
template <class T, class Container = deque <T> >
class stack
{
public:
    explicit stack(const Container& cnt = Container());
    // Default constructor; initializes an empty stack.
```

```
                        // Precondition: None.
                        // Postcondition: An empty stack exists.

                        bool empty() const;
                        // Determines whether the stack is empty.
                        // Precondition: None.
                        // Postcondition: Returns true if the stack is empty,
                        // otherwise returns false.

                        size_type size() const;
                        // Determines the size of the stack. The return type
                        // size_type is an integral type.
                        // Precondition: None.
                        // Postcondition: Returns the number of items that
                        // are currently on the stack.

                        T &top();
                        // Returns a reference to the top of the stack.
                        // Precondition: None.
                        // Postcondition: The item remains on the stack.

                        void pop();
                        // Removes the top item in the stack.
                        // Precondition: None.
                        // Postcondition: The item most recently added is removed
                        // from the stack.


                        void push(const T& x);
                        // Adds an item to the top of the stack.
                        // Precondition: None.
                        // Postcondition: Item x is on top of the stack.

} // end STL stack
```

Note that the template specification has two parameters. The first parameter, *T*, is the data type for the items contained in the stack. This parameter is just like the parameter in the STL *list* class that specifies the data type for the items in a list. The second parameter, *Container*, is

The *stack* template also specifies a container class

a container class that the STL uses in its implementation of the STL class *stack*, much as we used our class *List* to implement our class *Stack*. You will note that the *stack* constructor mentions this container type in its formal parameter list. At this time, you need not worry about this container class since defaults are provided on both the template specification and the constructor. Chapter 7 expands on these ideas and describes the default container class *deque* in the section on the STL class *queue*.

Notice the keyword **explicit** in the constructor's declaration. This limits how you can use the constructor to create new instances of the stack. In particular, you cannot use the assignment operator to invoke the constructor.

Here is an example of how the STL *stack* type is used:

```cpp
#include <iostream>
#include <stack>
using namespace std;

int main()
{
   stack<int> aStack;
   int item;

   // Right now, the stack is empty
   if (aStack.empty())
      cout << "The stack is empty" << endl;

   for (int j = 0; j < 5; j++)
      aStack.push(j); // places items on top of stack

   while (!aStack.empty())
   {
      cout << aStack.top() << " ";
      aStack.pop();
   }  // end while
   return 0;
} // end main
```

The output of this program is

```
The stack is empty
4 3 2 1 0
```

The keyword *explicit* in a constructor disallows the use of the assignment operator to invoke the constructor

6.4 Application: Algebraic Expressions

This section contains two more problems that you can solve neatly by using the ADT stack. Keep in mind throughout that you are using the ADT stack to solve the problems. You can use the stack operations, but you may not assume any particular implementation. You choose a specific implementation only as a last step.

Chapter 5 presented recursive grammars that specified the syntax of algebraic expressions. Recall that prefix and postfix expressions avoid

Your use of an ADT's operations should not depend on its implementation

the ambiguity inherent in the evaluation of infix expressions. We will now consider stack-based solutions to the problems of evaluating infix and postfix expressions. To avoid distracting programming issues, we will allow only the binary operators *, /, +, and −, and disallow exponentiation and unary operators.

To evaluate an infix expression, first convert it to postfix form and then evaluate the postfix expression

The strategy we shall adopt here is first to develop an algorithm for evaluating postfix expressions and then to develop an algorithm for transforming an infix expression into an equivalent postfix expression. Taken together, these two algorithms provide a way to evaluate infix expressions. This strategy eliminates the need for an algorithm that directly evaluates infix expressions, a somewhat more difficult problem, which Programming Problem 8 considers.

Evaluating Postfix Expressions

As we mentioned in Chapter 5, some calculators require you to enter postfix expressions. For example, to compute the value of

$$2 * (3 + 4)$$

by using a postfix calculator, you would enter the sequence 2, 3, 4, +, *, which corresponds to the postfix expression

$$2\ 3\ 4 + *$$

Recall that an operator in a postfix expression applies to the two operands that immediately precede it. Thus, the calculator must be able to retrieve the operands entered most recently. The ADT stack provides this capability. In fact, each time you enter an operand, the calculator pushes it onto a stack. When you enter an operator, the calculator applies it to the top two operands on the stack, pops the operands from the stack, and pushes the result of the operation onto the stack. Figure 6-8 shows the action of the calculator for the previous sequence of operands and operators. The final result, 14, is on the top of the stack.

You can formalize the action of the calculator to obtain an algorithm that evaluates a postfix expression, which is entered as a string of characters. To avoid issues that cloud the algorithm with programming details, assume that

Simplifying assumptions

- The string is a syntactically correct postfix expression
- No unary operators are present
- No exponentiation operators are present
- Operands are single uppercase letters that represent integer values

The pseudocode algorithm is then

A pseudocode algorithm that evaluates postfix expressions

```
for (each character ch in the string)
{   if (ch is an operand)
        Push value that operand ch represents onto stack
```

Key entered	Calculator action		After stack operation: Stack (bottom to top)
2	push 2		2
3	push 3		2 3
4	push 4		2 3 4
+	operand2 = pop stack	(4)	2 3
	operand1 = pop stack	(3)	2
	result = operand1 + operand2	(7)	2
	push result		2 7
*	operand2 = pop stack	(7)	2
	operand1 = pop stack	(2)	
	result = operand1 * operand2	(14)	
	push result		14

FIGURE 6-8   The action of a postfix calculator when evaluating the expression
2 * (3 + 4)

```
else  // ch is an operator named op
{   // evaluate and push the result
    operand2 = top of stack
    Pop the stack
    operand1 = top of stack
    Pop the stack
    result = operand1 op operand2
    Push result onto stack
}  // end if
}  // end for
```

Upon termination of the algorithm, the value of the expression will be on the top of the stack. Programming Problem 5 at the end of this chapter asks you to implement this algorithm.

Converting Infix Expressions to Equivalent Postfix Expressions

Now that you know how to evaluate a postfix expression, you will be able to evaluate an infix expression, if you first can convert it into an equivalent postfix expression. The infix expressions here are the familiar ones, such as $(a + b) * c / d - e$. They allow parentheses, operator precedence, and left-to-right association.

Will you ever want to evaluate an infix expression? Certainly, you have written such expressions in programs. The compiler that translated your programs had to generate machine instructions to evaluate the expressions. To do so, the compiler first transformed each infix expression into postfix form. Knowing how to convert an expression from infix to postfix notation not only will lead to an algorithm to evaluate infix expressions, but also will give you some insight into the compilation process.

If you manually convert a few infix expressions to postfix form, you will discover three important facts:

Facts about converting from infix to postfix

- The operands always stay in the same order with respect to one another.

- An operator will move only "to the right" with respect to the operands; that is, if, in the infix expression, the operand x precedes the operator op, it is also true that in the postfix expression the operand x precedes the operator op.

- All parentheses are removed.

As a consequence of these three facts, the primary task of the conversion algorithm is determining where to place each operator.

The following pseudocode describes a first attempt at converting an infix expression to an equivalent postfix expression *postfixExp*:

First draft of an algorithm to convert an infix expression to postfix form

```
Initialize postfixExp to the null string
for (each character ch in the infix expression)
{ switch (ch)
  { case ch is an operand:
        Append ch to the end of postfixExp
        break
    case ch is an operator:
        Store ch until you know where to place it
        break
    case ch is '(' or ')':
        Discard ch
        break
  } // end switch
} //  end for
```

You may have guessed that you really do not want simply to discard the parentheses, as they play an important role in determining the placement of the operators. In any infix expression a set of matching parentheses defines an isolated subexpression that consists of an operator and its two operands. Therefore, the algorithm must evaluate the subexpression independently of the rest of the expression. Regardless of what the rest of the expression looks like, the operator within the subexpression belongs with the operands in that subexpression. The parentheses tell the rest of the expression

> *You can have the value of this subexpression after it is evaluated; simply ignore everything inside.*

Parentheses, operator precedence, and left-to-right association determine where to place operators in the postfix expression

Parentheses are thus one of the factors that determines the placement of the operators in the postfix expression. The other factors are precedence and left-to-right association.

In Chapter 5, you saw a simple way to convert a fully parenthesized infix expression to postfix form. Because each operator corresponded to a pair of parentheses, you simply moved each operator to the position marked by its closed parenthesis, and finally removed the parentheses.

The actual problem is more difficult, however, because the infix expression is not always fully parenthesized. Instead, the problem allows precedence and left-to-right association, and therefore requires a more complex algorithm. The following is a high-level description of what you must do when you encounter each character as you read the infix string from left to right.

1. When you encounter an operand, append it to the output string *postfixExp*. *Justification*: The order of the operands in the postfix expression is the same as the order in the infix expression, and the operands that appear to the left of an operator in the infix expression also appear to its left in the postfix expression.

Five steps in the process to convert from infix to postfix form

2. Push each "(" onto the stack.

3. When you encounter an operator, if the stack is empty, push the operator onto the stack. However, if the stack is not empty, pop operators of greater or equal precedence from the stack and append them to *postfixExp*. You stop when you encounter either a "(" or an operator of lower precedence or when the stack becomes empty. You then push the new operator onto the stack. Thus, this step orders the operators by precedence and in accordance with left-to-right association. Notice that you continue popping from the stack until you encounter an operator of strictly lower precedence than the current operator in the infix expression. You do not stop on equality, because the left-to-right association rule says that in case of a tie in precedence, the leftmost operator is applied first—and this operator is the one that is already on the stack.

4. When you encounter a ")", pop operators off the stack and append them to the end of *postfixExp* until you encounter the matching "(". *Justification*: Within a pair of parentheses, precedence and left-to-right association determine the order of the operators, and Step 3 has already ordered the operators in accordance with these rules.

5. When you reach the end of the string, you append the remaining contents of the stack to *postfixExp*.

For example, Figure 6-9 traces the action of the algorithm on the infix expression $a-(b+c*d)/e$, assuming that the stack *aStack* and the string *postfixExp* are initially empty. At the end of the algorithm, *postfixExp* contains the resulting postfix expression $abcd*+e/-$.

You can use the previous five-step description of the algorithm to develop a fairly concise pseudocode solution, which follows. The symbol $+$ means concatenate (append), so *postfixExp* $+ x$ means concatenate

ch	Stack (bottom to top)	postfixExp	
a		a	
–	–	a	
(	– (	a	
b	– (	ab	
+	– (+	ab	
c	– (+	abc	
*	– (+ *	abc	
d	– (+ *	abcd	
)	– (+	abcd*	Move operators
	– (	abcd*+	from stack to
	–	abcd*+	postfixExp until " ("
/	– /	abcd*+	
e	– /	abcd*+e	Copy operators from
		abcd*+e/–	stack to postfixExp

FIGURE 6-9   A trace of the algorithm that converts the infix expression
$a - (b + c * d)/e$ to postfix form

the string currently in *postfixExp* and the character *x*—that is, follow
the string in *postfixExp* with the character *x*.

A pseudocode algorithm that
converts an infix expression
to postfix form

```
for (each character ch in the infix expression)
{  switch (ch)
   {  case operand:  // append operand to end of PE
         postfixExp = postfixExp + ch
         break
      case '(':       // save '(' on stack
         aStack.push(ch)
         break
      case ')':       // pop stack until matching '('
         while (top of stack is not '(')
         {  postfixExp = postfixExp + (top of aStack)
            aStack.pop()
         }  // end while

         aStack.pop()       // remove the open parenthesis
         break
      case operator:    // process stack operators of
                        // greater precedence
         while (!aStack.isEmpty() and
                top of stack is not '(' and
                precedence(ch) <= precedence(top of aStack))
         {  postfixExp = postfixExp + (top of aStack)
            aStack.pop()
         }  // end while

         aStack.push(ch)  // save new operator
         break
   }  // end switch
}  // end for
```

```
// append to postfixExp the operators remaining in the stack
while (!aStack.isEmpty())
{  postfixExp = postfixExp + (top of aStack)
   aStack.pop()
}  // end while
```

Because this algorithm assumes that the given infix expression is syntactically correct, it can ignore the exception *StackException*. Programming Problem 7 at the end of this chapter asks you to remove this assumption. In doing so, you will find that you must include *try-catch* blocks with each use of a stack operation.

6.5 Application: A Search Problem

This final application of stacks will introduce you to a general type of search problem. In this particular problem, you must find a path from some point of origin to some destination point. We shall solve this problem first by using stacks and then by using recursion. The recursive solution will bring to light the close relationship between stacks and recursion.

The High Planes Airline Company (HPAir) wants a program to process customer requests to fly from some origin city to some destination city. So that you can focus on the issue at hand—the use of stacks during problem solving—we will simplify the problem: For each customer request, just indicate whether a sequence of HPAir flights from the origin city to the destination city exists. The more realistic problem of actually producing an itinerary—that is, the sequence of flights—is considered in Programming Problem 13 at the end of this chapter.

Determine whether HPAir flies from one city to another

Imagine three input text files that specify all of the flight information for the airline as follows:

- The names of cities that HPAir serves

- Pairs of city names, each pair representing the origin and destination of one of HPAir's flights

- Pairs of city names, each pair representing a request to fly from some origin to some destination

The program should then produce output such as

```
Request is to fly from Providence to San Francisco.
HPAir flies from Providence to San Francisco.

Request is to fly from Philadelphia to Albuquerque.
Sorry. HPAir does not fly from Philadelphia to
Albuquerque.

Request is to fly from Salt Lake City to Paris.
Sorry. HPAir does not serve Paris.
```

Representing the flight data. The flight map in Figure 6-10 represents the routes that HPAir flies. An arrow from city C_1 to city C_2 indicates a flight from C_1 to C_2. In this case C_2 is adjacent to C_1 and the path from C_1 to C_2 is called a **directed path**. Notice that if C_2 is adjacent to C_1, it does not follow that C_1 is adjacent to C_2. For example, in Figure 6-10, there is a flight from city R to city X, but not from city X to city R. As you will see in Chapter 13, the map in Figure 6-10 is called a **directed graph**.

C_2 is adjacent to C_1 if there is a directed path from C_1 to C_2

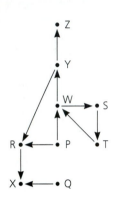

FIGURE 6-10   Flight map for HPAir

Use a stack to organize an exhaustive search

A Nonrecursive Solution That Uses a Stack

When processing a customer's request to fly from some origin city to some destination city, you must determine from the flight map whether there is a route from the origin to the destination. For example, by examining the flight map in Figure 6-10, you can see that a customer could fly from city P to city Z by flying first to city W, then to city Y, and finally to city Z; that is, there is a directed path from P to Z: $P \rightarrow W, W \rightarrow Y, Y \rightarrow Z$. Thus, you must develop an algorithm that searches the flight map for a directed path from the origin city to the destination city. Such a path might involve either a single flight or a sequence of flights. The solution developed here performs an **exhaustive search**. That is, beginning at the origin city, the solution will try every possible sequence of flights until either it finds a sequence that gets to the destination city or it determines that no such sequence exists. You will see that the ADT stack is useful in organizing this search.

First consider how you might perform the search by hand. One approach is to start at the origin city C_0 and select an arbitrary path to travel—that is, select an arbitrary flight departing from the origin city. This flight will lead you to a new city, C_1. If city C_1 happens to be the destination city, you are done; otherwise, you must attempt to get from C_1 to the destination city. To do this, you select a path to travel out of C_1. This path will lead you to a city C_2. If C_2 is the destination, you are done; otherwise, you must attempt to get from C_2 to the destination city, and so on.

Consider the possible outcomes of applying the previous strategy:

Possible outcomes of the exhaustive search strategy

1. You eventually reach the destination city and can conclude that it is possible to fly from the origin to the destination.

2. You reach a city C from which there are no departing flights.

3. You go around in circles. For example, from C_1 you go to C_2, from C_2 you go to C_3, and from C_3 you go back to C_1. You might continue this tour of the three cities forever; that is, the algorithm might enter an infinite loop.

If you always obtained the first outcome, everyone would be happy. However, because HPAir does not fly between all pairs of cities, you certainly cannot expect that the algorithm will always find a path from the origin city to the destination. For example, if city P in Figure 6-10 is the origin city and city Q is the destination city, the algorithm could not possibly find a path from city P to city Q.

Even if there were a sequence of flights from the origin city to the destination, it would take a bit of luck for the previous strategy to discover it—the algorithm would have to select a "correct" flight at each step. For example, even though there is a way to get from city P to city Z in Figure 6-10, the algorithm might not find it and instead might reach outcome 2 or 3. That is, suppose that from city P the algorithm chose to go to city R. From city R the algorithm would have to go to city X, from which there are no flights out (outcome 2). On the other hand, suppose that the algorithm chose to go to city W from city P. From city W the algorithm might choose to go to city S. It would then have to go to city T and then back to W. From W it might once again choose to go to city S and continue to go around in circles (outcome 3).

You thus need to make the algorithm more sophisticated, so that it always finds a path from the origin to the destination, if such a path exists, and otherwise terminates with the conclusion that there is no such path. Suppose that the earlier strategy results in outcome 2: You reach a city C from which there are no departing flights. This certainly does not imply that there is no way to get from the origin to the destination; it implies only that there is no way to get from city C to the destination. In other words, it was a mistake to go to city C. After discovering such a mistake, the algorithm can retrace its steps, or *backtrack*, to the city C' that was visited just before city C was visited. Once back at city C', the algorithm can select a flight to some city other than C. Notice that it is possible that there are no other flights out of city C'. If this were the case, it would mean that it was a mistake to visit city C', and thus you would want to backtrack again, this time to the city that was visited just before city C'.

For example, you saw that, in trying to get from city P to city Z in Figure 6-10, the algorithm might first choose to go from city P to city R and then on to city X. As there are no departing flights from city X, the algorithm must backtrack to city R, the city visited before city X. Once back at city R, the algorithm would attempt to go to some city other than city X, but would discover that this is not possible. The algorithm would thus backtrack once more, this time to city P, which was visited just before city R. From city P the algorithm would choose to go to city W, which is a step in the right direction!

For the algorithm to implement this new strategy, it must maintain information about the order in which it visits the cities. First notice that when the algorithm backtracks from a city C, it must retreat to the city that it visited most recently before C. This observation suggests that you maintain the sequence of visited cities in a stack. That is, each time you decide to visit a city, you push its name onto the stack, as parts a, b, and c of Figure 6-11 illustrate for the flights from P to R to X in the previous example. You select the next city to visit from those adjacent to the city on the top of the stack. When you need to backtrack from the city C at the top of the stack (for example, because

Use backtracking to recover from a wrong choice

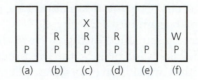

(a)   (b)   (c)   (d)   (e)   (f)

FIGURE 6-11   The stack of cities as you travel (a) from *P*; (b) to *R*; (c) to *X*; (d) back to *R*; (e) back to *P*; (f) to *W*

there are no flights out of the city), you simply pop a city from the stack, as shown in Figure 6-11d. After the pop, the city on the top of the stack is the city on the current path that you visited most recently before *C*. Parts *e* and *f* of Figure 6-11 illustrate the backtrack to city *P* and the subsequent flight to *W*.

The algorithm, as developed so far, is

```
aStack.createStack()

aStack.push(originCity)   // push origin city onto aStack

while (a sequence of flights from the origin to the
                         destination has not been found)
{  if (you need to backtrack from the city on the
        top of the stack)
      aStack.pop()
   else
   {  Select a destination city C for a flight from
        the city on the top of the stack
      aStack.push(C)
   }  // end if
}  // end while
```

Notice that at any point in the algorithm, the contents of the stack correspond to the sequence of flights currently under consideration. The city on the top of the stack is the city you are visiting currently, directly "below" it is the city visited previously, and so forth down to the bottom city, which is the first city visited in the sequence, or the origin city. In other words, an invariant of the `while` loop is that

Invariant

> *The stack contains a directed path from the origin city at the bottom of the stack to the city at the top of the stack.*

You can, therefore, always retrace your steps as far back through the sequence as needed.

Now consider the question of when to backtrack from the city on the top of the stack. You have already seen one case when backtracking is necessary. You must backtrack from the city on the top of the stack when there are no flights out of that city. Another time when you need to backtrack is related to the problem of going around in circles, described previously as the third possible outcome of the original strategy.

A key observation that will tell you when to backtrack is, *You never want to visit a city that the search has already visited.* As a consequence, you must backtrack from a city whenever there are no more unvisited cities to fly to. To see why you never want to visit a city a second time, consider two cases:

- If you have visited city C and it is still somewhere in the stack—that is, it is part of the sequence of cities that you are exploring currently—you do not want to visit C again. Any sequence that goes from C through $C_1, C_2, \ldots, C_k$, back to C, and then to C' might just as well skip the intermediate cities and go from C directly to C'.

  For example, suppose that the algorithm starts at P in Figure 6-10 and, in trying to find a path to Y, visits W, S, and T. There is now no reason for the algorithm to consider the flight from T to W because W is already in the stack. Anywhere you could fly to by going from W to S, from S to T, and then back to W, such as city Y, you could fly to directly from W without first going through S and T. Because you do not allow the algorithm to visit W a second time, it will backtrack from S and T to W and then go from W directly to Y. Figure 6-12 shows how the stack would appear if revisits were allowed and how it looks after backtracking when revisits are not allowed. Notice that backtracking to W is very different from visiting W for a second time.

- If you have visited city C, but it is no longer in the stack—because you backtracked from it and popped it from the stack—you do not want to visit C again. This situation is subtle; consider two cases that depend on why you backtracked from the city.

  If you backtracked from C because there were no flights out of it, then you certainly do not ever want to try going through C again. For example, if, starting at P in Figure 6-10, the algorithm goes to R and then to X, it will backtrack from X to R. At this point, although X is no longer in the stack, you certainly do not want to visit it again, because you know there are no flights out of X.

  Now suppose that you backtracked from city C because all cities adjacent to it had been visited. This situation implies that you have already tried all possible flights from C and have failed to find a way to get to the destination city. There is thus no reason to go to C again. For example, suppose that starting from P in Figure 6-10, the algorithm executes the following sequence: Visit R, visit X, backtrack to R (because there are no flights out of X), backtrack to P (because there are no more unvisited cities adjacent to R), visit W, visit Y. At this point the stack contains P-W-Y, with Y on top, as Figure 6-12b shows. You need to choose a

Backtrack when there are no more unvisited cities

Two reasons for not visiting a city more than once

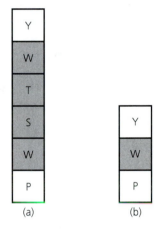

FIGURE 6-12 The stack of cities (a) allowing revisits and (b) after backtracking when revisits are not allowed

flight out of *Y*. You do not want to fly from *Y* to *R*, because you have visited *R* already and tried all possible flights out of *R*.

In both cases, visiting a city a second time does not gain you anything, and in fact it may cause you to go around in circles.

Mark the visited cities

To implement the rule of not visiting a city more than once, you simply mark a city when it has been visited. When choosing the next city to visit, you restrict consideration to unmarked cities adjacent to the city on the top of the stack. The algorithm thus becomes

Next draft of the search algorithm

```
aStack.createStack()
Clear marks on all cities

aStack.push(originCity)  // push origin city onto aStack
Mark the origin as visited

while (a sequence of flights from the origin to the
                           destination has not been found)
{  // Loop invariant: The stack contains a directed path
   // from the origin city at the bottom of the stack to
   // the city at the top of the stack
   if (no flights exist from the city on the
        top of the stack to unvisited cities)
     aStack.pop()  // backtrack
   else
   {  Select an unvisited destination city C for a
        flight from the city on the top of the stack
      aStack.push(C)
      Mark C as visited
   }  // end if
}  // end while
```

Finally, you need to refine the condition in the `while` statement. That is, you need to refine the algorithm's final determination of whether a path exists from the origin to the destination. The loop invariant, which states that the stack contains a directed path from the origin city to the city on the top of the stack, implies that the algorithm can reach an affirmative conclusion if the city at the top of the stack is the destination city. On the other hand, the algorithm can reach a negative conclusion only after it has exhausted all possibilities—that is, after the algorithm has backtracked to the origin and there remain no unvisited cities to fly to from the origin. At that point, the algorithm will pop the origin city from the stack and the stack will become empty.

With this refinement, the algorithm appears as follows:

The final version of the search algorithm

```
+searchS(in originCity:City,
         in destinationCity:City):boolean
// Searches for a sequence of flights from
// originCity to destinationCity
```

```
aStack.createStack()
Clear marks on all cities

aStack.push(originCity)   // push origin onto aStack
Mark the origin as visited

while (!aStack.isEmpty() and
                destinationCity is not at the top of the stack)

{   // Loop invariant: The stack contains a directed path
    // from the origin city at the bottom of the stack to
    // the city at the top of the stack
// originCity to destinationCity
    if (no flights exist from the city on the
          top of the stack to unvisited cities)
       aStack.pop()   // backtrack

    else
    {  Select an unvisited destination city C for a
          flight from the city on the top of the stack
       aStack.push(C)
       Mark C as visited
    }  // end if
}  // end while

if (aStack.isEmpty())
   return false   // no path exists
else
   return true    // path exists
```

Notice that the algorithm does not specify the order of selection for the unvisited cities. It really does not matter what selection criteria the algorithm uses, because the choice will not affect the final outcome: Either a sequence of flights exists or it does not. The choice, however, will affect the specific flights that the algorithm considers. For example, suppose that the algorithm always flies to the alphabetically earliest unvisited city from the city on the top of the stack. Under this assumption, Figure 6-13 contains a trace of the algorithm's action, given the map in Figure 6-10, with P as the origin city and Z as the destination city. The algorithm terminates with success.

Now consider the operations that the search algorithm must perform on the flight map. The algorithm marks cities as it visits them, determines whether a city has been visited, and determines which cities are adjacent to a given city. You can treat the flight map as an ADT that has at least these operations, in addition to the search operation itself. Other desirable operations include placing data into the flight map, inserting a city adjacent to another city, displaying the flight map, displaying a list of all cities, and displaying all cities that are

Action	Reason	Contents of stack (bottom to top)
Push P	Initialize	P
Push R	Next unvisited adjacent city	P R
Push X	Next unvisited adjacent city	P R X
Pop X	No unvisited adjacent city	P R
Pop R	No unvisited adjacent city	P
Push W	Next unvisited adjacent city	P W
Push S	Next unvisited adjacent city	P W S
Push T	Next unvisited adjacent city	P W S T
Pop T	No unvisited adjacent city	P W S
Pop S	No unvisited adjacent city	P W
Push Y	Next unvisited adjacent city	P W Y
Push Z	Next unvisited adjacent city	P W Y Z

FIGURE 6-13   A trace of the search algorithm, given the flight map in
Figure 6-10

adjacent to a given city. Thus, the ADT flight map could include the
following operations:

ADT flight map operations

```
+createFlightMap()
// Creates an empty flight map.

+destroyFlightmap()
// Destroys a flight map.

+readFlightMap(in cityFileName:string,
              in flightFileName:string)
// Reads flight information into the flight map.

+displayFlightMap()
// Displays flight information.

+displayAllCities()
// Displays the names of all cities that HPAir serves.

+displayAdjacentCities(in aCity:City)
// Displays all cities that are adjacent to a given city.

+markVisited(in aCity:City)
// Marks a city as visited.

+unvisitAll()
// Clears marks on all cities.

+isVisited(in aCity:City):boolean
// Determines whether a city was visited.

+insertAdjacent(in aCity:City, in adjCity:City)
// Inserts a city adjacent to another city in a flight map.
```

```
+getNextCity(in fromCity:City, out nextCity:City):boolean
// Determines the next unvisited city, if any, that is
// adjacent to a given city. Returns true if an unvisited
// adjacent city was found, false otherwise.

+isPath(in originCity:City, in destinationCity:City):boolean
// Determines whether a sequence of flights exists between
// two cities.
```

The following C++ function implements the *isPath* operation by using the *searchS* algorithm. It assumes that the class *Stack* implements the stack operations and the class *Map* implements the ADT flight map operations just described. Notice that to improve efficiency, integers represent cities, so a stack of integers is sufficient for this function.

```cpp
bool Map::isPath(int originCity, int destinationCity)
// ---------------------------------------------------
// Determines whether a sequence of flights between two
// cities exists. Nonrecursive stack version.
// Precondition: originCity and destinationCity are the city
// numbers of the origin and destination cities,
// respectively.
// Postcondition: Returns true if a sequence of flights
// exists from originCity to destinationCity; otherwise
// returns false. Cities visited during the search are
// marked as visited in the flight map.
// Implementation notes: Uses a stack for the city
// numbers of a potential path. Calls unvisitAll,
// markVisited, and getNextCity.
// ---------------------------------------------------
{
   Stack aStack;
   int    topCity, nextCity;
   bool   success;

   unvisitAll();  // clear marks on all cities

   // push origin city onto aStack, mark it visited
   aStack.push(originCity);
   markVisited(originCity);

   aStack.getTop(topCity);
   while (!aStack.isEmpty() && (topCity != destinationCity))
   {  // Loop invariant: The stack contains a directed path
      // from the origin city at the bottom of the stack to
      // the city at the top of the stack

      // find an unvisited city adjacent to the city on the
```

C++ implementation of *searchS*

```
                       // top of the stack
                       success = getNextCity(topCity, nextCity);

                       if (!success)
                          aStack.pop();   // no city found; backtrack

                       else                    // visit city
                       {  aStack.push(nextCity);
                          markVisited(nextCity);
                       }  // end if
                  if (!aStack.isEmpty())
                     aStack.getTop(topCity);
                  }  // end while

                  if (aStack.isEmpty())
                     return false;   // no path exists
                  else
                     return true;    // path exists
               }  // end isPath
```

Programming Problem 11 at the end of this chapter provides implementation details that will enable you to complete the solution to the
HPAir problem.

A Recursive Solution

Recall the initial attempt at a solution to the HPAir problem of searching for a sequence of flights from some origin city to some destination
city. Consider how you might perform the search "by hand." One
approach is to start at the origin city and select an arbitrary flight that
departs from the origin city. This flight will lead you to a new city, C_1.
If city C_1 happens to be the destination city, you are done; otherwise,
you must attempt to get from C_1 to the destination city by selecting a
flight out of C_1. This flight will lead you to city C_2. If C_2 is the destination, you are done; otherwise, you must attempt to get from C_2 to the
destination city, and so on. There is a distinct recursive flavor to this
search strategy, which can be restated as follows:

A recursive search strategy

```
To fly from the origin to the destination:

   Select a city C adjacent to the origin
   Fly from the origin to city C
   if (C is the destination city)
      Terminate -- the destination is reached
   else
      Fly from city C to the destination
```

This statement of the search strategy makes its recursive nature very
apparent. The first step in flying from the origin city to the destination

city is to fly from the origin city to city *C*. Once at city *C*, you are confronted with another problem of the same type—you now must fly from city *C* to the destination.

This recursive formulation is nothing more than a restatement of the initial (incomplete) strategy developed previously. As such it has the same three possible outcomes:

1. You eventually reach the destination city and can conclude that it is possible to fly from the origin to the destination.

2. You reach a city *C* from which there are no departing flights.

3. You go around in circles.

Possible outcomes of the recursive search strategy

The first of these outcomes corresponds to a base case of the recursive algorithm. If you ever reach the destination city, no additional problems of the form "fly from city *C* to the destination" are generated, and the algorithm terminates. However, as was observed previously, the algorithm might not produce this outcome; that is, it might not reach this base case. The algorithm might reach a city *C* that has no departing flights. (Notice that the algorithm does not specify what to do in this case—in this sense the algorithm is incomplete.) Or the algorithm might repeatedly cycle through the same sequence of cities and thus never terminate.

You can resolve these problems by mirroring what you did in the previous solution. Consider the following refinement, in which you mark visited cities and never fly to a city that has been visited already:

```
+searchR(in originCity:City,
         in destinationCity:City):boolean
// Searches for a sequence of flights from
// originCity to destinationCity.

   Mark originCity as visited

   if (originCity is destinationCity)
      Terminate -- the destination is reached

   else
      for (each unvisited city C adjacent to originCity)
         searchR(C, destinationCity)
```

A refinement of the recursive search algorithm

Now consider what happens when the algorithm reaches a city that has no unvisited city adjacent to it. For example, consider the piece of a flight map in Figure 6-14. When *searchR* reaches city *X*—that is, when the argument *originCity* has the value *X*—the *for* loop will not be entered, because no unvisited cities are adjacent to *X*. Hence, the function *searchR* returns. This return has the effect of backtracking to city *W*, from which the flight to *X* originated. In terms of the previous pseudocode, the return is made to the point from which the call *searchR(X, destinationCity)* occurred. This point is within the

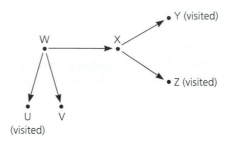

FIGURE 6-14   A piece of a flight map

for loop, which iterates through the unvisited cities adjacent to *W*; that is, the argument *originCity* has the value *W*.

After backtracking from *X* to *W*, the *for* loop will again execute. This time the loop chooses city *V*, resulting in the recursive call *searchR(V, destinationCity)*. From this point, the algorithm either will eventually reach the destination city and terminate, or it will backtrack once again to city *W*. If it backtracks to *W*, the *for* loop will terminate because there are no more unvisited cities adjacent to *W*, and a return from *searchR* will occur. The effect is to backtrack to the city where the flight to *W* originated. If the algorithm ever backtracks to the origin city and no remaining unvisited cities are adjacent to it, the algorithm will terminate, and you can conclude that no sequence of flights from the origin to the destination exists. Notice that the algorithm will always terminate in one way or another, because it will either reach the destination city or run out of unvisited cities to try.

The following C++ function implements the *searchR* algorithm:

C++ implementation of searchR

```
bool Map::isPath(int originCity, int destinationCity)
{
    int  nextCity;
    bool success, done;

    // mark the current city as visited
    markVisited(originCity);

    // base case: the destination is reached
    if (originCity == destinationCity)
        return true;

    else  // try a flight to each unvisited city
    {   done = false;
        success = getNextCity(originCity, nextCity);

        while (success && !done)
        {   done = isPath(nextCity, destinationCity);
            if (!done)
```

```
            success = getNextCity(originCity, nextCity);
    }  // end while

    return done;
  }  // end if
}  // end isPath
```

You have probably noticed a close parallel between this recursive algorithm and the earlier stack-based algorithm *searchS*. In fact, the two algorithms simply employ different techniques to implement the identical search strategy. The next section will elaborate on the relationship between the two algorithms.

6.6 The Relationship Between Stacks and Recursion

The previous section solved the HPAir problem once by using the ADT stack and again by using recursion. The goal of this section is to relate the way that the stack organizes the search for a sequence of flights to the way a recursive algorithm organizes the search. You will see that the ADT stack has a hidden presence in the concept of recursion and, in fact, that stacks have an active role in most computer implementations of recursion.

Consider how the two search algorithms implement three key aspects of their common strategy.

- **Visiting a new city.** The recursive algorithm *searchR* visits a new city *C* by calling *searchR(C, destinationCity)*. The algorithm *searchS* visits city *C* by pushing *C* onto a stack. Notice that if you were to use the box method to trace the execution of *searchR*, the call *searchR(C, destinationCity)* would generate a box in which the city *C* is associated with the formal argument *originCity* of *searchR*.

  For example, Figure 6-15 shows both the state of the box trace for *searchR* and the stack for *searchS* at corresponding points of their search for a path from city *P* to city *Z* in Figure 6-10.

A comparison of key aspects of two search algorithms

(a) Box trace:

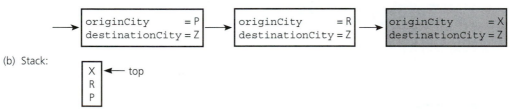

(b) Stack:

FIGURE 6-15   Visiting city *P*, then *R*, then *X*: (a) box trace versus (b) stack

- **Backtracking.** Both search algorithms attempt to visit an unvisited city that is adjacent to the current city. Notice that this current city is the value associated with the formal argument *originCity* in the deepest (rightmost) box of *searchR*'s box trace. Similarly, the current city is on the top of *searchS*'s stack. In Figure 6-15, this current city is *X*. If no unvisited cities are adjacent to the current city, the algorithms must backtrack to the previous city. The algorithm *searchR* backtracks by returning from the current recursive call. You represent this action in the box method by crossing off the deepest box. The algorithm *searchS* backtracks by explicitly popping from its stack. For example, from the state depicted in Figure 6-15, both algorithms backtrack to city *R* and then to city *P,* as Figure 6-16 illustrates.

- **Termination.** The search algorithms terminate either when they reach the destination city or when they exhaust all possibilities. All possibilities are exhausted when, after backtracking to the origin city, no unvisited adjacent cities remain. This situation occurs for *searchR* when all boxes have been crossed off in the box trace and a return occurs to the point of the original call to the function. For *searchS*, no unvisited cities are adjacent to the origin when the stack becomes empty.

Thus, the two search algorithms really do perform the identical action. In fact, provided that they use the same rule to select an unvisited city—for example, traverse the current city's list of adjacent cities alphabetically—they will always visit the identical cities in the identical order. The similarities between the algorithms are far more than coincidence. In fact, it is always possible to capture the actions of a recursive function by using a stack.

An important context in which the close tie between stacks and recursion is explicitly utilized is a compiler's implementation of a recursive function. It is common for a compiler to use a stack to implement a recursive function in a manner that greatly resembles the box method.

Typically, stacks are used to implement recursive functions

(a) Box trace:

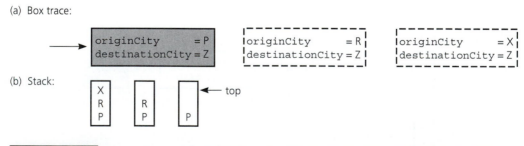

(b) Stack:

FIGURE 6-16   Backtracking from city *X* to *R* to *P*: (a) box trace versus (b) stack

When a recursive call to a function occurs, the implementation must remember certain information. This information consists essentially of the same local environment that you place in the boxes—values of both arguments and local variables, and a reference to the point from which the recursive call was made.

During execution, the compiled program must manage these boxes of information, or activation records, just as you must manage them on paper. As the HPAir example has indicated, the operations needed to manage the activation records are those that a stack provides. When a recursive call occurs, a new activation record is created and pushed onto a stack. This action corresponds to the creation of a new box at the deepest point in the sequence. When a return is made from a recursive call, the stack is popped, bringing the activation record that contains the appropriate local environment to the top of the stack. This action corresponds to crossing off the deepest box and following the arrow back to the preceding box. Although we have greatly simplified the process, most implementations of recursion are based on stacks of activation records.

Each recursive call generates an activation record that is pushed onto a stack

You can use a similar strategy to implement a nonrecursive version of a recursive algorithm. You might need to recast a recursive algorithm into a nonrecursive form to make it more efficient, as mentioned in Chapter 2. The previous discussion should give you a taste of the techniques for removing recursion from a program. You will encounter recursion removal as a formal topic in more advanced courses, such as compiler construction.

You can use stacks when implementing a nonrecursive version of a recursive algorithm

Summary

1. The ADT stack operations have a last-in, first-out (LIFO) behavior.

2. Algorithms that operate on algebraic expressions are an important application of stacks. The LIFO nature of stacks is exactly what the algorithm that evaluates postfix expressions needs to organize the operands. Similarly, the algorithm that transforms infix expressions to postfix form uses a stack to organize the operators in accordance with precedence rules and left-to-right association.

3. You can use a stack to determine whether a sequence of flights exists between two cities. The stack keeps track of the sequence of visited cities and enables the search algorithm to backtrack easily. However, displaying the sequence of cities in their normal order from origin to destination is awkward, because the origin city is at the bottom of the stack and the destination is at the top.

4. A strong relationship between recursion and stacks exists. Most implementations of recursion maintain a stack of activation records in a manner that resembles the box method.

Cautions

1. Operations such as *getTop* and *pop* must take reasonable action when the stack is empty. One possibility is to ignore the operation and throw an exception *StackException*.

2. Algorithms that evaluate an infix expression or transform one to postfix form must determine which operands apply to a given operator. Doing so allows for precedence and left-to-right association so that you can omit parentheses.

3. When searching for a sequence of flights between cities, you must take into account the possibility that the algorithm will make wrong choices. For example, the algorithm must be able to backtrack when it hits a dead end, and you must eliminate the possibility that the algorithm will cycle.

Self-Test Exercises

1. If you push the letters A, B, C, and D in order onto a stack of characters and then pop them, in what order will they be deleted from the stack?

2. What do the initially empty stacks *stack1* and *stack2* "look like" after the following sequence of operations:

```
stack1.push(1)
stack1.push(2)
stack2.push(3)
stack2.push(4)
stack1.pop()
stack2.getTop(stackTop)
stack1.push(stackTop)
stack1.push(5)
stack2.pop(stackTop)
stack2.push(6)
```

3. The algorithms that appear in the section "Simple Applications of the ADT Stack" involve strings. Under what conditions would you choose an array-based implementation for the stack in these algorithms? Under what conditions would you choose a pointer-based implementation?

4. List the changes that you must make to convert a program that uses an array-based implementation of a stack to one that uses a pointer-based implementation of a stack.

5. For each of the following strings, trace the execution of the balanced-braces algorithm and show the contents of the stack at each step.

   a. x{{yz}}}

   b. {x{y{{z}}}

   c. {{{x}}}

6. Use the stack algorithms in this chapter to evaluate the postfix expression $ab-c+$. Assume the following values for the identifiers: $a = 7$; $b = 3$; $c = -2$. Show the status of the stack after each step.

7. Use the stack algorithms in this chapter to convert the infix expression $a / b*c$ to postfix form. Be sure to account for left-to-right association. Show the status of the stack after each step.

8. Explain the significance of the precedence tests in the infix-to-postfix conversion algorithm. Why is a $\geq$ test used rather than a $>$ test?

9. Execute the HPAir algorithm with the map in Figure 6-17 for the following requests. Show the state of the stack after each step.

   a. Fly from A to B.

   b. Fly from A to D.

   c. Fly from C to G.

Exercises

1. Suppose that you have a stack *aStack* and an empty auxiliary stack *auxStack*. Show how you can do each of the following tasks by using only the ADT stack operations:

   a. Display the contents of *aStack* in reverse order; that is, display the top last.

   b. Count the number of items in *aStack*, leaving *aStack* unchanged.

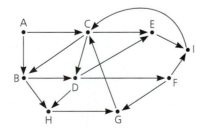

FIGURE 6-17 Flight map for Self-Test Exercise 9 and Exercise 14

c. Delete every occurrence of a specified item from *aStack*, leaving the order of the remaining items unchanged.

2. The diagram of a railroad switching system in Figure 6-18 is commonly used to illustrate the notion of a stack. Identify three stacks in the figure and show how they relate to one another. How can you use this system to construct any possible permutation of railroad cars?

3. An operation that displays the contents of a stack can be useful during program debugging. Add a *display* method to the ADT stack such that

    a. The method uses only ADT stack operations; that is, it is independent of the stack's implementation

    b. The method assumes and uses the pointer-based implementation of the ADT stack

4. To the ADT stack given in this chapter, add a function called *popAndDiscard* that removes and discards the user-specified number of elements from the top of the stack. This function does not return a value and accepts a parameter called *count* of data type *int*. Write a pointer-based implementation for this function.

5. Repeat the previous exercise, but write an array-based implementation instead.

6. Discuss the efficiency of the implementation of the ADT stack that uses the ADT list, when the list has an array-based implementation.

7. The section "Developing an ADT During the Design of a Solution" described an algorithm *readAndCorrect* that reads a string of characters, correcting mistakes along the way.

    a. For the following input line, trace the execution of *readAnd-Correct* and show the contents of the stack at each step:

        abc←de←←fg←h

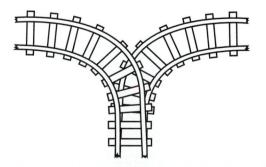

FIGURE 6-18   Railroad switching system for Exercise 2

b. The nature of the stack-based algorithm makes it simple to display the string in reverse order, but somewhat harder to display it in its correct order. Write a pseudocode algorithm that displays the string in its correct forward order.

c. Implement `readAndCorrect` as a C++ function, but make the stack local to the function instead of an argument. Let the function construct a string that contains the corrected input characters in forward order and return it as an argument.

8. Revise the solution to the balanced-braces problem so that the expression can contain three types of delimiters: ( ), [ ], and { }. Thus, {ab(c[d])e} is valid, but {ab(c)) is not.

9. For each of the following strings, trace the execution of the language-recognition algorithm described in the section "Recognizing Strings in a Language," and show the contents of the stack at each step.

   a. xy$xy   **c.** y$yx   **e.** xy$y
   b. xy$x   **d.** xx$xx

10. Write a pseudocode function that uses a stack to determine whether a string is in the language L, where

   a. $L = \{w : w \text{ contains equal numbers of A's and B's}\}$

   b. $L = \{w : w \text{ is of the form } A^n B^n \text{ for some } n \geq 0\}$

11. Write a function that uses a stack to determine whether a string is in the language L, where:

   $$L = \{ww' : w \text{ is a string of characters}$$

   $$w' = \text{reverse } (w) \}$$

   Note: The empty string, a string with fewer than 2 characters, or a string with an odd number of characters will not be in the language.

12. Evaluate the following postfix expressions by using the algorithm given in this chapter. Show the status of the stack after each step of the algorithm. Assume the following values for the identifiers: $a = 7; b = 3; c = 12; d = -5; e = 1$.

   a. $abc+-$ **b.** $abc-d*+$ **c.** $ab+c-de*+$

13. Convert the following infix expressions to postfix form by using the algorithm given in this chapter. Show the status of the stack after each step of the algorithm.

   a. $a-b+c$ **e.** $a-(b/c*d)$
   b. $a/(b*c)$ **f.** $a/b/c-(d+e)*f$
   c. $(a+b)*c$ **g.** $a*(b/c/d)+e$
   d. $a-(b+c)$ **h.** $a-(b+c*d)/e$

14. Execute the HPAir algorithm with the map in Figure 6-17 (see Self–Test Exercise 9) for the following requests. Show the state of the stack after each step.

a. Fly from *A* to *F.*   **c.** Fly from *A* to *G.*   **e.** Fly from *F* to *H.*
b. Fly from *D* to *A.*   **d.** Fly from *I* to *G.*

★**15.** As Chapter 3 pointed out, you can define ADT operations in a mathematically formal way by using axioms. For example, the following axioms formally define the ADT stack, where `aStack` is an arbitrary stack and `item` is an arbitrary stack item. To simplify the notation, `getTop` is treated as a valued function that returns the top of the stack.

```
(aStack.createStack()).isEmpty() = true
(aStack.push(item)).isEmpty() = false
(aStack.createStack()).pop() = error
(aStack.push(item)).pop() = aStack
(aStack.createStack()).getTop() = error
(aStack.push(item)).getTop() = item
```

You can use these axioms, for example, to prove that the stack defined by the sequence of operations

```
Create an empty stack
Push a 5
Push a 7
Push a 3
Pop (the 3)
Push a 9
Push a 4
Pop (the 4)
```

which you can write as

```
(((((((aStack.createStack()).push(5)).push(7)).push(3)).
  pop()).push(9)).push(4)).pop()
```

is exactly the same as the stack defined by the sequence

```
Create an empty stack
Push a 5
Push a 7
Push a 9
```

which you can write as

```
(((aStack.createStack()).push(5)).push(7)).push(9)
```

Similarly, you can use the axioms to show that

```
((((((aStack.createStack()).push(1)).push(2)).pop()).
   push(3)).pop()).pop()).isEmpty()
```

is true.

a. The following representation of a stack as a sequence of *push* operations without any *pop* operations is called a *canonical form*:

```
(···(aStack.createStack()).push()).push())··· ).push()
```

Prove that any stack is equal to a stack that is in canonical form.

b. Prove that the canonical form is unique. That is, a stack is equal to exactly one stack that is in canonical form.

c. Use the axioms to show formally that

```
((((((((((aStack.createStack()).push(6)).push(9)).
   pop()).pop()).push(2)).pop()).push(3)).push(1)).
   pop()).stackTop()
```

equals 3.

16. The destructor given for the pointer-based implementation of the ADT stack calls *pop*. Although easy to write, this destructor can be inefficient due to repeated function calls. Write another implementation for the destructor that deallocates the linked list directly without calling *pop*.

Programming Problems

1. Write an implementation of the ADT stack that uses a dynamically allocated array to represent the stack items. Anytime the stack becomes full, double the size of the array.

2. Add member functions to the ADT stack to do the following:

   a. Return the number of elements in the stack.

   b. Remove all elements from the stack.

   The existing ADT stack may be modified in order to add this functionality.

3. Implement the solution to the expanded balanced-braces problem in Exercise 8.

4. The section "Recognizing Strings in a Language" describes a recognition algorithm for the language

$$L = \{w\$w' : w \text{ is a possibly empty string of characters other than \$,}$$
$$w' = \text{reverse}(w) \}$$

Implement this algorithm.

5. Design and implement a class of postfix calculators. Use the algorithm given in this chapter to evaluate postfix expressions, as entered into the calculator. Use only the operators $+$, $-$, $*$, and $/$. Assume the postfix expressions are syntactically correct.

6. Consider simple infix expressions that consist of single-digit operands; the operators $+$, $-$, $*$, and $/$; and parentheses. Assume that unary operators are illegal and that the expression contains no embedded spaces.

    Design and implement a class of infix calculators. Use the algorithms given in this chapter to evaluate infix expressions, as entered into the calculator. You must first convert the infix expression to postfix form and then evaluate the resulting postfix expression.

7. The infix-to-postfix conversion algorithm described in this chapter assumes that the given infix expression is syntactically correct. Modify Programming Problem 6 without this assumption.

8. Repeat Programming Problem 6, but use the following algorithm to evaluate an infix expression *infixExp*. The algorithm uses two stacks: One stack *opStack* contains operators, and the other stack *valStack* contains values of operands and intermediate results. Note that the algorithm treats parentheses as operators with the lowest precedence.

```
for (each character ch in infixExp)
{  switch (ch)
   {  case ch is an operand, that is, a digit
         valStack.push(ch)
         break
      case ch is '('
         opStack.push(ch)
         break
      case ch is an operator
         if (opStack.isEmpty())
            opStack.push(ch)

         else if (precedence(ch) >
                              precedence(top of opStack))
            opStack.push(ch)
```

```
        else
        {  while (!opStack.isEmpty() and
                   precedence(ch) <=
                   precedence(top of opStack))
              Execute
           opStack.push(ch)
        }  // end if
        break

    case ch is ')'
        while (top of opStack is not '(')
           Execute
        opStack.pop()
        break
    }  // end switch
}  // end for

while (!opStack.isEmpty())
   Execute
valStack.getTop(result)
```

Note that *Execute* means:

```
valStack.pop(operand2)
valStack.pop(operand1)
opStack.Pop(op)
result = operand1 op operand2
valStack.push(result)
```

Choose one of the following two approaches for your implementation:

- The operator stack *opStack* contains characters, but the operand stack *valStack* contains integers.

- The stack *opStack* contains integer codes that represent the operators, so both stacks contain integers.

(Programming Problem 12 of Chapter 8 asks you to reconsider this problem in light of class templates.)

9. The infix evaluation algorithm given in Programming Problem 8 assumes that the given infix expression is syntactically correct. Repeat Programming Problem 8 without this assumption.

10. Using stacks, write a nonrecursive version of the function *solveTowers*, as defined in Chapter 2.

11. Complete the solution to the HPAir problem. The input to the program consists of three text files, as follows:

cityFile   Each line contains the name of a city that HPAir serves. The names are in alphabetical order.

flightFile   Each line contains a pair of city names that represents the origin and destination of one of HPAir's flights.

requestFile   Each line contains a pair of city names that represents a request to fly from some origin to some destination.

You can make the following assumptions:

- Each city name contains at most 15 characters. Pairs of city names are separated by a comma.

- HPAir serves at most 20 cities.

- The input data is correct.

For example, the input files could appear as

```
cityFile:       Albuquerque
                Chicago
                San Diego

flightFile:     Chicago,      San Diego
                Chicago,      Albuquerque
                Albuquerque,  Chicago

requestFile:    Albuquerque,  San Diego
                Albuquerque,  Paris
                San Diego,    Chicago
```

For this input, the program should produce the following output:

```
Request is to fly from Albuquerque to San Diego.
HPAir flies from Albuquerque to San Diego.

Request is to fly from Albuquerque to Paris.
Sorry. HPAir does not serve Paris.

Request is to fly from San Diego to Chicago.
Sorry. HPAir does not fly from San Diego to Chicago.
```

Begin by implementing the ADT flight map as the C++ class *Map*. Use the nonrecursive version of *isPath*. Since *getNextCity* is the primary operation that the search algorithm performs on the flight map, you should choose an implementation that will efficiently determine which cities are adjacent to a given city. If there are *N* cities numbered 1, 2, ..., *N*, you can use *N* linked lists to represent the flight map. You place a node on list *i* for city *j* if and only if there is a directed path from city *i* to city *j*. Such a data structure is called an **adjacency list**; Figure 6-19 illustrates an adjacency list for the flight map in Figure 6-10. Chapter 13 discusses adjacency lists further when it presents ways to represent graphs. At that time, you will learn why an adjacency list is a good choice for the present program.

Although you can implement the adjacency list from scratch, you should also consider using *N* instances of the class *List*, which has a pointer-based implementation.

To improve efficiency, you can associate each city name with an integer. To do so, you can read the names of the cities that HPAir serves into consecutive locations of the array *namesOfCities*. You can then refer to *namesOfCities[i]* as city *i*. This scheme allows you to place integers rather than strings in the stack. Thus, *namesOfCities* and the previously described adjacency list are the underlying data structures for the ADT flight map.

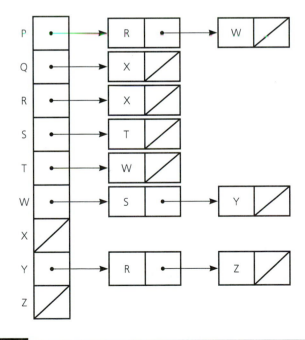

FIGURE 6-19   Adjacency list for the flight map in Figure 6-10

Because you will be using integers to identify cities, you will have to convert between integer labels and city names. This need suggests that you add the following operations to the ADT flight map:

```
+cityName(in number:integer):string
// Determines the name of a city, given its number.
```

```
+cityNumber(in name:string):integer
// Determines the number of a city, given its name.
```

Requiring the cities in the input file `cityFile` to be in alphabetical order causes the array `namesOfCities` to be sorted. This requirement allows `cityNumber` to perform a binary search on the array for a given name and then to associate the name with the correct city number.

To simplify reading the input text files, define a class that includes the following member functions:

```
+getName(out name:string)
// Gets a name from the next line in a text file.
```

```
+getNamePair(out name1:string, out name2:string)
// Gets two names from the next line in a text file.
```

12. In the implementation of the HPAir problem (see Programming Problem 11), the search for the next unvisited city adjacent to a city i always starts at the beginning of the ith linked list in the adjacency list. This approach is actually a bit inefficient, because once the search visits a city, the city can never become unvisited. Modify the program so that the search for the next city begins where the last search left off. That is, maintain an array of `tryNext` pointers into the adjacency list.

13. Implement an expanded version of the HPAir problem. In addition to the "from" and "to" cities, each line of input contains a flight number (an integer) and the cost of the flight (an integer). Modify the HPAir program so that it will produce a complete itinerary for each request, including the flight number of each flight, the cost of each flight, and the total cost of the trip.

    For example, the input files could appear as

cityFile:	Albuquerque			
	Chicago			
	San Diego			

flightFile:	Chicago,	San Diego	703	325
	Chicago,	Albuquerque	111	250
	Albuquerque,	Chicago	178	250

```
requestFile:     Albuquerque,     San Diego
                 Albuquerque,     Paris
                 San Diego,       Chicago
```

For this input, the program should produce the following output:

```
Request is to fly from Albuquerque to San Diego.
Flight #178 from Albuquerque to Chicago    Cost: $250
Flight #703 from Chicago to San Diego      Cost: $325
Total Cost .............  $575
Request is to fly from Albuquerque to Paris.
Sorry. HPAir does not serve Paris.
Request is to fly from San Diego to Chicago.
Sorry. HPAir does not fly from San Diego to Chicago.
```

When the nonrecursive *isPath* function finds a sequence of flights from the origin city to the destination city, its stack contains the corresponding path of cities. The stumbling block to reporting this path is that the cities appear in the stack in reverse order; that is, the destination city is at the top of the stack and the origin city is at the bottom. For example, if you use the program to find a path from city P to city Z in Figure 6-10, the final contents of the stack will be P-W-Y-Z, with Z on top. You want to display the origin city P first, but it is at the bottom of the stack. If you restrict yourself to the stack operations, the only way that you can write the path in its correct order is first to reverse the stack by popping it onto a temporary stack and then to write the cities as you pop them off the temporary stack. Note that this approach requires that you process each city on the path twice.

Evidently a stack is not the appropriate ADT for the problem of writing the path of cities in the correct order; the appropriate ADT is a traversable stack. In addition to the standard stack operations, *isEmpty*, *push*, *pop*, and *getTop*, a traversable stack includes the operation *traverse*. The *traverse* operation begins at one end of the stack and *visits* each item in the stack until it reaches the other end of the stack. For this project, you want *traverse* to begin at the bottom of the stack and move toward the top.

14. What modifications to Programming Problem 13 are required to find a least-cost trip for each request? How can you incorporate time considerations into the problem?

CHAPTER 7

Queues

PREVIEW

Whereas a stack's behavior is characterized as last in, first out, a queue's behavior is characterized as first in, first out. This chapter defines the queue's operations and discusses strategies for implementing them. As you will see, queues are common in everyday life. Their first-in, first-out behavior makes them appropriate ADTs for situations that involve waiting. Queues are also important in simulation, a technique for analyzing the behavior of complex systems. This chapter uses a queue to model the behavior of people in a line.

7.1 The Abstract Data Type Queue

A queue is like a line of people. The first person to join a line is the first person served, that is, to leave the line. New items enter a queue at its **back**, or **rear**, and items leave a queue from its **front**. Operations on a queue occur only at its two ends. This characteristic gives a queue its first-in, first-out (FIFO) behavior. In contrast, you can think of a stack as having only one end, because all operations are performed at the top of the stack. This characteristic gives a stack its last-in, first-out behavior.

As an abstract data type, the queue has the following operations:

FIFO: The first item inserted into a queue is the first item out

---

KEY CONCEPTS

ADT Queue Operations

1. Create an empty queue.

2. Destroy a queue.

3. Determine whether a queue is empty.

4. Add a new item to the queue.

5. Remove from the queue the item that was added earliest.

6. Retrieve from the queue the item that was added earliest.

Queues are appropriate for many real-world situations. You wait in a queue—that is, a line—to buy a movie ticket, to check out at the book store, or to use an automatic teller machine. The person at the front of the queue is served, while new people join the queue at its back. Even when you call an airline to make a reservation, your call actually enters a queue while you wait for the next available agent.

Queues occur in everyday life

Queues also have applications in computer science. When you print an essay, the computer sends lines faster than the printer can print them. The lines are held in a queue for the printer, which removes them in FIFO order. If you share the printer with other computers, your request to print enters a queue to wait its turn.

Queues have applications in computer science

Since all of these applications involve waiting, people study them to see how to reduce the wait. Such studies are called **simulations**, and they typically use queues. Later, this chapter examines a simulation of a line of customers at a bank.

The following pseudocode specifies the operations for the ADT queue in more detail, and Figure 7-1 shows a UML diagram for the class *Queue*. As we did for the ADT stack, we have included an operation that both retrieves and then removes the item at the front of the queue.

KEY CONCEPTS

Pseudocode for the ADT Queue Operations

```
// QueueItemType is the type of the items stored in the queue

+createQueue()
// Creates an empty queue.

+destroyQueue()
// Destroys a queue.

+isEmpty():boolean {query}
// Determines whether a queue is empty.

+enqueue(in newItem:QueueItemType) throw QueueException
// Inserts newItem at the back of a queue. Throws
// QueueException if the insertion is not successful.

+dequeue() throw QueueException
// Removes the front of a queue; that is, removes the item
// that was added earliest. Throws QueueException if
// the deletion is not successful.

+dequeue(out queueFront:QueueItemType) throw QueueException
// Retrieves into queueFront and then removes the front of
// a queue. That is, retrieves and removes the item that
// was added earliest. Throws QueueException if the
// deletion is not successful.

+getFront(out queueFront:QueueItemType) throw QueueException
// Retrieves into queueFront the front of a queue. That is,
// retrieves the item that was added earliest. Throws
// QueueException if the retrieval is not successful. The
// queue is unchanged.
```

Figure 7-2 illustrates these operations with a queue of integers. Notice that *enqueue* inserts an item at the back of the queue and that *getFront* looks at the item at the front of the queue, whereas *dequeue* deletes the item at the front of the queue.

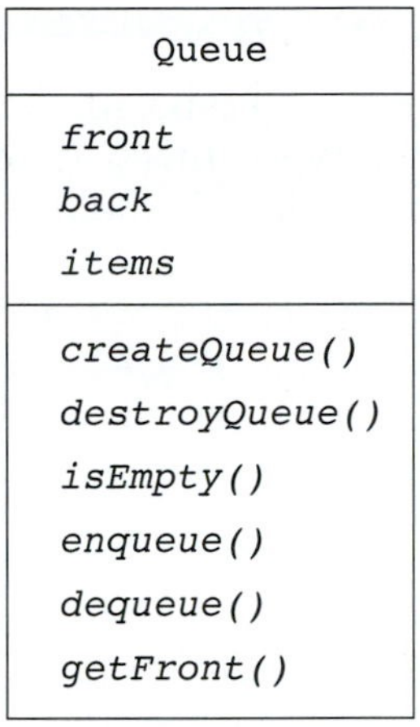

```
┌─────────────────────────────┐
│           Queue             │
├─────────────────────────────┤
│   front                     │
│   back                      │
│   items                     │
├─────────────────────────────┤
│   createQueue()             │
│   destroyQueue()            │
│   isEmpty()                 │
│   enqueue()                 │
│   dequeue()                 │
│   getFront()                │
└─────────────────────────────┘
```

FIGURE 7-1   UML diagram for the class *Queue*

Operation	Queue after operation
	┌──────────── front
aQueue.createQueue()	▼
aQueue.enqueue(5)	5
aQueue.enqueue(2)	5 2
aQueue.enqueue(7)	5 2 7
aQueue.getFront(queueFront)	5 2 7 (queueFront is 5)
aQueue.dequeue(queueFront)	2 7 (queueFront is 2)
aQueue.dequeue(queueFront)	7 (queueFront is 7)

FIGURE 7-2   Some queue operations

7.2 Simple Applications of the ADT Queue

This section presents two simple applications of the ADT queue. The applications use the ADT queue operations independently of their implementations.

Reading a String of Characters

When you enter characters at a keyboard, the system must retain them in the order in which you typed them. It could use a queue for this purpose, as the following pseudocode indicates:

A queue can retain characters in the order in which you type them

```
// read a string of characters from a
// single line of input into a queue
aQueue.createQueue()
while (not end of line)
{   Read a new character ch
    aQueue.enqueue(ch)
}  // end while
```

Once the characters are in a queue, the system can process them as necessary. For example, if you had typed an integer—without any mistakes, but possibly preceded or followed by blanks—the queue would contain digits and possibly blanks. If the digits are 2, 4, and 7, the system could convert them into the decimal value 247 by computing

$$10 * (10 * 2 + 4) + 7$$

The following pseudocode performs this conversion in general:

```
// convert digits in a queue aQueue into a
// decimal integer n

// get first digit, ignoring any leading blanks
do
{ aQueue.dequeue(ch)
} while (ch is blank)

// Assertion: ch contains first digit

// compute n from digits in queue
n = 0
done = false
do
{ n = 10 * n + integer that ch represents
   if (!aQueue.isEmpty())
      aQueue.dequeue(ch)
   else
      done = true
} while (!done and ch is a digit)

// Assertion: n is result
```

Recognizing Palindromes

Recall from Chapter 5 that a palindrome is a string of characters that reads the same from left to right as it does from right to left. In Chapter 6, you learned that you can use a stack to reverse the order of occurrences. You should realize by now that you can use a queue to preserve the order of occurrences. Thus, you can use both a queue and a stack to determine whether a string is a palindrome.

As you traverse the character string from left to right, you can insert each character into both a queue and a stack. Figure 7-3 illustrates the result of this action for the string *abcbd*, which is not a palindrome. You can see that the first character in the string is at the front of the queue and the last character in the string is at the top of the stack. Thus, characters removed from the queue will occur in the order in which they appear in the string; characters removed from the stack will occur in the opposite order.

Knowing this, you can compare the characters at the front of the queue and the top of the stack. If the characters are the same, you can delete them. You repeat this process until either the ADTs become empty, in which case the original string is a palindrome, or the two characters are not the same, in which case the string is not a palindrome.

The following is a pseudocode version of a nonrecursive recognition algorithm for the language of palindromes:

You can use a queue in conjunction with a stack to recognize palindromes

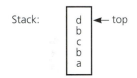

FIGURE 7-3 The results of inserting a string into both a queue and a stack

```
isPal(in str:string):boolean
// Determines whether str is a palindrome.

    // create an empty queue and an empty stack
    aQueue.createQueue()
    aStack.createStack()

    // insert each character of the string into both
    // the queue and the stack
    length = length of str
    for (i = 1 through length)
    {   nextChar = ith character of str
        aQueue.enqueue(nextChar)
        aStack.push(nextChar)
    }  // end for

    // compare the queue characters with the stack
    // characters
    charactersAreEqual = true
    while (aQueue is not empty and charactersAreEqual)
    {   aQueue.getFront(queueFront)
        aStack.getTop(stackTop)
```

```
    if (queueFront equals stackTop)
    {  aQueue.dequeue()
       aStack.pop()
    }
    else
       charactersAreEqual = false
}  // end while

return charactersAreEqual
```

7.3 Implementations of the ADT Queue

Like stacks, queues can have an array-based or a pointer-based implementation. All of the implementations can use the following definition of *QueueException*:

```
#include <stdexcept>
#include <string>
using namespace std;

class QueueException: public logic_error
{
public:
   QueueException(const string & message="")
          : logic_error(message.c_str())
   {}
};  // end QueueException
```

For queues, the pointer-based implementation is a bit more straightforward than the array-based one, so we start with it.

A Pointer-Based Implementation

A pointer-based implementation of a queue could use a linear linked list with two external pointers, one to the front and one to the back, as Figure 7-4a illustrates. Figure 7-4b shows that you can actually get by with a single external pointer—to the back—if you make the linked list circular. Programming Problem 1 at the end of the chapter asks you to consider the details of this second implementation. Here, we will develop the first implementation.

Insertion at the back and deletion from the front are straightforward. Figure 7-5 illustrates the addition of an item to a nonempty queue. Inserting the new node, to which *newPtr* points, at the back of the queue requires three pointer changes: the next pointer in the new node, the next pointer in the current back node, and the external pointer *backPtr*. Figure 7-5 depicts these changes and indicates the

A linear linked list or a circular linked list can represent a queue

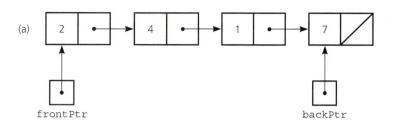

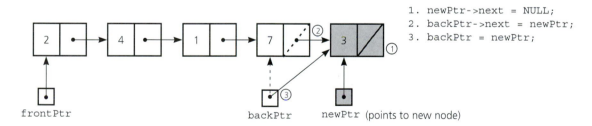

FIGURE 7-4 A pointer-based implementation of a queue: (a) a linear linked list with two external pointers; (b) a circular linked list with one external pointer

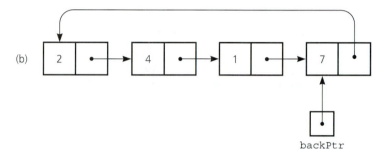

FIGURE 7-5 Inserting an item into a nonempty queue

order in which they can occur. (The dashed lines indicate pointer values before the changes.) The addition of an item to an empty queue is a special case, as Figure 7-6 illustrates.

Deletion from the front of the queue is simpler than insertion at the back. Figure 7-7 illustrates the removal of the front item of a queue that contains more than one item. Notice that you need to change only the external pointer *frontPtr*. Deletion from a queue of one item is a special case that sets the external pointers *backPtr* and *frontPtr* to *NULL*.

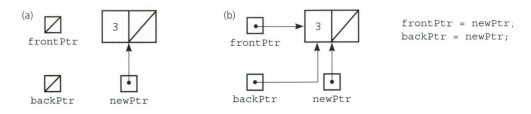

FIGURE 7-6 Inserting an item into an empty queue: (a) before insertion; (b) after insertion

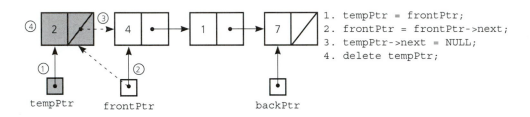

FIGURE 7-7 Deleting an item from a queue of more than one item

The following files contain a pointer-based implementation of the ADT queue. Because the data are stored in dynamically allocated memory, you must write both a copy constructor and a destructor.

```
// **********************************************************
// Header file QueueP.h for the ADT queue.
// Pointer-based implementation.
// **********************************************************
#include "QueueException.h"
typedef desired-type-of-queue-item QueueItemType;

class Queue
{
public:
// constructors and destructor:
   Queue();                          // default constructor
   Queue(const Queue& Q);            // copy constructor
   ~Queue();                         // destructor

// Queue operations:
   bool isEmpty() const;
   // Determines whether the queue is empty.
   // Precondition: None.
   // Postcondition: Returns true if the queue is empty;
   // otherwise returns false.
```

```
    void enqueue(QueueItemType newItem) throw(QueueException);¹
    // Inserts an item at the back of a queue.
    // Precondition: newItem is the item to be inserted.
    // Postcondition: If the insertion is successful, newItem
    // is at the back of the queue.
    // Exception: Throws QueueException if newItem cannot
    // be placed on the queue.

    void dequeue() throw(QueueException);
    // Dequeues the front of a queue.
    // Precondition: None.
    // Postcondition: If the queue is not empty, the item
    // that was added to the queue earliest is deleted.
    // Exception: Throws QueueException if the queue is
    // empty.

    void dequeue(QueueItemType& queueFront)
            throw(QueueException);
    // Retrieves and deletes the front of a queue.
    // Precondition: None.
    // Postcondition: If the queue is not empty, queueFront
    // contains the item that was added to the queue
    // earliest, and the item is deleted.
    // Exception: Throws QueueException if the queue is
    // empty.

    void getFront(QueueItemType& queueFront) const
            throw(QueueException);
    // Retrieves the item at the front of a queue.
    // Precondition: None.
    // Postcondition: If the queue is not empty, queueFront
    // contains the item that was added to the queue
    // earliest.
    // Exception: Throws QueueException if the queue is
    // empty.

private:
    // The queue is implemented as a linked list
    // with one external pointer to the front of the queue
    // and a second external pointer to the back of the
    // queue.
    struct QueueNode
    { QueueItemType  item;
```

---

[1] If *newItem* is an instance of a class, pass it as a constant reference argument instead of a value argument to avoid making an expensive copy.

```
      QueueNode      *next;
   }; // end struct
   QueueNode *backPtr;
   QueueNode *frontPtr;
};  // end class
// End of header file.

// ********************************************************
// Implementation file QueueP.cpp for the ADT queue.
// Pointer-based implementation.
// ********************************************************
#include "QueueP.h"  // header file
#include <cstddef>
#include <cassert>

Queue::Queue() : backPtr(NULL), frontPtr(NULL)
{
}  // end default constructor

Queue::Queue(const Queue& Q)
{  // Implementation left as an exercise (Exercise 6).
}  // end copy constructor

Queue::~Queue()
{
   while (!isEmpty())
      dequeue();
   assert ((backPtr == NULL) && (frontPtr == NULL));
}  // end destructor

bool Queue::isEmpty() const
{
   return backPtr == NULL;
}  // end isEmpty

void Queue::enqueue(QueueItemType newItem)
                              throw(QueueException)
{
   // create a new node
   QueueNode *newPtr = new QueueNode;

   if (newPtr == NULL)  // check allocation
      throw QueueException(
         "QueueException: enqueue cannot allocate memory");
   else
   {  // allocation successful; set data portion of new node
      newPtr->item = newItem;
      newPtr->next = NULL;
```

```cpp
      // insert the new node
   if (isEmpty())
      // insertion into empty queue
      frontPtr = newPtr;
   else
      // insertion into nonempty queue
      backPtr->next = newPtr;

   backPtr = newPtr;  // new node is at back
   }  // end if
}  // end enqueue

void Queue::dequeue() throw(QueueException)
{
   if (isEmpty())
      throw QueueException(
         "QueueException: empty queue, cannot dequeue");
   else
   {  // queue is not empty; remove front
      QueueNode *tempPtr = frontPtr;
      if (frontPtr == backPtr)   // special case?
      {  // yes, one node in queue
         frontPtr = NULL;
         backPtr = NULL;
      }
      else
         frontPtr = frontPtr->next;

      tempPtr->next = NULL;  // defensive strategy
      delete tempPtr;
   } // end if
}  // end dequeue

void Queue::dequeue(QueueItemType& queueFront)
                              throw(QueueException)
{
   if (isEmpty())
      throw QueueException(
         "QueueException: empty queue, cannot dequeue");
   else
   {  // queue is not empty; retrieve front
      queueFront = frontPtr->item;
      dequeue();  // delete front
   } // end if
}   // end dequeue

void Queue::getFront(QueueItemType& queueFront) const
                              throw(QueueException)
{
   if (isEmpty())
```

```
        throw QueueException(
            "QueueException: empty queue, cannot getFront");
     else
        // queue is not empty; retrieve front
        queueFront = frontPtr->item;
}  // end getFront
// End of implementation file.
```

A program that uses this implementation could begin as follows:

```
#include "QueueP.h"

int main()
{
   Queue aQueue;

   aQueue.enqueue(15);
   . . .
```

An Array-Based Implementation

For applications in which a fixed-sized queue does not present a problem, you can use an array to represent a queue. As Figure 7-8a illustrates, a naive array-based implementation of a queue might include the following definitions:

A naive array-based implementation of a queue

```
const int MAX_QUEUE = maximum-size-of-queue;
typedef desired-type-of-queue-item QueueItemType;

QueueItemType items[MAX_QUEUE];
int           front;
int           back;
```

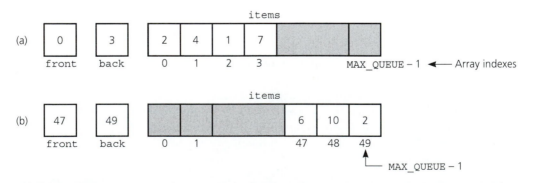

FIGURE 7-8   (a) A naive array-based implementation of a queue; (b) rightward drift can cause the queue to appear full

Here *front* and *back* are the indexes of the front and back items, respectively, in the queue. Initially, *front* is 0 and *back* is −1. To insert a new item into the queue, you increment *back* and place the item in *items[back]*. To delete an item, you simply increment *front*. The queue is empty whenever *back* is less than *front*. The queue is full when *back* equals *MAX_QUEUE* − 1.

The problem with this strategy is rightward drift—that is, after a sequence of additions and removals, the items in the queue will drift toward the end of the array, and *back* could equal *MAX_QUEUE* − 1 even when the queue contains only a few items. Figure 7-8b illustrates this situation.

One possible solution to this problem is to shift array elements to the left, either after each deletion or whenever *back* equals *MAX_QUEUE* − 1. This solution guarantees that the queue can always contain up to *MAX_QUEUE* items. Shifting is not really satisfactory, however, as it would dominate the cost of the implementation.

A much more elegant solution is possible by viewing the array as circular, as Figure 7-9 illustrates. You advance the queue indexes *front* (to delete an item) and *back* (to insert an item) by moving them clockwise around the array. Figure 7-10 illustrates the effect of a sequence of three queue operations on *front*, *back*, and the array. When either *front* or *back* advances past *MAX_QUEUE* − 1, it wraps around to 0. This wrap-around eliminates the problem of rightward drift, which occurred in the previous implementation, because here the circular array has no end.

The only difficulty with this scheme involves detecting the queue-empty and queue-full conditions. It seems reasonable to select as the queue-empty condition

> *front* is *one slot ahead* of *back*

since this appears to indicate that *front* "passes" *back* when the queue becomes empty, as Figure 7-11a depicts. However, it is also possible that this condition signals a full queue: Because the queue is circular, *back* might in fact "catch up" with *front* as the queue becomes full; Figure 7-11b illustrates this situation.

Rightward drift can cause a queue-full condition even though the queue contains few entries

Shifting elements to compensate for rightward drift is expensive

A circular array eliminates rightward drift

front and back cannot be used to distinguish between queue-full and queue-empty conditions

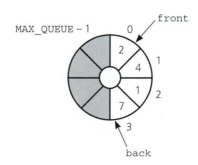

FIGURE 7-9   A circular implementation of a queue

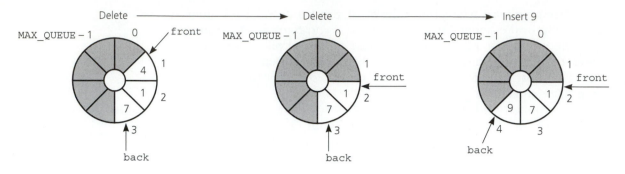

The effect of some operations on the queue in Figure 7-9

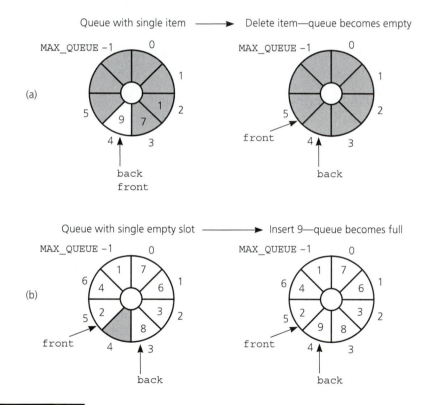

(a) *front* passes *back* when the queue becomes empty;
(b) *back* catches up to *front* when the queue becomes full

Obviously, you need a way to distinguish between the two situations. One way is to keep a count of the number of items in the queue. Before inserting an item into the queue, you check to see if the count is equal to *MAX_QUEUE*: if it is, the queue is full. Before deleting an item from the queue, you check to see if the count is equal to zero; if it is, the queue is empty.

By counting queue items, you can detect queue-full and queue-empty conditions

To initialize the queue, you set *front* to 0, *back* to *MAX_QUEUE* − 1, and *count* to 0. You obtain the wraparound effect of a circular queue by using modulo arithmetic (that is, the C++ % operator) when incrementing *front* and *back*. For example, you can insert *newItem* into the queue by using the statements

Initialize *front*, *back*, and *count*

```
back = (back+1) % MAX_QUEUE;
items[back] = newItem;
++count;
```

Inserting into a queue

Notice that if *back* equaled *MAX_QUEUE* − 1 before the insertion of *newItem*, the first statement, *back = (back+1) % MAX_QUEUE*, would have the effect of wrapping *back* around to location 0.

Similarly, you can delete the item at the front of the queue by using the statements

```
front = (front+1) % MAX_QUEUE;
--count;
```

Deleting from a queue

The following C++ files contain an array-based implementation of the ADT queue that uses a circular array as just described. Since the data are stored in statically allocated memory, the compiler-generated destructor and copy constructor are sufficient.[2] Preconditions and postconditions have been omitted to save space but are the same as those given for the previous pointer-based implementation.

```
// ***********************************************************
// Header file QueueA.h for the ADT queue.
// Array-based implementation.
// ***********************************************************
#include "QueueException.h"
const int MAX_QUEUE = maximum-size-of-queue;
typedef desired-type-of-queue-item QueueItemType;

class Queue
{
public:
// constructors and destructor:
   Queue();  // default constructor
   // copy constructor and destructor are
   // supplied by the compiler

// Queue operations:
   bool isEmpty() const;
```

---

[2] If you use a dynamically allocated array, you must provide a destructor and copy constructor.

```
    void enqueue(QueueItemType newItem)³
          throw(QueueException);
    void dequeue() throw(QueueException);
    void dequeue(QueueItemType& queueFront)
          throw(QueueException);
    void getFront(QueueItemType& queueFront) const
          throw(QueueException);

private:
    QueueItemType items[MAX_QUEUE];
    int           front;
    int           back;
    int           count;
};  // end Queue class
// End of header file.


// ********************************************************
// Implementation file QueueA.cpp for the ADT queue.
// Circular array-based implementation.
// The array has indexes to the front and back of the
// queue. A counter tracks the number of items currently
// in the queue.
// ********************************************************

#include "QueueA.h"  // header file

Queue::Queue():front(0), back(MAX_QUEUE-1), count(0)
{
}  // end default constructor

bool Queue::isEmpty() const
{
    return count == 0;
}  // end isEmpty

void Queue::enqueue(QueueItemType newItem) throw(QueueException)
{
    if (count == MAX_QUEUE)
        throw QueueException(
             "QueueException: queue full on enqueue");
    else
    {  // queue is not full; insert item
        back = (back+1) % MAX_QUEUE;
```

---

[3] If the items in the queue are instances of another class, copying them can be expensive. You can avoid making a copy of *newItem* by passing it as a constant reference argument instead of a value argument.

```
      items[back] = newItem;
      ++count;
   }  // end if
}  // end enqueue

void Queue::dequeue() throw(QueueException)
{
   if (isEmpty())
      throw QueueException(
             "QueueException: empty queue, cannot dequeue");
   else
   {  // queue is not empty; remove front
      front = (front+1) % MAX_QUEUE;
      --count;
   }  // end if
}  // end dequeue

void Queue::dequeue(QueueItemType& queueFront)
                                 throw(QueueException)
{
   if (isEmpty())
      throw QueueException(
          "QueueException: empty queue, cannot dequeue");
   else
   {  // queue is not empty; retrieve and remove front
      queueFront = items[front];
      front = (front+1) % MAX_QUEUE;
      --count;
   }  // end if
}  // end dequeue

void Queue::getFront(QueueItemType& queueFront) const
                                 throw(QueueException)
{
   if (isEmpty())
      throw QueueException(
          "QueueException: empty queue, cannot getFront");
   else
      // queue is not empty; retrieve front
      queueFront = items[front];
}  // end getFront
// End of implementation file.
```

Several commonly used variations of this implementation do not require a count of the number of items in the queue. One approach uses a flag *isFull* to distinguish between the full and empty conditions. The expense of maintaining an *isFull* flag is about the same as that of maintaining a counter, however. A faster implementation declares *MAX_QUEUE* + 1 locations for the array *items*, but uses only

An *isFull* flag can replace the counter

MAX_QUEUE of them for queue items. You sacrifice one array location and make *front* the index of the location before the front of the queue. As Figure 7-12 illustrates, the queue is full if

$$front \text{ equals } (back+1) \text{ \% } (MAX\_QUEUE+1)$$

but the queue is empty if

$$front \text{ equals } back$$

Using an extra array location is more time-efficient

This implementation does not have the overhead of maintaining a counter or flag, and so is more efficient time-wise. For the standard data types, the implementation requires the same space as either the counter or the flag implementation. However, for more complex data, the memory wasted on an extra array location can be significant. Programming Problems 3 and 4 discuss these two alternate implementations further.

An Implementation That Uses the ADT List

You can use the ADT list to represent the items in a queue, as Figure 7-13 illustrates. If the item in position 1 of a list represents the front of the queue,

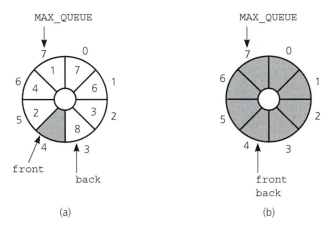

(a)   (b)

FIGURE 7-12   A more efficient circular implementation: (a) a full queue; (b) an empty queue

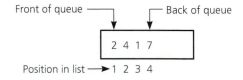

FIGURE 7-13   An implementation that uses the ADT list

you can implement the operation *dequeue()* as the list operation *remove(1)* and the operation *getFront(queueFront)* as the list operation *retrieve(1, queueFront)*. Similarly, if you let the item at the end of the list represent the back of the queue, you can implement the operation *enqueue(newItem)* as the list operation *insert(getLength()+1, newItem)*.

Recall that Chapters 3 and 4 presented the ADT list as the class *List*. (See, for example, pages 189–190.) The following class for the ADT queue uses an instance of *List* to represent the queue. Preconditions and postconditions in the header file are omitted to save space but are the same as those given earlier in this chapter.

```cpp
// *********************************************************
// Header file QueueL.h for the ADT queue.
// ADT list implementation.
// *********************************************************
#include "ListP.h"  //  ADT list operations
#include "QueueException.h"
typedef ListItemType QueueItemType;

class Queue
{
public:
// constructors and destructor:
   Queue();                      // default constructor
   Queue(const Queue& Q);        // copy constructor
   ~Queue();                     // destructor

// Queue operations:
   bool isEmpty() const;
   void enqueue(QueueItemType newItem)
         throw(QueueException);
   void dequeue() throw(QueueException);
   void dequeue(QueueItemType& queueFront)
         throw(QueueException);
   void getFront(QueueItemType& queueFront) const
         throw(QueueException);

private:
   List aList;  // list of queue items
};  // end queue class
// End of header file.

// *********************************************************
// Implementation file QueueL.cpp for the ADT queue.
// ADT list implementation.
// *********************************************************
#include "QueueL.h"  // header file
```

```
Queue::Queue()
{
}  // end default constructor

Queue::Queue(const Queue& Q): aList(Q.aList)
{
}  // end copy constructor

Queue::~Queue()
{
}  // end destructor

bool Queue::isEmpty() const
{
   return (aList.getLength() == 0);
}  // end isEmpty

void Queue::enqueue(QueueItemType newItem)
                                throw(QueueException)
{
   try
   {
     aList.insert(aList.getLength()+1, newItem);
   } // end try
   catch (ListException e)
   {
     throw QueueException(
        "QueueException: cannot enqueue item");
   } // end catch
}  // end enqueue

void Queue::dequeue() throw(QueueException)
{
   if (aList.isEmpty())
     throw QueueException(
        "QueueException: empty queue, cannot dequeue");
   else
     aList.remove(1);
}  // end dequeue

void Queue::dequeue(QueueItemType& queueFront)
                                throw(QueueException)
{
   if (aList.isEmpty())
     throw QueueException(
        "QueueException: empty queue, cannot dequeue");
   else
   {
     aList.retrieve(1, queueFront);
     aList.remove(1);
```

```
      } // end if
  }  // end dequeue

  void Queue::getFront(QueueItemType& queueFront) const
                              throw(QueueException)
  {
     if (aList.isEmpty())
        throw QueueException(
           "QueueException: empty queue, cannot getFront");
     else
        aList.retrieve(1, queueFront);
  }  // end getFront
  // End of implementation file.
```

As was true for the analogous implementation of the ADT stack in Chapter 6, implementing the queue is simple once you have implemented the ADT list. Exercise 9 at the end of this chapter asks you to consider the efficiency of this implementation.

The Standard Template Library Class *queue*

The Standard Template Library (STL) provides a container class *queue* similar to the class *Queue* presented in this chapter. Like the class *Queue*, the STL class *queue* provides operations for adding and removing items from the front of the queue, but it names them *push* and *pop*, just like the corresponding stack operations. This is a poor choice of names, since the locations where items are added and deleted in stacks and queues differ.

The STL class *queue*, like our class *Queue*, provides a function that retrieves the first item in the queue. In the STL, the function is *front*; in our class it is *getFront*. Two functions in the STL class not found in our version of a queue are *back*, which returns a reference to the last item placed in the queue, and *size*, which returns the number of items in the queue. Here is a slightly simplified specification for the STL *queue* container:

```
template <class T, class Container = deque <T> >
class queue
{
public:
   explicit queue(const Container& cnt = Container());
   // Default constructor, initializes an empty queue.
   // Precondition: None.
   // Postcondition: An empty queue exists.

   bool empty() const;
   // Determines if the queue is empty.
   // Precondition: None.
   // Postcondition: Returns true if the queue is empty,
   // otherwise returns false.
```

```
size_type size() const;
// Determines the size of the queue. size_type is
// an integral type.
// Precondition: None.
// Postcondition: Returns the number of items that
// are currently in the queue.

T &front();
// Returns a reference to the first item in the queue.
// Precondition: None.
// Postcondition: The item is not removed from the queue.

T &back();
// Returns a reference to the last item in the queue.
// Precondition: None.
// Postcondition: The item is not removed from the queue.

void pop();
// Removes the first item in the queue.
// Precondition: None.
// Postcondition: The item at the front of the queue is
// removed.

void push(const T& x);
// Inserts an item at the back of the queue.
// Precondition: None.
// Postcondition: The item x is at the back of the queue.

} // end STL queue
```

The STL class *queue*, like the STL class *stack*, is implemented by using a more basic container type. Classes whose implementations use other classes are called **adapter containers**. An adapter container provides a restricted interface to another container used in its implementation.

Adapter containers are based upon basic container classes

In the STL, there are three basic container types that are used by adapter containers: *vector*, *list*, and *deque*. We have already seen the *list* class in Chapter 4. The *vector* class supports a dynamic array. The *deque* type supports a double-ended queue, which is a slight variation of the ADT queue. In this variation, items can be added to or deleted from either end. These three basic container classes are typically implemented directly, since it is not efficient for one of them to be built on another.

The container classes *stack* and *queue*, however, do have simple and efficient implementations that are based on one of the three basic container types. For example, the implementation of the STL *queue* class could use the STL *list* class. You cannot use the basic container type *vector* as the basis for the implementation of a queue, since it does not provide some necessary operations. However, you can base the *stack* class on any of the three basic container classes.

When you declare an instance of an STL *stack* or *queue* and do not provide a container class in the declaration, the default basic container class *deque* is used. For example, the declaration

```
queue<int> myQueue;
```

creates an empty queue *myQueue* that is implemented by using a *deque*. Alternatively, you can base the queue on a *list* by using the following declaration:

```
queue<int, list<int> > myQueue;
```

This creates an empty queue *myQueue* that is implemented by using a *list*.

You can provide an initial set of values for a queue or stack by providing an existing container in the constructor. The following program creates a queue and a stack from an existing list:

```
#include <iostream>
#include <list>
#include <queue>
#include <stack>
using namespace std;

int main()
{
   list<int> myList;   // create an empty list
   list<int>::iterator i = myList.begin();

   for (int j = 1; j < 5; j++)
   {  i = myList.insert(i, j);
      i++;
   }  // end for



   cout << "myList:  ";
   i = myList.begin();
   while (i != myList.end())
   {  cout << *i << " ";
      i++;
   }  // end while
   cout << endl;

   // assumes the front of the list is the front of the
   // queue
   queue<int, list<int> > myQueue(myList);

   // assumes the back of the list is the top of the stack
   stack<int, list<int> > myStack(myList);
```

```
    cout << "myQueue: ";
    while (!myQueue.empty())
    {   cout << myQueue.front() << " ";
        myQueue.pop();
    }   // end while
    cout << endl;

    cout << "myStack: ";
    while (!myStack.empty())
    {   cout << myStack.top() << " ";
        myStack.pop();
    }   // end while
    cout << endl;
    return 0;
}   // end main
```

This program produces the following output:

```
    myList:  1 2 3 4
    myQueue: 1 2 3 4
    myStack: 4 3 2 1
```

As you can see, the queue assumes that the front of the list is also the front of the queue, whereas the stack assumes that the back of the list is the top of the stack.

Comparing Implementations

We have suggested implementations of the ADT queue that use either a linear linked list, a circular linked list, an array, a circular array, or the ADT list to represent the items in a queue. You have seen the details of three of these implementations. All of our implementations of the ADT queue are ultimately either array based or pointer based.

The reasons for making the choice between array-based and pointer-based implementations are the same as those discussed in earlier chapters. The discussion here is similar to the one in Chapter 6 in the section "Comparing Implementations." We repeat the highlights here in the context of queues.

Fixed size versus dynamic size

An implementation based on a statically allocated array prevents the *enqueue* operation from adding an item to the queue if the array is full. If this restriction is not acceptable, you must use either a dynamically allocated array or a pointer-based implementation.

Reuse of an already implemented class saves you time

Suppose that you decide to use a pointer-based implementation. Should you choose the implementation that uses a linked list, or should you choose a pointer-based implementation of the ADT list? Because a linked list actually represents the items on the ADT list, using the ADT list to represent a queue is not as efficient as using a linked list directly. However, the ADT list approach is much simpler to write.

If you decide to use a linked list instead of the ADT list to represent the queue, should you use a linear linked list or a circular linked list? We leave this question for you to answer in Programming Problem 1.

7.4 A Summary of Position-Oriented ADTs

So far, we have seen three abstract data types—the list, the stack, and the queue—that have a common theme: All of their operations are defined in terms of the positions of their data items. Stacks and queues greatly restrict the positions that their operations can affect; only their end positions can be accessed. The list removes this restriction.

Stacks are really quite similar to queues. This similarity becomes apparent if you pair off their operations, as follows:

- *createStack* and *createQueue*. These operations create an empty ADT of the appropriate type.

- **Stack** *isEmpty* **and queue** *isEmpty*. These operations determine whether any items exist in the ADT.

- *push* **and** *enqueue*. These operations insert a new item into one end (the top and back, respectively) of the ADT.

- *pop* **and** *dequeue*. The *pop* operation deletes the most recent item, which is at the top of the stack, and *dequeue* deletes the first item, which is at the front of the queue.

- **Stack** *getTop* **and queue** *getFront*. Stack *getTop* retrieves the most recent item, which is at the top of the stack, and queue *get-Front* retrieves the first item, which is at the front of the queue.

The ADT list, introduced in Chapter 3, allows you to insert into, delete from, and inspect the item at any position of the list. Thus, it has the most flexible operations of the three **position-oriented ADTs**. You can view the list operations as general versions of the stack and queue operations, as follows:

- *getLength*. If you remove the restriction that stack and queue versions of *isEmpty* can tell only when an item is present, you obtain an operation that can count the number of items that are present.

- *insert*. If you remove the restriction that *push* and *enqueue* can insert new items into only one position, you obtain an operation that can insert a new item into any position of the list.

- *remove*. If you remove the restriction that *pop* and *dequeue* can delete items from only one position, you obtain an operation that can delete an item from any position of the list.

Operations for the ADTs list, stack, and queue reference the position of items

A comparison of stack and queue operations

ADT list operations generalize stack and queue operations

- *retrieve.* If you remove the restriction that stack `getTop` and queue `getFront` can retrieve items from only one position, you obtain an operation that can retrieve the item from any position of the list.

Because each of these three ADTs defines its operations in terms of an item's position in the ADT, this book has presented implementations for them that can provide easy access to specified positions. For example, the stack implementations allow the first position (top) to be accessed quickly, while the queue implementations allow the first position (front) and the last position (back) to be accessed quickly.

7.5 Application: Simulation

Simulation models the behavior of systems

Simulation—a major application area for computers—is a technique for modeling the behavior of both natural and human-made systems. Generally, the goal of a simulation is to generate statistics that summarize the performance of an existing system or to predict the performance of a proposed system. In this section we will consider a simple example that illustrates one important type of simulation.

Consider the following problem. Ms. Simpson, president of the First City Bank of Springfield, has heard her customers complain about how long they have to wait for service. Because she fears that they may move their accounts to another bank, she is considering whether to hire a second teller.

Before Ms. Simpson hires another teller, she would like an approximation of the average time that a customer has to wait for service from First City's only teller. How can Ms. Simpson obtain this information? She could stand with a stopwatch in the bank's lobby all day, but she does not find this prospect particularly exciting. Besides, she would like to use a method that also allows her to predict how much improvement she could expect if the bank hired a given number of additional tellers. She certainly does not want to hire the tellers on a trial basis and monitor the bank's performance before making a final decision.

Ms. Simpson concludes that the best way to obtain the information she wants is to use a computer model to simulate the behavior of her bank. The first step in simulating a system such as a bank is to construct a mathematical model that captures the relevant information about the system. For example, how many tellers does the bank employ? How often do customers arrive? If the model accurately describes the real-world system, a simulation can derive accurate predictions about the system's overall performance. For example, a simulation could predict the average time a customer has to wait before receiving service. A simulation can also evaluate proposed changes to the real-world system. For example, it could predict the effect of hiring more tellers in the bank. A large decrease in the time predicted for the average wait of a customer might justify the cost of hiring additional tellers.

Central to a simulation is the concept of simulated time. Envision a stopwatch that measures time elapsed during a simulation. For example, suppose that the model of the bank specifies only one teller. At time 0, which is the start of the banking day, the simulated system would be in its initial state with no customers. As the simulation runs, the stopwatch ticks away units of time—perhaps minutes—and certain events occur. At time 12 the bank's first customer arrives. Since there is no line, the customer goes directly to the teller and begins her transaction. At time 20, a second customer arrives. Because the first customer has not yet completed her transaction, the second customer must wait in line. At time 38, the first customer completes her transaction and the second customer can begin his. Figure 7-14 illustrates these four times in the simulation.

Simulated time

To gather the information you need, you run this simulation for a specified period of simulated time. During the course of the run, you need to keep track of certain statistics, such as the average time a customer has to wait for service. Notice that in the small example of Figure 7-14, the first customer had to wait 0 minutes to begin a transaction and the second customer had to wait 18 minutes to begin a transaction—an average wait of 9 minutes.

One point not addressed in the previous discussion is how to determine when certain events occur. For example, why did we say that the first customer arrived at time 12 and the second at time 20? After studying real-world systems like our bank, mathematicians learned to model events such as the arrival of people by using techniques from probability theory. This statistical information is incorporated into the mathematical model of the system and is used to generate events in a way that reflects the real world. The simulation uses these events and is thus called an **event-driven simulation**. Note that the goal is to reflect long-term average behavior of the system rather than to predict occurrences of specific events. This goal is sufficient for the needs of the simulation.

Although the techniques for generating events to reflect the real world are interesting and important, they require a good deal of mathematical sophistication. Therefore, simply assume that you already have a list of events available for your use. In particular, for the bank problem, assume that a file contains the time of each customer's arrival—an arrival event—and the duration of that customer's transaction once the customer reaches the teller. For example, the data

20	5
22	4
23	2
30	3

Sample arrival and transaction times

indicates that the first customer arrives 20 minutes into the simulation and that the transaction—once begun—requires 5 minutes; the second customer arrives 22 minutes into the simulation and the transaction requires 4 minutes; and so on. Assume that the input file is ordered by arrival time.

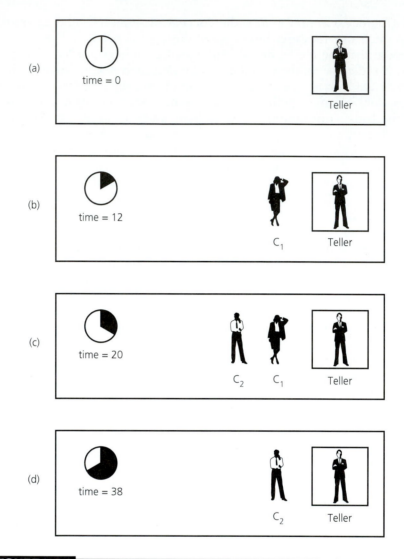

FIGURE 7-14   A bank line at time (a) 0; (b) 12; (c) 20; (d) 38

Notice that the file does not contain departure events; the data does not specify when a customer will complete the transaction and leave. Instead, the simulation must determine when departures occur. By using the arrival time and the transaction length, the simulation can easily determine the time at which a customer departs. To see how to make this determination, you can conduct a simulation by hand with the previous data as follows:

Time	Event
20	Customer 1 enters bank and begins transaction.
22	Customer 2 enters bank and stands at end of line
23	Customer 3 enters bank and stands at end of line
25	Customer 1 departs; customer 2 begins transaction
29	Customer 2 departs; customer 3 begins transaction
30	Customer 4 enters bank and stands at end of line
31	Customer 3 departs; customer 4 begins transaction
34	Customer 4 departs

The results of a simulation

A customer's wait time is the elapsed time between arrival in the bank and the start of the transaction. The average of this wait time over all the customers is the statistic that you want to obtain.

To summarize, this simulation is concerned with two types of events:

- **Arrival events.** These events indicate the arrival at the bank of a new customer. The input file specifies the times at which the arrival events occur. As such, they are **external events**. When a customer arrives at the bank, one of two things happens. If the teller is idle when the customer arrives, the customer enters the line and begins the transaction immediately. If the teller is busy, the new customer must stand at the end of the line and wait for service.

- **Departure events.** These events indicate the departure from the bank of a customer who has completed a transaction. The simulation determines the times at which the departure events occur. As such, they are **internal events**. When a customer completes the transaction, he or she departs and the next person in line—if there is one—begins a transaction.

The main tasks of an algorithm that performs the simulation are to determine the times at which the events occur and to process the events when they do occur. The algorithm is stated at a high level as follows:

```
// initialize
currentTime = 0
Initialize the line to "no customers"

while (currentTime ≤ time of the final event)
{  if (an arrival event occurs at time currentTime)
      Process the arrival event

   if (a departure event occurs at time currentTime)
      Process the departure event
```

A first attempt at a simulation algorithm

```
// when an arrival event and departure event
// occur at the same time, arbitrarily process
// the arrival event first

++currentTime
} // end while
```

But do you really want to increment *currentTime* by 1? You would for a **time-driven simulation**, where you would determine arrival and departure times at random and compare those times to *currentTime*. In such a case, you would increment *currentTime* by 1 to simulate the ticking of a clock. Recall, however, that this simulation is event driven, so you have a file of arrival times and transaction times. Because you are interested only in those times at which arrival and departure events occur and because no action is required between events, you can advance *currentTime* from the time of one event directly to the time of the next.

Thus, you can revise the pseudocode solution as follows:

A time-driven simulation simulates the ticking of a clock

An event-driven simulation considers only times of certain events, in this case, arrivals and departures

First revision of the simulation algorithm

```
// Initialize the line to "no customers"

while (events remain to be processed)
{   currentTime = time of next event

    if (event is an arrival event)
        Process the arrival event
    else
        Process the departure event

    // when an arrival event and departure event
    // occur at the same time, arbitrarily process
    // the arrival event first
} // end while
```

You must determine the time of the next arrival or departure event so that you can implement the statement

```
        currentTime = time of next event
```

An event list contains all future events

To make this determination, you must maintain an **event list**. An event list contains all arrival and departure events that will occur but have not occurred yet. The times of the events in the event list are in ascending order, and thus the next event to be processed is always at the beginning of the list. The algorithm simply gets the event from the beginning of the list, advances to the time specified, and processes the event. The difficulty, then, lies in successfully managing the event list.

Since each arrival event generates exactly one departure event, you might think that you should read the entire input file and create an event list of all arrival and departure events sorted by time. Self-Test

Exercise 5 asks you to explain why this approach is impractical. As you will see, you can instead manage the event list for this particular problem so that it always contains at most one event of each kind.

Recall that the arrival events are specified in the input file in ascending time order. You thus never need to worry about an arrival event until you have processed all the arrival events that precede it in the file. You simply keep the earliest unprocessed arrival event in the event list. When you eventually process this event—that is, when it is time for this customer to arrive—you replace it in the event list with the next unprocessed arrival event, which is the next item in the input file.

Similarly, you need to place only the next departure event to occur on the event list. But how can you determine the times for the departure events? Observe that the next departure event always corresponds to the customer that the teller is currently serving. As soon as a customer begins service, the time of his or her departure is simply

time of next departure = time service begins + length of transaction

Recall that the length of the customer's transaction is in the input file, along with the arrival time. Thus, as soon as a customer begins service, you place a departure event corresponding to this customer in the event list. Figure 7-15 illustrates a typical instance of the event list for this simulation.

Now consider how you can process an event when it is time for the event to occur. You must perform two general types of actions:

- **Update the line:** Add or remove customers.

- **Update the event list:** Add or remove events.

As customers arrive, they go to the back of the line. The current customer, who is at the front of the line, is being served, and it is this customer that you remove from the system next. It is thus natural to use a queue to represent the line of customers in the bank. For this problem, the only information that you must store in the queue about each customer is the time of arrival and the length of the transaction. The event

> This event list contains at most one arrival event and one departure event

> Two tasks are required to process each event

> A queue represents the customers in line

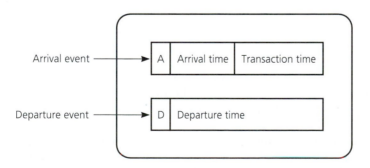

FIGURE 7-15 A typical instance of the event list

The event list is not a queue

list, since it is sorted by time, is not a queue. We will examine it in more detail shortly.

To summarize, you process an event as follows:

The algorithm for arrival events

TO PROCESS AN ARRIVAL EVENT

```
// Update the event list
Delete the arrival event for customer C from
  the event list

if (new customer C begins transaction immediately)
   Insert a departure event for customer C into the
      event list (time of event = current time +
      transaction length)

if (not at the end of the input file)
   Read a new arrival event and add it to the event list
      (time of event = time specified in file)
```

A new customer always enters the queue and is served while at the queue's front

Because a customer is served while at the front of the queue, a new customer always enters the queue, even if the queue is empty. You then delete the arrival event for the new customer from the event list. If the new customer is served immediately, you insert a departure event into the event list. Finally, you read a new arrival event into the event list. This arrival event can occur either before or after the departure event.

The algorithm for departure events

TO PROCESS A DEPARTURE EVENT

```
// Update the line
Delete the customer at the front of the queue
if (the queue is not empty)
   The current front customer begins transaction

// Update the event list
Delete the departure event from the event list
if (the queue is not empty)
   Insert into the event list the departure event for
      the customer now at the front of the queue
      (time of event = current time + transaction length)
```

After processing the departure event, you do not read another arrival event from the file. Assuming that the file has not been read completely, the event list will contain an arrival event whose time is earlier than any arrival still in the input file.

Examining the event list more closely will help explain the workings of the algorithm. There is no typical form that an event list takes. For this simulation, however, the event list has four possible configurations:

- Initially, the event list contains an arrival event A after you read the first arrival event from the input file but before you process it:

  Event list: A (initial state)

- Generally, the event list for this simulation contains exactly two events: one arrival event A and one departure event D. Either the departure event is first or the arrival event is first as follows:

  Event list: $D\ A$ (general case—next event is a departure)

  or

  Event list: $A\ D$ (general case—next event is an arrival)

- If the departure event is first and that event leaves the teller's line empty, a new departure event does not replace the just-processed event. Thus, in this case, the event list appears as

  Event list: A (a departure leaves the teller's line empty)

  Notice that this instance of the event list is the same as its initial state.

- If the arrival event is first and if, after it is processed, you are at the end of the input file, the event list contains only a departure event:

  Event list: D (the input has been exhausted)

Four configurations of the event list for this simulation

Other situations result in an event list that has one of the previous four configurations.

You insert new events either at the beginning of the event list or at the end, depending on the relative times of the new event and the event currently in the event list. For example, suppose that the event list contains only an arrival event A and that another customer is now at the front of the line and beginning a transaction. You need to generate a departure event D for this customer. If the customer's departure time is before the time of the arrival event A, you must insert the departure event D before the event A in the event list. However, if the departure time is after the time of the arrival event, you must insert the departure event D after the arrival event A. In the case of a tie, you need a rule to determine which event should take precedence. In this solution we arbitrarily choose to place the departure event after the arrival event.

You can now combine and refine the pieces of the solution into an algorithm that performs the simulation by using the ADT queue operations to manage the bank line:

```
+simulate()
// Performs the simulation.

    Create an empty queue bankQueue to represent the
        bank line
    Create an empty event list eventList
```

The final pseudocode for the event-driven simulation

```
    Get the first arrival event from the input file
    Place the arrival event in eventList

    while (eventList is not empty)
    {  newEvent = the first event in eventList

       if (newEvent is an arrival event)
          processArrival(newEvent, arrivalFile,
                         eventList, bankQueue)
       else
          processDeparture(newEvent, eventList, bankQueue)
    }  // end while

+processArrival(in arrivalEvent:Event,
               in arrivalFile:File,
               inout anEventList:EventList,
               inout bankQueue:Queue)
// Processes an arrival event.

    atFront = bankQueue.isEmpty()  // present queue status

    // update the bankQueue by inserting the customer, as
    // described in arrivalEvent, into the queue
    bankQueue.enqueue(arrivalEvent)

    // update the event list
    Delete arrivalEvent from anEventList

    if (atFront)
    {  // the line was empty, so new customer is at front
       // of line and begins transaction immediately
       Insert into anEventList a departure event that
         corresponds to the new customer and has
         currentTime = currentTime + transaction length
    }  // end if

    if (not at end of input file)
    {  Get the next arrival event from arrivalFile
       Add the event -- with time as specified in the input
         file -- to anEventList
    }  // end if

+processDeparture(in departureEvent:Event,
                 inout anEventList:EventList,
                 inout bankQueue:Queue)
// Processes a departure event.
```

```
// update the line by deleting the front customer
bankQueue.dequeue()

// update the event list
Delete departureEvent from anEventList
if (!bankQueue.isEmpty())
{  // customer at front of line begins transaction
   Insert into anEventList a departure event that
      corresponds to the customer now at the front of the
      line and has currentTime = currentTime +
      transaction length
}  // end if
```

Figure 7-16 begins a trace of this algorithm for the data on page 365 and shows the changes to the queue and event list. Self-Test Exercise 6 at the end of this chapter asks you to complete the trace.

Time	Action	bankQueue (front to back)	anEventList (beginning to end)
0	Read file, place event in `anEventList`	*(empty)*	A 20 5
20	Update `anEventList` and `bankQueue`: Customer 1 enters bank	20 5	*(empty)*
	Customer 1 begins transaction, create departure event	20 5	D 25
	Read file, place event in `anEventList`	20 5	A 22 4 D 25
22	Update `anEventList` and `bankQueue`: Customer 2 enters bank	20 5 22 4	D 25
	Read file, place event in `anEventList`	20 5 22 4	A 23 2 D 25
23	Update `anEventList` and `bankQueue`: Customer 3 enters bank	20 5 22 4 23 2	D 25
	Read file, place event in `anEventList`	20 5 22 4 23 2	D 25 A 30 3
25	Update `anEventList` and `bankQueue`: Customer 1 departs	22 4 23 2	A 30 3
	Customer 2 begins transaction, create departure event	22 4 23 2	D 29 A 30 3

Self-Test Exercise 6 asks you to complete this trace.

FIGURE 7-16   A partial trace of the bank simulation algorithm for the data

20 5
22 4
23 2
30 3

The event list is, in fact, an ADT. By examining the previous pseudocode, you can see that this ADT must include at least the following operations:

ADT event list operations

```
+createEventList()
// Creates an empty event list.

+destroyEventList()
// Destroys an event list.

+isEmpty():boolean {query}
// Determines whether an event list is empty.

+insert(in anEvent:Event)
// Inserts anEvent into the event list so that events
// are ordered by time. If an arrival event and a
// departure event have the same time, the arrival
// event precedes the departure event.

+delete()
// Deletes the first event from an event list.

+retrieve(out anEvent:Event)
// Sets anEvent to the first event in an event list.
```

Programming Problem 8 at the end of this chapter asks you to complete the implementation of this simulation.

Summary

1. The definition of the queue operations gives the ADT queue first-in, first-out (FIFO) behavior.

2. The insertion and deletion operations for a queue require efficient access to both ends of the queue. Therefore, a pointer-based implementation of a queue uses either a circular linked list or a linear linked list that has both a head pointer and a tail pointer.

3. An array-based implementation of a queue is prone to rightward drift. This phenomenon can make a queue look full when it really is not. Shifting the items in the array is one way to compensate for rightward drift. A more efficient solution uses a circular array.

4. If you use a circular array to implement a queue, you must be able to distinguish between the queue-full and queue-empty conditions. You can make this distinction by counting the number of items in the queue, using an *isFull* flag, or leaving one array location empty.

5. Models of real-world systems often use queues. The event-driven simulation in this chapter used a queue to model a line of customers in a bank.

6. Central to a simulation is the notion of simulated time. In a time-driven simulation, simulated time is advanced by a single time unit, whereas in an event-driven simulation, simulated time is advanced to the time of the next event. To implement an event-driven simulation, you maintain an event list that contains events that have not yet occurred. The event list is ordered by the time of the events so that the next event to occur is always at the head of the list.

Cautions

1. If you use a linear linked list with only a head pointer to implement a queue, the insertion operation will be inefficient. Each insertion requires a traversal to the end of the linked list. As the queue increases in length, the traversal time—and hence the insertion time—will increase.

2. The management of an event list in an event-driven simulation is typically more difficult than it was in the example presented in this chapter. For instance, if the bank had more than one teller line, the structure of the event list would be much more complex.

Self-Test Exercises

1. If you add the letters A, B, C, and D in sequence to a queue of characters and then remove them, in what order will they be deleted from the queue?

2. What do the initially empty queues *queue1* and *queue2* "look like" after the following sequence of operations?

```
queue1.enqueue(1)
queue1.enqueue(2)
queue2.enqueue(3)
queue2.enqueue(4)
queue1.dequeue()
queue2.getFront(queueFront)
queue1.enqueue(queueFront)
queue1.enqueue(5)
queue2.dequeue(queueFront)
queue2.enqueue(6)
```

Compare these results with Self-Test Exercise 2 in Chapter 6.

3. Trace the palindrome-recognition algorithm described in the section "Simple Applications of the ADT Queue" for each of the following strings:

   a. abcda

   b. radar

4. For each of the following situations, which of these ADTs (1 through 4) would be most appropriate: (1) a queue; (2) a stack; (3) a list; (4) none of these?

   a. The customers at a deli counter who take numbers to mark their turn

   b. An alphabetic list of names

   c. Integers that need to be sorted

   d. The boxes in a box trace of a recursive function

   e. A grocery list ordered by the occurrence of the items in the store

   f. The items on a cash register tape

   g. A word processor that allows you to correct typing errors by using the backspace key

   h. A program that uses backtracking

   i. A list of ideas in chronological order

   j. Airplanes that stack above a busy airport, waiting to land

   k. People who are put on hold when they call an airline to make reservations

   l. An employer who fires the most recently hired person

5. In the bank simulation problem that this chapter discusses, why is it impractical to read the entire input file and create a list of all the arrival and departure events before the simulation begins?

6. Complete the hand trace of the bank-line simulation that Figure 7-16 began with the data given on page 365. Show the state of the queue and the event list at each step.

Exercises

1. Consider the palindrome-recognition algorithm described in the section "Simple Applications of the ADT Queue." Is it necessary for the algorithm to look at the entire queue and stack? That is, can you reduce the number of times that the loop must execute?

2. Consider the language

   $L = \{w\$w' : w$ is a possibly empty string of characters other than $\$$,
   $$w' = \text{reverse}(w)\}$$

   as defined in Chapter 6. Write a recognition algorithm for this language that uses both a queue and a stack. Thus, as you traverse the input string, you insert each character of w into a queue and each character of w' into a stack. Assume that each input string contains exactly one $\$$.

3. What is the output of the following pseudocode, where *num1*, *num2*, and *num3* are integer variables?

```
num1 = 5
num2 = 1
num3 = 4

aQueue.enqueue(num2)
aQueue.enqueue(num3)
aQueue.dequeue()
aQueue.enqueue(num1 - num2)

num1 = aQueue.dequeue()
num2 = aQueue.dequeue()
cout << num2 << " " << num1 << " " << num3 << endl
```

4. Consider a function called *getNumberOfElements* that returns the number of elements in a queue without changing the queue. The return type is *int* and it does not accept any parameters.

   a. Add *getNumberOfElements* to the array-based ADT queue given in this chapter.

   b. Add *getNumberOfElements* to the pointer-based ADT queue given in this chapter.

5. Revise the infix-to-postfix conversion algorithm of Chapter 6 so that it uses a queue to represent the postfix expression.

6. Implement the copy constructor for the pointer-based implementation of the ADT queue. *Hint*: Look at the copy constructor for the ADT stack in Chapter 6.

7. The destructor given for the pointer-based implementation of the ADT queue calls *dequeue*. Although easy to write, this destructor can be inefficient due to repeated function calls. Write another implementation for the destructor that deallocates the linked list directly without calling *dequeue*.

8. Write a client function that returns the last element of a queue while leaving the queue unchanged. This function can call any of the member functions of the ADT queue. It can also declare new *Queue* objects. The return type is *QueueItemType* and it accepts a *Queue* object as a parameter.

9. Consider the queue implementation that uses the ADT list to represent the items in the queue. Discuss the efficiency of the queue's insertion and deletion operations when the ADT list's implementation is

   a. Array based

   b. Pointer based

10. An operation that displays the contents of a queue can be useful during program debugging. Add a *display* operation to the ADT queue such that

    a. *display* uses only ADT queue operations, so it is independent of the queue's implementation

    b. *display* assumes and uses the pointer-based implementation of the ADT queue

11. Consider a slight variation of the ADT queue. In this variation, new items can be added to and deleted from either end. This ADT is commonly called a double-ended queue, or deque. Use a deque to solve the read-and-correct problem that Chapter 6 describes. In that problem, you enter text at a keyboard and correct typing mistakes by using the backspace key. Each backspace erases the most recently entered character. Your pseudocode solution should provide a corrected string of characters in the order in which they were entered at the keyboard.

12. With the following data, hand-trace the execution of the bank-line simulation that this chapter describes. Each line of data contains an arrival time and a transaction time. Show the state of the queue and the event list at each step.

5	9
7	5
14	5
30	5
32	5
34	5

   Note that at time 14 there is a tie between the execution of an arrival event and a departure event.

13. In the solution to the bank simulation problem, can the event list be an ADT queue? Can the event list be an ADT list or sorted list?

14. Consider the stack–based search of the flight map in the HPAir problem of Chapter 6. You can replace the stack that *searchS* uses with a queue. That is, you can replace every call to *push* with a call to *enqueue,* every call to *pop* with a call to *dequeue,* and every call to *getTop* with a call to *getFront.* Trace the resulting algorithm when you fly from P to Z in the flight map in Figure 6-10. Indicate the contents of the queue after every operation on it.

15. As Chapter 3 pointed out, you can define ADT operations in a mathematically formal way by using axioms. Consider the following axioms for the ADT queue, where *aQueue* is an arbitrary queue and *item* is an arbitrary queue item. To simplify the notation, *getFront* is treated as a valued function that returns the front of the queue.

```
(aQueue.createQueue()).isEmpty() = true
(aQueue.enqueue(item)).isEmpty() = false
(aQueue.createQueue()).dequeue() = aQueue.create-
Queue() (or error)
((aQueue.createQueue()).enqueue(item)).dequeue()
                                    = aQueue.createQueue()
aQueue.isEmpty() = false ⇒
  (aQueue.enqueue(item)).dequeue() =
                  (aQueue.dequeue()).enqueue(item)
(aQueue.createQueue()).getFront() = error
((aQueue.createQueue()).enqueue(item)).getFront() = item
aQueue.isEmpty() = false ⇒
  (aQueue.enqueue(item)).getFront() = aQueue.getFront()
```

a. Note the recursive nature of the definition of *getFront.* What is the base case? What is the recursive step? What is the significance of the *isEmpty* test? Why is the queue operation *getFront* recursive in nature while the stack operation *getTop* for the ADT stack is not?

b. The representation of a stack as a sequence of *push* operations without any *pop* operations was called a canonical form. (See Exercise 15 in Chapter 6.) Is there a canonical form for the ADT queue that uses only *enqueue* operations? That is, is every queue equal to a queue that can be written with only *enqueue*? Prove your answer.

Programming Problems

1. Write a pointer-based implementation of a queue that uses a circular linked list to represent the items in the queue. You will need a single tail pointer. When you are done, compare your implementation to the one given in this chapter that uses a linear linked list with two external pointers. Which implementation is easier to write? Which is easier to understand? Which is more efficient?

2. Write an array-based implementation of a queue that uses a dynamically allocated, circular array to represent the items in the queue.

3. Consider the array-based implementation of a queue given in the text. Instead of counting the number of items in the queue, you could maintain a flag *isFull* to distinguish between the full and empty conditions. Revise the array-based implementation by using the *isFull* flag.

4. This chapter described another array-based implementation of a queue that uses no special data member—such as *count* or *isFull* (see Programming Problem 3)—to distinguish between the full and empty conditions. In this implementation, you declare *MAX_QUEUE* + 1 locations for the array *items*, but use only *MAX_QUEUE* of them for queue items. You sacrifice one array location by making *front* the index of the location before the front of the queue. The queue is full if *front* equals *(back+1) % (MAX_QUEUE+1)*, but the queue is empty if *front* equals *back*.

   a. For a queue whose items have a standard data type, why does this implementation have the same space requirements as the *count* or *isFull* implementations?

   b. Implement this array-based approach.

5. Implement the palindrome-recognition algorithm described in the section "Simple Applications of the ADT Queue."

6. Implement the recognition algorithm in Exercise 2 using the STL *stack* and *queue* classes.

7. Exercise 11 mentioned the double-ended queue, or deque. New items can be added to and deleted from either end of a deque. Construct array-based and pointer-based implementations of the deque.

8. Implement the event-driven simulation of a bank that this chapter described. A queue of arrival events will represent the line of customers in the bank. Maintain the arrival events and departure events in an ADT event list, sorted by the time of the event. Use a pointer-based implementation for the ADT event list.

   The input is a text file of arrival and transaction times. Each line of the file contains the arrival time and required transaction time for a customer. The arrival times are ordered by increasing time.

Your program must count customers and keep track of their cumulative waiting time. These statistics are sufficient to compute the average waiting time after the last event has been processed.

Display a trace of the events executed and a summary of the computed statistics (total number of arrivals and average time spent waiting in line). For example, the input file shown in the left columns of the following table should produce the output shown in the right column.

Input	File	Output
1	5	Simulation Begins
2	5	Processing an arrival event at time: 1
4	5	Processing an arrival event at time: 2
20	5	Processing an arrival event at time: 4
22	5	Processing a departure event at time: 6
24	5	Processing a departure event at time: 11
26	5	Processing a departure event at time: 16
28	5	Processing an arrival event at time: 20
30	5	Processing an arrival event at time: 22
88	3	Processing an arrival event at time: 24
		Processing a departure event at time: 25
		Processing an arrival event at time: 26
		Processing an arrival event at time: 28
		Processing an arrival event at time: 30
		Processing a departure event at time: 30
		Processing a departure event at time: 35
		Processing a departure event at time: 40
		Processing a departure event at time: 45
		Processing a departure event at time: 50
		Processing an arrival event at time: 88
		Processing a departure event at time: 91
		Simulation Ends

```
Final Statistics:
   Total number of people processed: 10
   Average amount of time spent waiting: 5.6
```

9. Modify and expand the event-driven simulation program that you wrote in Programming Problem 8. Here are a few suggestions:

   a. Add an operation that displays the event list, and use it to check your hand trace in Exercise 12.

   b. Add some statistics to the simulation. For example, compute the maximum wait in line, the average length of the line, and the maximum length of the line.

   c. Modify the simulation so that it accounts for three tellers, each with a distinct line. You should keep in mind that there should be

- Three queues, one for each teller
- A rule that chooses a line when processing an arrival event (for example, enter the shortest line)
- Three distinct departure events, one for each line
- Rules for breaking ties in the event list

Run both this simulation and the original simulation on several sets of input data. How do the statistics compare?

d. The bank is considering the following change: Instead of having three distinct lines (one for each teller), there will be a single line for the three tellers. The person at the front of the line will go to the first available teller. Modify the simulation of Part c to account for this variation. Run both simulations on several sets of input data. How do the various statistics compare (averages and maximums)? What can you conclude about having a single line as opposed to having distinct lines?

10. The people that run the Motor Vehicle Department (MVD) have a problem. They are concerned that people do not spend enough time waiting in lines to appreciate the privilege of owning and driving an automobile. The current arrangement is as follows:

- When people walk in the door, they must wait in a line to sign in.
- Once they have signed in, they are told either to stand in line for registration renewal or to wait until they are called for license renewal.
- Once they have completed their desired transaction, they must go and wait in line for the cashier.
- When they finally get to the front of the cashier's line, if they expect to pay by check, they are told that all checks must get approved. To do this, it is necessary to go to the check-approver's table and then reenter the cashier's line at the end.

Write an event-driven simulation to help the Motor Vehicle Department gather statistics.

Each line of input will contain

- A desired transaction code (*L* for license renewal, *R* for registration renewal)
- A method-of-payment code ($ for cash, *C* for check)
- An arrival time (integer)
- A name

Write out the specifics of each event (when, who, what, and so on). Then display these final statistics:

- The total number of license renewals and the average time spent in MVD (arrival until completion of payment) to renew a license

- The total number of registration renewals and the average time spent in MVD (arrival until completion of payment) to renew a registration

Incorporate the following details into your program:

- Define the following events: arrive, sign in, renew license, renew registration, and cope with the cashier (make a payment or find out about check approval).

- In the case of a tie, let the order of events be determined by the list of events just given—that is, arrivals have the highest priority.

- Assume that the various transactions take the following amounts of time:

Sign in	10 seconds
Renew license	90 seconds
Register automobile	60 seconds
See cashier (payment)	30 seconds
See cashier (check not approved)	10 seconds

- As ridiculous as it may seem, the people waiting for license renewal are called in alphabetical order. Note, however, that people are not pushed back once their transactions have started.

- For the sake of this simulation, you can assume that checks are approved instantly. Therefore, the rule for arriving at the front of the cashier's line with a check that has not been approved is to go to the back of the cashier's line with a check that has been approved.

CHAPTER 8

Advanced C++ Topics

PREVIEW

C++ classes provide a way to enforce the walls of data abstraction by encapsulating an abstract data type's data and operations. An object-oriented approach, however, goes well beyond encapsulation. Inheritance and polymorphism allow you to derive new classes from existing classes. This chapter describes techniques that make collections of reusable software components possible. Realize that much more can and should be said about these techniques. Consider this chapter as an introduction to this material.

8.1 Inheritance Revisited

When you think of inheritance, you might imagine a bequest of one million dollars from some long-lost wealthy relative. In the object-oriented world, however, inheritance describes the ability of a class to derive properties from a previously defined class. These properties are like the genetic characteristics you received from your parents: Some traits are the same, some are similar but different, and some are new.

Inheritance, in fact, is a relationship among classes. One class can derive the behavior and structure of another class. For example, Figure 8-1 illustrates some relationships among various timepieces. Digital clocks, for example, include the clock in the dashboard of your car, the clock on the sign of the downtown bank, and the clock on your microwave oven. All digital clocks have the same underlying structure and perform operations such as

A class can derive the behavior and structure of another class

```
Set the time
Advance the time
Display the time
```

A digital alarm clock is a digital clock that also has alarm functions, such as

A digital alarm clock is a digital clock

```
Set the alarm
Enable the alarm
Sound the alarm
Silence the alarm
```

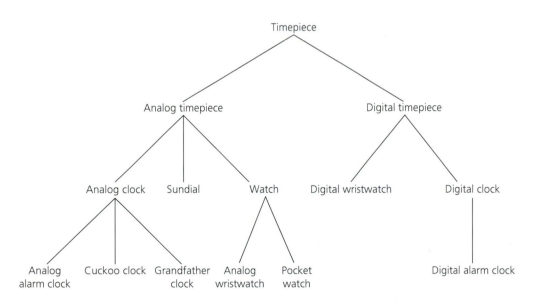

FIGURE 8-1 Inheritance: Relationships among timepieces

That is, a digital alarm clock has the structure and operations of a digital clock and, in addition, has an alarm and operations to manipulate the alarm.

You can think of the group of digital clocks and the group of digital alarm clocks as classes. The class of digital alarm clocks is a derived class, or subclass, of the class of digital clocks. The class of digital clocks is a base class, or superclass, of the class of digital alarm clocks.

In C++, a derived class inherits all the members of its base class, except the constructors and destructor. That is, a derived class has the data members and member functions of the base class in addition to the members it defines. A derived class can also revise any inherited member function. For example, according to Figure 8-1, a cuckoo clock is a descendant of an analog clock, like the one on a classroom wall. The cuckoo clock inherits the structure and behavior of the analog clock, but revises the way it reports the time each hour by adding a cuckoo.

Sometimes a derived class has more than one base class. For example, as Figure 8-2 illustrates, you can derive a class of clock radios from the class of digital clocks and the class of radios. These relationships are known as **multiple inheritance**. We will not consider this kind of inheritance further.

Inheritance enables you to reuse software components when you define a new class. For example, you can reuse your design and implementation of an analog clock when you design a cuckoo clock. A simpler example will demonstrate the details of such reuse and show you how C++ implements inheritance.

Chapter 3 spoke of volleyballs and soccer balls as objects. While designing a class of balls—*Ball*—you might decide that a ball is simply a sphere with a name. This realization is significant in that *Sphere*—the class of spheres—already exists. Thus, if you let *Sphere* be a base class of *Ball*, you can implement *Ball* without reinventing the sphere. Toward that end, recall the definition of the class *Sphere* from Chapter 3:

A derived class inherits the members of its base class

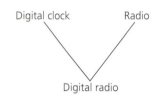

FIGURE 8-2   Multiple inheritance

Inheritance enables the reuse of existing classes

Inheritance reduces the effort necessary to add features to an existing object

```cpp
class Sphere
{
public:
// constructors:
   Sphere();
   Sphere(double initialRadius);
   // copy constructor and destructor supplied
   // by the compiler

// Sphere operations:
   void setRadius(double newRadius);
   double getRadius() const;
   double getDiameter() const;
   double getCircumference() const;
   double getArea() const;
   double getVolume() const;
```

```
   void displayStatistics() const;

private:
   double theRadius;   // the sphere's radius
};   // end class
```

The derived class *Ball* will inherit all the members of the class *Sphere*—except the constructors and destructor—and make some changes. It could add a data member that names the ball; add member functions to access this name, set this name, and alter an existing ball's radius and name; and revise *displayStatistics* to display the ball's name in addition to its statistics as a sphere.

A derived class can add new members to those it inherits

You can add as many new members to a derived class as you like. Although you cannot revise an ancestor's private data members and should not reuse their names, you can **redefine** other inherited member functions. A member function in a derived class redefines a member function in the base class if the two functions have the same parameter declarations. Here, the class *Ball* redefines *displayStatistics*. Figure 8-3 illustrates the relationship between *Sphere* and *Ball*.

A derived class can redefine an inherited member function of its base class

You can declare *Ball* as follows:

```
class Ball: public Sphere
{
public:
// constructors:
   Ball();
```

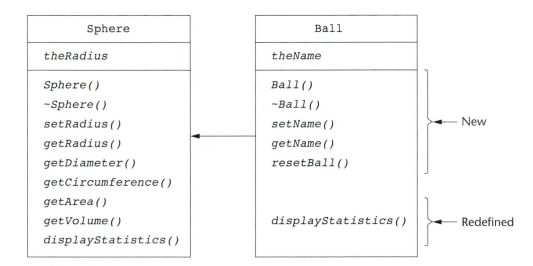

FIGURE 8-3   The derived class *Ball* inherits members of the base class *Sphere* and redefines and adds member functions

```
Ball(double initialRadius,
     const string& initialName);
// Creates a ball with radius initialRadius and
// name initialName.

// copy constructor and destructor supplied
// by the compiler

// additional or revised operations:
  void getName(string& currentName) const;
  // Determines the name of a ball.

  void setName(const string& newName);
  // Sets (alters) the name of an existing ball.

  void resetBall(double newRadius,
                 const string& newName);
  // Sets (alters) the radius and name of an existing
  // ball to newRadius and newName, respectively.

  void displayStatistics() const;
  // Displays the statistics of a ball.

private:
  string theName;  // the ball's name
};  // end class
```

Adding a colon and *public Sphere* after *class Ball* indicates that *Sphere* is a base class of *Ball* or, equivalently, that *Ball* is a derived class of *Sphere*.

An instance of the class *Ball* has two data members—*theRadius*, which is inherited, and *theName*, which is new. Since an instance of a derived class can invoke any public member function in the base class, an instance of *Ball* has all the methods that *Sphere* defines; new constructors; a new, compiler-generated destructor; new member functions *getName*, *setName*, and *resetBall*; and a revised method *displayStatistics*. Although an instance of a derived class contains copies of inherited data members, the code for inherited member functions is not copied.

A derived class cannot access the private members of the base class directly, even though they are inherited. Inheritance does not imply access. After all, you can inherit a locked vault but be unable to open it. In the current example, the data member *theRadius* of *Sphere* is private, so you can reference it only within the definition of the class *Sphere* and not within the definition of *Ball*. However, the class *Ball*

An instance of a derived class has all the behaviors of its base class

A derived class inherits private members from the base class, but cannot access them directly can use *Sphere*'s public member functions *setRadius* and *getRadius* to set or obtain the value of *theRadius* indirectly.

You implement the additional member functions of the class *Ball* as follows:

```
Ball::Ball() : Sphere()
{
   setName("");
} // end default constructor

Ball::Ball(double initialRadius,
           const string& initialName)
          : Sphere(initialRadius)
{
   setName(initialName);
}  // end constructor

void Ball::getName(string& currentName) const
{
   currentName = theName;
}  // end getName

void Ball::setName(const string& newName)
{
   theName = newName;
}  // end setName

void Ball::resetBall(double newRadius,
                     const string& newName)
{
   setRadius(newRadius);
   setName(newName);
}  // end resetBall

void Ball::displayStatistics() const
{
   cout << "Statistics for a " << theName << ":";
   Sphere::displayStatistics();
}  // end displayStatistics
```

The constructors for *Ball* invoke the corresponding constructors of *Sphere* by using an initializer syntax. Within the implementation of *Ball*, you can use the member functions that *Ball* inherits from *Sphere*. For example, the new member function *resetBall* calls the inherited function *setRadius*. Also, *Ball*'s *displayStatistics* calls the inherited version of *displayStatistics*, which you indicate by

A derived class's member functions can call the base class's public member functions

writing *Sphere::displayStatistics*. This notation is necessary to differentiate between the two versions of the function. Thus, you can access a base member, even though it has been redefined, by using the scope resolution operator *::*.

Clients of a derived class can invoke the public members of the base class. For example, if you write

```
Ball myBall(5.0, "Volleyball");
```

myBall.getDiameter() returns *myBall*'s diameter, 10.0 (2 times *myBall*'s radius), by using the member function *getDiameter* that *Ball* inherits from *Sphere*. If a new function has the same name as an ancestor function—*displayStatistics*, for example—instances of the new class will use the new function, while instances of the ancestor class will use the original function. Therefore, if *mySphere* is an instance of *Sphere*, the call *mySphere.displayStatistics()* will invoke *Sphere*'s *displayStatistics*, whereas *myBall.displayStatistics()* will invoke *Ball*'s *displayStatistics*, as Figure 8-4 illustrates. Because the compiler can determine which form of *displayStatistics* to use at compilation time—as opposed to at execution time—this situation is called **early binding**, or **static binding**.

Finally, a derived class's constructor executes after the base class's constructor. For example, if you define an instance of *Ball*, its constructor executes after *Sphere*'s constructor. The destructor of a derived class executes before the destructor of the base class. For example,

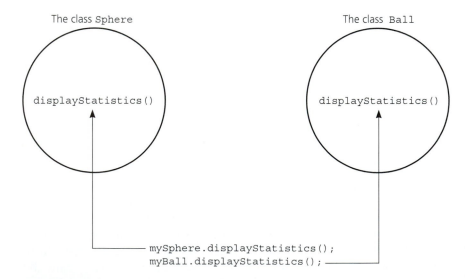

FIGURE 8-4   Early, or static, binding: The compiler determines which version of a method to invoke

Ball's destructor executes before *Sphere*'s destructor. This is true for constructors and destructors that you write as well as those generated by the compiler.

Public, private, and protected sections of a class. In addition to its public and private sections, a class can have a **protected section**. By creating a protected section, a class designer can hide members from a class's clients but make them available to a derived class. That is, a derived class can reference the protected members of its base class directly, but clients of the base class or derived class cannot.

For example, *Sphere* has a private member *theRadius*, which the derived class *Ball* cannot reference directly. If, instead, you declared *theRadius* as protected, *Ball* would be able to access *theRadius* directly. Clients of *Ball* or *Sphere*, however, would not have direct access to *theRadius*. Figure 8-5 illustrates the access of public, private, and protected members of a class.

As a general stylistic guideline, you should make all data members of a class private and, if desired, provide indirect access to them by defining member functions that are either public or protected. Although a class's public members are available to anyone, its protected members are available exclusively to either its own member functions (and friends[1]) or the member functions (and friends) of a derived class. The following summary distinguishes among the sections of a class:

In general, a class's data members should be private

KEY CONCEPTS

Membership Categories of a Class

1. Public members can be used by anyone.

2. Private members can be used only by member functions (and friends) of the class.

3. Protected members can be used only by member functions (and friends) of both the class and any derived class.

Public, Private, and Protected Inheritance

Several kinds of inheritance are possible. Regardless of the kind of inheritance, a derived class can access all of the base class's public and protected members, but not its private members. You can control how

---

[1] Friends of a class are nonmember functions that can access its private and protected members. Friends are discussed later in this chapter.

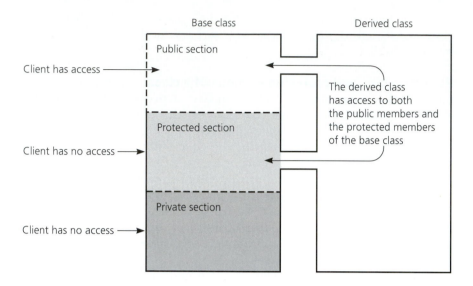

Access to public, private, and protected sections of a class by a client and a derived class

a class's inherited members are passed to subsequent derived classes by specifying one of three kinds of inheritance. You begin the definition of the derived class as follows:

class DerivedClass : *kind* BaseClass

where *kind* is one of *public*, *private*, or *protected*. The inheritance that you saw earlier in this chapter is public inheritance. The following summary describes the three kinds of inheritance:

KEY CONCEPTS

Kinds of Inheritance

1. **Public inheritance:** Public and protected members of the base class remain, respectively, public and protected members of the derived class.

2. **Protected inheritance:** Public and protected members of the base class are protected members of the derived class.

3. **Private inheritance:** Public and protected members of the base class are private members of the derived class.

In all cases, private members of a base class remain private to the base class and cannot be accessed by a derived class.

Of the three types of inheritance, public inheritance is the most important and the one that we will use in subsequent chapters. You use public inheritance to extend the definition of a class. You use private inheritance to implement one class in terms of another class. Protected inheritance is not often used, so we will not cover it.

The following section describes when it is appropriate to use public and private inheritance.

Is-a, Has-a, and *As-a* Relationships

As you just saw, inheritance provides for ancestor/descendant relationships among classes. Other relationships are also possible. When designing new classes from existing ones, it is important to identify their relationship so that you can determine whether to use inheritance and, if so, the kind of inheritance that best reflects the relationship. Three basic kinds of relationships are possible: *is-a*, *has-a*, and *as-a*.

Is-a relationships.   Earlier in this chapter, we used public inheritance to derive the class *Ball* from *Sphere*. You should use public inheritance only when an *is-a* relationship exists between the base class and the derived class. In this example, a ball *is a* sphere, as Figure 8-6 illustrates. That is, whatever is true of the base class *Sphere* is also true of the derived class *Ball*. Wherever you can use an object of type *Sphere*, you can also use an object of type *Ball*. This feature is called **object type compatibility**. In general, a derived class is type-compatible with all of its ancestor classes. Thus, you can use an instance of a derived class instead of an instance of its base class, but not the other way around.

In particular, the object type of an actual argument in a call to a function can be a descendant of the object type of the corresponding

Public inheritance should imply an is-a relationship

You can use an instance of a derived class anywhere you can use an instance of the base class

FIGURE 8-6   A ball *is a* sphere

formal argument. For example, suppose your program uses the classes *Sphere* and *Ball* and contains the following ordinary function, which is not a member of any class:

```
void displayDiameter(Sphere thing)
{
   cout << "The diameter is "
        << thing.getDiameter() << ".\n";
}  // end displayDiameter
```

If you define *mySphere* and *myBall* as

```
Sphere mySphere(2.0);
Ball   myBall(5.0, "Volleyball");
```

the following calls to *displayDiameter* are legal:

```
displayDiameter(mySphere);  // mySphere's diameter
displayDiameter(myBall);    // myBall's diameter
```

The first call is unremarkable because both the actual argument *mySphere* and the formal argument *thing* have the same data type. The second call is more interesting: The data type of the actual argument *myBall* is a descendant of the data type of the formal argument *thing*. Because a ball is a sphere, it can behave like a sphere. That is, *myBall* can perform sphere behaviors, so you can use *myBall* anywhere you can use *mySphere*. Note that object type compatibility applies to both value and reference arguments.

> Since a ball is a sphere, you can use it anywhere you can use a sphere

***Has-a* relationships.**   A ball-point pen *has a* ball as its point, as Figure 8-7 illustrates. Although you would want to use *Ball* in your definition

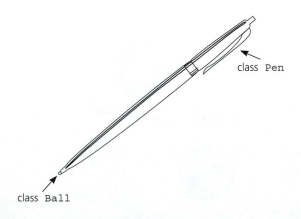

class Pen

class Ball

FIGURE 8-7   A pen *has a* or *contains a* ball

of a class *Pen*, you should not use public inheritance, because a pen is not a ball. In fact, you do not use inheritance at all to implement a *has-a* relationship. Instead, you can define a data member *point*—whose type is *Ball*—within the class *Pen*, as follows:

```
class Pen
{
   ...
private:
   Ball point;
};
```

If the relationship between two classes is not is-a, you should not use public inheritance

Recall that a data member can be an instance of any class other than the one currently being defined—*Pen*, in this example. An instance of *Pen* has, or *contains*, an instance of *Ball*. Thus, another name for the *has-a* relationship is containment.

Has-a, or containment, means a class has an object as a data member

The constructors for a class's member objects execute before the class's constructor. For example, *Ball*'s constructor executes before *Pen*'s constructor. The destructors of a class's member objects execute after the class's destructor. For example, *Ball*'s destructor executes after *Pen*'s.

You have already seen two other examples of the *has-a* relationship among classes in the preceding two chapters: Chapter 6 presented an implementation of the class *Stack* that used the ADT list to represent the items in a stack, while Chapter 7 used a similar implementation for the ADT queue. The class *Stack*, for example, contains a private member *aList* of type *List*. That is, an instance of *Stack* has, or contains, an instance of *List* that manages the stack's items.

As-a relationships. Finally, we examine one last way to view the relationship among classes. In particular, consider again the relationship between the classes *Stack* and *List*. You can implement the ADT stack *as a* list by using private inheritance. If you began your class definition with

```
class Stack: private List
```

List's public members—and protected members, if *List* had any—would be private members of *Stack*. Thus, within the implementation of *Stack*, you would be able to manipulate the items on the stack by using *List*'s methods. Both the descendants and clients of *Stack*, however, would not be able to access any members of *List*. Thus, the underlying list would be hidden from the clients of the stack.

Both *has-a* and *as-a* relationships between two classes are possible when public inheritance is inappropriate. If your class needs access to the protected members of another class, or if you need to redefine functions in that class, use *as-a*, that is, private inheritance. For other cases, *has-a* is preferable and simpler to use. Later, this chapter implements the ADT sorted list by using the three relationships just discussed.

8.2 Virtual Functions and Late Binding

As you saw earlier, if *mySphere* is an instance of *Sphere* and *myBall* is an instance of *Ball*, *mySphere.displayStatistics()* invokes *Sphere*'s version of *displayStatistics*, whereas *myBall.display-Statistics()* invokes *Ball*'s version of *displayStatistics*. (See Figure 8-4.) Again, the compiler chooses the correct version of *displayStatistics* to invoke. These choices, which are examples of early binding, cannot be altered during execution.

Early binding can lead to problems. For example, if you write

```
Sphere *spherePtr = &mySphere;
```

spherePtr points to *mySphere*. As you would expect,

```
spherePtr->displayStatistics();
```

invokes *Sphere*'s version of *displayStatistics*. Unfortunately, if *spherePtr* points to *myBall*—for example, if you write

Early binding can cause problems

```
spherePtr = &myBall;
```

the statement

```
spherePtr->displayStatistics();
```

still invokes *Sphere*'s version of *displayStatistics*, instead of *Ball*'s version. In this case, the compiler determined the version of the method to invoke from the type of the pointer *spherePtr* instead of from the type of object to which *spherePtr* points.

Simply redefining *displayStatistics* in *Ball*—as we did earlier—is insufficient. You also need to tell the compiler that derived classes of *Sphere* might revise *displayStatistics* so that the compiler can make accommodations for such an occurrence. You do this by making *displayStatistics* a **virtual function**. To indicate that a particular member function is virtual, you simply write the keyword *virtual* before the function's declaration within the definition of the base class. For example, the class *Sphere* appears as follows:

```
class Sphere
{
public:
   // everything as before, except displayStatistics
   . . .
   virtual void displayStatistics() const;
   . . .
}; // end class
```

The implementation of *displayStatistics* is the same as given earlier.
Now, if *spherePtr* points to *myBall*, the statement

```
spherePtr->displayStatistics();
```

invokes *Ball*'s version of *displayStatistics*. Thus, the appropriate
version of a member function is decided at execution time, instead of at
compilation time, based on the type of object to which *spherePtr*
points. This situation is called **late binding**, or **dynamic binding**,
and a function such as *displayStatistics* is called polymorphic.
Polymorphism—which literally means "many forms"—enables this
determination to be made at execution time. That is, the outcome of a
particular operation depends upon the objects on which the operation
acts. We also say that *Ball*'s version of *displayStatistics* overrides
Sphere's version.

> Late binding means that
> the appropriate version of a
> member function is decided
> at execution time
>
> A polymorphic function has
> multiple meanings

A virtual member function in a derived class can override a virtual
member function in the base class if they have the same declarations.
Overriding a function is similar to redefining a function. However, you
can override only virtual functions.

> A virtual function is one that
> you can override

If you want the derived class *Ball* to override *displayStatistics*,
you can write the class *Ball* exactly as it appeared earlier. That is, you can
omit *virtual* in the derived class. Any member function in a derived
class that has the same declaration as an ancestor's virtual function—such
as *displayStatistics*—is also virtual without explicit identification,
although tagging it with *virtual* is desirable stylistically.

We will now examine a more subtle example of early and late
binding. Suppose you wanted *Ball* to have a method *getArea* that
behaved differently than *Sphere*'s *getArea*. Just as *Ball* overrides *displayStatistics*, it could override *getArea* to compute, for example,
the ball's cross-sectional area. Thus, you would add

> A function that is virtual in a
> base class is virtual in any
> derived class

```
double getArea() const;
```

as a public member of the class *Ball* and implement *getArea* as

```
double Ball::getArea() const
{
   double r = getRadius();
   return PI * r * r;  // PI is a global constant
}  // end getArea
```

Since you are overriding *Sphere*'s *getArea*, it should be virtual,
but observe what would happen if it is not. Consider

```
class Sphere
{
public:
   · · ·        // everything as before
```

Although *getArea* should be virtual, consider what would happen if it was not

```cpp
    double getArea() const;   // surface area
    virtual void displayStatistics() const;
    . . .
};  // end class


class Ball: public Sphere
{
public:
    · · ·   // everything as before, except
            // displayStatistics is omitted
            // and getArea is revised:
    double getArea() const;   // cross-sectional area
    · · ·
};  // end class
```

Let *mySphere* be an instance of *Sphere* and *myBall* be an instance of *Ball*.

Although *mySphere.getArea()* returns the sphere's surface area and *myBall.getArea()* returns the ball's cross-sectional area, as desired, a problem will occur when you omit *displayStatistics* from *Ball*. This omission is reasonable because *Ball* will inherit—and can use—*Sphere*'s *displayStatistics*, which, recall, is defined as

```cpp
void Sphere::displayStatistics() const
{   cout << "\nRadius = " << getRadius()
         << "\nDiameter = " << getDiameter()
         << "\nCircumference = " << getCircumference()
         << "\nArea = " << getArea()
         << "\nVolume = " << getVolume() << endl;
}   // end displayStatistics
```

If *getArea* is not virtual, the compiler chooses a version of *getArea* and it is wrong

This function invokes *getArea*, but the statement *myBall.display-Statistics()* displays *myBall*'s surface area instead of its cross-sectional area. That is, *Sphere*'s *getArea* is invoked, as Figure 8-8 illustrates. Since *getArea* is not virtual, the compiler chooses *Sphere*'s version of *getArea*, not *Ball*'s version of *getArea*, when it compiles *Sphere::displayStatistics*.

Early binding is again the problem here. The base class *Sphere* should make *getArea* virtual so that the derived class *Ball* can properly override it. (*displayStatistics* should also be virtual, as you saw earlier, but that does not affect this example.) Thus, the classes should be as follows:

```cpp
class Sphere
{
public:
    . . .
    virtual double getArea() const; // surface area
```

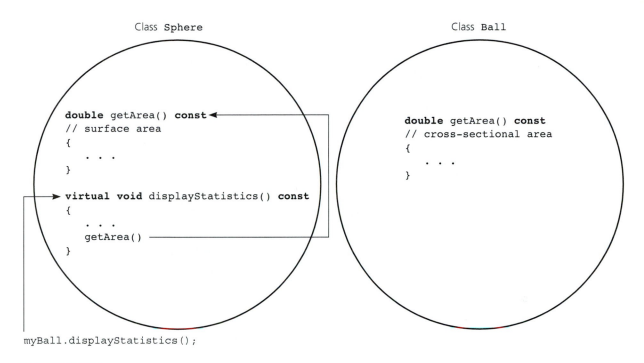

```
myBall.displayStatistics();
```

FIGURE 8-8   *getArea* is not virtual: *myBall.displayStatistics()* calls *Sphere::getArea*

```
    virtual void displayStatistics() const;
    . . .
};  // end class

class Ball: public Sphere
{
public:
    . . .
    virtual double getArea() const; // cross-sectional area
    // virtual is redundant but stylistic;
    // displayStatistics is omitted
    . . .
};  // end class
```

Now when an instance of *Sphere* calls *displayStatistics*, *displayStatistics* will call *Sphere::getArea* (Figure 8-9a), yet when an instance of *Ball* calls *displayStatistics*, *displayStatistics* will call *Ball::getArea* (Figure 8-9b). Thus, the meaning of *displayStatistics* depends on the type of object that invokes it.

The use of virtual functions has a significant impact on the future use of a class. Imagine that you had compiled the class *Sphere* and its implementation before you wrote the derived class *Ball*. If you then wrote *Ball*, assuming access to the compiled class *Sphere*, you could

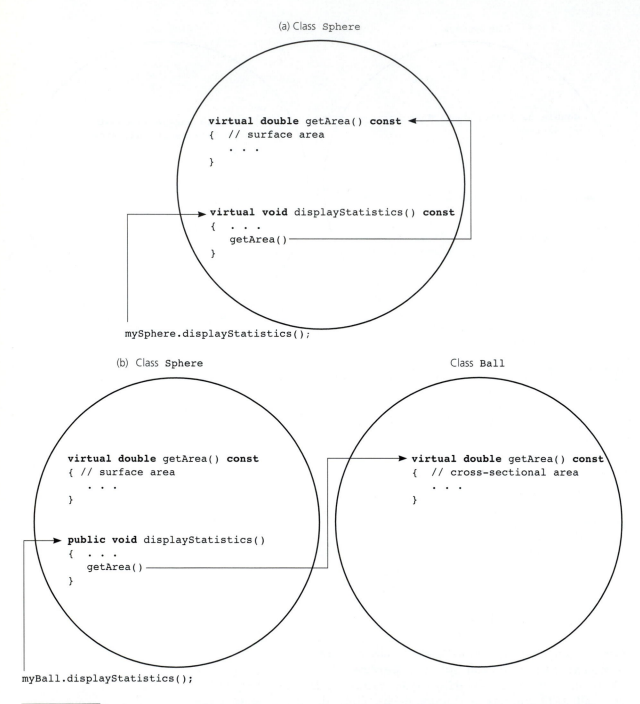

getArea is virtual: (a) *mySphere.displayStatistics()* calls *Sphere::getArea;* (b) *myBall.displayStatistics()* calls *Ball::getArea*

override *getArea* because it is virtual in *Sphere*. As a result, you would change the behavior of *Sphere*'s *displayStatistics* for instances of *Ball*, even though *Sphere* was already compiled. That is, classes that define virtual functions are **extensible**: You can add capabilities to a derived class without having access to the ancestor's source statements.

A class is extensible if it contains virtual functions

Generally, your classes should use virtual functions. However, if you do not want a derived class to override a particular member function, the function should not be virtual. For example, *Sphere::getRadius* should always return the value of *theRadius*, so you would not want a derived class to override the function.

Every class that defines a virtual function has a **virtual method table**, or VMT, which remains invisible to the programmer. For each virtual function in the class, the VMT contains a pointer to the actual instructions that implement the method. A call to the constructor establishes this pointer. That is, when a constructor for an object is called, the constructor establishes within the VMT pointers to the versions of the virtual functions that are appropriate for the object. Thus, the VMT is the mechanism that enables late binding.

The following summary provides some facts about virtual functions:

KEY CONCEPTS

Virtual Functions

1. A virtual function is one that a derived class can override.

2. You must implement a class's virtual functions. (Pure virtual functions, which the next section defines, are not included in this requirement.)

3. A derived class does not need to override an existing implementation of an inherited virtual function.

4. Generally, a class's member functions should be virtual, unless you do not want any derived class to override them.

5. Constructors cannot be virtual.

6. Destructors can and should be virtual. Virtual destructors ensure that future descendants of the object can deallocate themselves correctly.

7. A virtual function's return type cannot be overridden.

Abstract Base Classes

Imagine a CD player (CDP) and a DVD player (DVDP). Both devices share several characteristics. Each involves a compact disc. You can insert, remove, play, and stop such discs. You can also skip forward or skip backward from the current position on the disc. Some of these operations are essentially the same for both devices, while others—in particular, the play function—are different but similar.

If you were specifying both devices, you might begin by describing the common operations:

Disc transport operations

```
+insert()
// Inserts a disc into the player.

+remove()
// Removes a disc from the player.

+play()
// Plays the disc.

+stop()
// Stops playing the disc.

+skipForward()
// Skip ahead to another section of the disc.

+skipBackward()
// Skip back to an earlier section of the disc.
```

These operations could constitute a generic disc player (GDP).

If GDP, CDP, and DVDP were classes, GDP could be the base class of CDP and DVDP, as Figure 8-10 illustrates. While GDP could implement operations such as *insert* and *remove* that would be suitable for

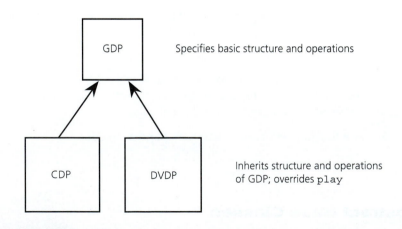

FIGURE 8-10   CDP and DVDP have an abstract base class GDP

both a CDP and a DVDP, it could only indicate that these devices have a *play* operation. So CDP, for example, inherits the operations provided by GDP but overrides the *play* operation to suit CDs, as Figure 8-11 illustrates. If necessary, CDP could override any of GDP's operations or define additional ones. We can make similar comments about DVDP. Thus,

- A CDP is a GDP that plays sound.

- A DVDP is a GDP that plays sound and video.

Because GDP cannot implement its play operation, we would not want instances of it. So GDP is simply a class without instances that forms the basis of other classes. If a class never has instances, its member functions need not be implemented. Such functions, however, must be virtual so that derived classes can supply their own implementations. A virtual function with an undefined body is called a **pure virtual function**, and is written as

virtual *prototype* = 0;

A pure virtual function has an undefined body

within a class definition. The implementation of a pure virtual function is deferred to a derived class.

A class that contains at least one pure virtual function is called an **abstract base class**. An abstract base class has no instances and is used only as the basis of other classes. Thus, the GDP class is an abstract base class because it does not implement all of its functions. Any derived class that fails to implement all of the pure virtual functions is also an abstract base class and cannot have instances.

A class that contains at least one pure virtual function is an abstract base class

An abstract base class has descendants but no instances

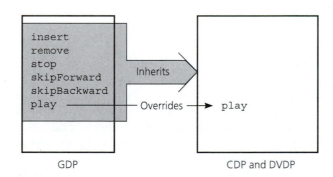

GDP

CDP and DVDP

FIGURE 8-11 CDP and DVDP are derived from GDP

Another example. The previous classes *Sphere* and *Ball* describe points that are equidistant from the origin of a three-dimensional coordinate system. The following class, *EquidistantShape*, which declares operations to set and return the distance of a point from the origin, could be an abstract base class of *Sphere*:

An abstract base class
for *Sphere*

```cpp
class EquidistantShape  // abstract base class
{
public:
   virtual void setRadius(double newRadius) = 0;
   virtual double getRadius() const = 0;
   virtual void displayStatistics() const = 0;
};  // end class
```

This class declares the pure virtual functions *setRadius*, *getRadius*, and *displayStatistics*.

Now you could define *Sphere* as a descendant of *EquidistantShape*:

```cpp
class Sphere: public EquidistantShape
{
public:
   Sphere();
   Sphere(double initialRadius);
   Sphere(const Sphere& aSphere);
   virtual ~Sphere();

   virtual void setRadius(double newRadius);
   virtual double getRadius() const;
   virtual double getDiameter() const;
   virtual double getCircumference() const;
   virtual double getArea() const;
   virtual double getVolume() const;
   virtual void displayStatistics() const;

private:
   double theRadius;
};  // end class
```

By including pure virtual functions—such as *setRadius*, *getRadius*, and *displayStatistics*—in an abstract base class, you force some derived class—like *Sphere*—to implement them. The class *Ball* can now be a descendant of *Sphere*, just as it appeared earlier in this chapter.

You could define *theRadius* to be a private data member of *EquidistantShape* instead of *Sphere*. If you do, derived classes will be unable to access *theRadius* directly by name. Thus, *EquidistantShape* must contain the methods *setRadius* and *getRadius*, and you must provide default implementations for the derived classes to inherit.

That is, *setRadius* and *getRadius* cannot be pure. In addition, they should not be virtual, because a derived class should not override them. The following class contains these changes:

```
class EquidistantShape  // abstract base class
{
public:
   void setRadius(double newRadius);
   double getRadius() const;
   virtual void displayStatistics() const = 0;

private:
   double theRadius;
};  // end class
```

Another abstract base class for *Sphere*; *setRadius* and *getRadius* are not pure, so they must be implemented

Alternatively, you could define *theRadius* to be a protected data member of *EquidistantShape*, enabling the derived class to both access *theRadius* directly and define *setRadius* and *getRadius*. Generally, however, data members should be private.

An abstract base class can provide a constructor, which, because constructors cannot be virtual, cannot be pure. A destructor in an abstract base class should not be pure, because derived classes will call it and thus it should be implemented. Generally, virtual destructors are recommended.

Virtual destructors are recommended for all objects

The key points about abstract base classes are summarized as follows:

KEY CONCEPTS

Abstract Base Classes

An abstract base class

1. By definition is a class that contains at least one pure virtual function.

2. Is used only as the basis for derived classes and thus defines a minimum interface for its descendants.

3. Has no instances.

4. Should, in general, omit implementations except for the destructor and functions that provide access to private data members. That is, virtual functions in an abstract base class usually should be pure.

5. Must implement any virtual function that is not pure, thereby providing a default implementation if a derived class chooses not to supply its own.

8.3 Friends

Functions and classes can be friends of a class

In C++, a class can provide additional access to its private and protected parts by declaring other functions and classes as **friends**. Declaring a nonmember function as a friend to a class allows that function to access all of the private and protected members of the class. For example, input and output functions are often defined as friend functions:

Functions that are friends of the class *Sphere*

```
class Sphere
{
public:
// constructors and operations as before
   . . .
   friend void readSphereData(Sphere& s);
   friend void writeSphereData(Sphere& s);
private:
   double theRadius;  // the sphere's radius
};  // end class
```

Friend functions

The functions *readSphereData* and *writeSphereData* are not members of the class *Sphere*; they are functions that are defined outside of the class *Sphere*. For example, if the data for a *Sphere* object can be read from standard input and written to standard output, the functions are as follows:

Friend functions are not members of *Spheres*

```
void readSphereData(Sphere& s)
{
   cout << "Enter sphere radius: ";
   cin >> s.theRadius;
}  // end readSphereData

void writeSphereData(Sphere& s)
{
   cout << "The radius of the sphere is "
        << s.theRadius << endl;
}  // end writeSphereData
```

Note that the functions access the private data member *theRadius* of the class *Sphere*. This seems to violate the principle of information hiding, but it is done in a controlled fashion. The class *Sphere* must explicitly grant this access by declaring the function as a friend function.

The functions *readSphereData* and *writeSphereData* could be members of the class *Sphere* instead of friends. However, performing input and output outside of a class provides more flexibility. When you know the context in which you will use a class, you can decide exactly how the input and output will occur. Also, recompiling the class is not necessary each time you use a different method of input and output.

Declaring a class as a friend of a class *c* allows all of the functions contained in the friend class to have access to the private and protected parts of the class *c*. This feature is particularly useful when one class is used in the implementation of another class. For example, we have seen pointer-based implementations of ADTs that have a node declared as a structure within the private part of the class. An alternative is to implement the node as a separate class and declare the ADT's class as a friend class. For example, you could define a node for the ADT list as follows:

A friend class is a class that is a friend of another class

```
#include <cstddef>
typedef desired-type-of-list-item ListItemType;

class ListNode                  // a node on the list
{
private:
   ListNode(): next(NULL) {};
   ListNode(const ListItemType& nodeItem, ListNode *ptr)
            :item(nodeItem), next(ptr) {};
   ListItemType item;           // a data item on the list
   ListNode      *next;         // pointer to next node

   // friend class - can access private parts
   friend class List;
};   // end class
```

The class *List* is a friend of *ListNode*

The class *List* has the same access privileges to the node's data members *item* and *next* as when *ListNode* is a *struct*. It also now has a constructor available for initializing the list node (a constructor could have also been provided in the *struct*).

Friends of a base class do not have access to the private and protected parts added by the derived class—only to the private and protected members that appear in the base class. For example, the following uses our *Sphere* class with the friends defined earlier:

A friend of a base class is not a friend of a derived class

```
class Sphere
{
public:
// constructors and operations as before
   . . .
   friend void readSphereData(Sphere& s);
   friend void writeSphereData(Sphere& s);
private:
   double theRadius;   // the sphere's radius
};   // end class

class Ball: public Sphere
{
```

```
public:
   Ball();
   Ball(double initialRadius,
        const string initialName);
   void getName(string currentName) const;
   void setName(const string newName);
   void resetBall(double newRadius,
                  const string newName);
   void displayStatistics() const;
private:
   string theName;   // the ball's name
};   // end class
```

Since the friend functions *readSphereData* and *writeSphereData* have a formal argument of type *Sphere*, you can pass them *Ball* objects as arguments. However, the functions will have access only to the private data member *theRadius*, and not to *Ball*'s private data member *theName*. The following list summarizes the key points about friends.

KEY CONCEPTS

Friends

1. Friend functions can access the private and protected parts of the class.

2. Friend functions are not members of the class.

3. When a class is declared as a friend of a class *C*, all of its member functions have access to the private and protected parts of the class *C*.

4. Friendship is not inherited. The private and protected members declared in a derived class are not accessible by friends of the base class.

8.4 The ADTs List and Sorted List Revisited

Chapter 3 introduced the ADT list and the ADT sorted list. As you know, these lists have some characteristics and operations in common. For example, each ADT can determine its length and determine whether it is empty. You can organize such commonalities into an abstract base class, which can be the basis of these and other lists. For example,

```
class BasicADT  // abstract base class
{
public:
   virtual ~BasicADT();  // destructor
   virtual bool isEmpty() const = 0;
   virtual int getLength() const = 0;
};  // end class
```

An abstract base class for lists

Because the destructor is not pure, you need to implement it. The other members are pure virtual functions, so some derived class must provide their implementations. That is, the designer of this base class wants all descendant classes to have the operations *isEmpty* and *getLength*, and so includes them in the abstract base class, thus imposing them on all descendant classes.

Notice that *BasicADT* could be used as the base class for the three ADTs that we have studied thus far: list, stack, and queue. All of these ADTs have the function *isEmpty* defined, and they could easily have had the function *getLength* specified as well. Using *BasicADT* as the base class would be a way to guarantee that all of the derived ADT classes minimally have an *isEmpty* function and a *getLength* function.

The following class for the ADT list publicly inherits this abstract base class and assumes that *ListItemType* is the desired type of list item. The class reflects its anticipated pointer-based implementation. Since you have already seen the preconditions and postconditions for the ADT list methods in Chapter 3, they are omitted here.

```
// ***********************************************************
// Header file List.h for the ADT list.
// Uses ListNode and BasicADT.
// ***********************************************************
#include "ListNode.h"    // as specified in previous section,
                         // also specifies ListItemType
#include "ListException.h"
#include "ListIndexOutOfRangeException.h"
#include "BasicADT.h"

class List : public BasicADT
{
public:
// constructors and destructor:
   List();
   List(const List& aList);
   virtual ~List();

// list operations:
   virtual bool isEmpty() const;
```

```cpp
    virtual int getLength() const;
    virtual void insert(int index, ListItemType newItem)
         throw(ListIndexOutOfRangeException, ListException);
    virtual void remove(int index)
         throw(ListIndexOutOfRangeException);
    virtual void retrieve(int index,
                           ListItemType& dataItem) const
         throw(ListIndexOutOfRangeException);

protected:
    void setSize(int newSize);          // sets size
    ListNode *getHead() const;          // returns head pointer
    void setHead(ListNode *newHead); // sets head pointer

    // the next two functions return the list item or
    // next pointer of a node in the linked list
    ListItemType getNodeItem(ListNode *ptr) const;
    ListNode *getNextNode(ListNode *ptr) const;

private:
    int       size;    // number of items in the list
    ListNode *head;    // pointer to the linked list

    ListNode *find(int index) const;
};  // end class
```

You must implement at least the functions *isEmpty* and *getLength*, which *List* publicly inherits from *BasicADT*, because the methods are pure in the abstract base class. Failure to do so would make *List* an abstract base class as well.

Because *List* defines its data members *size* and *head* as private, only member functions within this class can access them. We can give a descendant class of *List* indirect access to these data members by defining protected member functions *setSize*, *getHead*, and *setHead*. (Notice that we do not need a protected member function to return the value of *size*, because the public method *getLength* already accomplishes that task.) Protected member functions *getNodeItem* and *getNextNode* are also defined to enable a derived class to access nodes in the implementation's underlying linked list. You will see these functions used in the next section.

The function *find* is private, and so a descendant class cannot use it. You could, however, decide to make *find* protected so that it would be available to descendant classes.

Because you have already seen the pointer-based implementations of the ADT list in Chapter 4, the implementation of *List* is omitted here.

Protected member functions enable a derived class to access private data members

Implementations of the ADT Sorted List That Use the ADT List

Now suppose you want to define and implement a class for the ADT sorted list, whose operations are

```
+createSortedList()
+destroySortedList()
+sortedIsEmpty():boolean {query}
+sortedLength():integer {query}
+sortedInsert(in newItem:ListItemType)
            throw ListException
+sortedRemove(in anItem:ListItemType)
            throw ListException
+sortedRetrieve(in index:integer,
            out dataItem:ListItemType) {query}
            throw ListIndexOutOfRangeException
+locatePosition(in anItem:ListItemType,
            out isPresent:boolean):integer {query}
```

ADT sorted list operations

You could, of course, use an array or a linked list to implement a sorted list, but such an approach would force you to repeat much of the corresponding implementations of *List*.

Fortunately, you can avoid this repetition by using the previously defined class *List* to implement the class *SortedList*. Three approaches are possible by using the *is-a*, *has-a*, and *as-a* relationships between these two classes. In most cases, one or more of the three approaches will not be applicable to a particular problem; usually, one of the approaches will be best, with the *as-a* relationship often the least desirable choice. However, we will use the sorted list to demonstrate all three approaches.

You can reuse List *to implement* SortedList

A sorted list *is a* list. Chapter 3 stated that the ADT list is simply a list of items that you reference by position number. If you maintained those items in sorted order, would you have a sorted list? Ignoring name differences, most operations for the ADT list *are* the same as the corresponding operations for the ADT sorted list. The insertion and deletion operations differ, however, and the ADT sorted list has an additional operation, *locatePosition*.

You can insert an item into a sorted list by first using *locatePosition* to determine the position in the sorted list where the new item belongs. You then use *List*'s *insert* operation to insert the item into that position in the list. You use a similar approach to delete an item from a sorted list.

Thus, a sorted list *is a* list, so you can use public inheritance. That is, the class *SortedList* can be a descendant of the class *List*, inherit-

An is-a *relationship implies public inheritance*

ing *List*'s members, adding the member function *locatePosition*, and revising the insertion and deletion operations, as follows:

```
#include "List.h"
class SortedList: public List
{
public:
// constructors and destructor:
   SortedList();
   SortedList(const SortedList& sList);
   virtual ~SortedList();

// new operations:
   virtual void sortedInsert(ListItemType newItem)
                               throw(ListException);
   virtual void sortedRemove(ListItemType anItem)
                               throw(ListException);
   virtual int locatePosition(ListItemType anItem,
                               bool& isPresent);
};   // end SortedList class
```

The implementations of the sorted list member functions are as follows:

```
SortedList::SortedList()
{
}  // end default constructor

SortedList::SortedList(const SortedList& sList):
                       List(sList)
{
}  // end copy constructor

SortedList::~SortedList()
{
}  // end destructor

void SortedList::sortedInsert(ListItemType newItem)
                               throw(ListException)
{
   bool found;
   int newPosition = locatePosition(newItem, found);
   insert(newPosition, newItem);
}  // end sortedInsert

void SortedList::sortedRemove(ListItemType anItem)
                               throw(ListException)
{
   bool found;
```

```
   int position = locatePosition(anItem, found);
   if (found) // item actually found
      remove(position);
   else
      throw ListException(
         "ListException: Item to remove not found");
}  // end sortedRemove

int SortedList::locatePosition(ListItemType anItem,
                               bool& isPresent)
{
   ListNode *trav = getHead();
   int position = 1;
   while ((trav != NULL) && (getNodeItem(trav) < anItem))
   {
      trav = getNextNode(trav);
      position++;
   }  // end while
   if ((trav != NULL) && (anItem == getNodeItem(trav)))
      isPresent = true;
   else
      isPresent = false;
   return position;
}  // end locatePosition
```

Note the use of *List*'s protected member functions *getHead*, *get-NodeItem*, and *getNextNode*.

The class *SortedList* now has operations such as *isEmpty*, *getLength*, and *retrieve*—which it inherits from the class *List*—and *sortedInsert* and *sortedRemove*. This set of operation names is confusing at best. You can improve this situation in one of two ways:

You use List's protected member functions to access the underlying data structure

1. You can add to *SortedList* member functions such as *sortedGetLength*, which you implement as

   ```
   int SortedList::sortedGetLength()
   {
      return getLength();
   }  // end sortedGetLength
   ```

   Although this approach provides a set of reasonable function names, it allows you to insert into a sorted list either by value (by using *sortedInsert*) or by position (by using the inherited function *insert*). This flexibility might or might not be desirable for your particular application.

   This approach allows list operations on a sorted list

2. You can change the names of the insertion and deletion operations for the sorted list to *insert* and *remove*. You would then implement *insert*, for example, as

   One set of function names is best

```
void SortedList::insert(ListItemType newItem)
                                throw(ListException)
{
   bool found;
   int newPosition = locatePosition(newItem, found);

   List::insert(newPosition, newItem);
}  // end insert
```

Because the insertion operation for both *List* and *SortedList* is named *insert*, you must write *List::insert* to invoke *List*'s insertion operation.

   This approach is in the spirit of polymorphism because it overrides *List*'s insertion and deletion operations, if they are virtual. Thus, you have only one insertion operation and one deletion operation for the sorted list. To enable a derived class to override inherited member functions, similar operations within related classes should really have the same names.

A sorted list *has a* list as a member.   If you do not have an *is-a* relationship between your new class and an existing class, public inheritance is inappropriate. You may, however, be able to use an instance of the existing class to implement the new class. The following declaration of the class *SortedList has a* private data member that is an instance of *List* and that contains the items in the sorted list:

An instance of *List* can implement the sorted list

```
class SortedList
{
public:
// constructors and destructor:
   SortedList();
   SortedList(const SortedList& sList);
   virtual ~SortedList();

// sorted List operations:
   virtual bool sortedIsEmpty() const;
   virtual int  sortedGetLength() const;
   virtual void sortedInsert(ListItemType newItem)
                            throw(ListException);
   virtual void sortedRemove(ListItemType anItem)
                            throw(ListException);
   virtual void sortedRetrieve(int index,
               ListItemType anItem) const
               throw(ListIndexOutOfRangeException);
   virtual int locatePosition(ListItemType anItem,
                            bool& isPresent);

private:
   List aList;
};  // end class
```

You need to implement the constructor, the copy constructor, the destructor, and each method in the class. For example, you implement the insertion operation as follows:

```
void SortedList::sortedInsert(ListItemType newItem)
                            throw(ListException)
{
   bool found;
   int newPosition = locatePosition(newItem, found);
   aList.insert(newPosition, newItem);
}  // end sortedInsert
```

SortedList's data member *aList* is an instance of *List*. The notation *aList.insert* indicates an invocation of *List*'s insertion operation.

Programming Problem 3 at the end of this chapter asks you to complete this implementation. In doing so, you will realize that *locatePosition* needs *retrieve* to access items in *aList*; that is, *List*'s implementation is hidden from *SortedList*. Notice also that a client of *SortedList* cannot access *aList* and has only the sorted list operations available.

A sorted list is implemented *as a* list. Once again, if you do not have an *is-a* relationship between your new class and an existing class, you should not use public inheritance. If, however, you want to inherit members from the existing class, you can instead use private inheritance, as follows:

```
class SortedList: private List
{
public:
     · · · same as public section of the class for previous has-a example
};  // end class
```

The public section of this derived class is the same as the one for the class in the previous *has-a* example. Because clients of *SortedList* do not have access to the member functions of the base class (*List*), you need to provide a complete set of sorted list operations. This was not necessary for public inheritance.

The implementation of *SortedList* can use the public and protected members of *List*. In fact, the member functions have the same implementations as they did with public inheritance.

In both this example and the *has-a* example, *List* is hidden from the clients of *SortedList*. That is, you can use either private inheritance or containment to hide the implementation of the sorted list. Realize, however, that unlike public inheritance, private inheritance does not allow you to use an instance of *SortedList* wherever you can use an instance of *List*; that is, *SortedList* and *List* are not type-compatible.

We will not pursue private inheritance further.

8.5 Class Templates

The ADTs developed in this text thus far manipulate items of a particular data type. For example, the class *List* in the previous section depends on the definition of *ListItemType* to specify the type of list items. You would use a statement such as

```
typedef double ListItemType;  // type of list item;
```

Suppose, however, that your algorithm required two lists: a list of real numbers and a list of characters, for example. An instance of the class *List*, with *ListItemType* defined as *double*, can contain only real numbers. You would need another list node class that was written in terms of a data type other than *ListItemType* to provide a list of characters.

You can avoid multiple class definitions, however, by using a C++ class template to specify a class in terms of a data-type parameter. When you (the client) declare instances of the class, you specify the actual data type that the parameter represents. Templates are used by all of the container classes in the Standard Template Library.

Consider a simple class definition written as a class template, where *T* is the data-type parameter:

A class template describes a class in terms of a data-type parameter

```
template <class T>
class NewClass
{
public:
    NewClass();
    NewClass(T initialData);

    void setData(T newData);
    T getData();

private:
    T theData;
};  // end class
```

You precede the class definition with *template <class T>* and use *T* to represent the data type that the client will specify. This class contains one data member, two member functions to set and access the data member, and two constructors.

A simple program that uses this class template could begin as follows:

```
int main()
{
    NewClass<int>      first;
    NewClass<double>   second(4.8);

    first.setData(5);
    cout << second.getData() << endl;
```

The client specifies an actual data type when declaring an instance of the class template

Notice that the declarations of *first* and *second* specify the data type that the parameter *T* represents within the template.

The implementation of this class template appears as follows:

```
template <class T>
NewClass<T>::NewClass()
{
}  // end default constructor

template <class T>
NewClass<T>::NewClass(T initialData)
                      :theData(initialData)

{
}  // end constructor

template <class T>
void NewClass<T>::setData(T newData)
{
    theData = newData;
}  // end setData

template <class T>
T NewClass<T>::getData()
{
    return theData;
}  // end getData
```

You precede each function definition with *template <class T>* and follow each occurrence of the object type *NewClass* with *<T>*.

You must be careful about what you do with objects of type *T* within the template class. For example, suppose you add a *display* function to the class *NewClass* as follows:

```
void display();
```

with the following implementation:

```
template <class T>
void NewClass<T>::display()
{
    cout << theData;
}  // end display
```

The *display* function assumes that the output stream operator *<<* has been defined for objects of type *T*. This is true when standard types such as *int*, *char*, and even *string* are used, but it may not be true for user-defined types. The next section will show you how to define such operators for an object type. A class template should clearly document the operations that objects of type *T* must support.

You place the class template and its implementation in two separate files, as you did for the classes you have seen before. However, you use them somewhat differently. Most compilers must see how the client uses the class template before they can compile the template's implementation file. That is, the compiler needs to know the actual data type that the parameter *T* represents. Therefore, you do not compile the class template's implementation separately from the program that uses it. Instead, include the implementation file at the end of the header file, and then include the header file in the client program. You will see this organization in the next example.

You do not compile a class template's implementation separately from the client program

The following files revise the pointer-based list class—which appears in Chapter 4 and was discussed again earlier in this chapter—as a class template. Differences between this template version and the earlier versions are shaded. The shorter notation *T* is used instead of *ListItemType* as the parameter that represents the data type of the list items. To avoid distracting detail, the abstract base class discussed earlier is not used.

Template version of a header file for a list node

```
// ********************************************************
// Header file ListNodeT.h for the ADT list.
// Pointer-based implementation -- TEMPLATE VERSION
// ********************************************************

#include <cstddef>
template <class T> class List;

template <class T>
class ListNode
{
private:
   ListNode(): next(NULL) {};
   ListNode(const T & nodeItem, ListNode *ptr)
            : item(nodeItem), next(ptr) {};
   T        item;          // a data item on the list
   ListNode *next;         // pointer to next node

   // friend class - can access private parts
   friend class List <T>;
};  // end class
```

Template version of a header file for ADT list

```
// ********************************************************
// Header file ListT.h for the ADT list.
// Pointer-based implementation -- TEMPLATE VERSION
// ********************************************************
#include "ListNodeT.h"
#include "ListException.h"
```

```cpp
#include "ListIndexOutOfRangeException.h"

template <class T>
class List
{
public:
// constructors and destructor:
    List();
    List(const List<T> & aList);
    virtual ~List();
    // List operations:
    virtual bool isEmpty() const;
    virtual int  getLength() const;
    virtual void insert(int index, T newItem)
            throw(ListIndexOutOfRangeException, ListException);
    virtual void remove(int index)
            throw(ListIndexOutOfRangeException);
    virtual void retrieve(int index, T & dataItem) const
            throw(ListIndexOutOfRangeException);
protected:
    void setSize(int newSize);
    ListNode<T> *getHead() const;
    void setHead(ListNode<T> *newHead);
    T getNodeItem(ListNode<T> *ptr) const;
    ListNode<T> *getNextNode(ListNode<T> *ptr) const;

private:
    int         size;
    ListNode<T> *head;

    ListNode<T> *find(int position) const;
};  // end class

#include "ListT.cpp"
```

If you compare this class template with the earlier declaration of
List, you will see little difference. The declarations

```cpp
class ListNode
```

and

```cpp
class List
```

in the header file are preceded by

```cpp
template <class T>
```

When used as object types, *List* and *ListNode* are followed by *<T>*.

The following excerpts from the implementation file show the differences between the template implementation and the implementation that you saw in Chapter 4. Again, these differences are shaded.

Template version of an implementation file for the ADT list

```cpp
// **********************************************************
// Excerpts from the implementation file ListT.cpp.
// **********************************************************
#include <cstddef>  // for NULL

template <class T>
List<T>::List(): size(0), head(NULL)
{
}  // end default constructor

template <class T>
void List<T>::insert(int index, T newItem)
        throw(ListIndexOutOfRangeException, ListException)
{
    int newLength = getLength() + 1;

    if ((index < 1) || (index > newLength))
        throw ListIndexOutOfRangeException(
        "ListOutOfRangeException: insert index out of range");
    else
    {  // create new node and place newItem in it
        ListNode<T> *newPtr = new ListNode<T>;
        if (newPtr == NULL)
            throw ListException(
            "ListException: insert cannot allocate memory");
        else
        {  size = newLength;
            newPtr->item = newItem;

            // attach new node to list
            if (index == 1)
            {  // insert new node at beginning of list
                newPtr->next = head;
                head = newPtr;
            }
            else
            {  ListNode<T> *prev = find(index-1);
                // insert new node after node
                // to which prev points
                newPtr->next = prev->next;
                prev->next = newPtr;
            }  // end if
```

```
      }   // end if
   }   // end if
} // end insert


template <class T>
ListNode<T> *List<T>::find(int index) const
{
   if ( (index < 1) || (index > getLength()) )
      return NULL;
   else  // count from the beginning of the list
   {  ListNode<T> *cur = head;
      for (int skip = 1; skip < index; ++skip)
         cur = cur->next;
      return cur;
   }   // end if
}   // end find
```

In the implementation file presented in Chapter 4, the *List* method *insert*, for example, begins with

```
void List::insert(int index, ListItemType newItem)
         throw(ListIndexOutOfRangeException, ListException)
```

whereas in the previous template implementation file, it begins with

```
template <class T>
void List<T>::insert(int index, T newItem)
         throw(ListIndexOutOfRangeException, ListException)
```

You precede *void* with *template <class T>*, follow *List* with *<T>*, and replace *ListItemType* with *T*.
   A program that uses the previous class template could begin as follows:

```
#include "ListT.h"
int main()
{
   List<double> floatList;
   List<char>   charList;

   floatList.insert(1, 1.1);
   floatList.insert(2, 2.2);

   charList.insert(1, 'a');
   charList.insert(2, 'b');
   . . .
```

Like our first simple example, the declarations of *floatList* and *charList* specify the data type of the list items.

Converting previous
classes into class
templates is
straightforward

Admittedly, the notation for a class template is imposing, particularly at first, but changing any of the classes that you saw earlier into a template is mechanical and rather straightforward. However, you should realize that the design of the class itself can be quite demanding. Although the previous examples use simple data types, the client could specify data that are instances of a class. The designer, therefore, must ensure that the class template will behave correctly for any data.

Finally, note that a class template can have more than one data-type parameter. The notation

```
template <class T1, class T2>
```

designates two data-type parameters, *T1* and *T2*.

The following list summarizes some key points about class templates.

KEY CONCEPTS

Class Templates

1. A C++ class template is used to specify a class in terms of a data-type parameter.

2. When you (the client) declare instances of a class template, you must specify the actual data type that the class template will use.

3. Any operation required of the actual data type should be clearly documented in the class template.

4. Templates can have more than one data-type parameter.

8.6 Overloaded Operators

The standard arithmetic operators in C++ actually have multiple meanings. Although the addition operators in the expressions *2 + 3* and *2.0 + 3.0* appear to be the same, they in fact are not. Because integers such as 2 and 3 have internal representations that differ from floating-point numbers such as 2.0 and 3.0, the algorithm to add two integers must differ from the algorithm to add two floating-point numbers. C++ could use two different symbols to designate integer addition and floating-point addition, but instead it uses only one symbol, +. The actual meaning of + —that is, the type of addition it designates—is implied by the data type of its operands. An operator with more than one meaning is said to be overloaded and is an example of a simple form of polymorphism.

An overloaded operator has
more than one meaning

You saw earlier that you define new data types within C++ by using classes. Clients of such data types should be able to use them as naturally as the standard data types of the language. In particular, a client should be able to combine instances of a class with C++ operators in meaningful ways. To enable a particular operator to operate correctly on instances of a class, you typically must define a new meaning for the operator; that is, you must overload it.

Suppose that *myList* and *yourList* are two instances of *List* and you write

```
if (myList == yourList)
        cout << "The lists are equal.\n";
```

You must provide *List* with a definition of ==, since the compiler will not provide a default interpretation. To this end, note that list *myList* is equal to list *yourList* if

- *myList* and *yourList* have the same size, and

- Every item on *myList* is the same as the corresponding item on *yourList*.

Two lists are equal if they have identical lengths and items

To overload an operator, you define an operator function whose name has the form

operator *symbol*

where *symbol* is the operator that you want to overload. For the **==** operator, you name the function *operator*== and declare one argument: the object that will appear on the right-hand side of the operator. For *List*, you would add the declaration

virtual bool operator==(const List& rhs**) const;**

to the class definition.[2]

To help you understand this notation, realize that you might have written

virtual bool isEqual**(const** List& rhs**) const;**

To use *isEqual* to compare the lists *myList* and *yourList*, you would write

```
if (myList.isEqual(yourList))
   cout << "The lists are equal.\n";
```

---

[2] In a class template, you would add
  virtual bool operator==(const List<T> & rhs**) const;**
  (assuming that the operator == is defined for type *T*).

You can treat *operator*== exactly as you do *isEqual*; you could write

```
if (myList.operator==(yourList))
   cout << "The lists are equal.\n";
```

because *operator*== is simply a function name. However, you can also use the more natural notation *myList == yourList* instead of *my-List.operator==(yourList)*.

The pointer-based implementation of this function is

```
bool List::operator==(const List& rhs) const
{
   bool isEqual;
   if (size != rhs.size)
      isEqual = false;  // lists have unequal lengths

   else if ( (head == NULL) && (rhs.head == NULL) )
      isEqual = true;  // both lists are empty

   else // lists have same length > 0;
        // head pointers not NULL
   {  // compare items
      ListNode *leftPtr = head;
      ListNode *rightPtr = rhs.head;
      for (int count = 1;
            (count <= size) &&
                    (leftPtr->item == rightPtr->item);
          ++count)
      {  leftPtr = leftPtr->next;
         rightPtr = rightPtr->next;
      }  // end for

      isEqual = count > size;
   }  // end if
   return isEqual;
}  // end operator==
```

The == operator must be defined for items on the list

Note that this function depends on the == operator for items on the list. If these items are themselves instances of a class, then that class must overload ==.

You can overload the relational operators (<, <=, >, >=) in a similar manner. The assignment operator (=), however, presents other concerns. Once again, suppose that *myList* and *yourList* are two instances of *List*. If you place several items in the list *yourList* and then write

```
myList = yourList;
```

you would expect *myList* to be an exact copy of *yourList*. Without an overloaded assignment operator, however, you would get a shallow copy of *yourList* instead of a deep copy (see Figure 4-18). That is, only the data members of *yourList* would be copied. While a shallow copy might be sufficient for a statically allocated data structure, a deep copy is necessary for a dynamically allocated one. For example, for a pointer-based implementation of *List*, a shallow copy would copy only the data members *size* (the length of the list *yourList*) and *head* (the pointer to *yourList*'s first item). The items in the list would not be copied.

Without an overloaded assignment operator, you get a shallow copy

To provide an assignment operator for the class *List*, you would add the declaration

virtual List & **operator**=(**const** List& rhs);

to the class definition.[3] The argument *rhs* represents the object to be copied, that is, the object that will appear on the right-hand side of the assignment operator. The function is valued instead of void to accommodate assignments such as *myList = yourList = theirList*. As you will see, the function returns a reference to the invoking object.

In implementing this function, you must deal with a few subtleties. Suppose that *myList* and *yourList*, our two instances of *List*, each contain several items. If you write

myList = yourList;

what happens to the items that were in *myList*? You might not care, as long as *myList* ultimately contains a copy of the items in *yourList*. You should care, however, if you have a pointer-based list. Before you can copy the linked list of items in *yourList*, you need to deallocate the linked list of items in *myList*. Failure to do so results in a memory leak; that is, memory that was allocated to *myList* is not returned to the system and is inaccessible. Thus, the assignment of *yourList* to *myList* must take these steps:

The assignment operator must first deallocate *myList*, the object on the left-hand side

```
Deallocate memory assigned to myList
for (each item in yourList)
{  Allocate a new node for myList
   Set the node's data portion to a copy of the
     item in yourList
}  // end for
```

---

[3] In a class template, you would add
 virtual List<T> & **operator**=(**const** List<T> & rhs);
 (assuming that the operator = is defined for type *T*).

The tasks necessary here are like those that you implemented when you wrote the destructor and copy constructor for *List*. To avoid redundancy, you can reorganize *List*, providing the member functions *removeAll* to delete all the items from a list and *copyListNodes* to copy the nodes in the underlying linked list of items. These functions can be used for other purposes besides the implementation of the assignment operator. The destructor can call *removeAll*, and the copy constructor can call *copyListNodes*. Although you want *copyList-Nodes* to be either private or protected, *removeAll* could be a useful public member. Programming Problem 1 asks you to implement these two functions.

Now suppose you write

Make the assignment opera-tor fail-safe by checking for a special case

```
myList = myList;
```

Notice what our previous pseudocode tells you to do here: Deallocate *myList* and then make a copy of *myList*. After you have deallocated *myList*, there is nothing left to copy! Your implementation should test for this special case by asking whether the invoking object on the left side of the = is the same as the object on the right. Your assignment operator should be fail-safe.

You can make this test by comparing the addresses of the two list objects rather than by comparing the items on the lists. In C++, *this* is a pointer to the invoking object. Thus, you write

```
if (this != &rhs)
```

to compare the addresses of the objects on the left and right of the =.

The pointer-based implementation of the overloaded assignment operator for *List* follows:

```
List & List::operator=(const List& rhs)
{
   // check for assignment to self
   if (this != &rhs)
   {  removeAll();    // deallocate left-hand side
      copyListNodes(rhs); // copy list nodes
      size = rhs.size;    // copy size of list
   }  // end if
   return *this;
} // end operator=
```

The function returns **this*, which is the invoking object.

The following list provides some guidelines for overloading operators.

Guidelines for Overloading Operators

1. You can overload any C++ operator except

   `.`   `.*`   `::`   `?:`   `sizeof`

2. You cannot define new operators by overloading symbols that are not already operators in C++.

3. You cannot change the standard precedence of a C++ operator or the number of its operands.

4. At least one operand of an overloaded operator must be an instance of a class.

5. A typical class should overload at least the assignment (=), the equality (== and !=), and the relational (<, <=, >, >=) operators.

6. You cannot change the number of arguments for an overloaded method.

8.7 Iterators

An iterator is an object that can access a collection of like objects one object at a time. That is, an iterator traverses the collection of objects. For example, the ADT list presented in Chapters 3 and 4 contains a collection of like objects. The list's index value, combined with the *retrieve* operation, acts as a primitive form of iterator. The index value indicates which item in the collection is accessed, and the *retrieve* operation returns that item. To access the next item in the list, you increment the index value and call the *retrieve* operation again.

An iterator is an object that traverses a collection of like objects

Typically, an iterator has an operation that accesses the item it currently references. Usually this operation is implemented by overloading the C++ dereferencing operator `*`. For example, you define the `*` operator for an iterator *i* so that `*i` is the item that *i* references.

Iterators also have operations that move the iterator forward and backward through the collection. Often, these operations take the form of the overloaded operators `++` and `--`. Lastly, the operators `==` and `!=` are usually overloaded to compare iterators for equality.

Here is the specification of a class *ListIterator* that you can use with a special version of the ADT list that uses iterators. You will see that version of the list in the next section. Note that *ListIterator* does not provide the `--` operator; you can only move forward through the list. Programming Problem 15 at the end of this chapter asks you to implement a bidirectional iterator with the `--` operator.

KEY CONCEPTS

Common Iterator Operations

Operation	Description
*	Return the item that the iterator currently references
++	Move the iterator to the next item in the list
--	Move the iterator to the previous item in the list
==	Compare two iterators for equality
!=	Compare two iterators for inequality

```cpp
// ************************************************************
// Header file ListIterator.h.
// Used in the iterator version of the ADT list.
// ************************************************************
#include "ListNode.h" // Definition of ListNode and
                      // ListItemType; ListNode declares
                      // ListIterator as a friend class
class ListIterator
{
public:
   ListIterator(List *container, ListNode *nodePtr);

   const ListItemType & operator*();
   ListIterator operator++();     // prefix ++

   bool operator==(const ListIterator& rhs) const;
   bool operator!=(const ListIterator& rhs) const;

   friend class List;

private:
   const List *container; // ADT associated with iterator
   ListNode *cur;         // current location in collection
}; // end class
```

The operator ++ is the prefix version of ++. It advances the iterator to the next item in the list. The operators == and != compare iterator objects for equality. The iterator has private variables that keep track of the list being iterated, and it has a pointer into the list that represents the current position of the iterator in the list. Since the *List* class will provide functions that return iterators, *List* must be able to access the private parts of an iterator. Thus, *List* is declared as a friend of the class *ListIterator*. Also assume that the *ListIterator* class is a friend of the class *ListNode*.

List is a friend class of *ListIterator*

List and *ListIterator* are friend classes of *ListNode*

The implementation of the *ListIterator*'s member functions are as follows:

```cpp
// ************************************************************
// Implementation file ListIterator.cpp.
// ************************************************************
#include "ListIterator.h"

ListIterator::ListIterator(const List *aList,
                           ListNode *nodePtr)
                         : container(aList),cur(nodePtr)
{
} //end constructor

const ListItemType & ListIterator::operator*()
{
   return cur->item;
} // end operator*

ListIterator ListIterator::operator++()
{
   cur = cur->next;
   return *this;
}  // end prefix operator++

bool ListIterator::operator==(const ListIterator& rhs) const
{
   return ((container==rhs.container) &&
           (cur == rhs.cur));
}  // end operator ==

bool ListIterator::operator!=(const ListIterator& rhs) const
{
   return !(*this == rhs);
}  // end operator !=
```

Implementing the ADT List Using Iterators

We are now ready to rewrite the *List* class, using the *ListIterator* class. Operations that previously used an index value use a list iterator here. Also note that many of the operations now return an iterator value.

```cpp
// ************************************************************
// Header file ListI.h for the ADT list.
// Implementation uses ListIterator.
// ************************************************************
```

```cpp
#include "ListIterator.h"
#include "ListException.h"

class List
{
public:
// constructors and destructor:
   List();
   List(const List& aList);
   ~List();

// List operations:
   bool isEmpty() const;
   int getLength() const;

   ListIterator insert(ListIterator iter,
                       ListItemType newItem)
         throw(ListException);
   // Inserts an item into a list after the item
   // specified by iter.  An iterator to the newly
   // added item is returned.
   // Precondition: Iterator iter specifies either an
   // item in the list or the end of the list.
   // Postcondition:  If iter equals the value returned
   // by end(), newItem is placed at the end of the
   // list. Returns an iterator to newItem within the list.
   // Exception: Throws ListException if the iterator is
   // not initialized properly for this list.

   void retrieve(ListIterator iter,
                 ListItemType& dataItem) const
         throw(ListException);
   // Retrieves an item in the list.
   // Precondition: Iterator iter specifies an item in
   // the list.
   // Postcondition: dataItem is the value of the
   // desired item.
   // Exception: Throws ListException if the iterator is
   // not initialized properly for this list.

   ListIterator remove(ListIterator iter) throw(ListException);
   // Removes an item from the list and returns an
   // iterator to the item after the removed item.
   // Precondition: Iterator iter specifies an item in
   // the list.
   // Postcondition: The item specified by iter is
   // removed from the list. Returns an iterator that
   // references the item after the one removed. If the last
```

```
// item in the list is removed, returns an iterator that
// is equal to the result returned by end().
// Exception: Throws ListException if the iterator is
// not initialized properly for this list.

ListIterator begin() const;
// Returns an iterator that references the first item
// in the list.
// Precondition: None.
// Postcondition: Returns an iterator to the first
// item in the list. If the list is empty, returns an
// iterator that is equal to the result returned by end().

ListIterator end() const;
// Returns an iterator value that can be used to
// determine whether an iterator has reached the end
// of the list.
// Precondition: None.
// Postcondition: None

private:
    int        size;    // number of items in the list
    ListNode *head;  // pointer to the linked list

    ListNode *findPrev(ListIterator iter);
    // Locates the node before the node specified by iter.
    // Precondition: The list is not empty (head != NULL).
    // Postcondition: Returns a pointer to the node
    // before the node referenced by iter.  If iter == end(),
    // returns a pointer to the last node in the list.
};  // end class
```

The member function *begin* allows the client to initialize an iterator to the beginning of the list. The function *end* returns a value that can be used to determine whether the end of the list has been reached.

Here is a simple program that demonstrates the use of the *List* class that utilizes the iterator class *ListIterator*:

```
#include "ListI.h"
#include <iostream>
using namespace std;

int main()
{
    List aList;

    ListIterator i = aList.begin();
    for (int j=1; j<=5; j++)
```

```
   {
      i = aList.insert(i, j);
   } // end for

   i = aList.begin();
   while (i != aList.end())
   {
      cout << *i << " ";
      ++i;
   } // end while
   cout << endl;

   return 0;
} // end main
```

The implementation of the member functions *begin*, *end*, and *insert* are as follows:

```
#include "ListI.h"
ListIterator List:: begin() const
{
   ListIterator iter(this, head);
   return iter;
} // end begin

ListIterator List::end() const
{
   ListIterator iter(this, NULL);
   return iter;
} // end end

ListIterator List::insert(ListIterator iter,
                          ListItemType newItem)
                   throw(ListException)
{ // Make sure iterator references this list
   if ((iter.container == this))
   { // create new node and place NewItem in it
      ListNode *newPtr = new ListNode(newItem, NULL);
      if (newPtr == NULL)
         throw ListException(
         "ListException: insert cannot allocate memory");

      else
      { size++;
         // attach new node to list
         if (iter == begin())
         { // insert new node at beginning of list
```

```
          newPtr->next = head;
          head = newPtr;
      }
      else
      {  ListNode *prev = findPrev(iter);
         // insert new node before node
         // to which iter references
         newPtr->next = prev->next;
         prev->next = newPtr;
      }  // end if
   }  // end if
   return ListIterator(this, newPtr);
   }  // end if
 else
    throw ListException(
    "ListException: insert has bad iterator value");
} // end insert
```

Programming Problem 14 at the end of this chapter asks you to add exception handling to the class and provide implementations for the other member functions.

Summary

1. Classes can have ancestor and descendant relationships. A derived, or descendant, class inherits all members of its previously defined base class but can access only the public and protected members. Private members of a class are accessible only by its member functions (and friends). Protected members can be accessed by member functions (and friends) of both the class and any derived classes, but not by clients of these classes.

2. With public inheritance, the public and protected members of the base class remain, respectively, public and protected members of the derived class. Such a derived class is type-compatible with its base class. That is, you can use an instance of a derived class wherever you can use an instance of its base class. This relationship between the base and derived classes is an *is-a* relationship.

3. A member function in a derived class redefines a member function in the base class if they have the same declarations. A virtual member function in a derived class overrides a virtual member function in the base class if they have the same declarations.

4. A virtual member function in a class is a function that you can override in a derived class. When a member function is virtual, you can either implement it or make it pure. A pure virtual function has an undefined body.

5. A derived class inherits the interface of each function that is in its base class. A derived class also inherits the implementation of each nonvirtual function that is in its base class.

6. A class with at least one pure virtual member function is called an abstract base class. An abstract base class specifies only the essential members necessary for its descendants and, therefore, can serve as the base class for a family of classes.

7. Early, or static, binding describes a situation whereby a compiler can determine at compilation time the correct member function to invoke. Late, or dynamic, binding describes a situation whereby the system makes this determination at execution time.

8. When you use a pointer to an object to invoke a method—for example, `spherePtr->displayStatistics()`—the type of pointer determines the appropriate version of the method under early binding, whereas the type of object is the determining factor under late binding.

9. Class templates enable you to parameterize the type of a class's data.

10. You can provide additional meaning to an existing C++ operator for instances of a class by overloading it. In general, a class should overload assignment, equality, and relational operators.

11. Iterators provide an alternative way to cycle through a collection of items.

Cautions

1. If a member function is not virtual, you must implement it. As a result, you force any derived class to inherit the implementation of each such function.

2. If a member function is virtual but not pure, you must implement it. A derived class can either use or override such an implementation. The advantage of a pure virtual function is that a derived class cannot accidentally inherit the function's implementation, because it does not have one.

3. You should use public inheritance only if the relationship between two classes is *is-a*.

4. Failure to overload the assignment, equality, and relational operators of a class can lead to errors when a client combines instances of the class with operators whose meaning has not been defined for the class.

Self-Test Exercises

Self-Test Exercises 1, 2, and 3 consider the classes *Sphere* and *Ball*, which this chapter describes in the section "Inheritance Revisited."

1. Write C++ statements for the following tasks:

    a. Declare an instance *mySphere* of *Sphere* with a radius 2.

    b. Declare an instance *myBall* of *Ball* whose radius is 6 and whose name is *Beach ball*.

    c. Display the diameters of *mySphere* and *myBall*.

2. Define a class *Planet* that publicly inherits *Ball*, as defined in this chapter. Your new class should have a private data member that specifies a planet's distance from the sun and public member functions that access or alter this distance.

3. **a.** Can *resetBall*, which is a member function of *Ball*, access *Sphere*'s data member *theRadius* directly, or must *resetBall* call *Sphere*'s *setRadius*? Explain.

    b. Repeat Part *a*, but assume that *theRadius* is a protected data member instead of a private data member of the class *Sphere*.

4. Consider the class GDP, as described in the section "Abstract Base Classes." Which member functions in the class GDP must be virtual in anticipation of the derived classes CDP and DVDP?

5. Consider the class *SortedList*, as described in this chapter. If *aList* is an alphabetical list of people's names, should *aList* be an instance of *SortedList*, or should it be an instance of a class that is derived from *SortedList*? Explain.

6. Consider a derived class of the abstract base class *BasicADT*, as given in this chapter. If *aList* is an instance of this derived class, must the derived class provide an implementation for the functions *isEmpty* and *getLength*? Explain.

7. Why should a class's private member functions never be virtual?

8. Given the class template *NewClass*, as described in the section "Class Templates," write a statement that defines an instance *myClass* of *NewClass* for character data. Write another statement that sets *myClass*'s data portion to '*c*'. Finally, write a statement that displays the data portion of *myClass*.

Exercises

1. Recall the classes *Sphere* and *Ball*, as described in this chapter in the section "Inheritance Revisited," and consider the following variation:

```
class Sphere
{
public:
   . . .
   double getArea() const;   // surface area
   void displayStatistics() const;
   . . .
}; // end class

class Ball: public Sphere
{
public:
   . . .
   double getArea() const;   // cross-sectional area
   void displayStatistics() const;
   . . .
}; // end class
```

Suppose that the implementation of each version of *display-Statistics* invokes the function *getArea*.

a. If *mySphere* is an instance of *Sphere* and *myBall* is an instance of *Ball*, which version of *getArea* does each of the following calls to *displayStatistics* invoke? Explain your answer.

```
mySphere.displayStatistics();
myBall.displayStatistics();
```

b. If the statements

```
Sphere *spherePtr;
Ball *ballPtr;
```

declare *spherePtr* and *ballPtr*, which version of *getArea* does each of the following calls to *displayStatistics* invoke? Explain your answer.

```
spherePtr->displayStatistics();
spherePtr = &myBall;
spherePtr->displayStatistics();
ballPtr->displayStatistics();
```

2. Define and implement a class *Pen* that has an instance of *Ball* as one of its members. Provide several members for the class *Pen*, such as the data member *color* and member functions *isEmpty* and *write*.

3. Consider the following classes:

   LandVehicle represents a vehicle that travels on land. Its public methods include *wheelCount* and *speed*.

   MotorizedLandVehicle represents a land vehicle that has a motor. Its public methods include *engineCapacity* and *fuelType*.

   a. Which of the methods mentioned above can the implementation of *speed* invoke?

   b. Which of the methods mentioned above can the implementation of *engineCapacity* invoke?

4. Assume the classes described in the previous question and consider a main method that contains the following statements:

   ```
   LandVehicle landVeh;
   MotorizedLandVehicle motorVeh;
   ```

   a. Which of these objects can invoke the method *wheelCount*?

   b. Which of these objects can invoke the method *fuelType*?

5. The section "Abstract Base Classes" gives a version of the abstract base class *EquidistantShape* that contains a private data member *theRadius*.

   a. Revise the class *Sphere*, which is a derived class of *EquidistantShape*. Which methods must you implement?

   b. Define a class of circles as a derived class of *EquidistantShape*.

   c. Revise the abstract base class *EquidistantShape* so that *theRadius* is a protected data member instead of a private data member. Which methods are virtual, and which methods must you implement?

   d. Repeat Parts a and b, assuming the revision you made in Part c.

6. Consider the following classes:

   ```
   class Expr
   {
   public:
       . . .
       int getLength() const;
   ```

```cpp
    virtual void display() const;
    . . .
private:
    char Array[MAX_STRING+1];
};   // end class


class AlgExpr: public Expr
{
public:

    . . .
    bool isExpression() const;
    bool isBlank(int first, int last) const;
};   // end class


class InfixExpr: public AlgExpr
{
public:

    . . .
    bool isExpression() const;
    int valueOf() const;
    void display() const;
    . . .
protected:
    int endFactor(int first, int last) const;
    int endTerm(int first, int last) const;
    int endExpression(int first, int last) const;

private:
    Stack<int>  values;
    Stack<char> operators;
};   // end class
```

The class *AlgExpr* represents algebraic expressions, including prefix, postfix, and infix expressions. Its member function *isExpression* simply examines the expression for valid characters but does not consider the order of the characters.

The class *InfixExpr* represents infix expressions. Its *isExpression* calls *isBlank*, and its *display* calls *valueOf*.

a. Should *isBlank* be public, protected, or private? Explain.

b. If *inExp* is an instance of *InfixExpr* in the main function, can *inExp* invoke *endExpression*? Explain.

c. What small change(s) would you make to the above classes to ensure that the correct version of *isExpression* is called?

7. Assume the classes described in the previous question, and consider a main function that contains

```
Expr exp;
AlgExpr aExp;
InfixExpr inExp;
```

    a. Which of these objects can correctly invoke the function `getLength`?

    b. Which of these objects can correctly invoke the function `isExpression`?

    c. Which of these objects can correctly invoke the function `valueOf`?

    d. Give an example of object type compatibility by writing a function declaration and a call to it that could appear in this main function.

8. Consider an ADT front list, which restricts insertions, deletions, and retrievals to the first item in the list.

    a. Define a class `FrontList` that will use a pointer-based implementation and that is a descendant of the abstract base class `BasicADT`.

    b. Define and implement a class for the ADT stack that is a descendant of `FrontList`.

9. Define an abstract base class `Person` that describes a typical person. Next, define a derived class `Student` that describes a typical student. Finally, derive from `Student` a class `GradStudent` for a typical graduate student.

10. Design and implement the following classes:

    a. An abstract class `Employee` that represents a generic employee. Include methods to retrieve information about an employee.

    b. A subclass of `Employee` called `HourlyEmployee` that describes an employee who gets paid by the hour. Include a public method called *pay* that returns the pay of the employee for that month, and any other relevant methods.

    c. A subclass of `Employee` called `NonHourlyEmployee` that describes an employee who gets paid a fixed salary every month. Include a public method called *pay* that returns the pay of the employee for that month. Include any other relevant methods.

11. The section "Class Templates" describes a class template for *List*. Using this template, write statements that define an ADT list of five user-specified integers.

12. Overload the assignment (=) operator for the pointer-based implementations of *Stack* (Chapter 6) and *Queue* (Chapter 7). *Hint*: Study the copy constructors.

Programming Problems

1. The section "Overloaded Operators" suggests a revision of *List* to include the public function *removeAll* and the private function *copyListNodes*. Complete a pointer-based implementation of *List* that includes these functions as well as overloaded equality (== and !=) and assignment (=) operators.

2. Define and implement an array-based version of the class *List* as a descendant of the abstract base class *BasicADT*.

3. Complete the implementation of *SortedList* that has an instance of *List* as a member.

4. The class *List*, as described in this chapter, does not contain a method *position* that returns the number of a particular item, given the item's value. Such a method enables you to pass the node's number to *remove*, for example, to delete the item.

   Define a descendant of *List* that has *position* as a member function as well as member functions that insert, delete, and retrieve items by their values instead of their positions. Always make insertions at the beginning of the list. Although the items in this list are not sorted, the new ADT is analogous to *SortedList*, which contains the method *locatePosition*.

5. Consider an ADT circular list, which is like the ADT list but treats its first item as being immediately after its last item. For example, if a circular list contains six items, retrieval or deletion of the eighth item actually involves the list's second item. Let insertion into a circular list, however, behave exactly like insertion into a list. Define and implement the ADT circular list as a derived class of *List*, as described in this chapter.

6. Programming Problem 13 in Chapter 6 describes the ADT traversable stack. In addition to the standard stack operations—*isEmpty*, *push*, *pop*, and *getTop*—a traversable stack includes the operation. This operation begins at the bottom of the stack and displays each item in the stack until it reaches the top of the stack.

   Define and implement the ADT traversable stack as a derived class of *Stack*, as given in Chapter 6.

7. Exercise 11 in Chapter 7 defined the doubly ended queue, or deque. Define and implement the ADT deque as a derived class of *Queue*, as given in Chapter 7.

8. Complete the implementation of the class template for *List* that this chapter describes in the section "Class Templates."

9. Define and implement a class template for the ADT stack, which Chapter 6 describes.

   a. Use an array–based implementation.

   b. Use a pointer–based implementation.

10. Define and implement a class template for the ADT queue, which Chapter 7 describes.

   a. Use an array–based implementation.

   b. Use a pointer–based implementation.

11. Define and implement a class template for the ADT sorted list that is derived from the template for *List*. A sorted list must compare items, so you need to allow for the comparison of objects of unknown types.

12. Since algebraic expressions are character strings, you can derive a class of algebraic expressions from a class of strings. Begin this problem by creating your own simple string class called *SimpleString*. (See Programming Problems 6 and 7 of Chapter 4.) You will need at least the following string operations:

   - String input and output

   - Determination of the string length

   - Access to the nth character, where the first character is numbered 1

   Overloaded operators =, ==, !=, <, >, <=, and >= are desirable.

   Programming Problem 8 of Chapter 5 describes a grammar and a recognition algorithm for infix algebraic expressions. That grammar makes left-to-right association illegal when consecutive operators have the same precedence. Thus, *a/b*c* is illegal, but both *a/(b*c)* and *(a/b)*c* are legal.

   Programming Problem 8 of Chapter 6 describes an algorithm to evaluate an infix expression that is syntactically correct by using two stacks.

   Design and implement a class of algebraic expressions derived from the class *SimpleString*. Include an *isExpression* operation—based on the recognition algorithm given in Chapter 5—and a *valueOf* operation—based on the evaluation algorithm given in Chapter 6. Use the class template for a stack that Programming Problem 9 describes.

13. Chapter 5 described the classes *Board* and *Queen* that were used in a solution to the Eight Queens problem. Programming Problem 1 of Chapter 5 asked you to write a program to solve the Eight Queens problem based on these classes. Revise that program to define one of these classes as a *friend* class.

14. Complete the iterator version of the *List* class presented in the last section of this chapter. Also add exception handling to the operations.

15. Define and implement a bidirectional iterator for the ADT circular doubly linked list described in Programming Problem 5 of Chapter 4. Revise the circular doubly linked list implementation to use the list iterator.

CHAPTER 9

Algorithm Efficiency and Sorting

PREVIEW

This chapter will show you how to analyze the efficiency of algorithms. The basic mathematical techniques for analyzing algorithms are central to more advanced topics in computer science and give you a way to formalize the notion that one algorithm is significantly more efficient than another. As examples, you will see analyses of some algorithms that you have studied before, including those that search data. In addition, this chapter examines the important topic of sorting data. You will study some simple algorithms, which you may have seen before, and some more-sophisticated recursive algorithms. Sorting algorithms provide varied and relatively easy examples of the analysis of efficiency.

9.1 Measuring the Efficiency of Algorithms

The comparison of algorithms is a topic that is central to computer science. Measuring an algorithm's efficiency is quite important because your choice of algorithm for a given application often has a great impact. Responsive word processors, grocery checkout systems, automatic teller machines, video games, and life support systems all depend on efficient algorithms.

Suppose two algorithms perform the same task, such as searching. What does it mean to compare the algorithms and conclude that one is better? Chapter 1 discussed the several components that contribute to the cost of a computer program. Some of these components involve the cost of human time—the time of the people who develop, maintain, and use the program. The other components involve the cost of program execution—that is, the program's efficiency—measured by the amount of computer time and space that the program requires to execute.

We have, up to this point, emphasized the human cost of a computer program. The early chapters of this book stressed style and readability. They pointed out that well-designed algorithms reduce the human costs of implementing the algorithm with a program, of maintaining the program, and of modifying the program. The primary concern has been to develop good problem-solving skills and programming style. Although we shall continue to concentrate our efforts in that direction, the efficiency of algorithms is also important. Efficiency is a criterion that you should use when selecting an algorithm and its implementation. The solutions in this book, in addition to illustrating good programming style, are frequently based on relatively efficient algorithms.

Consider efficiency when selecting an algorithm

The **analysis of algorithms** is the area of computer science that provides tools for contrasting the efficiency of different methods of solution. Notice the use of the term *methods of solution* rather than *programs*; it is important to emphasize that the analysis concerns itself primarily with *significant* differences in efficiency—differences that you can usually obtain only through superior methods of solution and rarely through clever tricks in coding. Reductions in computing costs due to clever coding tricks are often more than offset by reduced program readability, which increases human costs. An analysis should focus on gross differences in the efficiency of algorithms that are likely to dominate the overall cost of a solution. To do otherwise could lead you to select an algorithm that runs a small fraction of a second faster than another algorithm yet requires many more hours of your time to implement and maintain.

A comparison of algorithms should focus on significant differences in efficiency

The efficient use of both time and memory is important. Computer scientists use similar techniques to analyze an algorithm's time and space efficiency. Since none of the algorithms covered in this text has significant space requirements, our focus will be primarily on time efficiency.

How do you compare the time efficiency of two algorithms that solve the same problem? One possible approach is to implement the two algorithms in C++ and run the programs. This approach has at least three fundamental difficulties:

1. **How are the algorithms coded?** If algorithm A_1 runs faster than algorithm A_2, it could be the result of better programming. Thus, if you compare the running times of the programs, you are really comparing implementations of the algorithms rather than the algorithms themselves. You should not compare implementations, because they are sensitive to factors such as programming style that tend to cloud the issue of which algorithm is inherently more efficient.

Three difficulties with comparing programs instead of algorithms

2. **What computer should you use?** The particular computer on which the programs are run also obscures the issue of which algorithm is inherently more efficient. One computer may simply be much faster than the other, so clearly you should use the same computer for both programs. Which computer should you choose? The particular operations that the algorithms require can cause A_1 to run faster than A_2 on one computer, while the opposite is true on another computer. You should compare the efficiency of the algorithms independently of a particular computer.

3. **What data should the programs use?** Perhaps the most important difficulty on this list is the selection of the data for the programs to use. There is always the danger that you will select instances of the problem for which one of the algorithms runs uncharacteristically fast. For example, when comparing a sequential search and a binary search of a sorted array, you might search for an item that happens to be the smallest item in the array. In such a case, the sequential search will find the item more quickly than the binary search because the item is first in the array and so is the first item that the sequential search will examine. Any analysis of efficiency must be independent of specific data.

To overcome these difficulties, computer scientists employ mathematical techniques that analyze algorithms independently of specific implementations, computers, or data. You begin this analysis by counting the number of significant operations in a particular solution, as the next section describes.

Algorithm analysis should be independent of specific implementations, computers, and data

The Execution Time of Algorithms

Previous chapters have informally compared different solutions to a given problem by looking at the number of operations that each solution required. For example, Chapter 4 compared array-based and pointer-based implementations of the ADT list and found that an array-based list *retrieve* function could access the nth item in a list directly in one step, because the item is stored in *items[n-1]*. A

Counting an algorithm's operations is a way to assess its efficiency

pointer-based `retrieve`, however, must traverse the list from its beginning until the nth node is reached, and so would require n steps.

An algorithm's execution time is related to the number of operations it requires. Counting an algorithm's operations—if possible—is a way to assess its efficiency. Consider a few other examples.

Traversal of a linked list. Recall from Chapter 4 that you can display the contents of a linked list to which *head* points by using the following statements:[1]

```
Node *cur = head;               ← 1 assignment
while (cur != NULL)             ← n + 1 comparisons
{   cout << cur->item << endl;  ← n writes
    cur = cur->next;            ← n assignments
}  // end while
```

Assuming a linked list of n nodes, these statements require $n + 1$ assignments, $n + 1$ comparisons, and n write operations. If each assignment, comparison, and write operation requires, respectively, a, c, and w time units, the statements require $(n + 1) * (a + c) + n * w$ time units.[2] Thus, the time required to write n nodes is proportional to n. This conclusion makes sense intuitively: It takes longer to display, or traverse, a linked list of 100 items than it does a linked list of 10 items.

Displaying the data in a linked list of n nodes requires time proportional to n

The Towers of Hanoi. Chapter 5 proved recursively that the solution to the Towers of Hanoi problem with n disks requires $2^n - 1$ moves. If each move requires the same time m, the solution requires $(2^n - 1) * m$ time units. As you will soon see, this time requirement increases rapidly as the number of disks increases.

Nested loops. Consider an algorithm that contains nested loops of the following form:

```
for (i = 1 through n)
    for (j = 1 through i)
        for (k = 1 through 5)
            Task T
```

If task T requires t time units, the innermost loop on k requires $5 * t$ time units. The loop on j requires $5 * t * i$ time units, and the outermost loop on i requires

---

[1] Chapter 4 actually used a `for` statement. We use an equivalent `while` statement here to clarify the analysis.

[2] Although omitting multiplication operators is common in algebra, we indicate them explicitly here to facilitate counting them.

$$\sum_{i=1}^{n} (5 * t * i) = 5 * t * (1 + 2 + \cdots + n) = 5 * t * n * (n + 1)/2$$

time units.

Algorithm Growth Rates

As you can see, the previous examples derive an algorithm's time requirement as a function of the problem size. The way to measure a problem's size depends on the application—typical examples are the number of nodes in a linked list, the number of disks in the Tower of Hanoi problem, the size of an array, or the number of items in a stack. Thus, we reached conclusions such as

Measure an algorithm's time requirement as a function of the problem size

> *Algorithm A requires $n^2/5$ time units to solve a problem of size n*

> *Algorithm B requires 5 * n time units to solve a problem of size n*

The time units in these two statements must be the same before you can compare the efficiency of the two algorithms. Perhaps we should have written

> *Algorithm A requires $n^2/5$ seconds to solve a problem of size n*

Our earlier discussion indicates the difficulties with such a statement: On what computer does the algorithm require $n^2/5$ seconds? What implementation of the algorithm requires $n^2/5$ seconds? What data caused the algorithm to require $n^2/5$ seconds?

What specifically do you want to know about the time requirement of an algorithm? The most important thing to learn is how quickly the algorithm's time requirement grows as a function of the problem size. Statements such as

> *Algorithm A requires time proportional to n^2*

> *Algorithm B requires time proportional to n*

each express an algorithm's proportional time requirement, or growth rate, and enable you to compare algorithm *A* with another algorithm *B*. Although you cannot determine the exact time requirement for either algorithm *A* or algorithm *B* from these statements, you can determine that for large problems, *B* will require significantly less time than *A*. That is, *B*'s time requirement—as a function of the problem size *n*—increases at a slower rate than *A*'s time requirement, because *n* increases at a slower rate than n^2. Even if *B* actually requires 5 * *n* seconds and *A* actually requires $n^2/5$ seconds, *B* eventually will require significantly less time than *A*, as *n* increases. Figure 9-1 illustrates this fact. Thus, an assertion like "*A* requires time proportional to n^2" is exactly the kind of statement that characterizes the inherent efficiency of an algorithm independently of such factors as particular computers and implementations.

Compare algorithm efficiencies for large problems

Figure 9-1 also shows that A's time requirement does not exceed B's until n exceeds 25. Algorithm efficiency is typically a concern for large problems only. The time requirements for small problems are generally not large enough to matter. Thus, our analyses assume large values of n.

Order-of-Magnitude Analysis and Big O Notation

If

Algorithm A requires time proportional to f(n)

Algorithm A is said to be **order f(n)**, which is denoted as **O(f(n))**. The function $f(n)$ is called the algorithm's **growth-rate function**. Because the notation uses the capital letter O to denote *order*, it is called the **Big O notation**. If a problem of size n requires time that is directly proportional to n, the problem is $O(n)$—that is, order n. If the time requirement is directly proportional to n^2, the problem is $O(n^2)$, and so on.

The following definition formalizes these ideas:

KEY CONCEPTS

Definition of the Order of an Algorithm

Algorithm A is order $f(n)$ — denoted $O(f(n))$ — if constants k and n_0 exist such that A requires no more than $k * f(n)$ time units to solve a problem of size $n \geq n_0$.

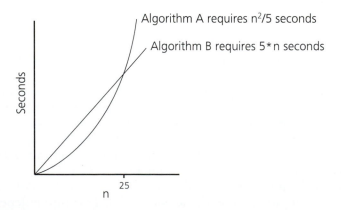

Algorithm A requires $n^2/5$ seconds

Algorithm B requires $5*n$ seconds

Seconds

25

n

FIGURE 9-1   Time requirements as a function of the problem size n

The requirement $n \geq n_0$ in the definition of $O(f(n))$ formalizes the notion of sufficiently large problems. In general, many values of k and n can satisfy the definition.

The following examples illustrate the definition:

- Suppose that an algorithm requires $n^2 - 3 * n + 10$ seconds to solve a problem of size n. If constants k and n_0 exist such that

$$k * n^2 > n^2 - 3 * n + 10 \text{ for all } n \geq n_0$$

the algorithm is order n^2. In fact, if k is 3 and n_0 is 2,

$$3 * n^2 > n^2 - 3 * n + 10 \text{ for all } n \geq 2$$

as Figure 9-2 illustrates. Thus, the algorithm requires no more than $k * n^2$ time units for $n \geq n_0$ so is $O(n^2)$.

- Previously, we found that displaying a linked list's first n items requires $(n + 1) * (a + c) + n * w$ time units. Since $2 * n \geq n + 1$ for $n \geq 1$,

$$(2 * a + 2 * c + w) * n \geq (n + 1) * (a + c) + n * w \text{ for } n \geq 1$$

Thus, this task is $O(n)$. Here, k is $2 * a + 2 * c + w$ and n_0 is 1.

- Similarly, the solution to the Towers of Hanoi problem requires $(2^n - 1) * m$ time units. Since

$$m * 2^n > (2^n - 1) * m \text{ for } n \geq 1$$

the solution is $O(2^n)$.

The requirement $n \geq n_0$ in the definition of $O(f(n))$ means that the time estimate is correct for sufficiently large problems. In other words, the time estimate is too small for at most a finite number of problem sizes. For example, the function $\log n$ takes on the value 0 when n is 1. Thus, the fact that $k * \log 1$ is 0 for all constants k implies an unrealistic

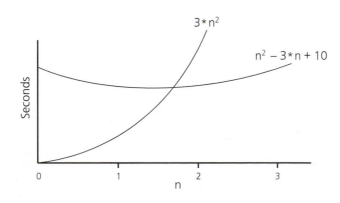

FIGURE 9-2 When $n \geq 2$, $3 * n^2$ exceeds $n^2 - 3 * n + 10$

time requirement; presumably, all algorithms require more than 0 time units even to solve a problem of size 1. Thus, you can discount problems of size $n = 1$ if $f(n)$ is log n.

To dramatize further the significance of an algorithm's proportional growth rate, consider the table and graph in Figure 9-3. The table (Figure 9-3a) gives, for various values of n, the approximate values of some common growth-rate functions, which are listed in order of growth:

(a)

Function	n					
	10	100	1,000	10,000	100,000	1,000,000
1	1	1	1	1	1	1
$\log_2 n$	3	6	9	13	16	19
n	10	10^2	10^3	10^4	10^5	10^6
$n * \log_2 n$	30	664	9,965	10^5	10^6	10^7
n^2	10^2	10^4	10^6	10^8	10^{10}	10^{12}
n^3	10^3	10^6	10^9	10^{12}	10^{15}	10^{18}
2^n	10^3	10^{30}	10^{301}	$10^{3,010}$	$10^{30,103}$	$10^{301,030}$

(b)

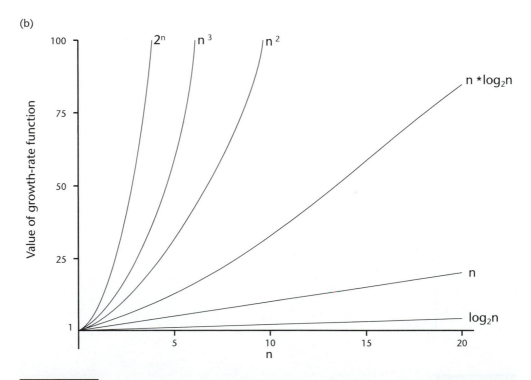

FIGURE 9-3   A comparison of growth-rate functions: (a) in tabular form; (b) in graphical form

$$O(1) < O(\log_2 n) < O(n) < O(n * \log_2 n) < O(n^2) < O(n^3) < O(2^n)$$

Order of growth
of some common functions

The table demonstrates the relative speed at which the values of the functions grow. (Figure 9-3b represents the growth-rate functions graphically.[3])

These growth-rate functions have the following intuitive interpretations:

1	A growth-rate function of 1 implies a problem whose time requirement is constant and, therefore, independent of the problem's size n.	Intuitive interpretations of growth-rate functions

$\log_2 n$ — The time requirement for a logarithmic algorithm increases slowly as the problem size increases. If you square the problem size, you only double its time requirement. Later you will see that the recursive binary search algorithm that you studied in Chapter 2 has this behavior. Recall that a binary search halves an array and then searches one of the halves. Typical logarithmic algorithms solve a problem by solving a smaller constant fraction of the problem.

The base of the log does not affect a logarithmic growth rate, so you can omit it in a growth-rate function. Exercise 6 at the end of this chapter asks you to show why this is true.

n — The time requirement for a linear algorithm increases directly with the size of the problem. If you square the problem size, you also square its time requirement.

$n * \log_2 n$ — The time requirement for an $n * \log_2 n$ algorithm increases more rapidly than a linear algorithm. Such algorithms usually divide a problem into smaller problems that are each solved separately. You will see an example of such an algorithm—the mergesort—later in this chapter.

n^2 — The time requirement for a quadratic algorithm increases rapidly with the size of the problem. Algorithms that use two nested loops are often quadratic. Such algorithms are practical only for small problems. Later in this chapter, you will study several quadratic sorting algorithms.

---

[3] The graph of $f(n) = 1$ is omitted because the scale of the figure makes it difficult to draw. It would, however, be a straight line parallel to the x axis through $y = 1$.

n^3 The time requirement for a cubic algorithm increases more rapidly with the size of the problem than the time requirement for a quadratic algorithm. Algorithms that use three nested loops are often cubic, and are practical only for small problems.

2^n As the size of a problem increases, the time requirement for an exponential algorithm usually increases too rapidly to be practical.

If algorithm A requires time that is proportional to function f and algorithm B requires time that is proportional to a slower-growing function g, it is apparent that B will always be significantly more efficient than A for large enough problems. For large problems, the proportional growth rate dominates all other factors in determining an algorithm's efficiency.

Several mathematical properties of Big O notation help to simplify the analysis of an algorithm. As we discuss these properties, you should keep in mind that $O(f(n))$ means "is of order $f(n)$" or "has order $f(n)$." O is not a function.

Some properties of growth-rate functions

1. **You can ignore low-order terms in an algorithm's growth-rate function.** For example, if an algorithm is $O(n^3 + 4 * n^2 + 3 * n)$, it is also $O(n^3)$. By examining the table in Figure 9-3a, you can see that the n^3 term is significantly larger than either $4 * n^2$ or $3 * n$, particularly for large values of n. For large n, the growth rate of $n^3 + 4 * n^2 + 3 * n$ is the same as the growth rate of n^3. It is the growth rate of $f(n)$, not the value of $f(n)$, that is important here. Thus, even if an algorithm is $O(n^3 + 4 * n^2 + 3 * n)$, we say that it is simply $O(n^3)$. In general, you can usually conclude that an algorithm is $O(f(n))$, where f is a function similar to the ones listed in Figure 9-3.

2. **You can ignore a multiplicative constant in the high-order term of an algorithm's growth-rate function.** For example, if an algorithm is $O(5 * n^3)$, it is also $O(n^3)$. This observation follows from the definition of $O(f(n))$, if you let $k = 5$.

3. **$O(f(n)) + O(g(n)) = O(f(n) + g(n))$.** You can combine growth-rate functions. For example, if an algorithm is $O(n^2) + O(n)$, it is also $O(n^2 + n)$, which you write simply as $O(n^2)$ by applying property 1. Analogous rules hold for multiplication.

These properties imply that you need only an estimate of the time requirement to obtain an algorithm's growth rate; you do not need an exact statement of an algorithm's time requirement, which is fortunate because deriving the exact time requirement is often difficult and sometimes impossible.

Worst-case and average-case analyses. A particular algorithm might require different times to solve different problems of the same size. For example, the time that an algorithm requires to search n items might depend on the nature of the items. Usually you consider the maximum amount of time that an algorithm can require to solve a problem of size n—that is, the worst case. Worst-case analysis concludes that algorithm A is $O(f(n))$ if, in the worst case, A requires no more than $k * f(n)$ time units to solve a problem of size n for all but a finite number of values of n. Although a worst-case analysis can produce a pessimistic time estimate, such an estimate does not mean that your algorithm will always be slow. Instead, you have shown that the algorithm will never be slower than your estimate. Realize, however, that an algorithm's worst case might happen rarely, if at all, in practice.

An **average-case analysis** attempts to determine the average amount of time that an algorithm requires to solve problems of size n. In an average-case analysis, A is $O(f(n))$ if the average amount of time that A requires to solve a problem of size n is no more than $k * f(n)$ time units for all but a finite number of values of n. Average-case analysis is, in general, far more difficult to perform than worst-case analysis. One difficulty is determining the relative probabilities of encountering various problems of a given size; another is determining the distributions of various data values. Worst-case analysis is easier to calculate and is thus more common.

An algorithm can require different times to solve different problems of the same size

Keeping Your Perspective

Before continuing with additional order-of-magnitude analyses of specific algorithms, a few words about perspective are appropriate. For example, consider an ADT list of n items. You saw earlier that an array-based list `retrieve` operation can access the nth item in the list directly. This access is independent of n; `retrieve` takes the same time to access the 100th item as it does to access the first item in the list. Thus, the array-based implementation of the retrieval operation is $O(1)$. However, the pointer-based implementation of the list `retrieve` operation requires n steps to traverse the list until it reaches the nth item, and so is $O(n)$.

An array-based list `retrieve` is $O(1)$

A pointer-based list `retrieve` is $O(n)$

Throughout the course of an analysis, you should always keep in mind that you are interested only in *significant* differences in efficiency. Is the difference in efficiency for the two implementations of `retrieve` significant? As the size of the list grows, the pointer-based implementation might require more time to retrieve the desired node, because the node can be farther away from the beginning of the list. In contrast, regardless of how large the list is, the array-based implementation always requires the same constant amount of time to retrieve any particular item. Thus, no matter what your notion of a significant difference in time is, you will reach this time difference if the list is large enough. In this example, observe that the difference in efficiency for the two implementations is worth considering only when the problem is large enough. If the list never has more than 25 items, for example, the difference in the implementations is not significant at all.

Now consider an application—such as a word processor's spelling checker—that frequently retrieves items from a list but rarely inserts or deletes an item. Since an array-based list `retrieve` is faster than a pointer-based list `retrieve`, you should choose an array-based implementation of the list for the application. On the other hand, if an application requires frequent insertions and deletions but rarely retrieves an item, you should choose a pointer-based implementation of the list. The most appropriate implementation of an ADT for a given application strongly depends on how frequently the application will perform the operations. You will see more examples of this point in the next chapter.

The response time of some ADT operations, however, can be crucial, even if you seldom use them. For example, an air traffic control system could include an emergency operation to resolve the impending collision of two airplanes. Clearly, this operation must occur quickly, even if it is rarely used. Thus, before you choose an implementation for an ADT, you should know what operations a particular application requires, approximately how often the application will perform each operation, and the response times that the application requires of each operation.

Soon we will compare a searching algorithm that is $O(n)$ with one that is $O(\log_2 n)$. While it is true that an $O(\log_2 n)$ searching algorithm requires significantly less time on large arrays than an $O(n)$ algorithm requires, on small arrays—say $n < 25$—the time requirements might not be significantly different at all. In fact, it is entirely possible that, because of factors such as the size of the constant k in the definition of Big O, the $O(n)$ algorithm will run faster on small problems. It is only on large problems that the slower growth rate of an algorithm necessarily gives it a significant advantage. Figure 9-1 illustrated this phenomenon.

Thus, in general, if the maximum size of a given problem is small, the time requirements of any two solutions for that problem likely will not differ significantly. If you know that your problem size will always be small, do not overanalyze; simply choose the algorithm that is easiest to understand, verify, and code.

Frequently, when evaluating an algorithm's efficiency, you have to weigh carefully the trade-offs between a solution's execution time requirements and its memory requirements. You are rarely able to make a statement as strong as "This method is the best one for performing the task." A solution that requires a relatively small amount of computer time often also requires a relatively large amount of memory. It may not even be possible to say that one solution requires less time than another. Solution *A* may perform some components of the task faster than solution *B,* while solution *B* performs other components of the task faster than solution *A*. Often you must analyze the solutions in light of a particular application.

In summary, it is important to examine an algorithm for both style and efficiency. The analysis should focus only on gross differences in efficiency and not reward coding tricks that save milliseconds. Any finer differences in efficiency are likely to interact with coding issues, which

When choosing an ADT's implementation, consider how frequently particular ADT operations occur in a given application

Some seldom-used but critical operations must be efficient

If the problem size is always small, you can probably ignore an algorithm's efficiency

Weigh the trade-offs between an algorithm's time requirements and its memory requirements

Compare algorithms for both style and efficiency

you should not allow to interfere with the development of your programming style. If you find a method of solution that is significantly more efficient than others, you should select it, unless you know that the maximum problem size is quite small. If you will be solving only small problems, it is possible that a less efficient algorithm would be more appropriate. That is, other factors, such as the simplicity of the algorithm, could become more significant than minor differences in efficiency. In fact, performing an order-of-magnitude analysis implicitly assumes that an algorithm will be used to solve large problems. This assumption allows you to focus on growth rates because, regardless of other factors, an algorithm with a slow growth rate will require less time than an algorithm with a fast growth rate, provided that the problems to be solved are sufficiently large.

Order-of-magnitude analysis focuses on large problems

The Efficiency of Searching Algorithms

As another example of order-of-magnitude analysis, consider the efficiency of two search algorithms: the sequential search and the binary search of an array.

Sequential search. In a sequential search of an array of n items, you look at each item in turn, beginning with the first one, until either you find the desired item or you reach the end of the data collection. In the best case, the desired item is the first one that you examine, so only one comparison is necessary. Thus, in the best case, a sequential search is $O(1)$. In the worst case, the desired item is the last one you examine, so n comparisons are necessary. Thus, in the worst case, the algorithm is $O(n)$. In the average case, you would find the desired item in the middle of the collection, making $n/2$ comparisons. Thus, the algorithm is $O(n)$ in the average case.

Sequential search. Worst case: $O(n)$; average case: $O(n)$; best case: $O(1)$

What is the algorithm's order when you do not find the desired item? Does the algorithm's order depend on whether or not the initial data are sorted? These questions are left for you in Self-Test Exercise 4 at the end of this chapter.

Binary search. Is a binary search of an array more efficient than a sequential search? The binary search algorithm, which Chapter 2 presents, searches a sorted array for a particular item by repeatedly dividing the array in half. The algorithm determines which half the item must be in—if it is indeed present—and discards the other half. Thus, the binary search algorithm searches successively smaller arrays: The size of a given array is approximately one-half the size of the array previously searched.

At each division, the algorithm makes a comparison. How many comparisons does the algorithm make when it searches an array of n items? The exact answer depends, of course, on where the sought-for item resides in the array. However, you can compute the maximum number of comparisons that a binary search requires—that is, the worst case. The number of comparisons is equal to the number of times that the algorithm divides the array in half. Suppose that $n = 2^k$ for some k. The search requires the following steps:

1. Inspect the middle item of an array of size n.

2. Inspect the middle item of an array of size $n/2$.

3. Inspect the middle item of an array of size $n/2^2$, and so on.

To inspect the middle item of an array, you must first divide the array in half. If you divide an array of n items in half, then divide one of those halves in half, and continue dividing halves until only one item remains, you will have performed k divisions. This is true because $n/2^k = 1$. (Remember, we assumed that $n = 2^k$.) In the worst case, the algorithm performs k divisions and, therefore, k comparisons. Because $n = 2^k$,

$$k = \log_2 n$$

Thus, the algorithm is $O(\log_2 n)$ in the worst case when $n = 2^k$.

What if n is not a power of 2? You can easily find the smallest k such that

$$2^{k-1} < n < 2^k$$

(For example, if n is 30, then $k = 5$, because $2^4 = 16 < 30 < 32 = 2^5$.) The algorithm still requires at most k divisions to obtain a subarray with one item. Now it follows that

$$k - 1 < \log_2 n < k$$

$$k < 1 + \log_2 n < k + 1$$

$$k = 1 + \log_2 n \text{ rounded down}$$

Binary search is $O(\log_2 n)$ in the worst case

Thus, the algorithm is still $O(\log_2 n)$ in the worst case when $n \neq 2^k$. In general, the algorithm is $O(\log_2 n)$ in the worst case for any n.

Is a binary search better than a sequential search? Much better! For example $\log_2 1{,}000{,}000 \approx 19$, so a sequential search of one million sorted items can require one million comparisons, but a binary search of the same items will require at most 20 comparisons. For large arrays, the binary search has an enormous advantage over a sequential search.

Realize, however, that maintaining the array in sorted order requires an overhead cost, which can be substantial. The next section examines the cost of sorting an array.

9.2 Sorting Algorithms and Their Efficiency

Sorting is a process that organizes a collection of data into either ascending[4] or descending order. The need for sorting arises in many sit-

---

[4] To allow for duplicate data items, *ascending* is used here to mean nondecreasing and *descending* to mean nonincreasing.

uations. You may simply want to sort a collection of data before includ-ing it in a report. Often, however, you must perform a sort as an initialization step for certain algorithms. For example, searching for data is one of the most common tasks performed by computers. When the collection of data to be searched is large, an efficient method for searching—such as the binary search algorithm—is desirable. However, the binary search algorithm requires that the data be sorted. Thus, sort-ing the data is a step that must precede a binary search on a collection of data that is not already sorted. Good sorting algorithms, therefore, are quite valuable.

You can organize sorting algorithms into two categories. An **inter-nal sort** requires that the collection of data fit entirely in the com-puter's main memory. The algorithms in this chapter are internal sorting algorithms. You use an **external sort** when the collection of data will not fit in the computer's main memory all at once but must reside in secondary storage, such as on a disk. Chapter 14 examines external sorts.

The sorts in this chapter are internal sorts

The data items to be sorted might be integers, character strings, or even objects. It is easy to imagine the results of sorting a collection of integers or character strings, but consider a collection of objects. If each object contains only one data member, sorting the objects is really no different than sorting a collection of integers. However, when each object contains several data members, you must know which data member determines the order of the entire object within the collection of data. This data member is called the **sort key**. For example, if the objects represent people, you might want to sort on their names, their ages, or their zip codes. Regardless of your choice of sort key, the sort-ing algorithm orders entire objects based on only one data member, the sort key.

For simplicity, this chapter assumes that the data items are quantities such as numbers or characters. Data items that are objects with several data members are considered in the exercises. All algorithms in this chapter sort the data into ascending order. Modifying these algorithms to sort data into descending order is simple. Finally, each example assumes that the data resides in an array.

Selection Sort

Imagine some data that you can examine all at once. To sort it, you could select the largest item and put it in its place, select the next larg-est and put it in its place, and so on. For a card player, this process is analogous to looking at an entire hand of cards and ordering it by selecting cards one at a time in their proper order. The **selection sort** formalizes these intuitive notions. To sort an array into ascending order, you first search it for the largest item. Because you want the largest item to be in the last position of the array, you swap the last item with the largest item, even if these items happen to be identical. Now, ignoring the last—and largest—item of the array, you search the

Select the largest item

rest of the array for its largest item and swap it with its last item, which is the next-to-last item in the original array. You continue until you have selected and swapped $n - 1$ of the n items in the array. The remaining item, which is now in the first position of the array, is in its proper order, so it is not considered further.

Figure 9-4 provides an example of a selection sort. Beginning with five integers, you select the largest—37—and swap it with the last integer—13. (As the items in this figure are ordered, they appear in boldface. This convention will be used throughout this chapter.) Next you select the largest integer—29—from among the first four integers in the array and swap it with the next-to-last integer in the array—13. Notice that the next selection—14—is already in its proper position, but the algorithm ignores this fact and performs a swap of 14 with itself. It is more efficient in general to occasionally perform an unnecessary swap than it is to continually ask whether the swap is necessary. Finally, you select the 13 and swap it with the item in the second position of the array—10. The array is now sorted into ascending order.

A C++ function that performs a selection sort on an array *theArray* of n items follows:

```
typedef type-of-array-item DataType;

void selectionSort(DataType theArray[], int n)
// ----------------------------------------------------
// Sorts the items in an array into ascending order.
// Precondition: theArray is an array of n items.
// Postcondition: The array theArray is sorted into
// ascending order; n is unchanged.
// Calls: indexOfLargest, swap.
// ----------------------------------------------------
{
   // last = index of the last item in the subarray of
   //        items yet to be sorted,
   // largest = index of the largest item found
```

Shaded elements are selected;
boldface elements are in order.

Initial array:	29	10	14	37	13
After 1st swap:	29	10	14	13	**37**
After 2nd swap:	13	10	14	**29**	**37**
After 3rd swap:	13	10	**14**	**29**	**37**
After 4th swap:	**10**	**13**	**14**	**29**	**37**

FIGURE 9-4   A selection sort of an array of five integers

```
    for (int last = n-1; last >= 1; --last)
    {  // Invariant: theArray[last+1..n-1] is sorted and
       // > theArray[0..last]

       // select largest item in theArray[0..last]
       int largest = indexOfLargest(theArray, last+1);

       // swap largest item theArray[largest] with
       // theArray[last]
       swap(theArray[largest], theArray[last]);
    }  // end for
}  // end selectionSort
```

The function *selectionSort* calls the following two functions:

```
int indexOfLargest(const DataType theArray[], int size)
// ------------------------------------------------
// Finds the largest item in an array.
// Precondition: theArray is an array of size items,
// size >= 1.
// Postcondition: Returns the index of the largest
// item in the array. The arguments are unchanged.
// ------------------------------------------------
{
    int indexSoFar = 0;  // index of largest item
                         // found so far

    for (int currentIndex = 1; currentIndex < size;
                               ++currentIndex)
    {  // Invariant: theArray[indexSoFar] >=
       //            theArray[0..currentIndex-1]
       if (theArray[currentIndex] > theArray[indexSoFar])
          indexSoFar = currentIndex;
    }  // end for

    return indexSoFar;  // index of largest item
}  // end indexOfLargest

void swap(DataType& x, DataType& y)
// -------------------------------------------------
// Swaps two items.
// Precondition: x and y are the items to be swapped.
// Postcondition: Contents of actual locations that x
// and y represent are swapped.
// -------------------------------------------------
{
    DataType temp = x;
    x = y;
    y = temp;
}  // end swap
```

Analysis. As you can see from the previous algorithm, sorting in general compares, exchanges, or moves items. As a first step in analyzing such algorithms, you should count these operations. Generally, such operations are more expensive than ones that control loops or manipulate array indexes, particularly when the data to be sorted are more complex than integers or characters. Thus, our approach ignores these incidental operations. You should convince yourself that by ignoring such operations we do not affect our final result. (See Exercise 7.)

Clearly, the *for* loop in the function *selectionSort* executes $n - 1$ times. Thus, *selectionSort* calls each of the functions *indexOfLargest* and *swap* $n - 1$ times. Each call to *indexOfLargest* causes its loop to execute *last* times (that is, *size* $- 1$ times when *size* is *last* $+$ 1). Thus, the $n - 1$ calls to *indexOfLargest*, for values of *last* that range from $n - 1$ down to 1, cause the loop in *indexOfLargest* to execute a total of

$$(n - 1) + (n - 2) + \cdots + 1 = n * (n - 1)/2$$

times. Because each execution of *indexOfLargest*'s loop performs one comparison, the calls to *indexOfLargest* require

$$n * (n - 1)/2$$

comparisons.

The $n - 1$ calls to *swap* result in $n - 1$ exchanges. Each exchange requires three assignments, or data moves. Thus, the calls to *swap* require

$$3 * (n - 1)$$

moves.

Together, a selection sort of n items requires

$$n * (n - 1)/2 + 3 * (n - 1)$$

$$= n^2/2 + 5 * n/2 - 3$$

Selection sort is O(n^2)

major operations. By applying the properties of growth-rate functions (see page 452), you can ignore low-order terms to get O($n^2/2$) and then ignore the multiplier $1/2$ to get O(n^2). Thus, selection sort is O(n^2).

Although a selection sort does not depend on the initial arrangement of the data, which is an advantage of this algorithm, it is appropriate only for small n because O(n^2) grows rapidly. While the algorithm requires O(n^2) comparisons, it requires only O(n) data moves. A selection sort could be a good choice over other methods when data moves are costly but comparisons are not. Such might be the case if each data item is lengthy but the sort key is short. Of course, storing the data in a linked list allows inexpensive data moves for any algorithm.

Bubble Sort

The next sorting algorithm is one that you may have seen already. That is precisely why it is analyzed here, because it is not a particularly good algorithm. The **bubble sort** compares adjacent items and exchanges them if they are out of order. This sort usually requires several passes over the data. During the first pass, you compare the first two items in the array. If they are out of order, you exchange them. You then compare the items in the next pair—that is, in positions 2 and 3 of the array. If they are out of order, you exchange them. You proceed, comparing and exchanging items two at a time until you reach the end of the array.

Figure 9-5a illustrates the first pass of a bubble sort of an array of five integers. You compare the items in the first pair—29 and 10—and exchange them because they are out of order. Next you consider the second pair—29 and 14—and exchange these items because they are out of order. The items in the third pair—29 and 37—are in order, and so you do not exchange them. Finally, you exchange the items in the last pair—37 and 13.

Although the array is not sorted after the first pass, the largest item has "bubbled" to its proper position at the end of the array. During the second pass of the bubble sort, you return to the beginning of the array and consider pairs of items in exactly the same manner as the first pass. You do not, however, include the last—and largest—item of the array. That is, the second pass considers the first $n-1$ items of the array. After the second pass, the second largest item in the array will be in its proper place in the next-to-last position of the array, as Figure 9-5b illustrates. Now, ignoring the last two items, which are in order, you continue with subsequent passes until the array is sorted.

Although a bubble sort requires at most $n-1$ passes to sort the array, fewer passes might be possible to sort a particular array. Thus, you could terminate the process if no exchanges occur during any pass. The

> When you order successive pairs of items, the largest item bubbles to the top (end) of the array

> Bubble sort usually requires several passes through the array

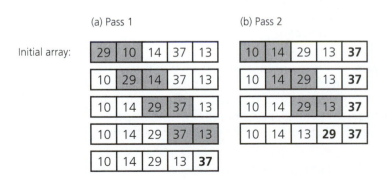

(a) Pass 1   (b) Pass 2

Initial array:

| 29 | 10 | 14 | 37 | 13 |
| 10 | 14 | 29 | 13 | **37** |

FIGURE 9-5   The first two passes of a bubble sort of an array of five integers: (a) pass 1; (b) pass 2

following C++ function *bubbleSort* uses a flag to signal when an exchange occurs during a particular pass. The function uses the previous *swap* function.

```cpp
void bubbleSort(DataType theArray[], int n)
// -------------------------------------------------
// Sorts the items in an array into ascending order.
// Precondition: theArray is an array of n items.
// Postcondition: theArray is sorted into ascending
// order; n is unchanged.
// Calls: swap.
// -------------------------------------------------
{
   bool sorted = false;  // false when swaps occur

   for (int pass = 1; (pass < n) && !sorted; ++pass)
   {  // Invariant: theArray[n+1-pass..n-1] is sorted
      //            and > theArray[0..n-pass]
      sorted = true;  // assume sorted
      for (int index = 0; index < n-pass; ++index)
      {  // Invariant: theArray[0..index-1] <=
         // theArray[index]
         int nextIndex = index + 1;
         if (theArray[index] > theArray[nextIndex])
         {  // exchange items
            swap(theArray[index], theArray[nextIndex]);
            sorted = false;  // signal exchange
         }  // end if
      }  // end for

      // Assertion: theArray[0..n-pass-1] <
      // theArray[n-pass]
   }  // end for
}  // end bubbleSort
```

Analysis. As was noted earlier, the bubble sort requires at most $n - 1$ passes through the array. Pass 1 requires $n - 1$ comparisons and at most $n - 1$ exchanges; pass 2 requires $n - 2$ comparisons and at most $n - 2$ exchanges. In general, pass i requires $n - i$ comparisons and at most $n - i$ exchanges. Therefore, in the worst case, a bubble sort will require a total of

$$(n - 1) + (n - 2) + \cdots + 1 = n * (n - 1)/2$$

comparisons and the same number of exchanges. Recall that each exchange requires three data moves. Thus, altogether there are

$$2 * n * (n - 1) = 2 * n^2 - 2 * n$$

major operations in the worst case. Therefore, the bubble sort algorithm is $O(n^2)$ in the worst case.

The best case occurs when the original data is already sorted: *bubbleSort* uses one pass, during which $n-1$ comparisons and no exchanges occur. Thus, the bubble sort is $O(n)$ in the best case.

Insertion Sort

Imagine once again arranging a hand of cards, but now you pick up one card at a time and insert it into its proper position; in this case you are performing an insertion sort. Chapter 4 introduced the insertion sort algorithm in the context of a linked list: You can create a sorted linked list from a file of unsorted integers, for example, by repeatedly calling a function that inserts an integer into its proper sorted order in a linked list.

You can use the insertion sort strategy to sort items that reside in an array. This version of the insertion sort partitions the array into two regions: sorted and unsorted, as Figure 9-6 depicts. Initially, the entire array is the unsorted region, just as the cards dealt to you sit in an unsorted pile on the table. At each step, the insertion sort takes the first item of the unsorted region and places it into its correct position in the sorted region. This step is analogous to taking a card from the table and inserting it into its proper position in your hand. The first step, however, is trivial: Moving *theArray[0]* from the unsorted region to the sorted region really does not require moving data. Therefore, you can omit this first step by considering the initial sorted region to be *theArray[0]* and the initial unsorted region to be *theArray[1..n-1]*. The fact that the items in the sorted region are sorted among themselves is an invariant of the algorithm. Because at each step the size of the sorted region grows by 1 and the size of the unsorted region shrinks by 1, the entire array will be sorted when the algorithm terminates.

Figure 9-7 illustrates an insertion sort of an array of five integers. Initially, the sorted region is *theArray[0]*, which is 29, and the unsorted region is the rest of the array. You take the first item in the unsorted region—the 10—and insert it into its proper position in the sorted region: This insertion requires you to shift array items to make room for the inserted item. You then take the first item in the

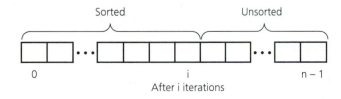

FIGURE 9-6   An insertion sort partitions the array into two regions

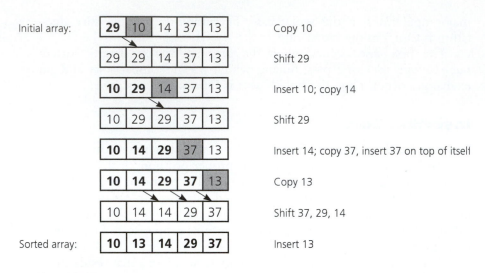

Initial array: 29 10 14 37 13   Copy 10

29 29 14 37 13   Shift 29

10 29 14 37 13   Insert 10; copy 14

10 29 29 37 13   Shift 29

10 14 29 37 13   Insert 14; copy 37, insert 37 on top of itself

10 14 29 37 13   Copy 13

10 14 14 29 37   Shift 37, 29, 14

Sorted array: 10 13 14 29 37   Insert 13

FIGURE 9-7   An insertion sort of an array of five integers

new unsorted region—the 14—and insert it into its proper position in the sorted region, and so on.

A C++ function that performs an insertion sort on an array of *n* items follows:

```
void insertionSort(DataType theArray[], int n)
// -------------------------------------------------
// Sorts the items in an array into ascending order.
// Precondition: theArray is an array of n items.
// Postcondition: theArray is sorted into ascending
// order; n is unchanged.
// -------------------------------------------------
{
   // unsorted = first index of the unsorted region,
   // loc = index of insertion in the sorted region,
   // nextItem = next item in the unsorted region

   // initially, sorted region is theArray[0],
   //           unsorted region is theArray[1..n-1];
   // in general, sorted region is
   //               theArray[0..unsorted-1],
   // unsorted region is theArray[unsorted..n-1]

   for (int unsorted = 1; unsorted < n; ++unsorted)
   {  // Invariant: theArray[0..unsorted-1] is sorted

      // find the right position (loc) in
      // theArray[0..unsorted] for theArray[unsorted],
```

```
            // which is the first item in the unsorted
            // region; shift, if necessary, to make room
            DataType nextItem = theArray[unsorted];
            int loc = unsorted;

            for (;(loc > 0) && (theArray[loc-1 ]> nextItem);
                  --loc)
               // shift theArray[loc-1] to the right
               theArray[loc] = theArray[loc-1];

            // Assertion: theArray[loc] is where nextItem
            // belongs

            // insert nextItem into Sorted region
            theArray[loc] = nextItem;
     }  // end for
}  // end insertionSort
```

Analysis. The outer *for* loop in the function *insertionSort* executes $n - 1$ times. This loop contains an inner *for* loop that executes at most *unsorted* times for values of *unsorted* that range from 1 to $n - 1$. Thus, in the worst case, the algorithm's comparison occurs

$$1 + 2 + \cdots + (n - 1) = n * (n - 1)/2$$

times. In addition, the inner loop moves data items at most the same number of times.

The outer loop moves data items twice per iteration, or $2 * (n - 1)$ times. Together, there are

$$n * (n - 1) + 2 * (n - 1) = n^2 + n - 2$$

major operations in the worst case.

Therefore, the insertion sort algorithm is $O(n^2)$ in the worst case. For small arrays—say, fewer than 25 items—the simplicity of the insertion sort makes it an appropriate choice. For large arrays, however, an insertion sort can be prohibitively inefficient.

Insertion sort is $O(n^2)$ in the worst case

Mergesort

Two important divide-and-conquer sorting algorithms, **mergesort** and **quicksort**, have elegant recursive formulations and are highly efficient. The presentations here are in the context of sorting arrays, but—as you shall see in Chapter 14—mergesort generalizes to external files. It will be convenient to express the algorithms in terms of the array *theArray[first..last]*.

Divide and conquer

Mergesort is a recursive sorting algorithm that always gives the same performance, regardless of the initial order of the array items. Suppose that you divide the array into halves, sort each half, and then merge the sorted halves into one sorted array, as Figure 9-8 illustrates.

Halve the array, recursively sort its halves, and then merge the halves

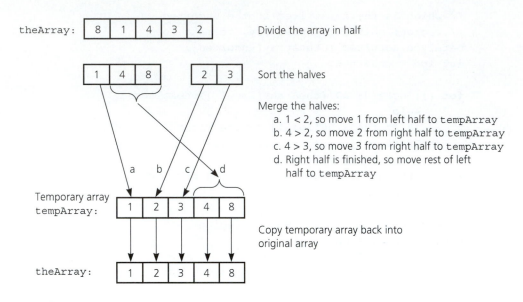

theArray: Divide the array in half

Sort the halves

Merge the halves:
   a. 1 < 2, so move 1 from left half to `tempArray`
   b. 4 > 2, so move 2 from right half to `tempArray`
   c. 4 > 3, so move 3 from right half to `tempArray`
   d. Right half is finished, so move rest of left half to `tempArray`

Temporary array
`tempArray`:

Copy temporary array back into original array

theArray:

FIGURE 9-8   A mergesort with an auxiliary temporary array

In the figure, the halves <1, 4, 8> and <2, 3> are merged to form the array <1, 2, 3, 4, 8>. This merge step compares an item in one half of the array with an item in the other half and moves the smaller item to a temporary array. This process continues until there are no more items to consider in one half. At that time, you simply move the remaining items to the temporary array. Finally, you copy the temporary array back into the original array.

Although the merge step of mergesort produces a sorted array, how do you sort the array halves prior to the merge step? Mergesort sorts the array halves by using mergesort—that is, by calling itself recursively. Thus, the pseudocode for mergesort is

```
mergesort(inout theArray:ItemArray,
          in first:integer, in last:integer)
// Sorts theArray[first..last] by
//   1. sorting the first half of the array
//   2. sorting the second half of the array
//   3. merging the two sorted halves

  if (first < last)
  {  mid = (first + last)/2          // get midpoint
     // sort theArray[first..mid]
     mergesort(theArray, first, mid)
     // sort theArray[mid+1..last]
     mergesort(theArray, mid + 1, last)
```

```
   // merge sorted halves theArray[first..mid] and
   // theArray[mid+1..last]
   merge(theArray, first, mid, last)
} // end if
// if first >= last, there is nothing to do
```

Clearly, most of the effort in the mergesort algorithm is in the merge step, but does this algorithm actually sort? The recursive calls continue dividing the array into pieces until each piece contains only one item; obviously an array of one item is sorted. The algorithm then merges these small pieces into larger sorted pieces until one sorted array results. Figure 9-9 (page 469) illustrates both the recursive calls and the merge steps in a mergesort of an array of six integers.

The following C++ functions implement the mergesort algorithm. To sort an array *theArray* of *n* items, you would invoke the function *mergesort* by writing *mergesort(theArray, 0, n-1)*.

```cpp
const int MAX_SIZE = maximum-number-of-items-in-array;

void merge(DataType theArray[],
           int first, int mid, int last)
// ----------------------------------------------------
// Merges two sorted array segments theArray[first..mid] and
// theArray[mid+1..last] into one sorted array.
// Precondition: first <= mid <= last. The subarrays
// theArray[first..mid] and theArray[mid+1..last] are each
// sorted in increasing order.
// Postcondition: theArray[first..last] is sorted.
// Implementation note: This function merges the two
// subarrays into a temporary array and copies the result
// into the original array theArray.
// ----------------------------------------------------
{
   DataType tempArray[MAX_SIZE];     // temporary array

   // initialize the local indexes to indicate the subarrays
   int first1 = first;        // beginning of first subarray
   int last1  = mid;          // end of first subarray
   int first2 = mid + 1;      // beginning of second subarray
   int last2  = last;         // end of second subarray

   // while both subarrays are not empty, copy the
   // smaller item into the temporary array
   int index = first1;     // next available location in
                           // tempArray
   for (; (first1 <= last1) && (first2 <= last2); ++index)
   {  // Invariant: tempArray[first1..index-1] is in order
```

```
      if (theArray[first1] < theArray[first2])
      {  tempArray[index] = theArray[first1];
         ++first1;
      }
      else
      {  tempArray[index] = theArray[first2];
         ++first2;
      }  // end if
   }  // end for

   // finish off the nonempty subarray

   // finish off the first subarray, if necessary
   for (; first1 <= last1; ++first1, ++index)
      // Invariant: tempArray[first1..index-1] is in order
      tempArray[index] = theArray[first1];

   // finish off the second subarray, if necessary
   for (; first2 <= last2; ++first2, ++index)
      // Invariant: tempArray[first1..index-1] is in order
      tempArray[index] = theArray[first2];

   // copy the result back into the original array
   for (index = first; index <= last; ++index)
      theArray[index] = tempArray[index];
}  // end merge

void mergesort(DataType theArray[], int first, int last)
// --------------------------------------------------------
// Sorts the items in an array into ascending order.
// Precondition: theArray[first..last] is an array.
// Postcondition: theArray[first..last] is sorted in
// ascending order.
// Calls: merge.
// --------------------------------------------------------
{
   if (first < last)
   {  // sort each half
      int mid = (first + last)/2;    // index of midpoint
      // sort left half theArray[first..mid]
      mergesort(theArray, first, mid);
      // sort right half theArray[mid+1..last]
      mergesort(theArray, mid+1, last);

      // merge the two halves
      merge(theArray, first, mid, last);
   }  // end if
}  // end mergesort
```

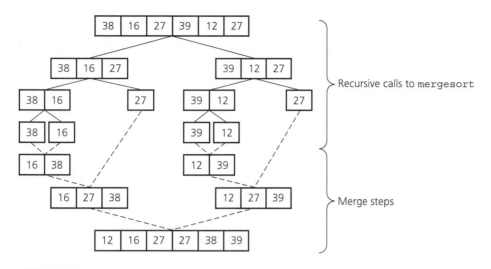

FIGURE 9-9 A mergesort of an array of six integers

Analysis. Because the merge step of the algorithm requires the most effort, let's begin the analysis there. Each merge step merges *theArray[first..mid]* and *theArray[mid+1..last]*. Figure 9-10 provides an example of a merge step that requires the maximum number of comparisons. If the total number of items in the two array segments to be merged is *n*, then merging the segments requires at most $n - 1$ comparisons. (For example, in Figure 9-10 there are six items in the segments and five comparisons.) In addition, there are *n* moves from the original array to the temporary array, and *n* moves from the temporary array back to the original array. Thus, each merge step requires $3 * n - 1$ major operations.

Each call to *mergesort* recursively calls itself twice. As Figure 9-11 illustrates, if the original call to *mergesort* is at level 0, two calls to *mergesort* occur at level 1 of the recursion. Each of these calls then calls *mergesort* twice, so four calls to *mergesort* occur at level 2 of

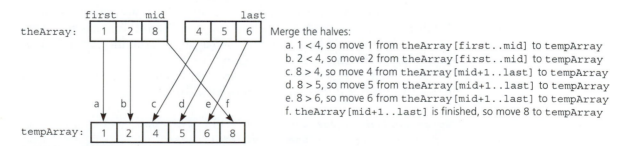

FIGURE 9-10 A worst-case instance of the merge step in *mergesort*

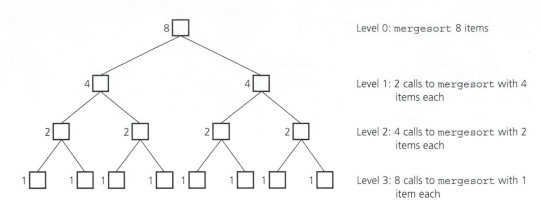

FIGURE 9-11   Levels of recursive calls to *mergesort*, given an array of eight items

the recursion, and so on. How many levels of recursion are there? We can count them, as follows.

Each call to *mergesort* halves the array. Halving the array the first time produces two pieces. The next recursive calls to *mergesort* halve each of these two pieces to produce four pieces of the original array; the next recursive calls halve each of these four pieces to produce eight pieces, and so on. The recursive calls continue until the array pieces each contain one item—that is, until there are n pieces, where n is the number of items in the original array. If n is a power of 2 ($n = 2^k$), then the recursion goes $k = \log_2 n$ levels deep. For example, in Figure 9-11, there are three levels of recursive calls to *mergesort* because the original array contains eight items and $8 = 2^3$. If n is not a power of 2, there are $1 + \log_2 n$ (rounded down) levels of recursive calls to *mergesort*.

The original call to *mergesort* (at level 0) calls *merge* once. Then *merge* merges all n items and requires $3 * n - 1$ operations, as was shown earlier. At level 1 of the recursion, two calls to *mergesort,* and hence to *merge*, occur. Each of these two calls to *merge* merges $n/2$ items and requires $3 * (n/2) - 1$ operations. Together these two calls to *merge* require $2 * (3 * (n/2) - 1)$, or $3 * n - 2$ operations. At level m of the recursion, 2^m calls to *merge* occur; each of these calls merges $n/2^m$ items and so requires $3 * (n/2^m) - 1$ operations. Together the 2^m calls to *merge* require $3 * n - 2^m$ operations. Thus, each level of the recursion requires $\mathrm{O}(n)$ operations. Because there are either $\log_2 n$ or $1 + \log_2 n$ levels, *mergesort* is $\mathrm{O}(n * \log n)$ in both the worst and average cases. You should look at Figure 9-3 again to convince yourself that $\mathrm{O}(n * \log n)$ is significantly faster than $\mathrm{O}(n^2)$.

Although mergesort is an extremely efficient algorithm with respect to time, it does have one drawback: To perform the step

Mergesort is O($n * \log n$)

```
Merge sorted halves theArray[first..mid] and
                     theArray[mid+1..last]
```

the algorithm requires an auxiliary array whose size equals the size of the original array. In situations where storage is limited, this requirement might not be acceptable.

Mergesort requires a second array as large as the original array

Quicksort

Consider the first two steps of the solution to the problem of finding the kth smallest item of the array `theArray[first..last]` that was discussed in Chapter 2:

Another divide-and-conquer algorithm

```
Choose a pivot item p from theArray[first..last]
Partition the items of theArray[first..last] about p
```

Recall that this partition, which is pictured again in Figure 9-12, has the property that all items in S_1 = `theArray[first..pivotIndex-1]` are less than the pivot p, and all items in S_2 = `theArray[pivotIndex+1..last]` are greater than or equal to p. Though this property does not imply that the array is sorted, it does imply an extremely useful fact: The items in positions `first` through `pivotIndex` − 1 remain in positions `first` through `pivotIndex` − 1 when the array is properly sorted, although their positions relative to one another may change. Similarly, the items in positions `pivotIndex` + 1 through `last` will remain in positions `pivotIndex` + 1 through `last` when the array is sorted, although their relative positions may change. Finally, the pivot item remains in its position in the final, sorted array.

Quicksort partitions an array into items that are less than the pivot and those that are greater than or equal to the pivot

The partition induces relationships among the array items that are the ingredients of a recursive solution. Arranging the array items around the pivot p generates two smaller sorting problems—sort the left section of the array (S_1), and sort the right section of the array (S_2). The relationships between the pivot and the array items imply that once you solve the left and right sorting problems, you will have solved the original sorting problem. That is, partitioning the array before making the recursive calls places the pivot in its correct position and ensures that when the smaller array segments are sorted their items will be in the proper relation to the rest of the array. Also, the quicksort algorithm will eventually terminate: The left and right sorting problems are

Partitioning places the pivot in its correct position within the array

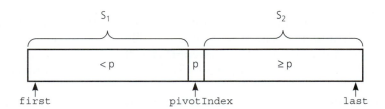

FIGURE 9-12 A partition about a pivot

indeed smaller problems and are each closer than the original sorting problem to the base case—which is an array containing one item—because the pivot is not part of either S_1 or S_2.

The pseudocode for the quicksort algorithm follows:

```
quicksort(inout theArray:ItemArray,
          in first:integer, in last:integer)
// Sorts theArray[first..last].

  if (first < last)
  {  Choose a pivot item p from theArray[first..last]

     Partition the items of theArray[first..last]
        about p
     // the partition is
     // theArray[first..pivotIndex..last]

     // sort S₁
     quicksort(theArray, first, pivotIndex-1)
     // sort S₂
     quicksort(theArray, pivotIndex+1, last)
  }  // end if
  // if first >= last, there is nothing to do
```

It is worth contrasting *quicksort* with the pseudocode function given for the kth smallest integer problem in Chapter 2:

```
kSmall(in k:integer, in theArray:ItemArray,
       in first:integer, in last:integer):ItemType
// Returns the kᵗʰ smallest value in theArray[first..last].

  Choose a pivot item p from theArray[first..last]
  Partition the items of theArray[first..last] about p
  if (k < pivotIndex - first + 1)
     return kSmall(k, theArray, first, pivotIndex-1)
  else if (k == pivotIndex - first + 1)
     return p
  else
     return kSmall(k-(pivotIndex-first+1), theArray,
                   pivotIndex+1, last)
```

Difference between *kSmall* and *quicksort*

kSmall is called recursively only on the section of the array that contains the desired item, and it is not called at all if the desired item is the pivot. On the other hand, *quicksort* is called recursively on both unsorted sections of the array. Figure 9-13 illustrates this difference.

Using an invariant to develop a partition algorithm. Now consider the partition function that both *kSmall* and *quicksort* must call. Partitioning an array section about a pivot item is actually the most difficult part of these two problems.

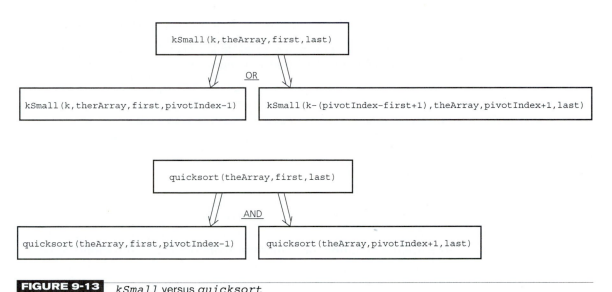

FIGURE 9-13   *kSmall* versus *quicksort*

The partition function will receive an array segment *theArray-[first..last]* as an argument. The function must arrange the items of the array segment into two regions: S_1, the set of items less than the pivot, and S_2, the set of items greater than or equal to the pivot. Thus, as you saw in Figure 9-12, S_1 is *theArray[first..pivotIndex-1]* and S_2 is *theArray[pivotIndex+1..last]*.

What pivot should you use? If the items in the array are arranged randomly, you can choose a pivot at random. For example, you can choose *theArray[first]* as the pivot. (The choice of pivot will be discussed in more detail later.) While you are developing the partition, it is convenient to place the pivot in the *theArray[first]* position, regardless of which pivot you choose.

Place your choice of pivot in *theArray[first]* before partitioning

The items that await placement into either S_1 or S_2 are in another region of the array, called the unknown region. Thus, you should view the array as shown in Figure 9-14. The array indexes *first*, *lastS1*, *firstUnknown*, and *last* divide the array as just described. The relationships between the pivot and the items in the unknown region—which is *theArray[firstUnknown..last]*—are, simply, unknown!

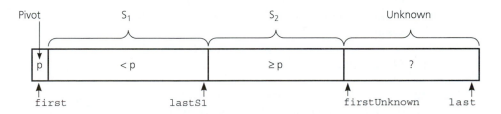

FIGURE 9-14   Invariant for the partition algorithm

Throughout the entire partitioning process, the following is true:

Invariant for the partition
algorithm

> *The items in the region S_1 are all less than the pivot, and those in S_2
> are all greater than or equal to the pivot.*

This statement is the invariant for the partition algorithm. For the invariant to be true at the start of the partition algorithm, the array's indexes must be initialized as follows so that the unknown region spans all of the array segment to be partitioned except the pivot:

Initially, all items except the pivot *theArray[first]* constitute the unknown region

```
lastS1 = first
firstUnknown = first + 1
```

Figure 9-15 shows the initial status of the array.

At each step of the partition algorithm, you examine one item of the unknown region, determine in which of the two regions, S_1 or S_2, it belongs, and place it there. Thus, the size of the unknown region decreases by 1 at each step. The algorithm terminates when the size of the unknown region reaches 0—that is, when *firstUnknown > last*.

The following pseudocode describes the partitioning algorithm:

The partition algorithm

```
partition(inout theArray:ItemArray,
          in first:integer, in last:integer,
          out pivotIndex:integer)
// Partitions theArray[first..last].

   // initialize
   Choose the pivot and swap it with theArray[first]
   p = theArray[first]              // p is the pivot

   // set S₁ and S₂ to empty, set unknown region
   // to theArray[first+1..last]
   lastS1 = first
   firstUnknown = first + 1

   // determine the regions S₁ and S₂
   while (firstUnknown <= last)
   {  // consider the placement of the "leftmost"
      // item in the unknown region
      if (theArray[firstUnknown] < p)
         Move theArray[firstUnknown] into S₁
      else
         Move theArray[firstUnknown] into S₂
   }  // end while

   // place pivot in proper position between
   // S₁ and S₂, and mark its new location
   swap theArray[first] with theArray[lastS1]
   pivotIndex = lastS1
```

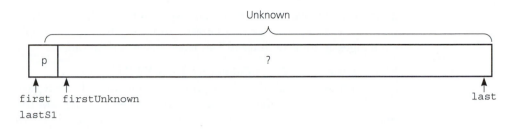

FIGURE 9-15   Initial state of the array

The algorithm is straightforward enough, but its move operations need clarifying. Consider the two possible actions that you need to take at each iteration of the *while* loop:

> **Move `theArray[firstUnknown]` into S_1.** S_1 and the unknown region are, in general, not adjacent: S_2 is between the two regions. However, you can perform the required move efficiently. You swap `theArray[firstUnknown]` with the first item of S_2—which is `theArray[lastS1 + 1]`, as Figure 9-16 illustrates. Then you increment `lastS1` by 1. The item that was in `theArray[firstUnknown]` will then be at the rightmost position of S_1. What about the item of S_2 that was moved to `theArray[firstUnknown]`? If you increment `firstUnknown` by 1, that item becomes the rightmost member of S_2. Thus, you should perform the following steps to move `theArray[firstUnknown]` into S_1:

```
swap theArray[firstUnknown] with theArray[lastS1+1]
Increment lastS1
Increment firstUnknown
```

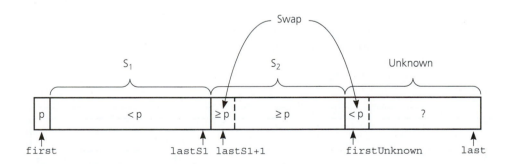

FIGURE 9-16   Moving `theArray[firstUnknown]` into S_1 by swapping it with `theArray[lastS1+1]` and by incrementing both `lastS1` and `firstUnknown`

This strategy works even when S_2 is empty. In that case, $lastS1 + 1$ equals $firstUnknown$, and thus the swap simply exchanges an item with itself. *This move preserves the invariant.*

Move $theArray[firstUnknown]$ into S2. This move is simple to accomplish. Recall that the rightmost boundary of the region S_2 is at position $firstUnknown - 1$; that is, regions S_2 and the unknown region are adjacent, as Figure 9-17 illustrates. Thus, to move $theArray[firstUnknown]$ into S_2, simply increment $firstUnknown$ by 1: S_2 expands to the right. *This move preserves the invariant.*

After you have moved all items from the unknown region into S_1 and S_2, one final task remains. You must place the pivot between the segments S_1 and S_2. Observe that $theArray[lastS1]$ is the rightmost item in S_1. By interchanging this item with the pivot, which is $theArray[first]$, you will place the pivot in its correct location. Then the statement

```
pivotIndex = lastS1
```

allows the function to return the location of the pivot. You can use this index to determine the boundaries of S_1 and S_2. Figure 9-18 traces the partition algorithm for an array of six integers when the pivot is the first item.

Before continuing the implementation of quicksort, we will establish the correctness of the partition algorithm by using invariants. Again, the loop invariant for the algorithm is

> *All items in S_1 ($theArray[first+1..lastS1]$) are less than the pivot, and all items in S_2 ($theArray[lastS1+1..firstUnknown-1]$) are greater than or equal to the pivot.*

Recall that when you use invariants to establish the correctness of an iterative algorithm, a four-step process is required:

The proof that the partition algorithm is correct uses an invariant and requires four steps

1. The invariant must be true initially, before the loop begins execution. In the partition algorithm, before the loop that swaps array items is entered, the pivot is $theArray[first]$, the unknown region is $theArray[first+1..last]$, and S_1 and S_2 are empty. The invariant is clearly true initially.

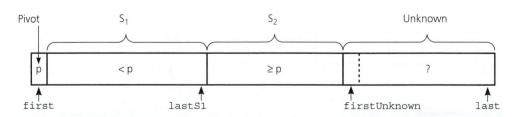

FIGURE 9-17   Moving $theArray[firstUnknown]$ into S_2 by incrementing $firstUnknown$

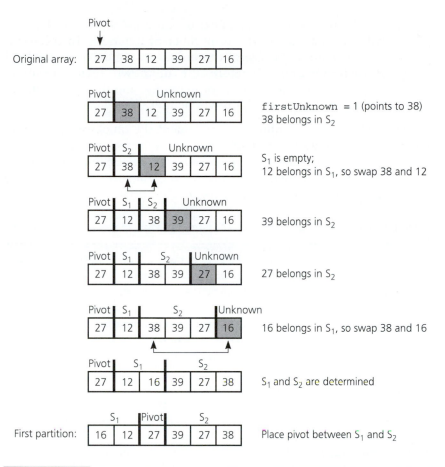

Pivot

Original array: | 27 | 38 | 12 | 39 | 27 | 16 |

Pivot | Unknown
| 27 | 38 | 12 | 39 | 27 | 16 |

firstUnknown = 1 (points to 38)
38 belongs in S_2

Pivot | S_2 | Unknown
| 27 | 38 | 12 | 39 | 27 | 16 |

S_1 is empty;
12 belongs in S_1, so swap 38 and 12

Pivot | S_1 | S_2 | Unknown
| 27 | 12 | 38 | 39 | 27 | 16 |

39 belongs in S_2

Pivot | S_1 | S_2 | Unknown
| 27 | 12 | 38 | 39 | 27 | 16 |

27 belongs in S_2

Pivot | S_1 | S_2 | Unknown
| 27 | 12 | 38 | 39 | 27 | 16 |

16 belongs in S_1, so swap 38 and 16

Pivot | S_1 | S_2
| 27 | 12 | 16 | 39 | 27 | 38 |

S_1 and S_2 are determined

S_1 | Pivot | S_2
First partition: | 16 | 12 | 27 | 39 | 27 | 38 |

Place pivot between S_1 and S_2

FIGURE 9-18 Developing the first partition of an array when the pivot is the first

2. An execution of the loop must preserve the invariant. That is, if the invariant is true before any given iteration of the loop, you must show that it is true after the iteration. In the partition algorithm, at each iteration of the loop a single item moves from the unknown region into either S_1 or S_2, depending on whether or not the item is less than the pivot. Thus, if the invariant was true before the move, it will remain true after the move.

3. The invariant must capture the correctness of the algorithm. That is, you must show that if the invariant is true when the loop terminates, the algorithm is correct. In the partition algorithm, the termination condition is that the unknown region is empty. But if the unknown region is empty, each item of *theArray[first+1..last]* must be in either S_1 or S_2—in which case the invariant implies that the partition algorithm has done what it was supposed to do.

4. The loop must terminate. That is, you must show that the loop will terminate after a finite number of iterations. In the partition algorithm, the size of the unknown region decreases by 1 at each iteration. Therefore, the unknown region becomes empty after a finite number of iterations, and thus the termination condition for the loop will be met.

The following C++ functions implement the quicksort algorithm. The function *choosePivot* enables you to try various pivots easily; the function *swap* is the same one that *selectionSort* uses. To sort an array *theArray* of *n* items, you invoke the function *quicksort* by writing *quicksort(theArray, 0, n-1)*.

```cpp
void choosePivot(DataType theArray[], int first, int last);
// ---------------------------------------------------------
// Chooses a pivot for quicksort's partition algorithm and
// swaps it with the first item in an array.
// Precondition: theArray[first..last] is an array;
// first <= last.
// Postcondition: theArray[first] is the pivot.
// ---------------------------------------------------------
// Implementation left as an exercise.

void partition(DataType theArray[],
               int first, int last, int& pivotIndex)
// ---------------------------------------------------------
// Partitions an array for quicksort.
// Precondition: theArray[first..last] is an array;
// first <= last.
// Postcondition: Partitions theArray[first..last] such
// that:
//    S1 = theArray[first..pivotIndex-1] <  pivot
//         theArray[pivotIndex]          == pivot
//    S2 = theArray[pivotIndex+1..last]  >= pivot
// Calls: choosePivot and swap.
// ---------------------------------------------------------
{
   // place pivot in theArray[first]
   choosePivot(theArray, first, last);
   DataType pivot = theArray[first];     // copy pivot

   // initially, everything but pivot is in unknown
   int lastS1 = first;          // index of last item in S1
   int firstUnknown = first + 1; // index of first item in
                                 // unknown

   // move one item at a time until unknown region is empty
```

```
   for (; firstUnknown <= last; ++firstUnknown)
   {  // Invariant: theArray[first+1..lastS1] < pivot
      //            theArray[lastS1+1..firstUnknown-1] >= pivot

      // move item from unknown to proper region
      if (theArray[firstUnknown] < pivot)
      {  // item from unknown belongs in S1
         ++lastS1;
         swap(theArray[firstUnknown], theArray[lastS1]);
      }  // end if

      // else item from unknown belongs in S2
   }  // end for

   // place pivot in proper position and mark its location
   swap(theArray[first], theArray[lastS1]);
   pivotIndex = lastS1;
}  // end partition


void quicksort(DataType theArray[], int first, int last)
// ---------------------------------------------------------
// Sorts the items in an array into ascending order.
// Precondition: theArray[first..last] is an array.
// Postcondition: theArray[first..last] is sorted.
// Calls: partition.
// ---------------------------------------------------------
{
   int pivotIndex;

   if (first < last)
   {  // create the partition: S1, pivot, S2
      partition(theArray, first, last, pivotIndex);

      // sort regions S1 and S2
      quicksort(theArray, first, pivotIndex-1);
      quicksort(theArray, pivotIndex+1, last);
   }  // end if
}  // end quicksort
```

In the analysis to follow, you will learn that it is desirable to avoid a pivot that makes either S_1 or S_2 empty. A good choice of pivot is one that is near the median of the array items. Exercise 20 at the end of this chapter considers this choice of pivot.

The *quicksort* and *mergesort* algorithms are similar in spirit, but whereas *quicksort* does its work before its recursive calls, *mergesort* does its work after its recursive calls. That is, while *quicksort* has the form

```
quicksort(inout theArray:ItemArray,
          in first:integer, in last:integer)

  if (first < last)
  { Prepare array theArray for recursive calls
     quicksort(S₁ region of theArray)
     quicksort(S₂ region of theArray)
  } // end if
```

mergesort has the general form

```
mergesort(inout theArray:ItemArray,
          in first:integer, in last:integer)
  if (first < last)
  { mergesort(Left half of theArray)
     mergesort(Right half of theArray)
     Tidy up array after the recursive calls
  } // end if
```

The preparation in *quicksort* is to partition the array into regions S_1 and S_2. The algorithm then sorts S_1 and S_2 independently, because every item in S_1 belongs to the left of every item in S_2. In *mergesort*, on the other hand, no work is done before the recursive calls: The algorithm sorts each half of the array with respect to itself. However, the algorithm must still deal with the interaction between the items in the two halves. That is, the algorithm must merge the two halves of the array after the recursive calls.

Analysis.   The major effort in the *quicksort* function occurs during the partitioning step. As you consider each item in the unknown region, you compare *theArray[firstUnknown]* with the pivot and move *theArray[firstUnknown]* into either S_1 or S_2. It is possible for one of S_1 or S_2 to remain empty. For example, if the pivot is the smallest item in the array segment, S_1 will remain empty. This occurrence is the worst case because S_2 decreases in size by only 1 at each recursive call to *quicksort*. Thus, the maximum number of recursive calls to *quicksort* will occur.

quicksort is slow when the array is already sorted and you choose the smallest item as the pivot

Notice what happens when the array is already sorted into ascending order and you choose the first array item as the pivot. Figure 9-19 shows the results of the first call to *partition* for this situation. The pivot is the smallest item in the array, and S_1 remains empty. The *partition* function requires $n - 1$ comparisons to partition the n items in this array. On the next recursive call to *quicksort*, *partition* is passed $n - 1$ items, so it will require $n - 2$ comparisons to partition them. Again S_1 will remain empty. Because the array segment that *quicksort* considers at each level of recursion decreases in size by only 1, $n - 1$ levels of recursion are required. Therefore, *quicksort* requires

$$1 + 2 + \cdots + (n - 1) = n * (n - 1)/2$$

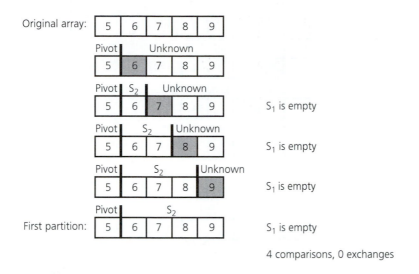

Original array:

| 5 | 6 | 7 | 8 | 9 |

Pivot | Unknown

| 5 | 6 | 7 | 8 | 9 |

Pivot | S_2 | Unknown

| 5 | 6 | 7 | 8 | 9 | S_1 is empty

Pivot | S_2 | Unknown

| 5 | 6 | 7 | 8 | 9 | S_1 is empty

Pivot | S_2 | Unknown

| 5 | 6 | 7 | 8 | 9 | S_1 is empty

Pivot | S_2

First partition:
| 5 | 6 | 7 | 8 | 9 | S_1 is empty

4 comparisons, 0 exchanges

FIGURE 9-19 A worst-case partitioning with `quicksort`

comparisons. However, recall that a move into S_2 does not require an exchange of array items; it requires only a change in the index `firstUnknown`.

Similarly, if S_2 remains empty at each recursive call, $n * (n - 1)/2$ comparisons are required. In addition, however, an exchange is necessary to move each unknown item to S_1. Thus, $n * (n - 1)/2$ exchanges are necessary. (Again, each exchange requires three data moves.) Thus, you can conclude that `quicksort` is $O(n^2)$ in the worst case.

In contrast, Figure 9-20 shows an example in which S_1 and S_2 contain the same number of items. In the average case, when S_1 and S_2 contain the same—or nearly the same—number of items arranged at random, fewer recursive calls to `quicksort` occur. As in the previous analysis of `mergesort`, you can conclude that there are either $\log_2 n$ or $1 + \log_2 n$ levels of recursive calls to `quicksort`. Each call to `quicksort` involves m comparisons and at most m exchanges, where m is the number of items in the subarray to be sorted. Clearly $m \leq n - 1$.

A formal analysis of `quicksort`'s average-case behavior would show that it is $O(n * \log n)$. Thus, on large arrays you can expect `quicksort` to run significantly faster than `insertionSort`, although in its worst case `quicksort` will require roughly the same amount of time as `insertionSort`.

It might seem surprising, then, that `quicksort` is often used to sort large arrays. The reason for `quicksort`'s popularity is that it is usually extremely fast in practice, despite its unimpressive theoretical worst-case behavior. Although a worst-case situation is not typical, even if the worst case occurs, `quicksort`'s performance is acceptable for moderately large arrays.

Quicksort. Worst case: $O(n^2)$; average case: $O(n * \log n)$

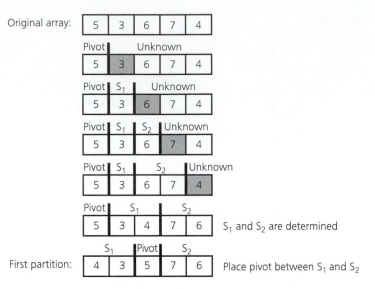

FIGURE 9-20   An average-case partitioning with `quicksort`

The fact that `quicksort`'s average-case behavior is far better than its worst-case behavior distinguishes it from the other sorting algorithms considered in this chapter. If the original arrangement of data in the array is "random," `quicksort` performs at least as well as any known sorting algorithm that involves comparisons. Unless the array is already ordered, `quicksort` is best.

The efficiency of `mergesort` is somewhere between the possibilities for `quicksort:` Sometimes `quicksort` is faster, and sometimes `mergesort` is faster. While the worst-case behavior of `mergesort` is of the same order of magnitude as `quicksort`'s average-case behavior, in most situations `quicksort` will run somewhat faster than `mergesort`. However, in its worst case `quicksort` will be significantly slower than `mergesort`.

Radix Sort

The radix sorting algorithm is included here because it is quite different from the others.

Imagine again that you are sorting a hand of cards. This time you pick up the cards one at a time and arrange them by rank into 13 possible groups in this order: 2, 3, . . . , 10, J, Q, K, A. Combine these groups and place the cards face down on the table so that the 2s are on top and the aces are on the bottom. Now pick up the cards one at a time and arrange them by suit into four possible groups in this order: clubs, diamonds, hearts, and spades. When taken together, the groups result in a sorted hand of cards.

A **radix sort** uses this idea of forming groups and then combining them to sort a collection of data. The sort treats each data item as a character string. As a first simple example of a radix sort, consider this collection of three-letter strings:

ABC, XYZ, BWZ, AAC, RLT, JBX, RDT, KLT, AEO, TLJ

The sort begins by organizing the data according to their rightmost (least significant) letters. Although none of the strings ends in A or B, two strings end in C. Place those two strings into a group. Continuing through the alphabet, you form the following groups:

(AB**C**, AA**C**) (TL**J**) (AE**O**) (RL**T**, RD**T**, KL**T**) (JB**X**) (XY**Z**, BW**Z**)

Group strings by rightmost letter

The strings in each group end with the same letter, and the groups are ordered by that letter. The strings within each group retain their relative order from the original list of strings.

Now combine the groups into one as follows. Take the items in the first group in their present order, follow them with the items in the second group in their present order, and so on. The following group results:

ABC, AAC, TLJ, AEO, RLT, RDT, KLT, JBX, XYZ, BWZ

Combine groups

Next, form new groups as you did before, but this time use the middle letter of each string instead of the last letter:

(A**A**C) (A**B**C, J**B**X) (R**D**T) (A**E**O) (T**L**J, R**L**T, K**L**T) (B**W**Z) (X**Y**Z)

Group strings by middle letter

Now the strings in each group have the same middle letter, and the groups are ordered by that letter. As before, the strings within each group retain their relative order from the previous group of all strings.

Combine these groups into one group, again preserving the relative order of the items within each group:

AAC, ABC, JBX, RDT, AEO, TLJ, RLT, KLT, BWZ, XYZ

Combine groups

Now form new groups according to the first letter of each string:

(**A**AC, **A**BC, **A**EO) (**B**WZ) (**J**BX) (**K**LT) (**R**DT, **R**LT) (**T**LJ) (**X**YZ)

Group strings by first letter

Finally, combine the groups, again maintaining the relative order within each group:

AAC, ABC, AEO, BWZ, JBX, KLT, RDT, RLT, TLJ, XYZ

Sorted strings

The strings are now in sorted order.

In the previous example, all character strings had the same length. If the character strings have varying lengths, you can treat them as if they were the same length by padding them on the right with blanks as necessary.

To sort numeric data, the radix sort treats a number as a character string. You can treat numbers as if they were padded on the left with zeros, making them all appear to be the same length. You then form groups according to the rightmost digits, combine the groups, form groups according to the next-to-last digits, combine them, and so on, just as you did in the previous example. Figure 9-21 shows a radix sort of eight integers.

The following pseudocode describes the algorithm for a radix sort of n decimal integers of d digits each:

```
radixSort(inout theArray:ItemArray,
          in n:integer, in d:integer)
// Sorts n d-digit integers in the array theArray.

  for (j = d down to 1)
  {  Initialize 10 groups to empty
     Initialize a counter for each group to 0
     for (i = 0 through n-1)
     {  k = jth digit of theArray[i]
        Place theArray[i] at the end of group k
        Increase kth counter by 1
     }  // end for i

     Replace the items in theArray with all the
        items in group 0, followed by all the items
        in group 1, and so on.
  }  // end for j
```

Analysis. From the pseudocode for the radix sort, you can see that this algorithm requires n moves each time it forms groups and n moves to combine them again into one group. The algorithm performs these $2 * n$ moves d times. Therefore, the radix sort requires $2 * n * d$ moves to sort n strings of d characters each. However, notice that no comparisons are necessary. Thus, radix sort is $O(n)$.

Despite its efficiency, radix sort has some difficulties that make it inappropriate as a general-purpose sorting algorithm. For example, to

Even though radix sort is $O(n)$, it is not appropriate as a general-purpose sorting algorithm

0123, 2154, 0222, 0004, 0283, 1560, 1061, 2150	Original integers
(156**0**, 215**0**) (106**1**) (022**2**) (012**3**, 028**3**) (215**4**, 000**4**)	Grouped by fourth digit
1560, 2150, 1061, 0222, 0123, 0283, 2154, 0004	Combined
(00**0**4) (02**2**2, 01**2**3) (21**5**0, 21**5**4) (15**6**0, 10**6**1) (02**8**3)	Grouped by third digit
0004, 0222, 0123, 2150, 2154, 1560, 1061, 0283	Combined
(0**0**04, 1**0**61) (0**1**23, 2**1**50, 2**1**54) (0**2**22, 0**2**83) (1**5**60)	Grouped by second digit
0004, 1061, 0123, 2150, 2154, 0222, 0283, 1560	Combined
(**0**004, **0**123, **0**222, **0**283) (**1**061, **1**560) (**2**150, **2**154)	Grouped by first digit
0004, 0123, 0222, 0283, 1061, 1560, 2150, 2154	Combined (sorted)

FIGURE 9-21   A radix sort of eight integers

perform a radix sort of strings of uppercase letters, you need to accommodate 27 groups—one group for blanks and one for each letter. If the original data collection contains n strings, each group must be able to hold n strings. For large n this requirement demands substantial memory, if you use arrays for both the original data and the resulting groups. However, you can save memory by using a linked list for each of the 27 groups. Thus, a radix sort is more appropriate for a linked list than for an array.

A Comparison of Sorting Algorithms

Figure 9-22 summarizes the worst-case and average-case orders of magnitude for the sorting algorithms that appear in this chapter. For reference purposes, two other algorithms—treesort and heapsort—are included here, even though you will not study them until Chapters 10 and 11, respectively.

The Standard Template Library Sorting Algorithms

The Standard Template Library (STL) provides several sort functions in the library header `<algorithm>`. Recall that the STL class *list* has its own built-in *sort* function. The *sort* for *list* is faster than the generic sort for containers because it is optimized for a list and swaps pointers rather than copying objects. When sorting deques, strings, arrays, or vectors, use the generic *sort* function. Note that this *sort* is not stable; that is, the elements with the same value are not guaranteed to remain in the same relative order. To preserve ordering, use *stable_sort* instead.

Other sorting algorithms are more efficient when only a range of elements needs to be sorted, or even simply distinguished. If only a range of elements needs to be sorted, use *partial_sort*. The range is specified in the arguments. The *partial_sort_copy* function produces a resulting container with elements in the specified range. The *nth_element* function partially sorts a range of elements as well, but it only guarantees that the nth will be a dividing point. All of the elements

	Worst case	Average case
Selection sort	n^2	n^2
Bubble sort	n^2	n^2
Insertion sort	n^2	n^2
Mergesort	$n * \log n$	$n * \log n$
Quicksort	n^2	$n * \log n$
Radix sort	n	n
Treesort	n^2	$n * \log n$
Heapsort	$n * \log n$	$n * \log n$

FIGURE 9-22   Approximate growth rates of time required for eight sorting algorithms

in the array below the nth element will be less than or equal to the nth element, and all the elements above the nth element will be greater than the value of the nth element. Note that neither range is required to be in any particular order. The `nth_element` function is useful for determining medians or percentiles.

When sorting elements according to a certain criteria (for example, elements less than the value 10), instead of sorting the top n elements, as in *nth-element*, use the *partition* or *stable_partition* functions instead of *nth_element*. These functions divide the container into two ranges; the first range contains elements that satisfy a particular criterion, and the second range contains those that do not. Finally, *<algorithm>* contains the *merge* and *inplace_merge* functions as well. However, both these functions take sorted ranges as arguments, so they perform only a single pass of the mergesort algorithm.

The functions *partition* and *stable_partition* require bidirectional iterators, while the other STL sorting functions require random-access iterators. The function specifications are listed below. Note that each function has the option of an additional parameter that determines the ordering of the sort. The default comparison operator is <.

```
void sort(RandomIter first, RandomIter last);
void sort(RandomIter first, RandomIter last, Compare cmp);
// Sorts first to last into ascending order by default.
// A comparison function object may be supplied.


void stable_sort(RandomIter first, RandomIter last);
void stable_sort(RandomIter first, RandomIter last,
                                    Compare cmp);
// Sorts first to last into ascending order by default.
// A comparison function object may be supplied.
// Preserves original ordering of equivalent elements.


void partial_sort(RandomIter first, RandomIter middle,
                  RandomIter last);
void partial_sort(RandomIter first, RandomIter middle,
                  RandomIter last, Compare cmp);
// Sorts the number of elements from first to last
// and places them in the range from first to middle.
// Elements from middle to last are not ordered.
// Default sort is in ascending order.
// A comparison function object may be supplied.


RandomIter partial_sort_copy(InputIter first, InputIter last,
                  RandomIter first2, RandomIter last2);
RandomIter partial_sort_copy(InputIter first, InputIter last,
                  RandomIter first2, RandomIter last2,
                  Compare cmp);
```

```
// Sorts the number of elements from first to last
// and copies them into a container in the range
// from first2 to last2.
// Default sort is in ascending order.
// A comparison function object may be supplied.

void nth_element(RandomIter first, RandomIter nth,
                 RandomIter, last);
void nth_element(RandomIter first, RandomIter nth,
                 RandomIter last, Compare cmp);
// The nth element becomes a dividing point for the container.
// The ranges from first to nth and nth to last are not sorted.
// All elements from first to nth are less than or equal to nth.
// All elements from nth to last are greater than nth.
// A comparison function object may be supplied.

BiIter partition(BiIter first, BiIter last,
                 Predicate p);
// The container is partitioned to place all elements that
// satisfy a particular predicate p before every element that
// does not satisfy the predicate p.
// The two ranges are not sorted.
// The return iterator points to either the first element that
// does not satisfy the predicate p or the end.
// Relative order of equivalent elements is not maintained.

BiIter stable_partition(BiIter first, BiIter last,
                        Predicate p);
// The container is partitioned to place all elements that
// satisfy a particular predicate p before every element that
// does not satisfy the predicate p.
// The two ranges are not sorted.
// The return iterator points to either the first element that
// does not satisfy the predicate p or the end.
// Relative order of equivalent elements is maintained.

OutputIter merge(InputIter first, InputIter last,
                 InputIter2 first2, InputIter2 last2,
                 OutIter res);
OutputIter merge(InputIter first, InputIter last,
                 InputIter2 first2, InputIter2 last2,
                 OutputIter res, Compare cmp);
// Takes two sorted ranges and
// merges them into another sorted container.
// A comparison function object may be supplied.
// For equivalent elements, elements from the first range will
// precede elements from the second.
```

```
void inplace_merge(BiIter  first, BiIter middle, BiIter last);
void inplace_merge(BiIter  first, BiIter middle, BiIter last,
                   Compare cmp);
// Takes two parts of a sorted container
// and merges them in place.
// The two ranges are first to middle and middle to last.
// A comparison function object may be supplied.
// For equivalent elements, elements from the first range will
// precede elements from the second.
```

The performance of the sorts depends on how many items need to be sorted. Therefore, algorithms that perform partial sorts, or simply divide the ranges, run faster than the full *sort* or *stable_sort*. In general, the stable sort algorithms are less efficient than sorts that do not preserve ordering of elements. The function *sort*, on average, has a performance of $O(n \log n)$, while the worst-case performance, which is rare, is $O(n^2)$.

The following program demonstrates how to use some of the STL sorts. The *inplace_merge* is used in Programming Problem 9 at the end of this chapter.

```
#include <algorithm>
#include <functional>
#include <ctime>
#include <vector>
#include <iostream>

using namespace std;

// number of elements in the vectors
const SIZE = 25;

int main()
{

    // create four vectors for sorting algorithms
    vector<int> v1;
    vector<int> v2(SIZE);
    vector<int> v3(SIZE);
    vector<int> v4(SIZE);

    // create an iterator for the vectors
    vector<int>::iterator iter;

    // seed the random number generator
    srand(time(0));
```

```cpp
// fill the first vector with random numbers from 1 to 50
for (int i = 0; i < SIZE; i++)
   v1.push_back(rand() % 50);

// print the original vector
cout << "original vector: " << endl;
for (iter = v1.begin(); iter != v1.end(); iter++)
   cout << *iter << " ";

// copy vectors
copy(v1.begin(), v1.end(), v2.begin());
copy(v1.begin(), v1.end(), v3.begin());
copy(v1.begin(), v1.end(), v4.begin());

// perform a stable_sort on the first vector
stable_sort(v1.begin(), v1.end());

// print out the stable_sort vector
cout << endl << "stable sort: " << endl;
for (iter = v1.begin(); iter != v1.end(); iter++)
   cout << *iter << " ";

// perform a partial_ sort on the second vector
partial_sort(v2.begin(), v2.begin() + v2.size()/2, v2.end());

// print out the partial_sort vector
cout << endl << "partial sort to the " << v2.size()/2
     << "th element: " << endl;
for (iter = v2.begin(); iter != v2.end(); iter++)
   cout << *iter << " ";

// perform a nth_element sort on the third vector
int n = 15;
iter = v3.begin() + n;  // iterator points to the nth element
nth_element(v3.begin(), iter, v3.end());

// print out the nth_element vector
cout<< endl << "nth element sort on the " << n
    << "th element with nth value " << v3[n-1]
    << ": " << endl;
for (iter = v3.begin(); iter != v3.end(); iter++)
   cout << *iter << " ";

// perform a stable_partition sort on the fourth vector
// iterator points to the first element that does not meet the
// criterion - odd numbers
```

```
        // bind2nd is an C++ library function that creates a
        // unary predicate from two arguments
        iter = stable_partition(v4.begin(), v4.end(),
                                bind2nd(modulus<int>(), 2));

        // print out the stable_partition vector
        cout << endl
             << "stable_partition sort for odd and even numbers — "
             <<  "the partition element is "
             << *iter << ": " << endl;
        for (iter = v4.begin(); iter != v4.end(); iter++)
              cout << *iter << " ";

        return 0;
}   // end main
```

Here is a sample run of this program:

```
original vector:
31 35 1 19 38 35 26 24 11 34 7 36 23 11 29 40 8 26 49 24 31
8 49 11 32
stable sort:
1 7 8 8 11 11 11 19 23 24 24 26 26 29 31 31 32 34 35 35 36
38 40 49 49
partial sort to the 12th element:
1 7 8 8 11 11 11 19 23 24 24 26 38 36 35 40 35 34 49 31 31
29 49 26 32
nth element sort on the 10th element begins with value 24:
1 7 8 8 11 11 11 19 23 24 24 26 26 29 31 40 36 34 49 35 38
35 49 31 32
stable partition sort for odd and even numbers - the
partition element is 38:
31 35 1 19 35 11 7 23 11 29 49 31 49 11 38 26 24 34 36 40 8
26 24 8 32
```

Summary

1. Order–of–magnitude analysis and Big O notation measure an algorithm's time requirement as a function of the problem size by using a growth-rate function. This approach enables you to analyze the efficiency of an algorithm without regard for such factors as computer speed and programming skill that are beyond your control.

2. When you compare the inherent efficiency of algorithms, you examine their growth-rate functions when the problems are large. Only significant differences in growth-rate functions are meaningful.

3. Worst-case analysis considers the maximum amount of work an algorithm will require on a problem of a given size, while average-case analysis considers the expected amount of work that it will require.

4. You can use order-of-magnitude analysis to help you choose an implementation for an abstract data type. If your application frequently uses particular ADT operations, your implementation should be efficient for at least those operations.

5. Selection sort, bubble sort, and insertion sort are all $O(n^2)$ algorithms. Although in a particular case one might be faster than another, for large problems they all are slow.

6. Quicksort and mergesort are two very efficient recursive sorting algorithms. In the "average" case, quicksort is among the fastest known sorting algorithms. However, quicksort's worst-case behavior is significantly slower than mergesort's. Fortunately, quicksort's worst case rarely occurs in practice. Mergesort is not quite as fast as quicksort in the average case, but its performance is consistently good in all cases. Mergesort has the disadvantage of requiring extra storage equal to the size of the array to be sorted.

Cautions

1. In general, you should avoid analyzing an algorithm solely by studying the running times of a specific implementation. Running times are influenced by such factors as programming style, the particular computer, and the data on which the program is run.

2. When comparing the efficiency of various solutions, look only at significant differences. This rule is consistent with the multidimensional view of the cost of a computer program.

3. While manipulating the Big O notation, remember that $O(f(n))$ represents an inequality. It is not a function but simply a notation that means "is of order $f(n)$" or "has order $f(n)$."

4. If a problem is small, do not overanalyze it. In such a situation, the primary concern should be simplicity. For example, if you are sorting an array that contains only a small number of items—say, fewer than 25—a simple $O(n^2)$ algorithm such as an insertion sort is appropriate.

5. If you are sorting a very large array, an $O(n^2)$ algorithm is probably too inefficient to use.

6. Quicksort is appropriate when you are confident that the data in the array to be sorted are arranged randomly. Although quicksort's worst-case behavior is $O(n^2)$, the worst case rarely occurs in practice.

Self-Test Exercises

1. How many comparisons of array items do the following loops contain?

   ```
   for (j = 1; j <= n-1; ++j)
   {  i = j + 1;
      do
      {  if (theArray[i] < theArray[j])
            swap(theArray[i], theArray[j]);
         ++i;
      }  while (i <= n);
   }  // end for
   ```

2. Repeat Self-Test Exercise 1, replacing the statement $i = j + 1$ with $i = j$.

3. What order is an algorithm that has as a growth-rate function

   a. $8 * n^3 - 9 * n$ **b.** $7 * \log_2 n + 20$ **c.** $7 * \log_2 n + n$

4. Consider a sequential search of n data items.

   a. If the data items are sorted into ascending order, how can you determine that your desired item is not in the data collection without always making n comparisons?

   b. What is the order of the sequential search algorithm when the desired item is not in the data collection? Do this for both sorted and unsorted data, and consider the best, average, and worst cases.

   c. Show that if the sequential search algorithm finds the desired item in the data collection, the algorithm's order does not depend upon whether or not the data items are sorted.

5. Trace the selection sort as it sorts the following array into ascending order: 20 80 40 25 60 30.

6. Repeat Self-Test Exercise 5, but instead sort the array into descending order.

7. Trace the bubble sort as it sorts the following array into ascending order: 25 30 20 80 40 60.

8. Trace the insertion sort as it sorts the array in Self-Test Exercise 7 into ascending order.

9. Show that the mergesort algorithm satisfies the four criteria of recursion that Chapter 2 describes.

10. Trace quicksort's partitioning algorithm as it partitions the following array. Use the first item as the pivot.

    38 16 40 39 12 27

11. Suppose that you sort a large array of integers by using mergesort. Next you use a binary search to determine whether a given integer occurs in the array. Finally, you display all the integers in the sorted array.

   a. Which algorithm is faster, in general: the mergesort or the binary search? Explain in terms of Big O notation.

   b. Which algorithm is faster, in general: the binary search or displaying the integers? Explain in terms of Big O notation.

Exercises

1. What is the order of each of the following tasks in the worst case?

   a. Computing the sum of the first n even integers by using a `for` loop

   b. Displaying all n integers in an array

   c. Displaying all n integers in a sorted linked list

   d. Displaying all n names in a circular linked list

   e. Displaying one array element

   f. Displaying the last integer in a linked list

   g. Searching an array of n integers for a particular value by using a binary search

   h. Sorting an array of n integers into descending order by using a mergesort

   i. Adding an item to a stack of n items

   j. Adding an item to a queue of n items

2. Suppose that your implementation of a particular algorithm appears in C++ as

```
for (int pass = 1; pass <= n; ++pass)
{   for (int index = 0; index < n; ++index)
    {   for (int count = 1; count < 10; ++count)
        {
            . . .
        } // end for
    } // end for
} // end for
```

The previous code shows only the repetition in the algorithm, not the computations that occur within the loops. These computations, however, are independent of n. What is the order of the algorithm? Justify your answer.

3. Consider the following C++ function f, which calls the function *swap*. Assume that *swap* exists and simply swaps the contents of its two arguments. Do not be concerned with f's purpose.

```
void f(int theArray[], int n)
{
    for (int j = 0; j < n; ++j)
    {   int i = 0;
        while (i <= j)
        {   if (theArray[i] < theArray[j])
                swap(theArray[i], theArray[j]);
            ++i;
        }  // end while
    }  // end for
}  // end f
```

How many comparisons does f perform?

4. For large arrays and in the worst case, is selection sort faster than insertion sort? Explain.

5. Show that any polynomial $f(x) = c_n x^n + c_{n-1} x^{n-1} + \cdots + c_1 x + c_0$ is $O(x^n)$.

6. Show that for all constants $a, b > 1, f(n)$ is $O(\log_a n)$ if and only if $f(n)$ is $O(\log_b n)$. Thus, you can omit the base when you write $O(\log n)$. *Hint:* Use the identity $\log_a n = \log_b n / \log_b a$ for all constants $a, b > 1$.

7. This chapter's analysis of selection sort ignored operations that control loops or manipulate array indexes. Revise this analysis by counting *all* operations, and show that the algorithm is still $O(n^2)$.

8. Trace the insertion sort as it sorts the following array into ascending order: 20 80 40 25 60 40.

9. Trace the selection sort as it sorts the following array into ascending order: 7 12 24 4 19 32.

10. Trace the bubble sort as it sorts the following array into descending order: 12 23 5 10 34.

11. Apply the selection sort, bubble sort, and insertion sort to

   a. An inverted array: 8 6 4 2

   b. An ordered array: 2 4 6 8

12. How many comparisons would be needed to sort an array containing 25 elements using the bubble sort in

   a. The worst case

   b. The best case

13. Find an array that makes the bubble sort exhibit its worst behavior.

14. Revise the function `selectionSort` so that it sorts an array of C++ structures according to one `int` data member, which is the sort key. Repeat this exercise for an array of instances of a class. Assume that this class contains a member function `sortKey` that returns the integer sort key.

15. Write recursive versions of `selectionSort`, `bubbleSort`, and `insertionSort`.

16. Trace the mergesort algorithm as it sorts the following array into ascending order. List the calls to `mergesort` and to `merge` in the order in which they occur.

    20 80 40 25 60 30

17. When sorting an array by using mergesort,

    a. Do the recursive calls to `mergesort` depend on the values in the array, the number of items in the array, or both? Explain.

    b. In what step of `mergesort` are the items in the array actually swapped (that is, sorted)? Explain.

18. Trace the quicksort algorithm as it sorts the following array into ascending order. List the calls to `quicksort` and to `partition` in the order in which they occur.

    20 80 40 25 60 10 15

19. Suppose that you remove the call to `merge` from the `mergesort` algorithm to obtain

```
mystery(inout theArray:ItemArray, in n:integer)
// Mystery algorithm for theArray[0..n-1].

   if (n > 1)
   {  mystery(lefthalf(theArray))
      mystery(righthalf(theArray))
   }  // end if
```

What does this new algorithm do?

20. You can choose any array item as the pivot for `quicksort`. Simply interchange items so that your pivot is in `theArray[first]`. One way to choose a pivot is to take the middle value of the three values `theArray[first]`, `theArray[(first + last)/2]`, and `theArray[last]`. How many recursive calls are necessary to sort an array of size *n* if you always choose the pivot in this way?

21. The partition algorithm that `quicksort` uses moves one item at a time from the unknown region into the appropriate region S_1 or

S_2. If the item to be moved belongs in region S_1, and if S_2 is empty, the algorithm will swap an array item with itself. Modify the partition algorithm to eliminate this unnecessary swapping.

22. Use invariants to show that the function *selectionSort* is correct.

23. Describe an iterative version of *mergesort*. Define an appropriate invariant and show the correctness of your algorithm.

24. One criterion used to evaluate sorting algorithms is stability. A sorting algorithm is stable if it does not exchange items that have the same sort key. Thus, items with the same sort key (possibly differing in other ways) will maintain their positions relative to one another. For example, you might want to take an array of students sorted by name and sort it by year of graduation. Using a stable sorting algorithm to sort the array by year will ensure that within each year the students will remain sorted by name. Some applications mandate a stable sorting algorithm. Others do not. Which of the sorting algorithms described in this chapter are stable?

25. When we discussed the radix sort, we sorted a hand of cards by first ordering the cards by rank and then by suit. To implement a radix sort for this example, you could use two characters to represent a card, if you used T to represent a 10. For example, S2 is the 2 of spades and HT is the 10 of hearts.

    a. Trace the radix sort for this example.

    b. Suppose that you did not use T to represent a 10—that is, suppose that H10 is the 10 of hearts—and that you padded the two-character strings on the right with a blank to form three-character strings. How would a radix sort order the entire deck of cards in this case?

Programming Problems

1. Add a counter to the functions *insertionSort* and *mergesort* that counts the number of comparisons that are made. Run the two functions with arrays of various sizes. On what size does the difference in the number of comparisons become significant? How does this size compare with the size that the orders of these algorithms predict?

2. The function *quicksort* uses the function *choosePivot* to choose a pivot and place it into the first array location. Implement *choosePivot* in two ways:

    a. Always choose the first item in the array as pivot.

    b. Choose a pivot as Exercise 20 describes.

Add a counter to the function *partition* that counts the number of comparisons that are made. Run *quicksort* with each pivot selection strategy and with arrays of various sizes. On what size array does the difference in the number of comparisons become significant? For which pivot selection strategy does the difference in the number of comparisons become significant?

3. **a.** Modify the partition algorithm for *quicksort* so that S_1 and S_2 will never be empty.

   b. Another partitioning strategy for *quicksort* is possible. Let an index *low* traverse the array segment *theArray[first..last]* from *first* to *last* and stop when it encounters the first item that is greater than the pivot item. Similarly, let a second index *high* traverse the array segment from *last* to *first* and stop when it encounters the first item that is smaller than the pivot item. Then swap these two items, increment *low,* decrement *high,* and continue until *high* and *low* meet somewhere in the middle. Implement this version of *quick-sort* in C++. How can you ensure that the regions S_1 and S_2 are not empty?

   c. There are several variations of this partitioning strategy. What other strategies can you think of? How do they compare to the two that have been given?

4. Implement the radix sort of an array by using an ADT queue for each group.

5. Implement a radix sort of a linked list of integers.

6. **a.** Implement a mergesort of a linked list of integers.

   b. Implement any other sorting algorithms that are appropriate for a linked list.

7. You can sort a large array of integers that are in the range 1 to 100 by using an array *count* of 100 items to count the number of occurrences of each integer in the array. Fill in the details of this sorting algorithm, which is called a bucket sort, and write a C++ function that implements it. What is the order of the bucket sort? Why is the bucket sort not useful as a general sorting algorithm?

8. Shellsort (named for its inventor, Donald Shell) is an improved insertion sort. Rather than always exchanging adjacent items—as in insertion sort—Shellsort can exchange items that are far apart in the array. Shellsort arranges the array so that every h^{th} item forms a sorted subarray for every h in a decreasing sequence of values. For example, if h is 5, every fifth item forms a sorted subarray. Ultimately, if h is 1, the entire array will be sorted.

   One possible sequence of h's begins at $n/2$ and halves n until it becomes 1. By using this sequence, and by replacing 1 with h and

0 with $h - 1$ in *insertionSort*, we get the following function for Shellsort:

```
void shellsort(DataType theArray[], int n)
{
    for (int h = n/2; h > 0; h = h/2)
    {  for (int unsorted = h; unsorted < n; ++unsorted)
        {  DataType nextItem = theArray[unsorted];
           int loc = unsorted;

           for (; (loc >= h) && (theArray[loc-h] > nextItem);
                   loc = loc - h)
              theArray[loc] = theArray[loc-h];
           theArray[loc] = nextItem;
        }  // end for
    }  // end for
}  // end shellsort
```

Add a counter to the functions *insertionSort* and *shellsort* that counts the number of comparisons that are made. Run the two functions with arrays of various sizes. On what size does the difference in the number of comparisons become significant?

9. Implement the mergesort algorithm for an unsorted STL container using the *inplace_merge* function in *<algorithm>*.

10. Write a program to display the running time, in terms of CPU ticks, of the STL sorts described in this chapter. Test the sorts on vectors of 100, 1,000, and 5,000 elements. Vectors of the same size should contain identical elements. Use the *clock_t* variable and *clock* function from *<ctime>* to time each sort.

10

CHAPTER

Trees

PREVIEW

The data organizations presented in previous chapters are linear in that items are one after another. The ADTs in this chapter organize data in a nonlinear, hierarchical form, whereby an item can have more than one immediate successor. In particular, this chapter discusses the specifications, implementations, and relative efficiency of the ADT binary tree and the ADT binary search tree. These ADTs are basic to the next three chapters.

The previous chapters discussed ADTs whose operations fit into at least one of these general categories:

- Operations that insert data into a data collection
- Operations that delete data from a data collection
- Operations that ask questions about the data in a data collection

The ADTs list, stack, and queue are all position oriented, and their operations have the form

- Insert a data item into the ith *position* of a data collection.
- Delete a data item from the ith *position* of a data collection.
- Ask a question about the data item in the ith *position* of a data collection.

As you have seen, the ADT list places no restriction on the value of i, while the ADTs stack and queue do impose some restrictions. For example, the operations of the ADT stack are restricted to inserting into, deleting from, and asking a question about one end—the top—of the stack. Thus, although they differ with respect to the flexibility of their operations, lists, stacks, and queues manage an association between data items and *positions*.

The ADT sorted list is **value oriented**. Its operations are of the form

- Insert a data item containing the *value x*.
- Delete a data item containing the *value x*.
- Ask a question about a data item containing the *value x*.

Although these operations, like position-oriented operations, fit into the three general categories of operations listed earlier—they insert data, delete data, and ask questions about data—they are based on *values* of data items instead of *positions*.

This chapter discusses two major ADTs: the binary tree and the binary search tree. As you will see, the binary tree is a position-oriented ADT, but it is not linear as are lists, stacks, and queues. Thus, you will not reference items in a binary tree by using a position number. Our discussion of the ADT binary tree provides an important background for the more useful binary search tree, which is a value-oriented ADT. Although a binary search tree is also not linear, it has operations similar to those of a sorted list, which is linear.

In the next chapter, you will see two more value-oriented ADTs: the ADT table and the ADT priority queue. The implementations of both of these ADTs can use the ideas presented in this chapter.

10.1 Terminology

You use *trees* to represent relationships. Previous chapters informally used tree diagrams to represent the relationships between the calls of a recursive algorithm. For example, the diagram of the *rabbit* algorithm's recursive calls in Figure 2-11 of Chapter 2 is actually a tree. Each call to *rabbit* is represented by a box, or node, or **vertex**, in the tree. The lines between the nodes (boxes) are called **edges**. For this tree, the edges indicate recursive calls. For example, the edges from *rabbit*(7) to *rabbit*(6) and *rabbit*(5) indicate that subproblem *rabbit*(7) makes calls to *rabbit*(6) and *rabbit*(5).

All trees are **hierarchical** in nature. Intuitively, hierarchical means that a "parent-child" relationship exists between the nodes in the tree. If an edge is between node *n* and node *m*, and node *n* is above node *m* in the tree, then *n* is the **parent** of *m*, and *m* is a **child** of *n*. In the tree in Figure 10-1, nodes *B* and *C* are children of node *A*. Children of the same parent—for example, *B* and *C*—are called **siblings**. Each node in a tree has at most one parent, and exactly one node—called the **root** of the tree—has no parent. Node *A* is the root of the tree in Figure 10-1. A node that has no children is called a *leaf* of the tree. The leaves of the tree in Figure 10-1 are *C, D, E,* and *F.*

The parent-child relationship between the nodes is generalized to the relationships **ancestor** and **descendant**. In Figure 10-1, *A* is an ancestor of *D,* and thus *D* is a descendant of *A*. Not all nodes are related by the ancestor or descendant relationship: *B* and *C,* for instance, are not so related. However, the root of any tree is an ancestor of every node in that tree. A **subtree** in a tree is any node in the tree together with all of its descendants. A **subtree of a node** *n* is a subtree rooted at a child of *n*. For example, Figure 10-2 shows a subtree of the tree in Figure 10-1. This subtree has *B* as its root and is a subtree of the node *A*.

Because trees are hierarchical in nature, you can use them to represent information that itself is hierarchical in nature—for example, organization charts and family trees, as Figure 10-3 depicts. It may be disconcerting to discover, however, that the nodes in the family tree in Figure 10-3b that represent Caroline's parents (John and Jacqueline) are the children of the node that represents Caroline! That is, the nodes that represent Caroline's ancestors are the descendants of Caroline's node. It's no wonder that computer scientists often seem to be confused by reality.

Formally, a **general tree** *T* is a set of one or more nodes such that *T* is partitioned into disjoint subsets:

- A single node *r*, the root

- Sets that are general trees, called subtrees of *r*

Thus, the trees in Figures 10-1 and 10-3a are general trees.

Trees are hierarchical

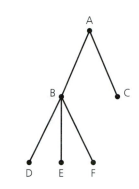

FIGURE 10-1   A general tree

A subtree is any node and its descendants

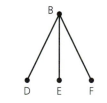

FIGURE 10-2   A subtree of the tree in Figure 10-1

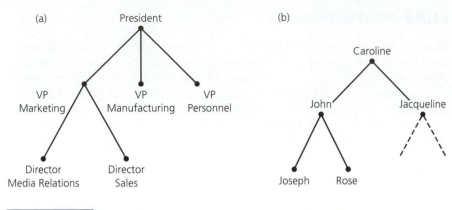

FIGURE 10-3   (a) An organization chart; (b) a family tree

The primary focus of this chapter will be on binary trees. Formally, a **binary tree** is a set T of nodes such that either

Formal definition of a binary tree

- T is empty, or

- T is partitioned into three disjoint subsets:

- A single node r, the root

- Two possibly empty sets that are binary trees, called **left** and **right subtrees** of r

The trees in Figures 2-11 and 10-3b are binary trees. Notice that each node in a binary tree has no more than two children. A binary tree is not a special kind of general tree, because a binary tree can be empty, whereas a general tree cannot.

The following intuitive restatement of the definition of a binary tree is useful:

T is a binary tree if either

Intuitive definition of a binary tree

- T has no nodes, or

- T is of the form

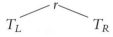

where r is a node and T_L and T_R are both binary trees.

Notice that the formal definition agrees with this intuitive one: If r is the root of T, then the binary tree T_L is the left subtree of node r and T_R is the right subtree of node r. If T_L is not empty, its root is the **left child** of r, and if T_R is not empty, its root is the **right child** of r. Notice that if both subtrees of a node are empty, that node is a leaf.

As an example of how you can use a binary tree to represent data in a hierarchical form, consider Figure 10-4. The binary trees in this figure represent algebraic expressions that involve the binary operators $+$, $-$, $*$, and $/$. To represent an expression such as $a - b$, you place the operator in the root node and the operands a and b into left and right children, respectively, of the root. (See Figure 10-4a.) Figure 10-4b represents the expression $a - b/c$; a subtree represents the subexpression b/c. A similar situation exists in Figure 10-4c, which represents $(a - b) * c$. The leaves of these trees contain the expression's operands, while other tree nodes contain the operators. Parentheses do not appear in these trees. The binary tree provides a hierarchy for the operations—that is, the tree specifies an unambiguous order for evaluating an expression.

The nodes of a tree typically contain values. A **binary search tree** is a binary tree that is in a sense sorted according to the values in its nodes. For each node n, a binary search tree satisfies the following three properties:

- n's value is greater than all values in its left subtree T_L.

- n's value is less than all values in its right subtree T_R.

- Both T_L and T_R are binary search trees.

Properties of a binary search tree

Figure 10-5 is an example of a binary search tree. As its name suggests, a binary search tree organizes data in a way that facilitates searching it for a particular data item. Later, this chapter discusses binary search trees in detail.

The height of trees. Trees come in many shapes. For example, although the binary trees in Figure 10-6 all contain the same nodes, their structures are quite different. Although each of these trees has seven nodes, some are "taller" than others. The **height of a tree** is the

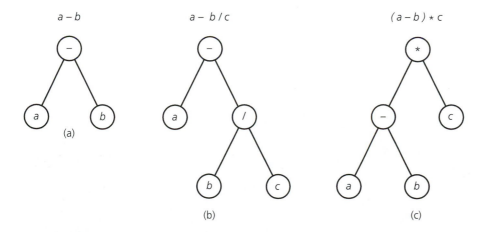

FIGURE 10-4 Binary trees that represent algebraic expressions

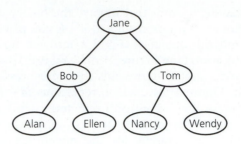

FIGURE 10-5   A binary search tree of names

number of nodes on the longest path from the root to a leaf. For exam‐
ple, the trees in Figure 10-6 have respective heights of 3, 5, and 7.
Many people's intuitive notion of height would lead them to say that
these trees have heights of 2, 4, and 6. Indeed, many authors define
height to agree with this intuition. However, the definition of height
used in this book leads to a cleaner statement of many algorithms and
properties of trees.

There are other equivalent ways to define the height of a tree *T*.
One way uses the following definition of the **level of a node** *n*:

Level of a node

- If *n* is the root of *T*, it is at level 1.

- If *n* is not the root of *T*, its level is 1 greater than the level of
  its parent.

For example, in Figure 10-6a, node *A* is at level 1, node *B* is at level 2,
and node *D* is at level 3.

The **height** of a tree *T* in terms of the levels of its nodes is defined
as follows:

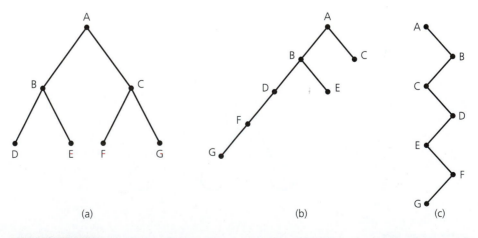

FIGURE 10-6   Binary trees with the same nodes but different heights

- If T is empty, its height is 0.

- If T is not empty, its height is equal to the maximum level of its nodes.

Apply this definition to the trees in Figure 10-6 and show that their heights are, respectively, 3, 5, and 7, as was stated earlier.

For binary trees, it is often convenient to use an equivalent recursive definition of height:

- If T is empty, its height is 0.

- If T is a nonempty binary tree, then because T is of the form

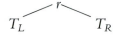

the height of T is 1 greater than the height of its root's taller subtree; that is,

$$height(T) = 1 + max\{height(T_L), height(T_R)\}$$

Later, when we discuss the efficiency of searching a binary search tree, it will be necessary to determine the maximum and minimum heights of a binary tree of n nodes.

Full, complete, and balanced binary trees. In a **full binary tree** of height h, all nodes that are at a level less than h have two children each. Figure 10-7 depicts a full binary tree of height 3. Each node in a full binary tree has left and right subtrees of the same height. Among binary trees of height h, a full binary tree has as many leaves as possible, and they all are at level h. Intuitively, a full binary tree has no missing nodes.

When proving properties about full binary trees—such as how many nodes they have—the following recursive definition of a full binary tree is convenient:

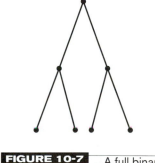

FIGURE 10-7 A full binary tree of height 3

- If T is empty, T is a full binary tree of height 0.

- If T is not empty and has height $h > 0$, T is a full binary tree if its root's subtrees are both full binary trees of height $h - 1$.

This definition closely reflects the recursive nature of a binary tree.

A **complete binary tree** of height h is a binary tree that is full down to level $h - 1$, with level h filled in from left to right, as Figure 10-8 illustrates. More formally, a binary tree T of height h is complete if

1. All nodes at level $h - 2$ and above have two children each, and

2. When a node at level $h - 1$ has children, all nodes to its left at the same level have two children each, and

3. When a node at level $h - 1$ has one child, it is a left child

Parts 2 and 3 of this definition formalize the requirement that level h be filled in from left to right. Note that a full binary tree is complete.

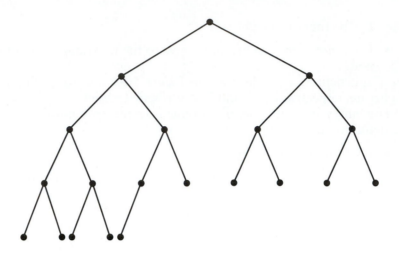

FIGURE 10-8   A complete binary tree

Finally, a binary tree is **height balanced**, or simply **balanced**, if the height of any node's right subtree differs from the height of the node's left subtree by no more than 1. The binary trees in Figures 10-8 and 10-6a are balanced, but the trees in Figures 10-6b and 10–6c are not balanced. A complete binary tree is balanced.

Complete binary trees are balanced

The following is a summary of the major tree terminology presented so far.

KEY CONCEPTS

Summary of Tree Terminology

General tree	A set of one or more nodes, partitioned into a root node and subsets that are general subtrees of the root.
Parent of node *n*	The node directly above node *n* in the tree.
Child of node *n*	A node directly below node *n* in the tree.
Root	The only node in the tree with no parent.
Leaf	A node with no children.
Siblings	Nodes with a common parent.
Ancestor of node *n*	A node on the path from the root to *n*.

continued on next page

continued from previous page

Descendant of node *n*	A node on a path from *n* to a leaf.
Subtree of node *n*	A tree that consists of a child (if any) of *n* and the child's descendants.
Height	The number of nodes on the longest path from the root to a leaf.
Binary tree	A set of nodes that is either empty or partitioned into a root node and one or two subsets that are binary subtrees of the root. Each node has at most two children, the left child and the right child.
Left (right) child of node *n*	A node directly below and to the left (right) of node *n* in a binary tree.
Left (right) subtree of node *n*	In a binary tree, the left (right) child (if any) of node *n* plus its descendants.
Binary search tree	A binary tree where the value in any node *n* is greater than the value in every node in *n*'s left subtree, but less than the value of every node in *n*'s right subtree.
Empty binary tree	A binary tree with no nodes.
Full binary tree	A binary tree of height *h* with no missing nodes. All leaves are at level *h* and all other nodes each have two children.
Complete binary tree	A binary tree of height *h* that is full to level *h* − 1 and has level *h* filled in from left to right.
Balanced binary tree	A binary tree in which the left and right subtrees of any node have heights that differ by at most 1.

10.2 The ADT Binary Tree

As an abstract data type, the binary tree has operations that add and remove nodes and subtrees. By using these basic operations, you can build any binary tree. Other operations set or retrieve the data in the root of the tree and determine whether the tree is empty.

Traversal operations that *visit* every node in a binary tree are typical. "Visiting" a node means "doing something with or to" the node. Chapter 4 introduced the concept of traversal for a linked list: Beginning with the list's first node, you visit each node sequentially until you reach the end of the linked list. Traversal of a binary tree, however, visits the tree's nodes in one of several different orders. The three standard orders are called preorder, inorder, and postorder, and they are described in the next section.

To summarize, the ADT binary tree has the following operations:

KEY CONCEPTS

ADT Binary Tree Operations

1. Create an empty binary tree.

2. Create a one-node binary tree, given an item.

3. Create a binary tree, given an item for its root and two binary trees for the root's subtrees.

4. Destroy a binary tree.

5. Determine whether a binary tree is empty.

6. Determine or change the data in the binary tree's root.

7. Attach a left or right child to the binary tree's root.

8. Attach a left or right subtree to the binary tree's root.

9. Detach the left or right subtree of the binary tree's root.

10. Return a copy of the left or right subtree of the binary tree's root.

11. Traverse the nodes in a binary tree in preorder, inorder, or postorder.

The following pseudocode specifies these operations in more detail, and a UML diagram for a class of binary trees appears in Figure 10-9.

Pseudocode for the ADT Binary Tree Operations

```
// TreeItemType is the type of the items stored in the
// binary tree

+createBinaryTree()
// Creates an empty binary tree.

+createBinaryTree(in rootItem:TreeItemType)
// Creates a one-node binary tree whose root contains
// rootItem.

+createBinaryTree(in rootItem:TreeItemType,
                  inout leftTree:BinaryTree,
                  inout rightTree:BinaryTree)
// Creates a binary tree whose root contains rootItem and
// has leftTree and rightTree, respectively, as its left
// and right subtrees. Makes leftTree and rightTree empty
// so they can't be used to gain access to the new tree.

+destroyBinaryTree()
// Destroys a binary tree.

+isEmpty():boolean {query}
// Determines whether a binary tree is empty.

+getRootData():TreeItemType throw TreeException
// Returns the data item in the root of a nonempty
// binary tree. Throws TreeException if the tree is empty.

+setRootData(in newItem:TreeItemType) throw TreeException
// Replaces the data item in the root of a binary tree
// with newItem, if the tree is not empty. However, if the
// tree is empty, creates a root node whose data item
// is newItem and inserts the new node into the tree.
// If a new node cannot be created, TreeException is
// thrown.

+attachLeft(in newItem:TreeItemType) throw TreeException
// Attaches a left child containing newItem to the root of
// a binary tree. Throws TreeException if a new child node
// cannot be allocated. Also throws TreeException if the
```

continued on next page

continued from previous page

```
// binary tree is empty (no root node to attach to) or a
// left subtree already exists (should explicitly detach it
// first).

+attachRight(in newItem:TreeItemType) throw TreeException
// Attaches a right child containing newItem to the root of
// a binary tree. Throws TreeException if a new child node
// cannot be allocated. Also throws TreeException if the
// binary tree is empty (no root node to attach to) or a
// right subtree already exists (should explicitly detach
// it first).

+attachLeftSubtree(inout leftTree:BinaryTree)
      throw TreeException
// Attaches leftTree as the left subtree of the
// root of a binary tree and makes leftTree empty so
// that it cannot be used to access this tree.
// Throws TreeException if the binary tree is empty
// (no root node to attach to) or a left subtree already
// exists (should explicitly detach it first).

+attachRightSubtree(inout rightTree:BinaryTree)
      throw TreeException
// Attaches rightTree as the right subtree of the
// root of a binary tree and makes rightTree empty so
// that it cannot be used to access this tree.
// Throws TreeException if the binary tree is empty (no
// root node to attach to) or a right subtree already
// exists (should explicitly detach it first).

+detachLeftSubtree(out leftTree:BinaryTree)
      throw TreeException
// Detaches the left subtree of a binary tree's root
// and retains it in getLeftTree. Throws TreeException if the
// binary tree is empty (no root node to detach from).

+detachRightSubtree(out rightTree:BinaryTree)
      throw TreeException
// Detaches the right subtree of a binary tree's root
// and retains it in getRightTree. Throws TreeException if the
// binary tree is empty (no root node to detach from).
```

continued on next page

continued from previous page

```
+leftSubtree():BinaryTree
// Returns a copy of the left subtree of a binary tree's
// root without detaching the subtree. Returns an empty
// tree if the binary tree is empty (no root node to copy
// from).

+rightSubtree():BinaryTree
// Returns a copy of the right subtree of a binary tree's
// root without detaching the subtree. Returns an empty
// tree if the binary tree is empty (no root node to copy
// from).

+preorderTraverse(in visit:FunctionType)
// Traverses a binary tree in preorder and calls the
// function visit() once for each node.

+inorderTraverse(in visit:FunctionType)
// Traverses a binary tree in inorder and calls the
// function visit() once for each node.

+postorderTraverse(in visit:FunctionType)
// Traverses a binary tree in postorder and calls the
// function visit() once for each node.
```

You can use these operations, for example, to build the binary tree in Figure 10-6b, where the node labels represent character data. The following pseudocode constructs the tree from the subtree *tree1* rooted at '*F*', the subtree *tree2* rooted at '*D*', the subtree *tree3* rooted at '*B*', and the subtree *tree4* rooted at '*C*'. Initially, these subtrees exist but are empty.

```
tree1.setRootData('F')
tree1.attachLeft('G')

tree2.setRootData('D')
tree2.attachLeftSubtree(tree1)

tree3.setRootData('B')
tree3.attachLeftSubtree(tree2)
tree3.attachRight('E')

tree4.setRootData('C')
// tree in Fig 10-6b
binTree.createBinaryTree('A', tree3, tree4)
```

Using ADT binary tree operations to build a binary tree

```
┌─────────────────────────────────┐
│           Binary tree           │
├─────────────────────────────────┤
│ root                            │
│ left subtree                    │
│ right subtree                   │
├─────────────────────────────────┤
│ createTree()                    │
│ destroyBinaryTree()             │
│ isEmpty()                       │
│ getRootData()                   │
│ setRootData()                   │
│ attachLeft()                    │
│ attachRight()                   │
│ attachLeftSubtree()             │
│ attachRightSubtree()            │
│ detachLeftSubtree()             │
│ detachRightSubtree()            │
│ getLeftSubtree()                │
│ getRightSubtree()               │
│ preorderTraverse()              │
│ inorderTraverse()               │
│ postorderTraverse()             │
└─────────────────────────────────┘
```

FIGURE 10-9   UML diagram for the class *BinaryTree*

Note that

binTree.getLeftSubtree()

is a copy of the subtree *tree3* (rooted at *'B'*), and that

binTree.detachLeftSubtree(leftTree)

detaches that same subtree from *binTree* and names it *leftTree*.
    The traversal operations are considered in detail next.

Traversals of a Binary Tree

A traversal algorithm for a binary tree visits each node in the tree. While visiting a node, you do something with or to the node such as display or modify the contents of the node. For the purpose of this discussion, assume that visiting a node simply means displaying the data portion of the node.

With the recursive definition of a binary tree in mind, you can construct a recursive traversal algorithm as follows. According to the definition, the binary tree T is either empty or is of the form

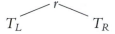

If T is empty, the traversal algorithm takes no action—an empty tree is the base case. If T is not empty, the traversal algorithm must perform three tasks: It must display the data in the root r, and it must traverse the two subtrees T_L and T_R, each of which is a binary tree smaller than T.

Thus, the general form of the recursive traversal algorithm is

```
traverse(in binTree:BinaryTree)
// Traverses the binary tree binTree.

    if (binTree is not empty)
    {   traverse(Left subtree of binTree's root)
        traverse(Right subtree of binTree's root)
    }
```

The general form of a recursive traversal algorithm

This algorithm is not quite complete, however. What is missing is the instruction to display the data in the root. When traversing any binary tree, the algorithm has three choices of when to visit the root r. It can visit r before it traverses both of r's subtrees, it can visit r after it has traversed r's left subtree T_L but before it traverses r's right subtree T_R, or it can visit r after it has traversed both of r's subtrees. These are called **preorder**, **inorder**, and **postorder traversals**, respectively. Figure 10-10 shows the results of these traversals for a given binary tree.

The preorder traversal algorithm is as follows:

```
preorder(in binTree:BinaryTree)
// Traverses the binary tree binTree in preorder.
// Assumes that "visit a node" means to display
// the node's data item.

    if (binTree is not empty)
    {   Display the data in the root of binTree
        preorder(Left subtree of binTree's root)
        preorder(Right subtree of binTree's root)
    }
```

Preorder traversal

The preorder traversal of the tree in Figure 10-10a visits the nodes in this order: 60, 20, 10, 40, 30, 50, 70. If you apply preorder traversal to a binary tree that represents an algebraic expression, such as any tree in

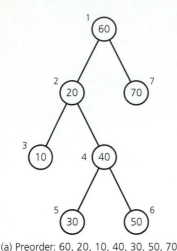
(a) Preorder: 60, 20, 10, 40, 30, 50, 70

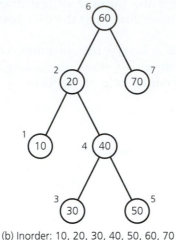
(b) Inorder: 10, 20, 30, 40, 50, 60, 70

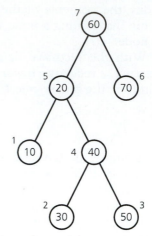
(c) Postorder: 10, 30, 50, 40, 20, 70, 60

(Numbers beside nodes indicate traversal order.)

FIGURE 10-10   Traversals of a binary tree: (a) preorder; (b) inorder; (c) postorder

Figure 10-4, and display the nodes as you visit them, you will obtain the prefix form of the expression.[1]

The inorder traversal algorithm is as follows:

Inorder traversal

```
inorder(in binTree:BinaryTree)
// Traverses the binary tree binTree in inorder.
// Assumes that "visit a node" means to display
// the node's data item.

    if (binTree is not empty)
    {  inorder(Left subtree of binTree's root)
       Display the data in the root of binTree
       inorder(Right subtree of binTree's root)
    }
```

The result of the inorder traversal of the tree in Figure 10-10b is 10, 20, 30, 40, 50, 60, 70. If you apply inorder traversal to a binary search tree, you will visit the nodes in order according to their data values. Such is the case for the tree in Figure 10-10b.

Finally, the postorder traversal algorithm is as follows:

Postorder traversal

```
postorder(in binTree:BinaryTree)
// Traverses the binary tree binTree in postorder.
```

---

[1] The prefix expressions are (a) $-ab$; (b) $-a/bc$; (c) $*-abc$.

```
// Assumes that "visit a node" means to display
// the node's data item.

   if (binTree is not empty)
   {  postorder(Left subtree of binTree's root)
      postorder(Right subtree of binTree's root)
      Display the data in the root of binTree
   }
```

The result of the postorder traversal of the tree in Figure 10-10c is 10, 30, 50, 40, 20, 70, 60. If you apply postorder traversal to a binary tree that represents an algebraic expression, such as any tree in Figure 10-4, and display the nodes as you visit them, you will obtain the postfix form of the expression.[2]

Each of these traversals visits every node in a binary tree exactly once. Thus, n visits occur for a tree of n nodes. Each visit performs the same operations on each node, independently of n, so it must be O(1). Thus, each traversal is O(n).

Traversal is O(n)

Although traversal means to visit each item in the ADT, traversal can be more difficult than you might imagine if you do more than simply display each item when you visit it. For example, you might copy the item into another data structure or even alter it. The details of traversal are thus quite application dependent, which makes traversal a difficult operation to define within the framework of an ADT. You could have a different traversal operation for each desired task, such as *preorderTraverse-AndDisplay*, *preorderTraverseAndCopy*, and so on. Or a traversal operation could call a function, which the client defines and passes as an argument, for each item in the table. For example, the ADT operation

bintree.preorderTraverse(visit)

specifies the function *visit* as an argument. If you define a function *display* to display the data item in a node, you could invoke the traversal operation for the binary tree *bintree* by writing

bintree.preorderTraverse(display)

A client-defined function, which the traversal functions call, defines the meaning of "visit"

The traversal operation would call *display* each time it visited a node in the tree.

Despite the fact that the ADT operation *preorderTraverse* calls a client-supplied function, the wall between the program and the implementation of the ADT has not been violated. Because *display* is on the client's side of the wall, the function can access the data only by using the ADT operations.

---

[2] The postfix expressions are (a) $ab-$; (b) $abc/-$; (c) $ab-c\star$.

The implementation details of the traversal operations will be discussed shortly.

Possible Representations of a Binary Tree

You can implement a binary tree by using the constructs of C++ in one of three general ways. Two of these approaches use arrays, but the typical implementation uses pointers. In each case, the described data structures would be private data members of a class of binary trees.

To illustrate the three approaches, we will implement a binary tree of names. Each node in this tree contains a name, and, because the tree is a binary tree, each node has at most two descendant nodes.

An array-based representation. If you use a C++ class to define a node in the tree, you can represent the entire binary tree by using an array of tree nodes. Each tree node contains a data portion—a name in this case—and two indexes, one for each of the node's children, as the following C++ statements indicate:

```cpp
const int MAX_NODES = 100; // maximum number of nodes
typedef string TreeItemType;

class TreeNode          // node in the tree
{
private:
   TreeNode();
   TreeNode(const TreeItemType& nodeItem,
            int left, int right);
   TreeItemType item;       // data portion
   int          leftChild;  // index to left child
   int          rightChild; // index to right child

   // friend class - can access private parts
   friend class BinaryTree;
};  // end class TreeNode

TreeNode[MAX_NODES] tree;  // array of tree nodes
int                 root;  // index of root
int                 free;  // index of free list
```

The class *TreeNode* has all of its members declared private, but specifies that the binary tree class *BinaryTree* is a friend class so that members of *BinaryTree* have direct access to all of the members of *TreeNode*. The *TreeNode* class is used only by the implementation of the *BinaryTree* class; it is not appropriate for other classes to have access to its members.

The variable *root* is an index to the tree's root within the array *tree*. If the tree is empty, *root* is −1. Both *leftChild* and *rightChild* within a node are indexes to the children of that node. If a node has no left child, `leftChild` is −1; if a node has no right child, `rightChild` is −1.

As the tree changes due to insertions and deletions, its nodes may not be in contiguous elements of the array. Therefore, this implementation requires you to establish a list of available nodes, which is called a **free list**. To insert a new node into the tree, you first obtain an available node from the free list. If you delete a node from the tree, you place it into the free list so that you can reuse the node at a later time. The variable *free* is the index to the first node in the free list and, arbitrarily, the *rightChild* member of each node in the free list is the index of the next node in the free list.[3] Figure 10-11 contains a binary tree and the data members for its array-based implementation.

A free list keeps track of available nodes

For this implementation, if *root* is the index of the root *r* of a binary tree, then *tree[root].leftChild* is the index of the root of

(a)

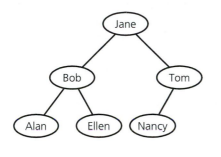

(b)   tree

	item	leftChild	rightChild	root
0	Jane	1	2	0
1	Bob	3	4	free
2	Tom	5	−1	6
3	Alan	−1	−1	
4	Ellen	−1	−1	
5	Nancy	−1	−1	
6	?	−1	7	
7	?	−1	8	
8	?	−1	9	Free list
.	.	.	.	
.	.	.	.	
.	.	.	.	

FIGURE 10-11   (a) A binary tree of names; (b) its array-based implementation

---

[3] This free list is actually an array-based linked list, as Programming Problem 11 of Chapter 4 describes.

the left subtree of *r*, and `tree[root].rightChild` is the index of the root of the right subtree of *r*.

An array-based representation of a complete tree.   The previous implementation works for any binary tree, even though the tree in Figure 10-11 is complete. If you know that your binary tree is complete, you can use a simpler array-based implementation that saves memory. As you saw earlier in this chapter, a complete tree of height *h* is full to level $h - 1$ and has level *h* filled from left to right.

Figure 10-12 shows the complete binary tree of Figure 10-11a with its nodes numbered according to a standard level-by-level scheme. The root is numbered 0, and the children of the root (the next level of the tree) are numbered, left to right, 1 and 2. The nodes at the next level are numbered, left to right, 3, 4, and 5. You place these nodes into the array `tree` in numeric order. That is, `tree[i]` contains the node numbered *i*, as Figure 10-13 illustrates. Now, given any node `tree[i]`, you can easily locate both of its children and its parent: Its left child (if it exists) is `tree[2*i+1]`, its right child (if it exists) is `tree[2*i+2]`, and its parent (if `tree[i]` is not the root) is `tree[(i-1)/2]`.

This array-based representation requires a complete binary tree. If nodes were missing from the middle of the tree, the numbering scheme would be thrown off, and the parent-child relationship among nodes would be ambiguous. This requirement implies that any changes to the tree must maintain its completeness.

As you will see in the next chapter, an array-based representation of a binary tree is useful in the implementation of the ADT priority queue.

A pointer-based representation.   You can use C++ pointers to link the nodes in the tree. Thus, you can represent a tree by using the following C++ statements:

> If the binary tree is complete and remains complete, you can use a memory-efficient array-based implementation

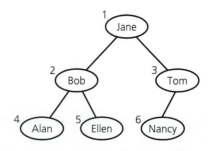

FIGURE 10-12   Level-by-level numbering of a complete binary tree

```
typedef string TreeItemType;

class TreeNode                    // node in the tree
{
private:
   TreeNode() {};
   TreeNode(const TreeItemType& nodeItem,
            TreeNode *left = NULL,
            TreeNode *right = NULL):
      item(nodeItem),leftChildPtr(left),
      rightChildPtr(right) {}
   TreeItemType item;         // data portion
   TreeNode *leftChildPtr;    // pointer to left child
   TreeNode *rightChildPtr;   // pointer to right child
   friend class BinaryTree;
}; // end TreeNode class
```

0	Jane
1	Bob
2	Tom
3	Alan
4	Ellen
5	Nancy
6	
7	

FIGURE 10-13 An array-based implementation of the complete binary tree in Figure 10-12

The external pointer *root* points to the tree's root. If the tree is empty, *root* is *NULL*. Figure 10-14 illustrates this implementation.

The root of a nonempty binary tree has a left subtree and a right subtree, each of which is a binary tree. In a pointer-based implementation, *root* points to the root *r* of a binary tree, *root->leftChildPtr* points to the root of the left subtree of *r*, and *root->rightChildPtr* points to the root of the right subtree of *r*.

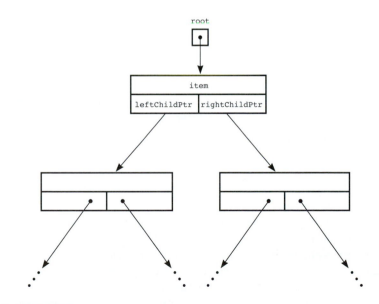

FIGURE 10-14 A pointer-based implementation of a binary tree

The following section provides the details for a pointer-based implementation of the ADT binary tree.

A Pointer-Based Implementation of the ADT Binary Tree

The following header and implementation files contain a pointer-based implementation of the ADT binary tree, as just described. A discussion of several implementation details follows these files. The specification of pre- and postconditions is left as an exercise.

```
// ********************************************************
// Header file TreeException.h for the ADT binary tree.
// ********************************************************
#include <stdexcept>
#include <string>
using namespace std;

class TreeException: public logic_error
{
public:
   TreeException(const string & message = "")
                           : logic_error(message.c_str())
   { }
};  // end TreeException
```

Header file

```
// ********************************************************
// Header file BinaryTree.h for the ADT binary tree.
// ********************************************************
#include "TreeException.h"
#include "TreeNode.h" // contains definitions for TreeNode
                      // and TreeItemType

typedef void (*FunctionType)(TreeItemType& anItem);

class BinaryTree
{
public:
// constructors and destructor:
   BinaryTree();
   BinaryTree(const TreeItemType& rootItem);
   BinaryTree(const TreeItemType& rootItem,
               BinaryTree& leftTree,
               BinaryTree& rightTree);
   BinaryTree(const BinaryTree& tree);
   virtual ~BinaryTree();[4]

// binary tree operations:
```

More constructors than usual

```
    virtual bool isEmpty() const;

    virtual TreeItemType getRootData() const
        throw(TreeException);
    virtual void setRootData(const TreeItemType& newItem)
        throw(TreeException);

    virtual void attachLeft(const TreeItemType& newItem)
        throw(TreeException);
    virtual void attachRight(const TreeItemType& newItem)
        throw(TreeException);

    virtual void attachLeftSubtree(BinaryTree& leftTree)
        throw(TreeException);
    virtual void attachRightSubtree(BinaryTree& rightTree)
        throw(TreeException);

    virtual void detachLeftSubtree(BinaryTree& leftTree)
        throw(TreeException);
    virtual void detachRightSubtree(BinaryTree& rightTree)
        throw(TreeException);

    virtual BinaryTree getLeftSubtree() const;
    virtual BinaryTree getRightSubtree() const;

    virtual void preorderTraverse(FunctionType visit);
    virtual void inorderTraverse(FunctionType visit);
    virtual void postorderTraverse(FunctionType visit);

// overloaded operator:
    virtual BinaryTree& operator=(const BinaryTree& rhs);

protected:
    BinaryTree(TreeNode *nodePtr);  // constructor

    void copyTree(TreeNode *treePtr,
                  TreeNode *& newTreePtr) const;
    // Copies the tree rooted at treePtr into a tree rooted
    // at newTreePtr. Throws TreeException if a copy of the
    // tree cannot be allocated.

    void destroyTree(TreeNode *& treePtr);
    // Deallocates memory for a tree.
```

An overloaded assignment operator

A protected constructor

---

[4] If you studied Chapter 8, you learned about inheritance, virtual member functions, and protected members. However, if you did not study Chapter 8, simply ignore *virtual* in this and subsequent implementations. Also, read *protected* as *private*. Doing so will not affect your understanding of the implementation.

```
                    // The next two functions retrieve and set the value
                    // of the private data member root.

                    TreeNode *rootPtr() const;
                    void setRootPtr(TreeNode *newRoot);

                    // The next two functions retrieve and set the values
                    // of the left and right child pointers of a tree node.
                    void getChildPtrs(TreeNode *nodePtr,
                                      TreeNode *& leftChildPtr,
                                      TreeNode *& rightChildPtr) const;
                    void setChildPtrs(TreeNode *nodePtr,
                                      TreeNode *leftChildPtr,
                                      TreeNode *rightChildPtr);
```

Protected member functions
that enable recursive
traversals

```
                    void preorder(TreeNode *treePtr, FunctionType visit);
                    void inorder(TreeNode *treePtr, FunctionType visit);
                    void postorder(TreeNode *treePtr, FunctionType visit);

                private:
                    TreeNode *root;  // pointer to root of tree
                };  // end class
                // End of header file.
```

Implementation file

```
                // ********************************************************
                // Implementation file BinaryTree.cpp for the ADT binary
                // tree.
                // ********************************************************

                #include "BinaryTree.h"      // header file
                #include <cstddef>  // definition of NULL
                #include <cassert>  // for assert()

                BinaryTree::BinaryTree() : root(NULL)
                {
                }  // end default constructor

                BinaryTree::BinaryTree(const TreeItemType& rootItem)
                {
                   root = new TreeNode(rootItem, NULL, NULL);
                   assert(root != NULL);
                }  // end constructor

                BinaryTree::BinaryTree(const TreeItemType& rootItem,
                                       BinaryTree& leftTree,
                                       BinaryTree& rightTree)
                {
```

```
   root = new TreeNode(rootItem, NULL, NULL);
   assert(root != NULL);

   attachLeftSubtree(leftTree);
   attachRightSubtree(rightTree);
}  // end constructor

BinaryTree::BinaryTree(const BinaryTree& tree)
{
   copyTree(tree.root, root);
}  // end copy constructor

BinaryTree::BinaryTree(TreeNode *nodePtr):
   root(nodePtr)
{
}  // end protected constructor

BinaryTree::~BinaryTree()
{
   destroyTree(root);
}  // end destructor

bool BinaryTree::isEmpty() const
{
   return (root == NULL);
}  // end isEmpty

TreeItemType BinaryTree::getRootData() const
               throw(TreeException)
{
   if (isEmpty())
      throw TreeException("TreeException: Empty tree");
   return root->item;
}  // end getRootData

void BinaryTree::setRootData(const TreeItemType& newItem)
               throw(TreeException)
{
   if (!isEmpty())
      root->item = newItem;
   else
   { root = new TreeNode(newItem, NULL, NULL);
      if (root == NULL)
         throw TreeException(
                  "TreeException: Cannot allocate memory");
   }  // end if
```

Note that the copy constructor must copy every node in the tree

```cpp
   }  // end setRootData

void BinaryTree::attachLeft(const TreeItemType& newItem)
              throw(TreeException)
{
   if (isEmpty())
      throw TreeException("TreeException: Empty tree");
   else if (root->leftChildPtr != NULL)
      throw TreeException(
         "TreeException: Cannot overwrite left subtree");
   else  // Assertion: nonempty tree; no left child
   {  root->leftChildPtr = new TreeNode(newItem, NULL, NULL);

      if (root->leftChildPtr == NULL)
         throw TreeException(
                  "TreeException: Cannot allocate memory");
   }  // end if
}  // end attachLeft

void BinaryTree::attachRight(const TreeItemType& newItem)
              throw(TreeException)
{
   if (isEmpty())
      throw TreeException("TreeException: Empty tree");
   else if (root->rightChildPtr != NULL)
      throw TreeException(
         "TreeException: Cannot overwrite right subtree");
   else  // Assertion: nonempty tree; no right child
   {  root->rightChildPtr = new TreeNode(newItem, NULL, NULL);

      if (root->rightChildPtr == NULL)
         throw TreeException(
                  "TreeException: Cannot allocate memory");
   }  // end if
}  // end attachRight

void BinaryTree::attachLeftSubtree(BinaryTree& leftTree)
              throw(TreeException)
{
   if (isEmpty())
      throw TreeException("TreeException: Empty tree");
   else if (root->leftChildPtr != NULL)
      throw TreeException(
         "TreeException: Cannot overwrite left subtree");
   else  // Assertion: nonempty tree; no left child
   {  root->leftChildPtr = leftTree.root;
      leftTree.root = NULL;
   }
}  // end attachLeftSubtree
```

```
void BinaryTree::attachRightSubtree(BinaryTree& rightTree)
                throw(TreeException)
{
   if (isEmpty())
      throw TreeException("TreeException: Empty tree");
   else if (root->rightChildPtr != NULL)
      throw TreeException(
         "TreeException: Cannot overwrite right subtree");
   else  // Assertion: nonempty tree; no right child
   {  root->rightChildPtr = rightTree.root;
      rightTree.root = NULL;
   }  // end if
}  // end attachRightSubtree

void BinaryTree::detachLeftSubtree(BinaryTree& leftTree)
                throw(TreeException)
{
   if (isEmpty())
      throw TreeException("TreeException: Empty tree");
   else
   {  leftTree = BinaryTree(root->leftChildPtr);
      root->leftChildPtr = NULL;
   }  // end if
}  // end detachLeftSubtree

void BinaryTree::detachRightSubtree(BinaryTree& rightTree)
                throw(TreeException)
{
   if (isEmpty())
      throw TreeException("TreeException: Empty tree");
   else
   {  rightTree = BinaryTree(root->rightChildPtr);
      root->rightChildPtr = NULL;
   }  // end if
}  // end detachRightSubtree

BinaryTree BinaryTree::getLeftSubtree() const
{
   TreeNode *subTreePtr;

   if (isEmpty())
      return BinaryTree();
   else
   {  copyTree(root->leftChildPtr, subTreePtr);
      return BinaryTree(subTreePtr);        ┤ Protected constructor invoked
   }  // end if
}  // end getLeftSubtree
```

```
BinaryTree BinaryTree::getRightSubtree() const
{
   TreeNode *subTreePtr;

   if (isEmpty())
      return BinaryTree();
   else
   {  copyTree(root->rightChildPtr, subTreePtr);
      return BinaryTree(subTreePtr);
   }  // end if
}  // end getRightSubtree

void BinaryTree::preorderTraverse(FunctionType visit)
{
   preorder(root, visit);
}  // end preorderTraverse

void BinaryTree::inorderTraverse(FunctionType visit)
{
   inorder(root, visit);
}  // end inorderTraverse

void BinaryTree::postorderTraverse(FunctionType visit)
{
   postorder(root, visit);
}  // end postorderTraverse

BinaryTree& BinaryTree::operator=(const BinaryTree& rhs)
{
   if (this != &rhs)
   {  destroyTree(root);  // deallocate left-hand side
      copyTree(rhs.root, root);  // copy right-hand side
   }  // end if
   return *this;
}  // end operator=

void BinaryTree::copyTree(TreeNode *treePtr,
                          TreeNode *& newTreePtr) const
{
   // preorder traversal
   if (treePtr != NULL)
   {  // copy node
      newTreePtr = new TreeNode(treePtr->item, NULL, NULL);
      if (newTreePtr == NULL)
         throw TreeException(
            "TreeException: Cannot allocate memory");

      copyTree(treePtr->leftChildPtr, newTreePtr->leftChildPtr);
      copyTree(treePtr->rightChildPtr, newTreePtr->rightChildPtr);
```

```
   }
   else
      newTreePtr = NULL;   // copy empty tree
}  // end copyTree

void BinaryTree::destroyTree(TreeNode *& treePtr)
{
   // postorder traversal
   if (treePtr != NULL)
   {  destroyTree(treePtr->leftChildPtr);
      destroyTree(treePtr->rightChildPtr);
      delete treePtr;
      treePtr = NULL;
   }  // end if
}  // end destroyTree

TreeNode *BinaryTree::rootPtr() const
{
   return root;
}  // end rootPtr

void BinaryTree::setRootPtr(TreeNode *newRoot)
{
   root = newRoot;
}  // end setRoot

void BinaryTree::getChildPtrs(TreeNode *nodePtr,
                              TreeNode *& leftPtr,
                              TreeNode *& rightPtr) const
{
   leftPtr = nodePtr->leftChildPtr;
   rightPtr = nodePtr->rightChildPtr;
}  // end getChildPtrs

void BinaryTree::setChildPtrs(TreeNode *nodePtr,
                              TreeNode *leftPtr,
                              TreeNode *rightPtr)
{
   nodePtr->leftChildPtr = leftPtr;
   nodePtr->rightChildPtr = rightPtr;
}  // end setChildPtrs

void BinaryTree::preorder(TreeNode *treePtr,
                          FunctionType visit)
{
   if (treePtr != NULL)
   {  visit(treePtr->item);
      preorder(treePtr->leftChildPtr, visit);
      preorder(treePtr->rightChildPtr, visit);
```

```
      } // end if
   } // end preorder

   void BinaryTree::inorder(TreeNode *treePtr,
                                   FunctionType visit)
   {
      if (treePtr != NULL)
      {  inorder(treePtr->leftChildPtr, visit);
         visit(treePtr->item);
         inorder(treePtr->rightChildPtr, visit);
      } // end if
   } // end inorder

   void BinaryTree::postorder(TreeNode *treePtr,
                                   FunctionType visit)
   {
      if (treePtr != NULL)
      {  postorder(treePtr->leftChildPtr, visit);
         postorder(treePtr->rightChildPtr, visit);
         visit(treePtr->item);
      } // end if
   } // end postorder
// End of implementation file.
```

The class *BinaryTree* has more constructors than previous classes you have seen. They allow you to define binary trees in a variety of circumstances. You can construct a binary tree

- That is empty
- From data for its root, which is its only node
- From data for its root and the root's two subtrees

For example, the following statements invoke these three constructors:

Sample uses of public constructors

```
BinaryTree tree1;
BinaryTree tree2(root2);
BinaryTree tree3(root3);
BinaryTree tree4(root4, tree2, tree3);
```

Here *tree1* is an empty binary tree; *tree2* and *tree3* have only root nodes, whose data is *root2* and *root3*, respectively; and *tree4* is a binary tree whose root contains *root4* and has subtrees *tree2* and *tree3*. Note that *tree2* and *tree3* are instances of *BinaryTree*, not pointers to trees.

The class also contains a protected constructor, which creates a tree from a pointer to a root node. For example,

Some member functions should not be public

```
BinaryTree tree5(nodePtr);
```

constructs a tree *tree5* whose root is the node to which *nodePtr* points. Although the member functions *getLeftSubtree* and *getRightSubtree* use this constructor, it should not be available to clients of the class, because they do not have access to node pointers. Thus, this constructor is not public. We also have not made this constructor private, so that a derived class can use it. These comments also apply to the other protected member functions in *BinaryTree*.

Items in a binary tree are often instances of another class. Several member functions require these items as input arguments. To avoid expensive copying of these objects, we pass them as constant reference arguments instead of value arguments.

You must implement the recursive traversal operations carefully so that you do not violate the wall of the ADT. For example, the function *inorder*, whose declaration is

```
void inorder(TreeNode *treePtr, FunctionType visit);
```

has as an argument the pointer *treePtr*, which eventually points to every node in the tree. Because this argument clearly depends on the tree's pointer-based implementation, *inorder* is not suitable as a public member. In fact, *inorder* is a protected member, which the public member function *inorderTraverse* calls.

Both *inorder* and *inorderTraverse* have *visit* as a formal argument. The function *visit* has the type *FunctionType*, which the header file defines as

Implement traversals so that *visit* *remains on the client's side of the wall*

```
typedef void (*FunctionType)(TreeItemType& anItem);
```

Note that the function *visit* specifies the tree item as a reference parameter. This allows you (the client) not only to view the item but to modify it as well.

To invoke *inorderTraverse*, the client first defines a function that will "visit" a node in the tree. According to the definition of *FunctionType*, this function must have an argument of type *TreeItemType*. The client then passes this function to *inorderTraverse* as the argument that corresponds to *visit*.

For example, if you (as the client) want to display a node's data item as the traversal visits it, you could write a function whose declaration is

```
void display(TreeItemType& anItem);
```

The following statement then performs an inorder traversal of the tree *tree4*:

```
tree4.inorderTraverse(display);
```

Finally, this class contains virtual member functions so that a derived class can override them and thereby change their effect, as Chapter 8 described.

To demonstrate how to use *BinaryTree*, we build and then traverse the binary tree in Figure 10-10:

A sample program

```cpp
#include "BinaryTree.h"  // binary tree operations
#include <iostream>
using namespace std;

void display(TreeItemType& anItem);

int main()
{
   BinaryTree tree1, tree2, left; // empty trees
   BinaryTree tree3(70);     // tree with only a root 70

// build the tree in Figure 10-10
   tree1.setRootData(40);
   tree1.attachLeft(30);
   tree1.attachRight(50);

   tree2.setRootData(20);
   tree2.attachLeft(10);
   tree2.attachRightSubtree(tree1);

   // tree in Fig 10-10
   BinaryTree binTree(60, tree2, tree3);

   binTree.inorderTraverse(display);
   binTree.getLeftSubtree().inorderTraverse(display);
   binTree.detachLeftSubtree(left);
   left.inorderTraverse(display);
   binTree.inorderTraverse(display);
   return 0;
}  // end main
```

The tree *binTree* is shown in Figure 10-10. Its inorder traversal is 10, 20, 30, 40, 50, 60, 70. The inorder traversal of the left subtree of *binTree*'s root (the subtree rooted at 20) is 10, 20, 30, 40, 50. The inorder traversal of the subtree *left* produces the same result. Since *left* is actually detached from *binTree*, the final traversal of *binTree* is 60, 70.

The copy constructor and the destructor implicitly use traversal. The protected member function *copyTree*, which the copy constructor calls, uses a recursive preorder traversal to copy each node in the tree. By copying—that is, visiting—each node as soon as the traversal reaches it, *copyTree* can make an exact copy of the original tree. Similarly, the protected member function *destroyTree*, which the destructor calls, uses a recursive postorder traversal to delete each node in the tree. A postorder traversal is appropriate here because you can delete a node only after you have first traversed and deleted both of its subtrees.

Nonrecursive traversal (*optional*). Before leaving the topic of traversals, let's develop a nonrecursive traversal algorithm to illustrate further the relationship between stacks and recursion that was discussed in Chapter 6. In particular, we will develop a nonrecursive inorder traversal for the pointer-based implementation of a binary tree.

The conceptually difficult part of a nonrecursive traversal is determining where to go next after a particular node has been visited. To gain some insight into this problem, consider how the recursive *inorder* function works:

```
void BinaryTree::inorder(TreeNode *treePtr,
                         FunctionType visit)
{  if (treePtr != NULL)
   {  inorder(treePtr->leftChildPtr, visit); // Point 1
      visit(treePtr->item);
      inorder(treePtr->rightChildPtr, visit); // Point 2
   } // end if
} // end inorder
```

Recursive calls from points 1 and 2

The function has its recursive calls marked as points 1 and 2.

During the course of the function's execution, the value of the pointer *treePtr* actually marks the current position in the tree. Each time *inorder* makes a recursive call, the traversal moves to another node. In terms of the stack that is implicit to recursive functions, a call to *inorder* pushes the new value of *treePtr*—that is, a pointer to the new current node—onto the stack. At any given time, the stack contains pointers to the nodes along the path from the tree's root to the current node *n*, with the pointer to *n* at the top of the stack and the pointer to the root at the bottom. Note that *n* is possibly "empty"—that is, it may be indicated by a *NULL* value for *treePtr* at the top of the stack.

Figure 10-15 partially traces the execution of *inorder* and shows the contents of the implicit stack. The first four steps of the trace show the stack as *treePtr* points first to 60, then to 20, then to 10, and then becomes *NULL*. The recursive calls for these four steps are from point 1 in *inorder*.

Study recursive inorder's implicit stack to gain insight into a nonrecursive traversal algorithm

Now consider what happens when *inorder* returns from a recursive call. The traversal retraces its steps by backing up the tree from a node *n* to its parent *p*, from which the recursive call to *n* was made. Thus, the pointer to *n* is popped from the stack and the pointer to *p* comes to the top of the stack, as occurs in Step 5 of the trace in Figure 10-15. (In this case, *n* happens to be empty, so *NULL* is popped from the stack.)

What happens next depends on which subtree of *p* has just been traversed. If you have just finished traversing *p*'s left subtree (that is, if *n*

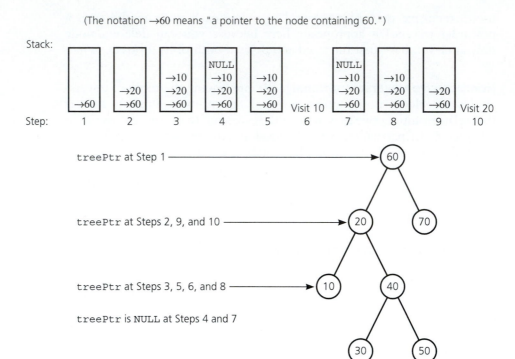

FIGURE 10-15 Contents of the implicit stack as *treePtr* progresses through a given tree during a recursive inorder traversal

is the left child of *p* and thus the return is made to point 1 in *inorder*), control is returned to the statement that displays the data in node *p*. Such is the case for Steps 6 and 10 of the trace in Figure 10-15. Figure 10-16a illustrates Steps 9 and 10 in more detail.

After the data in *p* has been displayed, a recursive call is made from point 2 and the right subtree of *p* is traversed. However, if, as Figure 10-16b illustrates, you have just traversed *p*'s right subtree (that is, if *n* is the right child of *p* and thus the return is made to point 2), control is returned to the end of the function. As a consequence another return is made, the pointer to *p* is popped off the stack, and you go back up the tree to *p*'s parent, from which the recursive call to *p* was made. In this latter case, the data in *p* is not displayed—it was displayed before the recursive call to *n* was made from point 2.

Thus, two facts emerge from the recursive version of *inorder* when a return is made from a recursive call:

Actions at a return from a recursive call to *inorder*

- The implicit recursive stack of pointers is used to find the node *p* to which the traversal must go back.

- Once the traversal backs up to node *p*, it either visits *p* (for example, displays its data) or backs farther up the tree. It visits *p* if *p*'s left subtree has just been traversed; it backs up if its right

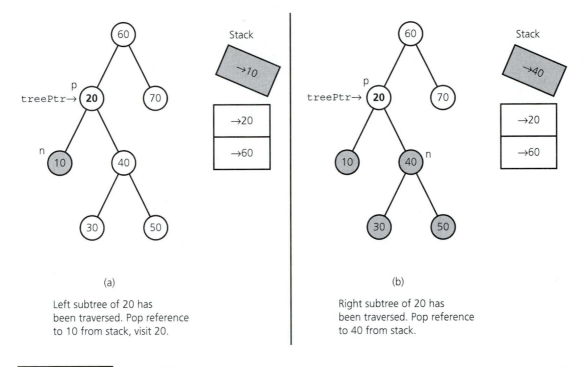

(a)

Left subtree of 20 has
been traversed. Pop reference
to 10 from stack, visit 20.

(b)

Right subtree of 20 has
been traversed. Pop reference
to 40 from stack.

FIGURE 10-16   Traversing (a) the left and (b) the right subtrees of 20

subtree has just been traversed. The appropriate action is taken simply as a consequence of the point—1 or 2—to which control is returned.

You could directly mimic this action by using an iterative function and an explicit stack, as long as some bookkeeping device kept track of which subtree of a node had just been traversed. However, you can use the following observation both to eliminate the need for the book-keeping device and to speed up the traversal somewhat. Consider the tree in Figure 10-17. After you have finished traversing the subtree rooted at node *R*, there is no need to return to nodes *C* and *B*, because the right subtrees of these nodes have already been traversed. You can instead return directly to node *A*, which is the nearest ancestor of *R* whose right subtree has not yet been traversed.

This strategy of not returning to a node after its right subtree has been traversed is simple to implement: You place a pointer to a node in the stack only before the node's left subtree is traversed, but not before its right subtree is traversed. Thus, in Figure 10-17, when you are at node *R*, the stack contains *A* and *R*, with *R* on top. Nodes *B* and *C* are not in the stack, because you have visited them already and are currently traversing their right subtrees. On the other hand, *A* is in the stack because you are currently traversing its left subtree. When you return from node *R*, nodes *B* and *C* are thus bypassed because you have

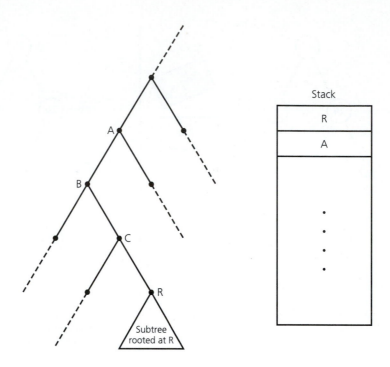

FIGURE 10-17   Avoiding returns to nodes *B* and *C*

finished with their right subtrees and do not need to return to these nodes. Thus, you pop *R*'s pointer from the stack and go directly to node *A,* whose left subtree has just been traversed. You then visit *A*, pop its pointer from the stack, and traverse *A*'s right subtree.

This nonrecursive traversal strategy is captured by the following pseudocode, assuming a pointer-based implementation. Exercise 17 at the end of this chapter asks you to trace this algorithm for the tree in Figure 10-15.

Nonrecursive inorder traversal

```
traverse(in visit:FunctionType)
// Nonrecursively traverses a binary tree inorder.


    // initialize
    Create an empty stack s
    cur = rootPtr()          // start at root
    done = false


    while (!done)
    {  if (cur != NULL)
        {  // place pointer to node on stack before
```

```
        // traversing node's left subtree
        s.push(cur)


        // traverse the left subtree
        cur = cur->leftChildPtr
    }


    else  // backtrack from the empty subtree and visit
          // the node at the top of the stack; however,
          // if the stack is empty, you are done
    { if (!s.isEmpty())
      { s.getTop(cur)
        visit(cur->item)
        s.pop()


        // traverse the right subtree
        // of the node just visited
        cur = cur->rightChildPtr
      }


      else
        done = true
    }  // end else backtrack
}  // end while
```

Eliminating recursion can be more complicated than the example given here. However, the general case is beyond the scope of this book.

10.3 The ADT Binary Search Tree

Searching for a particular item is one operation for which the ADT binary tree is ill suited. The binary search tree is a binary tree that corrects this deficiency by organizing its data by value. Recall that each node n in a binary search tree satisfies the following three properties:

- n's value is greater than all values in its left subtree T_L.

- n's value is less than all values in its right subtree T_R.

- Both T_L and T_R are binary search trees.

This organization of data enables you to search a binary search tree for a particular data item, given its value instead of its position. As you will see, certain conditions make this search efficient.

A binary search tree is often more useful if the items in the tree are instances of a class. For example, each item in a binary search tree might contain a person's name, ID number, address, telephone number, and so on. In general, such an item is called a **record** and will be an instance of a C++ class. To determine whether a particular person is in the tree, you could provide the data for all components, or **fields**, of the record, but typically you would provide only one field—the ID number, for example. Thus, the request

> *Find the record for the person whose ID number is 123456789*

is feasible if the ID number uniquely describes the person. By making this request, not only can you determine whether a person is in a binary search tree, but, once you find the person's record, you can also access the other data about the person.

A field such as an ID number is called a **search key**, or simply a **key**, because it identifies the record that you seek. The record, or item, in the tree would be an instance of a C++ class of the form

A data item in a binary search tree has a specially designated search key

```
class KeyedItem
{
public:
   KeyedItem() {};
   KeyedItem(const KeyType& keyValue)
      :searchKey(keyValue) { }
   KeyType getKey() const  // returns search key
   {
      return searchKey;
   }  // end getKey
private:
   KeyType searchKey;
   … and possibly other data members
};
```

Sometimes one field will not uniquely identify a record. For example, the request

> *Find the record for Jane Brown*

is more difficult to fulfill if the tree contains data for several people named Jane Brown. You could modify your request, as follows:

> *Find the records for all people named Jane Brown*

or

> *Find the record for the Jane Brown whose telephone number is 401-555-1212*

For simplicity, we will assume that a single-field search key uniquely identifies the records in your binary search tree. In this case, you can restate the recursive definition of a binary search tree as follows:

For each node N, a binary search tree satisfies the following three properties:

- N's search key is greater than all search keys in N's left subtree T_L.

- N's search key is less than all search keys in N's right subtree T_R.

- Both T_L and T_R are binary search trees.

A recursive definition of a binary search tree

As an ADT, the binary search tree has operations that are like the operations for the ADTs you studied in previous chapters in that they involve inserting, deleting, and retrieving data. In fact, the earlier ADTs also allowed their data items to be records. In the implementations of the position-oriented ADTs list, stack, and queue, you could define their items to be objects, and the operations would still make sense without modification. Because the ADT binary search tree is value oriented, however, the fact that its items can be objects has greater significance. The insertion, deletion, and retrieval operations for a binary search tree are by search-key value, not by position. On the other hand, the traversal operations that you just saw for a binary tree apply to a binary search tree without change, because a binary search tree is a binary tree.

The operations that define the ADT binary search tree are as follows:

KEY CONCEPTS

ADT Binary Search Tree Operations

1. Create an empty binary search tree.

2. Destroy a binary search tree.

3. Determine whether a binary search tree is empty.

4. Insert a new item into a binary search tree.

5. Delete the item with a given search key from a binary search tree.

6. Retrieve the item with a given search key from a binary search tree.

7. Traverse the items in a binary search tree in preorder, inorder, or postorder.

```
                    BinarySearchTree

              root
              left subtree
              right subtree

              createBinarySearchTree()
              destroyBinarySearchTree()
              isEmpty()
              searchTreeInsert()
              searchTreeDelete()
              searchTreeRetrieve()
              preorderTraverse()
              inorderTraverse()
              postorderTraverse()
```

FIGURE 10-18   UML diagram for the class *BinarySearchTree*

The following pseudocode specifies these operations in more detail. A UML diagram for a class of binary search trees appears in Figure 10-18.

KEY CONCEPTS

Pseudocode for the ADT Binary Search Tree Operations

```
// TreeItemType is the type of the items stored in the
// binary search tree. It should be based upon KeyedItem,
// which has a search key field of type KeyType.
+createSearchTree()
// Creates an empty binary search tree.

+destroySearchTree()
// Destroys a binary search tree.

+isEmpty():boolean {query}
// Determines whether a binary search tree is empty.
```

continued on next page

continued from previous page

```
+searchTreeInsert(in newItem:TreeItemType) throw TreeException
// Inserts newItem into a binary search tree whose items
// have distinct search keys that differ from newItem's
// search key. Throws TreeException if the insertion is not
// successful.

+searchTreeDelete(in searchKey:KeyType) throw TreeException
// Deletes from a binary search tree the item whose search
// key equals searchKey. If no such item exists, the
// operation fails and throws TreeException.

+searchTreeRetrieve(in searchKey:KeyType,
                   out treeItem:TreeItemType) throw TreeException
// Retrieves into treeItem the item in a binary search
// tree whose search key equals searchKey.
// If no such item exists, the operation fails and throws
// TreeException.

+preorderTraverse(in visit:FunctionType)
// Traverses a binary search tree in preorder and calls the
// function visit() once for each item.

+inorderTraverse(in visit:FunctionType)
// Traverses a binary search tree in inorder and calls the
// function visit() once for each item.

+postorderTraverse(in visit:FunctionType)
// Traverses a binary search tree in postorder and calls the
// function visit() once for each item.
```

Figure 10-19 is a binary search tree *nameTree* of names. Each node in the tree actually is a record that represents the named person. That is, if the search key for each record is the person's name, you see only the search keys in the picture of the tree.

For example,

```
nameTree.searchTreeRetrieve("Nancy", nameRecord)
```

retrieves Nancy's record into *nameRecord*. If you insert a record into *nameTree* that describes Hal by invoking

```
nameTree.searchTreeInsert(HalRecord)
```

you will be able to retrieve that record later and still be able to retrieve Nancy's record. If you delete Jane's record by using

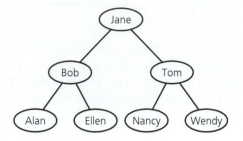

FIGURE 10-19   A binary search tree

```
nameTree.searchTreeDelete("Jane")
```

you will still be able to retrieve the records for Nancy and Hal. Finally, if *displayName* is a function that displays the name portion of a record,

```
nameTree.inorderTraverse(displayName)
```

will display in alphabetical order the names of the people that *nameTree* represents.

Algorithms for the ADT Binary Search Tree Operations

Consider again the binary search tree in Figure 10-19. Each node in the tree contains data for a particular person. The person's name is the search key, and that is the only data item you see in the figure. The following C++ statements describe the data in a tree node:

```cpp
#include <string>
using namespace std;

typedef string KeyType;

class KeyedItem
{
public:
   KeyedItem() {};
   KeyedItem(const KeyType& keyValue)
      :searchKey(keyValue) { }
   KeyType getKey() const
   {
      return searchKey;
   }  // end getKey
private:
   KeyType searchKey;
};  // end class
```

```
class Person : public KeyedItem
{
public:
   Person() {}
   Person(const string& name,
          const string& id,
          const string& phone):
      KeyedItem(name), idNum(id),
      phoneNumber(phone) { }
private:
   // Key item is the person's name
   string idNum;
   string phoneNumber;
   //... and other data about the person
}; // end class
```

A data item in a binary search tree can be an instance of a class

Because a binary search tree is recursive by nature, it is natural to formulate recursive algorithms for operations on the tree. Suppose that you want to locate Ellen's record in the binary search tree of Figure 10-19. Jane is in the root node of the tree, so if Ellen's record is present in the tree, it must be in Jane's left subtree because the search key Ellen is before the search key Jane alphabetically. From the recursive definition, you know that Jane's left subtree is also a binary search tree, so you use exactly the same strategy to search this subtree for Ellen. Bob is in the root of this binary search tree, and, because the search key Ellen is greater than the search key Bob, Ellen's record must be in Bob's right subtree. Bob's right subtree is also a binary search tree, and it happens that Ellen is in the root node of this tree. Thus, the search has located Ellen's record.

The following pseudocode summarizes this search strategy:

```
search(in binTree:BinarySearchTree,
       in searchKey:KeyType)
// Searches the binary search tree binTree for the
// item whose search key is searchKey.

   if (binTree is empty)
      The desired record is not found

   else if (searchKey == search key of root's item)
      The desired record is found

   else if (searchKey < search key of root's item)
      search(Left subtree of binTree, searchKey)

   else
      search(Right subtree of binTree, searchKey)
```

A search algorithm for a binary search tree

As you will see, this *search* algorithm is the basis of the insertion, deletion, and retrieval operations on a binary search tree.

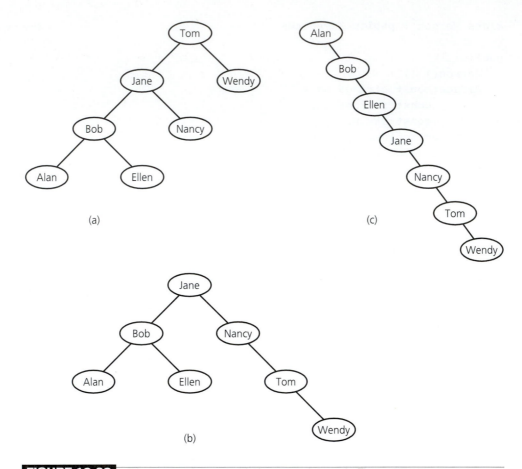

FIGURE 10-20   Binary search trees with the same data as in Figure 10-19

Several different binary search trees are possible for the same data

Many different binary search trees can contain the names Alan, Bob, Ellen, Jane, Nancy, Tom, and Wendy. For example, in addition to the tree in Figure 10-19, each tree in Figure 10-20 is a valid binary search tree for these names. Although these trees have different shapes, the shape of the tree in no way affects the validity of the *search* algorithm. The algorithm requires only that a tree be a binary search tree.

The *search* algorithm works more efficiently on some trees than on others, however. For example, with the tree in Figure 10-20c, *search* inspects every node before locating Wendy. In fact, this binary tree really has the same structure as a sorted linear linked list and offers no advantage in efficiency. In contrast, with the full tree in Figure 10-19, the *search* algorithm inspects only the nodes that contain the names Jane, Tom, and Wendy. These names are exactly the names that a binary search of the sorted array in Figure 10-21 would inspect. Later in this chapter, you will learn more about how the shape of a binary search tree affects *search*'s efficiency and how the insertion and deletion operations affect this shape.

The algorithms that follow for insertion, deletion, retrieval, and traversal assume the pointer-based implementation of a binary tree that was discussed earlier in this chapter. With minor changes, the basic algorithms also apply to other implementations of the binary tree. Also keep in mind the assumption that the items in the tree have unique search keys.

Insertion. Suppose that you want to insert a record for Frank into the binary search tree of Figure 10-19. As a first step, imagine that you instead want to *search* for the item with a search key of Frank. The *search* algorithm first searches the tree rooted at Jane, then the tree rooted at Bob, and then the tree rooted at Ellen. It then searches the tree rooted at the right child of Ellen. Because this tree is empty, as Figure 10-22 illustrates, the *search* algorithm has reached a base case and will terminate with the report that Frank is not present. What does it mean that *search* looked for Frank in the right subtree of Ellen? For one thing, it means that if Frank were the right child of Ellen, *search* would have found Frank there.

This observation indicates that a good place to insert Frank is as the right child of Ellen. Because Ellen has no right child, the insertion is simple, requiring only that Ellen's *rightChildPtr* pointer point to

Alan	Bob	Ellen	Jane	Nancy	Tom	Wendy
0	1	2	3	4	5	6

FIGURE 10-21   An array of names in sorted order

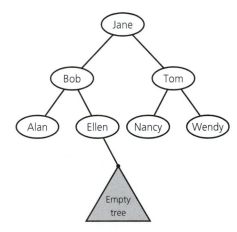

FIGURE 10-22   Empty subtree where *search* terminates

Frank. More important, Frank belongs in this location—*search* will look for Frank here. Specifically, inserting Frank as the right child of Ellen will preserve the tree's binary search tree property. Because *search,* when searching for Frank, would follow a path that leads to the right child of Ellen, you are assured that Frank is in the proper relation to the names above it in the tree.

Using *search* to determine where in the tree to insert a new name always leads to an easy insertion. No matter what new item you insert into the tree, *search* will always terminate at an empty subtree. Thus, *search* always tells you to insert the item as a new leaf. Because adding a leaf requires only a change of the appropriate pointer in the parent, the work required for an insertion is virtually the same as that for the corresponding search.

The following high-level pseudocode describes this insertion process:

> *Use* search *to determine the insertion point*

> *First draft of the insertion algorithm*

```
insertItem(in treePtr:TreeNodePtr,
           in newItem:TreeItemType)
// Inserts newItem into the binary search tree to
// which treePtr points.

   Let parentNode be the parent of the empty subtree
     at which search terminates when it seeks
     newItem's search key

   if (Search terminated at parentNode's left subtree)
      Set leftChildPtr of parentNode to point to newItem
   else
      Set rightChildPtr of parentNode to point to newItem
```

The appropriate pointer—*leftChildPtr* or *rightChildPtr*—of node *parentNode* must be set to point to the new node. The recursive nature of the *search* algorithm provides an elegant means of setting the pointer, provided that you pass *treePtr* as a reference argument, as you will see. Thus, *insertItem* is refined as follows:

> *Refinement of the insertion algorithm*

```
insertItem(inout treePtr:TreeNodePtr,
           in newItem:TreeItemType)
// Inserts newItem into the binary search tree to
// which treePtr points.

   if (treePtr is NULL)
   {  Create a new node and let treePtr point to it
      Copy newItem into new node's data portion
      Set the pointers in the new node to NULL
   }

   else if (newItem.getKey() < treePtr->item.getKey())
      insertItem(treePtr->leftChildPtr, newItem)
```

```
else
    insertItem(treePtr->rightChildPtr, newItem)
```

How does this recursive algorithm set *leftChildPtr* and *right-ChildPtr* to point to the new node? The situation is quite similar to the recursive insertion function for the sorted linked list that you saw in Chapter 4. If the tree was empty before the insertion, the external pointer to the root of the tree would be *NULL* and the function would not make a recursive call. Because *treePtr* is a reference argument, when it points to the new node, the actual argument—the external pointer to the root of the tree—points to the new node. Figure 10-23a illustrates insertion into an empty tree.

The general case of *insertItem* is similar to the special case for an empty tree. When the formal argument *treePtr* becomes *NULL*, the corresponding actual argument is the *leftChildPtr* or *rightChildPtr* pointer in the parent of the empty subtree; that is, this pointer has the value *NULL*. The pointer was passed to the *insertItem* function by one of the recursive calls

```
insertItem(treePtr->leftChildPtr, newItem)
```

or

```
insertItem(treePtr->rightChildPtr, newItem)
```

Thus, when *treePtr* points to the new node, the actual argument—which is the appropriate pointer within the parent—points to the new node. Parts b and c of Figure 10-23 illustrate the general case of insertion.

You can use *insertItem* to create a binary search tree. For example, beginning with an empty tree, if you insert the names Jane, Bob, Alan, Ellen, Tom, Nancy, and Wendy in order, you will get the binary search tree in Figure 10-19. It is interesting to note that the names Jane, Bob, Alan, Ellen, Tom, Nancy, and Wendy constitute the preorder traversal of the tree in Figure 10-19. Thus, if you take the output of a preorder traversal of a binary search tree and use it with *insertItem* to create a binary search tree, you will obtain a duplicate tree. This result should not surprise you, as the copy constructor for the ADT binary tree used a preorder traversal to copy the tree.

By inserting the previous names in a different order, you will get a different binary search tree. For example, by inserting the previous names in alphabetic order, you will get the binary search tree in Figure 10-20c.

To copy a tree, traverse it in preorder and insert each item visited into a new tree

Deletion. The deletion operation is a bit more involved than insertion. First, you use the *search* algorithm to locate the item with the specified search key and then, if it is found, you must remove the item from the tree. A first draft of the algorithm follows:

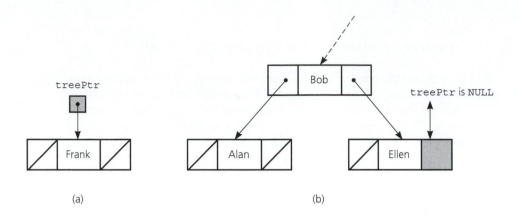

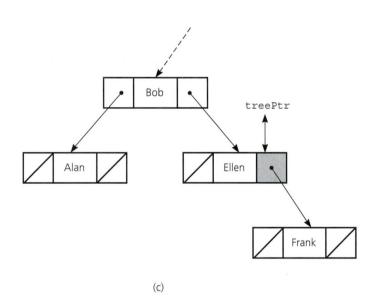

(c)

FIGURE 10-23   (a) Insertion into an empty tree; (b) search terminates at a leaf;
(c) insertion at a leaf

First draft of the deletion
algorithm

```
deleteItem(inout treePtr:TreeNodePtr,
            in searchKey:KeyType) throw TreeException
// Deletes from the binary search tree to which
// treePtr points the item whose search key equals
// searchKey. If no such item exists, the operation
// fails and throws TreeException.

    Locate (by using the search algorithm) the item i
      whose search key equals searchKey
```

```
if (item i is found)
    Remove item i from the tree
else
    Throw a tree exception
```

The essential task here is

```
Remove item i from the tree
```

Assuming that `deleteItem` locates item *i* in a particular node *N*, there are three cases to consider:

1. *N* is a leaf.

2. *N* has only one child.

3. *N* has two children.

Three cases for the node *N* containing the item to be deleted

The first case is the easiest. To remove the leaf containing item *i*, you need only set the pointer in its parent to *NULL*. The second case is a bit more difficult. If *N* has only one child, you have two possibilities:

Case 1: Set the pointer in a leaf's parent to *NULL*

- *N* has only a left child.

- *N* has only a right child.

Case 2: Two possibilities for a node with one child

The two possibilities are symmetrical, so it is sufficient to illustrate the solution for a left child. In Figure 10-24a, *L* is the left child of *N*, and *P* is the parent of *N*. *N* can be either the left or right child of *P*. If you deleted *N* from the tree, *L* would be without a parent, and *P* would be without one of its children. Suppose you let *L* take the place of *N* as

Let *N*'s parent adopt *N*'s child

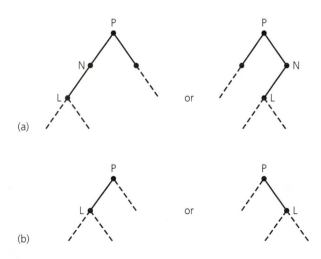

FIGURE 10-24   (a) *N* with only a left child—*N* can be either the left or right child of *P*; (b) after deleting node *N*

one of *P*'s children, as in Figure 10-24b. Does this adoption preserve the binary search tree property?

If *N* is the left child of *P*, for example, all of the search keys in the subtree rooted at *N* are less than the search key in *P*. Thus, all of the search keys in the subtree rooted at *L* are less than the search key in *P*. Therefore, after *N* is removed and *L* is adopted by *P*, all of the search keys in *P*'s left subtree are still less than the search key in *P*. This deletion strategy thus preserves the binary search tree property. A parallel argument holds if *N* is a right child of *P*, and therefore the binary search tree property is preserved in either case.

The most difficult of the three cases occurs when the item to be deleted is in a node *N* that has two children, as in Figure 10-25. As you just saw, when *N* has only one child, the child replaces *N*. However, when *N* has two children, these children cannot both replace *N*: *N*'s parent has room for only one of *N*'s children as a replacement for *N*. A different strategy is necessary.

In fact, you will not delete *N* at all. You can find another node that is easier to delete and delete it instead of *N*. This strategy may sound like cheating. After all, the programmer who requests

```
nameTree.searchTreeDelete(searchKey)
```

expects that the item whose search key equals *searchKey* will be deleted from the ADT binary search tree. However, the programmer expects only that the *item* will be deleted and has no right, because of the wall between the program and the ADT implementation, to expect a particular *node* in the tree to be deleted.

Consider, then, an alternate strategy. To delete from a binary search tree an item that resides in a node *N* that has two children, take the following steps:

Case 3: *N* has two children

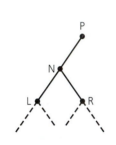

FIGURE 10-25   *N* with two children

Deleting an item whose node has two children

1. Locate another node *M* that is easier to remove from the tree than the node *N*.

2. Copy the item that is in *M* to *N*, thus effectively deleting from the tree the item originally in *N*.

3. Remove the node *M* from the tree.

What kind of node *M* is easier to remove than the node *N*? Because you know how to delete a node that has no children or one child, *M* could be such a node. You have to be careful, though. Can you choose any node and copy its data into *N*? No, because you must preserve the tree's status as a binary search tree. For example, if in the tree of Figure 10-26, you copied the data from *M* to *N*, the result would no longer be a binary search tree.

What data item, when copied into the node *N*, will preserve the tree's status as a binary search tree? All of the search keys in the left subtree of *N* are less than the search key in *N*, and all of the search keys in the right subtree of *N* are greater than the search key in *N*. You must

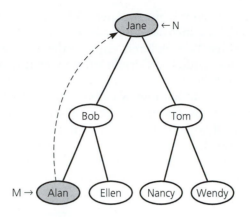

FIGURE 10-26 Not any node will do

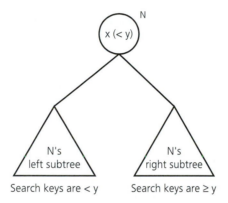

FIGURE 10-27 Search key *x* can be replaced by *y*

retain this property when you replace the search key x in node N with the search key y. There are two suitable possibilities for the value y: It can come immediately after or immediately before x in the sorted order of search keys. If y comes immediately after x, then clearly all search keys in the left subtree of N are smaller than y, because they are all smaller than x, as Figure 10-27 illustrates. Further, all search keys in the right subtree of N are greater than or equal to y, because they are greater than x and, by assumption, there are no search keys in the tree between x and y. A similar argument illustrates that if y comes immediately before x in the sorted order, it is greater than or equal to all search keys in the left subtree of N and smaller than all search keys in the right subtree of N.

You can thus copy into N either the item whose search key is immediately after N's search key[5] or the item whose search key is immediately before it. Suppose that, arbitrarily, you decide to use the node

The inorder successor of *N*'s search key is in the leftmost node in *N*'s right subtree

whose search key *y* comes immediately after *N*'s search key *x*. This search key is called *x*'s **inorder successor**.[6] How can you locate this node? Because *N* has two children, the inorder successor of its search key is in the leftmost node of *N*'s right subtree. That is, to find the node that contains *y*, you follow *N*'s `rightChildPtr` pointer to its right child *R*, which must be present because *N* has two children. You then descend the tree rooted at *R* by taking left branches at each node until you encounter a node *M* with no left child. You copy the item in this node *M* into node *N* and then, because *M* has no left child, you can remove *M* from the tree as one of the two easy cases. (See Figure 10-28.)

A more detailed high-level description of the deletion algorithm follows:

Second draft of the deletion algorithm

```
deleteItem(inout treePtr:TreeNodePtr,
           in searchKey:KeyType) throw TreeException
// Deletes from the binary search tree to which
// treePtr points the item whose search key equals
// searchKey. If no such item exists, the operation
// fails and throws TreeException.

    Locate (by using the search algorithm) the
      item whose search key equals searchKey; it
      occurs in node N

    if (item is found in node N)
```

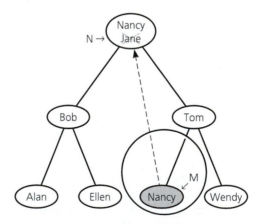

FIGURE 10-28 Copying the item whose search key is the inorder successor of *N*'s search key

---

[5] *N*'s search key is the search key of the data item in *N*.

[6] We also will use the term **N's inorder successor** to mean the inorder successor of *N*'s search key.

```
         deleteNodeItem(N)  // defined next
     else
        Throw a tree exception

deleteNodeItem(inout N:TreeNode)
// Deletes the item in a node N of a binary search
// tree

   if (N is a leaf)
      Remove N from the tree

   else if (N has only one child C)
   { if (N was a left child of its parent P)
        Make C the left child of P
     else
        Make C the right child of P
   }

   else  // node has two children
   { Find M, the node that contains N's inorder
        successor
     Copy the item from node M into node N
     Remove M from the tree by using the previous
        technique for a leaf or a node with one child
   }  // end if
```

In the following refinement, *search*'s algorithm is adapted and inserted directly into *deleteItem*. Also, the function *deleteNodeItem* uses the function *processLeftmost* to find the node, *M*, that contains the inorder successor of node *N*. The function *processLeftmost* returns the item in *M* and then deletes *M* from the tree. The returned item then replaces the item in node *N*, thus deleting it from the binary search tree.

```
deleteItem(inout treePtr:TreeNodePtr,
          in searchKey:KeyType) throw TreeException
// Deletes from the binary search tree, to which treePtr
// points, the item whose search key equals searchKey.
// If no such item exists, the operation fails and throws
// TreeException.

   if (treePtr == NULL)
      throw TreeException // item not found

   else if (searchKey == treePtr->item.getKey())
      // item is in the root of some subtree
      deleteNodeItem(treePtr)  // delete the item
```

Final draft of the deletion algorithm

```
       else if (searchKey < treePtr->item.getKey())
          // search the left subtree
          deleteItem(treePtr->leftChildPtr, searchKey)

       else  // search the right subtree
          deleteItem(treePtr->rightChildPtr, searchKey)

deleteNodeItem(inout nodePtr:TreeNodePtr)
// Deletes the item in node N to which nodePtr points.

   if (N is a leaf)
   {  // remove leaf from the tree
     delete nodePtr
     nodePtr = NULL
   }

   else if (N has only one child C)
   {  // C replaces N as the child of N's parent
      delPtr = nodePtr
      if (C is the left child of N)
         nodePtr = nodePtr->leftChildPtr
      else
         nodePtr = nodePtr->rightChildPtr
      delete delPtr
   }

   else  // N has two children
   {  // find the inorder successor of the search key in N:
      // it is in the leftmost node of the subtree
      // rooted at N's right child
      processLeftmost(nodePtr->rightChildPtr, replacementItem)

      Put replacementItem in node N
   }  // end if

processLeftmost(inout nodePtr:TreeNodePtr,
                out treeItem:TreeItemType)
// Retrieves into treeItem the item in the leftmost
// descendant of the node to which nodePtr points.
// Deletes the node that contains this item.

   if (nodePtr->leftChildPtr == NULL)
   {  // this is the node you want; it has no left
      // child, but it might have a right subtree
      treeItem = nodePtr->item
      delPtr = nodePtr

      // the actual argument corresponding to nodePtr is a
      // child pointer of nodePtr's parent; thus, the
```

```
// following "moves up" nodePtr's right subtree
nodePtr = nodePtr->rightChildPtr

delete delPtr
}

else
    processLeftmost(nodePtr->leftChildPtr, treeItem)
```

Observe that, as in the case of the *insertItem* function, the actual argument that corresponds to *treePtr* either is one of the pointers of the parent of *N*, as Figure 10-29 depicts, or is the external pointer to the root, in the case where *N* is the root of the original tree. In either case *treePtr* points to *N*. Thus, any change you make to *treePtr* by calling the function *deleteNodeItem* with actual argument *treePtr* changes the pointer in the parent of *N*. The recursive function *processLeftmost*, which is called by *deleteNodeItem* if *N* has two children, also uses this strategy to remove the inorder successor of the node containing the item to be deleted.

Exercise 30 at the end of this chapter describes an easier deletion algorithm. However, that algorithm tends to increase the height of the tree, and, as you will see later, an increase in height can decrease the efficiency of searching the tree.

Retrieval. By refining the *search* algorithm, you can implement the retrieval operation. Recall that the *search* algorithm is

```
search(in bst:BinarySearchTree, in searchKey:KeyType)
// Searches the binary search tree bst for the item
// whose search key is searchKey.

if (bst is empty)
    The desired record is not found
```

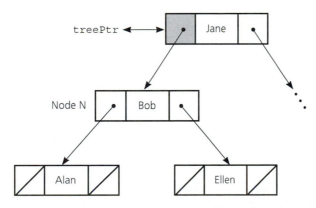

Any change to treePtr while deleting node N (Bob) changes leftChildPtr of Jane

FIGURE 10-29 Recursive deletion of node *N*

```
    else if (searchKey == search key of root's item)
        The desired record is found

    else if (searchKey < search key of root's item)
        search(Left subtree of bst, searchKey)

    else
        search(Right subtree of bst, searchKey)
```

The retrieval operation must return the item with the desired search key if it exists; otherwise it must throw an exception *TreeException*. The retrieval algorithm, therefore, appears as follows:

retrieveItem is a refinement of *search*

```
retrieveItem(in treePtr:TreeNodePtr,
             in searchKey:KeyType,
             out treeItem:TreeItemType)
             throw TreeException
// Retrieves into treeItem the item whose search
// key equals searchKey from the binary search
// tree to which treePtr points. The operation
// throws TreeException if no such item exists.

    if (treePtr == NULL)
        Throw a tree exception indicating item not found
    else if (searchKey == treePtr->item.getKey())
        // item is in the root of some subtree
        treeItem = treePtr->item

    else if (searchKey < treePtr->item.getKey())
        // search the left subtree
        retrieveItem(treePtr->leftChildPtr,
                     searchKey, treeItem)

    else  // search the right subtree
        retrieveItem(treePtr->rightChildPtr,
                     searchKey, treeItem)
```

Traversal. The traversals for a binary search tree are the same as the traversals for a binary tree. You should be aware, however, that an inorder traversal of a binary search tree will visit the tree's nodes in sorted search-key order. Before seeing the proof of this statement, recall the inorder traversal algorithm:

```
inorder(in bst:BinarySearchTree)
// Traverses the binary tree bst in inorder.

    if (bst is not empty)
```

```
{   inorder(Left subtree of bst's root)
    visit the root of T
    inorder(Right subtree of bst's root)
}
```

THEOREM 10-1. The inorder traversal of a binary search tree T will visit its nodes in sorted search-key order.

PROOF. The proof is by induction on h, the height of T.

Basis: $h = 0$. When T is empty, the algorithm does not visit any nodes. This is the proper sorted order for the zero names that are in the tree!

Inductive hypothesis: Assume that the theorem is true for all k, $0 < k < h$. That is, assume for all k ($0 < k < h$) that the inorder traversal visits the nodes in sorted search-key order.

Inductive conclusion: You must show that the theorem is true for $k = h > 0$. T has the form

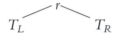

Because T is a binary search tree, all the search keys in the left subtree T_L are less than the search key in the root r, and all the search keys in the right subtree T_R are greater than the search key in r. The `inorder` algorithm will visit all the nodes in T_L, then visit r, and then visit all the nodes in T_R. Thus, the only concern is that `inorder` visit the nodes within each of the subtrees T_L and T_R in the correct sorted order. But because T is a binary search tree of height h, each subtree is a binary search tree of height less than h. Therefore, by the inductive hypothesis, `inorder` visits the nodes in each subtree T_L and T_R in the correct sorted search-key order. **(End of proof.)**

It follows from this theorem that `inorder` visits a node's inorder successor immediately after it visits the node.

Use inorder traversal to visit nodes of a binary search tree in search-key order

A Pointer-Based Implementation of the ADT Binary Search Tree

A C++ pointer-based implementation of the ADT binary search tree follows. Notice the protected member functions that implement the recursive algorithms. These functions are not public, because clients do not have access to node pointers. The functions could be private, but making them protected enables a derived class to use them directly.

```
// ***********************************************************
// Header file KeyedItem.h for the ADT binary search tree.
// ***********************************************************
typedef desired-type-of-search-key KeyType;

class KeyedItem
```

```
{
public:
   KeyedItem() {};
   KeyedItem(const KeyType& keyValue)
      :searchKey(keyValue) {}
   KeyType getKey() const
   {   return searchKey;
   }  // end getKey
private:
   KeyType searchKey;
   //... and other data about the person
};  // end class


// ********************************************************
// Header file TreeNode.h for the ADT binary search tree.
// ********************************************************
#include "KeyedItem.h"
typedef KeyedItem TreeItemType;


class TreeNode         // a node in the tree
{
private:
   TreeNode() { }
   TreeNode(const TreeItemType& nodeItem,
            TreeNode *left = NULL, TreeNode *right = NULL)
      :item(nodeItem), leftChildPtr(left),
      rightChildPtr(right) { }

   TreeItemType item;            // a data item in the tree
   // pointers to children
   TreeNode *leftChildPtr, *rightChildPtr;

   // friend class - can access private parts
   friend class BinarySearchTree;
};  // end class
```

Header file

```
// ********************************************************
// Header file BST.h for the ADT binary search tree.
// Assumption: A tree contains at most one item with a given
//             search key at any time.
// ********************************************************
#include "TreeException.h"
#include "TreeNode.h"
typedef void (*FunctionType)(TreeItemType& anItem);


class BinarySearchTree
{
public:
// constructors and destructor:
```

```
    BinarySearchTree();
    BinarySearchTree(const BinarySearchTree& tree);
    virtual ~BinarySearchTree();

// binary search tree operations:
// Precondition for all methods: No two items in a binary
// search tree have the same search key.

    virtual bool isEmpty() const;
    // Determines whether a binary search tree is empty.
    // Postcondition: Returns true if the tree is empty;
    // otherwise returns false.
    virtual void searchTreeInsert(const TreeItemType& newItem);


    // Inserts an item into a binary search tree.
    // Precondition: The item to be inserted into the tree
    // is newItem.
    // Postcondition: newItem is in its proper order in the
    // tree.

    virtual void searchTreeDelete(KeyType searchKey)
                                        throw(TreeException);
    // Deletes an item with a given search key from a binary
    // search tree.
    // Precondition: searchKey is the search key of the item
    // to be deleted.
    // Postcondition: If the item whose search key equals
    // searchKey existed in the tree, the item is deleted.
    // Otherwise, the tree is unchanged and TreeException
    // is thrown.

    virtual void searchTreeRetrieve(KeyType searchKey,
                          TreeItemType& treeItem) const
                          throw(TreeException);
    // Retrieves an item with a given search key from a
    // binary search tree.
    // Precondition: searchKey is the search key of the item
    // to be retrieved.
    // Postcondition: If the retrieval was successful,
    // treeItem contains the retrieved item.
    // If no such item exists, throws TreeException.

    virtual void preorderTraverse(FunctionType visit);
    // Traverses a binary search tree in preorder,
    // calling function visit() once for each item.
    // Precondition: The function represented by visit()
    // exists outside of the class implementation.
    // Postcondition: visit's action occurred once for each
    // item in the tree.
```

```
    // Note: visit() can alter the tree.

    virtual void inorderTraverse(FunctionType visit);
    // Traverses a binary search tree in sorted order,
    // calling function visit() once for each item.

    virtual void postorderTraverse(FunctionType visit);
    // Traverses a binary search tree in postorder,
    // calling function visit() once for each item.

// overloaded operator:
    virtual BinarySearchTree& operator=(
                              const BinarySearchTree& rhs);


protected:
    void insertItem(TreeNode *& treePtr,
                    const TreeItemType& newItem)
                    throw(TreeException);
    // Recursively inserts an item into a binary search tree.
    // Precondition: treePtr points to a binary search tree,
    // newItem is the item to be inserted.
    // Postcondition: Same as searchTreeInsert.

    void deleteItem(TreeNode *& treePtr, KeyType searchKey)
                                 throw(TreeException);
    // Recursively deletes an item from a binary search tree.
    // Precondition: treePtr points to a binary search tree,
    // searchKey is the search key of the item to be deleted.
    // Postcondition: Same as searchTreeDelete.

    void deleteNodeItem(TreeNode *& nodePtr);
    // Deletes the item in the root of a given tree.
    // Precondition: nodePtr points to the root of a
    // binary search tree; nodePtr != NULL.
    // Postcondition: The item in the root of the given
    // tree is deleted.

    void processLeftmost(TreeNode *& nodePtr,
                         TreeItemType& treeItem);
    // Retrieves and deletes the leftmost descendant of a
    // given node.
    // Precondition: nodePtr points to a node in a binary
    // search tree; nodePtr != NULL.
    // Postcondition: treeItem contains the item in the
    // leftmost descendant of the node to which nodePtr
    // points. The leftmost descendant of nodePtr is
    // deleted.

    void retrieveItem(TreeNode *treePtr, KeyType searchKey,
                      TreeItemType& treeItem) const
```

```
                    throw(TreeException);
  // Recursively retrieves an item from a binary search
  // tree.
  // Precondition: treePtr points to a binary search tree,
  // searchKey is the search key of the item to be
  // retrieved.
  // Postcondition: Same as searchTreeRetrieve.

// The following 9 methods are the same as for the ADT
// binary tree, and so their specifications are abbreviated.
  void copyTree(TreeNode *treePtr, TreeNode *& newTreePtr) const;

  void destroyTree(TreeNode *& treePtr);

  void preorder(TreeNode *treePtr, FunctionType visit);
  void inorder(TreeNode *treePtr, FunctionType visit);
  void postorder(TreeNode *treePtr, FunctionType visit);

  TreeNode *rootPtr() const;
  void setRootPtr(TreeNode *newRoot);

  void getChildPtrs(TreeNode *nodePtr,
                    TreeNode *& leftChildPtr,
                    TreeNode *& rightChildPtr) const;
  void setChildPtrs(TreeNode *nodePtr,
                    TreeNode *leftChildPtr,
                    TreeNode *rightChildPtr);

private:
  TreeNode *root;  // pointer to root of tree
};  // end class
// End of header file.

// *********************************************************     Implementation file
// Implementation file BST.cpp.
// *********************************************************
#include "BST.h"     // header file
#include <cstddef>   // definition of NULL

BinarySearchTree::BinarySearchTree() : root(NULL)
{
}  // end default constructor

BinarySearchTree::BinarySearchTree(
                         const BinarySearchTree& tree)
{
   copyTree(tree.root, root);
}  // end copy constructor

BinarySearchTree::~BinarySearchTree()
```

```cpp
{
   destroyTree(root);
} // end destructor

bool BinarySearchTree::isEmpty() const
{
   return (root == NULL);
} // end searchTreeIsEmpty

void BinarySearchTree::searchTreeInsert(
                          const TreeItemType& newItem)
{
   insertItem(root, newItem);
} // end searchTreeInsert

void BinarySearchTree::searchTreeDelete(KeyType searchKey)
                          throw(TreeException)
{
   deleteItem(root, searchKey);
} // end searchTreeDelete

void BinarySearchTree::searchTreeRetrieve(KeyType searchKey,
                          TreeItemType& treeItem) const
                          throw(TreeException)
{
   // if retrieveItem throws a TreeException, it is
   // ignored here and passed on to the point in the code
   // where searchTreeRetrieve was called
   retrieveItem(root, searchKey, treeItem);
} // end searchTreeRetrieve

void BinarySearchTree::preorderTraverse(FunctionType visit)
{
   preorder(root, visit);
} // end preorderTraverse

void BinarySearchTree::inorderTraverse(FunctionType visit)
{
   inorder(root, visit);
} // end inorderTraverse

void BinarySearchTree::postorderTraverse(FunctionType visit)
{
   postorder(root, visit);
} // end postorderTraverse

void BinarySearchTree::insertItem(TreeNode *& treePtr,
                          const TreeItemType& newItem)
                          throw(TreeException)
```

```
{
   if (treePtr == NULL)
   {  // position of insertion found; insert after leaf

      // create a new node
      treePtr = new TreeNode(newItem, NULL, NULL);

      // was allocation successful?
      if (treePtr == NULL)
         throw TreeException("TreeException: insert failed");
   }
   // else search for the insertion position
   else if (newItem.getKey() < treePtr->item.getKey())
      // search the left subtree
      insertItem(treePtr->leftChildPtr, newItem);

   else  // search the right subtree
      insertItem(treePtr->rightChildPtr, newItem);
}  // end insertItem

void BinarySearchTree::deleteItem(TreeNode *& treePtr,
                                  KeyType searchKey)
                                     throw(TreeException)
// Calls: deleteNodeItem.
{
   if (treePtr == NULL)
      throw TreeException(
         "TreeException: delete failed");  // empty tree

   else if (searchKey == treePtr->item.getKey())
      // item is in the root of some subtree
      deleteNodeItem(treePtr);  // delete the item

   // else search for the item
   else if (searchKey < treePtr->item.getKey())
      // search the left subtree
      deleteItem(treePtr->leftChildPtr, searchKey);

   else  // search the right subtree
      deleteItem(treePtr->rightChildPtr, searchKey);
}  // end deleteItem

void BinarySearchTree::deleteNodeItem(TreeNode *& nodePtr)
// Algorithm note: There are four cases to consider:
//    1. The root is a leaf.
//    2. The root has no left child.
//    3. The root has no right child.
//    4. The root has two children.
// Calls: processLeftmost.
```

```
{
    TreeNode     *delPtr;
    TreeItemType replacementItem;

    // test for a leaf
    if ( (nodePtr->leftChildPtr == NULL) &&
         (nodePtr->rightChildPtr == NULL) )
    {  delete nodePtr;
       nodePtr = NULL;
    }  // end if leaf
    // test for no left child
    else if (nodePtr->leftChildPtr == NULL)
    {  delPtr = nodePtr;
       nodePtr = nodePtr->rightChildPtr;
       delPtr->rightChildPtr = NULL;
       delete delPtr;
    }  // end if no left child

    // test for no right child
    else if (nodePtr->rightChildPtr == NULL)
    {  delPtr = nodePtr;
       nodePtr = nodePtr->leftChildPtr;
       delPtr->leftChildPtr = NULL;
       delete delPtr;
    }  // end if no right child

    // there are two children:
    // retrieve and delete the inorder successor
    else
    {  processLeftmost(nodePtr->rightChildPtr,
                       replacementItem);
       nodePtr->item = replacementItem;
    }  // end if two children
}  // end deleteNodeItem

void BinarySearchTree::processLeftmost(TreeNode *& nodePtr,
                             TreeItemType& treeItem)

{
    if (nodePtr->leftChildPtr == NULL)
    {  treeItem = nodePtr->item;
       TreeNode *delPtr = nodePtr;
       nodePtr = nodePtr->rightChildPtr;
       delPtr->rightChildPtr = NULL;  // defense
       delete delPtr;
    }

    else
       processLeftmost(nodePtr->leftChildPtr, treeItem);
```

```
}   // end processLeftmost

void BinarySearchTree::retrieveItem(TreeNode *treePtr,
                                    KeyType searchKey,
                                    TreeItemType& treeItem) const
                                    throw(TreeException)
{
   if (treePtr == NULL)
      throw TreeException(
         "TreeException: searchKey not found");

   else if (searchKey == treePtr->item.getKey())
      // item is in the root of some subtree
      treeItem = treePtr->item;

   else if (searchKey < treePtr->item.getKey())
   // search the left subtree
      retrieveItem(treePtr->leftChildPtr,
                  searchKey, treeItem);

   else  // search the right subtree
      retrieveItem(treePtr->rightChildPtr,
                    searchKey, treeItem);
}   // end retrieveItem

// Implementations of copyTree, destroyTree, preorder,
// inorder, postorder, setRootPtr, rootPtr, getChildPtrs,
// setChildPtrs, and the overloaded assignment operator are
// the same as for the ADT binary tree.
// End of implementation file.
```

You should see some redundancy between the previous implementations of the ADT binary tree and that of the ADT binary search tree. Both the underlying data structure and the implementations of several of the methods (see the ending comments in the implementation file just given) are in fact identical. Because a binary search tree is a binary tree, this redundancy should not surprise you. You can avoid this duplication of effort by defining *BinarySearchTree* as a derived class of *BinaryTree*. Exercise 32 at the end of this chapter asks you to explore this possibility.

The Efficiency of Binary Search Tree Operations

You have seen binary search trees in many shapes. For example, even though the binary search trees in Figures 10-19 and 10-20c have seven nodes each, they have radically different shapes and heights. You saw that to locate Wendy in Figure 10-20c, you would have to inspect all seven nodes, but you can locate Wendy in Figure 10-19 by inspecting only three nodes (Jane, Tom, and Wendy). Consider now the relationship between the height of a binary search tree and the efficiency of the retrieval, insertion, and deletion operations.

Each of these operations compares the specified value *searchKey* to the search keys in the nodes along a **path** through the tree. This path always starts at the root of the tree and, at each node *n*, follows the left or right branch, depending on the comparison of *searchKey* to the search key in *n*. The path terminates at the node that contains *searchKey* or, if *searchKey* is not present, at an empty subtree. Thus, each retrieval, insertion, or deletion operation requires a number of comparisons equal to the number of nodes along this path. This means that the maximum number of comparisons that each operation can require is the number of nodes on the longest path through the tree. In other words, the *maximum number of comparisons that these operations can require is equal to the height of the binary search tree.* What, then, are the maximum and minimum heights of a binary search tree of *n* nodes?

The maximum number of comparisons for a retrieval, insertion, or deletion is the height of the tree

_n_ is the maximum height of a binary tree with *n* nodes

Except for the last level, each level of a minimum-height binary tree must contain as many nodes as possible

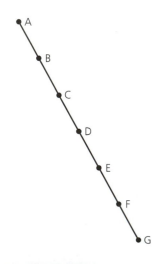

The maximum and minimum heights of a binary search tree. You can maximize the height of a binary tree with *n* nodes simply by giving each internal node (nonleaf) exactly one child, as shown in Figure 10-30. This process will result in a tree of height *n*. An *n*-node tree with height *n* strikingly resembles a linear linked list.

A minimum-height binary tree with *n* nodes is a bit more difficult to obtain. As a first step, consider the number of nodes that a binary tree with a given height *h* can have. For example, if *h* = 3, the possible binary trees include those in Figure 10-31. Thus, binary trees of height 3 can have between 3 and 7 nodes. In addition, Figure 10-31 shows that 3 is the minimum height for a binary tree with 4, 5, 6, or 7 nodes. Similarly, binary trees with more than 7 nodes require a height greater than 3.

Intuitively, to minimize the height of a binary tree given *n* nodes, you must fill each level of the tree as completely as possible. A complete tree meets this requirement (although it does not matter whether the nodes on the last level are filled left to right). In fact, trees *b*, *c*, *d*, and *e* of Figure 10-31 are complete trees. If a complete binary tree of a given height *h* is to have the maximum possible number of nodes, it should be full (as in Figure 10-31e). Figure 10-32 counts these nodes by level and shows the following:

THEOREM 10-2. A full binary tree of height $h \geq 0$ has $2^h - 1$ nodes.

A formal proof by induction of this theorem is left as an exercise.

It follows then that

THEOREM 10-3. The maximum number of nodes that a binary tree of height *h* can have is $2^h - 1$.

You cannot add nodes to a full binary tree of height *h* without increasing its height. The formal proof of this theorem, which closely parallels that of Theorem 10-2, is left as an exercise.

FIGURE 10-30   A maximum-height binary tree with seven nodes

The following theorem uses Theorems 10-2 and 10-3 to determine the minimum height of a binary tree that contains some given number of nodes.

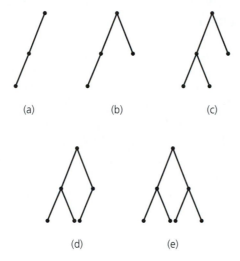

(a)   (b)   (c)

(d)   (e)

FIGURE 10-31   Binary trees of height 3

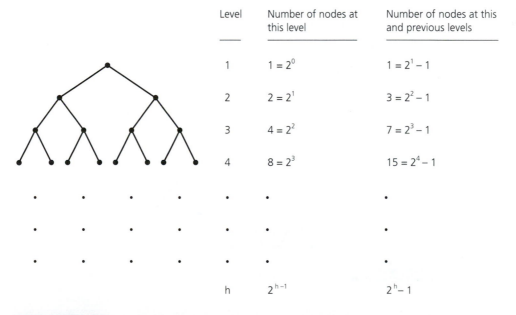

Level	Number of nodes at this level	Number of nodes at this and previous levels
1	$1 = 2^0$	$1 = 2^1 - 1$
2	$2 = 2^1$	$3 = 2^2 - 1$
3	$4 = 2^2$	$7 = 2^3 - 1$
4	$8 = 2^3$	$15 = 2^4 - 1$
.	.	.
.	.	.
.	.	.
h	2^{h-1}	$2^h - 1$

FIGURE 10-32   Counting the nodes in a full binary tree of height h

THEOREM 10-4. The minimum height of a binary tree with n nodes is $\lceil \log_2(n + 1) \rceil$.[7]

PROOF. Let h be the smallest integer such that $n \leq 2^h - 1$. To find the minimum height of a binary tree with n nodes, first establish the following facts:

1. *A binary tree whose height is $\leq h - 1$ has $< n$ nodes.*

   By Theorem 10-3, a binary tree of height $h - 1$ has at most $2^{h-1} - 1$ nodes. If it is possible that $n \leq 2^{h-1} - 1 < 2^h - 1$, then h is not the smallest integer such that $n \leq 2^h - 1$. Therefore, n must be greater than $2^{h-1} - 1$ or, equivalently, $2^{h-1} - 1 < n$. Because a binary tree of height $h - 1$ has at most $2^{h-1} - 1$ nodes, it must have fewer than n nodes.

2. *There exists a complete binary tree of height h that has exactly n nodes.*

   Consider the full binary tree of height $h - 1$. By Theorem 10-2, it has $2^{h-1} - 1$ nodes. As you just saw, $n > 2^{h-1} - 1$ because h was selected so that $n \leq 2^h - 1$. You can thus add nodes to the full tree from left to right until you have n nodes, as Figure 10-33 illustrates. Because $n \leq 2^h - 1$ and a binary tree of height h cannot have more than $2^h - 1$ nodes, you will reach n nodes by the time level h is filled up.

3. *The minimum height of a binary tree with n nodes is the smallest integer h such that $n \leq 2^h - 1$.*

   If h is the smallest integer such that $n \leq 2^h - 1$, and if a binary tree has height $\leq h - 1$, then by fact 1 it has fewer than n nodes. Because by fact 2 there is a binary tree of height h that has exactly n nodes, h must be as small as possible.

The previous discussion implies that

$$2^{h-1} - 1 < n \leq 2^h - 1$$

$$2^{h-1} < n + 1 \leq 2^h$$

$$h - 1 < \log_2(n + 1) \leq h$$

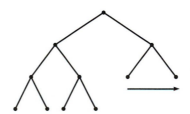

FIGURE 10-33   Filling in the last level of a tree

---

[7] The **ceiling of x**, which $\lceil x \rceil$ denotes, is x rounded up. For example, $\lceil 6 \rceil = 6$, $\lceil 6.1 \rceil = 7$, and $\lceil 6.8 \rceil = 7$.

If $\log_2(n + 1) = h$, the theorem is proven. Otherwise, $h - 1 < \log_2(n + 1) < h$ implies that $\log_2(n + 1)$ cannot be an integer. Therefore, round $\log_2(n + 1)$ up to get h.

Thus, $h = \lceil \log_2(n + 1) \rceil$ is the minimum height of a binary tree with n nodes. **(End of proof.)**

Complete trees and full trees with n nodes thus have heights of $\lceil \log_2(n + 1) \rceil$, which, as you just saw, is the theoretical minimum. This minimum height is the same as the maximum number of comparisons a binary search must make to search an array with n elements. Thus, if a binary search tree is complete and therefore balanced, the time it takes to search it for a value is about the same as that required for a binary search of an array. On the other hand, as you go from balanced trees toward trees with a linear structure, the height approaches the number of nodes n. This number is the same as the maximum number of comparisons that you must make when searching a linked list of n nodes.

Complete trees and full trees have minimum height

The height of an *n*-node binary search tree ranges from $\lceil \log_2(n + 1) \rceil$ to *n*

However, the outstanding efficiency of the operations on a binary search tree hinges on the assumption that the height of the binary search tree is $\lceil \log_2(n + 1) \rceil$. What will the height of a binary search tree actually be? The factor that determines the height of a binary search tree is the order in which you perform the insertion and deletion operations on the tree. Recall that, starting with an empty tree, if you insert names in the order Alan, Bob, Ellen, Jane, Nancy, Tom, Wendy, you would obtain a binary search tree of maximum height, as shown in Figure 10-20c. On the other hand, if you insert names in the order Jane, Bob, Tom, Alan, Ellen, Nancy, Wendy, you would obtain a binary search tree of minimum height, as shown in Figure 10-19.

Insertion in search-key order produces a maximum-height binary search tree

Which of these situations should you expect to encounter in the course of a real application? It can be proven mathematically that if the insertion and deletion operations occur in a random order, the height of the binary search tree will be quite close to $\log_2 n$. Thus, in this sense, the previous analysis is not unduly optimistic. However, in a real-world application, is it realistic to expect the insertion and deletion operations to occur in random order? In many applications, the answer is yes. There are, however, applications in which this assumption would be dubious. For example, the person preparing the previous sequence of names for the insertion operations might well decide to "help you out" by arranging the names to be inserted into sorted order. This arrangement, as has been mentioned, would lead to a tree of maximum height. Thus, while in many applications you can expect the behavior of a binary search tree to be excellent, you should be wary of the possibility of poor performance due to some characteristic of a given application.

Insertion in random order produces a near-minimum-height binary search tree

Is there anything you can do if you suspect that the operations might not occur in a random order? Similarly, is there anything you can do if you have an enormous number of items and need to ensure that the height of the tree is close to $\log_2 n$? Chapter 12 presents variations of the basic binary search tree that are guaranteed always to remain balanced.

Operation	Average case	Worst case
Retrieval	O(log n)	O(n)
Insertion	O(log n)	O(n)
Deletion	O(log n)	O(n)
Traversal	O(n)	O(n)

FIGURE 10-34   The order of the retrieval, insertion, deletion, and traversal operations for the pointer-based implementation of the ADT binary search tree

Figure 10-34 summarizes the order of the retrieval, insertion, deletion, and traversal operations for the ADT binary search tree.

Treesort

You can use the ADT binary search tree to sort an array of records efficiently into search-key order. To simplify the discussion, however, we will sort an array of integers into ascending order, as we did with the sorting algorithms in Chapter 9.

The basic idea of the algorithm is simple:

Treesort uses a binary search tree

```
treesort(inout anArray:ArrayType, in n:integer)
// Sorts the n integers in an array anArray into
// ascending order.

    Insert anArray's elements into a binary search tree
      bTree

    Traverse bTree in inorder. As you visit bTree's
      nodes, copy their data items into successive
      locations of anArray
```

An inorder traversal of the binary search tree *bTree* visits the integers in *bTree*'s nodes in ascending order.

A treesort can be quite efficient. As Figure 10-34 indicates, each insertion into a binary search tree requires $O(\log n)$ operations in the average case and $O(n)$ operations in the worst case. Thus, `treesort`'s n insertions require $O(n * \log n)$ operations in the average case and $O(n^2)$ operations in the worst case. The traversal of the tree involves one copy operation for each of the n elements and so is $O(n)$. Since $O(n)$ is less than $O(n * \log n)$ and $O(n^2)$, treesort is $O(n * \log n)$ in the average case and $O(n^2)$ in the worst case.

Treesort.
Average case: $O(n * \log n)$;
worst case: $O(n^2)$

Saving a Binary Search Tree in a File

Imagine a program that maintains the names, addresses, and telephone numbers of your friends and relatives. While the program is running, you can enter a name and get the person's address and phone number. If you terminate program execution, the program must save its database of people in a form that it can recover at a later time.

If the program uses a binary search tree to represent the database, it must save the tree's data in a file so that it can later restore the tree. Two different algorithms for saving and restoring a binary search tree will be considered here. The first algorithm restores a binary search tree to its original shape. The second restores a binary search tree to a shape that is balanced.

Saving a binary search tree and then restoring it to its original shape.
The first algorithm restores a binary search tree to exactly the same shape it had before it was saved. For example, consider the tree in Figure 10-35a. If you save the tree in preorder, you get the sequence 60, 20, 10, 40, 30, 50, 70. If you then use *searchTreeInsert* to insert these values into a tree that is initially empty, you will get the original tree. Figure 10-35b shows this sequence of insertion operations.

Use a preorder traversal and *searchTreeInsert* to save and then restore a binary search tree in its original shape

Saving a binary search tree and then restoring it to a balanced shape.
Can you do better than the previous algorithm? That is, do you necessarily want the restored tree to have its original shape? Recall that you can organize a given set of data items into binary search trees with many different shapes. Although the shape of a binary search tree has no effect whatsoever on the correctness of the ADT operations, it will affect the efficiency of those operations. Efficient operations are assured if the binary search tree is balanced.

A balanced binary search tree increases the efficiency of the ADT operations

The algorithm that restores a binary search tree to a balanced shape is surprisingly simple. In fact, you can even guarantee a restored tree of minimum height—a condition stronger than balanced. To gain some insight into the solution, consider a full tree, because it is balanced. If you save a full tree in a file by using an inorder traversal, the file will be

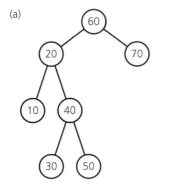

(a)

(b)
```
bst.searchTreeInsert(60);
bst.searchTreeInsert(20);
bst.searchTreeInsert(10);
bst.searchTreeInsert(40);
bst.searchTreeInsert(30);
bst.searchTreeInsert(50);
bst.searchTreeInsert(70);
```

FIGURE 10-35 (a) A binary search tree *bst* ; (b) the sequence of insertions that result in this tree

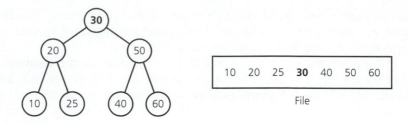

FIGURE 10-36   A full tree saved in a file by using inorder traversal

in sorted order, as Figure 10-36 illustrates. A full tree with exactly $n = 2^h - 1$ nodes for some height h has the exact middle of the data items in its root. The left and right subtrees of the root are full trees of $2^{h-1} - 1$ nodes each (that is, half of $n - 1$, since n is odd or, equivalently, $n/2$). Thus, you can use the following recursive algorithm to create a full binary search tree with n nodes, provided you either know or can determine n beforehand.

Building a full binary search tree

```
readFull(out treePtr:TreeNodePtr, in n:integer)
// Builds a full binary search tree from n sorted values
// in a file. treePtr will point to the tree's root.

   if (n > 0)
   {  // construct the left subtree
      treePtr = pointer to new node with NULL child pointers
      readFull(treePtr->leftChildPtr, n/2)

      // get the root
      Read item from file into treePtr->item

      // construct the right subtree
      readFull(treePtr->rightChildPtr, n/2)
   }  // end if
```

Surprisingly, you can construct the tree directly by reading the sorted data sequentially from the file.

This algorithm for building a full binary search tree is simple, but what can you do if the tree to be restored is not full (that is, if it does not have $n = 2^h - 1$ nodes for some h)? The first thing that comes to mind is that the restored tree should be complete—full up to the last level, with the last level filled in from left to right. Actually, because you care only about minimizing the height of the restored tree, it does not matter where the nodes on the last level go, as Figure 10-37 shows.

The function *readFull* is essentially correct even if the tree is not full. However, you do have to be a bit careful when computing the

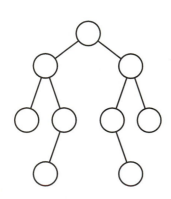

FIGURE 10-37   A tree of minimum height that is not complete

sizes of the left and right subtrees of the tree's root. If *n* is odd, both
subtrees are of size *n*/2, as before. (The root is automatically accounted
for.) If *n* is even, however, you have to account for the root and the fact
that one of the root's subtrees will have one more node than the other.
In this case, you can arbitrarily choose to put the extra node in the left
subtree. The following algorithm makes these compensations:

```
readTree(out treePtr:TreeNodePtr, in n:integer)
// Builds a minimum-height binary search tree from n sorted
// values in a file. treePtr will point to the tree's root.

   if (n > 0)
   {  // construct the left subtree
      treePtr = pointer to new node with NULL child pointers
      readTree(treePtr->leftChildPtr, n/2)

      // get the root
      Read item from file into treePtr->item

      // construct the right subtree
      readTree(treePtr->rightChildPtr, (n-1)/2)
   }  // end if
```

Building a minimum-height binary search tree

You should trace this algorithm and convince yourself that it is correct
for both even and odd values of *n*.

To summarize, you can easily restore a tree as a balanced binary
search tree if the data is sorted—that is, if it has been produced from
the inorder traversal—and you know the number *n* of nodes in the
tree. You need *n* so that you can determine the middle item and, in
turn, the number of nodes in the left and right subtrees of the tree's
root. Knowing these numbers is a simple matter of counting nodes as
you traverse the tree and then saving the number in a file that the
restore operation can read.

Note that *readTree* would be an appropriate protected member
function of *BinarySearchTree*, if you also had a public member function to call it.

The STL Search Algorithms

The Standard Template Library provides a group of operations to find
elements within sorted ranges. All of these functions assume the operator < unless a comparison function object is given as the last parameter.
In that case, the same comparison object must be used for finding the
elements as was used for sorting the elements.

The *binary_search* function returns true if a specified value
appears in the sorted range. Other algorithms are provided to find an
equal range of elements. The *lower_bound* function returns an iterator

to the first occurrence of a value, and *upper_bound* returns an iterator to one past the last occurrence of that value. They both return an iterator to the last element in the container if the value is not found. The function *equal_range* returns a pair of iterators that indicate the first occurrence and one past the last occurrence of a value. The iterators are returned in a *pair* class, which is defined in *<utility>*. This class contains a member function, *make_pair*, which creates a pair of items with previously defined types. The first element of the pair can be accessed by using the variable *first*, and the second element by using the variable *second*. Note that the STL also provides the *find*, *find_if*, and *count* operations to find elements on unsorted ranges. However, these functions run in linear time, whereas the search algorithms for sorted ranges run in logarithmic time. The STL functions listed below use a forward iterator to find an element:

```
bool binary_search(ForIter first, ForIter last, const T& value);
bool binary_search(ForIter first, ForIter last, const T& value,
                  Compare cmp);
// Returns true if value appears in the sorted range
// from first to last.
// Returns false if value is not found.
// A comparison function object may be supplied.

ForIter lower_bound(ForIter first, ForIter last, const T& value);
ForIter lower_bound(ForIter first, ForIter last, const T& value,
                  Compare cmp);
// Returns an iterator pointing to the first occurrence of value
// in the sorted range from first to last.
// Returns last if value is not found.
// A comparison function object may be supplied.

ForIter upper_bound(ForIter first, ForIter last, const T& value);
ForIter upper_bound(ForIter first, ForIter last, const T& value,
                  Compare cmp);
// Returns an iterator pointing to one past the last occurrence
// of value in the sorted range from first to last.
// Returns last if value is not found.
// A comparison function object may be supplied.

pair<ForIter, ForIter> equal_range(ForIter first, ForIter last,
                                 const T& value);
pair<ForIter, ForIter> equal_range(ForIter first, ForIter last,
                                 const T& value, Compare cmp);
// Combines lower_bound and upper_bound to return a pair
// of iterators to the first and one past the last occurrences
```

```
// of value.
// Both iterators point to last if value is not found.
// A comparison function object may be supplied.
```

The following program demonstrates the use of STL search algorithms on sorted ranges:

```cpp
#include <algorithm>
#include <vector>
#include <iostream>
#include <string>

using namespace std;

int main()
{
   //create a vector of strings
   vector<string> s;

   //create two vector iterators
   vector<string>::iterator iter1;
   vector<string>::iterator iter2;

   //add some items to the vector
   s.push_back("juice");
   s.push_back("apples");
   s.push_back("rice");
   s.push_back("juice");
   s.push_back("bread");
   s.push_back("oranges");
   s.push_back("juice");
   s.push_back("milk");
   s.push_back("ice cream");
   s.push_back("carrots");

   //display the vector
   for (iter1 = s.begin(); iter1 != s.end(); iter1++)
     cout << *iter1 <<  endl;

   // sort the vector
   sort(s.begin(), s.end());

   // search item
   string str("juice");

   // perform binary search for item
   // display whether item was found or not (1 or 0)
```

```cpp
      cout << endl << "binary search: "
          << binary_search(s.begin(), s.end(), str) << endl;

      // find range of equal items with lower and upper bounds
      iter1 = lower_bound(s.begin(), s.end(), str);
      iter2 = upper_bound(s.begin(), s.end(), str);

      // display occurrences of item
      cout << endl <<  "Finding lower and upper bounds for "
          << str <<": " << endl;
      int i = 0;
      for (iter1; iter1 != iter2; iter1++)
         ++i;
      cout << i << " occurrences of " << *(--iter1) << endl;

      // find range of equal items with equal_range
      pair<vector<string>::iterator, vector<string>::iterator> eq =
               equal_range(s.begin(), s.end(), str);

      // display occurrences of item
      cout << endl <<  "Finding equal_range for "
          << str << ": " << endl;
      i = 0;
      for (eq.first; eq.first != eq.second; eq.first++)
        ++i;
      cout << i << " occurrences of " << *(--eq.first) << endl;

      return 0;
   } // end main
```

This program produces the following output:

```
    juice
    apples
    rice
    juice
    bread
    oranges
    juice
    milk
    ice cream
    carrots

    binary search: 1

    Finding lower and upper bounds for juice:
    3 occurrences of juice
```

```
Finding equal_range for juice:
3 occurrences of juice
```

10.4 General Trees

This chapter ends with a brief discussion of general trees and their relationship to binary trees. Consider the general tree in Figure 10-38. The three children *B*, *C*, and *D* of node *A*, for example, are siblings. The leftmost child *B* is called the oldest child, or first child, of *A*. One way to implement this tree uses the same node structure that we used for a pointer-based binary tree. That is, each node has two pointers: The left pointer points to the node's oldest child and the right pointer points to the node's next sibling. Thus, you can use the data structure in Figure 10-39 to implement the tree in Figure 10-38. Notice that the structure in Figure 10-39 also represents the binary tree pictured in Figure 10-40.

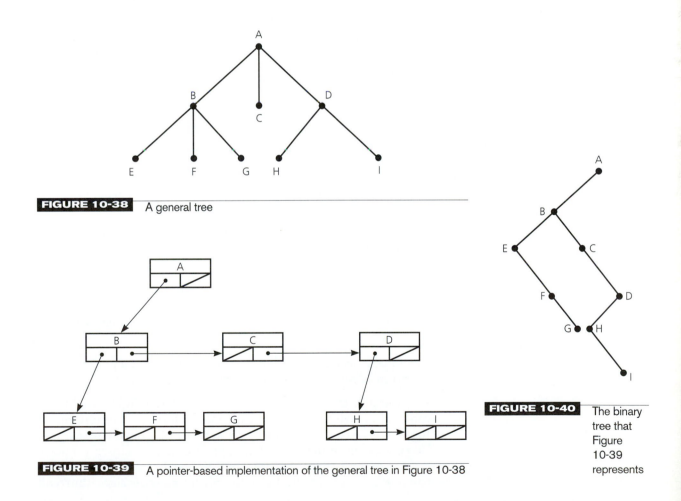

FIGURE 10-38 A general tree

FIGURE 10-39 A pointer-based implementation of the general tree in Figure 10-38

FIGURE 10-40 The binary tree that Figure 10-39 represents

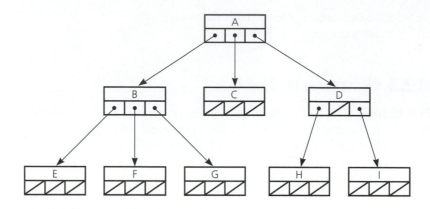

FIGURE 10-41   An implementation of the *n*-ary tree in Figure 10-38

An *n*-ary tree is a generalization of a binary tree whose nodes each can have no more than *n* children. The tree in Figure 10-38 is an *n*-ary tree with $n = 3$. You can, of course, use the implementation just described for an *n*-ary tree. However, because you know the maximum number of children for each node, you can let each node point directly to its children. Figure 10-41 illustrates such a representation for the tree in Figure 10-38. This tree is shorter than the tree in Figure 10-40.

Exercise 35 at the end of this chapter discusses general trees further.

Summary

1. Binary trees provide a hierarchical organization of data, which is important in many applications.

2. The implementation of a binary tree is usually pointer based. If the binary tree is complete, an efficient array-based implementation is possible.

3. Traversing a tree is a useful operation. Intuitively, traversing a tree means to visit every node in the tree. Because the meaning of "visit" is application dependent, you can pass a client-defined *visit* function to the traversal operation.

4. The binary search tree allows you to use a binary search–like algorithm to search for an item with a specified value.

5. Binary search trees come in many shapes. The height of a binary search tree with *n* nodes can range from a minimum of $\lceil \log_2(n+1) \rceil$ to a maximum of *n*. The shape of a binary search tree determines the efficiency of its operations. The closer a binary search tree is to a balanced tree (and the farther it is from a linear structure), the closer the behavior of the *search* algorithm will

be to a binary search (and the farther it will be from the behavior of a linear search).

6. An inorder traversal of a binary search tree visits the tree's nodes in sorted search-key order.

7. The treesort algorithm efficiently sorts an array by using the binary search tree's insertion and traversal operations.

8. If you save a binary search tree's data in a file while performing an inorder traversal of its nodes, you can restore the tree as a binary search tree of minimum height. If you save a binary search tree's data in a file while performing a preorder traversal of its nodes, you can restore the tree to its original form.

Cautions

1. If you use an array-based implementation of a complete binary tree, you must be sure that the tree remains complete as a result of insertions or deletions.

2. Operations on a binary search tree can be quite efficient. In the worst case, however—when the tree approaches a linear shape— the performance of its operations degrades and is comparable to that of a linear linked list. If you must avoid such a situation for a given application, you should use the balancing methods presented in Chapter 12.

Self-Test Exercises

1. Consider the tree in Figure 10-42. What node or nodes are

   a. The tree's root

   b. Parents

   c. Children of the parents in Part b

   d. Siblings

   e. Ancestors of 50

   f. Descendants of 20

   g. Leaves

2. What are the levels of all nodes in the tree in

   a. Figure 10-6b

   b. Figure 10-6c

3. What is the height of the tree in Figure 10-42?

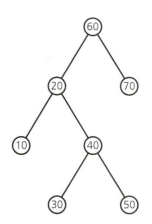

FIGURE 10-42 A tree for Self-Test Exercises 1, 3, 7, and 11, and for Exercises 7 and 14

4. Consider the binary trees in Figure 10-31. Which are complete? Which are full? Which are balanced?

5. What are the preorder, inorder, and postorder traversals of the binary tree in Figure 10-6a?

6. Beginning with an empty binary search tree, what binary search tree is formed when you insert the following values in the order given: J, N, B, A, W, E, T?

7. Starting with an empty binary search tree, in what order should you insert items to get the binary search tree in Figure 10-42?

8. Represent the full binary tree in Figure 10-36 with an array.

9. What complete binary tree does the array in Figure 10-43 represent?

5	1	2	8	6	10	3	9	4	7
0	1	2	3	4	5	6	7	8	9

FIGURE 10-43   An array for Self-Test Exercise 9

10. Is the tree in Figure 10-44 a binary search tree?

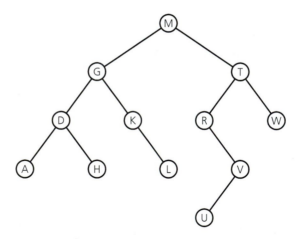

FIGURE 10-44   A tree for Self-Test Exercise 10 and for Exercise 2a

11. Using the tree in Figure 10-42, trace the algorithm that searches a binary search tree given a search key of

   a. 30

   b. 15

In each case, list the nodes in the order in which the search visits them.

12. Trace the treesort algorithm as it sorts the following array into ascending order: 20 80 40 25 60 30.

13. **a.** What binary search tree results when you execute `readTree` with a file of the six integers 2, 4, 6, 8, 10, 12?

   b. Is the resulting tree's height a minimum? Is the tree complete? Is it full?

Exercises

1. Write pre- and postconditions for the ADT binary tree operations.

2. What are the preorder, inorder, and postorder traversals of the binary trees in

   a. Figure 10-44   **b.** Figure 10-6b   **c.** Figure 10-6c

3. Consider the binary search tree in Figure 10-45. The numbers simply label the nodes so that you can reference them; they do not indicate the contents of the nodes.

   a. Which node must contain the inorder successor of the value in the root? Explain.

   b. In what order will an inorder traversal visit the nodes of this tree? Indicate this order by listing the labels of the nodes in the order that they are visited.

4. Beginning with an empty binary search tree, what binary search tree is formed when you insert the following values in the order given?

   a. W, T, N, J, E, B, A

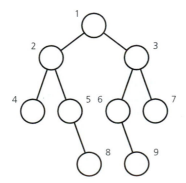

FIGURE 10-45   A binary search tree for Exercise 3

b. W, T, N, A, B, E, J

c. A, B, W, J, N, T, E

5. Draw the binary search tree that is formed when the following values are inserted in the order given: 4, 13, 5, 3, 7, 30.

6. Arrange nodes that contain the letters A, C, E, F, L, V, and Z into two binary search trees: one that has maximum height and one that has minimum height.

7. Consider the binary search tree in Figure 10-42.

   a. What tree results after you insert the nodes 80, 65, 75, 45, 35, and 25, in that order?

   b. After inserting the nodes mentioned in Part a, what tree results when you delete the nodes 50 and 20?

8. **a.** Beginning with an empty binary search tree, what binary search tree is formed when the following data is inserted in the order given? C, S, A, M, V, H.

   b. Assuming you have already made the insertions indicated in Part a, what does the tree look like after V and M are deleted?

9. **a.** Beginning with an empty binary search tree, what binary search tree is formed when the following data is inserted in the order given? 8, 13, 6, 10, 21, 19.

   b. Given a search key of 12, trace the algorithm that searches the binary search tree that you created in Part a. List the nodes in the order in which the search visits them.

10. If you delete an item from a binary search tree and then insert it back into the tree, will you ever change the shape of the tree?

11. Given the ADT binary tree operations as defined in this chapter, what tree or trees does the following sequence of statements produce?

```
typedef int TreeItemType;   // tree item
BinaryTree tree1, tree2;

tree2.setRootData(9);
tree2.attachLeft(10);
tree2.attachRight(8);
tree2.getLeftSubtree().attachLeft(2);
tree2.getLeftSubtree().getLeftSubtree().attachLeft(5);
tree2.getLeftSubtree().getLeftSubtree().attachRight(3);
tree2.getRightSubtree().attachLeft(6);
tree2.getRightSubtree().attachRight(7);
```

```
tree1.setRootData(1);
tree1.attachLeft(2);
tree1.attachRight(3);

BinaryTree bTree(4, tree2, tree1);
```

12. Consider a function *isLeaf()* that returns *true* if an instance of *BinaryTree* is a one-node tree—that is, if it consists of only a leaf—and returns *false* otherwise.

   a. Add a declaration of *isLeaf* to *BinaryTree* so that the function is available to clients of the class.

   b. Write the implementation of *isLeaf* as it would appear in the implementation file for *BinaryTree*.

   c. If *isleaf* were not a member of *BinaryTree*, would a client of the class be able to implement *isLeaf*? Explain.

13. The operation

   searchTreeReplace(in replacementItem:KeyType):boolean

   locates, if possible, the item in a binary search tree with the same search key as *replacementItem*. If the tree contains such an item, *searchTreeReplace* replaces it with *replacementItem*. Thus, all but the search key of the original item is updated.

   a. Add the operation *searchTreeReplace* to the pointer-based implementation of the ADT binary search tree given in this chapter. The operation should replace an item without altering the tree structure.

   b. Instead of adding *searchTreeReplace* as an operation of the ADT binary search tree, implement it as a client of *BinarySearchTree*. Will the shape of the binary tree remain the same?

14. Suppose that you traverse the binary search tree in Figure 10-42 and write the data item in each node visited to a file. You plan to read this file later and create a new binary search tree by using the ADT binary search tree operation *searchTreeInsert*. In creating the file, in what order should you traverse the tree so that the new tree will have exactly the same shape and nodes as the original tree? What does the file look like after the original tree is traversed?

15. Consider an array-based implementation of a binary search tree *bst*. Figure 10-11 presents such a representation for a particular binary search tree.

a. Depict the array in an array-based implementation for the binary search tree in Figure 10-20a.

b. Show the effect of each of the following sequential operations on the array in Part a of this exercise. For simplicity, assume that tree items are names instead of records.

```
bst.searchTreeInsert("Doug");
bst.searchTreeDelete("Nancy", Success);
bst.searchTreeDelete("Bob", Success);
bst.searchTreeInsert("Sarah");
```

c. Repeat Parts a and b of this exercise for the tree in Figure 10-20b.

d. Write an inorder traversal algorithm for this array-based implementation.

16. Duplicates in an ADT could mean either identical items or, more subtly, items that are records with identical search keys but with differences in other fields. If duplicates are allowed in a binary search tree, it is important to have a convention that determines the relationship between the duplicates. Items that duplicate the root of a tree should either all be in the left subtree or all be in the right subtree, and, of course, this property must hold for every subtree.

a. Why is this convention critical to the effective use of the binary search tree?

b. This chapter stated that you can delete an item from a binary search tree by replacing it with the item whose search key either immediately follows or immediately precedes the search key of the item to be deleted. If duplicates are allowed, however, the choice between inorder successor and inorder predecessor is no longer arbitrary. How does the convention of putting duplicates in either the left or right subtree affect this choice?

17. Complete the trace of the nonrecursive inorder traversal algorithm that Figure 10-15 began. Show the contents of the implicit stack as the traversal progresses.

18. Implement in C++ the nonrecursive inorder traversal algorithm for a binary tree that was presented in this chapter. (See Exercise 17.)

19. Given the recursive nature of a binary tree, a good strategy for writing a C++ function that operates on a binary tree is often first to write a recursive definition of the task. Given such a recursive definition, a C++ implementation is often straightforward.

Write recursive definitions that perform the following tasks on arbitrary binary trees. Implement the definitions in C++. Must your functions be members of *BinaryTree*? For simplicity, assume that each data item in the tree is a single integer and that there are no duplicates.

a. Count the number of nodes in the tree. (*Hint*: If the tree is empty, the count is 0. If the tree is not empty, the count is 1 plus the number of nodes in the root's left subtree plus the number of nodes in the root's right subtree.)

b. Compute the height of a tree.

c. Find the maximum element.

d. Find the sum of the elements.

⋆**e.** Find the average of the elements.

f. Find a specific item.

g. Determine whether one item is an ancestor of another (that is, whether one item is in the subtree rooted at the other item).

h. Determine the highest level that is full or, equivalently, has the maximum number of nodes for that level. (See Exercise 25.)

20. Consider a nonempty binary tree with two types of nodes: min nodes and max nodes. Each node has an integer value initially associated with it. You can define the value of such a minimax tree as follows:

▪ If the root is a min node, the value of the tree is equal to the *minimum* of

□ The integer stored in the root

□ The value of the left subtree, but only if it is nonempty

□ The value of the right subtree, but only if it is nonempty

▪ If the root is a max node, the value of the tree is equal to the *maximum* of the above three values.

a. Compute the value of the minimax tree in Figure 10–46. Each node is labeled with its initial value.

b. Write a general solution in C++ for representing and evaluating these trees.

⋆21. A binary search tree with a given set of data items can have several different structures that conform to the definition of a binary search tree. If you are given a list of data items, does at least one binary search tree whose preorder traversal matches the order of the items on your list always exist? Is there ever more than one binary search tree that has the given preorder traversal?

★22. How many differently shaped, n-node binary trees are possible? How many differently shaped, n-node binary search trees are possible? (Write recursive definitions.)

23. Write pseudocode for a function that performs a range query for a binary search tree. That is, the function should visit all items that have a search key in a given range of values (such as all values between 100 and 1,000).

24. Prove Theorems 10-2 and 10-3 by using induction.

25. What is the maximum number of nodes that a binary tree can have at level n? Prove your answer by using induction. Use this fact to do the following:

a. Rewrite the formal definition of a complete tree of height h.

b. Derive a closed form for the formula

$$\sum_{i=1}^{h} 2^{i-1}$$

What is the significance of this sum?

26. Prove by induction that a binary tree with n nodes has exactly $n + 1$ empty subtrees (or, in C++ terms, $n + 1$ *NULL* pointers).

27. A binary tree is strictly binary if every nonleaf node has exactly two children. Prove by induction on the number of leaves that a strictly binary tree with n leaves has exactly $2n - 1$ nodes.

28. Consider two algorithms for traversing a binary tree. Both are nonrecursive algorithms that use an extra ADT for bookkeeping. Both algorithms have the following basic form:

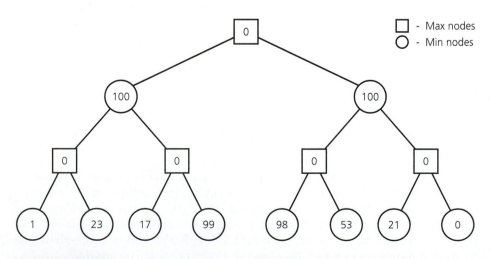

FIGURE 10-46   A minimax tree for Exercise 20

```
Put the root of the tree on the list
while (the ADT is not empty)
{   Remove a node from the ADT and call it n
    Visit n
    if (n has a left child)
        Put the child in the ADT
    if (n has a right child)
        Put the child in the ADT
}  // end while
```

The difference between the two algorithms is the method for choosing a node *n* to remove from the ADT.

Algorithm 1: Remove the newest (most recently added) node from the ADT.

Algorithm 2: Remove the oldest (earliest added) node from the ADT.

a. In what order would each algorithm visit the nodes of the tree in Figure 10-19?

b. For each algorithm, describe an appropriate ADT for doing the bookkeeping. What should the ADT data be? Do not use extra memory unnecessarily for the bookkeeping ADT. Also, note that the traversal of a tree should not alter the tree in any way.

29. Describe how to save a binary tree in a file so that you can later restore the tree to its original shape. Compare the efficiencies of saving and restoring a binary tree and a binary search tree.

30. Design another algorithm to delete nodes from a binary search tree. This algorithm differs from the one described in this chapter when the node *N* has two children. First let *N*'s right child take the place of the deleted node *N* in the same manner in which you delete a node with one child. Next reconnect *N*'s left child (along with its subtree, if any) to the left side of the node containing the inorder successor of the search key in *N*.

31. Write iterative functions to perform insertion and deletion operations on a binary search tree.

32. Use public inheritance to derive the class `BinarySearchTree` from the class `BinaryTree`. Is the definition of `BinaryTree` sufficient for this problem, or do you need to revise `BinaryTree`?

33. If you know in advance that you often access a given item in a binary search tree several times in a row before accessing a different item, you will search for the same item repeatedly. One way to address this problem is to add an extra bookkeeping component to your implementation. That is, you can maintain a last-accessed pointer that will always reference the last item that any binary search tree operation accessed. Whenever you perform

such an operation, you can check the search key of the item most recently accessed before performing the operation.

Revise the implementation of the ADT binary search tree to add this new feature by adding the data member `lastAccessed` to the class.

34. The motivation for a doubly linked list is the need to locate and delete a node in a list without traversing the list. The analogy for a binary search tree is to maintain parent pointers. That is, every node except the root will have a pointer to its parent in the tree. Write insertion and deletion operations for this tree.

35. A node in a general tree, such as the one in Figure 10-38, can have an arbitrary number of children.

   a. Describe a C++ implementation of a general tree in which every node contains an array of child pointers. Write a recursive preorder traversal method for this implementation. What are the advantages and disadvantages of this implementation?

   b. Consider the implementation of a general tree that this chapter described. Each node has two pointers: The left pointer points to the node's oldest child and the right pointer points to the node's next sibling. Write a recursive preorder traversal method for this implementation.

   c. Consider a binary tree T in which every node has at most two children. Compare the oldest-child/next-sibling representation of T, as Part b describes, to the left-child/right-child representation of a binary tree, as this chapter describes. Does one representation simplify the implementation of the ADT operations? Are the two representations ever the same?

★36. Implement an inorder traversal operation for a binary search tree that permits `visit` to delete the node visited.

★37. Write `BinaryTree` and `BinarySearchTree` as class templates.

★38. Add an overloaded == operator to the class `BinaryTree`.

Programming Problems

1. Write an array-based implementation of the ADT binary search tree that uses dynamic memory allocation. Use a data structure like the one in Figure 10-11.

2. Repeat Programming Problem 1 for complete binary trees.

3. Write a template version of the pointer-based binary search tree. Replace `TreeItemType` with the template parameter `<T>`.

4. Write a C++ program that learns about a universe of your choice by asking the user yes/no questions. For example, your program might learn about animals by having the following dialogue with its user. (User responses are in uppercase.)

```
Think of an animal and I will guess it.
Does it have legs? YES
Is it a cat? YES
I win! Continue? YES

Think of an animal and I will guess it.
Does it have legs? NO
Is it a snake? YES
I win! Continue? YES

Think of an animal and I will guess it.
Does it have legs? NO
Is it a snake? NO
I give up. What is it? EARTHWORM
Please type a question whose answer is yes for an
earthworm and no for a snake:
DOES IT LIVE UNDERGROUND?
Continue? YES

Think of an animal and I will guess it.
Does it have legs? NO
Does it live underground? NO
Is it a snake? NO
I give up. What is it? FISH
Please type a question whose answer is yes for a
fish and no for a snake:
DOES IT LIVE IN WATER?
Continue? NO

Good-bye.
```

The program begins with minimal knowledge about animals: It knows that cats have legs and snakes do not. When the program incorrectly guesses "snake" the next time, it asks for the answer and also asks for a way to distinguish between snakes and earthworms.

The program builds a binary tree of questions and animals. A YES response to a question is stored in the question's left child; a NO response is stored in the question's right child.

5. Write a program that maintains the names, addresses, and telephone numbers of your friends and relatives and thus serves as an address book. You should be able to enter, delete, modify, or search this data. The person's name should be the search key, and initially you can assume that the names are unique. The program should be able to save the address book in a file for use later.

Design a class to represent the people in the address book and another class to represent the address book itself. This class should contain a binary search tree of people as a data member.

You can enhance this problem by adding birth dates to the database and by adding an operation that lists everyone who satisfies a given criterion. For example, list people born in a given month or people who live in a given state. You should also be able to list everyone in the database.

6. Repeat Programming Problem 4 using an STL *vector* to represent the address book. Each element in the vector represents a person. Use the STL search algorithms presented in this chapter to perform the necessary operations. Note that a comparison function must be supplied for the vector elements. This can be accomplished by overriding an operator function as a member of the class representing a person.

7. Write a program that provides a way for you to store and retrieve telephone numbers. Design a user interface that provides the following operations:

Add: Adds a person's name and phone number to the phone book.

Delete: Deletes a given person's name and phone number from the phone book, given only the name.

Find: Locates a person's phone number, given only the person's name.

Change: Changes a person's phone number, given the person's name and new phone number.

Quit: Quits the application, after first saving the phone book in a text file.

You can proceed as follows:

- Design and implement the class *Person*, which represents the name and phone number of a person. You will store instances of this class in the phone book.

- Design and implement the class *Book*, which represents the phone book. The class should contain a binary search tree as a data member. This tree contains the people in the book.

- Add member functions that use a text file to save and restore the tree.

- Design and implement the class *UserInterface*, which provides the program's user interface.

The program should read data from a text file when it begins and save data into a text file when the user quits the program.

CHAPTER 11

Tables and Priority Queues

PREVIEW

This chapter considers the ADT table, which is appropriate for problems that must manage data by value. Several table implementations—which use arrays, linked lists, and binary search trees—will be presented, along with their advantages and disadvantages.

To make an intelligent choice among the various possible table implementations, you must analyze the efficiency with which each of the implementations supports the table operations. For example, this chapter analyzes the efficiency of array-based and pointer-based table implementations and concludes that, in many applications, the implementations do not support the table operations as efficiently as possible. This conclusion motivates the use of a more sophisticated table implementation based on the binary search tree.

This chapter also introduces an important variation of the table, the ADT priority queue. This ADT provides operations to retrieve and delete easily the item with the largest value. Although you can implement a priority queue by using a binary search tree, a simpler tree structure, known as a heap, is often more appropriate for this purpose.

11.1 The ADT Table

The previous chapter introduced value-oriented ADTs whose operations are of the form

- Insert a data item containing the value x.

- Delete a data item containing the value x.

- Ask a question about a data item containing the value x.

Applications that require such value-oriented operations are extremely prevalent, as you might imagine. For example, the tasks

- *Find the phone number of John Smith*

- *Delete all the information about the employee with ID number 12908*

involve values instead of positions. This section presents another example of a value-oriented ADT.

The name of an ADT often suggests images of familiar objects that possess properties resembling those of the ADT. For example, the name "stack" might remind you of a stack of dishes. What does the name "table" bring to mind? If you had heard the question before you began reading this book, you might have answered, "My favorite mahogany coffee table." However, your answer now should be something more like, "A table of the major cities of the world," such as the one in Figure 11-1.

This table of cities contains several pieces of information about each city. Its design allows you to look up this information. For example, if you wanted to know the population of London, you could scan the column of city names, starting at the top, until you came to London. Because the cities are listed in alphabetical order, you could also mimic a binary search. You could begin the search near the middle of the table, determine in which half London lies, and recursively apply the binary search to the appropriate half. As you know, a binary search is far more efficient than scanning the entire table from the beginning.

City	Country	Population
Athens	Greece	2,500,000
Barcelona	Spain	1,800,000
Cairo	Egypt	9,500,000
London	England	9,400,000
New York	U.S.A.	7,300,000
Paris	France	2,200,000
Rome	Italy	2,800,000
Toronto	Canada	3,200,000
Venice	Italy	300,000

FIGURE 11-1   An ordinary table of cities

If, however, you wanted to find which of the major cities are in Italy, you would have no choice but to scan the entire table. The alphabetical order of the city names does not help you for this problem at all. The table's arrangement facilitates the search for a given city, but other types of questions require a complete scan of the table.

The ADT **table**, or **dictionary**, also allows you to look up information easily and has a special operation for this purpose. Typically, the items in the ADT table are records that contain several pieces of data. You can facilitate the retrieval of an item by basing the search on a specified search key. In the table of cities, for example, you could designate `City` as the search key if you often needed to retrieve the information about a city. You can devise implementations of a table that allow the rapid retrieval of the item(s) whose search key matches some specified value. However, if you need to retrieve item(s) based on a value of a non-search-key portion of each record, you will have to inspect the entire table. Therefore, the choice of a search key sends the ADT implementer the following message:

The ADT table uses a search key to identify its items

> *Arrange the data to facilitate the search for an item, given the value of its search key.*

The basic operations that define the ADT table are as follows:

KEY CONCEPTS

ADT Table Operations

1. Create an empty table.

2. Destroy a table.

3. Determine whether a table is empty.

4. Determine the number of items in a table.

5. Insert a new item into a table.

6. Delete the item with a given search key from a table.

7. Retrieve the item with a given search key from a table.

8. Traverse the items in a table in sorted search-key order.

For simplicity, we will assume that all items in the table have distinct search keys. Under this assumption, the insertion operation must reject an attempt to insert an item whose search key is the same as an item already in the table. The following pseudocode specifies in more detail the operations for an ADT table of items with distinct search keys. Figure 11-2 shows a UML diagram for the class *Table*.

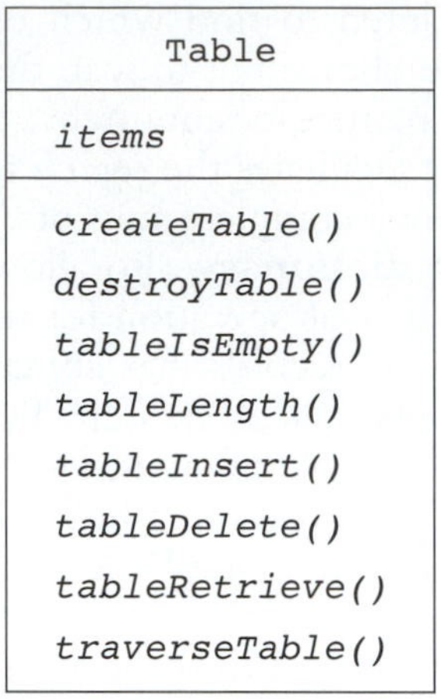

Table
items
createTable()
destroyTable()
tableIsEmpty()
tableLength()
tableInsert()
tableDelete()
tableRetrieve()
traverseTable()

FIGURE 11-2   UML diagram for class *Table*

KEY CONCEPTS

Pseudocode for the ADT Table Operations

```
// TableItemType is the type of the items stored in the table
+createTable()
// Creates an empty table.

+destroyTable()
// Destroys a table.

+tableIsEmpty():boolean {query}
// Determines whether a table is empty.

+tableLength():integer {query}
// Determines the number of items in a table.

+tableInsert(in newItem:TableItemType) throw TableException
// Inserts newItem into a table whose items have distinct
// search keys that differ from newItem's search key.
// Throws TableException if the insertion is not
// successful.
```

continued on next page

```
continued from previous page

+tableDelete(in searchKey:KeyType) throw TableException
// Deletes from a table the item whose search key equals
// searchKey. If no such item exists, the function throws
// TableException.

+tableRetrieve(in searchKey:KeyType,
             out tableItem:TableItemType)
             throw TableExeption {query}
// Retrieves into tableItem the item in a table whose search
// key equals searchKey. If no such item exists, the function
// throws TableException.

+traverseTable(in visit:FunctionType)
// Traverses a table in sorted search-key order
// and calls the function visit once for each item.
```

You should realize that these operations are only one possible set of table operations. The client may require either a subset of these operations or other operations not listed here to fit the application at hand. It may also be convenient to modify the definitions of some of the operations. For example, these operations assume that no two table items have the same values in their search keys. However, in many applications it is quite reasonable to expect duplicate search-key values. If this is the case, you must redefine several of the operations to eliminate the ambiguity that would arise from duplicate search-key values. For example, which item should *tableRetrieve* return if several items have the specified value in their search keys? You should tailor your definition of the ADT table to the problem at hand.

Various sets of table operations are possible

Our table assumes distinct search keys

Other tables could allow duplicate search keys

Although the operations *tableInsert*, *tableDelete*, and *tableRetrieve* in the previous set of operations are sufficient for some applications, you cannot do several significant things without additional operations. For instance, you cannot perform an important task such as

Display all the table items

because you cannot retrieve a data item unless you know the value of its search key. Thus, you cannot display the entire table unless you can traverse the table.

The *traverseTable* operation visits each item in the table once. In defining this operation, you must specify the order in which *traverse-Table* should visit the items. One common specification is to visit the items sorted by search key, but perhaps you do not care in what order *traverseTable* visits the items. As you will see, the way

traverseTable visits all table items in a specified order

you define *traverseTable*—if you request it at all—may affect the way that you implement the table.

Like the traversal operations in the previous chapter, *traverse-Table* has a *visit* function as its argument. Because *visit* can do any number of things—including access the table via the ADT operations—*traverseTable* is a versatile operation. This versatility is illustrated with three brief examples, in which the previous table of major cities is an ADT table.

The concept of a search key for the table items is essential to the implementation of the table. It is important that the value of the search key remain the same as long as the item is stored in the table. Changing the search key of an existing element in the table could make that element or other table elements impossible to find. Thus the search-key value should not be modifiable. This suggests the use of a class for items of the table; the class will contain the search key as a data member and a method for accessing it. This is the same class that appeared in Chapter 10:

```cpp
#include <string>
using namespace std;
typedef string KeyType;

class KeyedItem
{
public:
   KeyedItem() {};
   KeyedItem(const KeyType& keyValue):
      searchKey(keyValue) { }
   KeyType getKey() const
   {
      return searchKey;
   }  // end getKey
private:
   KeyType searchKey;
};  // end class
```

Note that classes that extend *KeyedItem* will have only the constructor available for initializing the search key. Thus the search-key value cannot be modified once an item is created, which meets our requirement.

Suppose that the items in the table are instances of the following class:

```cpp
#include <string>
using namespace std;

class City
{
public:
   . . .
```

```
    // functions for accessing private data members
private:
    string cityName; // city's name
    string country;  // city's country
    int    pop;      // city's population
};  // end class
```

and you want to perform tasks on this table such as

Tasks that use *City* as the search key

- *Display, in alphabetical order, the name of each city and its population*

- *Increase the population of each city by 10 percent*

- *Delete all cities with a population of less than 1,000,000*

Each task suggests that you designate *cityName* as the search key. The class *City* contains all of the information for a city, including the city name (returned by the inherited method *key*), country, and population. Here is a C++ definition of *City*:

```
class City : public KeyedItem
{
public:
    City() { }
    City(const string& name,
         const string& ctry,
         const int& num)
         :KeyedItem(name), country(ctry), pop(num) { }
    string cityName() const;
    int getPopulation() const;
    void setPopulation(int newPop);
private:
    // city's name is search-key value
    string country;  // city's country
    int    pop;      // city's population
};  // end class
```

The first task requires you to write the city names in alphabetical order. Thus, *traverseTable* must visit items alphabetically by search key. To perform the first task, you pass to *traverseTable* the name of the function *displayItem*, which appears in pseudocode as follows:

```
displayItem(in anItem:TableItemType)
```

First task

```
    Display anItem.cityName()
    Display anItem.getPopulation()
```

The visitation order that *traverseTable* uses is immaterial for the other two tasks. To perform the second task, you pass to *traverseTable* the name of the function *updatePopulation*:

Second task

```
updatePopulation(inout anItem:TableItemType)

    anItem.setPopulation(1.1 * anItem.getPopulation())
```

To perform the third task, you pass to *traverseTable* the name of the function *deleteSmall*:

Third task

```
deleteSmall(inout t:Table, in anItem::TableItemType)

    if (anItem.getPopulation() < 1,000,000)
        t.tableDelete(anItem)
```

However, this task is not as simple as it may seem. By deleting an item, you alter the table during the traversal. Which item will *traverseTable* visit next? Clearly it should visit the one after the deleted item, but will *traverseTable* skip that item? The traversal of a table while deleting parts of it is left as a difficult exercise.

Selecting an Implementation

In the previous chapters, ADT implementations were either array based or pointer based. That is, you used either an array or a linked list to store the ADT's items. Such implementations are called **linear** because they represent items one after another in a data structure and thus mirror the flat, listlike appearance of the table of cities in Figure 11-1.

Linear implementations of a table are certainly possible and fall into four categories:

Four categories of linear implementations

- Unsorted, array based

- Unsorted, pointer based

- Sorted (by search key), array based

- Sorted (by search key), pointer based

The unsorted implementations store the items in no particular order; they can insert a new item into any convenient location. The sorted implementations, however, must insert a new item into its proper position as determined by the value of its search key. Whether sorted or unsorted, the array-based and pointer-based linear implementations have the basic structures shown in Figure 11-3. Both implementations maintain a count of the present number of items in the table. As you will see, the unsorted and sorted implementations have their relative advantages and disadvantages.

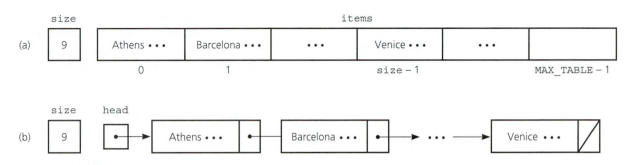

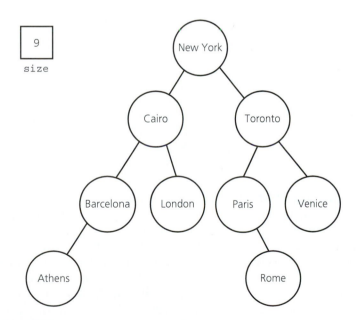

FIGURE 11-3 The data members for two sorted linear implementations of the ADT table for the data in Figure 11-1: (a) array based; (b) pointer based

At this point in your study of ADTs, you have other choices for a table implementation. For instance, you can implement the ADT table by using an ADT list, sorted list, or binary search tree. The binary search tree implementation, as illustrated in Figure 11-4, is an example of a nonlinear implementation and offers several advantages over linear implementations. Among these advantages is the opportunity to reuse the implementation of the ADT binary search tree given in Chapter 10. Implementations based on the ADTs list and sorted list also share this advantage, and they are left for you to consider as exercises.

A binary search tree implementation is nonlinear

FIGURE 11-4 The data members for a binary search tree implementation of the ADT table for the data in Figure 11-1

A major goal of this chapter is to indicate how the requirements of a particular application influence the selection of an implementation. The discussion here elaborates on the comments made in Chapter 9 in the section "Keeping Your Perspective." Some applications require all of the ADT table operations given earlier; others require either a subset of them or additional operations. Before choosing an implementation of the ADT table, you as problem solver should carefully analyze which operations you really need for the application at hand. It is tempting to want all possible operations, but this strategy is a poor one, because often one implementation supports some of the operations more efficiently than another implementation does. Therefore, if you include an operation that you never use, you might end up with an implementation of the ADT that does not best suit your purpose.

In addition to knowing what operations are needed for a given application, the ADT implementer should know approximately how often the application will perform each operation. Although some applications may require many occurrences of every operation, other applications may not. For example, if you maintained a table of major cities such as the one in Figure 11-1, you would expect to perform many more retrieval operations than insertions or deletions. Thus, if you seldom insert items, you can tolerate a table implementation that results in an inefficient insertion operation, as long as frequently used operations are efficient. Of course, as Chapter 9 mentioned, if an ADT operation is to be used in a life-or-death situation, that operation must be efficient, even if you rarely need it. The necessary operations, their expected frequency of occurrence, and their required response times are therefore some factors that influence which implementation of an ADT you should select for a particular application. You should, however, remain conscious of factors other than efficiency, as discussed in Chapter 9.

Consider now several different application scenarios, each of which requires a particular mix of the table operations. The analysis of various implementations of the ADT table will illustrate some of the basic concerns of the analysis of algorithms. You will see, given an application, how to select an implementation that supports in a reasonably efficient manner the required mix of table operations.

Scenario A: Insertion and traversal in no particular order. Mary's sorority plans to raise money for a local charity. Tired of previous fundraisers, Mary suggests a brainstorming session to discover a new money-making strategy. As sorority members voice their ideas, Mary records them by inserting each new thought into a table. Later, she will print a report of all the ideas currently in the table. Assume that the organization of the report is irrelevant—the items can be sorted or unsorted. Also assume that operations such as retrieval, deletion, or traversal in sorted order either do not occur or occur so infrequently that they do not influence your choice of an implementation.

For this application, maintaining the items in a sorted order has no advantage. In fact, by not maintaining a sorted order, the *tableInsert*

What operations are needed?

How often is each operation required?

An unsorted order is efficient

operation can be quite efficient. For either unsorted linear implementation, you can insert a new item into any convenient location. For an unsorted array-based implementation, you can easily insert a new item after the last item in the array—that is, at location $items[size]$. Figure 11-5a shows the result of this insertion after $size$ has been updated. For a pointer-based implementation, you can simply insert a new item at the beginning of the linked list. As Figure 11-5b illustrates, the head pointer points to the new item, and the new item points to the item previously first on the list. Thus, not only can you insert a new item quickly into either unsorted implementation of a table, but also the $tableInsert$ operation is O(1): It requires a constant time for either implementation regardless of the table size.

Should you choose the array-based or the pointer-based implementation? As you have seen with other ADTs, an implementation that uses dynamically allocated memory is appropriate if you do not have a good estimate of the maximum possible size of the table. Mary's brainstorming session likely falls into this category. On the other hand, if you know that the table's maximum size is not drastically larger than its expected size,[1] the choice is mostly a matter of style. An array-based implementation requires less space than a pointer-based implementation, because no explicit pointer is stored. The extra cost of this pointer relative to the length of the data records, however, is insignificant in most situations because long records are typical.

Array based versus pointer based

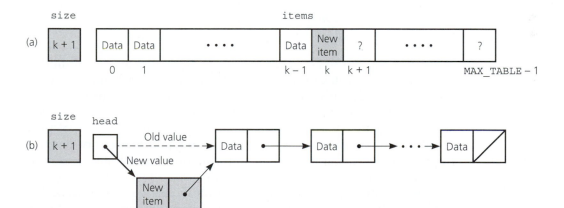

FIGURE 11-5   Insertion for unsorted linear implementations: (a) array based; (b) pointer based

---

[1] Chapter 4, in the section "Comparing Array-Based and Pointer-Based Implementations," discussed how the expected and maximum number of items in an ADT affect an array-based implementation.

Should you consider a binary search tree implementation for this application? Because such an implementation orders the table items, it does more work than the application requires. In fact, as you saw in Chapter 10, insertion into a binary search tree is $O(\log n)$ in the average case.

Scenario B: Retrieval.   When you use a word processor's thesaurus to look up synonyms for a word, you use a retrieval operation. If an ADT table represents the thesaurus, each table item is a record that contains both the word—which is the search key—and the word's synonyms. Frequent retrieval operations require a table implementation that allows you to search efficiently for an item, given its search-key value. Typically, you cannot alter the thesaurus, so no insertion or deletion operations are necessary.

A sorted array-based implementation can use a binary search

For an array-based implementation, you can use a binary search to retrieve a particular word's record, if the array is sorted. On the other hand, for a pointer-based implementation, you must traverse the linked list from its beginning until you encounter the word in the list. The binary search performs this retrieval in significantly less time than is required to traverse a linked list. Two questions come to mind at this point:

Questions

1. Is a binary search of a linked list possible?

2. How much more efficient is a binary search of an array than a sequential search of a linked list?

A binary search is impractical with a pointer-based implementation

Can you perform a binary search under a pointer-based implementation? Yes, but too inefficiently to be practical. Consider the very first step of the binary search algorithm:

```
Look at the "middle" item in the table
```

If n items are in a linked list, how can you possibly get to the middle item of the list? You can traverse the list from the beginning until you have visited $n/2$ items. But, as you will see in the answer to the second question, just this first step will often take longer than the entire binary search of an array. Further, you would have the same problem of finding the "middle" element at each recursive step. It is thus not practical to perform a binary search for the linear pointer-based implementation. This observation is extremely significant.

On the other hand, if n items are in an array *items*, the middle item is at location $n/2$ and can be accessed directly. Thus, a binary search of an array requires considerably less time than an algorithm that must inspect every item in the table. What does "considerably less time" mean? As you know, without the ability to perform a binary search, you may have to inspect every item in the table, either to locate an item with a particular value in its search key or to determine that such an item is not present. In other words, if a table has size n, you will have to inspect as many as n items; thus, such a search is $O(n)$. How much better can you do with a binary search? Recall from Chapter 9 that a binary search is $O(\log_2 n)$ in its worst case and that an $O(\log_2 n)$ algorithm is substantially more efficient than an $O(n)$ algorithm. For example, $\log_2 1024 = 10$ and $\log_2 1,048,576 = 20$. For a large table, the binary search has an enormous advantage.

Because a thesaurus is probably large, you must choose an implementation for which a binary search is practical. As you have just seen, this observation eliminates the linear pointer-based implementations. The sorted array-based implementation is fine here, because you know the size of the thesaurus.

If you know the table's maximum size, a sorted array-based implementation is appropriate for frequent retrievals

The binary search tree implementation is also a good choice for retrieval-dominated applications. As you saw in Chapter 10, searching a binary search tree is $O(\log n)$ if the tree is balanced. Because the thesaurus does not change, you can create a balanced tree that remains balanced and be assured of an efficient search. Although the pointers in a binary search tree add a space cost, as Scenario A mentioned, this cost is relatively insignificant when the data records are large.

If you do not know the table's maximum size, use a binary search tree implementation

Scenario C: Insertion, deletion, retrieval, and traversal in sorted order.

If your local library has computerized its catalog of books, you perform a retrieval operation when you access this catalog. The library staff uses insertion and deletion operations to update the catalog and a traversal to save the entire catalog in a file. Presumably, retrieval is the most frequent operation, but the other operations are not infrequent enough to ignore. (Otherwise, this scenario would be the same as Scenario B!)

To insert into a table an item that has the value *X* in its search key, you must first determine where the item belongs in the table's sorted order. Similarly, to delete from the table an item that has the value *X* in its search key, you must first locate the item. Thus, both the `table-Insert` and `tableDelete` operations perform the following steps:

1. Find the appropriate position in the table.

2. Insert into (or delete from) this position.

Both insertion and deletion perform these two steps

Step 1 is far more efficient if the table implementation is array based instead of pointer based. For an array-based implementation, you can use a binary search to determine—in the case of insertion—where the new item *X* belongs and—in the case of deletion—where the item is located. On the other hand, for a pointer-based implementation, you know from the discussion in Scenario B that a binary search is impractical, and so you must traverse the list from its beginning until you encounter the appropriate location in the list. You also saw in Scenario B that it takes significantly less time to perform a binary search of an array than it does to traverse a linked list.

Use an array-based implementation for Step 1

Thus, because it facilitates a binary search, the array-based implementation is superior with respect to Step 1 of `tableInsert` and `tableDelete`. However, as you may have guessed, the pointer-based implementation is better for Step 2, the actual insertion or deletion of

Use a pointer-based implementation for Step 2

the item. Under the array-based implementation, `tableInsert` must shift array items to make room for the new item (see Figure 11-6a), while `tableDelete` must shift array items to fill in the gap created when the item is removed. The worst case would require that every array item be shifted. On the other hand, under the pointer-based implementation, you can accomplish this second step simply by changing at most two pointers, as Figure 11-6b illustrates.

When you take Steps 1 and 2 together, you will find that the sorted array-based and sorted pointer-based implementations of `tableInsert` or `tableDelete` both require roughly the same amount of time—they are both O(*n*). Neither implementation supports these operations particularly well. The binary search tree implementation, however, combines the best features of the two linear implementations. Because it is pointer based, you avoid shifting data, and the table can grow dynamically as needed. You can also retrieve items from a binary search tree efficiently.

Summary. An unsorted array-based implementation of the ADT table can efficiently insert an item at the end of an array. A deletion, however, will usually require shifting data so that no hole remains in the array. Because the items are unsorted, retrieval will require a sequential search.

A sorted array-based implementation usually requires shifting data during both insertions and deletions. Retrieval, however, can use an efficient binary search because the items are sorted.

An unsorted pointer-based implementation can efficiently insert an item at the beginning of a linked list. A deletion will require a sequential search but no data shifts. Retrieval will also require a sequential search.

A sorted pointer-based implementation requires a sequential search but no data shifts during both insertions and deletions. Retrieval will also require a sequential search.

Although these linear implementations are less sophisticated and generally require more time than the binary search tree implementa-

A sorted array-based implementation shifts data during insertions and deletions

The sorted linear implementations are comparable here, but none are suitable

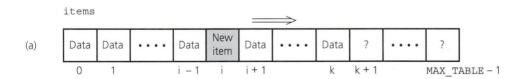

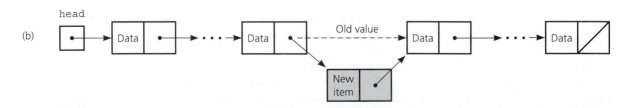

FIGURE 11-6   Insertion for sorted linear implementations: (a) array based; (b) pointer based

tion, they are nevertheless useful for many applications. Because linear implementations are easy to understand conceptually, they are appropriate for tables that will contain only a small number of items. In such cases efficiency is not as great a concern as simplicity and clarity. Even when a table is large, a linear implementation may still be appropriate for applications that can use an unsorted table and have few deletions.

The nonlinear, binary search tree implementation of the ADT table can be a better choice, in general. If an *n*-node binary search tree has minimum height—that is, has height $\lceil \log_2(n + 1) \rceil$—the binary search tree implementation of the ADT table certainly succeeds where the linear implementations failed: You can, with efficiency comparable to that of a binary search, locate an item in both the retrieval operation and the first steps of the insertion and deletion operations. In addition, the pointer-based implementation of the binary search tree permits dynamic allocation of its nodes, so that it can handle a table whose maximum size is unknown. This implementation also efficiently performs the second step of the insertion and deletion operations: The actual insertion and removal of a node requires only a few pointer changes (plus a short traversal to the inorder successor if the node to be removed has two children) rather than the possible shifting of all the table items, as the array-based implementations require. The binary search tree implementation therefore combines the best aspects of the two linear implementations, yet avoids their disadvantages.

As the previous chapter showed, however, the height of a binary search tree depends on the order in which you perform the insertion and deletion operations on the tree and can be as large as *n*. If the insertion and deletion operations occur in a random order, the height of the binary search tree will be quite close to its minimum value. You do need to watch for a possible increase in the tree's height, however, and the resulting decrease in performance. If instead you use a variation of the binary search tree that remains balanced—as Chapter 12 describes—you can keep the height of the tree near $\log_2 n$.

Figure 11-7 summarizes the order of the insertion, deletion, retrieval, and traversal operations for the table implementations discussed in this chapter.

	Insertion	Deletion	Retrieval	Traversal
Unsorted array based	O(1)	O(n)	O(n)	O(n)
Unsorted pointer based	O(1)	O(n)	O(n)	O(n)
Sorted array based	O(n)	O(n)	O(log n)	O(n)
Sorted pointer based	O(n)	O(n)	O(n)	O(n)
Binary search tree	O(log n)	O(log n)	O(log n)	O(n)

FIGURE 11-7   The average-case order of the ADT table operations for various implementations

A Sorted Array-Based Implementation of the ADT Table

If the binary search tree implementation of the ADT table is so good, you might wonder why you needed to study the linear implementations at all. There are three reasons. The first and foremost reason is perspective. Chapter 9 spoke of the dangers of overanalyzing a problem. If the size of the problem is small, the difference in efficiency among the possible solutions is likely insignificant. In particular, if the size of the table is small, a linear implementation is adequate and simple to understand.

Perspective, efficiency, and motivation are reasons for studying the linear implementations

The second reason is efficiency: A linear implementation can be quite efficient for certain situations. For example, a linear implementation was best for Scenario A, where the predominant operations are insertion and traversal in no particular order. For Scenario B, where the predominant operation is retrieval, the sorted array-based implementation is adequate, if the maximum number of items is known. For these situations, a concern for simplicity suggests that you use a linear implementation and not a binary search tree, even for large tables.

The third reason is motivation. By seeing scenarios for which the linear implementations are not adequate, you are forced to look beyond arrays and consider other implementations, such as the binary search tree. Actually looking at both a linear implementation and a binary search tree implementation allows you to see these inadequacies more clearly.

The following sorted array-based implementation assumes unique search keys. Exercises 7 and 8 at the end of this chapter ask you to remove this assumption.

Header file

```
// ***********************************************************
// Header file TableException.h for the ADT Table.
// ***********************************************************
#include <stdexcept>
#include <string>
using namespace std;

class TableException: public logic_error
{
public:
   TableException(const string & message = "")
                         : logic_error(message.c_str())
   { }
};  // end TableException
// ***********************************************************
// Header file TableA.h for the ADT table.
// Sorted array-based implementation.
// Assumption: A table contains at most one item with a
//             given search key at any time.
// ***********************************************************
#include "KeyedItem.h"  // definition of KeyedItem
                        // and KeyType
```

```cpp
#include "TableException.h"
const int MAX_TABLE = maximum-size-of-table;

typedef KeyedItem TableItemType;
typedef void (*FunctionType)(TableItemType& anItem);

class Table
{
public:
    Table();  // default constructor
    // copy constructor and destructor are
    // supplied by the compiler

// Table operations:
// Precondition for all operations:
// No two items of the table have the same search key.
// The table's items are sorted by search key.

    virtual bool tableIsEmpty() const;
    // Determines whether a table is empty.
    // Postcondition: Returns true if the table is empty;
    // otherwise returns false.

    virtual int tableLength() const;
    // Determines the length of a table.
    // Postcondition: Returns the number of items in the
    // table.

    virtual void tableInsert(const TableItemType& newItem)
                            throw(TableException);
    // Inserts an item into a table in its proper sorted
    // order according to the item's search key.
    // Precondition: The item to be inserted into the table
    // is newItem, whose search key differs from all search
    // keys presently in the table.
    // Postcondition: If the insertion is successful,
    // newItem is in its proper order in the table.
    // Exception: Throws TableException if the item cannot
    // be inserted.


    virtual void tableDelete(KeyType searchKey)
                            throw(TableException);
    // Deletes an item with a given search key from a table.
    // Precondition: searchKey is the search key of the item
    // to be deleted.
    // Postcondition: If the item whose search key equals
    // searchKey existed in the table, the item is deleted.
    // Exception: Throws TableException if the item does not
    // exist.
```

```
    virtual void tableRetrieve(KeyType searchKey,
                               TableItemType& tableItem) const
                               throw(TableException);
    // Retrieves an item with a given search key from a
    // table.
    // Precondition: searchKey is the search key of the item
    // to be retrieved.
    // Postcondition: If the retrieval is successful,
    // tableItem contains the retrieved item.
    // Exception: Throws TableException if the item
    // does not exist.

    virtual void traverseTable(FunctionType visit);
    // Traverses a table in sorted search-key order, calling
    // function visit() once for each item.
    // Precondition: The function represented by visit()
    // exists outside of the ADT implementation.
    // Postcondition: visit()'s action occurs once for each
    // item in the table.
    // Note: visit() can alter the table.

protected:
    void setSize(int newSize);
    // Sets the private data member size to newSize.

    void setItem(const TableItemType& newItem, int index);
    // Sets items[index] to newItem.

    int position(KeyType searchKey) const;
    // Finds the position of a table item or its insertion
    // point.
    // Precondition: searchKey is the value of the search key
    // sought in the table.
    // Postcondition: Returns the index (between 0 and
    // size - 1) of the item in the table whose search key
    // equals searchKey. If no such item exists, returns the
    // position (between 0 and size) that the item would
    // occupy if inserted into the table. The table is
    // unchanged.

private:
    TableItemType items[MAX_TABLE];  // table items
    int           size;              // table size

    int keyIndex(int first, int last, KeyType searchKey) const;
    // Searches a particular portion of the private array
    // items for a given search key by using a binary search.
    // Precondition: 0 <= first, last < MAX_TABLE, where
    // MAX_TABLE = max size of the array, and the array
```

```
   // items[first..last] is sorted in ascending order by
   // search key.
   // Postcondition: If searchKey is in the array, returns
   // the index of the array element that contains
   // searchKey; otherwise returns the index (between first
   // and last) of the array element that the item would
   // occupy if inserted into the array in its proper order.
   // The array is unchanged.
};  // end Table class
// End of header file.
```

Because much of the implementation of the previous class is straight-forward, only excerpts of the implementation file are presented here:

Implementation file

```
// ************************************************************
// Excerpts from the implementation file TableA.cpp.
// Sorted array-based implementation.
// ************************************************************
#include "TableA.h"  // header file

void Table::tableInsert(const TableItemType& newItem)
             throw(TableException)
// Note: Insertion is unsuccessful if the table is full,
// that is, if the table already contains MAX_TABLE items.
// Calls: position.
{
   if (size == MAX_TABLE)
      throw TableException("TableException: Table full");

   // there is room to insert;
   // locate the position where newItem belongs
   int spot = position(newItem.getKey());

   // shift up to make room for the new item
   for (int index = size-1; index >= spot; --index)
      items[index+1] = items[index];

   // make the insertion
   items[spot] = newItem;
   ++size;
}  // end tableInsert

void Table::tableDelete(KeyType searchKey)
             throw(TableException)
// Calls: position.
{
   // locate the position where searchKey exists/belongs
   int spot = position(searchKey);
```

```
      // is searchKey present in the table?
      if ((spot > size) || (items[spot].getKey() != searchKey))
         // searchKey not in table
         throw TableException(
            "TableException: Item not found on delete");
      else
      {  // searchKey in table
         --size;  // delete the item

         // shift down to fill the gap
         for (int index = spot; index < size; ++index)
            items[index] = items[index+1];
      }  // end if
   }  // end tableDelete


   void Table::tableRetrieve(KeyType searchKey,
                             TableItemType& tableItem) const
         throw(TableException)
   // Calls: position.
   {
      // locate the position where searchKey exists/belongs
      int spot = position(searchKey);

      // is searchKey present in table?
      if ((spot > size) || (items[spot].getKey() != searchKey))
         // searchKey not in table
         throw TableException(
            "TableException: Item not found on retrieve");
      else
         tableItem = items[spot];  // item present; retrieve it
   }  // end tableRetrieve


   void Table::traverseTable(FunctionType visit)
   {
      for (int index = 0; index < size; ++index)
         visit(items[index]);
   }  // end traverseTable
   // End of implementation file.
```

A Binary Search Tree Implementation of the ADT Table

Although linear implementations are suited to specific applications, they are not good as general-purpose implementations of the ADT table.

The following nonlinear pointer–based implementation uses a binary search tree to represent the items in the ADT table. That is, the class *Table* has a binary search tree as one of its data members. In this way, the class *Table* reuses the class *BinarySearchTree* from the previous chapter. In the header file, the pre- and postconditions are omitted to save space, but they are the same as those given earlier in this chapter.

```cpp
// ********************************************************
// Header file TableB.h for the ADT table.
// Binary search tree implementation.
// Assumption: A table contains at most one item with a
//             given search key at any time.
// ********************************************************
#include "BST.h"  // binary search tree operations
#include "TableException.h"

typedef TreeItemType TableItemType;

class Table
{
public:
   Table();  // default constructor
   // copy constructor and destructor are
   // supplied by the compiler

// Table operations:
   virtual bool tableIsEmpty() const;
   virtual int tableLength() const;
   virtual void tableInsert(const TableItemType& newItem)
                       throw(TableException);
   virtual void tableDelete(KeyType searchKey)
                       throw(TableException);
   virtual void tableRetrieve(KeyType searchKey,
                       TableItemType& tableItem) const
                       throw(TableException);
   virtual void traverseTable(FunctionType visit);

protected:
   void setSize(int newSize);

private:
   BinarySearchTree bst; // binary search tree that contains
                         // the table's items
   int          size;  // number of items in the table
};  // end Table class
// End of header file.
```

Header file

This table implementation has a binary search tree as a data member

Here again, only excerpts from the implementation file are presented:

Implementation file

```cpp
// ***********************************************************
// Excerpts from the implementation file TableB.cpp.
// Binary search tree implementation.
// ***********************************************************

#include "TableB.h"  // header file

void Table::tableInsert(const TableItemType& newItem)
          throw(TableException)
{
   try
   {
      bst.searchTreeInsert(newItem);
      ++size;
   }  // end try
   catch (TreeException e)
   {  throw TableException(
         "TableException: Cannot insert item");
   }  // end catch
}  // end tableInsert

void Table::tableDelete(KeyType searchKey)
          throw(TableException)
{
   try
   {  bst.searchTreeDelete(searchKey);
   }  // end try
   catch (TreeException e)
   {  throw TableException(
         "TableException: Item not found on delete");
   }  // end catch
}  // end tableDelete

void Table::tableRetrieve(KeyType searchKey,
                          TableItemType& tableItem) const
          throw(TableException)
{
   try
   {  bst.searchTreeRetrieve(searchKey, tableItem);
   }  // end try
   catch (TreeException e)
   {  throw TableException(
         "TableException: Item not found on retrieve");
   }  // end catch
}  // end tableRetrieve
```

```
void Table::traverseTable(FunctionType visit)
{
   bst.inorderTraverse(visit);
} // end traverseTable
// End of implementation file.
```

The following statements demonstrate how to use these files in a program that requires the ADT table:

```
#include <iostream>
#include "TableB.h"
using namespace std;

void displayKey(TableItemType& anItem)
{
   cout << anItem.getKey() << endl;
} // end displayKey

int main()
{
   Table        chart;
   TableItemType anItem;

   cin >> anItem;
   chart.tableInsert(anItem);

   . . .

   chart.traverseTable(displayKey);  // traversal in order
```

A sample program

11.2 The ADT Priority Queue: A Variation of the ADT Table

The ADT table organizes its data by search key, which facilitates the retrieval of a particular item. Thus, the ADT table is appropriate when you have a database to maintain and search by value, such as the table of cities described earlier in this chapter. Consider now applications for which another ADT, related to the ADT table, would be more appropriate.

Imagine a person who visits a hospital's emergency room (ER). When any patient enters the hospital, the staff creates a record about that person in a database for later retrieval by nurses, doctors, and the billing department. In addition, the staff must keep track of the ER patients and decide when each person will receive care.

The ADT table would be an appropriate choice for the hospital's general database. What ADT should the ER staff use for their patients?

The ADT table would facilitate the treatment of ER patients in alphabetical order by name or in numerical order by ID number. A queue would enable treatment of patients in the order of arrival. In either case, Ms. Zither, who was just rushed to the ER with acute appendicitis, would have to wait for Mr. Able to have a splinter removed. Clearly, the ER staff should assign some measure of urgency, or priority, to the patients waiting for treatment. The next available doctor should treat the patient with the highest priority. The ADT that the ER staff needs should produce this patient on request.

You can organize data by priorities

Another example of the use of priorities is your list of daily or weekly tasks. Suppose that your "to do" list for this week contains the following items:

You usually prioritize your list of tasks

Send a birthday card to Aunt Mabel.

Start the research paper for world history.

Finish reading Chapter 11 of *Walls and Mirrors*.

Make plans for Saturday night.

When you consult your list, you most likely will attend to the task that, for you, has the highest priority.

A **priority value** indicates, for example, a patient's priority for treatment or a task's priority for completion. What quantity should you use for this priority value? Many reasonable possibilities exist, including a simple ranking from 1 to 10. Let's arbitrarily decide that the largest priority value indicates the highest priority. The priority value becomes a part of the record that represents an item. You insert each item into an ADT and then ask the ADT for the item that has the highest priority.

A priority queue orders by priority values

Such an ADT is known as a **priority queue**. More formally, a priority queue is an ADT that provides the following operations:

KEY CONCEPTS

ADT Priority Queue Operations

1. Create an empty priority queue.

2. Destroy a priority queue.

3. Determine whether a priority queue is empty.

4. Insert a new item into a priority queue.

5. Retrieve and then delete the item in a priority queue with the highest priority value.

```
┌─────────────────────────────────┐
│          PriorityQueue          │
├─────────────────────────────────┤
│  items                          │
├─────────────────────────────────┤
│  createPriorityQueue()          │
│  destroyPriorityQueue()         │
│  pqIsEmpty()                    │
│  pqIsInsert()                   │
│  pqIsDelete()                   │
│                                 │
└─────────────────────────────────┘
```

FIGURE 11-8   UML diagram for the class *PriorityQueue*

Figure 11-8 shows a UML diagram for a class of priority queues. The following pseudocode specifies in more detail the operations for an ADT priority queue.

KEY CONCEPTS

Pseudocode for the ADT Priority Queue Operations

```
// PQItemType is the type of the items stored in the
// priority queue

+createPQueue()
// Creates an empty priority queue.

+destroyPQueue()
// Destroys a priority queue.

+pqIsEmpty():boolean
// Determines whether a priority queue is empty.

+pqInsert(in newItem:PQItemType) throw PQException
// Inserts newItem into a priority queue. Throws
// PQException if the priority queue is full.

+pqDelete(out priorityItem:PQItemType) throw PQException
// Retrieves into priorityItem and then deletes the item
// in a priority queue with the highest priority value.
// Throws PQException if the queue is empty.
```

pqDelete is the difference
between a priority queue
and a table

These operations resemble a subset of the ADT table operations. The significant difference is the *pqDelete* operation. Whereas the sequence of table operations *tableRetrieve-tableDelete* allows you to retrieve and delete an item that has a specified value in its search key, *pqDelete* allows you to retrieve and delete the item with the highest priority value. Notice that *pqDelete,* unlike *tableRetrieve* and *tableDelete,* is not told the value in question. Because in general you will not know what the highest priority value is, *tableRetrieve* and *tableDelete* could not easily perform this task. On the other hand, you could not use *pqDelete* to retrieve and delete an item with some specified value.

Possible implementations

The ADT priority queue and the ADT table are thus both similar and dissimilar, a fact that their implementations reflect. To begin, consider some of the table implementations as implementations for a priority queue. The sorted linear implementations are appropriate if the number of items in the priority queue is small. The array-based implementation maintains the items sorted in ascending order of priority value, so that the item with the highest priority value is at the end of the array, as Figure 11-9a illustrates. Thus, *pqDelete* simply returns the item in *items[size-1]* and decrements *size.* However, the *pqInsert* operation, after using a binary search to find the correct position for the insertion, must shift the array elements to make room for the new item.

The linear pointer-based implementation, shown in Figure 11-9b, maintains the items sorted in descending order of priority value, so that the item with the highest priority value is at the beginning of the linked list. Thus, *pqDelete* simply returns the item to which *pqHead* points and then changes *pqHead* to point to the next item. The *pqInsert* operation, however, must traverse the list to find the correct position for the insertion. Thus, the linear implementations of priority queues suffer from the same trade-offs as the linear implementations of tables.

Instead, consider a binary search tree as an implementation of a priority queue, as Figure 11-9c illustrates. Although the *pqInsert* operation is the same as *tableInsert*, the *pqDelete* operation has no direct analogue among the table operations. It must locate the item with the highest priority value, without knowing what that value is. The task is not difficult, however, because this item is always in the rightmost node of the tree. (Why?) You thus need only follow *rightChildPtr* pointers until you encounter a node with a *NULL rightChildPtr* pointer. (A function analogous to the binary search tree's *processLeftmost* can accomplish this task.) Removing this node from the tree is particularly easy because it has at most one child.

A binary search tree implementation is thus good for both a table and a priority queue. Tables and priority queues have different uses, however. Some table applications primarily involve retrieval and traversal operations and thus do not affect the balance of the binary search tree. Priority queues, on the other hand, do not have retrieval and traversal operations, so all their applications involve insertions and deletions, which can affect

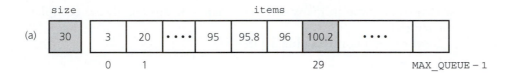

(a)

size   items

| 30 | 3 | 20 | • • • • | 95 | 95.8 | 96 | 100.2 | • • • • | |

0   1   29   MAX_QUEUE – 1

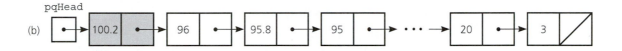

pqHead

(b)

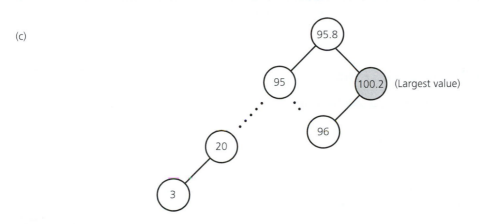

(c)

FIGURE 11-9   Some implementations of the ADT priority queue: (a) array based; (b) pointer based; (c) binary search tree

the shape of the binary search tree. You could use a balanced variation of the binary search tree from Chapter 12; however, if you know the maximum size of the priority queue, a better choice might be an array-based implementation of a heap, which is described next. The heap implementation is often the most appropriate one for a priority queue, but it is not at all appropriate as an implementation of a table.

Heaps

A **heap** is an ADT that is similar to a binary search tree, although it differs from a binary search tree in two significant ways. First, while you can view a binary search tree as sorted, a heap is ordered in a much weaker sense. This order, however, is sufficient for the efficient performance of the priority-queue operations. Second, while binary

A heap differs from a binary search tree in two ways

A heap is a special complete binary tree

search trees come in many different shapes, heaps are always complete binary trees.

A heap is a complete binary tree

1. That is empty

or

2a. Whose root contains a search key greater than or equal to the search key in each of its children, and

2b. Whose root has heaps as its subtrees

In our definition of a heap, the root contains the item with the largest search key. Such a heap is also known as a **maxheap**. A **minheap**, on the other hand, places the item with the smallest search key in its root. Exercise 19 considers the minheap further.

Figure 11-10 contains a UML diagram for the class *Heap*. The pseudocode for the heap operations follows.

KEY CONCEPTS

Pseudocode for the ADT Heap Operations

```
// HeapItemType is the type of the items stored in the
// priority queue

+createHeap()
// Creates an empty heap.

+destroyHeap()
// Destroys a heap.

+heapIsEmpty():boolean {query}
// Determines whether a heap is empty.

+heapInsert(in newItem:HeapItemType) throw HeapException
// Inserts newItem into a heap. Throws HeapException
// if the heap is full.

+heapDelete(out rootItem:HeapItemType) throw Heap Exception
// Retrieves and then deletes a heap's root item.
// This item has the largest search key. Throws
// HeapException if heap is empty.
```

Heap
items
createHeap() *destroyHeap()* *heapIsEmpty()* *heapInsert()* *heapDelete()*

FIGURE 11-10 UML diagram for the class *Heap*

Because a heap is a complete binary tree, you can use an array-based implementation of a binary tree, as you saw in Chapter 10, if you know the maximum size of the heap. For example, Figure 11-11 shows a heap along with its array representation. The search key in a heap node is greater than or equal to the search keys in each of the node's children. Further, in a heap the search keys of the children have no relationship; that is, you do not know which child contains the larger search key.

An array-based implementation of a heap. Let the following data members represent the heap:

- *items*: an array of heap items

- *size*: an integer equal to the number of items in the heap

An array and an integer counter are the data members for an array-based implementation of a heap

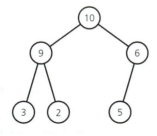

0	10
1	9
2	6
3	3
4	2
5	5

FIGURE 11-11 A heap with its array representation

The array *items* corresponds to the array-based representation of a tree. (To simplify the following discussion, assume that the heap items are integers.)

heapDelete. First consider the *heapDelete* operation. Where is the largest search key in the heap? Because the search key in every node is greater than or equal to the search key in either of its children, the largest search key must be in the root of the tree. Thus, the first step of the *heapDelete* operation is

heapDelete's first step

```
// return the item in the root
rootItem = items[0]
```

That was easy, but you must also remove the root. When you do so, you are left with two disjoint heaps, as Figure 11-12a indicates. Therefore, you need to transform the remaining nodes back into a

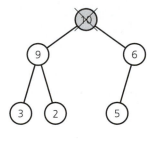

(a)

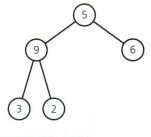

(b)

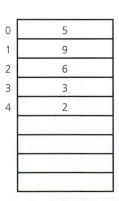

FIGURE 11-12   (a) Disjoint heaps; (b) a semiheap

heap. To begin this transformation, you take the item in the last node of the tree and place it in the root, as follows:

```
// copy the item from the last node into the root
items[0] = items[size-1]

// remove the last node
--size
```

heapDelete's second step produces a semiheap

As Figure 11-12b suggests, the result of this step is *not* necessarily a heap. It is, however, a complete binary tree whose left and right subtrees are both heaps. The only problem is that the item in the root may be (and usually is) out of place. Such a structure is called a **semiheap**. You thus need a way to transform a semiheap into a heap. One strategy allows the item in the root to *trickle down* the tree until it reaches a node in which it will not be out of place; that is, the item will come to rest in the first node where its search key would be greater than (or equal to) the search key of each of its children. To accomplish this, you first compare the search key in the root of the semiheap to the search keys in its children. If the root has a smaller search key than the larger of the search keys in its children, you swap the item in the root with that of the larger child. (The larger child is the child whose search key is greater than the search key of the other child.)

   Figure 11-13 illustrates the *heapDelete* operation. Although the value 5 trickles down to its correct position after only one swap, in general more swaps may be necessary. In fact, once the items in the root and the larger child *C* have been swapped, *C* becomes the root of a semiheap. (Notice that node *C* does not move; only its value changes.) This strategy suggests the following recursive algorithm:

```
heapRebuild(inout items:ArrayType, in root:integer,
            in size:integer)
// Converts a semiheap rooted at index root into a heap.
```

heapDelete's final step transforms the semiheap into a heap

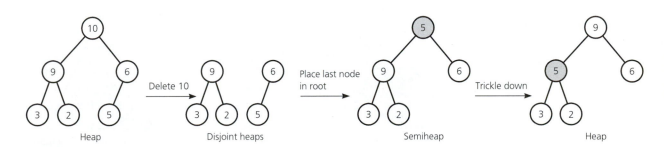

FIGURE 11-13   Deletion from a heap

```
// Recursively trickle the item at index root down to
// its proper position by swapping it with its larger
// child, if the child is larger than the item.
// If the item is at a leaf, nothing needs to be done.

if (the root is not a leaf)
{  // root must have a left child
   child = 2 * root + 1          // left child index

   if (the root has a right child)
   {  rightChild = child + 1  // right child index
      if (items[rightChild].getKey() > items[child].getKey())
         child = rightChild  // larger child index
   }  // end if

   // if the item in the root has a smaller search key
   // than the search key of the item in the larger
   // child, swap items
   if (items[root].getKey() < items[child].getKey())
   {  Swap items[root] and items[child]

      // transform semiheap rooted at child into a heap
      heapRebuild(items, child, size)
   }  // end if
}  // end if

// else root is a leaf, so you are done
```

Figure 11-14 illustrates *heapRebuild*'s recursive calls.

Now the *heapDelete* operation uses *heapRebuild* as follows:

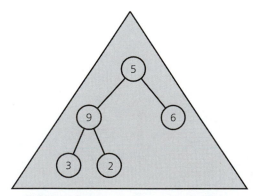
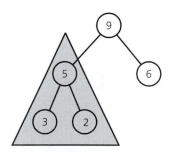

First semiheap passed to *heapRebuild*   Second semiheap passed to *heapRebuild*

FIGURE 11-14   Recursive calls to *heapRebuild*

```
// return the item in the root
rootItem = items[0]

// copy the item from the last node into the root
items[0] = items[size-1]

// remove the last node
--size

// transform the semiheap back into a heap
heapRebuild(items, 0, size)
```

Consider briefly the efficiency of *heapDelete*. Because the tree is stored in an array, the removal of a node requires you to swap array elements rather than simply to change a few pointers. These swaps may concern you, but they do not necessarily indicate that the algorithm is inefficient. At most, how many array elements will you have to swap? After *heapDelete* copies the item in the last node of the tree into the root, *heapRebuild* trickles this item down the tree until its appropriate place is found. This item travels down a single path from the root to, at worst, a leaf. Therefore, the number of array items that *heapRebuild* must swap is no greater than the height of the tree. The height of a complete binary tree with n nodes is always $\lceil \log_2(n + 1) \rceil$, as you know from Chapter 10. Each swap requires three data moves, so *heapDelete* requires

heapDelete's efficiency

$$3 * \lceil \log_2(n + 1) \rceil + 1$$

data moves. Thus, *heapDelete* is O(log n), which is in fact quite efficient.

heapDelete is O(log n)

heapInsert. The strategy for the *heapInsert* algorithm is the opposite of that for *heapDelete*. A new item is inserted at the bottom of the tree, and it trickles up to its proper place, as Figure 11-15 illustrates. It is easy to trickle up a node, because the parent of the node in *items[i]*—other than a root—is always stored in *items[(i-1)/2]*. The pseudocode for *heapInsert* is

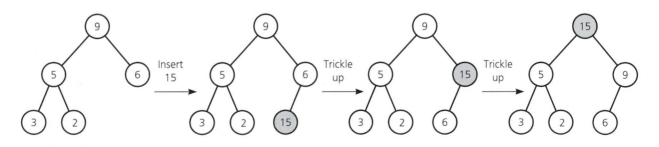

FIGURE 11-15 Insertion into a heap

Insertion strategy

```
// insert newItem into the bottom of the tree
items[size] = newItem

// trickle new item up to appropriate spot in the tree
place = size
parent = (place-1)/2
while ( (parent >= 0) and
        (items[place] > items[parent]) )
{ Swap items[place] and items[parent]
  place = parent
  parent = (place-1)/2
}  // end while

Increment size
```

The efficiency of *heapInsert* is like that of *heapDelete*. At worst, *heapInsert* has to swap array elements on a path from a leaf to the root. The number of swaps, therefore, cannot exceed the height of the tree. Because the height of the tree, which is complete, is always $\lceil \log_2(n + 1) \rceil$,

heapInsert is O(log *n*)

heapInsert is also O(log *n*).

The files that contain the array-based implementation of the ADT heap follow:

Header file

```
// *********************************************************
// Header file HeapException.h for the ADT heap.
// *********************************************************
#include <stdexcept>
#include <string>
using namespace std;

class HeapException: public logic_error
{
public:
   HeapException(const string & message = "")
                        : logic_error(message.c_str())
   { }
};  // end HeapException

// *********************************************************
// Header file Heap.h for the ADT heap.
// *********************************************************
const int MAX_HEAP = maximum-size-of-heap;
#include "HeapException.h"
#include "KeyedItem.h"  // definition of KeyedItem

typedef KeyedItem HeapItemType;
```

```cpp
class Heap
{
public:
    Heap();  // default constructor
    // copy constructor and destructor are
    // supplied by the compiler

// Heap operations:
    virtual bool heapIsEmpty() const;
    // Determines whether a heap is empty.
    // Precondition: None.
    // Postcondition: Returns true if the heap is empty;
    // otherwise returns false.

    virtual void heapInsert(const HeapItemType& newItem)
        throw(HeapException);
    // Inserts an item into a heap.
    // Precondition: newItem is the item to be inserted.
    // Postcondition: If the heap was not full, newItem is
    // in its proper position; otherwise HeapException is
    // thrown.

    virtual void heapDelete(HeapItemType& rootItem)
        throw(HeapException);
    // Retrieves and deletes the item in the root of a heap.
    // This item has the largest search key in the heap.
    // Precondition: None.
    // Postcondition: If the heap was not empty, rootItem
    // is the retrieved item, the item is deleted from the
    // heap. However, if the heap is empty, removal is
    // impossible and the function throws HeapException.

protected:
    void heapRebuild(int root);
    // Converts the semiheap rooted at index root
    // into a heap.

private:
    HeapItemType items[MAX_HEAP];  // array of heap items
    int          size;             // number of heap items
};  // end class
// End of header file.

// ***********************************************************    Implementation file
// Implementation file Heap.cpp for the ADT heap.
// ***********************************************************
#include "Heap.h"  // header file for class Heap
```

```
Heap::Heap() : size(0)
{
}  // end default constructor

bool Heap::heapIsEmpty() const
{
   return bool(size == 0);
}  // end heapIsEmpty

void Heap::heapInsert(const HeapItemType& newItem)
         throw(HeapException)
// Method: Inserts the new item after the last item in the
// heap and trickles it up to its proper position. The
// heap is full when it contains MAX_HEAP items.
{
   if (size > MAX_HEAP)
      throw HeapException("HeapException: Heap full");
   // place the new item at the end of the heap
   items[size] = newItem;

   // trickle new item up to its proper position
   int place = size;
   int parent = (place - 1)/2;
   while ( (parent >= 0) &&
           (items[place].getKey() > items[parent].getKey()) )
   {  // swap items[place] and items[parent]
      HeapItemType temp = items[parent];
      items[parent] = items[place];
      items[place] = temp;

      place = parent;
      parent = (place - 1)/2;
   }  // end while

   ++size;
}  // end heapInsert

void Heap::heapDelete(HeapItemType& rootItem)
         throw(HeapException)
// Method: Swaps the last item in the heap with the root
// and trickles it down to its proper position.
{
   if (heapIsEmpty())
      throw HeapException("HeapException: Heap empty");
   else
   {  rootItem = items[0];
```

```
        items[0] = items[--size];
        heapRebuild(0);
    }  // end if
}  // end heapDelete

void Heap::heapRebuild(int root)
{
   // if the root is not a leaf and the root's search key
   // is less than the larger of the search keys in the
   // root's children
   int child = 2 * root + 1;  // index of root's left
                              // child, if any
   if ( child < size )
   {  // root is not a leaf, so it has a left child at child
      int rightChild = child + 1;  // index of right child,
                                   // if any

      // if root has a right child, find larger child
      if ( (rightChild < size) &&
           (items[rightChild].getKey() > items[child].getKey()) )
         child = rightChild;  // index of larger child

      // if the root's value is smaller than the
      // value in the larger child, swap values
      if ( items[root].getKey() < items[child].getKey() )
      {  HeapItemType temp = items[root];
         items[root] = items[child];
         items[child] = temp;

         // transform the new subtree into a heap
         heapRebuild(child);
      }  // end if
   }  // end if

   // if root is a leaf, do nothing
}  // end heapRebuild
// End of implementation file.
```

A Heap Implementation of the ADT Priority Queue

Once you have implemented the ADT heap, the implementation of the ADT priority queue is straightforward, because priority-queue operations are exactly analogous to heap operations. The priority value in a priority-queue item corresponds to a heap item's search key. Thus,

Priority-queue operations and heap operations are analogous

the implementation of the priority queue can reuse *Heap*. That is, *PriorityQueue* has an instance of *Heap* as its data member. The following files contain this implementation:

Header file

```
// **********************************************************
// Header file PQueueException.h for the ADT priority queue.
// **********************************************************
#include <stdexcept>
#include <string>
using namespace std;

class PQueueException: public logic_error
{
public:
   PQueueException(const string & message = "")
                         : logic_error(message.c_str())
   { }
};  // end PQueueException


// **********************************************************
// Header file PQ.h for the ADT priority queue.
// Heap implementation.
// **********************************************************
#include "Heap.h"  // ADT heap operations
#include "PQueueException.h"
typedef HeapItemType PQueueItemType;

class PriorityQueue
{
public:
   // default constructor, copy constructor, and
   // destructor are supplied by the compiler

// priority-queue operations:
   virtual bool pqIsEmpty() const;
   virtual void pqInsert(const PQueueItemType& newItem)
      throw(PQueueException);
   virtual void pqDelete(PQueueItemType& PQueueItemType)
      throw(PQueueException);

private:
   Heap h;
};  // end PriorityQueue class
// End of header file.
```

This priority-queue implementation has a heap as a data member

Implementation file

```
// **********************************************************
// Implementation file PQ.cpp for the ADT priority queue.
```

```
// A heap represents the priority queue.
// *********************************************************
#include "PQ.h"    // header file for priority queue

bool PriorityQueue::pqIsEmpty() const
{
   return h.heapIsEmpty();
} // end pqIsEmpty

void PriorityQueue::pqInsert(const PQueueItemType& newItem)
               throw(PQueueException)
{
   try
   {
      h.heapInsert(newItem);
   } // end try
   catch (HeapException e)
   { throw PQueueException(
        "PQueueException: Priority queue full");
   } // end catch
} // end pqInsert

void PriorityQueue::pqDelete(PQueueItemType& priorityItem)
               throw(PQueueException)
{
   try
   {
      h.heapDelete(priorityItem);
   } // end try
   catch (HeapException e)
   { throw PQueueException(
        "PQueueException: Priority queue empty");
   } // end catch
} // end pqDelete
// End of implementation file.
```

How does a heap compare to a binary search tree as an implementation of a priority queue? If you know the maximum number of items in the priority queue, the heap is the better implementation.

Because a heap is complete, it is always balanced, which is its major advantage. If the binary search tree is balanced, both implementations will have the same average performance for n items: They both will be O($\log n$). The height of a binary search tree, however, can increase during insertions and deletions, greatly exceeding $\log_2 n$ and degrading the implementation's efficiency to O(n) in the worst case. The heap implementation avoids this decrease in performance.

In the next chapter, you will see how to keep a binary search tree balanced, but the operations that do this are far more complex than the

The heap implementation requires knowledge of the priority queue's maximum size

A heap is always balanced

heap operations. Do not think, however, that a heap can replace a binary search tree as a table implementation; as was stated earlier, a heap is not appropriate in this role. If this fact is not apparent to you, try to perform the table operation *tableRetrieve* on a heap, or try to traverse a heap in search-key order.

Finite, distinct priority values. If you have a finite number of distinct priority values, such as the integers 1 through 20, many items will likely have the same priority value. You could place items whose priority values are the same in the order in which you encounter them.

A heap of queues   A heap of queues accommodates this situation, one queue for each distinct priority value. To insert an item into the priority queue, you add a queue for the item's priority value to the heap, if it is not already there. Then you insert the item into the corresponding queue. To delete an item from a priority queue, you delete the item at the front of the queue that corresponds to the highest priority value in the heap. If this deletion leaves the queue empty, you remove it from the heap.

Programming Problem 7 at the end of this chapter treats distinct priority values further.

Heapsort

As its name implies, the **heapsort** algorithm uses a heap to sort an array *anArray* of items that are in no particular order. The first step of the algorithm transforms the array into a heap. One way to accomplish this transformation is to use the *heapInsert* function to insert the items into the heap one by one.

A more efficient method of building a heap out of the items of *anArray* is possible, however. For example, assume that the initial contents of *anArray* are as shown in Figure 11-16a. First you imagine the array as a binary tree by assigning the items of *anArray* to the tree's nodes, beginning with the root and proceeding left to right down the tree. Figure 11-16b shows the resulting tree. Next, you transform this tree into a heap by calling *heapRebuild* repeatedly. Each call to *heap-Rebuild* transforms a semiheap—a tree whose subtrees are both heaps but whose root may be out of place—into a heap. But are there any

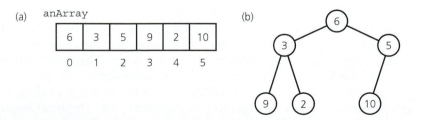

FIGURE 11-16   (a) The initial contents of *anArray*; (b) *anArray*'s corresponding binary tree

semiheaps in the tree for *heapRebuild* to work on? Although the tree in Figure 11-16b is not a semiheap, if you look at its leaves you will find semiheaps—that is, each leaf is a semiheap. (In fact, each leaf is a heap, but for the sake of simplicity, ignore this fact.) You first call *heapRebuild* on the leaves from right to left. You then move up the tree, knowing that by the time you reach a node *s*, its subtrees are heaps, and thus *heapRebuild* will transform the semiheap rooted at *s* into a heap.

The following algorithm transforms the array *anArray* of *n* items into a heap and is the first step of the heapsort algorithm:

```
for (index = n - 1 down to 0)
    // Assertion: the tree rooted at index is a semiheap
    heapRebuild(anArray, index, n)
    // Assertion: the tree rooted at index is a heap
```

Building a heap from an array of items

Actually, you can replace *n - 1* with *n/2* in the previous *for* statement. Exercise 23 at the end of this chapter asks you to explain why this improvement is possible. Figure 11-17 traces this algorithm for the array in Figure 11-16a.

After transforming the array into a heap, heapsort partitions the array into two regions—the Heap region and the Sorted region—as Figure 11-18 illustrates. The Heap region is in *anArray[0..last]*, and the Sorted region is in *anArray[last+1..n-1]*. Initially, the

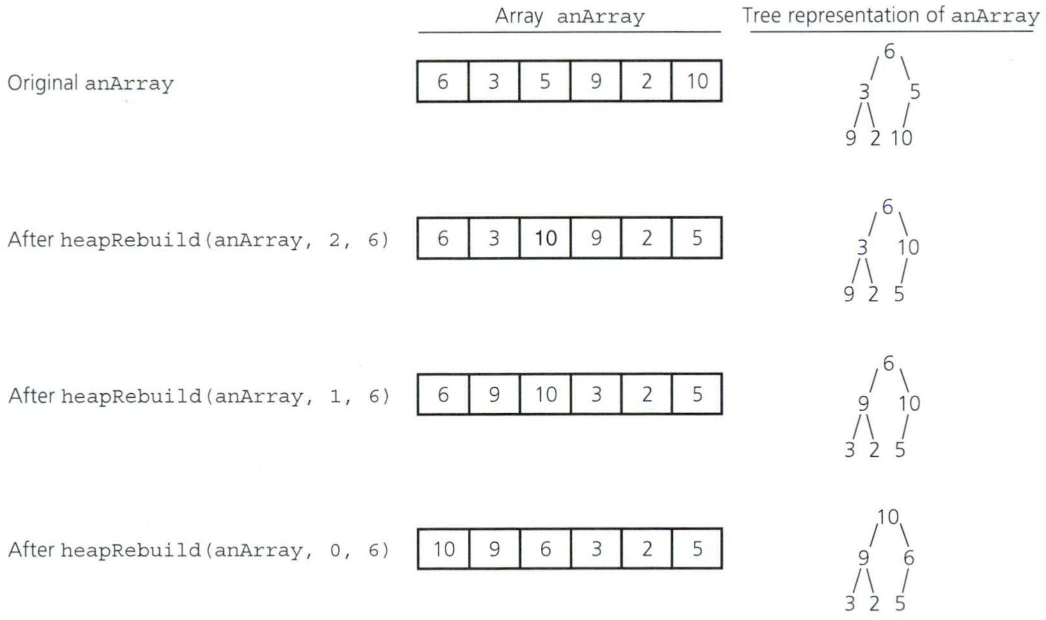

FIGURE 11-17   Transforming the array *anArray* into a heap

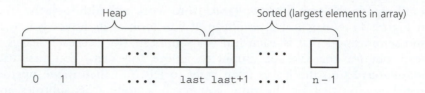

FIGURE 11-18   Heapsort partitions an array into two regions

Heap region is all of *anArray* and the Sorted region is empty—that is,
is equal to *n* − 1.

Each step of the algorithm moves an item *I* from the Heap region
to the Sorted region. The invariant of the heapsort algorithm is

Invariant for heapsort

- After Step *k*, the Sorted region contains the *k* largest values in
  anArray, and they are in sorted order—that is, *anArray[n − 1]*
  is the largest, *anArray[n − 2]* is the second largest, and so on.

- The items in the Heap region form a heap.

So that the invariant holds, *I* must be the item that has the largest value
in the Heap region, and therefore *I* must be in the root of the heap. To
accomplish the move, you exchange the item in the root of the heap
with the last item in the heap—that is, you exchange *anArray[0]*
with *anArray[last]*—and then decrement the value of *last*. As a
result, the item just swapped from the root into *anArray[last]*
becomes the smallest item in the Sorted region (and is in the first position of the Sorted region). After the move, you must transform the
Heap region back into a heap because the new root may be out of
place. You can accomplish this transformation by using *heapRebuild* to
trickle down the item now in the root so that the Heap region is once
again a heap.

The following algorithm summarizes these steps:

```
heapSort(inout anArray: ArrayType, in n:integer)
// Sorts anArray[0..n-1].

   // build initial heap
   for (index = n - 1 down to 0)
   {  // Invariant: the tree rooted at index is a semiheap
      heapRebuild(anArray, index, n)
      // Assertion: the tree rooted at index is a heap
   }  // end for
   // Assertion: anArray[0] is the largest item in heap
   // anArray[0..n-1]

   // initialize the regions
   last = n - 1
```

```
// Invariant: anArray[0..last] is a heap,
//            anArray[last+1..n-1] is
// sorted and contains the largest items of anArray

for (step = 1 through n)
{  // move the largest item in the Heap region -- that
   // is, the root anArray[0] -- to the beginning of the
   // region by swapping items
   Swap anArray[0] and anArray[last]

   // expand the Sorted region, shrink the Heap region
   Decrement last

   // make the Heap region a heap again
   heapRebuild(anArray, 0, last)
}  // end for
```

Figure 11-19 completes the trace of heapsort that Figure 11-17 began. The C++ implementation of heapsort is left as an exercise.

The analysis of the efficiency of heapsort is similar to that of mergesort, as given in Chapter 9. Both algorithms are $O(n * \log n)$ in both the worst and average cases. Heapsort has an advantage over mergesort in that it does not require a second array. Quicksort is also $O(n * \log n)$ in the average case but is $O(n^2)$ in the worst case. Even though quicksort has poor worst-case efficiency, it is generally the preferred sorting method.

Heapsort is $O(n * \log n)$

11.3 Tables and Priority Queues in the STL

The STL provides containers that act as tables. These classes are called **associative containers** because their elements are retrieved using a key that is not required to be an integral type. The STL also contains a `priority_queue` adapter container, as well as heap algorithms that can be applied to a container to transform it into a heap.

The STL Associative Containers

The associative containers in the STL are `map`, `multimap`, `set`, and `multiset`. The default comparison is the < operator, but a comparison function parameter is possible. These containers provide bidirectional iterators.

The `map` class stores (key, value) pairs, which are sorted based on unique keys. Recall that the `pair` class is defined in `<utility>`, as discussed in Chapter 10. A useful feature of `map` is that it provides

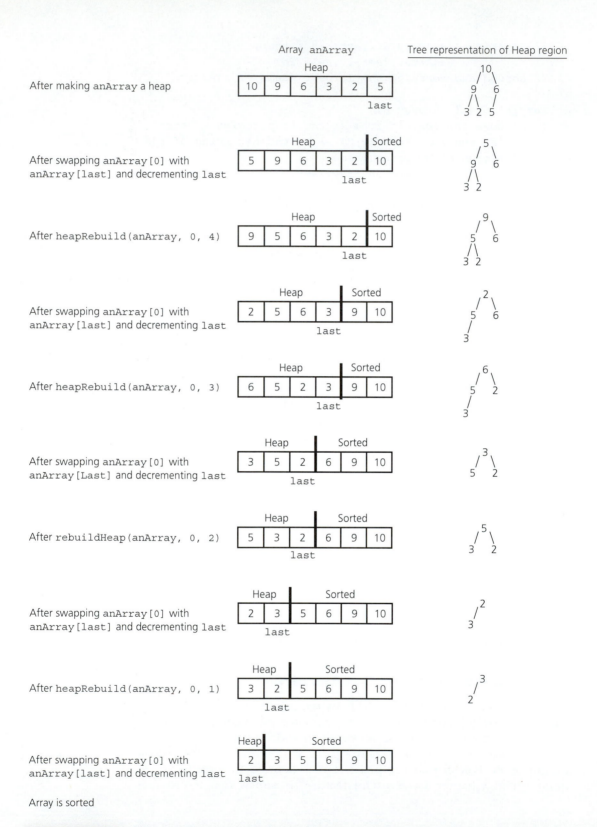

subscripting through its keys with the operator `[ ]`. Because of the subscripting functionality provided in *map*, values can be entered into a *map* either through the *insert* function or through array-type assignment, such as the following:

```
month["December"] = 31;
```

A partial specification for the map class is below.

```
template <class Key, class T, class Compare = less<Key>>
class map
{
public:
  explicit map(const Compare& cmp = Compare());
  // Default constructor
  // Precondition: None.
  // Postcondition: The map object is initialized to be empty.
  // The default comparison operator is <.
  // A comparison function object may be supplied.

   template <class InputIter>
   map(InputIter first, InputIter last,
       const Compare& comp = Compare());
  // Constructor: map is initialized with length last — first
  // and filled with all values from the dereferenced.
  // input iterators on the range [first, last].
  // Precondition: None.
  // Postcondition: The map contains input iterators in the
  // range [first, last].  If a function comp is supplied, it
  // is used to compare elements of the map.

  bool empty() const;
  // Determines whether the map is empty.
  // Precondition: None.
  // Postcondition: Returns true if the map is empty,
  // otherwise returns false.

  size_type size() const;
  // Determines the size of the map.
  // The return type size_type is an integral type.
  // Precondition: None.
  // Postcondition: Returns the number of items that
  // are currently in the map.

  size_type max_size() const;
  // Determines the maximum number of elements
  // the map can hold.
  // Precondition: None.
```

```
// Postcondition: Returns the maximum number of elements.

Iter (const value_type& e)
Iter insert(Iter i, const value_type& e);
// Inserts element pair e into the map if a value_type
// with the same key is not already present in the map.
// Takes an optional iterator parameter as a hint as to where
// to insert.
// Precondition: The iterator is initialized.
// Postcondition: Element e has been inserted into the map and
// an iterator to e is returned.

Iter erase(Iter i)
// Removes the map element pointed to by iterator i.
// Precondition: None.
// Postcondition: Returns an iterator pointing to the map
// element following the removed pair.
// If the pair was the last element, the value returned
// by end() was returned.

void erase(Iter first, Iter last);
// Removes all map elements in the range (first, last).
// Precondition: None.
// Postcondition: The map has no elements in the range
// [first, last].

Iter find(const key_value& e) const;
// Returns an iterator that points to the element
// equal to e.
// Precondition: None.
// Postcondition: If element e was in the map, an iterator
// that points to e was returned; otherwise, the value
// returned by end() was returned.

size_type count(const key_type& k);
// Returns number of elements equal to k.
// Precondition: None.
// Postcondition: Returns the number of elements equal to k.
// Since a map has unique keys, count will always return 1 or
// 0.

Iter lower_bound(const key_type& k) const;
// Returns an iterator that points to the first key
// that is equal to or greater than k.
// Precondition: None.
// Postcondition: Returns the comparison function object
// for the set.

Iter upper_bound(const key_type& k) const;
```

```
// Returns an iterator that points to the first key
// that is greater than e.
// Precondition: None.
// Postcondition: Returns the comparison function object
// for the set.

void swap(map<Key, T, Compare>& m);
// Exchanges maps.
// Precondition: None.
// Postcondition: Exchanges the contents of the map m
// with the current map, *this.

Iter begin();
// Returns an iterator to the first element in the
// map.
// Precondition: None.
// Postcondition: If the map was empty,
// the value returned by end() was returned.

Iter end();
// Returns an iterator to test for the end of the
// map.
// Precondition: None.
// Postcondition: The value for the end of the map was
// returned.
}   // end STL map
```

Note that associative containers have their own *find* and *count* functions to search for items. They can also use *lower_bound*, *upper_bound*, and *equal_range* functions to return a range of equivalent items. Items are added to associative containers using the *insert* function. In the case of *map* and *multimap*, elements can also be inserted using the subscript operator [ ].

The *multimap* and *multiset* containers are similar to their counterparts, *map* and *set*, except that they allow duplicate keys. This is useful in cases where a key might have two values associated with it. The following program creates a *map*, and then a *multimap*, to store names as keys and phone numbers as values. The *multimap* can store more than one phone number for a name, whereas the *map* will overwrite another entry with the same key.

```
#include <map>
#include <iostream>
#include <string>

using namespace std;

int main()
```

```cpp
{
   // declare a map to contain names and phone numbers
   map<string, string> phoneBook;

   // declare a map iterator
   map<string,string>::const_iterator it1;

   string name1 = "Smith, John";
   string name2 = "Thompson, Julia";
   string name3 = "Johnson, Mary";
   string name4 = "Little, Carol";
   string name5 = "Johnson, Mary";
   string phone1 = "212-555-4444";
   string phone2 = "806-555-6565";
   string phone3 = "445-555-7111";
   string phone4 = "745-555-6787";
   string phone5 = "745-555-7777";

   // assign elements to map using subscripts
   phoneBook[name1] = phone1;
   phoneBook[name2] = phone2;
   phoneBook[name3] = phone3;
   phoneBook[name4] = phone4;
   phoneBook[name5] = phone5;

   // print map elements
   // duplicate name keys are not listed
   for (it1 = phoneBook.begin(); it1 != phoneBook.end(); ++it1)
   {
      cout << it1->first<< '\t' << it1->second << endl;
   }  // end for

   // find a map element
   it1 = phoneBook.find(string(name3));

   // display found map element
   if (it1 != phoneBook.end())
     cout << " Search for " << it1->first
          << " - phone numbers" << endl
          << it1->second << endl << endl;

   // create a multimap to contain names and phone numbers
   // use the make_pair function to insert elements
   multimap<string, string> phoneBook2;
   phoneBook2.insert(make_pair(name1, phone1));
   phoneBook2.insert(make_pair(name2, phone2));
   phoneBook2.insert(make_pair(name3, phone3));
   phoneBook2.insert(make_pair(name4, phone4));
```

```
       phoneBook2.insert(make_pair(name5, phone5));

       typedef multimap<string,string>::const_iterator iter2;

       // print map elements
       for (iter2 it2 = phoneBook2.begin();
            it2 != phoneBook2.end(); ++it2)
       {
          cout << it2->first<< '\t' << it2->second << endl;
       }  // end for

       // returns map pairs with the same key
       pair<iter2,iter2>phoneNum = phoneBook2.equal_range(name3);

       // display pairs with same key
       cout << "Search for " << name3
            << " - phone numbers: " << endl;

       for(it2 = phoneNum.first; it2 != phoneNum.second; ++it2)
          cout << it2->second << endl;

       return 0;
    }  // end main
```

This program produces the following output:

```
       Johnson, Mary    745-555-7777
       Little, Carol    745-555-6787
       Smith, John      212-555-4444
       Thompson, Julia 806-555-6565
       Search for Johnson, Mary - phone numbers:
       745-555-7777

       Johnson, Mary    445-555-7111
       Johnson, Mary    745-555-7777
       Little, Carol    745-555-6787
       Smith, John      212-555-4444
       Thompson, Julia 806-555-6565
       Search for Johnson, Mary - phone numbers:
       445-555-7111
       745-555-7777
```

The *set*, like the *map*, is an ordered collection, but it stores only one object, which represents both the key and the value. Note that unlike *map*, *set* does not provide subscripting. Otherwise, the *set* member interface is comparable to the *map* member interface; therefore, the specification is not repeated below. The similar interfaces are possible through the definition of their container elements as a *value_type*. The *value_type* of a *set* is defined by its key type, whereas the *value_type* of a *map* is defined as a *pair*.

Standard set algorithms such as union, intersection, difference, and subset are provided externally in `<algorithm>`. A partial list of set algorithms is listed below:

```
OutputIter set_union(InputIter1 first, InputIter1 last,
                     InputIter2 first2, InputIter2 last2,
                     OutputIter result);
// Returns a set that is a union of two sets.
// Precondition: None.
// Postcondition: A set s3 contains the union of sets s1 and s2.


OutputIter set_difference(InputIter1 first, InputIter1 last,
                          InputIter2 first2, InputIter2 last2,
                          OutputIter result);
// Returns a set that has elements that belong to the
// first set, but not the second.
// Precondition:  None.
// Postcondition: A set s3 contains the difference of sets s1 and s2.


OutputIter set_intersection(InputIter1 first, InputIter1 last,
                            InputIter2 first2, InputIter2 last2,
                            OutputIter result);
// Returns a set that has elements that belong to both
// input sets.
// Precondition: None.
// Postcondition: A set s3 contains the intersection of sets s1 and s2.


bool includes(InputIter1 first, InputIter1 last,
              InputIter2 first2, InputIter2 last2);
// Tests whether set2 is a subset of set1.
// Precondition: None
// Postcondition: Returns true if s2 is a subset of s1; otherwise
// returns false
```

The following program creates two sets and performs set operations on them:

```
#include <set>
#include <iostream>
#include <string>
#include <algorithm>

using namespace std;

int main()
```

```cpp
{
    // declares three sets
    set<string> checkingAccounts;
    set<string> savingAccounts;
    set<string> bankAccounts;

    // declare a set iterator
    set<string>::const_iterator i;

    // insert customers with checking accounts
    checkingAccounts.insert("Marlow");
    checkingAccounts.insert("Johnson");
    checkingAccounts.insert("Garner");
    checkingAccounts.insert("Smith");

    // print checking account customers
    cout << "Checking accounts: " << endl;
    for (i = checkingAccounts.begin();
         i != checkingAccounts.end(); ++i)
    {
        cout << *i << " ";
    }  // end for
    cout << endl << endl;

    // insert customers with savings accounts
    savingAccounts.insert("Johnson");
    savingAccounts.insert("Abbott");
    savingAccounts.insert("Stricker");
    savingAccounts.insert("Marlow");

    // print saving account customers
    cout << "Savings accounts: " << endl;
    for (i = savingAccounts.begin();
         i != savingAccounts.end(); ++i)
    {
        cout << *i << " ";
    }  // end for
    cout << endl << endl;

    // Union of checking and savings accounts
    // The inserter is an output iterator that inserts elements
    // into a set before printing the set
    //
    set_union(checkingAccounts.begin(), checkingAccounts.end(),
              savingAccounts.begin(), savingAccounts.end(),
              inserter(bankAccounts,bankAccounts.begin()));
```

```
cout<< "All bank customers: " << endl;
for (i = bankAccounts.begin(); i != bankAccounts.end(); ++i)
{
    cout << *i << " ";
} // end for
cout << endl << endl;

// Erase all elements of the result set for the next operation
bankAccounts.erase(bankAccounts.begin(), bankAccounts.end());

// Intersection of checking and saving accounts
set_intersection(checkingAccounts.begin(),
                 checkingAccounts.end(),
                 savingAccounts.begin(),savingAccounts.end(),
                 inserter(bankAccounts,bankAccounts.begin()));

cout << "Customers with checking and savings accounts: "
    << endl;
for (i = bankAccounts.begin(); i != bankAccounts.end(); ++i)
{
    cout << *i << " ";
} // end for
cout << endl;

return 0;
} // end main
```

This program produces the following output:

```
Checking accounts:
Garner Johnson Marlow Smith

Savings accounts:
Abbott Johnson Marlow Stricker

All bank customers:
Abbott Garner Johnson Marlow Smith Stricker

Customers with checking and savings accounts:
Johnson Marlow
```

The STL *priority_queue* Class and Heap Algorithms

The STL provides a *priority_queue* class, which is an adapter container. The default underlying container type is a *vector*. The *priority_queue* allows for insertion of elements, but not iteration through its elements. Only the top element can be accessed. When an item is pushed or popped from the queue, the item with the highest priority, as determined by either the default operator $<$ or a comparison function object, is brought to the front of the queue. The *priority_queue* container uses a random-access iterator and adapts containers that support *front*, *push_back*, and *pop_back*, such as *deque* and *vector*. A *priority_queue* is most likely implemented as a heap. Here is a slightly simplified specification of the STL *priority_queue*:

```cpp
template <class T, class Container = vector<T>,
          class Compare = less<typename Container::value_type> >
class priority_queue

public:
   explicit priority_queue(const Compare& = Compare(),
                           const Container& = Container()) ;
   // Default constructor; initializes an empty priority queue.
   // The default comparison operator is <.
   // A comparison function object may be supplied.
   // Precondition: None.
   // Postcondition: An empty priority queue exists.

   bool empty() const;
   // Determines whether the priority queue is empty.
   // Precondition: None.
   // Postcondition: Returns true if the priority queue is empty,
   // otherwise returns false.

   size_type size() const;
   // Determines the size of the priority queue.
   // The return type size_type is an integral type.
   // Precondition: None.
   // Postcondition: Returns the number of items that
   // are currently in the priority queue.

   const value_type& top() const;
   // Returns a reference to the highest priority element in the
   // priority queue.
   // Precondition: None.
   // Postcondition: The item remains at the top of the
   // priority queue.

   void pop();
   // Removes the highest priority element in the
   // priority queue
   // Precondition: None.
   // Postcondition: The priority queue has the highest priority
   // element at the top.
```

```
        void push(const value_type& e);
        // Adds the item e to the priority queue
        // Precondition: None.
        // Postcondition: The priority queue has the highest priority
        // element at the top.
}   // end STL priority_queue
```

The STL also provides heap algorithms separately in *<algorithm>*. A container can be transformed into a heap using the *make_heap* function and then turned back into the container using *sort_heap*. The *push_heap* and *pop_heap* functions add and remove the first element of the heap, which is the element with the highest priority. Heap algorithms require random-access iterators. The function specifications are listed below:

```
void push_heap(RandomIter first, RandomIter last);
void push_heap(RandomIter first, RandomIter last, Compare cmp);
// Push an item onto the heap.
// The value pushed is *(last-1).
// A comparison function object may be supplied.

void pop_heap(RandomIter first, RandomIter last);
void pop_heap(RandomIter first, RandomIter last, Compare cmp);
// Push an item onto the heap.
// Swaps first element with *(last-1) and makes [first, last-1]
// into a heap.
// A comparison function object may be supplied.

void make_heap(RandomIter first, RandomIter last);
void make_heap(RandomIter first, RandomIter last, Compare cmp);
// Turns an existing container into a heap.
// A comparison function object may be supplied.

void sort_heap(RandomIter first, RandomIter last);
void sort_heap(RandomIter first, RandomIter last, Compare cmp);
// Turns the heap back into the original container.
// A comparison function object may be supplied.
```

The following program demonstrates the use of a priority queue and a vector that use heap operations:

```
#include <iostream>
#include <queue>
#include <vector>
#include <cstdlib>
#include <ctime>

using namespace std;
```

```
int main()
{
  //declare a priority queue
  priority_queue<int, vector<int> > pq;

  // declare a vector
  vector<int> vheap;

  // declare a vector iterator
  vector<int>::iterator iter;

  // seed the random number generator
  srand(time(0));

  // fill the priority queue and vector with the random numbers
  // push each number of the vector onto a heap
  // using the greater predicate
  for (int i=0; i < 25; i++)
  {
     int j = rand() % 25;
     pq.push(j);
     vheap.push_back(j);
     push_heap(vheap.begin(), vheap.end(), greater<int>() );
  }  // end for

  // show the generated numbers in their original order by
  // iterating through the vector
  cout << "Original numbers: " << endl;
  for (iter = vheap.begin(); iter != vheap.end(); iter++)
    cout << *iter << " ";

  // display the priority queue by popping the top off
  cout << endl << "Priority queue: " << endl;
  while (!pq.empty())
  {
    cout << pq.top() << " ";
    pq.pop();
  }  // end while

  // display the vector as a heap by popping the top off
  cout << endl << "Heap: " << endl;
  while (!vheap.empty())
  {
    cout << vheap[0] << " ";
    pop_heap(vheap.begin(), vheap.end(), greater<int>());
    vheap.pop_back();
  }  // end while

  cout << endl;
```

```
    return 0;
}  // end main
```

Here is the output of a sample run of the program:

```
Original numbers:
0 2 8 2 3 13 19 4 3 11 6 18 16 22 21 16 16 15 6 19 13 16 6 24 24
Priority queue:
24 24 22 21 19 19 18 16 16 16 16 15 13 13 11 8 6 6 6 4 3 3 2 2 0
Heap:
0 2 2 3 3 4 6 6 6 8 11 13 13 15 16 16 16 16 18 19 19 21 22 24 24
```

Summary

1. The ADT table supports value-oriented operations, such as

   Retrieve all the information about John Smith

2. The linear implementations (array based and pointer based) of a table are adequate only in limited situations, such as when the table is small or for certain operations. In those situations, the simplicity of a linear implementation may be an advantage. A linear implementation of a table, however, is not suitable as a general-purpose, reusable class.

3. A nonlinear pointer-based (binary search tree) implementation of the ADT table provides the best aspects of the two linear implementations. The pointer-based implementation allows the table to grow dynamically and allows insertions and deletions of data to occur through pointer changes instead of data movement. In addition, the binary search tree allows you to use a binary search-like algorithm when searching for an item with a specified value. These characteristics make a nonlinear table implementation far superior to the linear implementations in many applications.

4. A priority queue is a variation of the ADT table. Its operations allow you to retrieve and remove the item with the largest priority value.

5. A heap that uses an array-based representation of a complete binary tree is a good implementation of a priority queue when you know the maximum number of items that will be stored at any one time.

6. Heapsort, like mergesort, has good worst-case and average-case behaviors, but neither algorithm is as good in the average case as quicksort. Heapsort has an advantage over mergesort in that it does not require a second array.

Cautions

1. When defining an ADT to solve a particular problem, do not request unnecessary operations. The proper choice of an implementation depends on the mix of requested operations, and if you request an operation that you do not need, you might get an implementation that does not best support what you are really doing.

2. A linear array-based implementation of the ADT table must shift data during a deletion and during an insertion in sorted order. These shifts can be expensive, particularly for large tables.

3. Although a linear pointer-based implementation of the ADT table eliminates the need to shift data, it does not support the insertion and deletion operations any more efficiently than does an array-based implementation, because you cannot perform a binary search in a reasonable fashion.

4. Usually a binary search tree can support the ADT table operations quite efficiently. However, in the worst case, when the tree approaches a linear shape, the performance of the table operations is comparable to that of a linear pointer-based implementation. If a given application cannot tolerate poor performance, you should use the table implementations presented in Chapter 12.

5. Although a heap is a good implementation of a priority queue, it is not appropriate for a table. Specifically, a heap does not support the sorted `tableRetrieve` and `traverseTable` operations efficiently.

Self-Test Exercises

1. Using the ADT table operations, write pseudocode for a `tableReplace` operation that replaces the table item whose search key is *x* with another item whose search key is also *x*.

2. Does the array in Figure 11-20 represent a heap?

3. Is the full binary tree in Figure 10-36 a semiheap? Is it a heap?

4. Consider the heap in Figure 11-11. Draw the heap after you insert 12 and then remove 12.

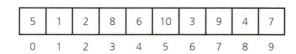

FIGURE 11-20   Array for Self-Test Exercises 2 and 7 and Exercise 24

5. What does the initially empty heap *h* contain after the following sequence of pseudocode operations?

```
h.heapInsert(2)
h.heapInsert(3)
h.heapInsert(4)
h.heapInsert(1)
h.heapInsert(9)
h.heapDelete(item)
h.heapInsert(7)
h.heapInsert(6)
h.heapDelete(item)
h.heapInsert(5)
```

6. What does the heap that represents the initially empty priority queue *pQueue* contain after the following sequence of pseudocode operations?

```
pQueue.pqInsert(5)
pQueue.pqInsert(9)
pQueue.pqInsert(6)
pQueue.pqInsert(7)
pQueue.pqInsert(3)
pQueue.pqInsert(4)
pQueue.pqDelete(item)
pQueue.pqInsert(9)
pQueue.pqInsert(2)
pQueue.pqDelete(item)
```

7. Execute the pseudocode statements

```
for (index = n - 1 down to 0)
    heapRebuild(anArray, index, n)
```

on the array in Figure 11-24.

Exercises

1. Complete the sorted array-based implementation of the ADT table.

2. The operation `tableReplace(replacementItem)` locates, if possible, the item in a table with the same search key as `replacement-Item`. If the table contains such an item, `tableReplace` replaces it with `replacementItem`. Thus, all but the search key of the original item is updated.

   a. Write implementations of `tableReplace` for the five implementations (four linear ones and the binary search tree) of the ADT table described in this chapter.

b. For the binary search tree implementation of the ADT table, under what circumstances can *tableReplace* replace an item without altering the structure of the binary search tree? (See Exercise 13 in Chapter 10.)

3. Imagine an application program that behaves like an English dictionary. The user types a word and the program provides the word's definition. Thus, the dictionary needs only a retrieval operation. Which implementation of the ADT table would be most efficient as an English dictionary?

4. When you use a word processor's spell checker, it compares the words in your document with words in a dictionary. You can add new words to the dictionary as necessary. Thus, this dictionary needs frequent retrievals and occasional insertions. Which implementation of the ADT table would be most efficient as a spell checker's dictionary?

5. A C++ compiler uses a symbol table to keep track of the identifiers that a program uses. When the compiler encounters an identifier, it searches the symbol table to see whether that identifier has already been encountered. If the identifier is new, it is inserted into the table. Thus, the symbol table needs only insertion and retrieval operations. Which implementation of the ADT table would be most efficient as a symbol table?

6. Revise *Table* as a class template.

7. The implementations of the ADT table given in this chapter make the following assumption: At any time, a table contains at most one item with a given search key. Although the ADT definition required for a specific application may not allow duplicates, it is probably wise to test for them rather than simply to assume that they will not occur. Why?

   Modify the table implementations so that they test for—and disallow—any duplicates. What table operations are affected? What are the implications for the unsorted linear implementations?

8. Although disallowing duplicates in the ADT table (see Exercise 7) is reasonable for some applications, it is just as reasonable to have an application that will allow duplicates.

   a. What are the implications of inserting duplicate items that are identical? What are the implications of duplicate items for the deletion and retrieval operations?

   b. What are the implications of inserting items that are not identical but have the same search key? Specifically, what would the implementations of *tableInsert*, *tableDelete*, and *tableRetrieve* do?

9. Suppose that you want to support table deletion operations for two different search keys (for example, *tableDeleteN* to delete by name and *tableDeleteS* to delete by Social Security number). Describe an efficient implementation.

10. Repeat Exercise 9, but instead organize one of the search keys with a binary search tree and the other with a sorted linked list.

★11. Implement a *traverseTable* operation that permits *visit()* to delete the item visited. Exercise 36 in Chapter 10 considered the analogous question for the ADT binary search tree.

12. Given the minheap *h* in Figure 11-21, show what the heap *h* would look like after each of the following pseudocode operations:

   a. h.heapInsert(8)
   b. h.heapInsert(5)
   c. h.heapDelete()

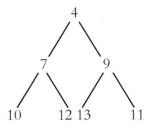

FIGURE 11-21   Minheap for Exercise 12

13. Given the maxheap *h* in Figure 11-22, show what the heap *h* would look like after each of the following pseudocode operations:

   a. h.heapInsert(16)
   b. h.heapInsert(14)
   c. h.heapDelete()

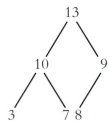

FIGURE 11-22   Maxheap for Exercise 13

14. Repeat Self-Test Exercise 7, but instead use the array 9, 12, 4, 8, 3, 11, 6, 15.

15. Prove that the root of a heap contains the largest search key in the tree.

16. Does the order in which you insert items into a heap affect the heap that results? Explain.

17. Revise the implementations of *heapInsert* and *heapRebuild* so that actual swaps of items are unnecessary.

18. Suppose that you have two items with the same priority value. How does the order in which you insert these items into a priority queue affect the order in which they will be deleted? What can you do if you need elements with equal priority value to be served on a first-come, first-served basis?

19. The heap that this chapter described is called a maxheap because the largest element is at the root. This organization is appropriate because the *pqDelete* operation for the heap implementation of the priority queue deletes the element with the highest priority value. Suppose that you wanted the *pqDelete* operation to delete the element with the lowest priority value instead. You would then use a minheap. Convert the maxheap implementation to a minheap implementation.

20. Suppose that you wanted to maintain the index of the item with the smallest priority value in a maxheap. That is, in addition to a *removeMax* operation, you might want to support a *retrieveMin* operation. How difficult would it be to maintain this index within the *pqInsert* and *removeMax* operations?

21. Suppose that after you have placed several items into a priority queue, you need to adjust one of their priority values. For example, a particular task in a priority queue of tasks could become either more or less urgent. How can you adjust a heap if a single priority value changes?

22. Revise *Heap* and *PriorityQueue* as class templates.

23. Show that within the pseudocode for the function *heapSort* you can replace the statement

```
for (index = n-1 down to 0)
```

with

```
for (index = n/2 down to 0)
```

24. Trace the action of *heapSort* on the array in Figure 11-20.

25. Implement *heapSort* in C++.

26. Revise *heapSort* so that it sorts an array into descending order.

Programming Problems

1. Write the sorted pointer-based, unsorted array-based, and unsorted pointer-based implementations of the ADT table described in this chapter.

2. Write unsorted and sorted implementations of the ADT table that use, respectively, the ADTs list and sorted list, which Chapter 3 described.

3. Repeat Programming Problem 5 of Chapter 10, using the ADT table as the address book.

4. Repeat Programming Problem 4 of Chapter 10, using the STL *map* or *multimap* container.

5. Implement the symbol table described in Exercise 5 by reusing *Table*.

6. As Figure 11-9 illustrates, you can use data structures other than a heap to implement the ADT priority queue.

a. Write the C++ class for the pointer-based implementation that Figure 11-9b represents.

b. Write the C++ class for the binary search tree implementation that Figure 11-9c represents.

c. Implement the classes that you wrote in Parts a and b.

7. Suppose that you wanted to implement a priority queue whose priority values are integers 1 through 20.

a. Implement the priority queue as a heap of queues, as described in this chapter.

b. Another solution uses an array of 20 queues, one for each priority value. Use this approach to implement the priority queue.

8. Implement the to-do list described at the beginning of the section "The ADT Priority Queue" in this chapter using the STL *priority_queue*.

9. Consider any collection of data that you can organize in at least two ways. For example, you can order a list of employees by name or by Social Security number and a list of books by title or by author. Note that other information about the employees or books is present in the database but is not used to organize these items. This program assumes that the search keys (for example, book title or book author) are unique and are strings. Thus, in the previous examples, the Social Security number must be a string instead of an integer, and only one book per author is permitted. Choose any set of data that conforms to these requirements, and create a text file.

Program behavior. When your program begins execution, it should read your text file. It then should provide some typical database management operations, all under user control via an interface of your design. For example, you should be able to add an item, delete an item, display (that is, retrieve) an item, and display all of the items in search-key order. You should be able to use either of two search keys to designate the item to be deleted or displayed.

Implementation notes. The items in the database should be objects that contain two search keys and additional data, all of which appear in the text file. Thus, you need to design and implement a class of these objects.

Although your program could create two tables from these objects—one organized by one search key (such as the employee name) and the other organized by another search key (such as the Social Security number)—this approach could waste a substantial amount of memory due to the duplication of all of the data in both tables.

A better approach revises the ADT table to provide operations according to two search keys. For example, you want to be able to delete by name and by Social Security number. The underlying data structure for the table's implementation should be a binary search tree. Actually, you will want two binary search trees so that you can organize the data in two ways: by name and by Social Security number, for example.

To avoid duplicated data, store the data in an ADT list and let each node in the binary search trees contain the position of the actual data item in the list, instead of the data item itself.

Your program can be specific to the type of database (employees, books, and so on) or it can be more general. For example, you could determine the search-key descriptions that the user interface displays by requiring that they be in the text file.

10. Write an interactive program that will monitor the flow of patients in a large hospital. The program should account for patients checking in and out of the hospital and should allow access to information about a given patient. In addition, the program should manage the scheduling of three operating rooms. Doctors make a request that includes a patient's name and a priority value between 1 and 10 that reflects the urgency of the operation. Patients are chosen for the operating room by priority value, and patients with the same priority are served on a first-come, first-served basis.

The user should use either one-letter or one-word commands to control the program. As you design your solution, try to identify the essential operations (excuse the pun) that you must perform on the data, and only then choose an appropriate data structure for implementation. This approach will allow you to maintain the wall between the main part of the program and the implementations. An interesting exercise would be to recast this problem as an event-driven simulation.

CHAPTER 12

Advanced Implementations of Tables

PREVIEW

Although Chapter 11 described the advantages of using the binary search tree to implement the ADT table, the efficiency of this implementation suffers when the tree loses its balance. This chapter introduces several advanced implementations of the table. First examined are various other search trees, which remain balanced in all situations and thus enable table operations whose efficiency is comparable to a binary search.

This chapter then considers a completely different implementation of the ADT table that, for many applications, is even more efficient than a search-tree implementation. In principle, the algorithm, which is called hashing, locates a data item by performing a calculation on its search-key value, rather than by searching for it.

Finally, the chapter considers data organizations that support diverse kinds of operations simultaneously. For example, you might want to organize data in first-in, first-out order, but you also might require the data to be in sorted order. The challenge is to store the data only once.

12.1 Balanced Search Trees

As you saw in the previous chapter, the efficiency of the binary search tree implementation of the ADT table is related to the tree's height. The operations *tableRetrieve*, *tableInsert*, and *tableDelete* follow a path from the root of the tree to the node that contains the desired item (or, in the case of the insertion operation, to the node that is to become the parent of the new item). At each node along the path, you compare a given value to the search key in the node and determine which subtree to search next. Because the maximum number of nodes on such a path is equal to the height of the tree, the maximum number of comparisons that the table operations can require is also equal to this height.

As you know, the height of a binary search tree of N items ranges from a maximum of N to a minimum of $\lceil \log_2(N + 1) \rceil$. As a consequence, locating a particular item in a binary search tree requires between N and $\lceil \log_2(N + 1) \rceil$ comparisons. Thus, a search of a binary search tree can be as inefficient as a sequential search of a linked list or as efficient as a binary search of an array. Efficiency was the primary reason for developing the binary search tree implementation of the table: We wanted to perform a search of a linked structure as efficiently as we could perform a binary search of an array. Thus, we certainly want the most optimistic behavior of the binary search tree.

The height of a binary search tree is sensitive to the order of insertions and deletions

What affects the height of a binary search tree? As you learned in Chapter 10, the height of the tree is quite sensitive to the order in which you insert or delete items. For example, consider a binary search tree that contains the items[1] 10, 20, 30, 40, 50, 60, and 70. If you inserted the items into the tree in ascending order, you would obtain a binary search tree of maximum height, as shown in Figure 12-1a. If, on the other hand, you inserted the items in the order 40, 20, 60, 10, 30, 50, 70, you would obtain a balanced binary search tree of minimum height, as shown in Figure 12-1b.

Various search trees can retain their balance despite insertions and deletions

As you can see, if you use the algorithms in Chapter 10 to maintain a binary search tree, insertions and deletions can cause the tree to lose its balance and approach a linear shape. Such a tree is no better than a linked list. For this reason, it is desirable in many applications to use one of several variations of the basic binary search tree. Such trees can absorb insertions and deletions without a deterioration of their balance and are easier to maintain than a minimum-height binary search tree. In addition, you can search these trees almost as efficiently as you can search a minimum-height binary search tree. This chapter discusses the better-known search trees to give you a sense of the possibilities. We continue to assume that the search keys in a tree are unique, that is, that there are no duplicates.

---

[1] As in Chapter 10, tree items are records that each contain a search key. The tree diagrams in this chapter will show only these search keys, and the discussions will often treat an item as if it consisted solely of its search key.

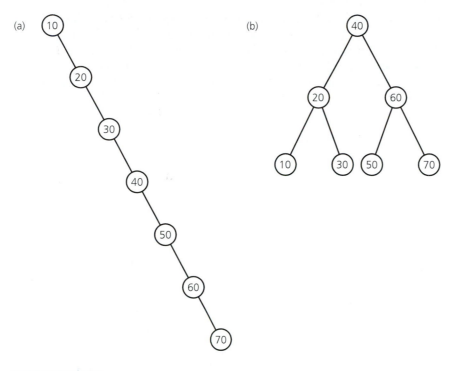

FIGURE 12-1   (a) A search tree of maximum height; (b) a search tree of minimum height

2-3 Trees

A **2-3 tree** is a tree in which each internal node (nonleaf) has either two or three children, and all leaves are at the same level. For example, Figure 12-2 shows a 2-3 tree of height 3. A node with two children is called a **2-node**—the nodes in a binary tree are all 2-nodes—and a node with three children is called a **3-node**.

A 2-3 tree is not a binary tree, because a node can have three chil-   A 2-3 tree is not binary
dren; nevertheless, a 2-3 tree does resemble a full binary tree. If a particular 2-3 tree does not contain 3-nodes—a possibility, according to the definition—it is like a full binary tree, because all of its internal

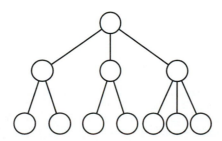

FIGURE 12-2   A 2-3 tree of height 3

nodes have two children and all of its leaves are at the same level. If, on the other hand, some of the internal nodes of a 2-3 tree do have three children, the tree will contain more nodes than a full binary tree of the same height. Therefore, a 2-3 tree of height h always has at least as many nodes as a full binary tree of height h; that is, it always has at least $2^h - 1$ nodes. To put this another way, a 2-3 tree with N nodes never has height greater than $\lceil \log_2(N + 1) \rceil$, the minimum height of a binary tree with N nodes.

A 2-3 tree is never taller than a minimum-height binary tree

Given these observations, a 2-3 tree might be useful as an implementation of the ADT table. Indeed, this is the case if the 2-3 tree orders its nodes to make it useful as a search tree. The following recursive definition[2] of a 2-3 tree specifies this order:

A 2-3 tree

T is a 2-3 tree of height h if

1. T is empty (a 2-3 tree of height 0).

or

2. T is of the form

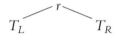

where r is a node that contains one data item and T_L and T_R are both 2-3 trees, each of height $h - 1$. In this case, the search key in r must be greater than each search key in the left subtree T_L and smaller than each search key in the right subtree T_R.

or

3. T is of the form

where r is a node that contains two data items and T_L, T_M, and T_R are 2-3 trees, each of height $h - 1$. In this case, the smaller search key in r must be greater than each search key in the left subtree T_L and smaller than each search key in the middle subtree T_M. The larger search key in r must be greater than each search key in the middle subtree T_M and smaller than each search key in the right subtree T_R.

This definition implies the following rules for how you may place data items in the nodes of a 2-3 tree.

---

[2] Just as we distinguish between a binary tree and a binary search tree, we could distinguish between a "2-3 tree" and a "2-3 search tree." The previous description would define a 2-3 tree, and the definition given here would define a 2-3 search tree. Most people, however, do not make such a distinction and use the term "2-3 tree" to mean "2-3 search tree"; we will also.

KEY CONCEPTS

Rules for Placing Data Items in the Nodes of a 2-3 Tree

1. A 2-node, which has two children, must contain a single data item whose search key is greater than the left child's search key(s) and less than the right child's search key(s), as Figure 12-3a illustrates.

2. A 3-node, which has three children, must contain two data items whose search keys S and L satisfy the following relationships, as Figure 12-3b illustrates: S is greater than the left child's search key(s) and less than the middle child's search key(s); L is greater than the middle child's search key(s) and less than the right child's search key(s).

3. A leaf may contain either one or two data items.

Thus, the items in a 2–3 tree are ordered by their search keys. For example, the tree in Figure 12-4 is a 2–3 tree.

Items in a 2-3 tree are ordered

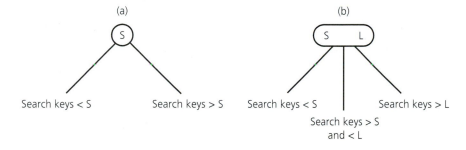

FIGURE 12-3 Nodes in a 2-3 tree: (a) a 2-node; (b) a 3-node

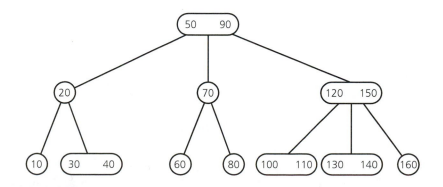

FIGURE 12-4 A 2-3 tree

The following C++ statements[3] describe any node in a 2-3 tree:

A node in a 2-3 tree

```cpp
class TreeNode
{
private:
   TreeItemType smallItem, largeItem;
   TreeNode *leftChildPtr, *midChildPtr, *rightChildPtr;

   // friend class-can access private class members
   friend class TwoThreeTree;
};  // end TreeNode
```

When a node contains only one data item, you can place it in *small-Item* and use *leftChildPtr* and *midChildPtr* to point to the node's children. To be safe, you can place *NULL* in *rightChildPtr*.

Now consider the traversal, retrieval, insertion, and deletion operations for a 2-3 tree. The algorithms for these operations are recursive. You can avoid distracting implementation details by defining the base case for these recursive algorithms to be a leaf rather than an empty subtree. As a result, the algorithms must assume that they are not passed an empty tree as an argument.

Traversing a 2-3 tree. You can traverse a 2-3 tree in sorted search-key order by performing the analogue of an inorder traversal:

Traversal in sorted order

```
inorder(in ttTree:TwoThreeTree)
// Traverses the nonempty 2-3 tree ttTree in sorted
// search-key order.

   if (ttTree's root node r is a leaf)
      Visit the data item(s)

   else if (r has two data items)
   {  inorder(left subtree of ttTree's root)
      Visit the first data item
      inorder(middle subtree of ttTree's root)
      Visit the second data item
      inorder(right subtree of ttTree's root)
   }

   else  // r has one data item
   {  inorder(left subtree of ttTree's root)
      Visit the data item
      inorder(right subtree of ttTree's root)
   }  // end if
```

---

[3] For simplicity, the constructor has been omitted.

Searching a 2-3 tree. The ordering of items in a 2-3 tree is analogous to the ordering for a binary search tree and allows you to search a 2-3 tree efficiently for a particular item. In fact, the retrieval operation for a 2-3 tree is quite similar to the retrieval operation for a binary search tree, as you can see from the following pseudocode:

Searching a 2-3 tree is efficient

```
retrieveItem(in ttTree:TwoThreeTree,
             in searchKey:KeyType,
             out treeItem:TreeItemType):boolean
// Retrieves into treeItem from a nonempty 2-3 tree ttTree
// the item whose search key equals searchKey. The
// operation fails if no such item exists. The function
// returns true if the item is found, false otherwise.


   if (searchKey is in ttTree's root node r)
   {  // the item has been found
      treeItem = the data portion of r
      return true
   }


   else if (r is a leaf)
      return false   // failure


   // else search the appropriate subtree
   else if (r has two data items)
   {  if (searchKey < smaller search key of r)
         return retrieveItem(r's left subtree, searchKey,
                                        treeItem)
      else if (searchKey < larger search key of r)
         return retrieveItem(r's middle subtree, searchKey,
                                        treeItem)
      else
         return retrieveItem(r's right subtree, searchKey,
                                        treeItem)
   }


   else  // r has one data item
   {  if (searchKey < r's search key)
         return retrieveItem(r's left subtree, searchKey,
                                        treeItem)

      else
         return retrieveItem(r's right subtree, searchKey,
                                        treeItem)
   }  // end if
```

Have you gained anything by using a 2–3 tree rather than a binary search tree to implement the ADT table? You can search the 2–3 tree and the shortest binary search tree with approximately the same efficiency, because

- A binary search tree with N nodes cannot be shorter than $\lceil \log_2(N + 1) \rceil$

- A 2–3 tree with N nodes cannot be taller than $\lceil \log_2(N + 1) \rceil$

- A node in a 2–3 tree has at most two items

Searching a 2–3 tree is not *more* efficient than searching a binary search tree, however. This observation may surprise you because, after all, the nodes of a 2–3 tree can have three children, and hence a 2–3 tree might indeed be shorter than the shortest possible binary search tree. Although true, this advantage in height is offset by the extra time required to compare a given value with two search-key values instead of only one. In other words, although you might visit fewer nodes when searching a 2–3 tree, you might have to make more comparisons at each node. As a consequence, the number of comparisons required to search a 2–3 tree for a given item is *approximately equal* to the number of comparisons required to search a binary search tree that is *as balanced as possible*. This number is approximately $\log_2 N$.

Searching a 2-3 tree is O(log *N*)

If you can search a 2–3 tree and a balanced binary search tree with approximately the same efficiency, why then should you use a 2–3 tree? Although maintaining the balance of a binary search tree is difficult in the face of insertion and deletion operations, maintaining the shape of a

Maintaining the shape of a 2-3 tree is relatively easy

2–3 tree is relatively simple. For example, consider the two trees in Figure 12-5. The first tree is a binary search tree and the second is a 2–3 tree. Both trees contain the same data items. The binary search tree is as balanced as possible, and thus you can search both it and the 2–3 tree for

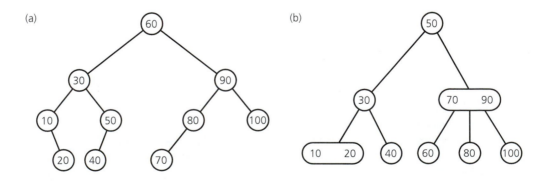

FIGURE 12-5   (a) A balanced binary search tree; (b) a 2-3 tree with the same elements

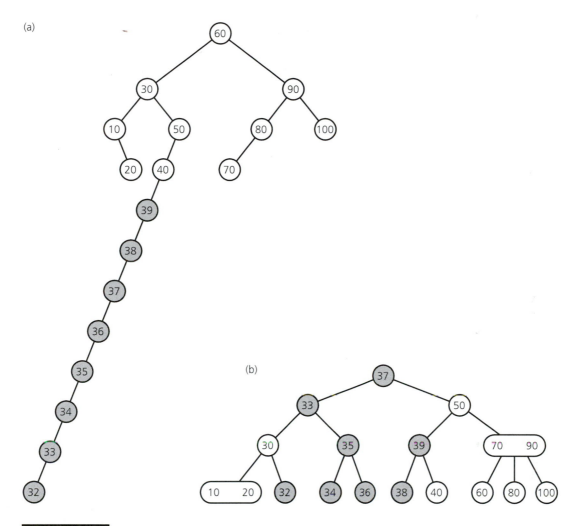

FIGURE 12-6 (a) The binary search tree of Figure 12-5a after a sequence of insertions; (b) the 2-3 tree of Figure 12-5b after the same insertions

an item with approximately the same efficiency. If, however, you perform a sequence of insertions on the binary search tree—by using the insertion algorithm of Chapter 10—the tree can quickly lose its balance, as Figure 12-6a indicates. As you soon will see, you can perform the same sequence of insertions on the 2-3 tree without a degradation in the tree's shape—it will retain its structure, as Figure 12-6b shows.

The new values (32 through 39) that were inserted into the binary search tree of Figure 12-5a appear along a single path in Figure 12-6a. The insertions increased the height of the binary search tree from 4 to 12—an increase of 8. On the other hand, the new values have been spread throughout the 2-3 tree in Figure 12-6b. As a consequence, the height of the resulting tree is only 1 greater than the height of the original

2-3 tree in Figure 12-5b. We demonstrate these insertions into the original 2-3 tree next.

Inserting into a 2-3 tree. Because the nodes of a 2-3 tree can have either two or three children and can contain one or two values, you can insert items into the tree while maintaining its shape. The following paragraphs informally describe the sequence of insertions that produced the 2-3 tree shown in Figure 12-6b. Figure 12-5b shows the original tree.

Insert 39.   As is true with a binary search tree, the first step in inserting a node into a 2-3 tree is to locate the node at which the search for 39 would terminate. To do this, you can use the search strategy of the *retrieveItem* algorithm given previously; an unsuccessful search will always terminate at a leaf. With the tree in Figure 12-5b, the search for 39 terminates at the leaf <40>.[4] Because this node contains only one item, you can simply insert the new item into this node. The result is the 2-3 tree in Figure 12-7.

Insertion into a 2-node leaf is simple

Insert 38.   In a similar manner, you would search the tree in Figure 12-7 for 38 and find that the search terminates at the node <39 40>. As a conceptual first step, you should place 38 in this node, as Figure 12-8a illustrates.

This placement is problematic because a node cannot contain three values. You divide these three values, however, into the smallest (38), middle (39), and largest (40) values. You can move the middle value (39) up to the node's parent p and separate the remaining values, 38 and 40, into two nodes that you attach to p as children, as Figure 12-8b indicates. Because you chose to move up the middle value of <38 39 40>, the parent correctly separates the values of its children; that is, 38 is less than 39, which is less than 40. The result of the insertion is the 2-3 tree in Figure 12-8c.

Insertion into a 3-node causes it to divide

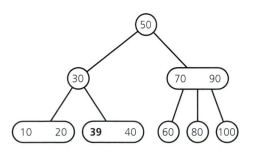

FIGURE 12-7   After inserting 39

---

[4] Here, the angle brackets denote a node and its contents.

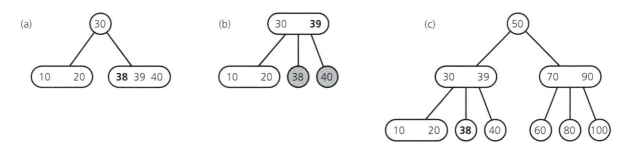

FIGURE 12-8   (a), (b) The steps for inserting 38; (c) the resulting tree

Insert 37. The insertion of 37 into the tree in Figure 12-8c is easy because 37 belongs in a leaf that currently contains only one value, 38. The result of this insertion is the 2-3 tree in Figure 12-9.

Insert 36. The search strategy determines that 36 belongs in the node <37 38> of the tree in Figure 12-9. Again, as a conceptual first step, place it there, as Figure 12-10a indicates.

 Because the node <36 37 38> now contains three values, you divide it—as you did previously—into the smallest (36), middle (37), and largest (38) values. You then move the middle value (37) up to the node's parent *p*, and attach to *p*—as children—nodes that contain the smallest (36) and largest (38) values, as Figure 12-10b illustrates.

 This time, however, you are not finished: You have a node <30 37 39> that contains three values and has four children. This situation is familiar, with the slight difference that the overcrowded node is not a leaf but rather has four children. As you did before, you divide the node into the smallest (30), middle (37), and largest (39) values and then move the middle value up to the node's parent. Because you are splitting an internal node, you now must account for its four children; that is, what happens to nodes <10 20>, <36>, <38>, and <40>, which were the children of node <30 37 39>? The solution is to attach the left pair of children (nodes <10 20> and <36>) to the smallest value

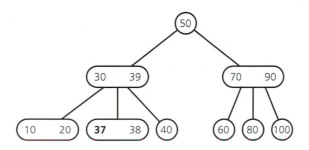

FIGURE 12-9   After inserting 37

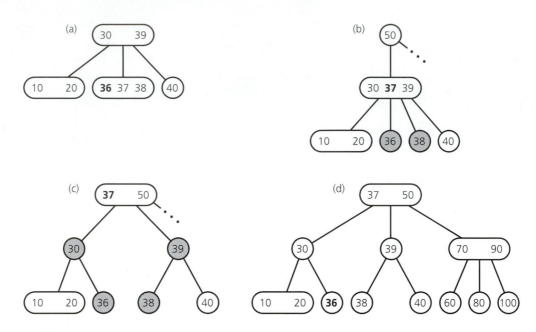

FIGURE 12-10   (a), (b), (c) The steps for inserting 36; (d) the resulting tree

(30) and attach the right pair of children (nodes <38> and <40>) to the largest value (39), as shown in Figure 12-10c. The final result of this insertion is the 2–3 tree in Figure 12-10d.

Insert 35, 34, and 33. Each of these insertions is similar to the previous ones. Figure 12-11 shows the tree after the three insertions.

Before performing the final insertion of the value 32, consider the 2–3 tree's insertion strategy.

The insertion algorithm. To insert an item *I* into a 2–3 tree, you first locate the leaf at which the search for *I* would terminate. You insert the new item *I* into the leaf, and if the leaf now contains only two items,

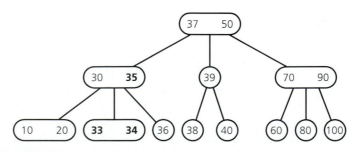

FIGURE 12-11   The tree after the insertion of 35, 34, and 33

you are done. However, if the leaf contains three items, you must split it into two nodes, n_1 and n_2. As Figure 12-12 illustrates, you place the smallest item[5] S into n_1, place the largest item L into n_2, and move the middle item M up to the original leaf's parent. Nodes n_1 and n_2 then become children of the parent. If the parent now has only three children (and contains two items)—as is true here—you are finished. On the other hand, if the parent now has four children (and contains three items), you must split it, as follows.

When a leaf contains three items, split it into two nodes

You split an internal node n that contains three items by using the process just described for a leaf, except that you must also take care of n's four children. As Figure 12-13 illustrates, you split n into n_1 and n_2, place n's smallest item S into n_1, attach n's two leftmost children to n_1, place n's largest item L into n_2, attach n's two rightmost children to n_2, and move n's middle item M up to n's parent.

When an internal node contains three items, split it into two nodes and accommodate its children

After this, the process of splitting a node and moving an item up to the parent continues recursively until a node is reached that had only one item before the insertion and thus has only two items after it takes on a new item. Notice in the previous sequence of insertions that the tree's height never increased from its original value of 3. In general, *an insertion will not increase the height of the tree* as long as there is at least one node containing only one item on the path from the root to the leaf into which the new item is inserted. The insertion strategy of a 2-3 tree has thus postponed the growth of the tree's height much more effectively than the strategy of a basic binary search tree did.

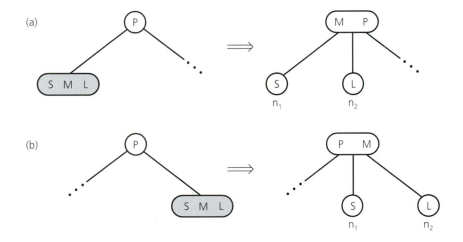

(a)

(b)

FIGURE 12-12 Splitting a leaf in a 2-3 tree

---

[5] "Smallest item" means the item with the smallest search key. Analogously, the terms "middle item" and "largest item" will also be used.

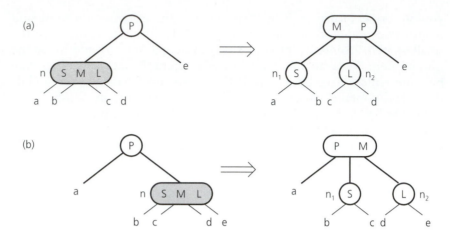

FIGURE 12-13   Splitting an internal node in a 2-3 tree

When the height of a 2–3 tree does grow, it does so from the top. An increase in the height of a 2–3 tree will occur if every node on the path from the root of the tree to the leaf into which the new item is inserted contains two items. In this case, the recursive process of splitting a node and moving an item up to the node's parent will eventually reach the root r. When this occurs you must split r into r_1 and r_2 exactly as you would any other internal node. However, you must create a new node that contains the middle item of r and becomes the parent of r_1 and r_2. Thus, the new node is the new root of the tree, as Figure 12-14 illustrates.

> **When the root contains three items, split it into two nodes and create a new root node**

The following algorithm summarizes the entire insertion strategy:

> **2-3 tree insertion algorithm**

```
insertItem(in ttTree:TwoThreeTree, in newItem:TreeItemType)

// Inserts newItem into a 2-3 tree ttTree whose items have
// distinct search keys that differ from newItem's search
// key.

    Let sKey be the search key of newItem
    Locate the leaf leafNode in which sKey belongs
```

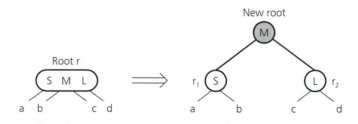

FIGURE 12-14   Splitting the root of a 2-3 tree

```
    Add newItem to leafNode

    if (leafNode now has three items)
        split(leafNode)


split(inout n:TreeNode)
// Splits node n, which contains 3 items. Note: if n is
// not a leaf, it has 4 children. Throws TreeException
// if node allocation fails.

    if (n is the root)
        Create a new node p (refine later to throw exception
                               if allocation fails)
    else
        Let p be the parent of n

    Replace node n with two nodes, n1 and n2, so that p is
      their parent

    Give n1 the item in n with the smallest search-key value
    Give n2 the item in n with the largest search-key value

    if (n is not a leaf)
    {   n1 becomes the parent of n's two leftmost children
        n2 becomes the parent of n's two rightmost children
    }

    Move the item in n that has the middle
      search-key value up to p

    if (p now has three items)
        split(p)
```

Insert 32. To be sure that you fully understand the insertion algorithm, go through the steps of inserting 32 into the 2-3 tree in Figure 12-11. The result should be the tree shown in Figure 12-6b.

Once again, compare this tree with the binary search tree in Figure 12-6a and notice the dramatic advantage of the 2-3 tree's insertion strategy.

Deleting from a 2-3 tree. The deletion strategy for a 2-3 tree is the inverse of its insertion strategy. Just as a 2-3 tree spreads insertions throughout the tree by splitting nodes when they become too full, it spreads deletions throughout the tree by merging nodes when they become empty. As an illustration of the 2-3 tree's deletion strategy, consider the deletion of 70, 100, and 80 from the tree in Figure 12-5b.

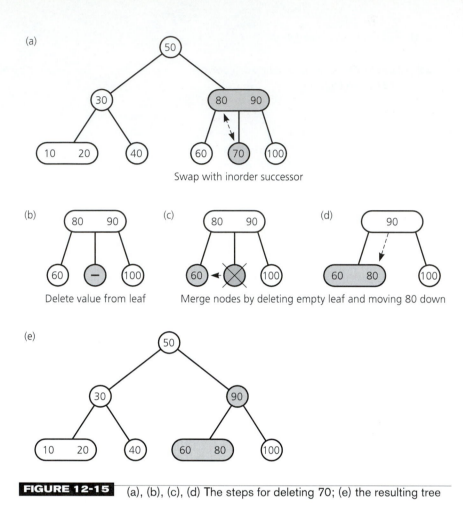

(a)

Swap with inorder successor

(b) Delete value from leaf

(c) (d) Merge nodes by deleting empty leaf and moving 80 down

(e)

(a), (b), (c), (d) The steps for deleting 70; (e) the resulting tree

Delete 70. By searching the tree, you will discover that 70 is in the node <70 90>. Because you always want to begin the deletion process at a leaf, the first step is to swap 70 with its inorder successor—the value that follows it in the sorted order. Because 70 is the smaller of the two values in the node, its inorder successor (80) is the smallest value in the node's middle subtree. (The inorder successor of an item in an internal node will always be in a leaf.) After the swap, the tree appears as shown in Figure 12-15a. The value 80 is in a legal position of the search tree because it is larger than all the values in its node's left subtree and smaller than all the values in its node's right subtree. The value 70 is not in a legal position, but this is of no concern, because the next step is to delete this value from the leaf.

In general, after you delete a value from a leaf, another value may remain in the leaf (because the leaf contained two values before the deletion). If this is the case, you are done, because a leaf of a 2-3 tree

Swap the value to be deleted with its inorder successor

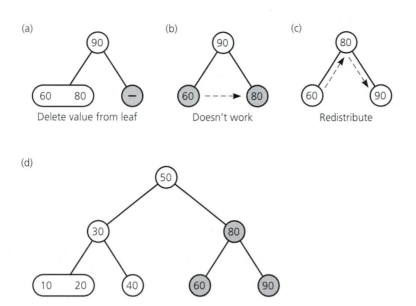

FIGURE 12-16   (a), (b), (c) The steps for deleting 100; (d) the resulting tree

can contain a single value. In this example, however, once you delete 70 from the leaf, the node is left without a value, as Figure 12-15b indicates.

You then delete the node, as Figure 12-15c illustrates. At this point you see that the parent of the deleted node contains two values (80 and 90) but has two children (60 and 100). This situation is not allowed in a 2-3 tree. (See rule 1.) You can remedy the problem by moving the smaller value (80) down from the parent into the left child, as Figure 12-15d illustrates. Deleting the leaf node and moving a value down to a sibling of the leaf is called merging the leaf with its sibling.   **Merge nodes**

The 2-3 tree that results from this deletion is shown in Figure 12-15e.

Delete 100.   The search strategy discovers that 100 is in the leaf <100> of the tree in Figure 12-15e. When you delete the value from this leaf, the node becomes empty, as Figure 12-16a indicates. In this case, however, no merging of nodes is required, because the sibling <60 80> can spare a value. That is, the sibling has two values, whereas a 2-3 tree requires only that it have at least one value. If you simply move the value 80 into the empty node—as Figure 12-16b illustrates—you find that the search-tree order is destroyed: The value in 90's right child is 80, whereas it should be greater than 90. The solution to this problem is to redistribute the values among the empty node, its sibling, and its parent.   **Redistribute values** Here you can move the larger value (80) from the sibling into the parent and move the value 90 down from the parent into the node that had been empty, as Figure 12-16c shows. This distribution preserves the search-tree order, and you have thus completed the deletion. The result- ing 2-3 tree is shown in Figure 12-16d.

Delete 80.   The search strategy finds that 80 is in an internal node of the tree in Figure 12-16d. You thus must swap 80 with its inorder successor, 90, as Figure 12-17a illustrates. When you delete 80 from the leaf, the node becomes empty. (See Figure 12-17b.) Because the sibling of the empty node has only one value, you cannot redistribute as you did in the deletion of 100. Instead you must merge the nodes, bringing the value 90 down from the parent and removing the empty leaf, as Figure 12-17c indicates.

You are not yet finished, however, because the parent now contains no values and has only one child. You must recursively apply the deletion

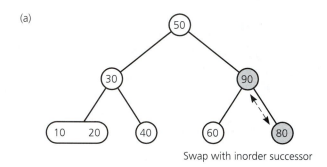

(a)

Swap with inorder successor

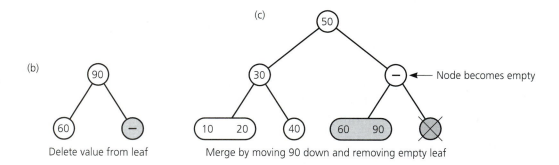

(b)

Delete value from leaf

(c)

← Node becomes empty

Merge by moving 90 down and removing empty leaf

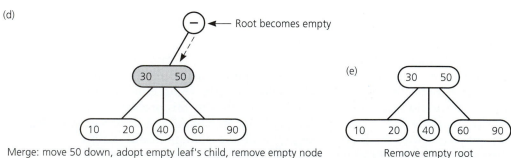

(d)

← Root becomes empty

(e)

Merge: move 50 down, adopt empty leaf's child, remove empty node

Remove empty root

FIGURE 12-17   The steps for deleting 80

strategy to this internal node without a value. First, you should check to see if the node's sibling can spare a value. Because the sibling <30> contains only the single value 30, you cannot redistribute—you must merge the nodes. The merging of two internal nodes is identical to the merging of leaves, except that the child <60 90> of the empty node must be adopted. Because the sibling of the empty node contains only one value (and hence can have only two children, as stated in rule 1), it can become the parent of <60 90> only if you bring the value 50 down from the sibling's parent. The tree now appears as shown in Figure 12-17d. Note that this operation preserves the search property of the tree.

Now the parent of the merged nodes is left with no values and only a single child. Usually, you would apply the recursive deletion strategy to this node, but this case is special because the node is the root. Because the root is empty and has only one child, you can simply remove it, allowing <30 50> to become the root of the tree, as Figure 12-17e illustrates. This deletion has thus caused the height of the tree to shrink by 1.

To summarize, we have deleted 70, 100, and 80 from the 2-3 tree in Figure 12-5b and obtained the 2-3 tree in Figure 12-18b. In contrast, after deleting 70, 100, and 80 from the balanced binary search tree in Figure 12-5a, you are left with the tree in Figure 12-18a. Notice that the deletions affected only one part of the binary search tree, causing it to lose its balance. The left subtree has not been affected at all, and thus the overall height of the tree has not been diminished.

The deletion algorithm. In summary, to delete an item *I* from a 2-3 tree, you first locate the node *n* that contains it. If *n* is not a leaf, you find *I*'s inorder successor and swap it with *I*. As a result of the swap, the deletion always begins at a leaf. If the leaf contains an item in addition to *I*, you simply delete *I* and you are done. On the other hand, if the leaf contains only *I*, deleting *I* would leave the leaf without a data item. In this case you must perform some additional work to complete the deletion.

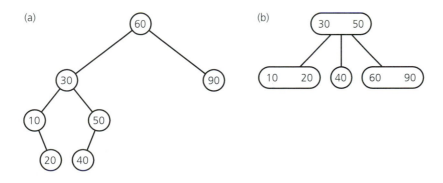

FIGURE 12-18 Results of deleting 70, 100, and 80 from (a) the binary search tree of Figure 12-5a and (b) the 2-3 tree of Figure 12-5b

You first check the siblings of the now-empty leaf. If a sibling has two items, you redistribute the items among the sibling, the empty leaf, and the leaf's parent, as Figure 12-19a illustrates. If no sibling of the leaf has two items, you merge the leaf with an adjacent sibling by moving an item down from the leaf's parent into the sibling—it had only one item before, so it has room for another—and removing the empty leaf. This case is shown in Figure 12-19b.

By moving an item down from a node *n*, as just described, you might cause *n* to be left without a data item and with only one child. If so, you recursively apply the deletion algorithm to *n*. Thus, if *n* has a sibling with two items (and three children), you redistribute the items among *n*, the sibling, and *n*'s parent. You also give *n* one of its sibling's children, as Figure 12-19c indicates.

If *n* has no sibling with two items, you merge *n* with a sibling, as Figure 12-19d illustrates. That is, you move an item down from the parent and let the sibling adopt *n*'s one child. (At this point you know that the sibling previously had only one item and two children.) You then remove the empty leaf. If the merge causes *n*'s parent to be without an item, you recursively apply the deletion process to it.

If the merging continues so that the root of the tree is without an item (and has only one child), you simply remove the root. When this step occurs, the height of the tree is reduced by 1, as Figure 12-19e illustrates.

A high-level statement of the algorithm for deleting from a 2-3 tree follows:

```
deleteItem(in ttTree:TwoThreeTree,
           in searchKey:KeyType)
           throw TwoThreeTreeException
// Deletes from the 2-3 tree ttTree the item whose search
// key equals searchKey. Throws TwoThreeTreeException
// if no such item exists.

   Attempt to locate item theItem whose search key
     equals searchKey

   if (theItem is present)
   {  if (theItem is not in a leaf)
         Swap item theItem with its inorder successor,
           which will be in a leaf leafNode

      // the deletion always begins at a leaf
      Delete item theItem from leaf leafNode

      if (leafNode now has no items)
         fix(leafNode)
   }
```

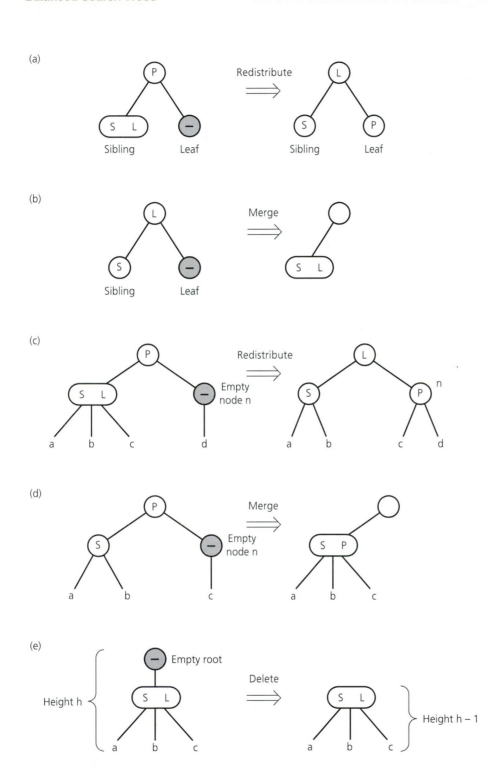

FIGURE 12-19 (a) Redistributing values; (b) merging a leaf; (c) redistributing values and children; (d) merging internal nodes; (e) deleting the root

```
    else
        Throw a TwoThreeTreeException


fix(in n:TreeNode)
// Completes the deletion when node n is empty by either
// removing the root, redistributing values, or merging
// nodes. Note: if n is internal, it has one child.


    if (n is the root)
        Remove the root


    else
    {  Let p be the parent of n

        if (some sibling of n has two items)
        {  Distribute items appropriately among n, the
              sibling, and p
           if (n is internal)
               Move the appropriate child from sibling to n
        }


        else  // merge the node
        {  Choose an adjacent sibling s of n
           Bring the appropriate item down from p into s


           if (n is internal)
               Move n's child to s


           Remove node n


           if (p is now empty)
               fix(p)
        }  // end if
    }  // end if
```

The details of the C++ implementation of the preceding insertion and deletion algorithms for 2-3 trees are rather involved. The implementation is left as a challenging exercise (Programming Problem 2).

You might be concerned about the overhead that the insertion and deletion algorithms incur in the course of maintaining the 2-3 structure of the tree. That is, after the search strategy locates either the item or the position for the new item, the insertion and deletion algorithms sometimes have to perform extra work, such as splitting and merging nodes. However, this extra work is not a real concern. A rigorous mathematical analysis would show that the extra work required to maintain the structure of a 2–3 tree after an insertion or a deletion is not significant. In other words, when analyzing the efficiency of the *insertItem* and *deleteItem* algorithms, it is sufficient to consider only the time required to locate the item (or the position for the insertion). Given that a 2–3 tree is always balanced, you can search a 2–3 tree in all situations with the logarithmic efficiency of a binary search. Thus, the 2–3 tree implementation of the ADT table is guaranteed to provide efficient table operations. Although a binary search tree that is as balanced as possible minimizes the amount of work required to implement the ADT table operations, its balance is difficult to maintain. A 2–3 tree is a compromise—although searching it may not be quite as efficient as searching a binary search tree of minimum height, it is relatively simple to maintain.

A 2-3 tree is always balanced

A 2-3 implementation of a table is O(log N) for all table operations

2-3-4 Trees

If a 2–3 tree is so good, are trees whose nodes can have more than three children even better? To an extent, the answer is yes. A **2–3–4 tree** is like a 2–3 tree, but it also allows **4-node trees**, which are nodes that have four children and three data items. For example, Figure 12-20 shows a 2–3–4 tree of height 3 that has the same items as the 2–3 tree in Figure 12-6b. As you will see, you can perform insertions and deletions on a 2–3–4 tree with fewer steps than a 2–3 tree requires.

T is a 2–3–4 tree of height *h* if

1. *T* is empty (a 2–3–4 tree of height 0).

or

2. *T* is of the form

$$T_L \quad \overset{r}{\diagup \diagdown} \quad T_R$$

A 2-3-4 tree

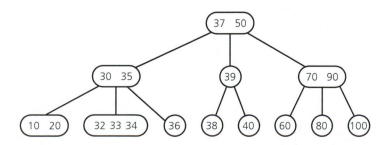

FIGURE 12-20   A 2-3-4 tree with the same items as the 2-3 tree in Figure 12-6b

where r is a node that contains one data item and T_L and T_R are both 2-3-4 trees, each of height $h - 1$. In this case, the search key in r must be greater than each search key in the left subtree T_L and smaller than each search key in the right subtree T_R.

or

3. T is of the form

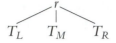

where r is a node that contains two data items and T_L, T_M, and T_R are 2-3-4 trees, each of height $h - 1$. In this case, the smaller search key in r must be greater than each search key in the left subtree T_L and smaller than each search key in the middle subtree T_M. The larger search key in r must be greater than each search key in T_M and smaller than each search key in the right subtree T_R.

or

4. T is of the form

where r is a node that contains three data items and T_L, T_{ML}, T_{MR}, and T_R are 2-3-4 trees, each of height $h - 1$. In this case, the smallest search key in r must be greater than each search key in the left subtree T_L and smaller than each search key in the middle-left subtree T_{ML}. The middle search key in r must be greater than each search key in T_{ML} and smaller than each search key in the middle-right subtree T_{MR}. The largest search key in r must be greater than each search key in T_{MR} and smaller than each search key in the right subtree T_R.

This definition implies the following rules for how you may place data items in the nodes of a 2-3-4 tree:

KEY CONCEPTS

Rules for Placing Data Items in the Nodes of a 2-3-4 Tree

1. A 2-node, which has two children, must contain a single data item whose search keys satisfy the relationships pictured earlier in Figure 12-3a.

2. A 3-node, which has three children, must contain two data items whose search keys satisfy the relationships pictured earlier in Figure 12-3b.

continued on next page

continued from previous page

3. A 4-node, which has four children, must contain three data items whose search keys *S*, *M*, and *L* satisfy the following relationships, as Figure 12-21 illustrates: *S* is greater than the left child's search key(s) and less than the middle-left child's search key(s); *M* is greater than the middle-left child's search key(s) and less than the middle-right child's search key(s); *L* is greater than the middle-right child's search key(s) and less than the right child's search key(s).

4. A leaf may contain either one, two, or three data items.

Although a 2-3-4 tree has more efficient insertion and deletion operations than a 2-3 tree, a 2-3-4 tree has greater storage requirements due to the additional data members in its 4-nodes, as the following C++ statements indicate:

A 2-3-4 tree requires more storage than a 2-3 tree

```
class TreeNode
{
private:
    TreeItemType smallItem, middleItem, largeItem;
    TreeNode *leftChildPtr, *lMidChildPtr,
            *rMidChildPtr, *rightChildPtr;

    friend class TwoThreeFourTree;
};  // end TreeNode
```

A node in a 2-3-4 tree

As you will see later, however, you can transform a 2-3-4 tree into a special binary tree that reduces the storage requirements.

Searching and traversing a 2-3-4 tree. The search algorithm and the traversal algorithm for a 2-3-4 tree are simple extensions of the corresponding algorithms for a 2-3 tree. For example, to search the tree in Figure 12-20 given the search key 31, you would search the left subtree of the root, because 31 is less than 37; search the middle subtree of the node <30 35>, because 31 is between 30 and 35; and terminate the search at the left child pointer of <32 33 34>, because 31 is less than 32,

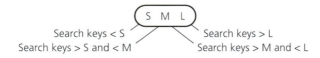

FIGURE 12-21   A 4-node in a 2-3-4 tree

deducing that no item in the tree has a search key of 31. Exercise 8 asks you to complete the details of searching and traversing a 2-3-4 tree.

Inserting into a 2-3-4 tree. The insertion algorithm for a 2-3-4 tree, like the insertion algorithm for a 2-3 tree, splits a node by moving one of its items up to its parent node. For a 2-3 tree, the search algorithm traces a path from the root to a leaf and then backs up from the leaf as it splits nodes. To avoid this return path after reaching a leaf, the insertion algorithm for a 2-3-4 tree splits 4-nodes as soon as it encounters them on the way down the tree from the root to a leaf. As a result, when a 4-node is split and an item is moved up to the node's parent, the parent cannot possibly be a 4-node and so can accommodate another item.

Split 4-nodes as they are encountered

As an example of the algorithm, consider the tree in Figure 12-22a. This one-node tree is the result of inserting 60, 30, and 10 into an initially empty 2-3-4 tree.

Insert 20. While determining the insertion point, you begin at the root and encounter the 4-node <10 30 60>, which you split by moving the middle value 30 up. Because the node is the root, you create a new root, move 30 into it, and attach two children, as Figure 12-22b illustrates. You continue the search for 20 by examining the left subtree of the root, because 20 is less than 30. The insertion results in the tree in Figure 12-22c.

Insert 50 and 40. The insertions of 50 and 40 do not require split nodes and result in the tree in Figure 12-23.

Insert 70. As you search Figure 12-23 for 70's insertion point, you encounter the 4-node <40 50 60>, because 70 is greater than 30. You split this 4-node by moving 50 up to the node's parent <30>, to get the tree in Figure 12-24a. You then insert 70 into the leaf <60>, as Figure 12-24b illustrates.

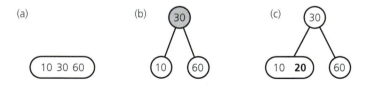

FIGURE 12-22   Inserting 20 into a one-node 2-3-4 tree

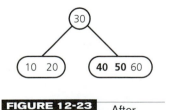

FIGURE 12-23   After inserting 50 and 40

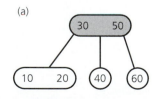

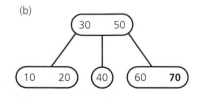

FIGURE 12-24   The steps for inserting 70

Insert 80 and 15. These insertions do not require split nodes and result in the tree in Figure 12-25.

Insert 90. As you search Figure 12-25 for 90's insertion point, you traverse the root's right subtree, because 90 is greater than 50, and encounter the 4-node <60 70 80>. You split this 4-node into two nodes and move 70 up to the root, as Figure 12-26a indicates. Finally, because 90 is greater than 70, you insert 90 into the leaf <80> to get the tree in Figure 12-26b.

Insert 100. As you begin to search Figure 12-26b, you immediately encounter a 4-node at the tree's root. You split this node into two nodes and move 50 up to a new root, as Figure 12-27a indicates. After continuing the search, you insert 100 into <80 90> to get the tree in Figure 12-27b.

(a)
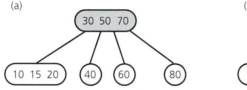

(b)
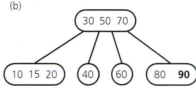

FIGURE 12-25   The steps for inserting 90

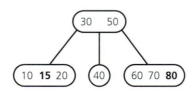

FIGURE 12-26   After inserting 80 and 15

(a)
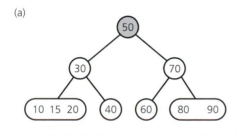

(b)
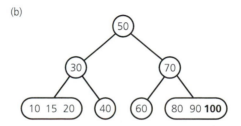

FIGURE 12-27   The steps for inserting 100

Splitting 4-nodes during insertion. As you have just seen, you split each 4-node as soon as you encounter it during your search from the root to a leaf that will accommodate the new item to be inserted. The 4-node will

- Be the root,

- Have a 2-node parent, or

- Have a 3-node parent

Figure 12-28 illustrates how to split a 4-node that is the tree's root. You have seen two previous examples of this: We split <10 30 60> in Figure 12-22a, resulting in the tree in Figure 12-22b. We also split <30 50 70> during the insertion of 100 into the tree in Figure 12-26b, giving us the tree in Figure 12-27a.

Figure 12-29 illustrates the two possible situations that you can encounter when you split a 4-node whose parent is a 2-node. For example, when you split <40 50 60> during the insertion of 70 into the tree in Figure 12-23, you get the tree in Figure 12-24a.

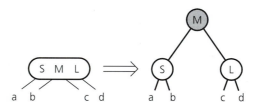

FIGURE 12-28   Splitting a 4-node root during insertion

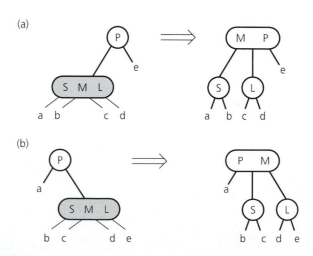

FIGURE 12-29   Splitting a 4-node whose parent is a 2-node during insertion

Figure 12–30 illustrates the three possible situations that you can encounter when you split a 4-node whose parent is a 3-node. For example, when you split <60 70 80> during the insertion of 90 into the tree in Figure 12–25, you get the tree in Figure 12–26a.

Deleting from a 2-3-4 tree. The deletion algorithm for a 2-3-4 tree has the same beginning as the deletion algorithm for a 2-3 tree. You first locate the node *n* that contains the item *I* that you want to delete. You then find *I*'s inorder successor and swap it with *I* so that the deletion will always be at a leaf. If that leaf is either a 3-node or a 4-node, you simply remove *I*. If you can ensure that *I* does not occur in a 2-node, you can perform the deletion in one pass through the tree from root to leaf, unlike deletion from a 2-3 tree. That is, you will not have to back away from the leaf and restructure the tree.

To accomplish this goal, you transform each 2-node that you encounter during the search for *I* into either a 3-node or a 4-node. Several cases are possible, depending on the configuration of the 2-node's parent and nearest sibling. (Arbitrarily, a node's nearest sibling is its left sibling, unless the node is a left child, in which case its nearest sibling is to its right.) That is, either the parent or the sibling could be a 2-node, a 3-node, or a 4-node. For example, if the next node that you

Transform each 2-node into
a 3-node or a 4-node

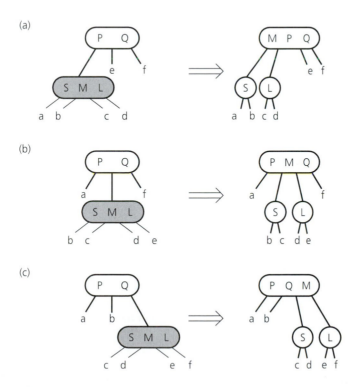

FIGURE 12-30 Splitting a 4-node whose parent is a 3-node during insertion

will encounter is a 2-node and both its parent and nearest sibling are 2-nodes, apply the transformation that Figure 12-28 illustrates, but in reverse; if the parent is a 3-node, apply the transformation that Figure 12-29 illustrates, but in reverse; and if the parent is a 4-node, apply the transformation that Figure 12-30 illustrates, but in reverse.

The details of deletion are left to you as a challenging exercise (Exercise 8).

2-3 and 2-3-4 trees are attractive because their balance is easy to maintain

Insertion and deletion algorithms for a 2-3-4 tree require fewer steps than those for a 2-3 tree

Allowing nodes with more than four children is counterproductive

A 2-3-4 tree requires more storage than a binary search tree

A red-black tree has the advantages of a 2-3-4 tree but requires less storage

Concluding remarks. The advantage of both 2-3 and 2-3-4 trees is their easy-to-maintain balance, not their shorter height. Even if a 2-3 tree is shorter than a balanced binary search tree, the reduction in height is offset by the increased number of comparisons that the search algorithm may require at each node. The situation is similar for a 2-3-4 tree, but its insertion and deletion algorithms require only one pass through the tree and so are simpler than those for a 2-3 tree. This decrease in effort makes the 2-3-4 tree more attractive than the 2-3 tree.

Should we consider trees whose nodes have even more than four children? Although a tree whose nodes can each have 100 children would be shorter than a 2-3-4 tree, its search algorithm would require more comparisons at each node to determine which subtree to search. Thus, allowing the nodes of a tree to have many children is counterproductive. Such a search tree is appropriate, however, when it is implemented in external storage, because moving from node to node is far more expensive than comparing the data values in a node. In such cases, a search tree with the minimum possible height is desirable, even at the expense of additional comparisons at each node. Chapter 14 will discuss external search trees further.

Red-Black Trees

A 2-3-4 tree is attractive because it is balanced and its insertion and deletion operations use only one pass from root to leaf. On the other hand, a 2-3-4 tree requires more storage than a binary search tree that contains the same data because a 2-3-4 tree has nodes that must accommodate up to three data items. A typical binary search tree is inappropriate, however, because it might not be balanced.

You can use a special binary search tree—a **red-black tree**—to represent a 2-3-4 tree and retain the advantages of a 2-3-4 tree without the storage overhead. The idea is to represent each 3-node and 4-node in a 2-3-4 tree by an equivalent binary tree. To distinguish between 2-nodes that appeared in the original 2-3-4 tree and 2-nodes that were generated from 3-nodes and 4-nodes, you use red and black child pointers. Let all the child pointers in the original 2-3-4 tree be black; use red child pointers to link the 2-nodes that result when you split 3-nodes and 4-nodes.

Figures 12-31 and 12-32 indicate how to represent, respectively, a 4-node and a 3-node as binary trees. Because there are two possible ways to represent a 3-node as a binary tree, a red-black representation

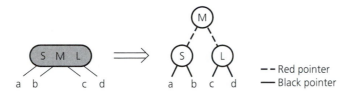

Red-black representation of a 4-node

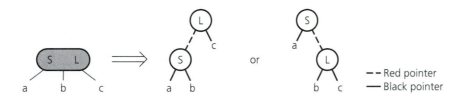

Red-black representation of a 3-node

of a 2–3–4 tree is not unique. Figure 12-33 gives a red–black representation for the 2–3–4 tree in Figure 12-20. In all of these figures, a dashed line represents a red pointer and a solid line represents a black pointer.

A node in a red–black tree is similar to a node in a binary search tree, but it must also store the pointer colors, as the following C++ statements indicate:

```
enum Color {RED, BLACK};

class TreeNode
{
private:
   TreeItemType Item;
```

A node in a red-black tree

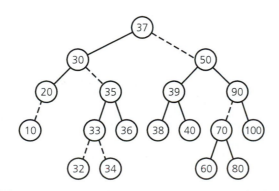

A red-black tree that represents the 2-3-4 tree in Figure 12-20

```
TreeNode *leftChildPtr, *rightChildPtr;
Color    leftColor, rightColor;

friend class RedBlackTree;
};  // end TreeNode
```

Even with the pointer colors, a node in a red-black tree requires less storage than a node in a 2-3-4 tree. (Why? See Self-Test Exercise 6.) Keep in mind that the transformations in Figures 12-31 and 12-32 imply a change in node structure.

Searching and traversing a red-black tree. Because a red-black tree is a binary search tree, you can search and traverse it by using the algorithms for a binary search tree. You simply ignore the color of the pointers.

Inserting into and deleting from a red-black tree. Because a red-black tree actually represents a 2-3-4 tree, you simply need to adjust the 2-3-4 insertion algorithms to accommodate the red-black representation. Recall that while searching a 2-3-4 tree, you split each 4-node that you encounter, so it is sufficient to reformulate that process in terms of the red-black representation. For example, Figure 12-31 shows the red-black representation of a 4-node. Thus, to identify a 4-node in its red-black form, you look for a node that has two red pointers.

Suppose that the 4-node is the root of the 2-3-4 tree. Figure 12-28 shows how to split the root into 2-nodes. By comparing this figure with Figure 12-31, you see that to perform an equivalent operation on a red-black tree, you simply change the color of its root's pointers to black, as Figure 12-34 illustrates.

Figure 12-29 shows how to split a 4-node whose parent is a 2-node. If you reformulate this figure by using the red-black notation given in Figures 12-31 and 12-32, you get Figure 12-35. Notice that this case also requires only color changes within the red-black tree.

Finally, Figure 12-30 shows how to split a 4-node whose parent is a 3-node. Note that each configuration before a split in Figure 12-30 has two red-black representations, as Figure 12-36 illustrates. (Apply the transformations that Figures 12-31 and 12-32 describe to Figure 12-30.) As you can see from Figure 12-36, each pair of representations

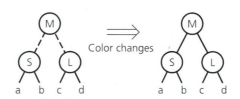

FIGURE 12-34   Splitting a red-black representation of a 4-node that is the root

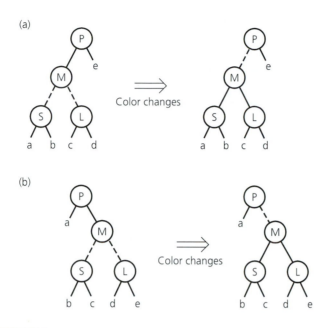

(a)

Color changes

(b)

Color changes

FIGURE 12-35 Splitting a red-black representation of a 4-node whose parent is a 2-node

transforms into the same red-black configuration. Of the six possibilities given in Figure 12-36, only two require simple color changes. The others also require changes to the pointers themselves. These pointer changes, which are called **rotations**, result in a shorter tree.

> Pointer changes called rotations result in a shorter tree

The deletion algorithm follows in an analogous fashion from the 2-3-4 deletion algorithm. Because insertion and deletion operations on a red-black tree frequently require only color changes, they are more efficient than the corresponding operations on a 2-3-4 tree.

Exercise 11 asks you to complete the details of the insertion and deletion algorithms.

AVL Trees

An **AVL tree**—named for its inventors, Adel'son-Vel'skii and Landis—is a balanced binary search tree. Because the heights of the left and right subtrees of any node in a balanced binary tree differ by no more than 1, you can search an AVL tree almost as efficiently as a minimum–height binary search tree. This section will simply introduce you to the notion of an AVL tree—which is the oldest form of balanced binary tree—and leave the details for another course.

> An AVL tree is a balanced binary search tree

It is, in fact, possible to rearrange any binary search tree of N nodes to obtain a binary search tree with the minimum possible height $\lceil \log_2(N + 1) \rceil$. Recall, for example, the algorithms developed in Chapter 10 that use a file to save and restore a binary search tree. You can

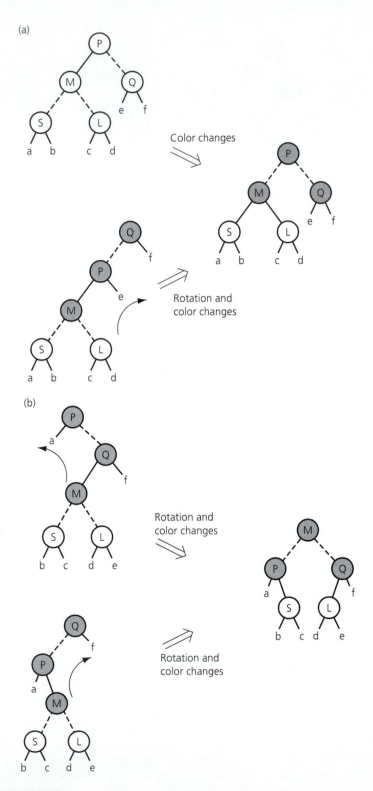

FIGURE 12-36   Splitting a red-black representation of a 4-node whose parent is a 3-node

(continues)

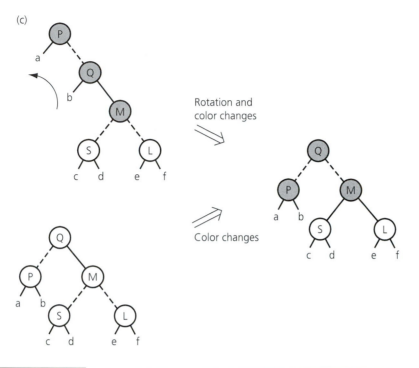

FIGURE 12-36

(continued)

start with an arbitrary binary search tree, save its values in a file, and then construct from these same values a new binary search tree of minimum height. Although this approach may be appropriate in the context of a table that occasionally is saved and restored, it requires too much work to be performed every time an insertion or deletion leaves the tree unbalanced. The cost of repeatedly rebuilding the tree could very well outweigh the benefit of searching a tree of minimum height.

The AVL method is a compromise. It maintains a binary search tree with a height close to the minimum, but it is able to do so with far less work than would be necessary to keep the height of the tree exactly equal to the minimum. The basic strategy of the AVL method is to monitor the shape of the binary search tree. You insert or delete nodes just as you would for any binary search tree, but after each insertion or deletion, you check that the tree is still an AVL tree. That is, you determine whether any node in the tree has left and right subtrees whose heights differ by more than 1. For example, suppose that the binary search tree in Figure 12-37a is the result of a sequence of insertions and deletions. The heights of the left and right subtrees of the root 30 differ by 2. You can restore this tree's AVL property—that is, its balance—by rearranging its nodes. For instance, you can rotate the tree so that the node 20 becomes the root, with left child 10 and right child 30, as in Figure 12-37b. Notice that you cannot arbitrarily rearrange the tree's

An AVL tree maintains a height close to the minimum

Rotations restore the balance

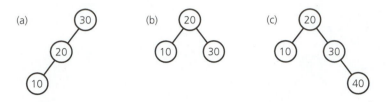

FIGURE 12-37   (a) An unbalanced binary search tree; (b) a balanced tree after rotation; (c) a balanced tree after insertion

nodes, because you must take care not to destroy the search tree's ordering property in the course of the rebalancing.

Rotations are not necessary after every insertion or deletion. For example, you can insert 40 into the AVL tree in Figure 12-37b and still have an AVL tree. (See Figure 12-37c.) However, when a rotation is necessary to restore a tree's AVL property, the rotation will be one of two possible types. Let's look at an example of each type.

Suppose that you have the tree in Figure 12-38a after the insertion or deletion of a node. (Perhaps you obtained this tree by inserting 60 into an AVL tree.) An imbalance occurs at the node 20; that is, 20's left and right subtrees differ in height by more than 1. A *single rotation* to the left is necessary to obtain the balanced tree in Figure 12-38b: 40 becomes the parent of 20, which adopts 30 as its right child. Figure 12-39 shows this rotation in a more general form. It shows, for example, that before the rotation the left and right subtrees of the node 40 have heights h and $h + 1$, respectively. After the rotation, the tree is balanced and, in this particular case, has decreased in height from $h + 3$ to $h + 2$. Figures 12-40 and 12-41 show examples of a single left rotation that restores a tree's balance but does not affect its height. An analogous single right rotation would produce a mirror image of these examples.

A more complex rotation may be necessary. For example, consider the tree in Figure 12-42a, which is the result of nodes being added to or deleted from an AVL tree. The left and right subtrees of 20 differ in height by more than 1. A double rotation is necessary to restore this

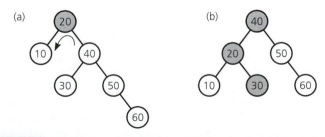

FIGURE 12-38   (a) An unbalanced binary search tree; (b) a balanced tree after a single left rotation

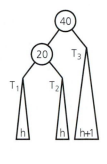
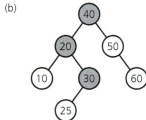

Before rotation   After rotation

FIGURE 12-39   Before and after a single left rotation that decreases the tree's height

(a)
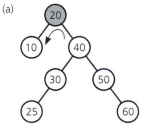

(b)
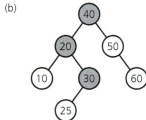

FIGURE 12-40   (a) An unbalanced binary search tree; (b) a balanced tree after a single left rotation

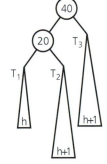

Before rotation   After rotation

FIGURE 12-41   Before and after a single left rotation that does not affect the tree's height

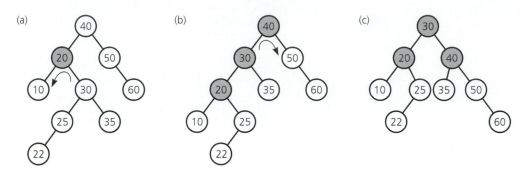

FIGURE 12-42   (a) Before; (b) during; and (c) after a double rotation

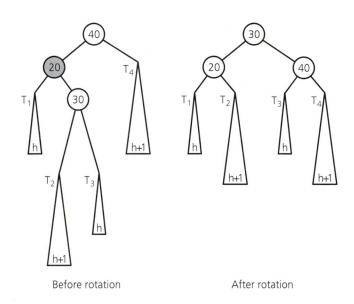

FIGURE 12-43   Before and after a double rotation that decreases the tree's height

tree's balance. Figure 12-42b shows the result of a left rotation about 20, and Figure 12-42c shows the result of a right rotation about 40. Figure 12-43 illustrates this double rotation in a more general form. Mirror images of these figures provide examples of other possible double rotations.

It can be proven that the height of an AVL tree with N nodes will always be very close to the theoretical minimum of $\lceil \log_2(N + 1) \rceil$. The AVL tree implementation of a table is, therefore, one implementation that guarantees a binary search-like efficiency. Usually, however, implementations that use either a 2-3-4 tree or a red-black tree will be simpler.

An AVL tree implementation of a table is more difficult than other implementations

12.2 Hashing

The binary search tree and its balanced variants, such as 2-3, 2-3-4, red-black, and AVL trees, provide excellent implementations of the ADT table. They allow you to perform all of the table operations quite efficiently. If, for example, a table contains 10,000 items, the operations *table-Retrieve, tableInsert,* and *tableDelete* each require approximately $\log_2 10,000 \approx 13$ steps. As impressive as this efficiency may be, situations do occur for which the search-tree implementations are not adequate.

As you know, time can be vital. For example, when a person calls the 911 emergency system, the system detects the caller's telephone number and searches a database for the caller's address. Similarly, an air traffic control system searches a database of flight information, given a flight number. Clearly these searches must be rapid.

A radically different strategy is necessary to locate (and insert or delete) an item virtually instantaneously. Imagine an array *table* of N items—with each array slot capable of holding a single table item—and a seemingly magical box called an "address calculator." Whenever you have a new item that you want to insert into the table, the address calculator will tell you where you should place it in the array. Figure 12-44 illustrates this scenario.

Table operations without searches

You can thus easily perform an insertion into the table as follows:

```
tableInsert(in newItem:TableItemType)

   i = the array index that the address calculator
       gives you for newItem's search key
   table[i] = newItem
```

An insertion is $O(1)$; that is, it requires constant time.

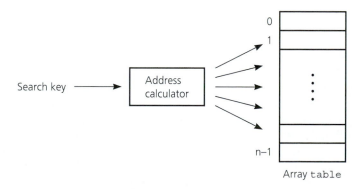

FIGURE 12-44 Address calculator

You also use the address calculator for the `tableRetrieve` and `tableDelete` operations. If you want to retrieve an item that has a particular search key, you simply ask the address calculator to tell you where it would insert such an item. Because you would have inserted the item earlier by using the `tableInsert` algorithm just given, if the desired item is present in the table, it will be in the array location that the address calculator specifies.

Thus, the retrieval operation appears in pseudocode as follows:

```
tableRetrieve(in searchKey:KeyType,
              out tableItem:TableItemType)
          throw TableException

i = the array index that the address calculator
        gives you for an item whose search key
        equals searchKey

if (table[i].getKey() != searchKey)
    Throw a TableException
else
    tableItem = table[i]
```

Similarly, the pseudocode for the deletion operation is

```
tableDelete(in searchKey:KeyType)
          throw TableException

i = the array index that the address calculator
        gives you for an item whose search key
        equals searchKey

if (table[i].getKey() != searchKey)
    Throw a TableException
else
    Delete the item from table[i]
```

It thus appears that you can perform the operations `tableRetrieve`, `tableInsert`, and `tableDelete` virtually instantaneously. You never have to search for an item; instead, you simply let the address calculator determine where the item should be. The amount of time required to carry out the operations is $O(1)$ and depends only on how quickly the address calculator can perform this computation.

If you are to implement such a scheme, you must, of course, be able to construct an address calculator that can, with very little work, tell you where a given item should be. Address calculators are actually not as mysterious as they seem; in fact, many exist that can approximate the idealized behavior just described. Such an address calculator is usually referred to as a **hash function**. The scheme just described is an

A hash function tells you where to place an item in an array called a hash table

idealized description of a method known as **hashing**, and the array `table` is called the **hash table**.

To understand how a hash function works, consider the 911 emergency system mentioned earlier. If, for each person, the system had a record whose search key was the person's telephone number, it could store these records in a search tree. Although searching a tree would be fast, faster access to a particular record would be possible by storing the records in an array `table`, as follows. You store the record for a person whose telephone number is *t* into `table[t]`. Retrieval of the record, then, is almost instantaneous given its search key *t*. For example, you can store the record for the telephone number 123-4567 in `table[1234567]`. If you can spare 10 million memory locations for `table`, this approach is fine. You need not use memory so extravagantly, however, since 911 systems are regional. If you consider only one telephone exchange, for example, you can store the record for the number 123-4567 in `table[4567]` and get by with an array `table` of 10,000 locations.

The transformation of 1234567 into an array index 4567 is a simple example of a hash function. A hash function *h* must take an arbitrary integer *x* and map it into an integer that you can use as an array index. In our example, such indexes would be in the range 0 through 9999. That is, *h* is a function such that for any integer *x*,

$$h(x) = i, \text{ where } i \text{ is an integer in the range 0 through 9999}$$

A hash function maps an integer into an array index

Because the database contains records for every telephone number in a particular exchange, the array `table` is completely full. In this sense, our example is not typical of hashing applications and serves only to illustrate the idea of a hash function. What if many fewer records were in the array? Consider, for example, an air traffic control system that stores a record for each current flight according to its four-digit flight number. You could store a record for Flight 4567 in `table[4567]`, but you still would need an array of 10,000 locations, even if only 50 flights were current.

A different hash function would save memory. If you allow space for a maximum of 101 flights, for example, so that the array `table` has indexes 0 through 100, the necessary hash function *h* should map any four-digit flight number into an integer in the range 0 through 100.

If you have such a hash function *h*—and you will see several suggestions for hash functions later—the table operations are easy to write. For example, in the `tableRetrieve` algorithm, the step

```
i = the array index that the address calculator
      gives you for an item whose search key
      equals searchKey
```

is implemented simply as

```
i = h(searchKey)
```

In the previous example, `searchKey` would be the flight number.

The table operations appear to be virtually instantaneous. But is hashing really as good as it sounds? If it really were this good, there would have been little reason for developing all those other table implementations. Hashing would beat them hands down!

Why is hashing not quite as simple as it seems? You might first notice that since the hashing scheme stores the items in an array, it would appear to suffer from the familiar problems associated with a fixed-size implementation. Obviously, the hash table must be large enough to contain all of the items that you want to store. This requirement is not the crux of the implementation's difficulty, however, for—as you will see later—there are ways to allow the hash table to grow dynamically. The implementation has a major pitfall, even given the assumption that the number of items to be stored will never exceed the size of the hash table.

Ideally, you want the hash function to map each x into a unique integer i. The hash function in the ideal situation is called a **perfect hash function**. In fact, it is possible to construct perfect hash functions if you know all of the possible search keys that *actually* occur in the table. You have this knowledge for the 911 example, since everyone is in the database, but not for the air traffic control example. Usually, you will not know the values of the search keys in advance.

In practice, a hash function can map two or more search keys x and y into the *same* integer. That is, the hash function tells you to store two or more items in the same array location `table[i]`. This occurrence is called a **collision**. Thus, even if fewer than 101 items were present in the hash table `table[0..100]`, h could very well tell you to place more than one item into the same array location. For example, if two items have search keys 4567 and 7597, and if

$$h(4567) = h(7597) = 22$$

h will tell you to place the two items into the same array location, `table[22]`. That is, the search keys 4567 and 7597 have collided.

Even if the number of items that can be in the array at any one time is small, the only way to avoid collisions completely is for the hash table to be large enough that each possible search-key value can have its own location. If, for example, Social Security numbers were the search keys, you would need an array location for each integer in the range 000000000 through 999999999. This situation would certainly require a good deal of storage! Because reserving vast amounts of storage is usually not practical, collision-resolution schemes are necessary to make hashing feasible. Such resolution schemes usually require that the hash function place items evenly throughout the hash table.

To summarize, a typical hash function must

- Be easy and fast to compute

- Place items evenly throughout the hash table

Note that the size of the hash table affects the ability of the hash function to distribute the items evenly throughout the table. The requirements of a hash function will be discussed in more detail later in this chapter.

Consider now several hash functions and **collision-resolution schemes**.

Hash Functions

It is sufficient to consider hash functions that have an arbitrary integer as an argument. Why? If a search key is not an integer, you can simply map the search key into an integer, which you then hash. At the end of this section, you will see one way to convert a string into an integer.

It is sufficient for hash functions to operate on integers

There are many ways to convert an arbitrary integer into an integer within a certain range, such as 0 through 100. Thus, there are many ways to construct a hash function. Many of these functions, however, will not be suitable. Here are several simple hash functions that operate on positive integers.

Selecting digits. If your search key is the nine-digit employee ID number 001364825, you could select the fourth digit and the last digit, to obtain 35 as the index to the hash table. That is,

$h(001364825) = 35$ (*select the fourth and last digits*)

Therefore, you would store the item whose search key is 001364825 in `table[35]`.

You do need to be careful about which digits you choose in a particular situation. For example, the first three digits of a Social Security number are based on the geographic region in which the number was assigned. If you select only these digits, you will map all people from the same state into the same location of the hash table.

Digit-selection hash functions are simple and fast, but generally they do not evenly distribute the items in the hash table. A hash function really should utilize the entire search key.

Digit selection does not distribute items evenly in the hash table

Folding. One way to improve on the previous method of selecting digits is to add the digits. For example, you can add all of the digits in 001364825 to obtain

$0 + 0 + 1 + 3 + 6 + 4 + 8 + 2 + 5 = 29$ (*add the digits*)

Therefore, you would store the item whose search key is 001364825 in `table[29]`. Notice that if you add all of the digits from a nine-digit search key,

$0 \leq h(\text{search key}) \leq 81$

That is, you would use only `table[0]` through `table[81]` of the hash table. To change this situation or to increase the size of the hash table, you can group the digits in the search key and add the groups. For example, you could form three groups of three digits from the search key 001364825 and add them as follows:

$$001 + 364 + 825 = 1,190$$

For this hash function,

$$0 \leq h(\text{search key}) \leq 3 * 999 = 2,997$$

Clearly, if 2,997 is larger than the size of the hash table that you want, you can alter the groups that you choose. Perhaps not as obvious is that you can apply more than one hash function to a search key. For example, you could select some of the digits from the search key before adding them, or you could either select digits from the previous result 2,997 or apply folding to it once again by adding 29 and 97.

Applying more than one hash function to a single search key

Modulo arithmetic. Modulo arithmetic provides a simple and effective hash function that we will use in the rest of this chapter. For example, consider the function[6]

$$h(x) = x \bmod tableSize$$

where the hash table `table` has *tableSize* elements. In particular, if *tableSize* is 101, $h(x) = x \bmod 101$ maps any integer x into the range 0 through 100. For example, h maps 001364825 into 12.

For $h(x) = x \bmod tableSize$, many x's map into `table[0]`, many x's map into `table[1]`, and so on. That is, collisions occur. However, you can distribute the table items evenly over all of `table`—thus reducing collisions—by choosing a prime number as *tableSize*. For instance, 101 in the previous example is prime. The choice of table size will be discussed in more detail later in this chapter. For now, realize that 101 is used here as a simple example of a prime table size. For the typical table, it is much too small.

The table size should be prime

Converting a character string to an integer. If your search key is a character string—such as a name—you could convert it into an integer before applying the hash function $h(x)$. To do so, you could first assign each character in the string an integer value. For example, for the word "NOTE" you could assign the ASCII values 78, 79, 84, and 69, to the letters N, O, T, and E, respectively. Or, if you assign the values 1 through 26 to the letters A through Z, you could assign 14 to N, 15 to O, 20 to T, and 5 to E.

If you now simply add these numbers, you will get an integer, but it will not be unique to the character string. For example, the string "TONE" will give you the same result. Instead, write the numeric value for each character in binary and concatenate the results. If you

---

[6] Remember that this book uses "mod" as an abbreviation for the mathematical operation modulo. In C++, the modulo operator is `%`.

assign the values 1 through 26 to the letters A through Z, you obtain the following for the string "NOTE":

N is 14, or 01110 in binary

O is 15, or 01111 in binary

T is 20, or 10100 in binary

E is 5, or 00101 in binary

Concatenating the binary values gives you the binary integer

01110011111010000101

which is 474,757 in decimal. You can apply the hash function x mod *tableSize* for $x = 474{,}757$.

Now consider a more efficient way to compute 474,757. Rather than converting the previous binary number to decimal, you can evaluate the expression

$$14 * 32^3 + 15 * 32^2 + 20 * 32^1 + 5 * 32^0$$

This computation is possible because we have represented each character as a 5-bit binary number, and 2^5 is 32.

By factoring this expression, you can minimize the number of arithmetic operations. This technique is called Horner's rule and results in

$$((14 * 32 + 15) * 32 + 20) * 32 + 5$$

Although both of these expressions have the same value, the result in either case could very well be larger than a typical computer can represent; that is, an overflow can occur.

Because we plan to use the hash function

$$h(x) = x \bmod tableSize$$

you can prevent an overflow by applying the modulo operator after computing each parenthesized expression in Horner's rule. The implementation of this algorithm is left as an exercise.

Horner's rule minimizes the number of computations

Resolving Collisions

Consider the problems caused by a collision. Suppose that you want to insert an item whose search key is 4567 into the hash table *table,* as was described previously. The hash function $h(x) = x$ mod 101 tells you to place the new item in *table[22]*, because 4567 mod 101 is 22. Suppose, however, that *table[22]* already contains an item, as Figure 12-45 illustrates. If earlier you had placed 7597 into *table[22]* because 7597 mod 101 equals 22, where do you place the new item? You certainly do not want to disallow the insertion on the grounds that the table is full: You could have a collision even when inserting into a table that contains only one item!

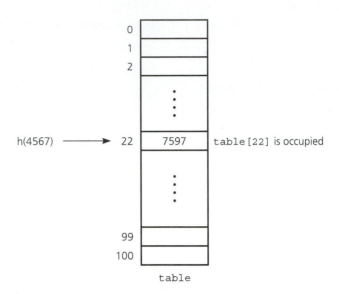

FIGURE 12-45   A collision

Two approaches to collision resolution

Two general approaches to collision resolution are common. One approach allocates another location *within* the hash table to the new item. A second approach changes the structure of the hash table so that each location `table[i]` can accommodate more than one item. The collision-resolution schemes described next exemplify these two approaches.

Approach 1: Open addressing.   During an attempt to insert a new item into a table, if the hash function indicates a location in the hash table that is already occupied, you probe for some other empty, or open, location in which to place the item. The sequence of locations that you examine is called the **probe sequence**.

Such schemes are said to use **open addressing**. The concern, of course, is that you must be able to find a table item efficiently after you have inserted it. That is, the `tableDelete` and `tableRetrieve` operations must be able to reproduce the probe sequence that `tableInsert` used and must do so efficiently.

The difference among the various open-addressing schemes is the method used to probe for an empty location. We briefly describe three such methods.

Linear probing.   In this simple scheme to resolve a collision, you search the hash table sequentially, starting from the original hash location. More specifically, if `table[h(searchKey)]` is occupied, you check `table[h(searchKey)+1]`, `table[h(searchKey)+2]`, and so on until you find an available location. Figure 12-46 illustrates the placement of four items that all hash into the same location `table[22]` of the hash table, assuming a hash function $h(x) = x$ mod 101. Typically, you *wrap around* from the last table location to the first table location if necessary.

Begin at the hash location and search the table sequentially

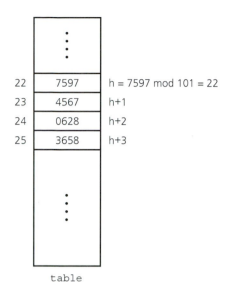

table

FIGURE 12-46   Linear probing with $h(x) = x \bmod 101$

In the absence of deletions, the implementation of `tableRetrieve` under this scheme is straightforward. You need only follow the same probe sequence that `tableInsert` used until you either find the item you are searching for, reach an empty location, which indicates that the item is not present, or visit every table location.

Deletions, however, add a slight complication. The `tableDelete` operation itself is no problem. You merely find the desired item, as in `tableRetrieve`, and delete it, making the location empty. But what happens to `tableRetrieve` after deletions? The new empty locations that `tableDelete` created along a probe sequence could cause `table-Retrieve` to stop prematurely, incorrectly indicating a failure. You can resolve this problem by allowing a table location to be in one of three states: occupied (currently in use), empty (has not been used), or deleted (was once occupied but is now available). You then modify the `tableRetrieve` operation to continue probing when it encounters a location in the deleted state. Similarly, you modify `tableInsert` to insert into either empty or deleted locations.

One of the problems with the linear-probing scheme is that table items tend to **cluster** together in the hash table. That is, the table contains groups of consecutively occupied locations. This phenomenon is called *primary clustering*. Clusters can get close to one another and, in fact, merge into a larger cluster. Large clusters tend to get even larger. ("The rich get richer.") Thus, one part of the table might be quite dense, even though another part has relatively few items. Primary clustering causes long probe searches and therefore decreases the overall efficiency of hashing.

Quadratic probing.   You can virtually eliminate primary clusters simply by adjusting the linear probing scheme just described. Instead of probing

Three states: occupied, empty, deleted

Clustering can be a problem

consecutive locations from the original hash location `table[h(search-Key)]`, you check locations `table[h(searchKey)+1²]`, `table[h(search-Key)+2²]`, `table[h(searchKey)+3²]`, and so on until you find an available location. Figure 12-47 illustrates this open-addressing scheme—which is called **quadratic probing**—for the same items that appear in Figure 12-46.

Unfortunately, when two items hash into the same location, quadratic probing uses the same probe sequence for each item. This phenomenon—called *secondary clustering*—delays the resolution of the collision. Although the analysis of quadratic probing remains incomplete, it appears that secondary clustering is not a problem.

Double hashing.   Double hashing, which is yet another open-addressing scheme, drastically reduces clustering. The probe sequences that both linear probing and quadratic probing use are *key independent*. For example, linear probing inspects the table locations sequentially no matter what the hash key is. In contrast, double hashing defines *key-dependent* probe sequences. In this scheme the probe sequence still searches the table in a linear order, starting at the location $h_1(key)$, but a second hash function h_2 determines the size of the steps taken.

Although you choose h_1 as usual, you must follow these guidelines for h_2:

$$h_2(key) \neq 0$$
$$h_2 \neq h_1$$

Clearly, you need a nonzero step size $h_2(key)$ to define the probe sequence. In addition, h_2 must differ from h_1 to avoid clustering.

> A hash address and a step size determine the probe sequence

> Guidelines for the step-size function h_2

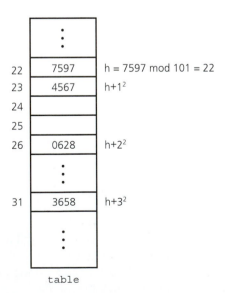

table

FIGURE 12-47   Quadratic probing with $h(x) = x \bmod 101$

For example, let h_1 and h_2 be the primary and secondary hash functions defined as

$$h_1(key) = key \bmod 11$$
$$h_2(key) = 7 - (key \bmod 7)$$

where a hash table of only 11 items is assumed, so that you can readily see the effect of these functions on the hash table. If $key = 58$, h_1 hashes key to table location 3 (58 mod 11), and h_2 indicates that the probe sequence should take steps of size 5 (7 − 58 mod 7). In other words, the probe sequence will be 3, 8, 2 (wraps around), 7, 1 (wraps around), 6, 0, 5, 10, 4, 9. On the other hand, if $key = 14$, h_1 hashes key to table location 3 (14 mod 11), and h_2 indicates that the probe sequence should take steps of size 7 (7 − 14 mod 7), and so the probe sequence would be 3, 10, 6, 2, 9, 5, 1, 8, 4, 0.

Each of these probe sequences visits *all* the table locations. This phenomenon always occurs if the size of the table and the size of the probe step are relatively prime, that is, if their greatest common divisor is 1. Because the size of a hash table is commonly a prime number, it will be relatively prime to all step sizes.

Figure 12-48 illustrates the insertion of 58, 14, and 91 into an initially empty hash table. Because $h_1(58)$ is 3, you place 58 into `table[3]`. You then find that $h_1(14)$ is also 3, so to avoid a collision, you step by $h_2(14) = 7$ and place 14 into `table[3 + 7]`, or `table[10]`. Finally, $h_1(91)$ is 3 and $h_2(91)$ is 7. Because `table[3]` is occupied, you probe `table[10]` and find that it, too, is occupied. You finally store 91 in `table[(10 + 7) % 11]`, or `table[6]`.

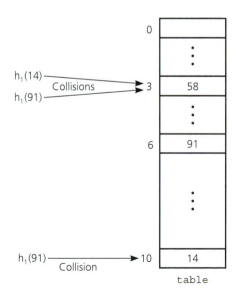

Double hashing during the insertion of 58, 14, and 91

Using more than one hash function is called rehashing. While more than two hash functions can be desirable, such schemes are difficult to implement.

Increasing the size of the hash table.   With any of the open-addressing schemes, as the hash table fills, the probability of a collision increases. At some point, a larger hash table becomes desirable. If you use a dynamically allocated array for the hash table, you can increase its size whenever the table becomes too full.

You cannot simply double the size of the array, as we did in earlier chapters, because the size of the hash table must remain prime. Secondly, you do not copy the items from the original hash table to the new hash table. If your hash function is x mod *tableSize*, it changes as *tableSize* changes. Thus, you need to apply your new hash function to every item in the old hash table before placing it into the new hash table.

Approach 2: Restructuring the hash table.   Another way to resolve collisions is to change the structure of the array `table`—the hash table—so that it can accommodate more than one item in the same location. We describe two such ways to alter the hash table.

Each hash-table location can accommodate more than one item

Buckets.   If you define the hash table `table` so that each location `table[i]` is itself an array called a **bucket**, you then can store the items that hash into `table[i]` in this array. The problem with this approach, of course, is choosing the size B of each bucket. If B is too small, you will only have postponed the problem of collisions until $B + 1$ items map into some array location. If you attempt to make B large enough so that each array location can accommodate the largest number of items that might map into it, you are likely to waste a good deal of storage.

A bucket is an element of a hash table that is itself an array

Separate chaining.   A better approach is to design the hash table as an array of linked lists. In this collision-resolution method, known as **separate chaining**, each entry `table[i]` is a pointer to a linked list—the **chain**—of items that the hash function has mapped into location i, as Figure 12-49 illustrates. The following classes for the ADT table assume an implementation that uses a hash table and separate chaining:

Each hash-table location is a linked list

```
// ************************************************************
// Header file TableH.h for the ADT table.
// Hash table implementation.
// Assumption: A table contains at most one item with a
//             given search key at any time.
// ************************************************************
#include "ChainNode.h"
#include "TableException.h"7
typedef KeyedItem TableItemType;
```

---

[7] See page 604 for a definition of the `TableException` class.

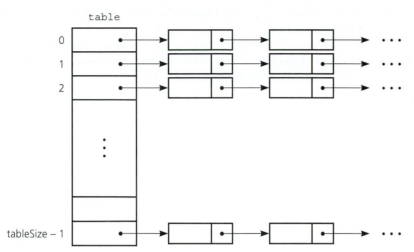

Each location of the hash table contains a pointer to a linked list

FIGURE 12-49 Separate chaining

```
class HashTable
{
public:
// constructors and destructor:
   HashTable();
   HashTable(const HashTable& table);
   ~HashTable();

// table operations:
   virtual bool tableIsEmpty() const;
   virtual int tableGetLength() const;
   virtual void tableInsert(const TableItemType& newItem)
                       throw(TableException);
   virtual bool tableDelete(KeyType searchKey);
                       throw(TableException);
   virtual bool tableRetrieve(KeyType searchKey,
                       TableItemType& tableItem) const;
                       throw(TableException);

protected:
   int hashIndex(KeyType searchKey);   // hash function

private:
   enum {HASH_TABLE_SIZE = 101};   // size of hash table
   typedef ChainNode * HashTableType[HASH_TABLE_SIZE];

   HashTableType table;             // hash table
   int           size;              // size of ADT table
};  // end HashTable class
// End of header file.
```

```
// **********************************************************
// Header file KeyedItem.h.
// Provides basis for classes that need a search key value.
// **********************************************************
typedef desired-type-of-search-key KeyType;

class KeyedItem
{
public:
   KeyedItem() {};
   KeyedItem(const KeyType& keyValue) : searchKey(keyValue) {}
   KeyType getKey() const // returns search key
   {
      return searchKey;
   }   // end getKey
private:
   KeyType searchKey;
};   // end KeyedItem class


// **********************************************************
// Header file ChainNode.h.
// Provides the chain node definition for the hash table.
// **********************************************************
#include "KeyedItem.h"

class ChainNode
{
private:
   ChainNode();
   ChainNode(const KeyedItem & nodeItem,
             ChainNode *nextNode = NULL)
             :item(nodeItem), next(nextNode) {}
   KeyedItem item;
   ChainNode *next;

   friend class HashTable;
};   // end ChainNode class
```

The class *KeyedItem* can be used as the base class for the items that are stored in the table. The *KeyedItem* class was first presented in Chapter 10 and provides a data field for the search key. The search key is used by the *hashIndex* method in the class *HashTable* to generate a hash index value.

When you insert a new item into the table, you simply place it at the beginning of the linked list that the hash function indicates. The following pseudocode describes the insertion algorithm:

```
tableInsert(in newItem:TableItemType)
          throw TableException

  searchKey = the search key of newItem
  i = hashIndex(searchKey)
  p = pointer to a new node
  Throw TableException according to whether the
    previous memory allocation is successful
  p->item = newItem
  p->next = table[i]
  table[i] = p
```

When you want to retrieve an item, you search the linked list that the hash function indicates. The following pseudocode describes the retrieval algorithm:

```
tableRetrieve(in searchKey:KeyType,
            in tableItem:TableItemType)
            throw TableException

  i = hashIndex(searchKey)
  p = table[i]

  while ( (p != NULL) &&
          (p->item.getKey() != searchKey) )
    p = p->next

  if (p == NULL)
    Throw a TableException
  else
    tableItem = p->item
```

The deletion algorithm is very similar to the retrieval algorithm and is left as an exercise. (See Exercise 14.)

Separate chaining is thus a successful method of resolving collisions. With separate chaining, the size of the ADT table is dynamic and can exceed the size of the hash table, because each linked list can be as long as necessary. As you will see in the next section, the length of these linked lists affects the efficiency of retrievals and deletions.

Separate chaining successfully resolves collisions

The Efficiency of Hashing

An analysis of the average-case efficiency of hashing involves the **load factor** α, which is the ratio of the current number of items in the table to the maximum size of the array `table`. That is,

$$\alpha = \frac{\textit{Current number of table items}}{\textit{tableSize}}$$

The load factor measures how full a hash table is

α is a measure of how full the hash table `table` is. As `table` fills, α increases and the chance of collision increases, so search times increase. Thus, hashing efficiency decreases as α increases.

Unlike the efficiency of earlier table implementations, the efficiency of hashing does not depend solely on the number N of items in the table. While it is true that for a fixed *tableSize*, efficiency decreases as N increases, for a given N you can choose *tableSize* to increase efficiency. Thus, when determining *tableSize*, you should estimate the largest possible N and select *tableSize* so that α is small. As you will see shortly, α should not exceed 2/3.

Hashing efficiency for a particular search also depends on whether the search is successful. An unsuccessful search requires more time in general than a successful search. The following analyses[8] enable a comparison of collision-resolution techniques.

Unsuccessful searches generally require more time than successful searches

Linear probing. For linear probing, the approximate average number of comparisons that a search requires is

$$\frac{1}{2}\left[1 + \frac{1}{1-\alpha}\right] \qquad \text{for a successful search, and}$$

$$\frac{1}{2}\left[1 + \frac{1}{1-\alpha}\right]^2 \qquad \text{for an unsuccessful search}$$

As collisions increase, the probe sequences increase in length, causing increased search times. For example, for a table that is two-thirds full ($\alpha = 2/3$), an average unsuccessful search might require at most five comparisons, or probes, while an average successful search might require at most two comparisons. To maintain efficiency, it is important to prevent the hash table from filling up.

Do not let the hash table get too full

Quadratic probing and double hashing. The efficiency of both quadratic probing and double hashing is given by

$$\frac{-\log_e\left(1-\alpha\right)}{\alpha} \qquad \text{for a successful search, and}$$

$$\frac{1}{1-\alpha} \qquad \text{for an unsuccessful search}$$

On average, both methods require fewer comparisons than linear probing. For example, for a table that is two-thirds full, an average unsuccessful search might require at most three comparisons, or probes, while an average successful search might require at most two comparisons. As a result, you can use a smaller hash table for both quadratic probing and double hashing than you can for linear probing. However,

---

[8] D. E. Knuth, *Searching and Sorting*, vol. 3 of *The Art of Computer Programming* (Menlo Park, CA: Addison-Wesley, 1973).

because they are open-addressing schemes, all three methods suffer when you are unable to predict the number of insertions and deletions that will occur. If your hash table is too small, it will fill up, and search efficiency will decrease.

Separate chaining. Because the `tableInsert` operation places the new item at the beginning of a linked list within the hash table, it is O(1). The `tableRetrieve` and `tableDelete` operations, however, are not as fast. They each require a search of the linked list of items, so ideally you would like for these linked lists to be short.

For separate chaining, *tableSize* is the number of linked lists, not the maximum number of table items. Thus, it is entirely possible, and even likely, that the current number of table items *N* exceeds *tableSize*. That is, the load factor α, or *N/tableSize*, can exceed 1. Because *tableSize* is the number of linked lists, *N/tableSize*—that is, α—is the average length of each linked list.

Some searches of the hash table are unsuccessful because the relevant linked list is empty. Such searches are virtually instantaneous. For an unsuccessful search of a nonempty linked list, however, `tableRetrieve` and `tableDelete` must examine the entire list, or α items in the average case. On the other hand, a successful search must examine a nonempty linked list. In the average case, the search will locate the item in the middle of the list. That is, after determining that the linked list is not empty, the search will examine $\alpha/2$ items.

Thus, the efficiency of the retrieval and deletion operations under the separate-chaining approach is

$$1 + \frac{\alpha}{2} \qquad \text{for a successful search, and}$$

$$\alpha \qquad \text{for an unsuccessful search}$$

Even if the linked lists typically are short, you should still estimate the worst case. If you seriously underestimate *tableSize* or if most of the table items happen to hash into the same location, the number of items in a linked list could be quite large. In fact, in the worst case, all *N* items in the table could be in the same linked list!

As you can see, the time that a retrieval or deletion operation requires can range from almost nothing—if the linked list to be searched either is empty or has only a couple of items in it—to the time required to search a linked list that contains all the items in the table, if all the items hashed into the same location.

Comparing methods. Figure 12-50 plots the relative efficiency of the collision-resolution schemes just discussed. When the hash table `table` is about half full—that is, when α is 0.5—the methods are nearly equal in efficiency. As the table fills and α approaches 1, separate chaining is the most efficient. Does this mean that we should discard all other search methods in favor of hashing with separate chaining?

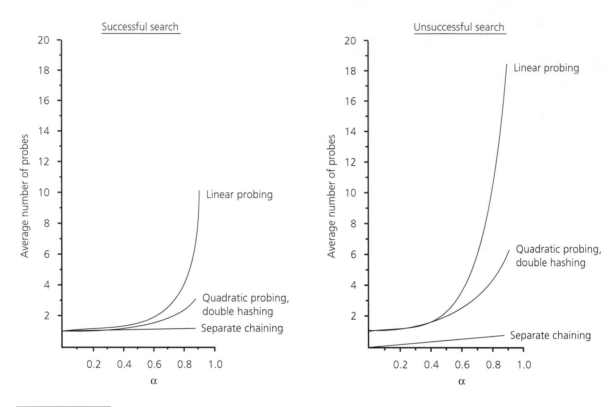

FIGURE 12-50   The relative efficiency of four collision-resolution methods

In the worst case, a hashing implementation of a table can be much slower than other implementations

No. The analyses here are average-case analyses. Although an implementation of the ADT table that uses hashing might often be faster than one that uses a search tree, in the worst case it can be much slower. If you can afford both an occasional slow search and a large *tableSize*—that is, a small α—then hashing can be an attractive table implementation. However, if you are performing a life-and-death search for your city's poison control center, a search-tree implementation would at least provide you with a guaranteed bound on its worst-case behavior.

Furthermore, while separate chaining is the most time-efficient collision-resolution scheme, you do have the storage overhead of the pointers in the linked list. If the data records in the table are small, the pointers add a significant overhead in storage, and you may want to consider a simpler collision-resolution scheme. On the other hand, if the records are large, the addition of a pointer is insignificant, so separate chaining is a good choice.

What Constitutes a Good Hash Function?

Before we conclude this introduction to hashing, consider in more detail the issue of choosing a hash function to perform the address calculations for a given application. A great deal has been written on this subject, most of which is beyond the mathematical level of this book. However, this section will present a brief summary of the major concerns.

- **A hash function should be easy and fast to compute.** If a hashing scheme is to perform table operations almost instantaneously and in constant time, you certainly must be able to calculate the hash function rapidly. Most of the common hash functions require only a single division (like the modulo function), a single multiplication, or some kind of "bit-level" operation on the internal representation of the search key. In all these cases, the requirement that the hash function be easy and fast to compute is satisfied.

- **A hash function should scatter the data evenly throughout the hash table.** Unless you use a perfect hash function—which is usually impractical to construct—you typically cannot avoid collisions entirely. For example, to achieve the best performance from a separate-chaining scheme, each entry *table[i]* should contain approximately the same number of items in its chain; that is, each chain should contain approximately *N/tableSize* items (and thus no chain should contain significantly more than *N/tableSize* items). To accomplish this goal, your hash function should scatter the search keys evenly throughout the hash table.

You cannot avoid collisions entirely

There are two issues to consider with regard to how evenly a hash function scatters the search keys.

- **How well does the hash function scatter random data?** If every search-key value is equally likely, will the hash function scatter the search keys evenly? For example, consider the following scheme for hashing nine-digit ID numbers:

  table[0..39] is the hash table, and
  the hash function is $h(x) = $ (first two digits of *x*) mod 40

  The question is, given the assumption that all employee ID numbers are equally likely, does a given ID number *x* have equal probability of hashing into any one of the 40 array locations? For this hash function, the answer is no. Only ID numbers that start with 19, 59, and 99 map into *table[19]*, while only ID numbers that start with 20 and 60 map into *table[20]*. In general, three different ID *prefixes*—that is, the first two digits of an ID number—map into each array location 0 through 19, while only two different prefixes map into each array location 20 through 39. Because all ID numbers are equally likely—and thus all prefixes 00 through 99 are equally likely—a given ID number is 50 percent more likely to hash into one of the locations 0 through 19 than it is to hash into one of the locations 20 through 39. As a result, each array location 0 through 19 would contain, on average, 50 percent more items than each location 20 through 39.

Thus, the hash function

A function that does not scatter random data evenly

$h(x) = $ (first two digits of x) mod 40

does not scatter random data evenly throughout the array `table[0..39]`. On the other hand, it can be shown that the hash function

A function that does scatter random data evenly

$h(x) = x$ mod 101

does, in fact, scatter random data evenly throughout the array `table[0..100]`.

■ **How well does the hash function scatter nonrandom data?** Even if a hash function scatters random data evenly, it may have trouble with nonrandom data. In general, no matter what hash function you select, it is always possible that the data will have some unlucky pattern that will result in uneven scattering. Although there is no way to guarantee that a hash function will scatter all data evenly, you can greatly increase the likelihood of this behavior.

As an example, consider the following scheme:

`table[0..99]` is the hash table, and
the hash function is $h(x) = $ first two digits of x

If every ID number is equally likely, h will scatter the search keys evenly throughout the array. But what if every ID number is not equally likely? For instance, a company might assign employee IDs according to department, as follows:

10xxxxxSales
20xxxxxCustomer Relations
. . .
90xxxxxData Processing

Under this assignment, only 9 out of the 100 array locations would contain any items at all. Further, those locations corresponding to the largest departments (Sales, for example, which corresponds to `table[10]`) would contain more items than those locations corresponding to the smallest departments. This scheme certainly does not scatter the data evenly. Much research has been done into the types of hash functions that you should use to guard against various types of patterns in the data. The results of this research are really in the province of more advanced courses, but two general principles can be noted here:

General requirements of a hash function

1. The calculation of the hash function should *involve the entire search key.* Thus, for example, computing a modulo of the entire ID number is much safer than using only its first two digits.

2. If a hash function uses modulo arithmetic, *the base should be prime;* that is, if h is of the form

$h(x) = x$ mod *tableSize*

then *tableSize* should be a prime number. This selection of *tableSize* is a safeguard against many subtle kinds of patterns in the data (for example, search keys whose digits are likely to be multiples of one another). Although each application can have its own particular kind of patterns and thus should be analyzed on an individual basis, choosing *tableSize* to be prime is an easy way to safeguard against some common types of patterns in the data.

Table Traversal: An Inefficient Operation Under Hashing

For many applications, hashing provides the most efficient implementation of the ADT table. One important table operation—traversal in sorted order—performs poorly when hashing implements the table. As was mentioned previously, a good hash function scatters items as randomly as possible throughout the array, so that no ordering relationship exists between the search keys that hash into `table[i]` and those that hash into `table[i+1]`. As a consequence, if you must traverse the table in sorted order, you first would have to sort the items. If sorting were required frequently, hashing would be a far less attractive implementation than a search tree.

Items hashed into `table[i]` and `table[i+1]` have no ordering relationship

Traversing a table in sorted order is really just one example of a whole class of operations that hashing does not support well. Many similar operations that you often wish to perform on a table require that the items be ordered. For example, consider an operation that must find the table item with the smallest or largest value in its search key. If you use a search-tree implementation, these items are in the leftmost and rightmost nodes of the tree, respectively. If you use a hashing implementation, however, you do not know where these items are—you would have to search the entire table. A similar type of operation is a **range query**, which requires that you retrieve all items whose search keys fall into a given range of values. For example, you might want to retrieve all items whose search keys are in the range 129 to 755. This task is relatively easy to perform by using a search tree (see Exercise 3), but if you use hashing, there is no efficient way to answer the range query.

In general, if an application requires any of these ordered operations, you should probably use a search tree. Although the *tableRetrieve, tableInsert,* and *tableDelete* operations are somewhat more efficient when you use hashing to implement the table instead of a balanced search tree, the balanced search tree supports these operations so efficiently itself that, in most contexts, the difference in speed for these operations is negligible (whereas the advantage of the search tree over hashing for the ordered operations is significant).

Hashing versus balanced search trees

In the context of external storage, however, the story is different. For data that is stored externally, the difference in speed between hashing's implementation of *tableRetrieve* and a search tree's implementation may well be significant, as you will see in Chapter 14. In an external setting, it is not uncommon to see a hashing implementation of the *tableRetrieve* operation and a search-tree implementation of the ordered operations used simultaneously.

Implementing a *HashMap* Class Using the STL

The standard C++ library does not contain a hash table class. However, there are several implementations of the STL that provide *hash_map* and *hash_set* classes. These classes will most likely be included in the next revision of the C++ STL. In the meantime, if programmers would like to provide a hash function to use with a table, they can either download one of the available implementations or write a hash table class themselves.

The following *HashMap* class is a template class derived from existing STL containers. It is implemented with separate chaining using a vector of *maps*. The vector holds the dynamic hash buckets, where each bucket is a map that holds elements with the same hash value. The hash function must be supplied as a template parameter, along with the key type, value, and the optional comparison function object for the *map* class.

The following files contain an ADT for a *HashMap*.

```
// **************************************************
// Header file HashMap.h
// The HashMap is derived from the STL vector and map
// **************************************************
#include <vector>
#include <map>
using namespace std;

template <class Key, class T, class Hash>
class HashMap : private vector<map<Key, T> >
{
   public:

       HashMap(const int maxBuckets);
       // Constructor
       // Precondition: The HashMap is empty.
       // Postcondition: The HashMap is initialized to hold
       // maxBuckets. The Hash template parameter is assigned to
       // the hash variable.

       T& operator[](Key& key);
       // Overloads the subscript operator for the HashMap class
       // Precondition: The HashMap contains a hash for type T.
       // Postcondition: The value of a hashed key is returned.
```

```
        map<Key, T>::const_iterator findItem(const Key& key);
        // Hashes the key to find the vector index.
        // Finds the map element using the key as the index.
        // Precondition: The HashMap contains a hash for type T.
        // Postcondition: An iterator to the (key, item) pair is
        // returned.
        // If the item is not in the map, the iterator points to
        // the end of the map.

        void insert (const Key& key, const T& item);
        // Hashes the key to find the vector index.
        // Inserts the (key, item) pair into the map at that index.
        // Precondition: The HashMap contains a hash for the
        // type T.
        // Postcondition: The (key, item) pair is inserted
        // at the hashed index.

        int erase(const Key& k);
        // Removes the item with the Key k in the hash table.
        // Precondition: The HashMap contains a hash for the
        // type T.
        // Postcondition: The (key, item) pair at the hashed index
        // is removed.
        // The number of items removed is returned (either 0 or 1).

        Hash hash;   // the hash function object
};  // end HashMap

#include "HashMap.cpp"
// End of header file

// ****************************************************
// Implementation file HashMap.cpp
// ****************************************************

template <class Key, class T, class Hash>
HashMap<Key, T, Hash>::HashMap(int maxBuckets)
{
    hash = Hash();
    resize(maxBuckets+1);
} // end constructor

template <class Key, class T, class Hash>
T& HashMap<Key, T, Hash>::operator[](Key& key)
{
    return at(hash(key))[key];
} // end operator[]
```

```cpp
template <class Key, class T, class Hash>
map<Key, T>::const_iterator HashMap<Key, T, Hash>::findItem
                                        (const Key& key)

{
   map<Key, T>::const_iterator it;
   int index = hash(key);
   it = at(index).find(key);

   return it;
} // end findItem

template <class Key, class T, class Hash>
void HashMap<Key, T, Hash>::insert (const Key& key,
                                    const T& item)

{
    int index = hash(key);
    at(index).insert(make_pair(key, item));
} // end insert

template <class Key, class T, class Hash>
int HashMap<Key, T, Hash>::erase(const Key& key)
{
    int index = hash(key);
    return at(index).erase(key);
} // end erase
// End of implementation file
```

Implementing a *Hash* class and adding exception handling and a display function to *HashMap* are left as programming problems at the end of this chapter.

12.3 Data with Multiple Organizations

Many applications require a data organization that simultaneously supports several different data-management tasks. One simple example involves a waiting list of customers, that is, a queue of customer records. In addition to requiring the standard queue operations *isEmpty*, *enqueue*, *dequeue*, and *getFront*, suppose that the application frequently requires a listing of the customer records in the queue. This listing is more useful if the records appear sorted by customer name. You thus need a *traverse* operation that visits the customer records in sorted order.

This scenario presents an interesting problem. If you simply store the customer records in a queue, they will not, in general, be sorted by name. If, on the other hand, you just store the records in sorted order, you will be unable to process the customers on a first-come, first-served basis. Apparently, this problem requires you to organize the data in two different ways.

One solution is to maintain two independent data structures, one organized to support the sorted traversal and the other organized to support the queue operations. Figure 12-51 depicts a sorted linked list of customer records and a pointer-based implementation of the queue. The pointer-based data structures are a good choice because they do not require a good estimate of the maximum number of customer records that must be stored.

One obvious disadvantage of this scheme is the space needed to store two copies of each customer record. In addition, not all of the required operations are supported as efficiently as possible. How well does this scheme support the required operations?

Several independent data structures waste space

The operations that only *retrieve* data—sorted `traverse` and `getFront`—are easy to perform. You can obtain a sorted listing of customer records by traversing the sorted linked list, and you can perform the queue `getFront` operation by inspecting the record at the front of the queue. The operations `enqueue` and `dequeue` are, however, more difficult to perform because they must *modify* the data.

The `enqueue` operation has two steps:

1. Insert a copy of the new customer record at the back of the queue. This step requires only a few pointer changes.

2. Insert a copy of the new customer record into its proper position in the sorted linked list. This step requires a traversal of the sorted linked list.

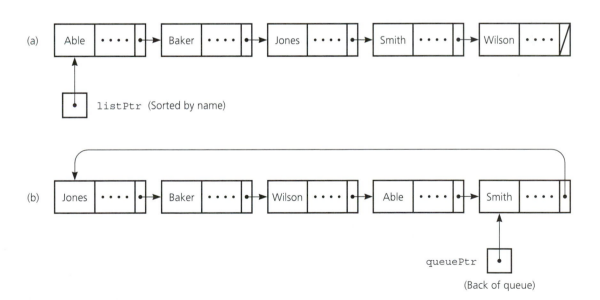

FIGURE 12-51   Independent data structures: (a) a sorted linked list; (b) a pointer-based queue

Similarly, the *dequeue* operation has two steps:

1. Delete the customer at the front of the queue, but retain a copy of the name for the next step. This step requires only a few pointer changes.

2. Search the sorted linked list for the name just removed from the queue, and delete from the list the customer record containing this name. This step requires a traversal of the sorted linked list.

Thus, although the scheme efficiently supports the *traverse* and *getFront* operations, *enqueue* and *dequeue* require a traversal of the sorted linked list (whereas in a queue alone *enqueue* and *dequeue* require only a small, constant number of steps). Can you improve on this scheme? One possibility is to store the customer records in a binary search tree rather than a sorted linked list. This approach would allow you to perform the second steps of the *enqueue* and *dequeue* operations much more efficiently. While the binary search tree strategy is certainly an improvement over the original scheme, the *enqueue* and *dequeue* operations would still require significantly more work than they would for a normal queue.

A different kind of scheme, one that supports the *dequeue* operation almost as efficiently as if you were maintaining only a queue, is possible by allowing the data structures to communicate with each other. This concept is demonstrated here first with a sorted linked list and a queue, and then with more-complex structures, such as a binary search tree.

In the data structure shown in Figure 12-52, the sorted linked list still contains customer records, but the queue now contains only pointers to customer records. That is, each entry of the queue points to the record in

> **Several independent data structures do not support all operations efficiently**

> **Interdependent data structures provide a better way to support a multiple organization of data**

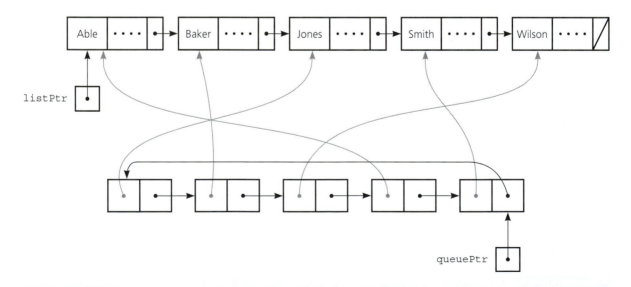

FIGURE 12-52   A queue pointing into a sorted linked list

the sorted linked list for the customer at the given queue position. An obvious advantage of storing only pointers in the queue is that the storage requirements are reduced, since a pointer is likely to be much smaller than a customer record. As you will soon see, this scheme also significantly improves the efficiency of the *dequeue* operation.

The efficiency of the *traverse*, *getFront*, and *enqueue* operations does not differ significantly from that of the original scheme that Figure 12-51 depicts. You still perform the *traverse* operation by traversing the sorted linked list. However, you perform *getFront* and *enqueue* as follows:

getFront(out queueFront:ItemType)


```
Let p be the pointer stored at the front of the
   queue (p points to the node, which is in the
   sorted linked list, that contains the record for
   the customer at the front of the queue)


queueFront = item in the node to which p points
```


enqueue(in newItem:ItemType)


```
Find the proper position for newItem in the sorted
   linked list
Insert a node that contains newItem into this
   position
Insert a pointer to the new node at the back of
   the queue
```


The real benefit of the new scheme is in the implementation of the *dequeue* operation:

dequeue()


```
Delete the item at the front of the queue and
   retain its value p (p points to the node that
   contains the customer record to be deleted)


Delete from the sorted linked list the node to
   which p points
```

Because the front of the queue contains a pointer to the customer record R that you want to delete, there is no need to search the sorted linked list. You have a pointer to the appropriate record, and all you need to do is delete it.

There is one big problem, however. Because you are able to go directly to R without traversing the linked list from its beginning, you have no trailing pointer to the record that precedes R on the list! Recall that you must have a trailing pointer to delete the record. As the scheme now stands, the only way to obtain the trailing pointer is to traverse the linked list from its beginning, but this requirement negates the advantage gained by having the queue point into the linked list. However, as you saw in Chapter 4, you can solve this problem by replacing the singly linked list in Figure 12-52 with a doubly linked list, as shown in Figure 12-53. (See Programming Problem 8.)

A doubly linked list is required

To summarize, you have seen a fairly good scheme for implementing the queue operations plus a sorted traversal. The only operation whose efficiency you might improve significantly is *enqueue*, since you still must traverse the linked list to find the proper place to insert a new customer record.

The choice to store the customer records in a linear linked list was made to simplify the discussion. A more efficient scheme has the queue point into a binary search tree rather than a linked list. This data structure allows you to perform the *enqueue* operation in logarithmic time, assuming that the tree remains balanced. To support the *dequeue* operation efficiently, however, you need a doubly linked tree. That is, each node in the tree must point to its parent so that you can easily delete the node to which the front of the queue points. Figure 12-54 illus-

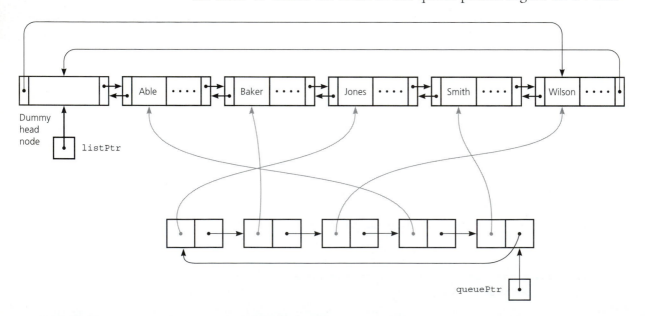

FIGURE 12-53   A queue pointing into a doubly linked list

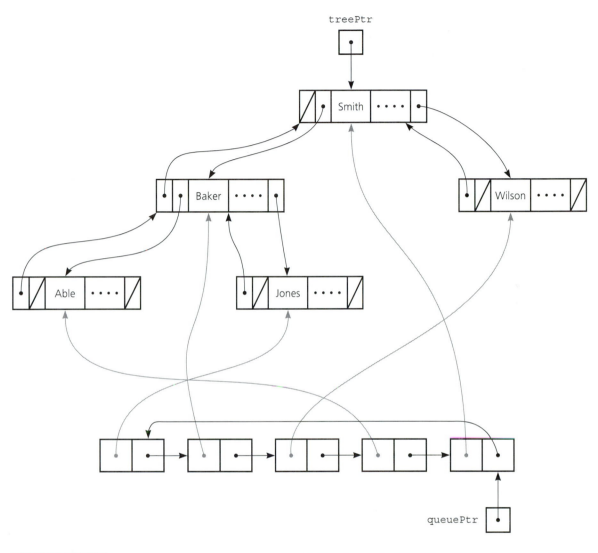

FIGURE 12-54   A queue pointing into a doubly linked binary search tree

trates this data structure; its implementation, which is somewhat difficult, is the subject of Programming Problem 9.

In general, you can impose several different organizations simultaneously on a set of data items. This concept is discussed further in
Chapter 14 in the context of indexing external storage.

Summary

1. A 2-3 tree and a 2-3-4 tree are variants of a binary search tree.
The internal nodes of a 2-3 tree can have either two or three chil-

dren. The internal nodes of a 2-3-4 tree can have either two, three, or four children. Allowing the number of children to vary permits the insertion and deletion algorithms to maintain the balance of the tree easily.

2. The insertion and deletion algorithms for a 2-3-4 tree require only a single pass from root to leaf and, therefore, are more efficient than the corresponding algorithms for a 2-3 tree.

3. A red-black tree is a binary tree representation of a 2-3-4 tree that requires less storage than a 2-3-4 tree. Insertions and deletions for a red-black tree are more efficient than the corresponding operations on a 2-3-4 tree.

4. An AVL tree is a binary search tree that is guaranteed to remain balanced. The insertion and deletion algorithms perform rotations in the event that the tree starts to stray from a balanced shape.

5. Hashing as a table implementation calculates where the data item should be rather than searching for it. Hashing allows for very efficient retrievals, insertions, and deletions.

6. The hash function should be extremely easy to compute—it should require only a few operations—and it should scatter the search keys evenly throughout the hash table.

7. A collision occurs when two different search keys hash into the same array location. Two ways to resolve collisions are through probing and chaining.

8. Hashing does not efficiently support operations that require the table items to be ordered—for example, traversing the table in sorted order.

9. When table operations such as traversal are not important to a particular application, if you know the maximum number of table items and if you have ample storage, hashing is a table implementation that is simpler and faster than balanced search tree implementations. Tree implementations, however, are dynamic and do not require you to estimate the maximum number of table items.

10. You can impose several independent organizations on a given set of data. For example, you can store records in a sorted doubly linked list and impose a first-in, first-out order by using a queue of pointers into the list.

Cautions

1. Even though search trees that allow their nodes to have more than two children are shorter than binary search trees, they are not

necessarily easier to search: More comparisons are necessary at each node to determine which subtree should be searched next.

2. A hashing scheme in general must provide a means of resolving collisions. Choose a hash function that keeps the number of collisions to a minimum. You should be careful to avoid a hash function that will map more items into one part of the hash table than into another.

3. To improve the performance of hashing, either change the hash function or increase the size of the hash table. Do not use complex collision-resolution schemes.

4. Hashing is not a good table implementation if you frequently require operations that depend on some order of the table's items. For example, if you frequently need to either traverse the table in sorted order or find the item with the largest search-key value, you probably should not use hashing.

Self-Test Exercises

1. What is the result of inserting 5, 40, 10, 20, 15, and 30—in the order given—into an initially empty 2-3 tree? Note that insertion of one item into an empty 2-3 tree will create a single node that contains the inserted item.

2. **a.** What is the result of deleting the 10 from the 2-3 tree that you created in Self-Test Exercise 1?

   b. What is the result of inserting 3 and 4 into the 2-3 tree that you created in Self-Test Exercise 1?

3. **a.** Repeat Self-Test Exercise 1 for a 2-3-4 tree.

   b. Insert 3 and 4 into the tree that you created in Part a.

4. What red-black tree represents the 2-3-4 tree in Figure 12-27a?

5. If your application of the ADT table involves only retrieval—such as the application in Scenario B of Chapter 11 that searched a thesaurus—what tree would provide for the most efficient table implementation: a balanced binary search tree, a 2-3 tree, a 2-3-4 tree, or a red-black tree?

6. Why does a node in a red-black tree require less memory than a node in a 2-3-4 tree?

7. Write the pseudocode for the `tableDelete` operation when linear probing is used to implement the hash table.

8. What is the probe sequence that double hashing uses when

$h_1(key) = key \bmod 11$, $h_2(key) = 7 - (key \bmod 7)$, and $key = 19$

9. If $h(x) = x$ mod 7 and separate chaining resolves collisions, what does the hash table look like after the following insertions occur: 8, 10, 24, 15, 32, 17? Assume that each table item contains only a search key.

Exercises

1. Execute the following sequence of operations on an initially empty ADT table *table* that is implemented as

   a. A binary search tree   **d.** A red-black tree

   b. A 2-3 tree   **e.** An AVL tree

   c. A 2-3-4 tree

and show the underlying tree after each operation:

```
table.tableInsert(10)
table.tableInsert(100)
table.tableInsert(30)
table.tableInsert(80)
table.tableInsert(50)
table.tableDelete(10)
table.tableInsert(60)
table.tableInsert(70)
table.tableInsert(40)
table.tableDelete(80)
table.tableInsert(90)
table.tableInsert(20)
table.tableDelete(30)
table.tableDelete(70)
```

2. What are the advantages of implementing the ADT table with a 2-3 tree instead of a binary search tree? Why do you not, in general, maintain a completely balanced binary search tree?

3. Write a pseudocode function that performs a range query for a 2-3 tree. That is, the function should visit all items that have a search key in a given range of values (such as all values between 100 and 1,000).

4. Given the 2-3 tree in Figure 12-55, draw the tree that results after inserting *k*, *b*, *c*, *y*, and *w* into the tree.

5. Given the 2-3 tree in Figure 12-56, draw the tree that results after removing *t*, *e*, *k*, and *d* from the tree.

6. Draw the 2-3-4 tree that results from inserting *o*, *d*, *j*, *h*, *s*, *g*, and *a*, in the order given, into a 2-3-4 tree that contains a single node whose value is *n*.

7. Assume that the tree in Figure 12-5b is a 2-3-4 tree, and insert 39, 38, 37, 36, 35, 34, 33, and 32 into it. What 2-3-4 tree results?

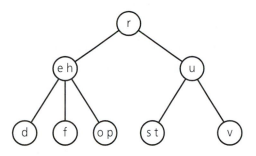

FIGURE 12-55 A 2-3 tree for Exercise 4

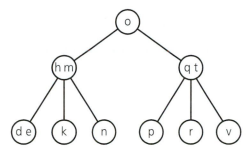

FIGURE 12-56 A 2-3 tree for Exercise 5

★**8.** Write pseudocode for the insertion, deletion, retrieval, and traversal operations for a 2–3–4 tree.

 9. Figure 12-33 is a red-black tree that represents the 2-3-4 tree in Figure 12-20. Draw another red-black tree that also represents the same 2-3-4 tree.

10. What 2-3-4 tree does the red-black tree in Figure 12-57 represent?

11. Write pseudocode for the insertion, deletion, retrieval, and traversal operations for a red-black tree.

12. Write a C++ function that converts a 2-3-4 tree to a red-black tree.

13. Write pseudocode for the table operations `tableInsert`, `tableDelete`, and `tableRetrieve` when the implementation uses hashing and linear probing to resolve collisions.

14. Write the pseudocode for the `tableDelete` operation when the implementation uses hashing and separate chaining to resolve collisions.

15. The success of a hash-table implementation of the ADT table is related to the choice of a good hash function. A good hash function is one that is easy to compute and will evenly distribute the possible data. Comment on the appropriateness of the following hash functions. What patterns would hash to the same location?

a. The hash table has size 2,048. The search keys are English words. The hash function is

$h(key)$ = (sum of positions in alphabet of *key*'s letters) mod 2048

b. The hash table has size 2,048. The keys are strings that begin with a letter. The hash function is

$h(key)$ = (position in alphabet of first letter of *key*) mod 2048

Thus, "BUT" maps to 2. How appropriate is this hash function if the strings are random? What if the strings are English words?

c. The hash table is 10,000 entries long. The search keys are integers in the range 0 through 9999. The hash function is

$h(key)$ = (*key* * *random*) truncated to an integer

where *random* represents a sophisticated random–number generator that returns a real value between 0 and 1.

d. The hash table is 10,000 entries long (*HASH_TABLE_SIZE* is 10000). The search keys are integers in the range 0 through 9999. The hash function is given by the following C++ function:

```
int hashIndex(int x)
{  for (int i = 1; i <= 1000000; ++i)
      x = (x * x) % HASH_TABLE_SIZE;
   return x;
}  // end hashIndex
```

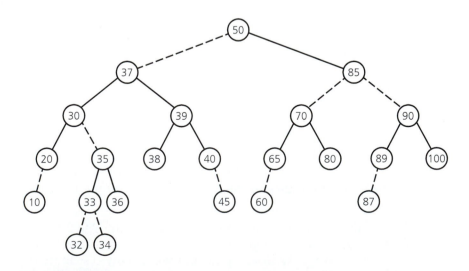

FIGURE 12-57   A red-black tree for Exercise 10

Programming Problems

1. Implement the ADT table by using a 2-3-4 tree.

2. Implement the ADT table by using a 2-3 tree. (This implementation is more difficult than the 2-3-4 implementation.)

3. Implement the ADT table by using a red-black tree.

4. Exercise 5 in Chapter 11 describes a compiler's symbol table, which keeps track of the program's identifiers. Write an implementation of a symbol table that uses hashing. Use the hash function $h(x) = x$ mod *tableSize* and the algorithm that involves Horner's rule, as described in the section "Hash Functions," to convert a variable into an integer x. Resolve collisions by using separate chaining.

   Because you add an item to the table only if it is not already present, does the time required for an insertion increase?

5. Repeat Programming Problem 4, but this time

   a. Use linear probing as the collision-resolution scheme.

   b. Use double hashing as the collision-resolution scheme.

   c. Use quadratic probing as the collision-resolution scheme.

6. Repeat Programming Problem 4, but allocate the hash table dynamically. If the hash table becomes more than half full, increase its size to the first prime number greater than 2 * *tableSize*.

7. Repeat Programming Problem 4, but experiment with variations of chaining. For example, you could use a binary search tree or a 2-3-4 tree instead of a linked list.

8. Implement the ADT queue operations as well as a sorted traversal operation for a queue that points into a doubly linked list, as shown in Figure 12-53.

9. Implement the ADT queue operations as well as a sorted traversal operation for a queue that points into a doubly linked binary search tree, as shown in Figure 12-54. You will need the insertion and deletion operations for a binary search tree that contains parent pointers, as discussed in Exercise 34 of Chapter 10.

10. Repeat Programming Problem 5 of Chapter 10, using the ADT table as the address book. Use a balanced search tree to implement the table.

11. Implement the symbol table described in Exercise 5 of Chapter 11 using hashing.

12. Implement a *Hash* class for use by the *HashMap* implementation in this chapter. The class will behave as a function object by overriding the *operator()* function. Write overloaded *operator()* functions: one for integers and one for strings. When *hash()* is called, the appropriate action will take place based on the parameter type in the function call.

13. Add exception handling to the *HashMap* class that is implemented in this chapter. Also, add a friend function to display the contents of the *HashMap*.

CHAPTER 13

Graphs

PREVIEW

Graphs are an important mathematical concept that have significant applications not only in computer science, but also in many other fields. You can view a graph as a mathematical construct, a data structure, or an abstract data type. This chapter provides an introduction to graphs that allows you to view a graph in any of these three ways. It also presents the major operations and applications of graphs that are relevant to the computer scientist.

13.1 Terminology

You are undoubtedly familiar with graphs: Line graphs, bar graphs, and pie charts are in common use. The simple line graph in Figure 13-1 is an example of the type of graph that this chapter considers: a set of points that are joined by lines. Clearly, graphs provide a way to illustrate data. However, graphs also represent the relationships among data items, and it is this feature of graphs that is important here.

G = {V, E}; that is, a graph is a set of vertices and edges

A **graph** G consists of two sets: a set V of vertices, or nodes, and a set E of edges that connect the vertices. For example, the campus map in Figure 13-2a is a graph whose vertices represent buildings and whose edges represent the sidewalks between the buildings. This definition of a graph is more general than the definition of a line graph. In fact, a line graph, with its points and lines, is a special case of the general definition of a graph.

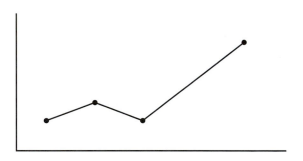

FIGURE 13-1   An ordinary line graph

(a)   (b)

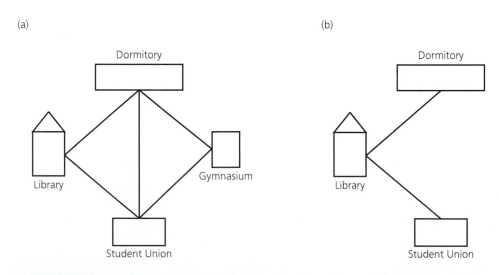

FIGURE 13-2   (a) A campus map as a graph; (b) a subgraph

A **subgraph** consists of a subset of a graph's vertices and a subset of its edges. Figure 13-2b shows a subgraph of the graph in Figure 13-2a. Two vertices of a graph are **adjacent** if they are joined by an edge. In Figure 13-2b, the Library and the Student Union are adjacent. A path between two vertices is a sequence of edges that begins at one vertex and ends at another vertex. For example, there is a path in Figure 13-2a that begins at the Dormitory, leads first to the Library, then to the Student Union, and finally back to the Library. Although a path may pass through the same vertex more than once, as the path just described does, a **simple path** may not. The path Dormitory–Library–Student Union is a simple path. A **cycle** is a path that begins and ends at the same vertex; a **simple cycle** is a cycle that does not pass through other vertices more than once. The path Library–Student Union–Gymnasium–Dormitory–Library is a simple cycle in the graph in Figure 13-2a. A graph is connected if each pair of distinct vertices has a path between them. That is, in a connected graph you can get from any vertex to any other vertex by following a path. Figure 13-3a shows a connected graph. Notice that a connected graph does not necessarily have an edge between every pair of vertices. Figure 13-3b shows a **disconnected** graph.

> Adjacent vertices are joined by an edge

> A path between two vertices is a sequence of edges

> A simple path passes through a vertex only once

> A cycle is a path that begins and ends at the same vertex

> A connected graph has a path between each pair of distinct vertices

In a **complete graph** each pair of distinct vertices has an edge between them. The graph in Figure 13-3c is complete. Clearly, a complete graph is also connected, but the converse is not true; notice that the graph in Figure 13-3a is connected but is not complete.

> A complete graph has an edge between each pair of distinct vertices

> A complete graph is connected

Since a graph has a *set* of edges, a graph cannot have duplicate edges between vertices. However, a **multigraph**, as illustrated in Figure 13-4a, does allow multiple edges. A graph's edges cannot begin and end at the same vertex. Figure 13-4b shows such an edge, which is called a **self** edge, or loop.

> A multigraph has multiple edges and so is not a graph

You can label the edges of a graph. When these labels represent numeric values, the graph is called a **weighted graph**. The graph in Figure 13-5a is a weighted graph whose edges are labeled with the distances between cities.

> The edges of a weighted graph have numeric labels

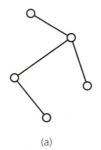   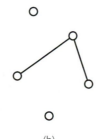   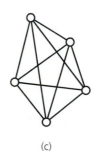

(a)   (b)   (c)

FIGURE 13-3   Graphs that are (a) connected; (b) disconnected; and (c) complete

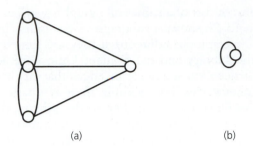

(a)   (b)

FIGURE 13-4   (a) A multigraph is not a graph; (b) a self edge is not allowed in a graph

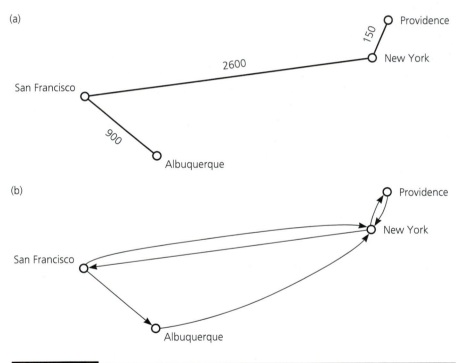

FIGURE 13-5   (a) A weighted graph; (b) a directed graph

All of the previous graphs are examples of **undirected graphs** because the edges do not indicate a direction. That is, you can travel in either direction along the edges between the vertices of an undirected graph. In contrast, each edge in a directed graph, or digraph, has a direction and is called a **directed edge**. Although each distinct pair of vertices in an undirected graph has only one edge between them, a directed graph can have two edges between a pair of vertices, one in each direction. For example, the airline flight map in Figure 13-5b is a directed graph. There are flights in both directions between Providence and New York, but, although there is a flight from San Francisco to

Each edge in a directed graph has a direction

Albuquerque, there is no flight from Albuquerque to San Francisco. You can convert an undirected graph to a directed graph by replacing each edge with two edges that point in opposite directions.

The definitions just given for undirected graphs apply also to directed graphs, with changes that account for direction. For example, a directed path is a sequence of directed edges between two vertices, such as the directed path in Figure 13-5b that begins in Providence, goes to New York, and ends in San Francisco. However, the definition of adjacent vertices is not quite as obvious for a digraph. If there is a directed edge from vertex x to vertex y, then y is adjacent to x. (Alternatively, y is a successor of x, and x is a predecessor of y.) It does not necessarily follow, however, that x is adjacent to y. Thus, in Figure 13-5b, Albuquerque is adjacent to San Francisco, but San Francisco is not adjacent to Albuquerque.

In a directed graph, vertex y is adjacent to vertex x if there is a directed edge from x to y

13.2 Graphs as ADTs

You can treat graphs as abstract data types. Insertion and deletion operations are somewhat different for graphs than for other ADTs that you have studied in that they apply to either vertices or edges. You can define the ADT graph so that its vertices either do or do not contain values. A graph whose vertices do not contain values represents only the relationships among vertices. Such graphs are not unusual, because many problems have no need for vertex values. However, the following ADT graph operations do assume that the graph's vertices contain values.

KEY CONCEPTS

ADT Graph Operations

1. Create an empty graph.

2. Destroy a graph.

3. Determine whether a graph is empty.

4. Determine the number of vertices in a graph.

5. Determine the number of edges in a graph.

6. Determine whether an edge exists between two given vertices.

7. Insert a vertex in a graph whose vertices have distinct search keys that differ from the new vertex's search key.

8. Insert an edge between two given vertices in a graph.

9. Delete a particular vertex from a graph and any edges between the vertex and other vertices.

10. Delete the edge between two given vertices in a graph.

11. Retrieve from a graph the vertex that contains a given search key.

Several variations of this ADT are possible. For example, if the graph is directed, you can replace occurrences of "edges" in the previous operations with "directed edges." You can also add traversal operations to the ADT. Graph-traversal algorithms are discussed in the section "Graph Traversals."

Implementing Graphs

Adjacency matrix

The two most common implementations of a graph are the adjacency matrix and the adjacency list. An **adjacency matrix** for a graph with n vertices numbered $0, 1, \ldots, n - 1$ is an n by n array `matrix` such that `matrix[i][j]` is 1 (`true`) if there is an edge from vertex i to vertex j, and 0 (`false`) otherwise. Figure 13-6 shows a directed graph and its adjacency matrix. Notice that the diagonal entries `matrix[i][i]` are 0, although sometimes it can be useful to set these entries to 1. You should choose the value that is most convenient for your application.

When the graph is weighted, you can let `matrix[i][j]` be the weight that labels the edge from vertex i to vertex j, instead of simply 1, and let `matrix[i][j]` equal ∞ instead of 0 when there is no edge from vertex i to vertex j. For example, Figure 13-7 shows a weighted undirected graph and its adjacency matrix. Notice that the adjacency matrix for an undirected graph is symmetrical; that is, `matrix[i][j]` equals `matrix[j][i]`.

(a)

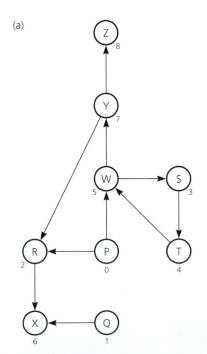

(b)

		0	1	2	3	4	5	6	7	8
		P	Q	R	S	T	W	X	Y	Z
0	P	0	0	1	0	0	1	0	0	0
1	Q	0	0	0	0	0	0	1	0	0
2	R	0	0	0	0	0	0	1	0	0
3	S	0	0	0	0	1	0	0	0	0
4	T	0	0	0	0	0	1	0	0	0
5	W	0	0	0	1	0	0	0	1	0
6	X	0	0	0	0	0	0	0	0	0
7	Y	0	0	1	0	0	0	0	0	1
8	Z	0	0	0	0	0	0	0	0	0

FIGURE 13-6   (a) A directed graph and (b) its adjacency matrix

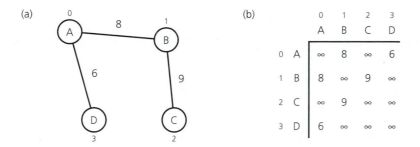

FIGURE 13-7 (a) A weighted undirected graph and (b) its adjacency matrix

Our definition of an adjacency matrix does not mention the value, if any, in a vertex. If you need to associate values with vertices, you can use a second array, *values*, to represent the *n* vertex values. The array *values* is one-dimensional, and *values[i]* is the value in vertex *i*.

Vertices can have values

An **adjacency list** for a graph with *n* vertices numbered 0, 1, . . . , *n* − 1 consists of *n* linked lists. The ith linked list has a node for vertex *j* if and only if the graph contains an edge from vertex *i* to vertex *j*. This node can contain the vertex *j*'s value, if any. If the vertex has no value, the node needs to contain some indication of the vertex's identity. Figure 13-8 shows a directed graph and its adjacency list. You can see, for example, that vertex 0 (*P*) has edges to vertex 2 (*R*) and vertex 5 (*W*). Thus, the first linked list in the adjacency list contains nodes for *R* and *W*.

Adjacency list

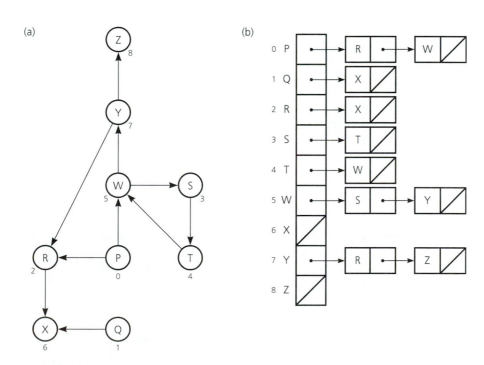

FIGURE 13-8 (a) A directed graph and (b) its adjacency list

Figure 13-9 shows an undirected graph and its adjacency list. The adjacency list for an undirected graph treats each edge as if it were two directed edges in opposite directions. Thus, the edge between A and B in Figure 13-9a appears as edges from A to B and from B to A in Figure 13-9b. The graph in 13-9a happens to be weighted; you can include the edge weights in the nodes of the adjacency list, given in Figure 13-9b.

Which of these two implementations of a graph—the adjacency matrix or the adjacency list—is better? The answer depends on how your particular application uses the graph. For example, the two most commonly performed graph operations are

Two common operations on graphs

1. Determine whether there is an edge from vertex i to vertex j

2. Find all vertices adjacent to a given vertex i

An adjacency matrix supports operation 1 more efficiently

The adjacency matrix supports the first operation somewhat more efficiently than does the adjacency list. To determine whether there is an edge from i to j by using an adjacency matrix, you need only examine the value of `matrix[i][j]`. If you use an adjacency list, however, you must traverse the ith linked list to determine whether a vertex corresponding to vertex j is present.

An adjacency list supports operation 2 more efficiently

The second operation, on the other hand, is supported more efficiently by the adjacency list. To determine all vertices adjacent to a given vertex i, given the adjacency matrix, you must traverse the ith row of the array; however, given the adjacency list, you need only traverse the ith linked list. For a graph with n vertices, the ith row of the adjacency matrix always has n entries, whereas the ith linked list has only as many nodes as there are vertices adjacent to vertex i, a number typically far less than n.

Consider now the space requirements of the two implementations. On the surface it might appear that the matrix implementation requires less memory than the linked list implementation, because each entry in the matrix is simply an integer, whereas each linked list node contains both a value to identify the vertex and a pointer. The adjacency matrix, however, always has n^2 entries, whereas the number of nodes in an

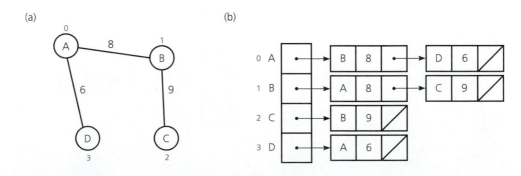

FIGURE 13-9   (a) A weighted undirected graph and (b) its adjacency list

adjacency list equals the number of edges in a directed graph or twice that number for an undirected graph. Even though the adjacency list also has *n* head pointers, it often requires less storage than an adjacency matrix.

Thus, when choosing a graph implementation for a particular application, you must consider such factors as what operations you will perform most frequently on the graph and the number of edges that the graph is likely to contain. For example, Chapter 6 presented the HPAir problem, which was to determine whether an airline provided a sequence of flights from an origin city to a destination city. The flight map for that problem is in fact a directed graph and appeared earlier in this chapter in Figure 13-8a. Figures 13-6b and 13-8b show, respectively, the adjacency matrix and adjacency list for this graph. Because the most frequent operation was to find all cities (vertices) adjacent to a given city (vertex), the adjacency list would be the more efficient implementation of the flight map. The adjacency list also requires less storage than the adjacency matrix, which you can demonstrate as an exercise.

Implementing a Graph Class Using the STL

Some C++ STL implementations provide a graph class; however, a graph class is not included as part of the STL. Graph classes and their accompanying algorithms can be implemented in many different ways. The *Graph* class in this section is an undirected, weighted graph. It is implemented with an adjacency list, which consists of a vector of maps. The vector elements represent the vertices of a graph. The map for each vertex contains element pairs, which consist of an adjacent vertex and an edge weight. The number of vertices in the graph is determined by an integer argument passed to the constructor. An *Edge* class holds both vertices of an edge, as well as the edge weight. The client application adds an edge to the graph by passing an *Edge* object to the *add* function. The following files contain an implementation for a graph.

```cpp
// **************************************************
// Header file Edge.h
// An Edge class for graph implementations.
// **************************************************
class Edge
{
    public:
        int v, w, weight;
        Edge(int firstVertex, int secondVertex, int edgeWeight)
        {
            v = firstVertex;
            w = secondVertex;
            weight = edgeWeight;
        }   // end constructor
};
// End of header file
```

```cpp
// *****************************************************
// Header file Graph.h
// An adjacency list representation of an undirected,
// weighted graph.
// *****************************************************
#include <vector>
#include <list>
#include <map>
#include "Edge.h"

using namespace std;

class Graph
{
   public:
       int numVertices;     // number of vertices in the graph
       int numEdges;        // number of edges in the graph

       // Adjacency list representation of the graph;
       // the map pair consists of the second vertex (key)
       // and the edge weight (value).
       vector<map<int, int> > adjList;

       Graph(int n);
       // Constructor.
       // Precondition: The graph is empty.
       // Postcondition: The graph is initialized to hold n
       // vertices.

       int getNumVertices() const;
       // Determines the number of vertices in the graph.
       // Precondition: None.
       // Postcondition: Returns the number of vertices in the
       // graph.


       int getNumEdges() const;
       // Determines the number of edges in the graph.
       // Precondition: None.
       // Postcondition: Returns the number of edges in the graph.


       int getWeight(Edge e) const;
       // Determines the weight of an edge.
       // Precondition: The edge exists in the graph.
       // Postcondition: Returns the weight of the edge parameter.

       void add(Edge e);
       // Creates an edge in the graph.
```

```cpp
      // Precondition: The vertices exist in the graph.
      // Postcondition: Adds to both v and w's list.

      void remove(Edge e);
      // Removes an edge from the graph.
      // Precondition: The vertices exist in the graph.
      // Postcondition: Removes edges from both v and w's list.

      map<int,int>::iterator findEdge(int v, int w);
      // Finds the edge connecting v and w.
      // Precondition: The edge exists.
      // Postcondition:  Returns an iterator to map key w in
      // vector[v].
};
// End of header file

// **************************************************
// Implementation file Graph.cpp
// An adjacency list representation of an undirected,
// weighted graph.
// **************************************************
#include "Graph.h"

Graph::Graph(int n)
{
   adjList.assign(n);
   numVertices = n;
}  // end constructor

int Graph::getNumVertices() const
{
   return numVertices;
}  // end getNumVertices

int Graph::getNumEdges() const
{
   return numEdges;
}  // end getNumEdges

int Graph::getWeight(Edge e) const
{
   return e.weight;
}  // end getWeight

void Graph::add(Edge e)
{
   int v = e.v,
       w = e.w,
       weight = e.weight;
```

```
        adjList[v].insert(make_pair(w, weight));
        adjList[w].insert(make_pair(v, weight));
        numEdges++;
    }  // end add

    void Graph::remove(Edge e)
    {
        int v = e.v,
            w = e.w,
            weight = e.weight;

        adjList[e.v].erase(w);
        adjList[e.w].erase(v);
        numEdges--;
    }  // end remove

    map<int,int>::iterator Graph::findEdge(int v, int w)
    {
        map<int,int> m = adjList[v];
        map<int,int>::iterator iter = m.find(w);

        return iter;
    }  // end findEdge
```

The programming problems at the end of the chapter ask you to add exception handling to the *Graph* class, modify the class to represent a directed graph, and to rewrite the *Graph* class as a template.

13.3 Graph Traversals

The solution to the HPAir problem in Chapter 6 involved an exhaustive search of the graph in Figure 13-8a to determine a directed path from the origin vertex (city) to the destination vertex (city). The algorithm *searchS* started at a given vertex and traversed edges to other vertices until it either found the desired vertex or determined that no (directed) path existed between the two vertices.

What distinguishes *searchS* from a standard graph traversal is that *searchS* stops when it first encounters the designated destination vertex. A **graph-traversal** algorithm, on the other hand, will not stop until it has visited *all of the vertices that it can reach*. That is, a graph traversal that starts at vertex v will visit all vertices w for which there is a path between v and w. Unlike a tree traversal, which always visits *all* of the nodes in a tree, a graph traversal does not necessarily visit all of the vertices in the graph unless the graph is connected. In fact, a graph traversal visits every vertex in the graph if and only if the graph is connected, regardless of where the traversal starts. (See Exercise 18.) Thus, you can use a graph traversal to determine whether a graph is connected.

A graph traversal visits all of the vertices that it can reach

A graph traversal visits all vertices if and only if the graph is connected

If a graph is not connected, a graph traversal that begins at vertex v will visit only a subset of the graph's vertices. This subset is called the **connected component** containing v. You can determine all of the connected components of a graph by repeatedly starting a traversal at an unvisited vertex.

If a graph contains a cycle, a graph-traversal algorithm can loop indefinitely. To prevent such a misfortune, the algorithm must mark each vertex during a visit and must never visit a vertex more than once.

Two basic graph-traversal algorithms, which apply to either directed or undirected graphs, are presented next. These algorithms visit the vertices in different orders, but if they both start at the same vertex, they will visit the same set of vertices. Figure 13-10 shows the traversal order for the two algorithms when they begin at vertex v.

> A connected component is the subset of vertices visited during a traversal that begins at a given vertex

Depth-First Search

From a given vertex v, the **depth-first search (DFS)** strategy of graph traversal proceeds along a path from v as deeply into the graph as possible before backing up. That is, after visiting a vertex, a DFS visits, if possible, an unvisited adjacent vertex.

The DFS strategy has a simple recursive form:

> DFS traversal goes as far as possible from a vertex before backing up

```
dfs(in v:Vertex)
// Traverses a graph beginning at vertex v by using a
// depth-first search: Recursive version.

    Mark v as visited
    for (each unvisited vertex u adjacent to v)
        dfs(u)
```

> Recursive DFS traversal algorithm

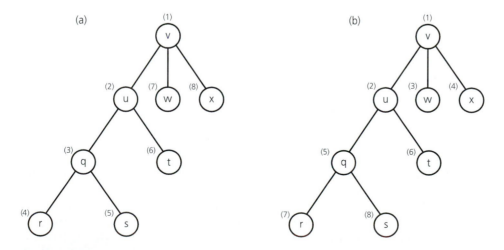

FIGURE 13-10   Visitation order for (a) a depth-first search; (b) a breadth-first search

Choose an order in which to
visit adjacent vertices

The depth-first search algorithm does not completely specify the order in which it should visit the vertices adjacent to *v*. One possibility is to visit the vertices adjacent to *v* in sorted (that is, alphabetic or numerically increasing) order. This possibility is natural either when an adjacency matrix represents the graph or when the nodes in each linked list of an adjacency list are linked in sorted order.

As Figure 13-10a illustrates, the DFS traversal algorithm marks and then visits each of the vertices *v, u, q,* and *r*. When the traversal reaches a vertex—such as *r*—that has no unvisited adjacent vertices, it backs up and visits, if possible, an unvisited adjacent vertex. Thus, the traversal backs up to *q* and then visits *s*. Continuing in this manner, the traversal visits vertices in the order given in the figure.

An iterative version of the DFS algorithm is also possible by using a stack:

An iterative DFS traversal
algorithm uses a stack

```
dfs(in v:Vertex)
// Traverses a graph beginning at vertex v by using a
// depth-first search: Iterative version.

   s.createStack()

   // push v onto the stack and mark it
   s.push(v)
   Mark v as visited

   // Loop invariant: there is a path from vertex v at the
   // bottom of the stack s to the vertex at the top of s
   while (!s.isEmpty())
   {
      if (no unvisited vertices are adjacent to
            the vertex on the top of the stack)
         s.pop()  // backtrack

      else
      {  Select an unvisited vertex u adjacent to
           the vertex on the top of the stack
         s.push(u)
         Mark u as visited
      }  // end if
   }  // end while
```

The *dfs* algorithm is similar to *searchS* of Chapter 6, but the *while* statement in *searchS* terminates when the top of the stack is *destination*.

For another example of a DFS traversal, consider the graph in Figure 13-11. Figure 13-12 shows the contents of the stack as the previous function *dfs* visits vertices in this graph, beginning at vertex *a*. Because the graph is connected, a DFS traversal will visit every vertex. In fact, the traversal visits the vertices in this order: *a, b, c, d, g, e, f, h, i*.

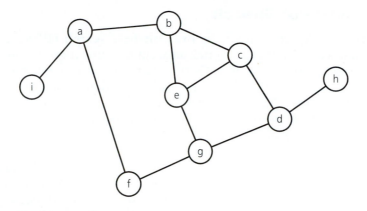

FIGURE 13-11 A connected graph with cycles

Node visited	Stack (bottom to top)
a	a
b	a b
c	a b c
d	a b c d
g	a b c d g
e	a b c d g e
(backtrack)	a b c d g
f	a b c d g f
(backtrack)	a b c d g
(backtrack)	a b c d
h	a b c d h
(backtrack)	a b c d
(backtrack)	a b c
(backtrack)	a b
(backtrack)	a
i	a i
(backtrack)	a
(backtrack)	(empty)

FIGURE 13-12 The results of a depth-first traversal, beginning at vertex *a*, of the graph in Figure 13-11

The vertex from which a depth-first traversal embarks is the vertex that it visited most recently. This *last visited, first explored* strategy is reflected both in the explicit stack of vertices that the iterative *dfs* uses and in the implicit stack of vertices that the recursive *dfs* generates with its recursive calls.

Breadth-First Search

BFS traversal visits all vertices adjacent to a vertex before going forward

After visiting a given vertex v, the **breadth-first search (BFS)** strategy of graph traversal visits every vertex adjacent to v that it can before visiting any other vertex. As Figure 13-10b illustrates, after marking and visiting v, the BFS traversal algorithm marks and then visits each of the vertices u, w, and x. Since no other vertices are adjacent to v, the BFS algorithm visits, if possible, all unvisited vertices adjacent to u. Thus, the traversal visits q and t. Continuing in this manner, the traversal visits vertices in the order given in the figure.

A BFS traversal will not embark from any of the vertices adjacent to v until it has visited all possible vertices adjacent to v. Whereas a DFS is a *last visited, first explored* strategy, a BFS is a *first visited, first explored* strategy. It is not surprising, then, that a breadth-first search uses a queue. An iterative version of this algorithm follows.

An iterative BFS traversal algorithm uses a queue

```
bfs(in v:Vertex)
// Traverses a graph beginning at vertex v by using a
// breadth-first search: Iterative version.


   q.createQueue()


   // add v to queue and mark it
   q.enqueue(v)
   Mark v as visited


   while (!q.isEmpty())
   {  q.dequeue(w)


      // Loop invariant: there is a path from vertex w to
      // every vertex in the queue q
      for (each unvisited vertex u adjacent to w)
      {  Mark u as visited
         q.enqueue(u)
      }  // end for
   }  // end while
```

Figure 13-13 shows the contents of the queue as `bfs` visits vertices in the graph in Figure 13-11, beginning at vertex a. In general, a breadth-first search will visit the same vertices as a depth-first search, but in a different order. In this example, the BFS traversal visits all of the vertices in this order: $a, b, f, i, c, e, g, d, h$.

A recursive BFS traversal algorithm is possible, but not simple

A recursive version of BFS traversal is not as simple as the recursive version of DFS traversal. Exercise 16 at the end of this chapter asks you to think about why this is so.

Node visited	Queue (front to back)
a	a
	(empty)
b	b
f	b f
i	b f i
	f i
c	f i c
e	f i c e
	i c e
g	i c e g
	c e g
	e g
d	e g d
	g d
	d
	(empty)
h	h
	(empty)

FIGURE 13-13 The results of a breadth-first traversal, beginning at vertex *a*, of the graph in Figure 13-11

Implementing a BFS Class Using the STL

A breadth-first search class for the *Graph* class in the previous section can be implemented with the STL *vector* and *queue* containers. The *BFS* class contains two vectors as members: one to store vertices that have been visited, and one to store the parent of each vertex. The parents of each vertex are stored for use by other graph algorithms. The constructor starts the BFS search with the first vertex. During the BFS search, a queue of *Edges* is maintained. The graph is searched by processing the edges from each vertex's adjacency list in the order that they were pushed onto the queue. The following files contain an ADT for a BFS class.

```
// ****************************************************
// Header file BFS.h
// A breadth-first search of the Graph class.
// ****************************************************

#include <queue>
#include "Graph.h"

using namespace std;
```

```cpp
class BFS
{
 protected:
   const Graph &g;
   int count;                // used to mark vertices as visited
   vector<int> mark;         // marked vertices
   vector<int> parents;      // parents of each vertex

   void search(Edge e);
   // Searches the adjacency list of each vertex breadth first.
   // Precondition:  The edge exists in the graph.
   // Postcondition: Performs a breadth first search of
   // the adjacency list of vertex w in Edge e.

 public:
   BFS(const Graph &g);
   // Constructor
   // Precondition: The graph exists.
   // Postcondition: Initializes arguments and starts the
   // breadth-first search.

   void startSearch();
   // Searches each unvisited vertex
   // Precondition:  The edge exists in the graph.
   // Postcondition: Starts a breadth first search with each
   // unvisited vertex.
};
// End of header file

// *************************************************
// Implementation file BFS.cpp
// A breadth-first search of the Graph class.
// *************************************************

#include "BFS.h"

BFS::BFS(const Graph &g) : g(g), mark(g.getNumVertices(), -1),
                    parents(g.getNumVertices(), 0), count(0)
{
   startSearch();

} // end constructor


void BFS::startSearch()
{
   for (int v = 0; v < g.getNumVertices(); v++)
      if (mark[v] == -1)
```

```
        search(Edge(v,v, 0));
} // end startSearch


void BFS::search(Edge e)
{
  // create a queue to push edges
  queue<Edge> q;

  map<int, int> m;     // holds adjacency list of current vertex
  map<int, int>::iterator iter;

  q.push(e);
  while (!q.empty())
  {
     // get the edge at the front if the queue
     e = q.front();

      // pop the edge off the queue
      q.pop();

       // if the vertex w has not visited yet, visit it
       if (mark[e.w] == -1)
       {
         int v = e.v,
             w = e.w,
             weight = e.weight;
         mark[w] = count++;  // mark w visited
         parents[w] = v;      // store w's parent

            // go through adjacency list of w
            m = g.adjList[w];
            for (iter = m.begin(); iter != m.end(); iter++)
              // if w's neighbor vertices have not been visited,
              // push the edge on the queue
              if (mark[iter->first] == -1)
                 q.push(Edge(w, iter->first, iter->second));
       }  // end if
   }  // end while
} // end search
// End of implementation file
```

13.4 Applications of Graphs

There are many useful applications of graphs. This section surveys some of these common applications.

Topological Sorting

A directed graph without cycles, such as the one in Figure 13-14, has a natural order. For example, vertex *a* precedes *b*, which precedes *c*. Such a graph has significance in ordinary life. If the vertices represent academic courses, the graph represents the prerequisite structure for the courses. For example, course *a* is a prerequisite to course *b*, which is a prerequisite to both courses *c* and *e*. In what order should you take all seven courses so that you will satisfy all prerequisites? There is a linear order, called a **topological order**, of the vertices in a directed graph without cycles that answers this question. In a list of vertices in topological order, vertex *x* precedes vertex *y* if there is a directed edge from *x* to *y* in the graph.

The vertices in a given graph may have several topological orders. For example, two topological orders for the vertices in Figure 13-14 are

> *a, g, d, b, e, c, f*

and

> *a, b, g, d, e, f, c*

If you arrange the vertices of a directed graph linearly and in a topological order, the edges will all point in one direction. Figure 13-15 shows two versions of the graph in Figure 13-14 that correspond to the two topological orders just given.

Arranging the vertices into a topological order is called **topological sorting**. There are several simple algorithms for finding a topological order. First, you could find a vertex that has no successor. You remove from the graph the vertex and all edges that lead to it, and add it to the beginning of a list of vertices. You add each subsequent vertex that has no successor to the beginning of the list. When the graph is empty, the list of vertices will be in topological order. The following pseudocode describes this algorithm:

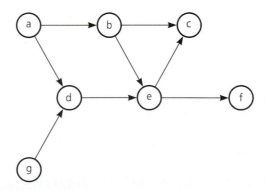

FIGURE 13-14   A directed graph without cycles

```
topSort1(in theGraph:Graph, out aList:List)
// Arranges the vertices in graph theGraph into a
// topological order and places them in list aList.


   n = number of vertices in theGraph
   for (step = 1 through n)
   {  Select a vertex v that has no successors
      aList.insert(1, v)
      Delete from theGraph vertex v and its edges
   }  // end for
```

A simple topological sorting algorithm

When the traversal ends, the list *aList* of vertices will be in topological order. Figure 13-16 traces this algorithm for the graph in Figure 13-14. The resulting topological order is the one that Figure 13-15a represents.

Another algorithm is a simple modification of the iterative depth-first search algorithm. First you push all vertices that have no predecessor onto a stack. Each time you pop a vertex from the stack, you add it to the beginning of a list of vertices. The pseudocode for this algorithm is

```
topSort2(in theGraph:Graph, out aList:List)
// Arranges the vertices in graph theGraph into a
// topological order and places them in list aList.


   s.createStack()
   for (all vertices v in the graph)
      if (v has no predecessors)
      {  s.push(v)
         Mark v as visited
      }  // end if/for

   while (!s.isEmpty())
   {  if (all vertices adjacent to the vertex on
            the top of the stack have been visited)
```

The DFS topological sorting algorithm

(a)

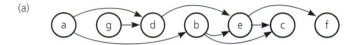

(b)

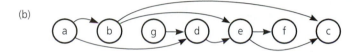

FIGURE 13-15   The graph in Figure 13-14 arranged according to the topological orders (a) *a, g, d, b, e, c, f* and (b) *a, b, g, d, e, f, c*

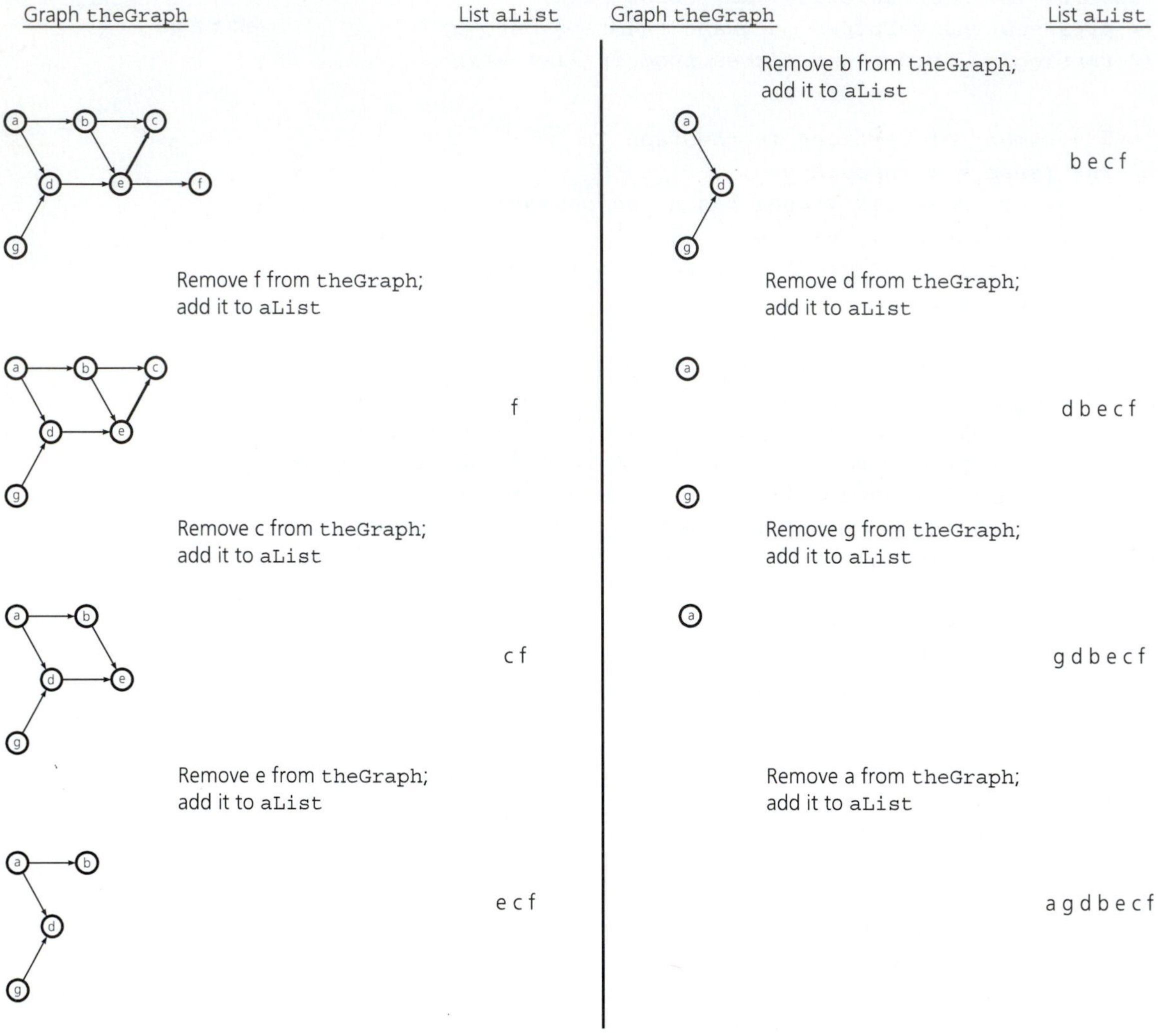

Graph theGraph	List aList	Graph theGraph	List aList

Remove b from theGraph;
add it to aList

b e c f

Remove f from theGraph;
add it to aList

f

Remove d from theGraph;
add it to aList

d b e c f

Remove c from theGraph;
add it to aList

c f

Remove g from theGraph;
add it to aList

g d b e c f

Remove e from theGraph;
add it to aList

e c f

Remove a from theGraph;
add it to aList

a g d b e c f

FIGURE 13-16 A trace of *topSort1* for the graph in Figure 13-14

```
{   s.pop(v)
    aList.insert(1, v)
}

else
{   Select an unvisited vertex u adjacent to
       the vertex on the top of the stack
    s.push(u)
    Mark u as visited
}   // end if
}   // end while
```

When the traversal ends, the list `aList` of vertices will be in topological order. Figure 13-17 traces this algorithm for the graph in Figure 13-14. The resulting topological order is the one that Figure 13-15b represents.

Spanning Trees

A tree is a special kind of undirected graph, one that is connected but has no cycles. Each vertex in the graph in Figure 13-3a could be the root of a different tree. Although all trees are graphs, not all graphs are trees. The nodes (vertices) of a tree have a hierarchical arrangement that is not required of all graphs.

A **spanning tree** of a connected undirected graph G is a subgraph of G that contains all of G's vertices and enough of its edges to form a tree. For example, Figure 13-18 shows a spanning tree for the graph in Figure 13-11. The dashed lines in Figure 13-18 indicate edges that were omitted from the graph to form the tree. There may be several spanning trees for a given graph.

If you have a connected undirected graph with cycles and you remove edges until there are no cycles, you will obtain a spanning tree for the graph. It is relatively simple to determine whether a graph contains a cycle. One way to make this determination is based on the following observations about undirected graphs:

1. **A connected undirected graph that has** *n* **vertices must have at least** *n* − **1 edges.** To establish this fact, recall that a connected graph has a path between every pair of vertices. Suppose that, beginning with *n* vertices, you choose one vertex and draw an edge between it and any other vertex. Next, draw an edge between this second vertex and any other unattached vertex. If you continue this process until you run out of unattached vertices, you will get a connected graph like the ones in Figure 13-19. If the graph has *n* vertices, it has *n* − 1 edges. In addition, if you remove an edge, the graph will not be connected.

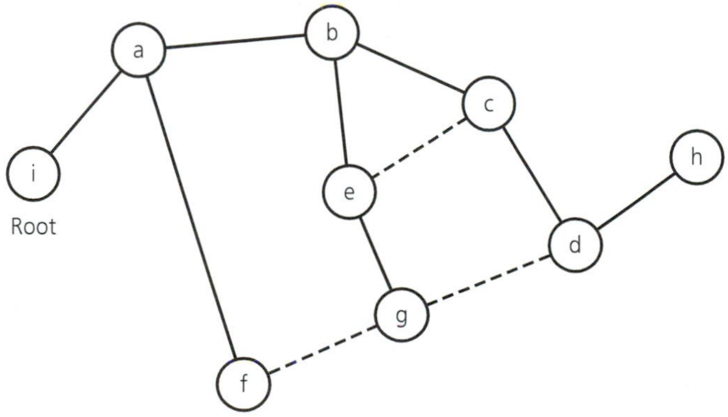

> A tree is an undirected connected graph without cycles

> Observations about undirected graphs that enable you to detect a cycle

FIGURE 13-17 A spanning tree for the graph in Figure 13-11

Action	Stack s (bottom to top)	List aList (beginning to end)
Push a	a	
Push g	a g	
Push d	a g d	
Push e	a g d e	
Push c	a g d e c	
Pop c, add c to aList	a g d e	c
Push f	a g d e f	c
Pop f, add f to aList	a g d e	f c
Pop e, add e to aList	a g d	e f c
Pop d, add d to aList	a g	d e f c
Pop g, add g to aList	a	g d e f c
Push b	a b	g d e f c
Pop b, add b to aList	a	b g d e f c
Pop a, add a to aList	*(empty)*	a b g d e f c

FIGURE 13-18   A trace of *topSort2* for the graph in Figure 13-14

2. **A connected undirected graph that has *n* vertices and exactly *n* − 1 edges cannot contain a cycle.** To see this, begin with the previous observation: To be connected, a graph with *n* vertices must have at least *n* − 1 edges. If a connected graph did have a cycle, you could remove any edge along that cycle and still have a connected graph. Thus, if a connected graph with *n* vertices and *n* − 1 edges did contain a cycle, removing an edge along the cycle would leave you with a connected graph with only *n* − 2 edges, which is impossible according to observation 1.

3. **A connected undirected graph that has *n* vertices and more than *n* − 1 edges must contain at least one cycle.** For example, if you add an edge to any of the graphs in Figure 13-19, you will create a cycle within the graph. This fact is harder to establish and is left as an exercise. (See Exercise 17 at the end of this chapter.)

FIGURE 13-19   Connected graphs that each have four vertices and three edges

Thus, you can determine whether a connected graph contains a cycle simply by counting its vertices and edges.

Simply count a graph's vertices and edges to determine whether it contains a cycle

It follows, then, that a tree, which is a connected undirected graph without cycles, must connect its n nodes with $n - 1$ edges. Thus, to obtain the spanning tree of a connected graph of n vertices, you must remove edges along cycles until $n - 1$ edges are left.

Two algorithms for determining a spanning tree of a graph are based on the previous traversal algorithms and are presented next. In general, these algorithms will produce different spanning trees for any particular graph.

The DFS spanning tree. One way to determine a spanning tree for a connected undirected graph is to traverse the graph's vertices by using a depth-first search. As you traverse the graph, mark the edges that you follow. After the traversal is complete, the graph's vertices and marked edges form a spanning tree, which is called the **depth-first search (DFS) spanning tree**. (Alternatively, you can remove the unmarked edges from the graph to form the spanning tree.) Simple modifications to the previous iterative and recursive versions of *dfs* result in algorithms to create a DFS spanning tree. For example, the recursive algorithm follows:

```
dfsTree(in v:Vertex)
// Forms a spanning tree for a connected undirected graph
// beginning at vertex v by using depth-first search:
// Recursive version.

   Mark v as visited

   for (each unvisited vertex u adjacent to v)
   {  Mark the edge from u to v
      dfsTree(u)
   }  // end for
```

DFS spanning tree algorithm

When you apply this algorithm to the graph in Figure 13-11, you get the DFS spanning tree rooted at vertex a shown in Figure 13-20. The figure indicates the order in which the algorithm visits vertices and marks edges. You should reproduce these results by tracing the algorithm.

The BFS spanning tree. Another way to determine a spanning tree for a connected undirected graph is to traverse the graph's vertices by using a breadth-first search. As you traverse the graph, mark the edges that you follow. After the traversal is complete, the graph's vertices and marked edges form a spanning tree, which is called the **breadth-first search (BFS) spanning tree**. (Alternatively, you can remove the unmarked edges from the graph to form the spanning tree.) You can modify the previous iterative version of *bfs* by marking the edge

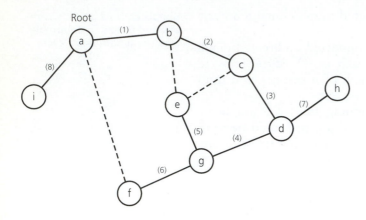

The DFS spanning tree algorithm visits vertices in this order: a, b, c, d, g, e, f, h, i. Numbers indicate the order in which the algorithm marks edges.

FIGURE 13-20   The DFS spanning tree rooted at vertex *a* for the graph in Figure 13-11

between *w* and *u* before you add *u* to the queue. The result is the following iterative algorithm to create a BFS spanning tree.

```
bfsTree(in v:Vertex)
// Forms a spanning tree for a connected undirected graph
// beginning at vertex v by using breadth-first search:
// Iterative version.

    q.createQueue()

    // add v to queue and mark it
    q.enqueue(v)
    Mark v as visited

    while (!q.isEmpty())
    {   q.dequeue(w)

        // Loop invariant: there is a path from vertex w to
        // every vertex in the queue q
        for (each unvisited vertex u adjacent to w)
        {   Mark u as visited
            Mark edge between w and u
            q.enqueue(u)
        }   // end for
    }   // end while
```

When you apply this algorithm to the graph in Figure 13-11, you get the BFS spanning tree rooted at vertex *a* shown in Figure 13-21. The figure indicates the order in which the algorithm visits vertices and marks edges. You should reproduce these results by tracing the algorithm.

Minimum Spanning Trees

Imagine that a developing country hires you to design its telephone system so that all the cities in the country can call one another. Obviously, one solution is to place telephone lines between every pair of cities. However, your engineering team has determined that due to the country's mountainous terrain, it is impossible to put lines between certain pairs of cities. The team's report contains the weighted undirected graph in Figure 13-22. The vertices in the graph represent *n* cities. An edge between two vertices indicates that it is feasible to place a telephone line between the cities that the vertices represent, and each edge's weight represents the installation cost of the telephone line. Note that if this graph is not connected, you will be unable to link all of the cities with a network of telephone lines. The graph in Figure 13-22 is connected, however, making the problem feasible.

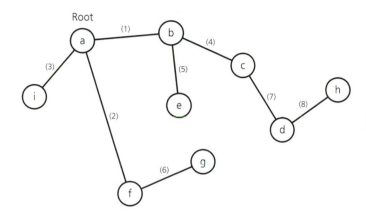

The BFS spanning tree algorithm visits vertices in this order: a, b, f, i, c, e, g, d, h. Numbers indicate the order in which the algorithm marks edges.

FIGURE 13-21   The BFS spanning tree rooted at vertex *a* for the graph in Figure 13-11

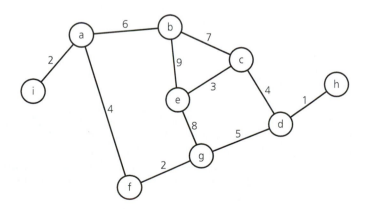

FIGURE 13-22   A weighted, connected, undirected graph

If you install a telephone line between each pair of cities that is connected by an edge in the graph, you will certainly solve the problem. However, this solution may be too costly. From observation 1 in the previous section, you know that $n - 1$ is the minimum number of edges necessary for a graph of n vertices to be connected. Thus, $n - 1$ is the minimum number of lines that can connect n cities.

If the cost of installing each line is the same, the problem is reduced to one of finding any spanning tree of the graph. The total installation cost—that is, the **cost of the spanning tree**—is the sum of the costs of the edges in the spanning tree. However, as the graph in Figure 13-22 shows, the cost of installing each line varies. Because there may be more than one spanning tree, and because the cost of different trees may vary, you need to solve the problem by selecting a spanning tree with the least cost; that is, you must select a spanning tree for which the sum of the edge weights (costs) is minimal. Such a tree is called the **minimum spanning tree**, and it need not be unique. Although there may be several minimum spanning trees for a particular graph, their costs are equal.

A minimum spanning tree of a connected undirected graph has a minimal edge-weight sum

One simple algorithm, called Prim's algorithm, finds a minimum spanning tree that begins at any vertex. Initially, the tree contains only the starting vertex. At each stage, the algorithm selects a least-cost edge from among those that begin with a vertex in the tree and end with a vertex not in the tree. The latter vertex and least-cost edge are then added to the tree. The following pseudocode describes this algorithm:

Minimum spanning tree algorithm

```
primsAlgorithm(in v:Vertex)
// Determines a minimum spanning tree for a weighted,
// connected, undirected graph whose weights are
// nonnegative, beginning with any vertex v.

  Mark vertex v as visited and include it in the minimum
    spanning tree

  while (there are unvisited vertices)
  {  Find the least-cost edge (v, u) from a visited
       vertex v to some unvisited vertex u
     Mark u as visited
     Add the vertex u and the edge (v, u) to the minimum
       spanning tree
  }  // end while
```

Figure 13-23 traces *primsAlgorithm* for the graph in Figure 13-22, beginning at vertex *a*. Edges added to the tree appear as solid lines, while edges under consideration appear as dashed lines.

It is not obvious that the spanning tree that *primsAlgorithm* determines will be minimal. However, the proof that *primsAlgorithm* is correct is beyond the scope of this book.

Shortest Paths

Consider once again a map of airline routes. A weighted directed graph can represent this map: The vertices are cities, and the edges indicate existing flights between cities. The edge weights represent the mileage between cities (vertices); as such, the weights are not negative. For example, you could combine the two graphs in Figure 13-5 to get such a weighted directed graph.

The shortest path between two vertices in a weighted graph has the smallest edge-weight sum

Often for weighted directed graphs you need to know the shortest path between two particular vertices. The **shortest path** between two given vertices in a weighted graph is the path that has the smallest sum of its edge weights. Although we use the term "shortest," realize that the weights could be a measure other than distance, such as the cost of each flight in dollars or the duration of each flight in hours. The sum of the weights of the edges of a path is called the path's **length** or **weight** or **cost**.

For example, the shortest path from vertex 0 to vertex 1 in the graph in Figure 13-24a is not the edge between 0 and 1—its cost is 8—but rather the path from 0 to 4 to 2 to 1, with a cost of 7. For convenience, the starting vertex, or origin, is labeled 0 and the other vertices are labeled from 1 to $n-1$. Notice the graph's adjacency matrix in Figure 13-24b.

The following algorithm, which is attributed to E. Dijkstra, actually determines the shortest paths between a given origin and *all* other vertices. The algorithm uses a set *vertexSet* of selected vertices and an array *weight*, where *weight[v]* is the weight of the shortest (cheapest) path from vertex 0 to vertex v that passes through vertices in *vertexSet*.

Finding the shortest paths between vertex 0 and all other vertices

If v is in *vertexSet*, the shortest path involves only vertices in *vertexSet*. However, if v is not in *vertexSet*, then v is the only vertex along the path that is not in *vertexSet*. That is, the path ends with an edge from a vertex in *vertexSet* to v.

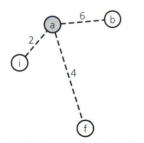

(a) Mark a, consider edges from a

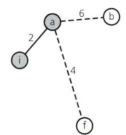

(b) Mark i, include edge (a, i)

FIGURE 13-23   A trace of `primsAlgorithm` for the graph in Figure 13-21, beginning at vertex *a*

(continues)

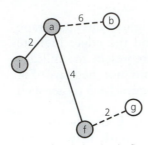

(c) Mark f, include edge (a, f)

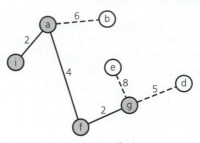

(d) Mark g, include edge (f, g)

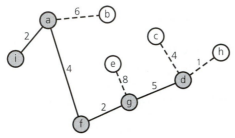

(e) Mark d, include edge (g, d)

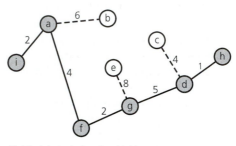

(f) Mark h, include edge (d, h)

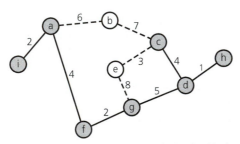

(g) Mark c, include edge (d, c)

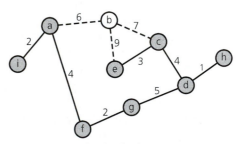

(h) Mark e, include edge (c, e)

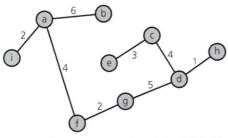

(i) Mark b, include edge (a, b)

FIGURE 13-23

(continued)

Initially, *vertexSet* contains only vertex 0, and *weight* contains the weights of the single-edge paths from vertex 0 to all other vertices. That is, *weight*[*v*] equals *matrix*[0][*v*] for all *v*, where *matrix* is the adjacency matrix. Thus, initially *weight* is the first row of *matrix*.

After this initialization step, you find a vertex *v* that is not in *vertexSet* and that minimizes *weight*[*v*]. You add *v* to *vertexSet*. For all (unselected)

(a) Origin

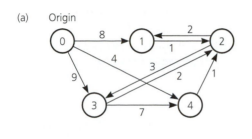

(b)

	0	1	2	3	4
0	∞	8	∞	9	4
1	∞	∞	1	∞	∞
2	∞	2	∞	3	∞
3	∞	∞	2	∞	7
4	∞	∞	1	∞	∞

FIGURE 13-24 (a) A weighted directed graph and (b) its adjacency matrix

vertices u not in *vertexSet*, you check the values *weight*[u] to ensure that they are indeed minimums. That is, can you reduce *weight*[u]—the weight of a path from vertex 0 to vertex u—by passing through the newly selected vertex v?

To make this determination, break the path from 0 to u into two pieces and find their weights as follows:

> *weight*[v] = weight of the shortest path from 0 to v
> *matrix*[v][u] = weight of the edge from v to u

Then compare *weight*[u] with *weight*[v] + *matrix*[v][u] and let

> *weight*[u] = the smaller of the values *weight*[u] and *weight*[v] +
> *matrix*[v][u]

The pseudocode for **Dijkstra's shortest-path algorithm** is as follows:

```
shortestPath(in theGraph:Graph, in weight:WeightArray)
// Finds the minimum-cost paths between an origin vertex
// (vertex 0) and all other vertices in a weighted directed
// graph theGraph; theGraph's weights are nonnegative.

   // Step 1: initialization
   Create a set vertexSet that contains only vertex 0
   n = number of vertices in theGraph
   for (v = 0 through n - 1)
      weight[v] = matrix[0][v]

   // Steps 2 through n
   // Invariant: For v not in vertexSet, weight[v] is the
   // smallest weight of all paths from 0 to v that pass
   // through only vertices in vertexSet before reaching
   // v. For v in vertexSet, weight[v] is the smallest
   // weight of all paths from 0 to v (including paths
   // outside vertexSet), and the shortest path
   // from 0 to v lies entirely in vertexSet.
   for (step = 2 through n)
   {  Find the smallest weight[v] such that v is not
         in vertexSet
      Add v to vertexSet
```

The shortest-path algorithm

Loop invariant

```
    // Check weight[u] for all u not in vertexSet
    for (all vertices u not in vertexSet)
        if (weight[u] > weight[v] + matrix[v][u])
            weight[u] = weight[v] + matrix[v][u]
}   // end for
```

The loop invariant states that once a vertex v is placed in *vertexSet*, *weight*[v] is the weight of the absolutely shortest path from 0 to v and will not change.

Figure 13-25 traces the algorithm for the graph in Figure 13-24a. The algorithm takes the following steps:

A trace of the shortest-path algorithm

Step 1. *vertexSet* initially contains vertex 0, and *weight* is initially the first row of the graph's adjacency matrix, shown in Figure 13-24b.

Step 2. *weight*[4] = 4 is the smallest value in *weight,* ignoring *weight*[0] because 0 is in *vertexSet.* Thus, v = 4, so add 4 to *vertexSet.* For vertices not in *vertexSet*—that is, for u = 1, 2, and 3—check whether it is shorter to go from 0 to 4 and then along an edge to u instead of directly from 0 to u along an edge. For vertices 1 and 3, it is not shorter to include vertex 4 in the path. However, for vertex 2 notice that *weight*[2] = ∞ > *weight*[4] + *matrix*[4][2] = 4 + 1 = 5. Therefore, replace *weight*[2] with 5. You can also verify this conclusion by examining the graph directly, as Figure 13-26a shows.

Step 3. *weight*[2] = 5 is the smallest value in *weight,* ignoring *weight*[0] and *weight*[4] because 0 and 4 are in *vertexSet.* Thus, v = 2, so add 2 to *vertexSet.* For vertices not in *vertexSet*—that is, for u = 1 and 3—check whether it is shorter to go from 0 to 2 and then along an edge to u instead of directly from 0 to u along an edge. (See parts b and c of Figures 13-26b and 13-26c.)

Notice that

weight[1] = 8 > *weight*[2] + *matrix*[2][1] = 5 + 2 = 7. Therefore, replace *weight*[1] with 7.

weight[3] = 9 > *weight*[2] + *matrix*[2][3] = 5 + 3 = 8. Therefore, replace *weight*[3] with 8.

				weight			
Step	v	vertexSet	[0]	[1]	[2]	[3]	[4]
1	–	0	0	8	∞	9	4
2	4	0, 4	0	8	5	9	4
3	2	0, 4, 2	0	7	5	8	4
4	1	0, 4, 2, 1	0	7	5	8	4
5	3	0, 4, 2, 1, 3	0	7	5	8	4

FIGURE 13-25	A trace of the shortest-path algorithm applied to the graph in Figure 13-24a

(a)

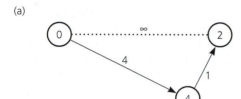

Step 2. The path 0–4–2 is
         shorter than 0–2

(b)

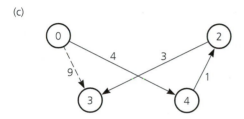

Step 3. The path 0–4–2–1 is
         shorter than 0–1

(c)

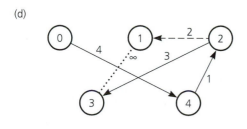

Step 3 continued. The path 0–4–2–3 is
                   shorter than 0–3

(d)

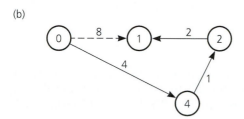

Step 4. The path 0–4–2–3 is
         shorter than
         0–4–2–1–3

FIGURE 13-26   Checking *weight*[*u*] by examining the graph: (a) *weight*[2] in
Step 2; (b) *weight*[1] in Step 3; (c) *weight*[3] in Step 3;
(d) *weight*[3] in Step 4

Step 4. *weight*[1] = 7 is the smallest value in *weight,* ignoring *weight*[0],
weight[2], and *weight*[4] because 0, 2, and 4 are in *vertexSet.* Thus,
$v = 1$, so add 1 to *vertexSet.* For vertex 3, which is the only vertex not in *vertexSet,* notice that *weight*[3] = 8 < *weight*[1] +
matrix[1][3] = 7 + ∞, as Figure 13-26d shows. Therefore, leave
weight[3] as it is.

Step 5. The only remaining vertex not in *vertexSet* is 3, so add it to
vertexSet and stop.

The final values in *weight* are the weights of the shortest paths. These values appear in the last line of Figure 13-25. For example, the shortest path from vertex 0 to vertex 1 has a cost of *weight*[1], which is 7. This result agrees with our earlier observation about Figure 13-24. We saw then that the shortest path is from 0 to 4 to 2 to 1. Also, the shortest path from vertex 0 to vertex 2 has a cost of *weight*[2], which is 5. This path is from 0 to 4 to 2.

The weights in *weight* are the smallest possible, as long as the algorithm's loop invariant is true. The proof that the loop invariant is true is by induction on `step`, and is left as a difficult exercise. (See Exercise 20.)

Circuits

A **circuit** is simply another name for a type of cycle that is common in the statement of certain problems. Recall that a cycle in a graph is a path that begins and ends at the same vertex. Typical circuits either visit every vertex once or visit every edge once.

Probably the first application of graphs occurred in the early 1700s when Euler proposed a bridge problem. Two islands in a river are joined to each other and to the river banks by several bridges, as Figure 13-27a illustrates. The bridges correspond to the edges in the multigraph in Figure 13-27b, and the land masses correspond to the vertices. The problem asked whether you can begin at a vertex *v*, pass through every edge exactly once, and terminate at *v*. Euler demonstrated that no solution exists for this particular configuration of edges and vertices.

For simplicity, we will consider an undirected graph rather than a multigraph. A path in an undirected graph that begins at a vertex *v*, passes through every edge in the graph exactly once, and terminates at *v* is called an **Euler circuit**. Euler showed that an Euler circuit exists if and only if each vertex touches an even number of edges. Intuitively, if you arrive at a vertex along one edge, you must be able to leave the

> An Euler circuit begins at a vertex *v*, passes through every edge exactly once, and terminates at *v*

(a)   (b)

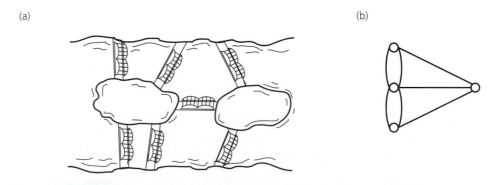

FIGURE 13-27   (a) Euler's bridge problem and (b) its multigraph representation

vertex along another edge. If you cannot, you will not be able to reach all of the vertices.

Finding an Euler circuit is like drawing each of the diagrams in Figure 13-28 without lifting your pencil or redrawing a line, and ending at your starting point. No solution is possible for Figure 13-28a, but you should be able to find one easily for Figure 13-28b. Figure 13-29 contains undirected graphs based on Figure 13-28. In Figure 13-29a, vertices *h* and *i* each touch an odd number of edges (three), so no Euler circuit is possible. On the other hand, each vertex in Figure 13-29b touches an even number of edges, making an Euler circuit feasible. Notice also that the graphs are connected. If a graph is not connected, a path through *all* of the vertices would not be possible.

Let's find an Euler circuit for the graph in Figure 13-29b, starting arbitrarily at vertex *a*. The strategy uses a depth-first search that marks edges instead of vertices as they are traversed. Recall that a depth-first search traverses a path from *a* as deeply into the graph as possible. By marking edges instead of vertices, you will return to the starting vertex; that is, you will find a cycle. In this example, the cycle is *a*, *b*, *e*, *d*, *a*, if

(a)   (b)

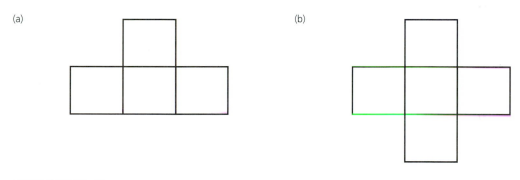

FIGURE 13-28   Pencil and paper drawings

(a)   (b)

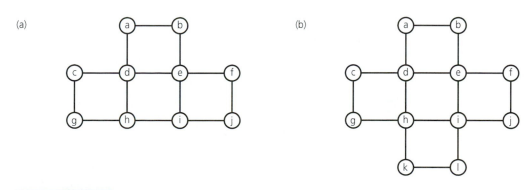

FIGURE 13-29   Connected undirected graphs based on the drawings in Figure 13-28

we visit the vertices in alphabetical order, as Figure 13-30a shows. Clearly this is not the desired circuit, because we have not visited every edge. We are not finished, however.

To continue, find the first vertex along the cycle *a, b, e, d, a* that touches an unvisited edge. In our example, the desired vertex is *e*. Apply our modified depth-first search, beginning with this vertex. The resulting cycle is *e, f, j, i, e*. Next you join this cycle with the one you found previously. That is, when you reach *e* in the first cycle, you travel along the second cycle before continuing in the first cycle. The resulting path is *a, b, e, f, j, i, e, d, a*, as Figure 13-30b shows.

The first vertex along our combined cycle that touches an unvisited edge is *i*. Beginning at *i*, our algorithm determines the cycle *i, l, k*,

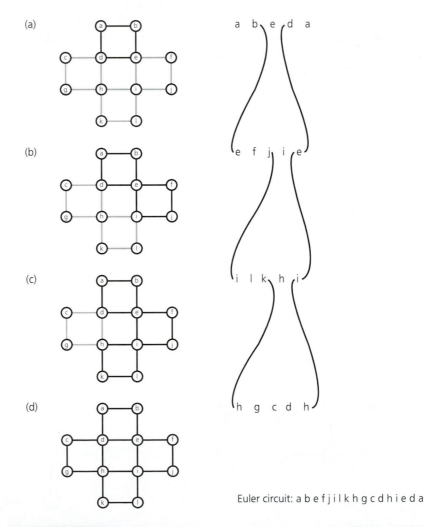

Euler circuit: a b e f j i l k h g c d h i e d a

FIGURE 13-30   The steps to determine an Euler circuit for the graph in Figure 13-29b

h, i. Joining this to our combined cycle results in the path *a, b, e, f, j, i, l, k, h, i, e, d, a.* (See Figure 13-30c.) The first vertex along this combined cycle that touches an unvisited edge is *h.* From *h,* we find the cycle *h, g, c, d, h.* Joining this to our combined cycle results in the Euler circuit *a, b, e, f, j, i, l, k, h, g, c, d, h, i, e, d, a.* (See Figure 13-30d.)

Some Difficult Problems

The next three applications of graphs have solutions that are beyond the scope of this book.

The traveling salesperson problem. A Hamilton circuit is a path that begins at a vertex *v,* passes through every vertex in the graph exactly once, and terminates at *v.* Determining whether or not an arbitrary graph contains a Hamilton circuit can be difficult. A well-known variation of this problem—the traveling salesperson problem—involves a weighted graph that represents a road map. Each edge has an associated cost, such as the mileage between cities or the time required to drive from one city to the next. The salesperson must begin at an origin city, visit every other city exactly once, and return to the origin city. However, the circuit traveled must be the least expensive.

A Hamilton circuit begins at a vertex *v,* passes through every vertex exactly once, and terminates at *v*

Unfortunately for this traveler, solving the problem is no easy task. Although a solution does exist, it is quite slow, and no better solution is known.

The three utilities problem. Imagine three houses *A, B,* and *C* and three utilities *X, Y,* and *Z* (such as telephone, water, and electricity), as Figure 13-31 illustrates. If the houses and the utilities are vertices in a graph, is it possible to connect each house to each utility with edges that do not cross one another? The answer to this question is no.

A graph is **planar** if you can draw it in a plane in at least one way so that no two edges cross. The generalization of the three utilities

A planar graph can be drawn so that no two edges cross

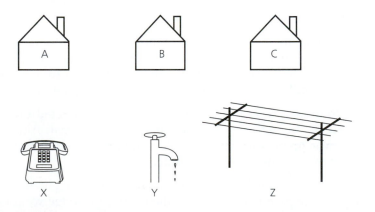

FIGURE 13-31   The three utilities problem

problem determines whether a given graph is planar. Making this determination has many important applications. For example, a graph can represent an electronic circuit where the vertices represent components and the edges represent the connections between components. Is it possible to design the circuit so that the connections do not cross? The solutions to these problems are also beyond the scope of this book.

The four-color problem. Given a planar graph, can you color the vertices so that no adjacent vertices have the same color, if you use at most four colors? For example, the graph in Figure 13-11 is planar because none of its edges cross. You can solve the coloring problem for this graph by using only three colors. Color vertices *a, c, g,* and *h* red, color vertices *b, d, f,* and *i* blue, and color vertex *e* green.

The answer to our question is yes, but it is difficult to prove. In fact, this problem was posed more than a century before it was solved in the 1970s with the use of a computer.

Summary

1. The two most common implementations of a graph are the adjacency matrix and the adjacency list. Each has its relative advantages and disadvantages. The choice should depend on the needs of the given application.

2. Graph searching is an important application of stacks and queues. Depth-first search is a graph-traversal algorithm that uses a stack to keep track of the sequence of visited vertices. It goes as deep into the graph as it can before backtracking. Breadth-first search uses a queue to keep track of the sequence of visited vertices. It visits all possible adjacent vertices before traversing further into the graph.

3. Topological sorting produces a linear order of the vertices in a directed graph without cycles. Vertex *x* precedes vertex *y* if there is a directed edge from *x* to *y* in the graph.

4. Trees are connected undirected graphs without cycles. A spanning tree of a connected undirected graph is a subgraph that contains all of the graph's vertices and enough of its edges to form a tree. DFS and BFS traversals produce DFS and BFS spanning trees.

5. A minimum spanning tree for a weighted undirected graph is a spanning tree whose edge-weight sum is minimal. Although a particular graph can have several minimum spanning trees, their edge-weight sums will be the same.

6. The shortest path between two vertices in a weighted directed graph is the path that has the smallest sum of its edge weights.

7. An Euler circuit in an undirected graph is a cycle that begins at vertex v, passes through every edge in the graph exactly once, and terminates at v.

8. A Hamilton circuit in an undirected graph is a cycle that begins at vertex v, passes through every vertex in the graph exactly once, and terminates at v.

Cautions

1. When searching a graph, realize that the algorithm might take wrong turns. For example, you must eliminate the possibility of cycling within the algorithm; the algorithm must be able to back-track when it hits a dead end.

Self-Test Exercises

1. Describe the graphs in Figure 13-32. For example, are they directed? Connected? Complete? Weighted?

2. Use the depth-first strategy and the breadth-first strategy to traverse the graph in Figure 13-32a, beginning with vertex 0. List the vertices in the order in which each traversal visits them.

3. Write the adjacency matrix for the graph in Figure 13-32a.

4. Add an edge to the directed graph in Figure 13-14 that runs from vertex d to vertex b. Write all possible topological orders for the vertices in this new graph.

5. Is it possible for a connected undirected graph with five vertices and four edges to contain a simple cycle? Explain.

6. Draw the DFS spanning tree whose root is vertex 0 for the graph in Figure 13-33.

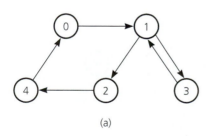
(a)

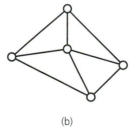
(b)

FIGURE 13-32   Graphs for Self-Test Exercises 1, 2, and 3

7. Draw the minimum spanning tree whose root is vertex 0 for the graph in Figure 13-33.

8. What are the shortest paths from vertex 0 to each vertex of the graph in Figure 13-24a? (Note the weights of these paths in Figure 13-25.)

Exercises

When given a choice of vertices to visit, the traversals in the following exercises should visit vertices in sorted order.

1. Give the adjacency matrix and adjacency list for

   a. The weighted graph in Figure 13-33

   b. The directed graph in Figure 13-34

2. Show that the adjacency list in Figure 13-8b requires less memory than the adjacency matrix in Figure 13-6b.

3. Consider Figure 13-35 and answer the following:

   a. Will the adjacency matrix be symmetrical?

   b. Provide the adjacency matrix.

   c. Provide the adjacency list.

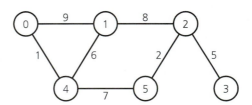

FIGURE 13-33 A graph for Self-Test Exercises 6 and 7 and for Exercises 1 and 4

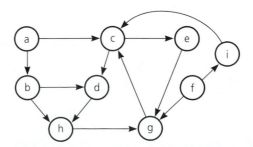

FIGURE 13-34 A graph for Exercise 1

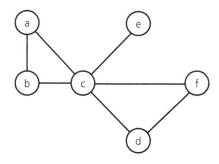

FIGURE 13-35 A graph for Exercise 3

4. Use both the depth-first strategy and the breadth-first strategy to traverse the graph in Figure 13-33, beginning with vertex 0, and the graph in Figure 13-36, beginning with vertex *a*. List the vertices in the order in which each traversal visits them.

5. By modifying the DFS traversal algorithm, write pseudocode for an algorithm that determines whether a graph contains a cycle.

6. Using the topological sorting algorithm *topSort1*, as given in this chapter, write the topological order of the vertices for each graph in Figure 13-37.

7. Trace the DFS topological sorting algorithm *topSort2*, and indicate the resulting topological order of the vertices for each graph in Figure 13-37.

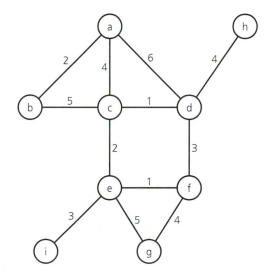

FIGURE 13-36 A graph for Exercises 4 and 10

8. Revise the topological sorting algorithm *topSort1* by removing predecessors instead of successors. Trace the new algorithm for each graph in Figure 13-37.

9. Trace the DFS and BFS spanning tree algorithms, beginning with vertex *a* of the graph in Figure 13-11, and show that the spanning trees are the trees in Figures 13-20 and 13-21, respectively.

10. Draw the DFS and BFS spanning trees rooted at *a* for the graph in Figure 13-36. Then draw the minimum spanning tree rooted at *a* for this graph.

11. For the graph in Figure 13-38

    a. Draw all the possible spanning trees.

    b. Draw the minimum spanning tree.

12. Write pseudocode for an iterative algorithm that determines a DFS spanning tree for an undirected graph. Base your algorithm on the traversal algorithm *dfs*.

13. Draw the minimum spanning tree for the graph in Figure 13-22 when you start with

    a. Vertex *g*   **b.** Vertex *c*

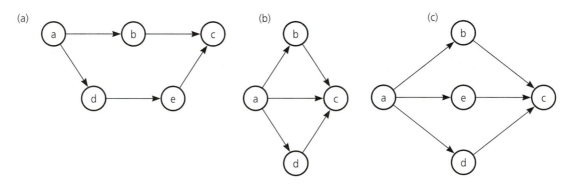

FIGURE 13-37   Graphs for Exercises 7 and 8

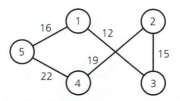

FIGURE 13-38   A graph for Exercise 11

*14. Trace the shortest-path algorithm for the graph in Figure 13–39, letting vertex 0 be the origin.

*15. Implement the shortest-path algorithm in C++. How can you modify this algorithm so that any vertex can be the origin?

*16. Determine an Euler circuit for the graph in Figure 13–40. Why is one possible?

*17. Prove that a connected undirected graph with n vertices and more than $n - 1$ edges must contain at least one simple cycle. (See observation 3 in the section "Spanning Trees.")

*18. Prove that a graph-traversal algorithm visits every vertex in the graph if and only if the graph is connected, regardless of where the traversal starts.

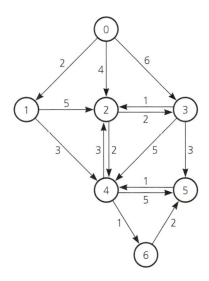

FIGURE 13-39 A graph for Exercise 14

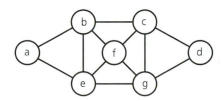

FIGURE 13-40 A graph for Exercise 16

*19. Although the DFS traversal algorithm has a simple recursive form, a recursive BFS traversal algorithm is not straightforward.

    a. Explain why this fact is true.

    b. Write the pseudocode for a recursive version of the BFS traversal algorithm.

*20. Prove that the loop invariant of Dijkstra's shortest-path algorithm is true by using a proof by induction on *step*.

Programming Problems

1. Modify the *Graph* class presented in the section "Graphs as ADTs" to represent a directed graph. Add exception handling to the class as well.

2. Implement a template version of the *Graph* class presented in the section "Graphs as ADTs." The template parameter will represent the value associated with each vertex. An additional vector of vertices will hold the data, and additional functions should be provided to allow the client application to add or remove vertex information.

3. Implement the ADT graph as a C++ class, first by using an adjacency matrix to represent the graph and then by using an adjacency list to represent the graph. Allow the graph to be either weighted or unweighted and either directed or undirected. Include DFS and BFS traversals.

4. Extend Programming Problem 3 by adding ADT operations such as *isConnected* and *hasCycle*. Also, include operations that perform a topological sort for a directed graph without cycles, determine the DFS and BFS spanning trees for a connected graph, and determine a minimum spanning tree for a connected undirected graph.

5. The HPAir problem was the subject of Programming Problems 11, 12, and 13 of Chapter 6. Revise these problems by implementing the ADT flight map as a derived class of the graph class that you wrote for Programming Problem 3.

CHAPTER 14

External Methods

PREVIEW

All of the previous table implementations assume that the data items reside in the computer's internal memory. Many real-world applications, however, require a table so large that it greatly exceeds the amount of available internal memory. In such situations, you must store the table on an external storage device such as a disk and perform table operations there.

This chapter considers the problem of data management in an external environment by using a direct access file as a model of external storage. In particular, this chapter discusses how to sort the data in an external file by modifying the mergesort algorithm and how to search an external file by using generalizations of the hashing and search-tree schemes developed previously.

14.1 A Look at External Storage

You use external storage when your program reads data from and writes data to a C++ file. Also, when you use a word processing program, for example, and choose *Save*, the program saves your current document in a file. This action enables you to exit the program and then use it later to retrieve your document for revision. This is one of the advantages of external storage: It exists beyond the execution period of a program. In this sense, it is "permanent" instead of volatile like internal memory.

External storage exists after program execution

Another advantage of external storage is that, in general, there is far more of it than internal memory. If you have a table of one million data items, each of which is a record of moderate size, you will probably not be able to store the entire table in internal memory at one time. On the other hand, this much data can easily reside on an external disk. As a consequence, when dealing with tables of this magnitude, you cannot simply read the entire table into memory when you want to operate on it and then write it back onto the disk when you are finished. Instead, you must devise ways to operate on data—for example, sort it and search it—while it resides externally.

Generally, there is more external storage than internal memory

In general you can create files for either sequential access or direct access. To access the data stored at a given position in a **sequential access file**, you must advance the file window beyond all the intervening data. In this sense, a sequential access file resembles a linked list. To access a particular node in the list, you must traverse the list from its beginning until you reach the desired node. In contrast, a **direct access file** allows you to access the data at a given position directly. A direct access file resembles an array in that you can access the element at $data[i]$ without first accessing the elements before $data[i]$.

Without direct access files, it would be impossible to support the table operations efficiently in an external environment. Many programming languages, including C++, support both sequential access and direct access of files. However, to permit a language-independent discussion, we will construct a model of direct access files that illustrates how a programming language that does not support such files might implement them. This model will be a simplification of reality but will include the features necessary for this discussion.

Direct access files are essential for external tables

Imagine that a computer's memory is divided into two parts: internal memory and external memory, as Figure 14-1 illustrates. Assume that an executing program, along with its nonfile data, resides in the computer's internal memory; the permanent files of a computer system reside in the external memory. Further assume that the external storage devices have the characteristics of a disk (although some systems use other devices).

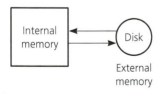

FIGURE 14-1 Internal and external memory

A file consists of **data records**. A data record can be anything from a simple value, such as an integer, to an aggregate structure, such as an employee record. For simplicity, assume that the data records in any one file are all of the same type.

The records of a file are organized into one or more **blocks**, as Figure 14-2 shows. The size of a block—that is, the number of bits of data it can contain—is determined by both the hardware configuration and the system software of the computer. In general, an individual program has no control over this size. Therefore, the number of records in a block is a function of the size of the records in the file. For example, a file of integer records will have more records per block than a file of employee records.

Much as you number the elements of an array, you can number the blocks of a file in a linear sequence. With a direct access file, a program can read a given block from the file by specifying its block number, and similarly, it can write data out to a particular block. In this regard a direct access file resembles an array of arrays, with each block of the file analogous to a single array entry, which is itself an array that contains several records.

In this direct access model, *all input and output is at the block level rather than at the record level.* That is, you can read and write a block of records, but you cannot read or write an individual record. Reading or writing a block is called a **block access**.

The algorithms in this chapter assume commands for reading and writing blocks. The statement

```
buf.readBlock(dataFile, i)
```

will read the ith block of file `dataFile` and place it in an object `buf`. The object must accommodate the many records that each block of file `dataFile` contains. For example, if each block contains 100 employee records, `buf` must store at least 100 employee records. The object `buf` is called a **buffer**, which is a location that temporarily stores data as it makes its way from one process or location to another.

Once the system has read a block into `buf,` the program can process—for example, inspect or modify—the records in the block. Also, because the records in the object `buf` are only copies of the

> A file contains records that are organized into blocks

> Direct access input and output involves blocks instead of records

> A buffer stores data temporarily

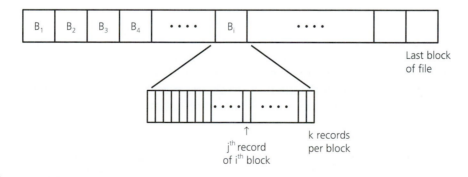

FIGURE 14-2 A file partitioned into blocks of records

records in the file *dataFile*, if a program does modify the records in *buf*, it must write *buf* back out to *dataFile*, so that the file also reflects the modifications. We assume that the statement

```
buf.writeBlock(dataFile, i)
```

will write the contents of *buf* to the ith block of the file *dataFile*. If *dataFile* contains *n* blocks, the statement

```
buf.writeBlock(dataFile, n + 1)
```

will append a new block to *dataFile*, and thus the file can grow dynamically, just as a C++ file can.

Again, realize that these input and output commands allow you to read and write only entire blocks. As a consequence, even if you need to operate on only a single record of the file, you must access an entire block. For example, suppose that you want to give employee Smith a $1,000 raise. If Smith's record is in block *i* (how to determine the correct block is discussed later in the chapter), you would perform the following steps:

Updating a portion of a record within a block

```
// read block i from file dataFile into buffer buf
buf.readBlock(dataFile, i)

Find the entry buf.getRecord(j) that contains the
    record whose search key is "Smith"

// increase the salary portion of Smith's record
(buf.getRecord(j)).setSalary((buf.getRecord(j)).getSalary() + 1000)

// write changed block back to file dataFile
buf.writeBlock(dataFile, i)
```

The time required to read or write a block of data is typically much longer than the time required to operate on the block's data once it is in the computer's internal memory.[1] For example, you typically can inspect every record in the buffer *buf* in less time than that required to read a block into the buffer. As a consequence, you should reduce the number of required block accesses. In the previous pseudocode, for instance, you should process as many records in *buf* as possible before writing it to the file. You should pay little attention to the time required to operate on a block of data once it has been read into internal memory.

Reduce the number of block accesses

---

[1] Data enters or leaves a buffer at a rate that differs from the record-processing rate. (Hence, a buffer between two processes compensates for the difference in the rates at which they operate on data.)

Interestingly, several programming languages, including C++, have commands to make it *appear* that you can access records one at a time. In general, however, the system actually performs input and output at the block level and perhaps hides this fact from the program. For example, if a programming language includes the statement

```
rec.readRecord(dataFile, i)
// Reads the ith record of file dataFile into rec.
```

the system probably accesses the entire block that contains the ith record. Our model of input and output therefore approximates reality reasonably well.

In most external data-management applications, the time required for block accesses typically dominates all other factors. The rest of the chapter discusses how to sort and search externally stored data. The goal will be to reduce the number of required block accesses.

File access time is the dominant factor when considering an algorithm's efficiency

14.2 Sorting Data in an External File

This section considers the following problem of sorting data that resides in an external file:

> An external file contains 1,600 employee records. You want to sort these records by Social Security number. Each block contains 100 records, and thus the file contains 16 blocks B_1, B_2, and so on to B_{16}. Assume that the program can access only enough internal memory to manipulate about 300 records (three blocks' worth) at one time.

A sorting problem

Sorting the file might not sound like a difficult task, because you have already seen several sorting algorithms earlier in this book. There is, however, a fundamental difference here in that the file is far too large to fit into internal memory all at once. This restriction presents something of a problem because the sorting algorithms presented earlier assume that all the data to be sorted is available at one time in internal memory (for example, that it is all in an array). Fortunately, however, we can remove this assumption for a modified version of mergesort.

The basis of the mergesort algorithm is that you can easily merge two sorted segments—such as arrays—of data records into a third sorted segment that is the combination of the two. For example, if S_1 and S_2 are sorted segments of records, the first step of the merge is to compare the first record of each segment and select the record with the smaller search key. If the record from S_1 is selected, the next step is to compare the second record of S_1 to the first record of S_2. This process is continued until all of the records have been considered. The key observation is that at any step, the merge never needs to look beyond the *leading edge* of either segment.

This observation makes a mergesort appropriate for the problem of sorting external files, if you modify the algorithm appropriately. Suppose that the 1,600 records to be sorted are in the file F and that you are not permitted to alter this file. You have two work files, F_1 and F_2. One of the work files will contain the sorted records when the algorithm terminates. The algorithm has two phases: Phase 1 sorts each block of records, and Phase 2 performs a series of merges.

External mergesort

Phase 1. Read a block from F into internal memory, sort its records by using an internal sort, and write the sorted block out to F_1 before you read the next block from F. After you process all 16 blocks of F, F_1 contains 16 **sorted runs** R_1, R_2, and so on to R_{16}; that is, F_1 contains 16 blocks of records, with the records within each block sorted among themselves, as Figure 14-3a illustrates.

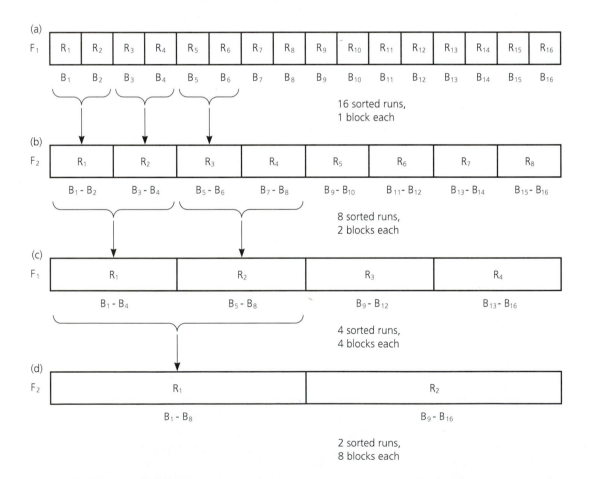

(a) Sixteen sorted runs, one block each, in file F1; (b) Eight sorted runs, two blocks each, in file F2; (c) Four sorted runs, four blocks each, in file F1; (d) Two sorted runs, eight blocks each, in file F2

Phase 2. Phase 2 is a sequence of merge steps. Each merge step merges pairs of sorted runs to form larger sorted runs. Each merge step doubles the number of blocks in each sorted run and thus halves the total number of sorted runs. For example, as Figure 14-3b shows, the first merge step merges eight pairs of sorted runs from F_1 (R_1 with R_2, R_3 with R_4, . . . , R_{15} with R_{16}) to form eight sorted runs, each two blocks long, which are written to F_2. The next merge step merges four pairs of sorted runs from F_2 (R_1 with R_2, R_3 with R_4, . . . , R_7 with R_8) to form four sorted runs, each four blocks long, which are written back to F_1, as Figure 14-3c illustrates. The next step merges the two pairs of sorted runs from F_1 to form two sorted runs, which are written to F_2. (See Figure 14-3d.) The final step merges the two sorted runs into one, which is written to F_1. At this point, F_1 will contain all of the records of the original file in sorted order.

Given this overall strategy, how can you merge the sorted runs at each step of Phase 2? The statement of the problem provides only sufficient internal memory to manipulate at most 300 records at once. However, in the later steps of Phase 2, runs contain more than 300 records each, so you must merge the runs a piece at a time. To accomplish this merge, you must divide the program's internal memory into three arrays, *in1, in2,* and *out,* each capable of holding 100 records (the block size). You read block-sized pieces of the runs into the two *in* arrays and merge them into the *out* array. Whenever an *in* array is exhausted—that is, when all of its elements have been copied to *out*— you read the next piece of the run into the *in* array; whenever the *out* array becomes full, you write this completed piece of the new sorted run to one of the files.

Consider how you can perform the first merge step. You start this step with the pair of runs R_1 and R_2, which are in the first and second blocks, respectively, of the file F_1. (See Figure 14-3a.) Because at this first merge step each run contains only one block, an entire run can fit into one of the *in* arrays. You can thus read R_1 and R_2 into the arrays *in1* and *in2,* and then merge *in1* and *in2* into *out*. However, although the result of merging *in1* and *in2* is a sorted run two blocks long (200 records), *out* can hold only one block (100 records). Thus, when in the course of the merge *out* becomes full, you write its contents to the first block of F_2, as Figure 14-4a illustrates. The merging of *in1* and *in2* into *out* then resumes. The array *out* will become full for a second time only after all of the records in *in1* and *in2* are exhausted. At that time, write the contents of *out* to the second block of F_2. You merge the remaining seven pairs from F in the same manner and append the resulting runs to F_2.

This first merge step is conceptually a bit easier than the others because the initial runs are only one block in size, and thus each can fit entirely into one of the *in* arrays. What do you do in the later steps

Merging sorted runs in Phase 2

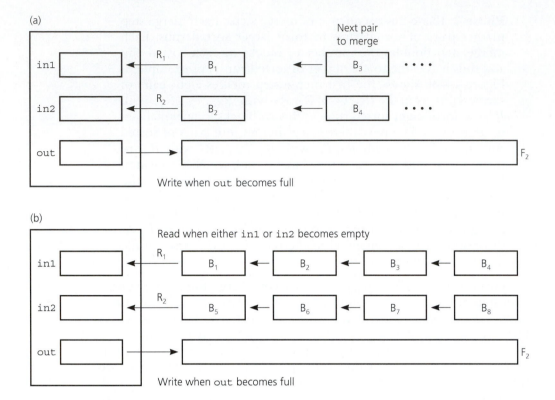

FIGURE 14-4   (a) Merging single blocks; (b) merging long runs

when the runs to be merged are larger than a single block? Consider, for example, the merge step in which you must merge runs of four blocks each to form runs of eight blocks each. (See Figure 14-3c.) The first pair of these runs to be merged is in blocks 1 through 4 and 5 through 8 of F_1.

The algorithm will read the first block of R_1—which is the first block B_1 of the file—into *in1*, and it will read the first block of R_2—which is B_5—into *in2*, as Figure 14-4b illustrates. Then, as it did earlier, the algorithm merges *in1* and *in2* into *out*. The complication here is that as soon as you finish moving all of the records from either *in1* or *in2*, you must read the next block from the corresponding run. For example, if you finish *in2* first, you must read the next block of R_2—which is B_6—into *in2* before the merge can continue. The algorithm thus must detect when the *in* arrays become exhausted as well as when the *out* array becomes full.

A high-level description of the algorithm for merging arbitrary-sized sorted runs R_i and R_j from F_1 into F_2 is as follows:

```
Read the first block of Rᵢ into in1
Read the first block of Rⱼ into in2
```

Pseudocode to merge sorted runs

```
while (either in1 or in2 is not exhausted)
{  Select the smaller "leading" record of in1 and in2
      and place it into the next position of out (if
      one of the arrays is exhausted, select the
      leading record from the other)

   if (out is full)
      Write its contents to the next block of F₂

   if (in1 is exhausted and blocks remain in Rᵢ)
      Read the next block into in1

   if (in2 is exhausted and blocks remain in Rⱼ)
      Read the next block into in2
}  // end while
```

A pseudocode version of the external sorting algorithm follows. Notice that it uses *readBlock* and *writeBlock,* as introduced in the previous section, and assumes a function *copyFile* that copies a file. To avoid further complications, the solution assumes that the number of blocks in the file is a power of 2. This assumption allows the algorithm always to pair off the sorted runs at each step of the merge phase, avoiding special end–of–file testing that would obscure the algorithm. Also note that the algorithm uses two temporary files and copies the final sorted temporary file to the designated output file.

```
externalMergesort(in unsortedFileName:String,
                  in sortedFileName:String)
// Sorts a file by using an external mergesort.
// Precondition: unsortedFileName is the name of an external
// file to be sorted. sortedFileName is the name that the
// function will give to the resulting sorted file.
// Postcondition: The new file named sortedFileName is
// sorted. The original file is unchanged. Both files are
// closed.
// Calls: blockSort, mergeFile, and copyFile.
// Simplifying assumption: The number of blocks in the
// unsorted file is an exact power of 2.


   Associate unsortedFileName with the file variable inFile
      and sortedFileName with the file variable outFile
```

A pseudocode mergesort function

```
// Phase 1: sort file block by block and count the blocks
blockSort(inFile, tempFile1, numberOfBlocks)


// Phase 2: merge runs of size 1, 2, 4, 8,...,
// numberOfBlocks/2 (uses two temporary files and a
// toggle that keeps files for each merge step)

toggle = 1
for (size = 1 through numberOfBlocks/2 with
                                    increments of size)
{   if (toggle == 1)
        mergeFile(tempFile1, tempFile2, size, numberOfBlocks)
    else
        mergeFile(tempFile2, tempFile1, size, numberOfBlocks)

    toggle = -toggle
}   // end for

// copy the current temporary file to outFile
if (toggle == 1)
    copyFile(tempFile1, outFile)
else
    copyFile(tempFile2, outFile)
```

Notice that *externalMergesort* calls *blockSort* and *mergeFile*, which calls *mergeRuns*. The pseudocode for these functions follows.

```
blockSort(in inFile:File, in outFile:File,
          in numberOfBlocks:integer)
// Sorts each block of records in a file.
// Precondition: The file variable inFile is associated
// with the file to be sorted.
// Postcondition: The file associated with the file variable
// outFile contains the blocks of inFile. Each block is
// sorted; numberOfBlocks is the number of blocks processed.
// Both files are closed.
// Calls: readBlock and writeBlock to perform direct access
// input and output, and sortBuffer to sort an array.

    Prepare inFile for input
    Prepare outFile for output

    numberOfBlocks = 0
    while (more blocks in inFile remain to be read)
    {   ++numberOfBlocks
        buffer.readBlock(inFile, numberOfBlocks)
```

```
        sortArray(buffer)  // sort with some internal sort

        buffer.writeBlock(outFile, numberOfBlocks)
   }  // end while

   Close inFile and outFile
// end blockSort


mergeFile(in inFile:File, in outFile:File,
          in runSize:integer, in numberOfBlocks:integer)
// Merges blocks from one file to another.
// Precondition: inFile is an external file that contains
// numberOfBlocks sorted blocks organized into runs of
// runSize blocks each.
// Postcondition: outFile contains the merged runs of
// inFile. Both files are closed.
// Calls: mergeRuns.

   Prepare inFile for input
   Prepare outFile for output

   for (next = 1 through numberOfBlocks with increments
                                      of 2 * runSize)
   {  // Invariant: runs in outFile are ordered
      mergeRuns(inFile, outFile, next, runSize)
   }  // end for
   Close inFile and outFile
// end mergeFile


mergeRuns(in fromFile:File, in toFile:File,
          in start:integer, in size:integer)
// Merges two consecutive sorted runs in a file.
// Precondition: fromFile is an external file of sorted runs
// open for input. toFile is an external file of sorted runs
// open for output. start is the block number of the first
// run on fromFile to be merged; this run contains size
// blocks.
//    Run 1: block start to block start + size - 1
//    Run 2: block start + size to start + (2 * size) - 1
// Postcondition: The merged runs from fromFile are appended
// to toFile. The files remain open.

   // initialize the input buffers for runs 1 and 2
   in1.readBlock(fromFile, first block of Run 1)
   in2.readBlock(fromFile, first block of Run 2)
```

```
// Merge until one of the runs is finished. Whenever an
// input buffer is exhausted, the next block is read.
// Whenever the output buffer is full, it is written.
while (neither run is finished) {
   // Invariant: out and each block in toFile are ordered
   Select the smaller "leading edge" of in1 and in2, and
      place it in the next position of out

   if (out is full)
      out.writeBlock(toFile, next block of toFile)

   if (in1 is exhausted and blocks remain in Run 1)
      in1.readBlock(fromFile, next block of Run 1)

   if (in2 is exhausted and blocks remain in Run 2)
      in2.readBlock(fromFile, next block of Run 2)
}  // end while

// Assertion: exactly one of the runs is complete

// append the remainder of the unfinished input
// buffer to the output buffer and write it

while (in1 is not exhausted)
   // Invariant: out is ordered
   Place next item of in1 into the next position of out

while (in2 is not exhausted)
   // Invariant: out is ordered
   Place next item of in2 into the next position of out

out.writeBlock(toFile, next block of toFile)

// finish off the remaining complete blocks

while (blocks remain in Run 1)
{  // Invariant: each block in toFile is ordered
   in1.readBlock(fromFile, next block of Run 1)
   in1.writeBlock(toFile, next block of toFile)
}  // end while

while (blocks remain in Run 2)
{  // Invariant: Each block in toFile is ordered
   in2.readBlock(fromFile, next block of Run 2)
   in2.writeBlock(toFile, next block of toFile)
}  // end while
// end mergeRuns
```

14.3 External Tables

This section discusses techniques for organizing records in external storage so that you can efficiently perform ADT table operations such as retrieval, insertion, deletion, and traversal. Although this discussion will only scratch the surface of this topic, you do have a head start: Two of the most important external table implementations are variations of the 2-3 tree and hashing, which you studied in Chapter 12.

Suppose you have a direct access file of records that are to be table items. The file is partitioned into blocks, as described earlier in this chapter. One of the simplest table implementations stores the records in order by their search key, perhaps sorting the file by using the external mergesort algorithm developed in the previous section. Once it is sorted, you can easily traverse the file in sorted order by using the following algorithm:

A simple external table implementation: records stored in search-key order

```
traverseTable(in dataFile:File, in numberOfBlocks:integer,
              in recordsPerBlock:integer, in visit:function)
// Traverses the sorted file dataFile in sorted order,
// calling function visit() once for each item.

   // read each block of file dataFile into an internal
   // buffer buf
   for (blockNumber = 1 through numberOfBlocks)
   {  buf.readBlock(dataFile, blockNumber)
      // visit each record in the block
      for (recordNumber = 1 through recordsPerBlock)
         Visit record buf.getRecord(recordNumber-1)
   }  // end for
```

Sorted-order traversal

To perform the *tableRetrieve* operation on the sorted file, you can use a binary search algorithm as follows:

```
tableRetrieve(in dataFile:File, in recordsPerBlock:integer,
              in first:integer, in last:integer,
              in searchKey:KeyItemType,
              out tableItem:TableItemType):boolean
// Searches blocks first through last of file dataFile,
// copies into tableItem the record whose search key equals
// searchKey, and returns true.  The function returns false
// if no such item exists.

   if (first > last or
       nothing is left to read from dataFile)
      return false

   else
```

```
{  // read the middle block of file dataFile into
   // array buf
   mid = (first + last)/2
   buf.readBlock(dataFile, mid)

   if ( (searchKey >= (buf.getRecord(0)).getKey()) &&
        (searchKey <=
           (buf.getRecord(recordsPerBlock-1)).getKey()) )
   {  // desired block is found
      Search buffer buf for record buf.getRecord(j)
         whose search key equals searchKey
      if (record is found)
      {  tableItem = buf.getRecord(j)
         return true
      }
      else
         return false
   }  // end if

   // else search appropriate half of the file
   else if (searchKey < (buf.getRecord(0)).getKey())
      return tableRetrieve(dataFile, recordsPerBlock,
                           first, mid-1, searchKey, tableItem)

   else
      return tableRetrieve(dataFile, recordsPerBlock,
                           mid+1, last, searchKey, tableItem)
}  // end if
```

The *tableRetrieve* algorithm recursively splits the file in half and reads the middle block into the internal object *buf*. Splitting a file segment requires that you know the numbers of the first and last blocks of the segment. You would pass these values as arguments, along with the file variable, to *tableRetrieve*.

Once you have read the middle block of the file segment into *buf*, you determine whether a record whose search key equals *searchKey* could be in this block. You can make this determination by comparing *searchKey* to the smallest search key in *buf*—which is in *buf.getRecord(0)* and to the largest search key in *buf*—which is in *buf.getRecord(recordsPerBlock-1)*. If *searchKey* does not lie between the values of the smallest and largest search keys in *buf*, you must recursively search one of the halves of the file (which half to search depends on whether *searchKey* is less than or greater than the search keys in the block you just examined). If, on the other hand, *search-Key* does lie between the values of the smallest and largest search keys of the block in *buf*, you must search *buf* for the record. Because the records within the block *buf* are sorted, you could use a binary search on the records within this block. However, the number of records in the block *buf* is typically small, and thus the time required to scan the block sequentially is insignificant compared to the time required to read the block from the file. It is therefore common simply to scan the block sequentially.

This external implementation of the ADT table is not very different from the internal sorted array-based implementation. As such, it has many of the same advantages and disadvantages. Its main advantage is that because the records are sorted sequentially, you can use a binary search to locate the block that contains a given search key. The main disadvantage of the implementation is that, as is the case with an array-based implementation, the *tableInsert* and *tableDelete* operations must shift table items. Shifting records in an external file is, in general, far more costly than shifting array items. A file may contain an enormous number of large records, which are organized as several thousand blocks. As a consequence, the shifting could require a prohibitively large number of block accesses.

tableInsert and *tableDelete* for an external implementation of the ADT table can require many costly file accesses due to shifting records

Consider, for example, Figure 14-5. If you insert a new record into block *k,* you must shift the records not only in block *k,* but also in every block after it. As a result, you must shift some records across block boundaries. Thus, for each of these blocks, you must read the block into internal memory, shift its records by using an assignment such as

```
buf.setRecord(i+1, buf.getRecord(i))
```

and write the block to the file so that the file reflects the change. This large number of block accesses makes the external sorted array-based implementation practical only for tables where insertions and deletions are rare. (See Exercise 1 at the end of this chapter.)

Indexing an External File

Two of the best external table implementations are variations of the internal hashing and search-tree schemes. The biggest difference between the internal and external versions of these implementations is that in the external versions, it is often advantageous to organize an **index** to the data file rather than to organize the data file itself. An

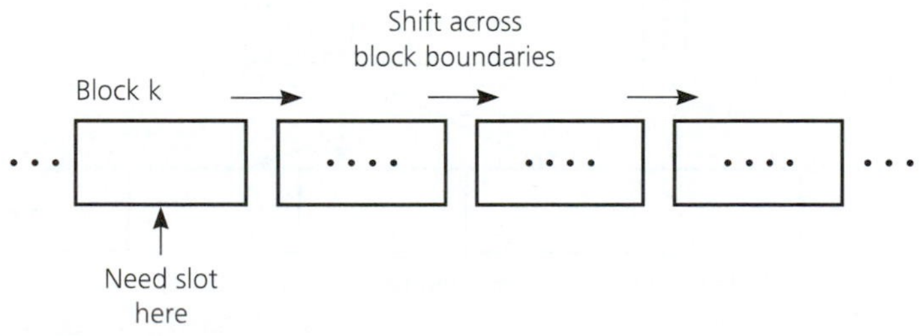

FIGURE 14-5 Shifting across block boundaries

index to a data file is conceptually similar to other indexes with which you are familiar. For example, consider a library catalog. Rather than looking all over the library for a particular title, you can simply search the catalog. The catalog is typically organized alphabetically by title (or by author), so it is a simple matter to locate the appropriate entry. The entry for each book contains an indication (for example, a Library of Congress number) of where on the shelves you can find the book.

Using a catalog to index the books in a library has at least three benefits:

Advantages of a library catalog

- Because each catalog entry is much smaller than the book it represents, the entire catalog for a large library can fit into a small space. A patron can thus locate a particular book quickly.

- The library can organize the books on the shelves in any way, without regard to how easy it will be for a patron to scan the shelves for a particular book. To locate a particular book, the patron searches the catalog for the appropriate entry.

- The library can have different types of catalogs to facilitate different types of searches. For example, it can have one catalog organized by title and another organized by author.

Now consider how you can use an index to a data file to much the same advantage as the library catalog. As Figure 14-6 illustrates, you can leave the data file in a disorganized state and maintain an organized index to it. When you need to locate a particular record in the data file, you search the index for the corresponding entry, which will tell you where to find the desired record in the data file.

An index to a data file

An index to the data file is simply a file, called the **index file**, that contains an **index record** for each record in the data file, just as a library catalog contains an entry for each book in the library. An index record has two parts: a key, which contains the same value as the search key of its corresponding record in the data file, and a pointer, which shows the number of the block in the data file that contains this data record. (Despite its name, an index record's pointer contains an integer, not a C++ pointer.) You thus can determine which block of the data

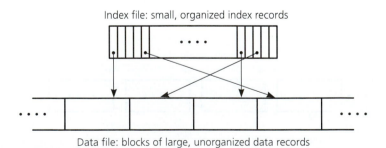

Index file: small, organized index records

Data file: blocks of large, unorganized data records

FIGURE 14-6   A data file with an index

file contains the record whose search key equals *searchKey* by search-ing the index file for the index record whose key equals *searchKey*.

Maintaining an index to a data file has benefits analogous to those provided by the library's catalog:

- In general, an index record will be much smaller than a data record. While the data record may contain many components, an index record contains only two: a key, which is also part of the data record, and a single integer pointer, which is the block number. Thus, just as a library catalog occupies only a small fraction of the space occupied by the books it indexes, an index file is only a fraction of the size of the data file. As you will see, the small size of the index file often allows you to manipulate it with fewer block accesses than you would need to manipulate the data file.

- Because you do not need to maintain the data file in any partic-ular order, you can insert new records in any convenient loca-tion, such as at the end of the file. As you will see, this flexibility eliminates the need to shift the data records during insertions and deletions.

- You can maintain several indexes simultaneously. Just as a library can have one catalog organized by title and another organized by author, you can have one index file that indexes the data file by one search key (for example, an index file that consists of <*name*, *pointer*> records), and a second index file that indexes the data file by another search key (for example, an index file that consists of <*socSec*, *pointer*> records). Such **multiple indexing** is discussed briefly at the end of this chapter.

Advantages of an index file

Although you do not organize the data file, you must organize the index file so that you can search and update it rapidly. Before consider-ing how to organize an index file by using either hashing or search-tree schemes, first consider a less complex organization that illustrates the concepts of indexing. In particular, let the index file simply store the index records sequentially, sorted by their keys, as shown in Figure 14-7.

Organize the index file but not the data file

To perform the *tableRetrieve* operation, for example, you can use a binary search on the index file as follows:

```
tableRetrieve(in tIndex:File, in tData:File,
              in searchKey:KeyItemType,
              out tableItem:TableItemType):boolean
// Retrieves into tableItem the record whose search key
// equals searchKey, where tIndex is the index file and
// tData is the data file. The operation returns true if
// the record exists, false otherwise.

   if (no blocks are left in tIndex to read)
      return false
```

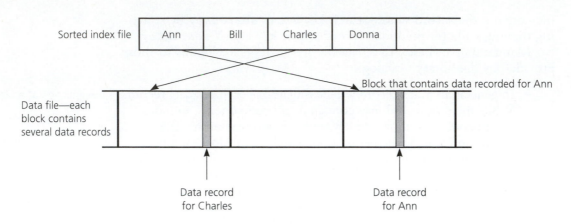

Sorted index file

| Ann | Bill | Charles | Donna | |

Block that contains data recorded for Ann

Data file—each
block contains
several data records

Data record
for Charles

Data record
for Ann

FIGURE 14-7   A data file with a sorted index file

```
else
{ // read the middle block of index file into object buf
   mid = number of middle block of index file tIndex
   buf.readBlock(tIndex, mid)

   if ((searchKey >= (buf.getRecord(0)).getKey()) &&
      (searchKey <=
         (buf.getRecord(indexrecordsPerBlock-1)).getKey()))
   { // desired block of index file found
      Search buf for index file record
        buf.getRecord(j) whose key value equals searchKey

      if (index record buf.getRecord(j) is found)
      { blockNum = number of the data-file block to
               which buf.getRecord(j) points
         data.readBlock(tData, blockNum)
         Find data record data.getRecord(k) whose search
           key equals searchKey
         tableItem = data.getRecord(k)
         return true
      }

      else
         return false
   }


   else if (tIndex is one block in size)
      return false  // no more blocks in file
```

```
        // else search appropriate half of index file
        else if (searchKey < (buf.getRecord(0)).getKey())
           return tableRetrieve(first half of tIndex, tData,
                                searchKey, tableItem)


        else
           return tableRetrieve(second half of tIndex, tData,
                                searchKey, tableItem)
    }  // end if
```

Because the index records are far smaller than the data records, the index file contains far fewer blocks than the data file. For example, if the index records are one-tenth the size of the data records and the data file contains 1,000 blocks, the index file will require only about 100 blocks. As a result, the use of an index cuts the number of block accesses in $tableRetrieve$ down from about $\log_2 1000 \approx 10$ to about $1 + \log_2 100 \approx 8$. (The one additional block access is into the data file once you have located the appropriate index record.)

An index file reduces the number of required block accesses for table operations

The reduction in block accesses is far more dramatic for the $tableInsert$ and $tableDelete$ operations. In the implementation of an external table discussed earlier in this section, if you insert a record into or delete a record from the first block of data, for example, you have to shift records in every block, requiring that you access all 1,000 blocks of the data file. (See Figure 14-5.)

However, when you perform an insertion or a deletion by using the index scheme, you have to shift only index records. When you use an index file, you do not keep the data file in any particular order, so you can insert a new data record into any convenient location in the data file. This flexibility means that you can simply insert a new data record at the end of the file or at a position left vacant by a previous deletion (as you will see). As a result, you never need to shift records in the data file. However, you do need to shift records in the index file to create an opening for a corresponding index entry in its proper sorted position. Because the index file contains many fewer blocks than the data file (100 versus 1,000 in the previous example), the maximum number of block accesses required is greatly reduced. A secondary benefit of shifting index records rather than data records is a reduction in the time requirement for a single shift. Because the index records themselves are smaller, the time required for the statement $buf.setRecord(i + 1, buf.getRecord(i))$ is decreased.

Shift index records instead of data records

Deletions under the index scheme reap similar benefits. Once you have searched the index file and located the data record to be deleted, you can simply leave its location vacant in the data file, and thus you need not shift any data records. You can keep track of the vacant locations in the data file (see Exercise 2), so that you can insert new data records into the vacancies, as was mentioned earlier. The only shifting required is in the index file to fill the gap created when you remove the index record that corresponds to the deleted data record.

Even though this scheme is an improvement over maintaining a sorted data file, in many applications it is far from satisfactory. The 100 block accesses that could be required to insert or delete an index record often would be prohibitive. Far better implementations are possible when you use either hashing or search trees to organize the index file.

An unsorted data file with a sorted index is more efficient than a sorted data file, but other schemes are even better

External Hashing

The external hashing scheme is quite similar to the internal scheme described in Chapter 12. In the internal hashing scheme, each entry of the array *table* contains a pointer to the beginning of the list of items that hash into that location. In the external hashing scheme, each entry of *table* still contains a pointer to the beginning of a list, but here each list consists of *blocks of index records*. In other words, you hash an index file rather than the data file, as Figure 14-8 illustrates. (In many applications the array *table* is itself so large that you must keep it in external storage—for example, in the first *K* blocks of the index file. To avoid this extra detail, you can assume here that the array *table* is an internal array.)

You hash the index file instead of the data file

Associated with each entry *table[i]* is a linked list of blocks of the index file, as you can see in Figure 14-8. Each block of *table[i]*'s

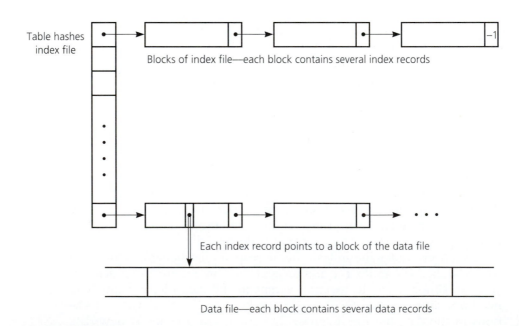

Table hashes index file

Blocks of index file—each block contains several index records

Each index record points to a block of the data file

Data file—each block contains several data records

FIGURE 14-8   A hashed index file

linked list contains index records whose keys (and thus whose corresponding data records' search keys) hash into location *i*. To form the linked lists, you must reserve space in each block for a block pointer—the integer block number of the next block in the chain—as Figure 14-9 illustrates. That is, in this linked list the pointers are integers, not C++ pointers. A pointer value of −1 is used as a *NULL* pointer.

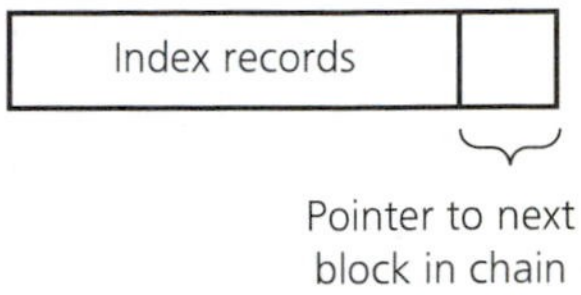

Pointer to next block in chain

FIGURE 14-9 A single block with a pointer

Retrieval under external hashing of an index file. The *tableRetrieve* operation appears in pseudocode as follows:

```
tableRetrieve(in tIndex:File, in tData:File,
              in searchKey:KeyItemType,
              out tableItem:TableItemType):boolean
// Retrieves into tableItem the item whose search key
// equals searchKey, where tIndex is the index file, which
// is hashed, and tData is the data file. The function
// returns true if the record exists, false otherwise.

   // apply the hash function to the search key
   i = h(searchKey)

   // find the first block in the chain of index blocks —
   // these blocks contain index records that hash into
   // location i
   p = table[i]

   // if p == -1, no values have hashed into location i
   if (p != -1)
      buf.readBlock(tIndex, p)

   // search for the block with the desired index record
   while (p != -1 and buf does not contain an index record
                          whose key value equals searchKey)
   {  p = number of next block in chain
      // if p == -1, you are at the last block in the chain
      if (p != -1)
         buf.readBlock(tIndex, p)
   }  // end while

   // retrieve the data item if present
   if (p != -1)
   {  // buf.getRecord(j) is the index record whose
      // key value equals searchKey
      blockNum = number of the data-file block to
                 which buf.getRecord(j) points
      data.readBlock(tData, blockNum)
      Find data record data.getRecord(k) whose search key
```

```
            equals searchKey
        tableItem = data.getRecord(k)
        return true
    }
    else
        return false
```

Insertion under external hashing of an index file.   The external hashing versions of `tableInsert` and `tableDelete` are also similar to the internal hashing versions. The major difference is that, in the external environment, you must insert or delete both a data record and the corresponding index record.

To insert a new data record whose search key is `searchKey`, you take the following steps:

1. **Insert the data record into the data file.** Because the data file is not ordered, the new record can go anywhere you want. If a previous deletion has left a free slot in the middle of the data file, you can insert it there. (See Exercise 2.)

    If no slots are free, you insert the new data record at the end of the last block, or, if necessary, you append a new block to the end of the data file and store the record there. In either case, let p denote the number of the block that contains this new data record.

2. **Insert a corresponding index record into the index file.** You need to insert into the index file an index record that has key value `searchKey` and pointer value p. (Recall that p is the number of the block in the data file into which you inserted the new data record.) Because the index file is hashed, you first apply the hash function to `searchKey`, letting

    ```
    i = h(searchKey)
    ```

    You then insert the index record $<searchKey, p>$ into the chain of blocks that the entry `table[i]` points to. You can insert this record into any block in the chain that contains a free slot, or, if necessary, you can allocate a new block and link it to the beginning of the chain.

Deletion under external hashing of an index file.   To delete the data record whose search key is `searchKey`, you take the following steps:

1. **Search the index file for the corresponding index record.** You apply the hash function to `searchKey`, letting

    ```
    i = h(searchKey)
    ```

You then search the chain of index blocks pointed to by the entry *table[i]* for an index record whose key value equals *searchKey*. If you do not find such a record, you can conclude that the data file does not contain a record whose search key equals *searchKey*. However, if you find an index record <*searchKey, p*>, you delete it from the index file after noting the block number *p*, which indicates where in the data file you can find the data record to be deleted.

2. **Delete the data record from the data file.** You know that the data record is in block *p* of the data file. You simply access this block, search the block for the record, delete the record, and write the block back to the file.

Observe that for each of the operations *tableRetrieve, tableInsert,* and *tableDelete* the number of block accesses is very low. You never have to access more than one block of the data file, and at worst you have to access all of the blocks along a single hash chain of the index file. You can take measures to keep the length of each of the chains quite short (for example, one or two blocks long), just as you can with internal hashing. You should make the size of the array *table* large enough so that the average length of a chain is near one block, and the hash function should scatter the keys evenly. If necessary, you can even structure each chain as an external search tree—a **B-tree**— by using the techniques described in the next section.

The hashing implementation is the one to choose when you need to perform the operations *tableRetrieve, tableInsert,* and *tableDelete* on a large external table. As is the case with internal hashing, however, this implementation is not practical for certain other operations, such as sorted traversal, retrieval of the smallest or largest item, and range queries that require ordered data. When these types of operations are added to the basic table operations *tableRetrieve, tableInsert,* and *tableDelete,* you should use a search-tree implementation instead of hashing.

Choose external hashing for *tableRetrieve, tableInsert,* and *tableDelete* operations

B-Trees

Another way to search an external table is to organize it as a balanced search tree. Just as you can apply external hashing to the index file, you can organize the index file, not the data file, as an external search tree. The implementation developed here is a generalization of the 2-3 tree of Chapter 12.

You can organize the blocks of an external file into a tree structure by using block numbers for child pointers. In Figure 14-10a, for example, the blocks are organized into a 2-3 tree. Each block of the file is a node in the tree and contains three child pointers, each of which is the integer block number of the child. A child pointer value of −1 plays the

(a)

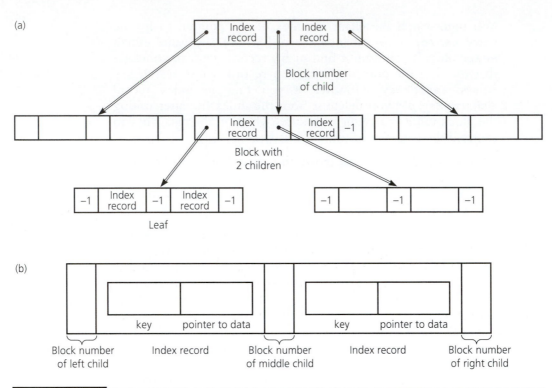

(b)

FIGURE 14-10   (a) Blocks organized into a 2-3 tree; (b) a single node of the 2-3 tree

role of a *NULL* pointer, and thus, for example, a leaf will contain three child pointers with the value −1.

Organize the index file as an external 2-3 tree

If you organized the index file into a 2-3 tree, each node (block of the index file) would contain either one or two index records, each of the form *<key, pointer>*, and three child pointers. The pointer portion of an index record has nothing to do with the tree structure of the index file; *pointer* indicates the block (in the data file) that contains the data record whose search key equals *key*. (See Figure 14-10b.) To help avoid confusion, the pointers in the tree structure of the index file will be referred to as child pointers.

You must organize the index records in the tree so that their keys obey the same search-tree ordering property as an internal 2-3 tree. This organization allows you to retrieve the data record with a given value in its search key as follows:

```
tableRetrieve(in tIndex:File, in tData:File,
              in rootNum:integer, in searchKey:KeyItemType,
              out tableItem:TableItemType):boolean
// Retrieves into tableItem the record whose search key
// equals searchKey. tIndex is the index file, which is
// organized as a 2-3 tree. rootNum is the block number (of
```

```
// the index file) that contains the root of the tree. tData
// is the data file. The function returns true if the
// record exists, false otherwise.

   if (no blocks are left in tIndex to read)
      return false

   else
   {  // read from index file into internal array buf the
      // block that contains the root of the 2-3 tree
      buf.readBlock(tIndex, rootNum)

      // search for the index record whose key value
      // equals searchKey
      if (searchKey is in the root)
      {  blockNum = number of the data-file block that
                        index record specifies
         data.readBlock(tData, blockNum)
         Find data record data.getRecord(k) whose
           search key equals searchKey
         tableItem = data.getRecord(k)
         return true
      }

      // else search the appropriate subtree
      else if (the root is a leaf)
         return false

      else
      {  child = block number of root of
                   appropriate subtree
         return tableRetrieve(tIndex, tData, child,
                                 searchKey, tableItem)
      }  // end if
   }  // end if
```

You also can perform insertions and deletions in a manner similar to the internal version, with the addition that you must insert records into and delete records from both the index file and the data file (as was the case in the external hashing scheme described earlier). In the course of insertions into and deletions from the index file, you must split and merge nodes of the tree just as you do for the internal version. You perform insertions into and deletions from the data file—which, recall, is not ordered in any way—exactly as described for the external hashing implementation. You thus can support the table operations fairly well by using an external version of the 2-3 tree.

However, you can generalize the 2-3 tree to a structure that is even more suitable for an external environment. Recall the discussion in

An external 2-3 tree is adequate, but an improvement is possible

Chapter 12 about search trees whose nodes can have many children. Adding more children per node reduces the height of the search tree but increases the number of comparisons at each node during the search for a value.

Keep an external search tree short

In an external environment, however, the advantage of keeping a search tree short far outweighs the disadvantage of performing extra work at each node. As you traverse the search tree in an external environment, you must perform a block access for each node visited. Because the time required to access a block of an external file is, in general, far greater than the time required to process the data in that block once it has been read in, the overriding concern is to reduce the number of block accesses required. This fact implies that you should attempt to reduce the height of the tree, even at the expense of requiring more comparisons at each node. In an external search tree, you should thus allow each node to have as many children as possible, with only the block size as a limiting factor.

How many children can a block of some fixed size accommodate? If a node is to have *m* children, clearly you must be able to fit *m* child pointers in the node. In addition to child pointers, however, the node must also contain index records.

Before you can answer the question of how many children a block can accommodate, you must first consider this related question: If a node *N* in a search tree has *m* children, how many key values—and thus how many index records—must it contain?

Binary search tree: the number of records and children per node

In a binary search tree, if the node *N* has two children, it must contain one key value, as Figure 14-11a indicates. You can think of the key

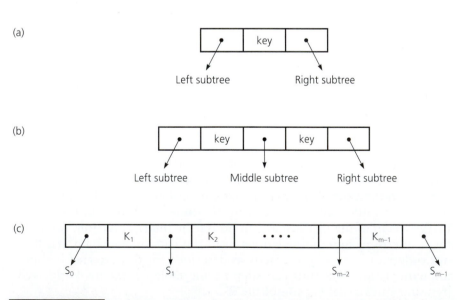

FIGURE 14-11   (a) A node with two children; (b) a node with three children; (c) a node with *m* children

value in node N as separating the key values in N's two subtrees—all of the key values in N's left subtree are less than N's key value, and all of the key values in N's right subtree are greater than N's key value. When you are searching the tree for a given key value, the key value in N tells you which branch to take.

Similarly, if a node N in a 2-3 tree has three children, it must contain two key values. (See Figure 14-11b.) These two values separate the key values in N's three subtrees—all of the key values in the left subtree are less than N's smaller key value, all of the key values in N's middle subtree lie between N's two key values, and all of the key values in N's right subtree are greater than N's larger key value. As is the case with a binary search tree, this requirement allows a search algorithm to know which branch to take at any given node.

In general, if a node N in a search tree is to have m children, it must contain $m - 1$ key values to separate the values in its subtrees correctly. (See Figure 14-11c.) Suppose that you denote the subtrees of N as S_0, S_1, and so on to S_{m-1} and denote the key values in N as K_1, K_2, and so on to K_{m-1} (with $K_1 < K_2 < \cdots < K_{m-1}$). The key values in N must separate the values in its subtrees as follows:

- All the values in subtree S_0 must be less than the key value K_1.

- For all i, $1 \leq i \leq m - 2$, all the values in subtree S_i must lie between the key values K_i and K_{i+1}.

- All the values in subtree S_{m-1} must be greater than the key value K_{m-1}.

If every node in the tree obeys this property, you can search the tree by using a generalized version of a search tree's retrieval algorithm. Thus, you can perform the *tableRetrieve* operation as follows:

```
tableRetrieve(in tIndex:File, in tData:File,
           in rootNum:integer, in searchKey:KeyItemType,
           out tableItem:TableItemType):boolean


// Retrieves into tableItem the record whose search key
// equals searchKey. tIndex is the index file, which is
// organized as a search tree. rootNum is the block number
// (of the index file) that contains the root of the tree.
// tData is the data file. The function returns true if
// the record exists, false otherwise.

   if (no blocks are left in tIndex to read)
     return false

   else
   { // read from index file into internal array buf the
     // block that contains the root of the tree
     buf.readBlock(tIndex, rootNum)
```

```
// search for the index record whose key value
// equals searchKey
if (searchKey is one of the Kᵢ in the root)
{   blockNum = number of the data-file block that
                index record specifies
    data.readBlock(tData, blockNum)
    Find data record data.getRecord(k) whose
      search key equals searchKey
    tableItem = data.getRecord(k)
    return true
}


// else search the appropriate subtree
else if (the root is a leaf)
    return false

else
{   Determine which subtree Sᵢ to search
    child = block number of the root of Sᵢ
    return tableRetrieve(tIndex, tData, child,
                         searchKey, tableItem)
}   // end if
}   // end if
```

Now return to the question of how many children the nodes of the search tree can have—that is, how big can m be? If you wish to organize the index file into a search tree, the items that you store in each node will be records of the form `<key, pointer>`. Thus, if each node in the tree (which, recall, is a block of the index file) is to have m children, it must be large enough to accommodate m child pointers and $m - 1$ records of the form `<key, pointer>`. You should choose m to be the largest integer such that m child pointers (which, recall, are integers) and $m - 1$ `<key, pointer>` records can fit into a single block of the file. Actually, the algorithms are somewhat simplified if you always choose an odd number for m. That is, you should choose m to be the largest odd integer such that m child pointers and $m - 1$ index records can fit into a single block.

Number of children per node

Ideally, then, you should structure the external search tree so that every internal node has m children, where m is chosen as just described, and all leaves are at the same level, as is the case with full trees and 2-3 trees. For example, Figure 14-12 shows a full tree whose internal nodes each have five children. Although this search tree has the minimum possible height, its balance is too difficult to maintain in the face of insertions and deletions. As a consequence, you must make a compromise. You can still insist that all the leaves of the search tree be at the same level—that is, that the tree be balanced—but you must allow

(a)

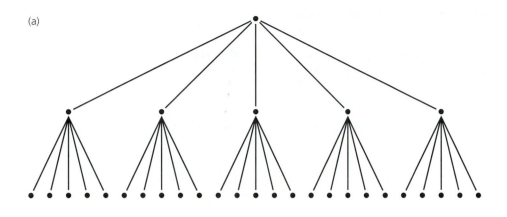

(b)

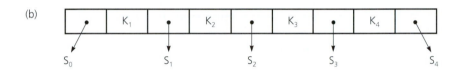

FIGURE 14-12 (a) A full tree whose internal nodes have five children; (b) the format of a single node

each internal node to have between m and $[m/2] + 1$ children. (The [] notation means *greatest integer in*. Thus, $[5/2]$ is 2, for example.)

This type of search tree is known as a B-tree of degree m and has the following characteristics:

- All leaves are at the same level.

B-tree of degree m

- Each node contains between $m - 1$ and $[m/2]$ records, and each internal node has one more child than it has records. An exception to this rule is that the root of the tree can contain as few as one record and can have as few as two children. This exception is necessitated by the insertion and deletion algorithms described next.

A 2-3 tree is a B-tree of degree 3. Furthermore, the manner in which the B-tree insertion and deletion algorithms maintain the structure of the tree is a direct generalization of the 2-3 tree's strategy of splitting and merging nodes.

A 2-3 tree is a B-tree of degree 3

The B-tree insertion and deletion algorithms are illustrated next by means of an example. Assume that the index file is organized into a B-tree of degree 5—that is, 5 is the maximum and 3 is the minimum number of children that an internal node (other than the root) in the tree can have. (Typically, a B-tree will be of a higher degree, but the diagrams would get out of hand!)

Insertion into a B-tree. To insert a data record with search key 55 into the tree shown in Figure 14-13, you take the following steps:

1. **Insert the data record into the data file.** First you find block p in the data file into which you can insert the new record. As was true with the external hashing implementation, block p is either any block with a vacant slot or a new block.

2. **Insert a corresponding index record into the index file.** You now must insert the index record $<55, p>$ into the index file, which is a B-tree of degree 5. The first step is to locate the leaf of the tree in which this index record belongs by determining where the search for 55 would terminate.

   Suppose that this is the leaf L shown in Figure 14-14a. Conceptually, you insert the new index record into L, causing it to contain five records (Figure 14-14b). Since a node can contain only four records, you must split L into L_1 and L_2. With an action analogous to the splitting of a node in a 2-3 tree, L_1 gets the two records with the smallest key values, L_2 gets the two records with the largest key values, and the record with the middle key value (56) is moved up to the parent P. (See Figure 14-14c.)

   In this example, P now has six children and five records, so it must be split into P_1 and P_2. The record with the middle key value (56) is moved up to P's parent, Q. Then P's children must be distributed appropriately, as happens with a 2-3 tree when an internal node is split. (See Figure 14-14d.)

   At this point the insertion is complete, since P's parent Q now contains only three records and has only four children. In general, though, an insertion might cause splitting to propagate all the way up to the root (Figure 14-14e). If the root must be split, the new root will contain only one record and have only two children—the definition of a B-tree allows for this eventuality.

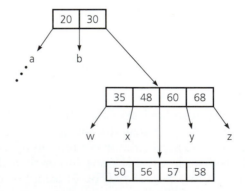

FIGURE 14-13   A B-tree of degree 5

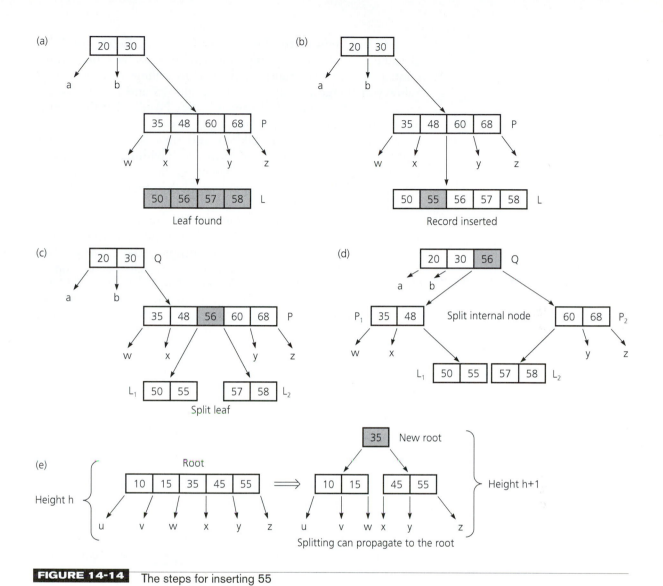

FIGURE 14-14 The steps for inserting 55

Deletion from a B-tree. To delete a data record with a given search key from a B-tree, you take the following steps:

1. **Locate the index record in the index file.** You use the search algorithm to locate the index record with the desired key value. If this record is not already in a leaf, you swap it with its inorder successor. (See Exercise 8.) Suppose that the leaf *L* shown in Figure 14-15a contains the index record with the desired key value, 73. After noting the value *p* of the pointer in this index record (you will need *p* in Step 2 to delete the data

record), you remove the index record from *L* (Figure 14–15b). Because *L* now contains only one value (recall that a node must contain at least two values), and since *L*'s siblings cannot spare a value, you merge *L* with one of the siblings and bring down a record from the parent *P* (Figure 14–15c). Notice that this step is analogous to the merge step for a 2-3 tree. However, *P* now has only one value and two children, and since its siblings cannot spare a record and child, you must merge *P* with its sibling P_1 and bring a record down from *P*'s parent, *Q*. Since *P* is an internal node, its children must be adopted by P_1. (See Figure 14–15d.)

After this merge, *P*'s parent *Q* is left with only two children and one record. In this case, however, *Q*'s sibling Q_1 can spare a record and a child, so you redistribute children and records among Q_1, *Q*, and the parent *S* to complete the deletion. (See Figure 14–15e.) If a deletion ever propagates all the way up to the root, leaving it with only one record and only two children, you are finished because the definition of a B-tree allows this situation. If a future deletion causes the root to have a single child

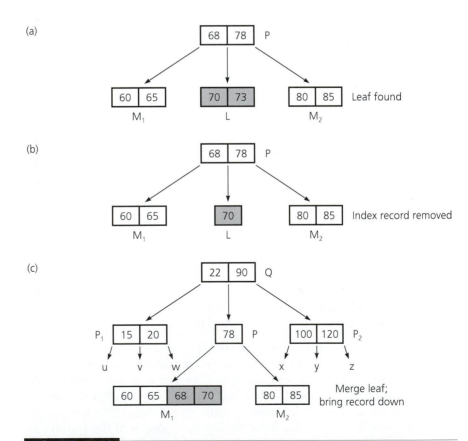

FIGURE 14-15 The steps for deleting 73

(continues)

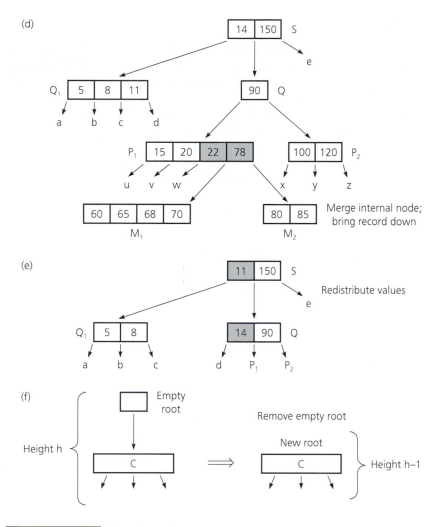

FIGURE 14-15

(*continued*)

and no records, you remove the root so that the tree's height decreases by 1, as Figure 14-15f illustrates. The deletion of the index record is complete, and you now must delete the data record.

2. **Delete the data record from the data file.** Prior to deleting the index record, you noted the value p of its pointer. Block p of the data file contains the data record to be deleted. Thus, you simply access block p, delete the data record, and write the block back to the file. The high-level pseudocode for the insertion and deletion algorithms parallels that of the 2-3 tree and is left as an exercise.

Traversals

Now consider the operation *traverseTable* in sorted order, which is one of the operations that hashing does not support at all efficiently. Often an application requires only that the traversal display the search keys of the records. If such is the case, the B-tree implementation can efficiently support the operation, because you do not have to access the data file. You can visit the search keys in sorted order by using an inorder traversal of the B-tree, as follows:

Accessing only the search key of each record, but not the data file

Inorder traversal of a B-tree index file

```
traverseTable(in blockNum:integer, in m:integer)
// Traverses in sorted order an index file that is organized
// as a B-tree of degree m. blockNum is the block number of
// the root of the B-tree in the index file.

    if (blockNum != -1)
    {  // read the root into internal array buf
       buf.readBlock(indexFile, blockNum)

       // traverse the children

       // traverse S₀
       Let p be the block number of the 0ᵗʰ child of buf
       traverseTable(p, m)

       for (i = 1 through m - 1)
       {  Display key Kᵢ of buf

          // traverse Sᵢ
          Let p be the block number of the iᵗʰ child of buf
          traverseTable(p, m)
       }  // end for
    }  // end if
```

This traversal accomplishes the task with the minimum possible number of block accesses because each block of the index file is read only once. This algorithm, however, assumes that enough internal memory is available for a recursive stack of h blocks, where h is the height of the tree. In many situations this assumption is reasonable—for example, a 255-degree B-tree that indexes a file of 16 million data records has a height of no more than 3. When internal memory cannot accommodate h blocks, you must use a different algorithm. (See Exercise 12.)

Accessing the entire data record

If the traversal must display the entire data record (and not just the search key), the B-tree implementation is less attractive. In this case, as you traverse the B-tree, you must access the appropriate block of the data file. The traversal becomes

Sorted-order traversal of a data file indexed with a B-tree

```
traverseTable(in blockNum:integer, in m:integer)
// Traverses in sorted order a data file that is indexed
```

```
// with a B-tree of degree m. blockNum is the block number
// of the root of the B-tree.

   if (blockNum != -1)
   {  // read the root into internal array buf
      buf.readBlock(indexFile, blockNum)

      // traverse S₀
      Let p be the block number of the 0ᵗʰ child of buf
      traverseTable(p, m)
      for (i = 1 through m - 1)
      {  Let p_i be the pointer in the iᵗʰ index
            record of buf
         data.readBlock(dataFile, p_i)
         Extract from data the data record whose search key
            equals Kᵢ
         Display the data record

         // traverse Sᵢ
         Let p be block number of the iᵗʰ child of buf
         traverseTable(p, m)
      }  // end for
   }  // end if
```

This traversal requires you to read a block of the data file before you display each data record; that is, the number of data-file block accesses is equal to the number of data records. In general, such a large number of block accesses would not be acceptable. If you must perform this type of traversal frequently, you probably would modify the B-tree scheme so that the data file itself was kept nearly sorted.

Generally, the previous traversal is unacceptable

Multiple Indexing

Before concluding the discussion of external implementations, let's consider the multiple indexing of a data file. Chapter 12 presented a problem in which you had to support multiple organizations for data stored in internal memory. Such a problem is also common for data stored externally. For example, suppose that a data file contains a collection of employee records on which you need to perform two types of retrievals:

```
retrieveN(in aName:NameType):ItemType
// Retrieves the item whose search key contains the
// name aName.

retrieveS(in ssn:SSNType):ItemType
// Retrieves the item whose search key contains the
// social security number ssn.
```

Multiple index files allow multiple data organizations

One solution to this problem is to maintain two independent index files to the data file. For example, you could have one index file that contains index records of the form <*name, pointer*> and a second index file that contains index records of the form <*socSec, pointer*>. These index files could both be hashed, could both be B-trees, or could be one of each, as Figure 14-16 indicates. The choice would depend on the operations you wanted to perform with each search key. (Similarly, if an application required extremely fast retrievals on *socSec* and also required operations such as traverse in sorted *socSec* order and range queries on *socSec*, it might be reasonable to have two *socSec* index files—one hashed, the other a B-tree.)

While you can perform each retrieval operation by using only one of the indexes (that is, use the *name* index for *retrieveN* and the *soc-Sec* index for *retrieveS*), insertion and deletion operations must update both indexes. For example, the delete-by-name operation *deleteN(Jones)* requires the following steps:

A deletion by name must update both indexes

1. Search the *name* index file for Jones and delete the index record.

2. Delete the appropriate data record from the data file, noting the *socSec* value *ssn* of this record.

3. Search the *socSec* index file for *ssn* and delete this index record.

In general, the price paid for multiple indexing is more storage space and an additional overhead for updating each index whenever you modify the data file.

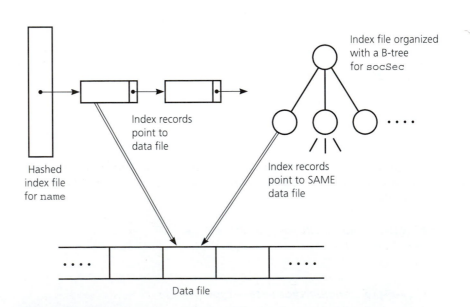

Index file organized with a B-tree for socSec

Index records point to data file

Hashed index file for name

Index records point to SAME data file

Data file

FIGURE 14-16   Multiple index files

This chapter has presented at a very high level the basic principles of managing data in external storage. The details of implementing the algorithms depend heavily on your specific computing system. Particular situations often mandate either variations of the methods described here or completely different approaches. In future courses and work experience, you will undoubtedly learn much more about these techniques.

Summary

1. An external file is partitioned into blocks. Each block typically contains many data records, and a block is generally the smallest unit of transfer between internal and external memory. That is, to access a record, you must access the block that contains it.

2. You can access the ith block of a direct access file without accessing the blocks that precede it. In this sense direct access files resemble arrays.

3. You can modify the mergesort algorithm, presented in Chapter 9, so that it can sort an external file of records without requiring all of the records to be in internal memory at one time.

4. An index to a data file is a file that contains an index record for each record in the data file. An index record contains both the search key of the corresponding data record and the number of the block in the data file that contains the data record.

5. You can organize the index file by using either hashing or a B-tree. These schemes allow you to perform the basic table operations by using only a few block accesses.

6. You can have several index files for the same data file. Such multiple indexing allows you to perform different types of operations efficiently, such as retrieve by name and retrieve by Social Security number.

Cautions

1. Before you can process (for example, inspect or update) a record, you must read it from an external file into internal memory. Once you modify a record, you must write it back to the file.

2. Block accesses are typically quite slow when compared to other computer operations. Therefore, you must carefully organize a file so that you can perform tasks by using only a few block accesses. Otherwise, response time can be very poor.

3. If a record is inserted into or deleted from a data file, you must make the corresponding change to the index file. If a data file has more than one index file, you must update each index file. Thus, multiple indexing has an overhead.

4. Although external hashing generally permits retrievals, insertions, and deletions to be performed more quickly than does a B-tree, it does not support such operations as sorted traversals or range queries. This deficiency is one motivation for multiple indexing.

Self-Test Exercises

1. Consider two files of 1,600 employee records each. The records in each file are organized into sixteen 100-record blocks. One file is sequential access and the other is direct access. Describe how you would append one record to the end of each file.

2. Trace `externalMergesort` with an external file of 16 blocks. Assume that the arrays `in1`, `in2`, and `out` are each one block long. List the calls to the various functions in the order in which they occur.

3. Trace the retrieval algorithm for an indexed external file when the search key is less than all keys in the index. Assume that the index file stores the index records sequentially, sorted by their search keys, and contains 20 blocks of 50 records each. Also, assume that the data file contains 100 blocks, and each block contains 10 employee records. List the calls to the various functions in the order in which they occur.

4. Repeat Self-Test Exercise 3, but this time assume that the search key equals the key in record 26 of block 12 of the index. Also assume that record 26 of the index points to block 98 of the data file.

Exercises

1. Assuming the existence of `readBlock` and `writeBlock` functions, write a pseudocode program for shifting data to make a gap at some specified location of a sorted file. Pay particular attention to the details of shifting the last item out of one block and into the first position of the next block. You can assume that the last record of the file is in record `lastRec` of block `lastBlock` and that `lastBlock` is not full. (Note that this assumption permits shifting without allocating a new block to the file.)

2. The problem of managing the blocks of an external data file indexed by either a B-tree or an external hashing scheme is similar to that of managing memory for internal structures. When an external structure such as a data file needs more memory (for example, to insert a new record), it gets a new block from a free list that the system manages. That is, if the file contains n blocks, the system can allocate to it an $(n + 1)^{\text{th}}$ block. When the file no longer needs a block, you can deallocate it and return it to the system.

The complication in the management of external storage is that a block allocated to a file may have available space interspersed with data. For example, after you have deleted a record from the middle of a data file, the block that contained that record will have space available for at least one record. Therefore, you must be able to keep track of blocks that have space available for one or more records as well as recognize when blocks are completely empty (so that you can return them to the system).

Assuming the existence of *allocateBlock* and *returnBlock* functions that get empty blocks from and return empty blocks to the system, write pseudocode implementations of the following external memory-management functions:

```
getSlot(in dataFile:File, out blockNum:integer,
        out recNum:integer)
// Determines the block number (blockNum) and record
// number (recNum) of an available slot in file
// dataFile. A new block is allocated to the file from
// the system if necessary.

freeSlot(in dataFile:File, in blockNum:integer,
         in recNum:integer)
// Makes record recNum in block blockNum of file
// dataFile available. The block is returned to the
// system if it becomes empty.
```

What data structure is appropriate to support these operations? You may assume that you can distinguish slots of a block that do not contain a record from those that do. You can make this distinction either by having a convention for *NULL* values within a record or by adding an empty/full flag.

3. Describe pseudocode algorithms for insertion into and deletion from a table implemented externally with a hashed index file.

4. Execute the following sequence of operations on an initially empty ADT table *t* that is implemented as a B-tree of degree 5. Note that insertion into an empty B-tree will create a single node that contains the inserted item.

```
t.tableInsert(10)
t.tableInsert(100)
t.tableInsert(30)
t.tableInsert(80)
t.tableInsert(50)
t.tableDelete(10)
t.tableInsert(60)
t.tableInsert(70)
t.tableInsert(40)
```

```
t.tableDelete(80)
t.tableInsert(90)
t.tableInsert(20)
t.tableDelete(30)
t.tableDelete(70)
```

5. Given a B-tree of degree 5 and a height of 3,

   a. What is the maximum number of nodes (including the root)?

   b. What is the maximum number of records that can be stored?

6. Given the B-tree of degree 7 in Figure 14-17, draw the B-tree that results after the insertion of *m, o, y, r, c, i, k, w,* and *h*.

7. Given the B-tree of degree 7 in Figure 14-18, draw the B-tree that results after the removal of *s, t, p, m, k,* and *e*.

8. Describe a pseudocode algorithm for finding an item's inorder successor in an external B-tree.

9. Describe pseudocode algorithms for insertion into and deletion from an ADT table implemented with an index file organized as a B-tree.

10. Write a *rangeQuery* function for a B-tree in pseudocode. (See Exercise 3 of Chapter 12.) Assume that only the key values are needed (as opposed to the entire data record).

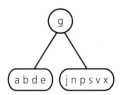

FIGURE 14-17   A B-tree for Exercise 6

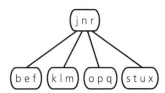

FIGURE 14-18   A B-tree for Exercise 7

11. Integrate calls to the appropriate memory-management functions (see Exercise 2) into the pseudocode for *tableInsert* and *table-Delete* under both the B-tree and hashing schemes. (See Exercises 3 and 9.)

12. The B-tree traversal algorithm presented in this chapter assumes that internal memory is large enough to accommodate the recursive stack that contains up to h blocks, where h is the height of the B-tree. If you are in an environment where this assumption is not true, modify the traversal algorithm so that the recursive stack contains block numbers rather than the actual blocks. How many block accesses does your algorithm have to perform?

13. a. Write pseudocode B-tree implementations of traversals and range queries that need to access entire data records, not simply the search keys. How many block accesses do your functions require?

b. To reduce the number of block accesses required by these operations, various modifications of the basic B-tree structure are frequently used. The central idea behind such structures is to keep the data file itself sorted. First, assume that you can keep the data file in sequential sorted order—that is, the records are sorted within each block and the records in B_{i-1} are less than the records in B_i for $i = 2, 3$, and so on to the number of blocks in the file. Rewrite your implementations of the traversal and range-query operations to take advantage of this fact. How many block accesses do these operations now require?

c. Because it is too inefficient to maintain a sequentially sorted data file in the face of frequent insertions and deletions, a compromise scheme is often employed. One such possible compromise is as follows. If a data record belongs in block B and B is full, a new block is allocated and linked to B, allowing the new record to be inserted into its proper sorted location. The difficulty is that you must now view each index record in the B-tree as indicating the first of possibly several blocks in a chain of blocks that might contain the corresponding data record. Rewrite the *tableInsert, tableDelete, tableRetrieve, traverseTable*, and *rangeQuery* operations in terms of this implementation. What is the effect on their efficiency?

14. Write an iterative (nonrecursive) version of *internalmergesort*, as given in Chapter 9, that is based on the external version that this chapter describes. That is, merge sorted runs that double in size at each pass of the array.

Programming Problems

1. a. Implement the *externalMergesort* algorithm in C++ by using the functions *seekg* and *seekp*. Assume that the file to be sorted is a file of type *int* and that each block contains one integer. Further assume that the file contains 2^n integers for some integer *n*.

   b. Now assume that each block contains many integers. Write C++ functions that simulate *readBlock* and *writeBlock*. Implement *externalMergesort* by using these functions.

   c. Extend your implementation of *externalMergesort* by removing the restriction that the file contains 2^n blocks.

2. Implement the ADT table by using a sorted index file, as described in the section "Indexing an External File."

3. Implement an ADT table that uses a sorted index file using the STL *map* container.

4. Implement a simple dictionary application, such as the one described in Exercise 4 of Chapter 11, using the external table of Programming Problem 3.

5. Implement the ADT table by using a hashed index file, as described in the section "External Hashing."

6. Implement the ADT table by using a B-tree, as described in the section "B-Trees."

7. Repeat Programming Problem 7 of Chapter 10, using an external table to implement *Book*.

APPENDIX A

Review of C++ Fundamentals

PREVIEW

This book assumes that you already know how to write programs in a modern programming language. If that language is C++, you can probably skip this appendix, returning to it for reference as necessary. If instead you know a language such as Java or C, this appendix will introduce you to C++.

It isn't possible to cover all of C++ in these pages. Instead this appendix focuses on the parts of the language used in this book. First we look at the basics of data types, variables, expressions, operators, and simple input/output. We continue with functions, decision constructs, looping constructs, arrays, strings, structures, exceptions, and files. C++ classes are covered in Chapters 3 and 8, and pointers are described in Chapter 4.

A.1 Language Basics

Let's begin with the elements of the language that allow you to perform simple computations. For example, the C++ program in Figure A-1 computes the volume of a sphere. Running this program produces the following output, where the user's response appears in boldface:

```
Enter the radius of the sphere: 19.1
The volume of a sphere of radius 19.1 is 29186.927734
```

A typical C++ program consists of several modules, some of which you write and some of which you use from standard libraries. C++ provides a **source-inclusion facility**, which allows the system to *include* the contents of a file automatically at a specified point in a program before the program is compiled. For example, our sample program uses a standard library to perform input and output operations. The first line of this program is an *include* directive that names a standard **header** *iostream*, which enables the program to use the input/output module. The second line informs the compiler to use the standard namespace (see page 144 in Chapter 3).

Each C++ program must contain a function *main*

A C++ program is a collection of functions, one of which must be called *main*. Program execution always begins with the function *main*. The following paragraphs provide an overview of the basics of C++ and refer to the simple program in Figure A-1 by line number. Note that this simple program contains only the function *main*.

Comments

Each comment line begins with two slashes

Each comment line in C++ begins with two slashes // and continues until the end of the line. You can also begin a multiple-line comment with the characters /* and end it with */. Although the programs in this book do not use /* and */, it is a good idea to use this notation

```
1. Enables input and output ------------>    #include <iostream.h>
2. Opens the standard namespace----->        using namespace std;
3. Begins the function main ----------->     int main()
4. A comment ----------------------------->  // Computes the volume of a sphere of a given radius.
5. Begins body of function ------------->    {
6. Defines a constant  -------------------->     const double PI = 3.14159;
7. Declares a variable  -------------------->    double radius;

8. Displays a prompt to the user ------->        cout << "Enter the radius of the sphere: ";
9. Reads radius ------------------------>        cin >> radius;

10. Declares and computes volume --->            double volume = 4 * PI * radius * radius * radius/3;
11. Displays results ---------------------->     cout << "The volume of a sphere of radius "
12. Statement continues ------------------>           << radius << " inches is " << volume
13. Statement continues ---------------->             << " cubic inches.\n";
14. Normal program termination ------->          return 0;
15. Ends body of function -------------->    }    // end program
```

FIGURE A-1   A simple C++ program

during debugging. That is, to isolate an error, you can temporarily ignore a portion of a program by enclosing it within /* and */. However, a comment that begins with /* and ends with */ cannot contain another comment that begins with /* and ends with */.

Identifiers and Keywords

A C++ identifier is a sequence of letters, digits, and underscores that must begin with either a letter or an underscore. C++ distinguishes between uppercase and lowercase letters, so be careful when typing identifiers.

C++ is case sensitive

You use identifiers to name various parts of the program. Certain identifiers, however, are reserved by C++ as keywords, and you should not use them for other purposes. A list of all C++ keywords appears inside the front cover of this book. The keywords that occur within C++ statements in this book are in boldface.

Fundamental Data Types

The fundamental data types in C++ are organized into four categories: Boolean, character, integer, and floating point. With the exception of Boolean, each category contains several data types. For most applications, you can use

bool	for Boolean values
char	for character values
int	for integer values
double	for floating-point values

A Boolean value can be either *true* or *false*. Characters are represented by their ASCII integer values, which are listed in Appendix B. Integer values are either signed, such as −5 and +98, or unsigned, such as 5 and 98. The floating-point types provide for real numbers that have both an integer portion and a fractional portion. Boolean, character, and integer types are called integral types. Integral and floating-point types are called arithmetic types.

Most of the data types are available in several forms and sizes. Although you will probably not need more than the four types given previously, Figure A-2 lists the available fundamental data types for your reference.

The size of a data type affects the range of its values. For example, a *long* integer can have a larger magnitude than a *short* integer. The sizes of—and therefore the specific ranges for—a data type depend on the particular computer and version of C++ that you use. C++, however, provides a way to determine these ranges, as you will see later in the section "Named Constants."

Variables

A variable, whose name is a C++ identifier, represents a memory location that contains a value of a particular data type. You declare a variable's data type by preceding the variable name with the data type, as in

```
double radius;  // radius of a sphere
```

Note that you can write a comment on the same line to describe the purpose of the variable.

Category	Available data types by category		
Boolean	bool		
Character	char	signed char	unsigned char
Signed integer	short	int	long
Unsigned integer	unsigned short	unsigned	unsigned long
Floating point	float	double	long double

FIGURE A-2   Fundamental data types

This declaration is also a definition in that it assigns memory for the variable *radius*. This memory, however, has no particular initial value and so is said to be uninitialized. The program in Figure A-1 declares *radius* without an initial value and later reads its value by using *cin >> radius*. You can declare several uninitialized variables of the same type in one statement, as in

```
int count, index;
```

When possible, you should avoid uninitialized variables. That is, you should initialize a variable when you first declare its data type or, alternatively, declare a variable's data type when you first assign it a value. For example, *volume* appears for the first time in line 9 of Figure A-1 in the statement

```
double volume = 4 * PI * radius * radius * radius/3;
```

Since we did not declare *volume*'s data type earlier in the program—thus avoiding an uninitialized value—we declare its data type *and* assign it a value in the same statement.

When possible, avoid uninitialized variables

Literal Constants

You use literal constants to indicate particular values within a program. The 4 and 3 in line 10 of Figure A-1 are examples of literal constants that are used within a computation. You can also use a literal constant to initialize the value of a variable. For example, you use *true* and *false* as the values of a Boolean variable, as mentioned previously.

You write decimal integer constants without commas, decimal points, or leading zeros.[1] The default data type of such a constant is either *int*, if small enough, or *long*.

You write floating constants, which have a default type of *double*, with a decimal point. You can specify an optional power-of-10 multiplier by writing *e* or *E* followed by the power of 10. For example, *1.2e-3* means 1.2×10^{-3}.

Character constants are enclosed in single quotes—for example, *'A'* and *'2'*—and have a default type of *char*. You write a literal character string as a sequence of characters enclosed in double quotes.

Several characters have names that use a backslash notation, as given in Figure A-3. This notation is useful when you want to embed one of these characters within a literal character string. For example, the program in Figure A-1 uses the new-line character *\n* in the string *"cubic inches.\n"* to end the line of output with a carriage return. You will learn about this use of *\n* in the discussion of output later in this appendix.

Do not begin a decimal integer constant with zero

Constant	Name
\n	New line
\t	Tab
\'	Single quote
\"	Double quote
\0	Zero

FIGURE A-3 Some special character constants

---

[1] Octal and hexadecimal constants are also available, but they are not used in this book. An octal constant begins with *0*, a hex constant with *0x* or *0X*.

You also use the backslash notation to specify either a single quote as a character constant ('\'') or a double quote within a character string.

Named Constants

Unlike variables, whose values can change during program execution, named constants have values that do not change. The declaration of a named constant is like that of an initialized variable, but the keyword *const* precedes the data type. For example, the statement

The value of a named constant does not change

```
const double PI = 3.14159;
```

declares *PI* as a named floating constant, as is the case in the sample program in Figure A-1. Once a named constant such as *PI* is declared, you can use it, but you cannot assign it another value. By using named constants, you make your program both easier to read and easier to modify.

Named constants make a program easier to read and modify

The standard header file *climits* contains named constants such as *INT_MIN* and *LONG_MAX* that specify installation-dependent maximum and minimum values for the integral data types. Likewise, the standard header file *cfloat* contains named constants that specify installation-dependent maximum and minimum values for the floating data types. You use the *include* directive to gain access to these header files.

Enumerations

Enumeration provides another way to name constants

Enumeration provides another way to name integer constants. For example, the statement

```
enum {SUN, MON, TUE, WED, THU, FRI, SAT};
```

is equivalent to the statements

```
const int SUN = 0;
const int MON = 1;
. . .
const int SAT = 6;
```

By default, the values assigned to the constants—called enumerators—begin with zero and are consecutive. You can, however, assign explicit values to any or all of the enumerators, as in

```
enum {PLUS = '+', MINUS = '−'};
```

An enumerator without an explicit value has a value that is 1 greater than the value of the previous enumerator. For example,

```
enum {WINTER = 1, SPRING, SUMMER, FALL};
```

assigns 2, 3, and 4 to *SPRING*, *SUMMER*, and *FALL*, respectively.

By naming an enumeration, you create a distinct integral type. For example,

```
enum Season {WINTER, SPRING, SUMMER, FALL};
```

You can create an integral data type by naming an enumeration

creates a type *Season*. The variable *whichSeason*, declared as

```
Season whichSeason;
```

can have values *WINTER* (0), *SPRING* (1), *SUMMER* (2), or *FALL* (3). This use of an enumeration instead of *int* can make your program easier to understand. However, it does have its limitations, as you will see in the section "Assignments and Expressions."

The *typedef* Statement

You use the *typedef* statement to give another name to an existing data type. In this way, you can make your program easier to modify and to read. For example, the statement

```
typedef double Real;
```

The *typedef* statement gives another name to an existing data type, making your program easier to change

declares *Real* as a synonym for *double* and allows you to use *Real* and *double* interchangeably.

Suppose that you revise the program in Figure A-1 by using *Real* as follows:

```
int main()
{
   typedef double Real;
   const Real PI = 3.14159;
   Real radius;

   cout << "Enter the radius of the sphere: ";
   cin >> radius;
   Real volume = 4 * PI * radius * radius * radius/3;
   . . .
```

At first glance, this program does not seem to be more advantageous than the original version, but suppose that you decide to increase the precision of your computation by declaring *PI*, *radius*, and *volume* as *long double* instead of *double*. In the original version of the program (Figure A-1), you would have to locate and change each occurrence of *double* to *long double*. In the revised program, you simply change the *typedef* statement to

```
typedef long double Real;
```

The `typedef` statement does not create a new data type

Realize that `typedef` does not create a new data type but simply declares a new name for a data type. A new data type requires more than a name; it requires a set of operations. C++, however, does provide a way to create your own data types, as described in Chapter 3.

Assignments and Expressions

You form an expression by combining variables, constants, operators, and parentheses. The assignment statement

```
volume = 4 * PI * radius * radius * radius/3;
```

assigns to the previously declared variable *volume* the value of the arithmetic expression on the right-hand side of the assignment operator =, assuming that *PI* and *radius* have values. The assignment statement

```
double volume = 4 * PI * radius * radius * radius/3;
```

which appears in line 10 of Figure A-1, also declares *volume*'s data type, since it was not declared previously.

The various kinds of expressions that you can use in an assignment statement are discussed next.

Arithmetic expressions. You can combine variables and constants with arithmetic operators and parentheses to form arithmetic expressions. The arithmetic operators are

- `*` Multiply
- `/` Divide
- `%` Remainder after division
- `+` Binary add or unary plus
- `-` Binary subtract or unary minus

The operators `*`, `/`, and `%` have the same precedence,[2] which is higher than that of `+` and `-`; unary operators[3] have a higher precedence than binary operators. The following examples demonstrate operator precedence:

Operators have a set precedence

a - b/c	means	*a - (b/c)*	(*precedence of / over -*)
-5/a	means	*(-5)/a*	(*precedence of unary operator -*)
a/-5	means	*a/(-5)*	(*precedence of unary operator -*)

Arithmetic operators and most other operators are left-associative. That is, operators of the same precedence execute from left to right within an expression. Thus,

---

[2] A list of all C++ operators and their precedences appears inside the back cover of this book.
[3] A unary operator requires only one operand, for example, the `-` in `-5`. A binary operator requires two operands, for example, the `+` in `2 + 3`.

```
a / b * c
```

means

```
(a / b) * c
```

Operators are either left- or right-associative

The assignment operator and all unary operators are right-associative, as you will see later. You can use parentheses to override operator precedence and associativity.

Relational and logical expressions.   You can combine variables and constants with parentheses; with the relational, or comparison, operators <, <=, >=, and >; and with the equality operators == (equal to) and != (not equal to) to form a relational expression. Such an expression evaluates to *false* if the specified relation is false and to *true* if it is true. For example, the expression *5 != 4* has a value of *true* because 5 is not equal to 4. Note that equality operators have a lower precedence than relational operators.

You can combine variables and constants of the arithmetic types, relational expressions, and the logical operators && (and) and || (or) to form logical expressions, which evaluate to *false* if false and to *true* if true. C++ evaluates logical expressions from left to right and stops as soon as the value of the entire expression is apparent; that is, C++ uses short-circuit evaluation. For example, C++ determines the value of each of the following expressions without evaluating *(a < b)*:

Logical expressions are evaluated from left to right

Sometimes the value of a logical expression is apparent before it is completely examined

```
(5 == 4) && (a < b)   // false since (5 == 4) is false
(5 == 5) || (a < b)   // true since (5 == 5) is true
```

Conditional expressions.   The expression

$$expression_1 \; ? \; expression_2 \; : \; expression_3$$

has the value of either *expression₂* or *expression₃* according to whether *expression₁* is *true* or *false*, respectively. For example, the statement

```
larger = ((a > b) ? a : b);
```

assigns the larger of *a* and *b* to *larger*, because the expression *a > b* is *true* if *a* is larger than *b* and *false* if not.

Implicit type conversions.   Automatic conversions from one data type to another can occur during assignment and during expression evaluation. For assignments, the data type of the expression on the right-hand side of the assignment operator is converted to the data type of the item on the left-hand side just before the assignment occurs. Floating-point values are truncated—not rounded—when they are converted to integral values.

Conversions from one data type to another occur during both assignment and expression evaluation

During the evaluation of an expression, any values of type *char* or *short* are converted to *int*. Similarly, any enumerator value is converted to *int* if *int* can represent all the values of that particular *enum*; otherwise, it is converted to *unsigned*. These conversions are called integral promotions. After these conversions, if the operands of an operator differ in data type, the data type that is lower in the following hierarchy is converted to one that is higher (*int* is lowest):

int → *unsigned* → *long* → *unsigned long* → *float* → *double* → *long double*

For example, if *a* is *long* and *b* is *float*, *a + b* is *float*. Only a copy of *a*'s *long* value is converted to *float* prior to the addition, so that the value stored at *a* is unchanged.

Explicit type conversions.   You can explicitly convert from one data type to another using a static cast, with the following notation:

```
static_cast<type>(expression)
```

which converts *expression* to data type *type*. For example, `static_cast<int>(14.9)` converts the double value 14.9 to the int value 14. Thus, the sequence

```
double volume = 14.9;
cout << static_cast<int>(volume);
```

displays 14 but does not change the value of *volume*.
Consider once again the enumeration

```
enum Season {WINTER, SPRING, SUMMER, FALL};
```

You can assign an instance of *Season* to an *int* variable, resulting in an implicit conversion from *enum* to *int*, as was noted earlier. Thus, the following is valid:

```
Season whichSeason = SUMMER;
int    result = whichSeason;    // result is 2
```

However, you must explicitly convert from an *int* to an enumeration, such as *Season*. Thus, for an integer *index*, you cannot write

```
whichSeason = index;  // incorrect
```

even if *index* has a value between 0 and 3. You instead must write

```
whichSeason = static_cast<Season>(index);
```

Use a static cast to convert explicitly from one data type to another

You can avoid explicit type conversion in this case by defining *Season* without *enum* as follows:

```
typedef int Season;
const int WINTER = 0;
const int SPRING = 1;
const int SUMMER = 2;
const int FALL = 3;
```

Multiple assignment.   If you omit the semicolon from an assignment statement, you get an assignment expression. You can embed assignment expressions within assignment expressions, as in

```
a = 5 + (b = 4)
```

This expression first assigns 4 to *b* and then 9 to *a*. This notation contributes to the terseness of C++ and is sometimes convenient, but it can be confusing. The assignment operator is right-associative. Thus, *a = b = c* means *a = (b = c)*.

Other assignment operators.   In addition to the assignment operator =, C++ provides several two-character assignment operators that perform another operation before assignment. For example,

```
    a += b  means a = a + b
```

Other operators, such as -=, *=, /=, and %=, have analogous meanings.
    Two more operators, ++ and --, provide convenient incrementing and decrementing operations:

```
    ++a  means  a += 1, which means  a = a + 1
```

Similarly,

```
    --a  means  a -= 1, which means  a = a - 1
```

The operators ++ and -- are useful for incrementing and decrementing a variable

The operators ++ and -- can either precede their operands, as you just saw, or follow them. Although *a++*, for instance, has the same effect as *++a*, the results differ when the operations are combined with assignment. For example,

```
    b = ++a  means a = a + 1; b = a
```

Here, the ++ operator acts on *a* *before* the assignment to *b* of *a*'s new value. In contrast,

```
    b = a++  means b = a; a = a + 1
```

The assignment operator assigns *a*'s old value to *b* before the ++ operator acts on *a*. That is, the ++ operator acts on *a* *after* the assignment. The operators ++ and -- are often used within loops and with array indexes, as you will see later in this appendix.

In addition to the operators described here, C++ provides several other operators. A summary of all C++ operators and their precedences appears inside the back cover of this book.

A.2 Input and Output Using *iostream*

A typical C++ program reads its input from a keyboard and writes its output to a monitor. Such input and output consist of streams, which are simply sequences of characters that either come from or go to an input or output (I/O) device.

The data type of an input stream is *istream*, and the data type of an output stream is *ostream*. The *iostream* library provides these data types and three default stream variables: *cin* for the standard input stream, *cout* for the standard output stream, and *cerr* for the standard error stream, which also is an output stream. Your program gains access to the *iostream* library by including the *iostream* header file. This section provides a brief introduction to simple input and output.

Input

The input operator >> reads from an input stream

C++ provides the input operator >> to read integers, floating-point numbers, and characters into variables whose data types are any of the fundamental data types. The input operator has the input stream as its left operand and the variable that will contain the value read as its right operand. Thus,

```
cin >> x;
```

reads a value for *x* from the standard input stream. The >> operator is left-associative. Thus,

```
cin >> x >> y
```

means

```
(cin >> x) >> y
```

That is, both of these expressions read characters for *x* from the input stream and then read subsequent characters for *y*.

The input operator >> skips whitespace

The input operator >> skips whitespace, such as blanks, tabs, and new-line characters, that might occur between values in the input data line. For example, after the program segment

```
int    ia, ib;
double da, db;
cin >> ia >> da >> ib;
cin >> db;
```

reads the data line

```
21    -3.45    -6   475.1e-2    <cr>
```

The variable *ia* contains 21, *da* contains −3.45, *ib* contains −6, and *db* contains 4.751. A subsequent attempt to read from *cin* will look beyond the carriage return (*<cr>*) and read from the next data line, if one exists. An error occurs if no data exists for a corresponding variable processed by >> or if the variable's data type does not match the type of the data available. For example, after the previous program segment reads the data line

```
-1.23    456.1e-2    -7   8 <cr>
```

the variable *ia* contains −1, *da* contains 0.23, *ib* contains 456, and *db* contains 0.001. The rest of the data line is left for a subsequent read, if any. As another example, if the segment attempts to read a data line that begins with *.21*, the read would terminate because *ia* is *int* and *.21* is not.

An expression such as *cin >> x* has a value after the read operation takes place. If the operation is successful, this value is *true*; otherwise the value is *false*. You can examine this value by using the selection and iteration statements that are described later in this appendix.

You can also use the >> operator to read individual characters from the input stream into character variables. Again, any whitespace is skipped. For example, after the program segment

```
char ch1, ch2, ch3;
cin >> ch1 >> ch2 >> ch3;
```

reads the data line

```
xy   z
```

ch1 contains *'x'*, *ch2* contains *'y'*, and *ch3* contains *'z'*.

You can read whitespace when reading individual characters into character variables by using the C++ function *get*. Either of the statements

```
cin.get(ch1);
```

Use *get* to read whitespace

or

```
ch1 = cin.get();
```

reads the next character, even if it is a blank, a tab, or a new-line character, from the input stream into the *char* variable *ch1*.

Later in this appendix, the section "Strings" describes how to read character strings.

Output

C++ provides the output operator << to write character strings and the contents of variables whose data types are any of the fundamental ones. For example, the program segment

```
int count = 5;
double average = 20.3;
cout << "The average of the " << count
     << " distances read is " << average
     << " miles.\n";
```

produces the following output:

```
The average of the 5 distances read is 20.3 miles.
```

Like the input operator, the output operator is left-associative. Thus, the previous statements append *The average of the* to the output stream, then append the characters that represent the value of *count*, and so on.

Note the use of the new-line character \n, which you can conveniently embed within a character string. Observe also that the output operator does not automatically introduce whitespace between values that are written; you must do so explicitly. The following statements provide another example of this:

```
int x = 2;
int y = 3;
char ch = 'A';
cout << x << y << ch << "\n";   // displays 23A
```

Although you can use the output operator to display individual characters, you can also use the *put* function for this task. Further, you can specify a character either as a *char* variable or in ASCII. Thus, the statements

```
char ch = 'a';
cout.put(ch);     // displays a
cout.put('b');    // displays b
cout.put(99);     // displays c, which is 99 in ASCII
cout.put(ch+3);   // displays d
cout.put('\n');   // carriage return
```

display *abcd* followed by a carriage return.

Later in this appendix, the section "Strings" provides further information about writing character strings.

Manipulators

C++ enables you to gain more control over the format of your output and the treatment of whitespace during input than the previous discussion has indicated. Most of these techniques apply to the format of output.

Suppose, for example, that you have computed your grade point average and you want to display it with one digit to the right of the decimal point. If the floating variable *gpa* contains 4.0, the statement

```
cout << "My GPA is " << gpa << "\n";
```

writes 4 without a decimal point. A number of **manipulators** affect the appearance of your output. You can use these with *cout*:

Use manipulators to specify the appearance of a program's output

```
cout << manipulator;
```

where *manipulator* has any of the values listed in Figure A-4. A manipulator is a predefined value or function that you use with the input and output operator. For example,

Manipulators also affect the appearance of a program's output

```
cout << showpoint;
```

uses the *showpoint* manipulator and causes all floating-point output to appear with a decimal point.

Even if you use the *showpoint* manipulator, *gpa* will likely appear as 4.00000 instead of 4.0. You can specify the number of digits that appear to the right of the decimal point by using the manipulator

Manipulator	Meaning
endl	Insert new line and flush stream
fixed	Use fixed decimal point in floating-point output
left	Left-align output
right	Right-align output
scientific	Use exponential (e) notation in floating-point output
setfill(*f*)	Set fill character to *f*
setprecision(*n*)	Set floating-point precision to integer *n*
setw(*n*)	Set field width to integer *n*
showpoint	Show decimal point in floating-point output
showpos	Show + with positive integers
ws	Extract whitespace characters

FIGURE A-4 Stream manipulators

function *setprecision*, and you can insert a new-line character and flush the output stream by using the manipulator value *endl*. Thus,

```
cout << showpoint;
cout << setprecision(1) << gpa << endl;
```

displays 4.0 followed by a carriage return.

The effect of *setprecision* on the output stream remains until another *setprecision* is encountered. Except for *setprecision*, however, a manipulator affects the appearance of only the next characters on which << (or >>) operates. For example,

```
cout << right;  // right-align output
cout << "abc" << setw(6) << "def" << "ghi";
```

displays

```
abc    defghi
```

While manipulator values, such as *endl*, are available when you include *iostream* in your program, you must also include *iomanip* to use any of the manipulator functions.

A.3 Functions

A C++ program is a collection of functions

As was mentioned earlier in this appendix, a C++ program is a collection of functions. Usually, each function should perform one well-defined task. For example, the following function returns the larger of two integers:

A function definition implements a function's task

```
int max(int x, int y)
{
   if (x > y)
      return x;
   else
      return y;
}  // end max
```

A function definition, like the one just given, has the following form:

type   name(formal argument declaration list)
{
    body
}

The portion of the definition before the left brace specifies a return type, the function name, and a list of **formal arguments**. The part of the definition that appears between the braces is the function's body.

The return type of a valued function—one that returns a value—is the data type of the value that the function will return. The body of a valued function must contain a statement of the form

return *expression*;

A valued function must use
return to return a value

where *expression* has the value to be returned.

Each formal argument represents either an input to or an output from the function. You declare a formal argument by writing a data type and an argument name, separating it from other formal argument declarations with a comma, as in

int x, **int** y

When you call, or invoke, the function *max*, you pass it **actual arguments** that correspond to the formal arguments with respect to number, order, and data type. For example, the following statements contain two calls to *max*:

When you call a function, you pass it actual arguments that correspond to the formal arguments in number, order, and data type

```
int a, b, c;
cin >> a >> b >> c;

int largerAB = max(a, b);
cout << "The largest of " << a << ", " << b << ", "
    << " and " << c << " is " << max(largerAB, c)
    << ".\n";
```

As written, the definition of *max* indicates that its arguments are passed by value. That is, the function makes local copies of the values of the actual arguments—*a* and *b*, for example—and uses these copies wherever *x* and *y* appear in the function definition. Thus, the function cannot alter the actual arguments that you pass to it. This restriction is desirable in this example because *x* and *y* are input arguments, which *max* does not change.

An actual argument passed by value is copied within the function

Alternatively, arguments can be passed by reference. The function does not copy such arguments; rather, it references the actual argument locations whenever the formal arguments appear in the function's definition. This allows a function to change the values of the actual arguments, thus implementing output arguments.

An actual argument passed by reference is not copied but is accessed directly within the function

As an example of arguments that are passed by reference, consider the following variation of the function *max*:

```
void computeMax(int x, int y, int& larger)
{
    larger = ((x > y) ? x : y);
}  // end computeMax
```

computeMax is a *void* function instead of a valued-function. That is, its return type is *void*, and it does not return a value by using a *return*

A *void* function does not use *return* to return a value

statement.[4] Instead, *computeMax* returns the larger of *x* and *y* in the output argument *larger*. The **&** that follows *larger*'s data type *int* indicates that *larger* is a reference argument. Thus, *computeMax* will access and alter the actual argument that corresponds to *larger*, whereas the function will make and use copies of the values of the actual arguments that correspond to the value arguments *x* and *y*.

An output argument should be a reference argument

The following statements demonstrate how to invoke *computeMax*:

```
int a, b, largerAB;
cin >> a >> b;
computeMax(a, b, largerAB);
cout << "The larger of " << a << " and " << b
    << " is " << largerAB << ".\n";
```

If a function's input argument is a large object, like the objects you will encounter in this book, you might not want the function to copy it. Thus, you would not pass the argument by value. Since it is an input argument, however, you do not want the function to be able to alter it. A constant reference argument is one that you pass by reference but tag as *const*. The function uses the actual argument, not a copy of it, yet cannot modify it.

An input argument should be either a value argument or a constant reference argument

For example, for the function *f* that begins

```
void f(const int& x, int y, int& z)
```

x is a constant reference argument, *y* is a value argument, and *z* is a reference argument. Here *x* and *y* are suitable as input arguments because *f* cannot change them, while *z* is an output argument. Note that *z* can also be an input argument. That is, an argument can both provide a value to a function and return a value from a function. Such arguments must be reference arguments.

An argument that is both an input to and an output from a function is passed by reference

If you write another function *f* that calls *computeMax*, you must either place the definition of *f* after the definition of *computeMax* or precede *f*'s definition with a function declaration for *computeMax*. For example, you can use either of the following statements to declare the function *computeMax*:

A function declaration ends with a semicolon

```
void computeMax(int x, int y, int& max);
```

or

```
void computeMax(int, int, int&);
```

---

[4] Whereas valued functions must contain a statement of the form
return *expression;*
void functions cannot. A *void* function can, however, contain
return;
without an expression. Such a statement causes the function to return to the statement that follows its call. This book does not use *return* with *void* functions.

A declaration for a function whose definition appears later in the program provides the data types of both the function's formal arguments and its return value. Argument names are optional in a function declaration, although they are helpful stylistically. However, argument names are required in the function's definition. Although a function declaration ends with a semicolon, this semicolon does not appear in a function definition.

A typical C++ program contains a function declaration for every function used in the program. These declarations appear first in the program, usually with comments that describe each function's purpose, arguments, and assumptions. The following program demonstrates the placement of a function declaration, function definition, and main function:

> Declarations for each function usually appear at the beginning of a program

```cpp
#include <iostream>
using namespace std;
int max(int x, int y);
// Returns the larger of x and y.

int main()
{
   int a, b;
   cout << "Please enter two integers: ";
   cin >> a >> b;

   int largerAB = max(a, b);
   cout << "The larger of " << a << " and " << b
        << " is " << largerAB << ".\n";
}  // end main

int max(int x, int y)
{
   return (x > y) ? x : y;
}  // end max
```

Standard Functions

C++ provides many standard functions, such as the square root function *sqrt* and the input function *get*. Appendix C provides a summary of the standard functions and indicates which header file you need to include in your program to gain access to them. For example, the standard functions listed in Figure A-5 facilitate character processing and require the header file *cctype*. Thus, you need to include the following statement in your program:

> Standard functions provide many common operations and require a specific header file

```cpp
#include <cctype>
```

when you want to use functions such as *isupper* and *toupper*. For the character variable *ch*, *isupper(ch)* is *true* if *ch* is an uppercase letter,

(a)

Function	Returns **true** if ch is
isalnum(ch)	A letter or digit
isalpha(ch)	A letter
isdigit(ch)	A digit
islower(ch)	A lowercase letter
isupper(ch)	An uppercase letter

(b)

Function	Returns
tolower(ch)	Lowercase version of ch
toupper(ch)	Uppercase version of ch
toascii(ch)	int ASCII code for ch

FIGURE A-5   A selection of (a) standard classification functions; and (b) standard conversion functions

and *toupper(ch)* returns the uppercase version of the letter *ch* without actually changing *ch*.

A.4 Selection Statements

Selection statements allow you to choose among several courses of action according to the value of an expression. In this category of statements, C++ provides the *if* statement and the *switch* statement.

The *if* Statement

You can write an *if* statement in one of two ways:

An *if* statement has two basic forms

```
if (expression)
    statement1
```

or

```
if (expression)
    statement1
else
    statement2
```

where *statement*$_1$ and *statement*$_2$ represent any C++ statement except a declaration. Such statements can be compound; a compound statement, or block, is a sequence of statements enclosed in braces. If the value of *expression* is `true`,[5] *statement*$_1$ is executed. Otherwise, the first form of the `if` statement does nothing, whereas the second form executes *statement*$_2$. Note that the parentheses around *expression* are required.

For example, the following `if` statements each compare the values of two integer variables *a* and *b*:

> Parentheses around the expression in an `if` statement are required

```
if (a > b)
   cout << a << " is larger than " << b << ".\n";
cout << "This statement is always executed.\n";

if (a > b)
{  largerAB = a;
   cout << a << " is larger than " << b << ".\n";
}

else
{  largerAB = b;
   cout << b << " is larger than " << a << ".\n";
}

cout << largerAB << " is the larger value.\n";
```

You can nest `if` statements in several ways, since either *statement*$_1$ or *statement*$_2$ can itself be an `if` statement. The following example, which determines the largest of three integer variables *a*, *b*, and *c*, shows a common way to nest `if` statements:

> You can nest `if` statements

```
if ((a >= b) && (a >= c))
   largest = a;
else if (b >= c)     // a is not largest at this point
   largest = b;
else
   largest = c;
```

The `switch` Statement

When you must choose among more than two courses of action, the `if` statement can become unwieldy. If your choice is to be made according to the value of an integral expression, you can use a `switch` statement.

> A `switch` statement provides a choice of several actions according to the value of an integral expression

For example, the following statement determines the number of days in a month. The `int` variable `month` designates the month as an integer from 1 to 12.

---

[5] Arithmetic nonzero values are treated as `true`.

Without a *break* statement, execution of a case will continue into the next case

```cpp
switch (month)
{  // 30 days hath Sept., Apr., June, and Nov.
   case 9: case 4: case 6: case 11:
      daysInMonth = 30;
      break;
   // all the rest have 31
   case 1: case 3: case 5: case 7:
   case 8: case 10: case 12:
      daysInMonth = 31;
      break;

   // except February
   case 2:  // assume leapYear is true if leap
            // year, else is false
      if (leapYear)
         daysInMonth = 29;
      else
         daysInMonth = 28;
      break;

   default:
      cout << "Incorrect value for month.\n";
}  // end switch
```

Parentheses must enclose the integral *switch* expression—*month*, in this example. The *case* labels have the form

case *expression*:

where *expression* is a constant integral expression. After the *switch* expression is evaluated, execution continues at the *case* label whose expression has the same value as the *switch* expression. Subsequent statements execute until either a *break* or a *return* is encountered or the *switch* statement ends.

Unless you terminate a *case* with either a *break* or a *return*, execution of the *switch* statement continues. Although this action can be useful, omitting the *break* statements in the previous example would be incorrect.

If no *case* label matches the current value of the *switch* expression, the statements that follow the *default* label, if one exists, are executed. If no *default* exists, the *switch* statement exits.

A.5 Iteration Statements

C++ has three statements—the *while*, *for*, and *do* statements—that provide for repetition by iteration, that is, loops. Each statement controls the number of times that another C++ statement—the body—is executed. The body cannot be a declaration and is often a compound statement.

The `while` Statement

The general form of the `while` statement is

while (*expression*)
   statement

A *while* statement executes as long as the expression is true

As long as the value of *expression* is `true`, *statement* is executed. Because *expression* is evaluated before *statement* is executed, it is possible that *statement* will not execute at all. Note that the parentheses around *expression* are required.

Suppose that you wanted to compute the sum of positive integers that you enter at the keyboard. Since the integers are positive, you can use a negative or zero value to indicate the end of the list of integers. The following `while` statement accomplishes this task:

```
int nextValue;
int sum = 0;

cin >> nextValue;
while (nextValue > 0)
{   sum += nextValue;
    cin >> nextValue;
}   // end while
```

If 0 was the first value read, the body of the `while` statement would not execute.

Recall that the expression `cin >> nextValue` has the value `true` if the input operation was successful and `false` otherwise. Thus, you could revise the previous statements as

```
int nextValue;
int sum = 0;

while ( (cin >> nextValue) && (nextValue > 0) )
    sum += nextValue;
```

The `break` and `continue` statements. You can use the `break` statement—which you saw earlier within a `switch` statement—within any of the iteration statements. A `break` statement within the body of a loop causes the loop to exit immediately. Execution continues with the statement that follows the loop. This use of `break` within a `while`, `for`, or `do` statement is generally considered poor style.

Use of a *break* statement within a loop is generally poor style

The `continue` statement stops only the current iteration of the loop and begins the next iteration at the top of the loop. The `continue` statement is valid only within *while*, *for*, or *do* statements.

The *for* Statement

The *for* statement provides for counted loops and has the general form

A *for* statement lists the initialization, testing, and updating steps in one location

for (*initialize*; *test*; *update*)
   statement

where *initialize*, *test*, and *update* are expressions. Typically, *initialize* is an assignment expression that initializes a counter to control the loop. This initialization occurs only once. Then if *test*, which is usually a logical expression, is `true`, *statement* executes. The expression *update* executes next, usually incrementing or decrementing the counter. This sequence of events repeats, beginning with the evaluation of *test*, until the value of *test* is `false`.

For example, the following *for* statement displays the integers from 1 to *n*:

```
for (int counter = 1; counter <= n; ++counter)
   cout << counter << " ";

cout << endl;  // this statement is always executed
```

If *n* is less than 1, the *for* statement does not execute at all. Thus, the previous statements are equivalent to the following *while* loop:

```
int counter = 1;
while (counter <= n)
{  cout << counter << " ";
   ++counter;
}  // end while

cout << endl;  // this statement is always executed
```

In general, the logic of a *for* statement is equivalent to

A *for* statement is equivalent to a *while* statement

```
initialize;
while (test)
{  statement;
   update;
}
```

with the understanding that if *statement* contains a `continue`, *update* will execute before *test* is evaluated again.

Note that the first expression *initialize* must have either an arithmetic type or a pointer type.[6] The following two examples demonstrate the flexibility of the *for* statement:

```
for (char ch = 'z'; ch >= 'a'; --ch)
// ch ranges from 'z' to 'a'


for (double x = 1.5; x < 10; x += 0.25)
// x ranges from 1.5 to 9.75 at steps of 0.25
```

The *initialize* and *update* portions of a *for* statement each can contain several expressions separated by commas, thus performing more than one action. For example, the following loop raises a floating-point value to an integer power by using multiplication:

```
// floating-point power equals floating-point x
// raised to int n; assumes int expon
for (power = 1.0, expon = 1; expon <= n; ++expon)
    power *= x;
```

Both *power* and *expon* are assigned values before the body of the loop executes for the first time. The comma here is an example of the comma operator, which evaluates its operand expressions from left to right.

Because the *for* statement consolidates the initialization, testing, and updating steps of a loop into one statement, C++ programmers tend to favor it over the *while* statement. For example, notice how the following *for* statement is equivalent to the *while* loop in the previous section that computed the sum of integers read:

> A *for* statement is usually favored over the *while* statement

```
for (int sum = 0;
     (cin >> nextValue) && (nextValue > 0);
     sum += nextValue);
```

In fact, this *for* statement has an empty body!

You can omit any of the expressions *initialize*, *test*, or *update* from a *for* statement, but you cannot omit the semicolons. For example, you can move the *update* step from the previous *for* statement to the body of the loop:

> You can omit any of the initialization, testing, and updating steps in a *for* statement, but you cannot omit the semicolons

```
for (int sum = 0; (cin >> nextValue) &&
                  (nextValue > 0); )
    sum += nextValue;
```

---

[6] Chapter 4 introduces pointer types.

You also could omit both the initialization and the update steps, as in the following loop to read and process positive integers:

```
for ( ; (cin >> nextValue) && (nextValue > 0); )
{
    statements to process nextValue
}
```

This *for* statement offers no advantage over the equivalent *while* statement:

```
while ( (cin >> nextValue) && (nextValue > 0) )
```

Although you can omit the *test* expression from *for*, you probably will not want to do so, because then the loop would be infinite.

The *do* Statement

Use the *do* statement when you want to execute a loop at least once. Its general form is

A *do* statement loops at least once

```
do
    statement
while (expression);
```

Here, *statement* executes until the value of *expression* is *false*.

For example, suppose that you execute a sequence of statements and then ask the user whether to execute them again. The *do* statement is appropriate, because you execute the statements before you decide whether to repeat them:

```
char response;
do
{  . . . (a sequence of statements)

    cout << "Do it again?";
    cin >> response;
} while ( (response == 'Y') || (response == 'y') );
```

A.6 Arrays

An array is a collection of data that has the same type

An array is a collection of elements or items or components that have the same data type. Array elements have an order: An array has a first element, a second element, and so on, as well as a last element. That is, an array contains a finite, limited number of elements. Therefore, you must know the maximum number of elements possible in a particular array when you write your program and *before* you execute it. Because you can access the array elements directly and in any order, an array is a direct access, or random access, data structure.

One-Dimensional Arrays

When you decide to use an array in your program, you must declare it and, in doing so, indicate the data type of its elements as well as its maximum size. The following statements declare a one-dimensional array, *maxTemps*, which contains the daily maximum temperatures for a given week:

```
const int DAYS_PER_WEEK = 7;
double maxTemps[DAYS_PER_WEEK];
```

The bracket notation [ ] declares *maxTemps* as an array. This array can contain at most seven floating-point elements.

You can refer to any of the floating-point elements in *maxTemps* directly by using an expression, which is called the index, or **subscript**, enclosed in square brackets. In C++, array indexes must have integer values in the range 0 to *size* − 1, where *size* is the number of elements in the array. The indexes for *maxTemps* range from 0 to *DAYS_PER_WEEK* − 1. For example, *maxTemps[4]* is the fifth element in the array. If *k* is an integer variable whose value is 4, *maxTemps[k]* is the fifth element in the array, and *maxTemps[k+1]* is the sixth element. Also, *maxTemps[++k]* adds 1 to *k* and then uses the new value of *k* to index *maxTemps*, whereas *maxTemps[k++]* accesses *maxTemps[k]* before adding 1 to *k*. Note that you use one index to refer to an element in a one-dimensional array.

Figure A-6 illustrates the array *maxTemps*, which at present contains only five temperatures. The last value in the array is *maxTemp[4]*; the values of *maxTemps[5]* and *maxTemps[6]* are not initialized and therefore are unknown.

You can use enumerators as indexes because they have integer values. For example, consider the following definition:

```
enum Day {SUN, MON, TUE, WED, THU, FRI, SAT};
```

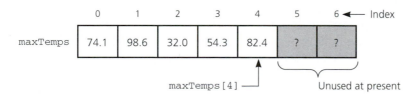

FIGURE A-6   A one-dimensional array of at most seven elements

Given this definition, *maxTemps[THU]* has the same meaning as *max-Temps[4]*. You can also use the enumerators within a loop that processes an array, as in the following *for* statement, which assumes that *dayIndex* has the data type *Day*:

```
for (dayIndex = SUN; dayIndex <= SAT;
                    dayIndex = static_cast<Day>(dayIndex+1))
    cout << maxTemps[dayIndex] << endl;
```

The expression *static_cast<Day>(dayIndex+1)* converts the integer sum *dayIndex+1* to the integral type *Day*.

Clearly, before you can retrieve an element of an array, you must assign it a value. You must assign values to array elements one at a time by using the previously described index notation. Note that, if *a* and *b* are arrays of the same type, the assignment *a = b* is illegal.[7]

The data type of *maxTemps* is a derived type, which is a type that you derive from the fundamental types by using a declaration operator such as [ ]. Naming a derived type by using a *typedef* is often useful. Thus, you can write

```
const int DAYS_PER_WEEK = 7;
typedef double ArrayType[DAYS_PER_WEEK];
ArrayType maxTemps;
```

and make *ArrayType* available for use throughout your program.

Initialization. You can initialize the elements of an array when you declare it for the first time. For example,

```
ArrayType maxTemps = {82.0, 71.5, 61.8, 75.0, 88.3};
```

You can initialize an array when you declare it

initializes the first five elements of *maxTemps* to the values listed and the last two elements to zero.

Passing an array to a function. If you wanted a function that computed the average of the first *n* elements in a one-dimensional array, you could declare the function as

```
double averageTemp(ArrayType temperatures, int n);
```

Since the compiler does not need the maximum number of items that the array can hold, you could also declare the function as follows:

---

[7] C++ enables you to define your own array data type and array operators so that this assignment would be valid. To do so, you need to use classes (Chapter 3) and overloaded operators (Chapter 8).

```
double averageTemp(double temperatures[], int n);
```

In either case, you can invoke the function by writing, for example,

```
double avg = averageTemp(maxTemps, 6);
```

where *maxTemps* is the previously defined array.

An array is never passed to a function by value, regardless of how you write its formal argument. An array is always passed by reference. This restriction avoids the copying of perhaps many array elements. Thus, the function *averageTemp* could modify the elements of *max-Temps*, even though the array is an input argument. To prevent such alteration, you can specify the formal array argument as a constant reference argument by preceding its type with *const*, as follows:

Arrays are always passed by reference to a function

```
double averageTemp(const double temperatures[], int n);
```

Multidimensional Arrays

You can use a one-dimensional array, which has one index, for a simple collection of data. For example, you can organize 52 temperatures linearly, one after another. A one-dimensional array of these temperatures can represent this organization.

You can also declare multidimensional arrays. You use more than one index to designate an element in a multidimensional array. Suppose that you wanted to represent the minimum temperature for each day during 52 weeks. The following statements declare a two-dimensional array, *minTemps*:

An array can have more than one dimension

```
const int DAYS_PER_WEEK = 7;
const int WEEKS_PER_YEAR = 52;

typedef double ArrayType[DAYS_PER_WEEK][WEEKS_PER_YEAR];
ArrayType minTemps;
```

These statements specify the ranges for two indexes: The first index can range from 0 to 6, while the second index can range from 0 to 51. Most people picture a two-dimensional array as a rectangular arrangement, or matrix, of elements that form rows and columns, as Figure A-7 indicates. The first dimension given in the definition of *Array-Type* is the number of rows. Thus, *minTemps* has 7 rows and 52 columns. Each column in this matrix represents the seven daily minimum temperatures for a particular week.

To reference an element in a two-dimensional array, you must indicate both the row and the column that contain the element. You make these indications of row and column by writing two indexes, each enclosed in brackets. For example, *minTemps[1][51]* is the element in the 2nd row and the 52nd column. In the context of the temperature

In a two-dimensional array, the first index represents the row, the second index represents the column

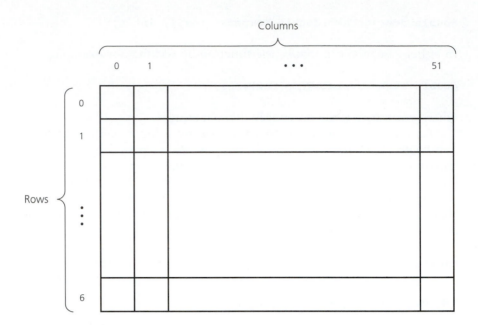

FIGURE A-7   A two-dimensional array

example, this element is the minimum temperature recorded for the 2nd day (Monday) of the 52nd week. The rules for the indexes of a one-dimensional array also apply to the indexes of multidimensional arrays.

As an example of how to use a two-dimensional array in a program, consider the following program segment, which determines the smallest value in the previously described array *minTemps*. We use enumerators to reference the days of the week.

```
enum Day {SUN, MON, TUES, WED, THURS, FRI, SAT};

// minTemps is a 2-dimensional array of daily minimum
// temperatures for 52 weeks, where each column of the
// array contains temperatures for one week.

// initially, assume the lowest temperature is
// first in the array
double lowestTemp = minTemps[0][0];
Day dayOfWeek = SUN;
int weekOfYear = 1;

// search array for lowest temperature
for (int weekIndex = 0; weekIndex < WEEKS_PER_YEAR;
                                    ++weekIndex)
    for (Day dayIndex = SUN; dayIndex <= SAT;
                    dayIndex = static_cast<Day>(dayIndex+1))
        if (lowestTemp > minTemps[dayIndex][weekIndex])
```

```
    {   lowestTemp = minTemps[dayIndex][weekIndex];
        dayOfWeek = dayIndex;
        weekOfYear = weekIndex+1;
    }   // end if, for
// Assertion: lowestTemp is the smallest value in
// minTemps and occurs on the day and week given by
// dayOfWeek and weekOfYear, that is, lowestTemp ==
// minTemps[dayOfWeek][weekOfYear-1].
```

It is entirely possible to declare *minTemps* as a one-dimensional array of 364 (7 * 52) elements, in which case you might use *minTemps[81]* instead of *minTemps[4][11]*. (Why? See Exercise 5 at the end of this appendix.) However, doing so will make your program harder to understand!

Although you can declare arrays with more than two dimensions, generally more than three dimensions is unusual. The techniques for working with such arrays, however, are analogous to those for two-dimensional arrays.

Initialization. You can initialize the elements of a two-dimensional array just as you initialize a one-dimensional array. You list the initial values row by row. For example, the statements

```
typedef int ArrayType[2][3];   // 2 rows, 3 columns
ArrayType x = {1,2,3,4,5,6};
```

initialize the two-dimensional array *x* so that it appears as

```
1   2   3

4   5   6
```

That is, the statements initialize the elements *x[0][0]*, *x[0][1]*, *x[0][2]*, *x[1][0]*, *x[1][1]*, and *x[1][2]* in that order. In general, when you assign initial values to a multidimensional array, it is the last, or rightmost, index that increases the fastest.

Arrays of Arrays

Consider again the daily minimum temperatures for 52 weeks. Instead of declaring a two-dimensional array to represent these temperatures, as was done previously, you could declare a one-dimensional array of 52 one-dimensional, 7-element arrays, as follows:

```
typedef double    WeekType[DAYS_PER_WEEK];
typedef WeekType  YearType[WEEKS_PER_YEAR];

YearType temps;
```

Here, *temps* is an array of arrays where *temps[11]*, for example, is an array of 7 temperatures for the 12th week. If it is useful to think about individual weeks, this organization is preferable to the previous two-dimensional array. For example, you could pass *temps[11]*, which is the data for week 12, to a function that calculates an average of the 7 temperatures in a one-dimensional array. (See Self-Test Exercise 7.)

You reference the temperature recorded for the 5th day of the 12th week by writing *temps[11][4]*; *temps[11]* is an array and *temps[11][4]* is its 5th component. C++ uses the same index notation for both an array of arrays and a two-dimensional array. In fact, C++ represents an array of arrays and a two-dimensional array in the same way. Even so, your choice of data structure should reflect your algorithm. Thus, if you will consider individual days rather than individual weeks, for example, you might prefer thinking of it as a two-dimensional array rather than as an array of arrays.

Initialization. You can initialize the elements of an array of arrays just as you initialize a multidimensional array. Given the definitions

```
typedef int       VectorType[3];
typedef VectorType ArrayType[2];
```

the statement

```
ArrayType x = {{1,2,3},{4,5,6}};
```

initializes the array *x[0]* to *{1,2,3}* and the array *x[1]* to *{4,5,6}*. The statement

```
ArrayType x = {1,2,3,4,5,6};
```

has the same effect, because the previous *typedef* statements have the same effect as

```
typedef int ArrayType[2][3];
```

A.7 Strings

Earlier, you saw that C++ provides literal character strings such as

```
"This is a string."
```

This section describes how you can create and use variables that contain such strings. C++ now provides a string data type that allows you to manipulate strings as naturally as you manipulate integers, by using familiar operators. C, which is a subset of C++, represents a string by using a one-dimensional array of characters. If we need to distinguish between

An array of arrays has the same representation and index notation as a multidimensional array

the two kinds of strings, we will use the terminology "C++ string" and "C string."

Our presentation includes only some of the possible operations on strings.

C++ Strings

The C++ Standard Library provides the data type *string*. With it, you can declare and use variables that contain strings. To use this library, you include the statements

```
#include <string>
using namespace std;
```

in your program.

You can declare a string variable *title* and initialize it to the empty string by writing

```
string title;
```

You can initialize a string variable to a string literal when you declare it by writing

```
string title = "Walls and Mirrors";
```

You can subsequently assign another string to *title* by using an assignment statement such as

```
title = "J Perfect's Diary";
```

In each of the previous examples, *title* has a length of 17. You use either of the functions *length* or *size* to determine the current length of a string. Thus, *title.length()* and *title.size()* are each 17.

You can reference the individual characters in a string by using the same index notation that you use for an array. Thus in the previous example, *title[0]* contains the character *J* and *title[16]* contains the character *y*.

You can compare strings by using the familiar comparison operators. Not only can you determine whether two strings are equal, but you can also determine which of two strings comes before the other. The ordering of two strings is analogous to alphabetic ordering, but you use the ASCII table instead of the alphabet. Thus, the following relationships are all true:

```
"dig" < "dog"
"Star" < "star"   (because 'S' < 's')
"start" > "star"
"d" > "abc"
```
Examples of true expressions

You can concatenate two strings to form another string by using the + operator. That is, you place one string after another to form another string. For example, if

```
string str1 = "Com";
```

the statements

```
string str2 = str1 + "puter";
str1 += "puter";
```

assign the string *"Computer"* to each of *str2* and *str1*. Similarly, you can append a single character to a string, as in

```
str1 += 's';
```

You can manipulate a portion of a string by using the function

Use *substr* to access part of a string

```
substr(position, length)
```

The first argument specifies the position of the beginning of the substring (remember that 0 is the position of the first character in the string). The second argument is the length of the substring. For example,

```
title.substr(2, 7)
```

is the string *"Perfect"*.

To perform input and output with C++ strings, you must use the modern version of *iostream*. To use this library, you include the statements

```
#include <iostream>
using namespace std;
```

in your program. This version of the iostream library works in much the same way as the old style library *iostream.h*. So just as you can use << to display a literal string, so can you display the contents of a string variable. For example,

You can use << to display a string

```
title = "Walls and Mirrors";
cout << "\"" << title << "\"\n";
```

writes *"Walls and Mirrors"*. Note the use of the special character \" within the literal strings to produce quotation marks in the output. The operator << writes the entire string, including the blanks.

You can read a string of characters into a string variable. When the statement

You can use >> to read a string without whitespace

```
cin >> title;
```

reads the data line

```
Jamie Perfect's Diary
```

it assigns the string `"Jamie"` to `title`. Whitespace in the input line terminates the read operation for a string. If you want to read a string that contains whitespace, use the function `getline(cin, title)`.

C Strings

You can represent a string by using a one-dimensional array of characters that is terminated by the null character `\0`, which has a value of zero. Thus, the array that represents the string `"abc"` actually contains four characters, not three. This use of the null character as a sentinel makes possible a library of standard functions that manipulate strings. To use this library, you include the statement

An array of characters that ends with a null character is a string

```
#include <cstring>
```

in your program. This section will demonstrate several functions in this library.

You can declare variables that will contain C strings, as follows:

```
const int MAX_LENGTH = 30;
typedef char StringType[MAX_LENGTH+1];

StringType title;
```

The variable `title` is an array of characters that you can treat as a string. Although you must allow for the terminating null character when you declare a string, it is convenient to ignore it when speaking of a string's length. Thus, the string `title` has a maximum length of `MAX_LENGTH`, even though the array `title` has `MAX_LENGTH` + 1 components. A string's maximum length is established at compilation time and, therefore, remains fixed. String variables also have a current length, which is the number of characters currently in the string, excluding the null character. A string's current length is dynamic—it changes as the string changes—and can range from a minimum of zero characters (the empty, or null, string) to the string's maximum length.

You can initialize a string variable when you declare it by assigning a string literal to it, as in

```
StringType title = "Walls and Mirrors";
```

You can use this syntax only when you declare the variable. If later you want to assign a new value to `title`, you must use the standard function `strcpy`, as in

```
strcpy(title, "J Perfect's Diary");
```

This function replaces the contents of its first argument with the contents of its second argument, assuming that the current length of the second argument does not exceed the maximum length of the first argument.

In each of the previous examples, *title* has a current length of 17. You use the standard function *strlen* to determine the current length of a string. Thus, *strlen(title)* is 17.

You can reference the individual characters in a string by using the same index notation that you use for an array. Thus, *title[0]* in the previous example contains the character *J*. Also, note that *title[17]* contains the null character *\0*.

You can compare strings by using the standard *int* function *strcmp*. Not only can you determine whether two strings are equal, but you can also determine which of two strings comes before the other. The ordering of two strings is analogous to alphabetic ordering, but you use the ASCII table instead of the alphabet. Thus, the following relationships are all true:

Examples of true expressions

```
"dig" < "dog"
"Star" < "star"    (because 'S' < 's')
"start" > "star"
"d" > "abc"
```

Use *strcmp* to compare strings

The function *strcmp(string₁, string₂)* returns an integer value that is

< 0 if *string₁* is less than *string₂*

= 0 if *string₁* and *string₂* are equal

> 0 if *string₁* is greater than *string₂*

You can concatenate two strings to form another string by using the standard function *strcat(string₁, string₂)*, which appends a copy of *string₂* to the end of *string₁* and returns the new *string₁*. For example, if

```
StringType str = "Com";
```

Use *strcat* to concatenate strings

the expression

```
strcat(str, "puter")
```

returns the string *"Computer"* and also assigns it to *str*. You need to ensure that the maximum length of *string₁* can accommodate the new string. In this example, the previous definition of *StringType* indicates that the maximum length of *str* is 30, which is ample.

Now, if *str2* is another variable of type *StringType*,

Use *strcpy* to assign one string to another

```
strcpy(str2, strcat(str, "s"));
```

assigns the string `"Computers"` to each of the strings `str` and `str2`. Notice the use of the one-character string `"s"` instead of the character constant `'s'`.

The following standard functions manipulate portions of strings. The function

strncmp(*string₁*, *string₂*, *count*)

behaves like `strcmp` but examines no more than the first *count* characters. The function

strncat(*string₁*, *string₂*, *count*)

appends a copy of no more than the first *count* characters of *string₂* to the end of *string₁* and then appends the null character `\0`. Because `strncat` appends a null character, you can append a character to a string. For example, if `ch` is a `char` variable, the expression

strncat(str, &ch, 1)

appends the character in `ch` to the end of the string `str` and returns this new string.

Just as you can use `<<` to display a literal string, so can you display the contents of a string variable. For example,

```
strcpy(title, "Walls and Mirrors");
cout << "\"" << title << "\"\n";
```

writes `"Walls and Mirrors"`. Note the use of the special character `\"` within the literal strings to produce quotation marks in the output. The operator `<<` writes characters until it detects the null character in the string, so the blanks in the title are written.

You can display part or all of a string by using the *write* function, as follows:

```
cout.write(title, 5);       // writes Walls
cout.write(&title[5], 12);  // writes ∆and∆Mirrors
```

Here, ∆ represents a space. The second statement places its output immediately after the output of the first statement and on the same line.

You can read a string of characters into a string variable. When the statement

```
cin >> title;
```

reads the data line

```
Jamie Perfect's Diary
```

getline, *get*, and *read* read strings that contain whitespace

it assigns the string *"Jamie"* to *title*. Whitespace in the input line terminates the read operation for a string. If you want to read whitespace, you can use one of the functions *getline*, *get*, or *read*, as follows:

- *cin.getline(s, count)* reads at most *count* – 1 characters into the string *s*. If the input line contains no more than *count* – 1 characters followed by a carriage return, *s* will contain the characters followed by \0. The carriage return will not be in *s*, but will be flushed from the input stream so that a subsequent read will not encounter it.

  If the input line contains more than *count* – 1 characters followed by a carriage return, *s* will contain *count* – 1 characters followed by \0. A subsequent read operation will encounter the characters that remain in the input line.

- *cin.get(s, count)* behaves like *getline*, but leaves the carriage return in the input line for a subsequent read operation to process.

- *cin.read(s, count)* reads *count* characters into the string *s*, but does not place \0 after the characters.

Three other functions are useful when processing characters or strings:

- *cin.peek()* returns the next character encountered in the input stream. The character, however, remains in the input stream and can be read again.

- *cin.ignore(n)* skips *n* characters in the input stream.

- *cin.ignore(n, ch)* either skips *n* characters in the input stream or skips characters until *ch* is skipped, whichever comes first.

- *cin.putback(ch)* places the character *ch* into the input stream so that it will be the next character read.

A.8 Structures

A structure is a group of related items of possibly different data types

Whereas an array is a collection of elements that are all of the same data type, a C++ structure is a group of related items that are not necessarily of the same data type. Each item in a structure is called a **member**. Although technically members can be either data or functions, structures typically contain only data members.[8]

A structure that describes you might contain your name, your age, and your grade point average. The following statements describe such a structure:

---

[8] Structures can, and often do, contain special member functions called constructors. Chapter 3 discusses constructors in the context of C++ classes.

```
struct Person
{  string name;
   int     age;
   double gpa;
}; // end struct
```

A semicolon follows the
closing brace of a structure
definition

The data members of this structure are *name*, *age*, and *gpa*. Notice the semicolon after the last brace.

You can use the data type *Person*—called an **aggregate data type**—to declare a structure *student*, as follows:

```
Person student;
```

This declaration does not initialize the data members associated with *student*.

You can initialize the data members of a structure much as you initialize an array. For example, you can replace the previous declaration with

```
Person student = {"Jamie Perfect", 21, 4.0};
```

Figure A-8 illustrates *student* after this initialization.

To reference the members within a particular structure, you **qualify** the member name by preceding it with the name of that structure and a dot operator—that is, a period. For example, the second data member in the structure *student* is

```
student.age
```

and the third letter in the first data member of *student* is

```
student.name[2]
```

You can make a copy of an entire structure by using the assignment operator. Thus, the following statement copies the structure *student* into a previously declared structure *studentCopy*:

```
studentCopy = student;
```

You can assign one structure
to another

student.name	student.age	student.gpa
Jamie Perfect	21	4.0

FIGURE A-8   The structure *student*

You can also pass a structure as an argument to a function. If the argument is a value argument, a copy of the structure is made. Finally, a valued function can return a structure as its result.

Structures Within Structures

A data member of a structure can be another structure

Sometimes it is desirable for a data member of a structure to be itself a structure. For example, suppose that you want the previous structure to contain an address. It is convenient to represent an address as a structure with data members such as house number, street, city, state, and zip code. The following definitions and declarations include these changes to *Person*:

```
struct Addr
{  int    number;
   string street;
   string city;
   string state;
   string zip;
};  // end struct

struct Person
{  string name;
   int    age;
   double gpa;
   Addr   address;
};  // end struct

Person student;
```

Note the order of the structure definitions: The definition of *Addr* must precede its use in *Person*. Now *student.address.zip*, for example, is *student*'s zip code.

Arrays of Structures

Given the structures *Addr* and *Person*, suppose that a teacher wants a structure for each student in a group of no more than *MAX_STUDENTS* students, where *MAX_STUDENTS* is a named constant. You can add the statements

```
typedef Person GroupType[MAX_STUDENTS];
GroupType csc212;
```

to the previous statements. The array *csc212* contains structures, and the following examples demonstrate how to reference this array:

csc212[9].name is the name of the 10th student in the array.
csc212[9].name[0] is the first letter in the 10th student's name.
csc212[9].address.state is the state in the 10th student's

A.9 C++ Exceptions

An exception is a mechanism used in C++ and other programming languages for handling errors. When an error occurs during execution of a function, the function can throw an exception. It can then deal with the error condition by catching the exception and executing appropriate code. Chapter 3 contains a basic explanation of the use of exceptions. This section elaborates on that discussion.

You may already have seen exceptions when you used some of the methods from the C++ Standard Library. For example, when an argument to a function is not in the required range, an *out_of_range* exception is thrown.

Catching Exceptions

To handle exceptions, C++ provides *try-catch* blocks. You place statements that might cause an exception within a *try* block. The *try* block must be followed by one or more *catch* blocks. Each *catch* block indicates the type of exception you want to handle. A *try* block can have many *catch* blocks associated with it, since even a single statement might cause more than one type of exception. A *try* block can also contain many statements, any of which might throw an exception. Here is the general syntax for a *try* block:

```
try
{    statement(s);
}
```

and here is the syntax for a *catch* block:

```
catch (ExceptionClass identifier)
{    statement(s);
}
```

When a statement in a *try* block causes an exception, the remainder of the *try* block is abandoned, and control passes to the statements in the *catch* block that corresponds to the type of exception thrown. The statements in the *catch* block then execute and, on completion of the *catch* block, execution resumes at the point following the last *catch* block. If an exception has no applicable *catch* block, abnormal program termination usually occurs.

Note that if an exception occurs in the middle of a *try* block, the destructors of all objects local to that block are called. This ensures that all resources allocated in that block are released, even if the block is not completely executed.

The compiler determines which *catch* block to use by iterating through the *catch* clauses in the order that they appear and using the first one that produces a legal assignment of the thrown exception and the argument specified in the *catch* clause. Thus, the *catch* clauses must be ordered so that the most specific exception classes appear before the more general exception classes; otherwise, the code will not compile. For example,

```cpp
string str = "Sarah";
try
{   str.substr(99, 1);
    // other statements appear here
}  // end try
catch (exception e)
{   cout << "Something else was caught" << endl;
}  // end catch
catch (out_of_range e)
{   cout << "out_of_range exception caught" << endl;
}  // end catch
```

compiles with the following warning message:

```
TestExceptionExample.cpp(11) : warning C4286:
'class std::out_of_range' : is caught by base class ('class
exception') on line 8


Linking . . .
```

To get the code to compile without warnings, you must interchange the two *catch* clauses.

The following program demonstrates what happens when an exception is thrown and not caught. The program encodes a string by doing a simple substitution. You replace each letter in the original string by the character that appears three positions later in the alphabet. When you reach the end of the alphabet, you wrap around to the beginning. For example, 'a' is replaced with 'd', 'b' is replaced with 'e', and 'x' is replaced with 'a'. Figure A-9 shows the flow of control when an exception occurs in this code.

```cpp
#include <iostream>
#include <string>
using namespace std;
```

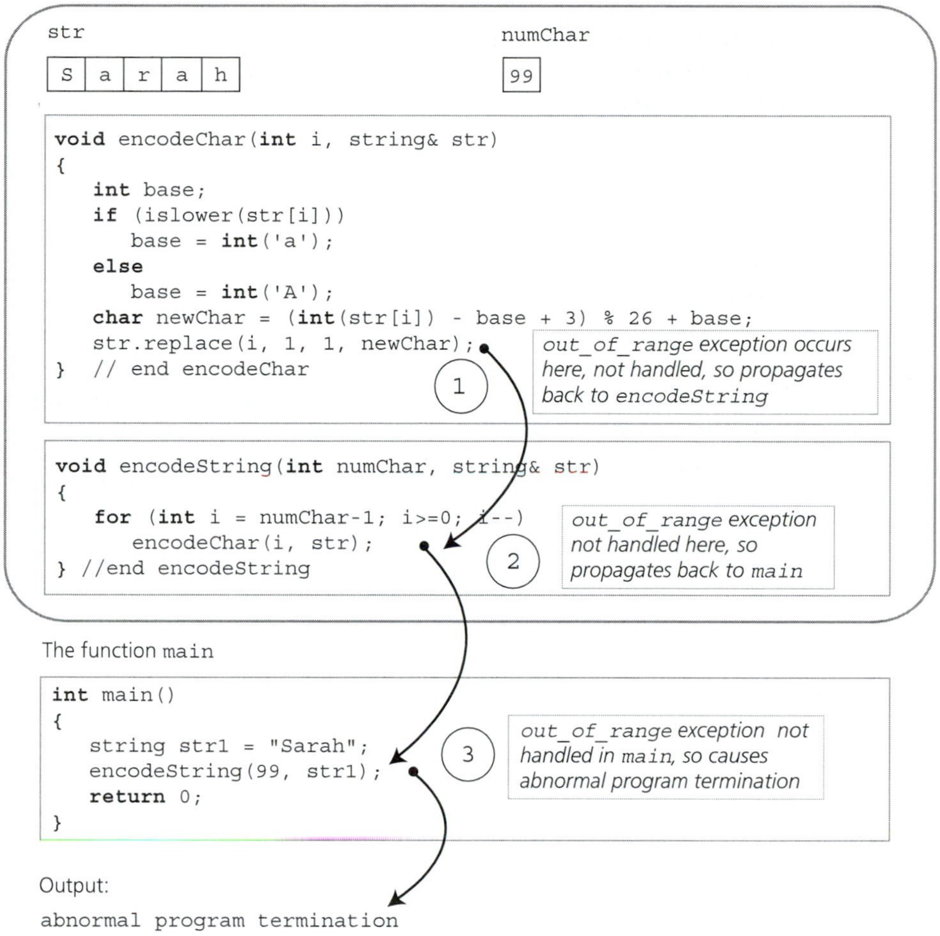

FIGURE A-9   Flow of control for an unhandled exception

```cpp
void encodeChar(int i, string& str)
{
   int base;
   if (islower(str[i]))
      base = int('a');
   else
      base = int('A');
   char newChar = (int(str[i]) - base + 3) % 26 + base;
   str.replace(i, 1, 1, newChar);
} // end encodeChar

void encodeString(int numChar, string& str)
```

```
{
   for (int i = numChar-1; i >= 0; i--)
      encodeChar(i, str);
} //end encodeString

int main()
{
   string str1 = "Sarah";
   encodeString(99, str1);
   return 0;
} // end main
```

The method *encodeChar* actually causes the *out_of_range* exception to be thrown when it attempts to access the 99th character in *str* with the function call *str.replace(99, 1, 1, newChar)*. Since *encode-Char* does not handle the exception, the function is terminated and the exception propagated back to *encodeString* at the point where *encode-Char* was called. The function *encodeString* also does not handle the exception, so it too is terminated and the exception propagated back to *main*. Since *main* is the main function of the program, and the exception is not handled in *main*, the program terminates with an error message indicating that the program has terminated abnormally.

This code contains no indication that the function *encodeChar* could throw the exception *out_of_range*. However, the documentation of *encodeChar* should indicate any exceptions it might throw. Thus, when documenting a function, as described in Chapter 1, you should also include any possible exceptions that could occur.

The exception *out_of_range* could be caught at any point in the sequence of function calls. For example, we could rewrite the function *encodeChar* as follows to catch the exception:

```
void encodeChar(int i, string& str)
{
   int base;
   if (islower(str[i]))
      base = int('a');
   else
      base = int('A');
   try
   {
      char newChar = (int(str[i]) - base + 3) % 26 + base;
      str.replace(i, 1, 1, newChar);
   }  // end try
   catch (out_of_range e)
   {
      cout << "No character at position " << i << endl;
   }  // end catch
} // end encodeChar
```

This version of *encodeChar* produces the following output:

```
No character at position 99
No character at position 98
No character at position 97

. . .
```

The function *encodeString* calls *encodeChar* 99 times, with the call *encodeString(99, str)*, and hence the exception is thrown 98-*str.length()* times. When the exception was not handled, the program terminated the first time the exception occurred. Handling the exception allows the code to continue execution.

Although the *out_of_range* exception is thrown in the *encodeChar* function, that is not necessarily the best place to handle the exception. For example, if the client had made the call *encodeString(10000, str)*, the message printed by *encodeChar* would have appeared 9999-*str.length()* times! In this case it makes more sense for the *try-catch* blocks to appear in the *encodeString* function and not in the *encodeChar* function. This means that *encodeChar* no longer handles the exception but propagates it back to *encodeString*. Here is the code for *encodeString* when it handles the exception:

```cpp
void encodeString(int numChar, string& str)
{   try
    {
        for (int i = numChar-1; i >= 0; i--)
            encodeChar(i, str);
    }  // end try
    catch (out_of_range e)
    {
        cout << "The string does not contain " << numChar ;
        cout << " characters." << endl;
        cout << e.what();
    }  // end catch
}  // end encodeString
```

This function produces the following output:

```
The string does not contain 10 characters.
invalid string position
```

Now when *encodeChar* throws the exception *out-of-range*, it is propagated back to *encodeString*. The function *encodeString* abandons execution of the statements in the *try* block, executes the statement in the *catch* block, and resumes execution after the last *catch* block. The message is printed only once, since the *for* loop is inside the *try* block, which is abandoned when the exception occurs. If the *try* block had been placed inside the *for* loop (surrounding the call to *encodeChar*), the exception would be thrown and handled at each iteration of the loop, causing the message to be printed multiple times.

The *catch* block also contains the function call *e.what()*. Recall that each *catch* block specifies the type of exception it will handle and an identifier. This identifier provides a name for the caught exception that can be used within the *catch* block. In this case, the function *what* for the exception *e* is called. The function *what* returns a pointer to a C string (terminated by the null character *\0*) that describes the exception. It is available for all exceptions defined in the Standard Library.

The header *<stdexcept>* defines several standard exceptions that can be thrown by the functions defined in the C++ Standard Library. This header contains two kinds of exceptions: runtime exceptions and logic exceptions. The runtime exceptions are as follows:

overflow_error	Arithmetic overflow has occurred
range_error	A range error has occurred
underflow_error	Arithmetic underflow has occurred

The logic exceptions are as follows:

domain_error	A domain error has occurred
invalid_argument	An invalid argument was used in a function call
length_error	An attempt was made to create an object that was too large
out_of_range	An argument to a function had a value that was not in the appropriate range

Throwing Exceptions

A function can indicate an error situation by throwing an exception. You throw an exception by executing a statement with the following form:

Use a throw statement to throw an exception

```
throw ExceptionClass(stringArgument);
```

Here *ExceptionClass* is the type of exception you want to throw, and *stringArgument* is an argument to the *ExceptionClass* constructor that provides a more detailed description of what may have caused the exception. When a *throw* statement executes, the remaining code within the function does not execute, and the exception is propagated back to the point where the function was called.

To restrict the exceptions that a function can throw, you include a *throw* clause in the function's header. A *throw* clause consists of the keyword *throw* followed by a list of exception types separated by commas and enclosed within parentheses. For example, the following function declares that it can throw the exceptions *BadDataException* and *MyException*:

```
void myFunction(int x)
                throw(BadDataException, MyException)
{
   if (x == MAX)
      throw BadDataException("BadDataException: reason");
   // some code here
   ...
   throw MyException("MyException: reason");
}  // end myFunction
```

A function whose code can throw exceptions

Including a *throw* clause in the function header insures that the function can throw only those exceptions. An attempt to throw any other exception will result in a runtime error. Omitting a *throw* clause allows a function to throw any exception.

You may find that the C++ Standard Library has an exception class already defined that will suit the exception needs of your program. For example, in our design of the ADT list in Chapter 3, we throw an exception when an index value is out of range. The C++ Standard Library has an exception *out_of_range* that you can use in this case. You will need to use the *std* namespace to use the exception classes within this library.

The C++ exception class *exception*, or one of its derived classes, is the base class for other exception classes. This provides a standardized interface for working with exceptions. In particular, all of the exceptions in the C++ Standard Library have a member function *what* that returns a message describing the exception. This function is useful within a *catch* clause.

You may also want to define your own exception class that you base on the standard class *exception*. You will need to use the *std* namespace in this case, too. An exception class typically consists of a constructor that has a string parameter. For example, you can define the class *MyException* as follows:

You can define your own exception class

```
#include <exception>
#include <string>
using namespace std;
class MyException : public exception
{
public:
   MyException(const string & Message = "")
             : exception(Message.c_str())
   { }
};  // end class
```

The constructor provides a way for a *throw* statement to identify the condition that caused the exception. For example:

```
throw MyException("MyException: Provide a reason");
```

invokes the constructor of *MyException*. The message given to the constructor is returned by the function *what* that is inherited from the class *exception*. Thus, a *catch* clause can access the message, as in the following example:

```
try
{  if (size > max)
        throw MyException("MyException: Size exceeded maximum");
}  // end try
catch (MyException e)
{  cout << e.what();
}  // end catch
```

A.10 File Input and Output

You have used **files** ever since you wrote your first program. In fact, your C++ source program is in a file that you probably created by using a text editor. You can create and access such files outside of and independently of any particular program. Files can also contain data that is either read or written by your program. It is this type of file that concerns us here.

A file is a *sequence* of components of the same data type that resides in auxiliary storage, often a disk. Files are useful because they can be large and can exist after program execution terminates. In contrast, variables of fundamental data types, for example, represent memory that is accessible only within the program that creates them. When program execution terminates, the operating system reuses this memory and changes its contents.

Since files can exist after program execution, they not only provide a permanent record for human users, they also allow communication between programs. Program *A* can write its output into a file that program *B* can use later for input. However, files that you discard after program execution are not unusual. You use such a file as a scratch pad during program execution when you have too much data to retain conveniently in memory all at once.

It is useful to contrast files with their closest C++ relatives, arrays. Files and arrays are similar in that they are both collections of components of the same type. For example, just as you can have an array of elements whose type is *char*, so also can you have a file of elements whose type is *char*. In both cases, the components are characters. However, in addition to the previous distinction between files and all

A file is a sequence of components of the same data type

other data types—files can exist after program execution and arrays cannot—files and arrays have two other differences:

- **Files grow in size as needed; arrays have a fixed size.** When you declare an array, you specify its maximum size. Thus, a fixed amount of memory represents the array. A well-written program always checks that an array can accommodate a new piece of data before attempting to insert it. If the array cannot accommodate the data, the program might have to terminate with a message of explanation. You can increase the array size—hopefully by changing the value of a named constant—and compile and run the program again.[9] On the other hand, if you declare the array's maximum size to be larger than you need, you waste memory. In contrast, the size of a file is not fixed. When the system first creates a file, the file requires almost no storage space. As a program adds data to the file, the file's size increases as necessary, up to the limit of the storage device. Thus, at any given time, the file occupies only as much space as it actually requires. This dynamic nature is a great advantage.

- **Files provide both sequential and direct access; arrays provide direct access.** If you want the 100th element in the one-dimensional array *anArray*, you can access it directly by writing *anArray[99]*; you do not need to look at the elements *anArray[0]* through *anArray[98]* first. You could choose, of course, to process an array's elements sequentially, but you would do so by accessing each successive element directly and independently of any other element.

  However, you can access elements in a file either directly or sequentially. If you want the 100th element in a file, you can access it directly by position without first reading past the 99 elements that precede it. On the other hand, you could read all of the first 100 elements one at a time, in sequential order, without specifying any element's position.

Files are classified as follows. A **text file** is a file of characters that are organized into lines. The files that you create—by using an editor—to contain your C++ programs are text files. Because text files consist of characters and accessing characters by position number is usually not convenient, you typically process a text file sequentially. A file that is not a text file is called a **binary file** or sometimes a **general file** or a **nontext file**.

---

[9] Chapter 4 describes dynamically allocated arrays. If you reach the end of such an array, you can increase its size during execution. However, this process requires copying the old array into the new array.

Text Files

Text files are designed for easy communication with people. As such, text files are flexible and easy to use, but they are not as efficient with respect to computer time and storage as binary files.

One special aspect of text files is that they *appear* to be divided into lines. This illusion is often the source of much confusion. In reality, a text file—like any other file—is a sequence of components of the same type. That is, a text file is a sequence of characters. A special end-of-line symbol creates the illusion that a text file contains lines by making the file *behave* as if it were divided into lines.

When you create a text file by typing data at your keyboard, each time you press the Enter, or Return, key, you insert one end-of-line symbol into the file. When an output device, such as a printer or monitor, encounters an end-of-line symbol in a text file, the device moves to the beginning of the next line. In C++, this end-of-line symbol is the character \n.

In addition, you can think of a special end-of-file symbol that follows the last component in a file. Such a symbol may or may not actually exist in the file, but C++ behaves as if one did. The predefined constant *EOF* represents this symbol within your program. This book assumes that all text files—including the empty file—end with both an end-of-line symbol and an end-of-file symbol. Figure A-10 depicts a text file with these special symbols.

Any program that uses files must access the standard C++ file stream library. You enable this access by including the following statements in your program:

```
#include <fstream>
using namespace std;
```

The C++ file stream library provides three stream types: *ifstream* for input file streams, *ofstream* for output file streams, and *fstream* for file streams that are for both input and output. You use a stream variable of one of these types to access a file.

A text file contains lines of characters

Files end with a special end-of-file symbol

Use a stream variable to access a file

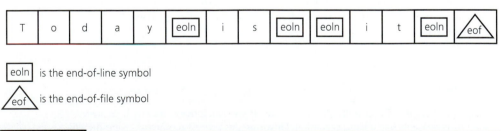

| eoln | is the end-of-line symbol |
| eof | is the end-of-file symbol |

FIGURE A-10   A text file with end-of-line and end-of-file symbols

Opening a file. Before you can read from or write to a file, you need to **open** it. That is, you need to initialize the file and associate its name with a stream variable. One way to open a file is to provide the file's name when you declare the file variable. For example,

```
ifstream inFile("Ages.DAT");   // input file
```

declares an input stream variable *inFile* and associates it with the file named *Ages.DAT*. The file name can be a literal constant, as it is here, or a string variable.

Alternatively, you can declare an input stream variable by writing

```
ifstream inFile;
```

and then later use the *open* function to associate it with the file's name:

```
inFile.open("Ages.DAT");
```

Regardless of how you open a file, you can check the stream variable to see if the process was successful by writing

```
if (!inFile)
   ProcessError();   // open was unsuccessful
```

Associated with each file in a program is a **file window**, which marks the current position within the file. Opening a file positions the file window over the first component in the file, as Figure A-11 illustrates. Because each component in a text file is a character, the file window for a text file moves from character to character. The following sections describe the behavior of the file window.

Character input. Suppose that you have declared an input stream variable *inFile* and associated it with the name of the text file by writing

```
ifstream inFile(fileName);
```

where *fileName* is a string variable. When you use a file for input, the file window is over the component that you will read next. Thus, after

You must initialize, or open, a file before you can use it

You can check whether a file was opened successfully

A file window marks the current position within a file

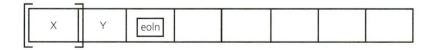

FIGURE A-11 The effect on the file window of opening an existing text file for input

you open a file, you are ready to read the first component, as you saw in Figure A-11. As you read the characters from a text file, the file window advances sequentially from one character to another. After reading several characters, you will see the file window shown in Figure A-12.

The input operator >> and functions such as *get*, whose use with *cin* was described earlier in this appendix, are also used with files. For the character variable *ch* and the stream variable *inFile*, either of the statements

```
inFile >> ch;
```

or

```
inFile.get(ch);
```

means

```
ch = the value at the file window
Advance the file window to the next component
```

as Figure A-13 illustrates.

If desired, you can also accomplish each of these actions separately. You can assign the current value at the file window to *ch*, without advancing the file window, by writing

```
ch = inFile.peek();
```

You can ignore the current value at the file window and simply advance the file window over the next *n* characters by writing

```
inFile.ignore(n);
```

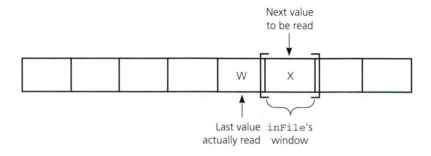

FIGURE A-12   A file window over the component to be read next

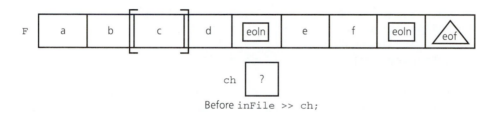

Before inFile >> ch;

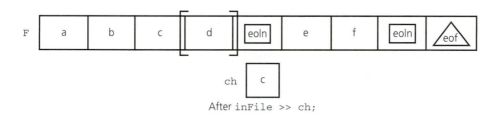

After inFile >> ch;

FIGURE A-13   The effect of *inFile* >> *ch* on a text file *inFile*

You can advance the file window either just beyond the next occurrence of a given character *ch* or over the next *n* characters, whichever occurs first, by writing

```
inFile.ignore(n, ch);
```

You can detect when the file window has reached either the end of a line or the end of the file by using the *peek* function. For example, the loop

```
while (inFile.peek() != '\n')  // loop until end of line
cout.put(inFile.get());
```

displays a line of a text file, and the loop

```
while (inFile.peek() != EOF)  // loop until end of file
cout.put(inFile.get());
```

displays the contents of an entire text file.

To summarize, consider the text file *inFile* that appears in Figure A-14. If *ch* is a character variable, the statements in the following sequence assign values to *ch* as indicated:

```
ifstream.inFile(fileName);
inFile >> ch;          // ch = 'a'
inFile.get(ch);        // ch = 'b'
ch = inFile.get();     // ch = 'c'
```

```
inFile.ignore(10, '\n');// skip 'd' and end-of-line symbol
inFile.get(ch);          // ch = 'e'
ch = inFile.peek();      // ch = 'f'
inFile.get(ch);          // ch = 'f'
inFile.get(ch);          // ch = '\n'
inFile.ignore(1);        // skip end-of-file symbol
inFile.get(ch);          // error: attempted read beyond
                         // end of file
```

You also can read the characters in the file as strings by using *get-line*, *get*, and *read* in the same way that you used them with *cin*.

Character output. Suppose that you have declared an output stream variable *outFile* and associated it with the name of the text file, as in

```
ofstream outFile(fileName);
```

If you are creating a new file, the file window will be positioned at the beginning (and the end) of the new file, which is empty. If the file already exists, opening it erases[10] the data in the file and positions the window at the beginning (and the end) of the now empty file.

The output operator << and functions such as *put*, whose use with *cout* was described earlier in this appendix, are also used with files. For the character variable *ch* and the file variable *outFile*, either of the statements

```
outFile << ch;
```

or

```
outFile.put(ch);
```

means

```
Write the value of ch at the file-window position
Advance the file window
```

Figure A-14 illustrates these steps when *ch* contains the character *X*. Note that if *ch* contains \n, either of the previous statements writes the end-of-line symbol to the file.

You can also write strings to a text file by using either << or the function *write*, as described in the section "Strings."

Closing a file. You close a particular file—that is, disassociate it from a stream variable *myFile*—by using the *close* function:

---

[10] The data might not actually be erased, but the file will behave as if it were empty.

```
myFile.close();
```

Such a file is no longer available for input or output until you open it again.

Numeric data within text files. As you know, you can read integer and floating-point values from the standard input stream into variables with arithmetic data types. You also know that the standard input stream is a sequence of characters. Likewise, a text file is a sequence of characters, so it should not surprise you that integer and floating-point values can be read from and written to a text file. Although this presentation uses *int* values to illustrate the concepts, the other arithmetic data types follow by analogy.

When your program reads from a text file into an *int* variable, the system expects a sequence of characters that it can convert into an integer. For example, if the text file contains the character sequence *2, 3, 4* and if you read from the text file into the *int* variable *x*, the system will convert these three characters into the computer's internal representation for the integer 234 and assign this value to *x*. More precisely, the text file contains the ASCII codes for the characters *2, 3*, and *4*— which are, respectively, the decimal values 50, 51, and 52. However, these codes appear in the file in binary, as Figure A-15a indicates. If you read those characters into the integer variable *x*, *x* will contain the computer's internal representation for the integer 234, which appears in binary as shown in Figure A-15b. Thus, the representation of digits in a text file differs from the representation in memory of the number that those digits symbolize.

To summarize, if *inFile* is an input stream variable that is associated with a text file of valid integers, and *x* is an *int* variable, the statement

```
inFile >> x;
```

has the following effect:

Skip to the first nonblank character
Convert into an integer the sequence of characters
  that begins at the current position of inFile's
  window and ends just before the next character c
  that is not a digit

Before `outFile << ch;`   After `outFile << ch;`

FIGURE A-14 The effect of *outFile* << *ch* on a text file *outFile* when *ch* contains the character *X*

(a)   Text file

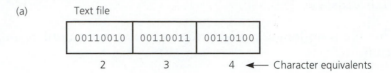

| 00110010 | 00110011 | 00110100 |

   2   3   4 ← Character equivalents

(b)   x

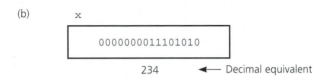

| 0000000011101010 |

234   ← Decimal equivalent

FIGURE A-15   (a) The ASCII characters 2, 3, and 4 represented in binary in a text file; (b) the internal binary representation of the integer 234

Assign this integer value to x
Advance the file window so that it is over the
*   character c*

Figure A-16 illustrates these steps. Observe that if the sequence begins with a character other than +, −, or 0 through 9, reading will terminate. For example, the system cannot convert the sequence *w123* into an integer. It will, however, read the integer 123 from the sequence *123wrt*.

When your program writes an integer value such as 234 to a text file, the system first converts the integer from the computer's internal

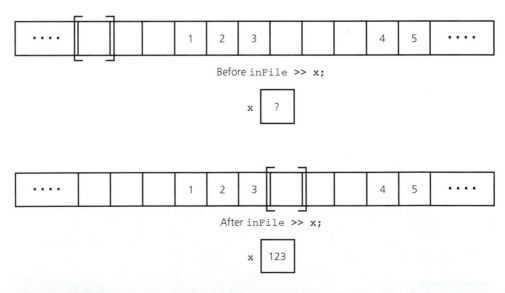

Before inFile >> x;

x ?

After inFile >> x;

x 123

FIGURE A-16   Reading an integer from a text file

binary representation (0000000011101010) to the character sequence
2, *3*, *4* and then writes these characters to the file. For the output
stream variable *outFile* and the integer variable *x*, the statement

```
outFile << x;
```

has the following effect:

Convert the value of x into a sequence of characters
Append this sequence of characters to the file
Position the file window just past the last character
  written

The following function reads and displays the contents of an entire
text file of integers:

```
void echoFile(string fileName)
{
    ifstream inFile(fileName);
    int x;

    while (inFile >> x)  // read to end of file
        cout << x << " ";
    cout << endl;

    inFile.close();
}   // end echoFile
```

The function ignores the end-of-line symbols in the file and displays
the integers all on one line.

Suppose that you want to display each line in the file. If each line of
the file contains the same number of integers, the solution is simple.
For example, if the file contains three integers per line and if *x*, *y*, and *z*
are integer variables, you could replace the previous *while* loop with

```
    while (inFile >> x >> y >> z)
        cout << x << " " << y << " " << z << endl;
```

Another solution that works regardless of the number of integers
per line is to use the *peek* and *ignore* functions. Thus, you can revise
the previous function as follows. Note that you always pass a file variable to a function as a reference argument.

```
void skipBlanks(ifstream& inFile)
// Skips blanks in a text file.
{
    while (inFile.peek() == ' ')
        inFile.ignore(1);
```

```
}   // end skipBlanks

void echoLine(ifstream& inFile)
// Displays one line of a text file.
{
   int x;

   while (inFile.peek() != '\n')
   {  inFile >> x;
      skipBlanks(inFile);
      cout << x << " ";
   }   // end while

   cout << "\n";
   inFile.ignore(1);   // advance beyond \n
}   // end echoLine

void echoFile(string fileName)
// Displays the contents of a text file.
{
   ifstream inFile(fileName);

   skipBlanks(inFile);
   while (inFile.peek() != EOF)
      echoLine(inFile);

   inFile.close();
}   // end echoFile
```

Copying a text file. Suppose that you wanted to make a copy of the
text file associated with the stream variable *originalFile*. Copying a
text file requires some work and provides a good example of the statements you have just studied. The approach taken by the following function copies the file one character at a time, taking into account both
the end-of-line symbols and the end-of-file symbol:

```
void copyTextFile(string originalFileName,
                  string copyFileName)
// -----------------------------------------------------------
// Makes a duplicate copy of a text file.
// Precondition: originalFileName is the name of an existing
// external text file, and copyFileName is the name of the
// text file to be created.
// Postcondition: The text file named copyFileName is a
// duplicate of the file named originalFileName.
// -----------------------------------------------------------
{
   ifstream originalFile(originalFileName);   // input file
```

```
   ofstream copyFile(copyFileName);           // output file
   char    ch;

   // copy characters one at a time from given file
   // to new file
   while (originalFile.get(ch))
      copyFile << ch;

   originalFile.close();  // close the files
   copyFile.close();
} // end copyTextFile
```

Notice that this function copies each end-of-line symbol just as it copies any other character. To do so, the expression

```
originalFile.get(ch)
```

is necessary because

```
originalFile >> ch
```

skips whitespace, including the end-of-line symbol.

Adding to a text file. When you open a file, you can specify a second argument in addition to the file's name. This second argument has the form

```
ios::mode
```

where *mode* has values such as *in*, *out*, or *app*. Until now, this argument has been omitted because *ifstream* files are by default opened for input, whereas *ofstream* files are opened for output. You can append a component to an *ofstream* file *outFile* by first opening it in append mode. Either the statement

```
ofstream outFile("Sample.DAT", ios::app);
```

or the statements

```
ofstream outFile;
outFile.open("Sample.DAT", ios::app);
```

prepare the file for output and position the file window after the file's last component. Thus, the old contents of the file are retained, and you can write additional components.

Exercise 13 at the end of this appendix asks you to write a function that appends data to a text file.

Searching a text file sequentially. Suppose that you have a text file of data about a company's employees. For simplicity, assume that this file contains two consecutive lines for each employee. The first line contains the employee's name, and the next line contains data such as salary.

Given the name of an employee, you can search the file for that name and then determine other information about this person. A sequential search examines the names in the order in which they appear in the file until the desired name is located. The following function performs such a sequential search:

```cpp
struct Person
{  string name;
   double salary;
};  // end struct

void searchFileSequentially(string fileName,
                            string desiredName,
                            person& desiredPerson,
                            bool& found)
// ----------------------------------------------------------
// Searches a text file sequentially for a desired person.
// Precondition: fileName is the name of a text file of
// names and data about people. Each person is represented
// by two lines in the file: The first line contains the
// person's name, and the second line contains the person's
// salary. desiredName is the name of the person sought.
// Postcondition: If desiredName was found in the file,
// desiredPerson is a structure that contains the person's
// name and data, and found is true. Otherwise, found is
// false and desiredPerson is unchanged. The file is
// unchanged and closed.
// ----------------------------------------------------------
{
   ifstream inFile(fileName);
   string   nextName;
   double   nextSalary;

   found = false;
   while ( !found && getline(inFile, nextName) )
   {  inFile >> nextSalary >> ws;  // skip trailing eoln

      if (nextName == desiredName)
         found = true;
   }  // end while

   if (found)
   {  desiredPerson.name = nextName;
      desiredPerson.salary = nextSalary;
```

```
    }  // end if

    inFile.close();
}  // end searchFileSequentially
```

This function needs to look at all the names in the file before determining that a particular name does not occur. If the names were in alphabetical order, you could determine when the search passed the place in the file that should have contained the desired name, if it existed. In this way, you could terminate the search before you needlessly searched the rest of the file. Exercise 10 asks you to make these changes to this function.

Accessing a text file directly. Although you usually process a text file sequentially, you can access the character stored at a given position directly without first reading the preceding characters.

The characters in a text file are numbered sequentially in order of appearance in the file, beginning with zero. The *seekg* function provides access to any character in the file, given the character's number. For example,

```
myFile.seekg(15)
```

advances the file window to the character numbered 15, which is actually the 16th character in the file. Immediately following this operation, you can read the character.

You can also locate a character relative to the beginning of the file, the current position in the file, or the end of the file by specifying, as the second argument to *seekg*,

```
ios::mode
```

where *mode* is one of *beg*, *cur*, or *end*. Thus,

```
myFile.seekg(2, ios::cur)
```

seeks the second character after the one at the present location of the file window.

Binary Files

Files that are not text files are called binary (or general or nontext) files. Like a text file, a binary file is a sequence of components of the same data type, which is any type other than a file. It is important to emphasize that each **file component** is an indivisible entity. For example, each component of a binary file of integers is an integer in the computer's internal representation. If you write the integer value 234 to a binary file, the system would write the computer's internal representation of 234, which is

0000000011101010 in binary, to the file, rather than the three ASCII characters *2*, *3*, *4*, which are, respectively, 00110010, 00110011, and 00110100 in binary. Similar comments are true for a binary file of floating-point numbers. If you could use a text editor to look at the file, you would see gibberish. You create a binary file not by using an editor—as you can for a text file—but rather by running a program.

The statement

```
ofstream outFile(myFileName, ios::binary);
```

associates the file variable *outFile* with the external binary file whose name is in the string variable *myFileName*. A binary file has an end-of-file symbol at its end, just as a text file does. However, the notion of lines does not exist for a binary file, although a binary file might contain data that coincidentally looks like an end-of-line symbol. Except for the differences noted here, C++ treats binary files in the same way that it treats text files.

A.11 Libraries

One of the advantages of modular programming is that you can implement functions independently of other functions. You may also find it possible for several different programs to use a particular function. As a result, you can build a library of functions that you can include in future programs.

The latest C++ standard supports both old-style libraries that are compatible with both C and C++ and new-style libraries that apply only to C++. Any library—an old-style library, a new-style library, or one that you write—has a corresponding header that provides information about the contents of the library. In the case of old-style libraries and user defined libraries, the header is usually a file and has a name that ends with *.h*. In new-style libraries, the header is simply an abstraction that the compiler may map to a filename or handle in a different manner. Thus, you do not see the *.h* extensions when using headers corresponding to the new-style libraries.

You have already seen some libraries, such as the one that provides input and output services. To use the functions contained in a library, you use the *include* directive with the name of the header associated with the library. For example, to use the old-style *iostream* library, you write

```
#include <iostream.h> // old-style iostream library
```

To indicate that you want to use the new-style library for input and output, you write the following lines in your program:

```
#include <iostream>  // new-style iostream library
using namespace std; // see Chapter 3, page 144 for
                     // an explanation of namespace
```

Though it is better to use the new-style headers, some older compilers may not support them. In this case, you would need to use the old-style libraries. Appendix C provides a list of new-style headers and any corresponding old-style headers.

User defined libraries are typically organized into two files. One file, the header file, contains a declaration for each function in the library that is available to your program. This file could also contain, for example, constant definitions, *typedef* statements, enumerations, structure declarations, and other *include* statements. By convention, the name of a header file associated with a user defined library ends in *.h*.[11] The other file—the implementation file—contains definitions of the functions that the header file declares. Typically, the name of an implementation file ends in *.cpp*.[12]

The assumption, of course, is that the files are in source form—that is, they need to be compiled. It certainly would be more efficient to compile the function definitions once, independently of any particular program, and then later merge the results of the compilation with any program that you desire. In fact, you should compile the implementation file and then include the header file in source form in your program by using an *include* directive such as

```
#include "MyHeader.h"
```

You use double quotes instead of angle brackets to enclose the name of a header file that you have written. The mechanics of incorporating the compiled implementation file into your program are system dependent.

Thus, your program can use previously compiled C++ statements, which are no longer available to you in source form. Maybe you did not even write these statements, just as you did not write the standard C++ functions such as *sqrt*. That is, you use a library in the same spirit in which you use standard functions. Because the header file indicates what is available to you, you must think of a library in terms of what it can do for you and not how it is implemented. You should think of all of your functions this way, even if you eventually implement them yourself.

---

[11] Other conventions, such as *.hpp* or *.hxx*, exist.

[12] Other conventions, such as *.c*, *.cp*, or *.cxx*, exist.

Avoiding Duplicate Header Files

Because header files can contain *include* directives, if you are not careful, your program could contain several copies of the same header file. Suppose you write a library of basic mathematical functions that has a header called *PI.h* and includes a constant declaration for π. You then write a series of more complex libaries that each include *PI.h*. If your program has several header files that each include *PI.h*, you will have multiple definitions of π, which, of course, is an error.

You can avoid this error by defining the header file *PI.h* as follows:

```
#ifndef _PI_
const double PI=3.14159;
#define _PI_
#endif
```

The directives *#ifndef*, *#define*, and *#endif* are commands to the C++ preprocessor, which can alter the source program before the compiler translates it. In this way, the preprocessor can determine whether more than one definition for *PI* occurs in the program, as follows:

> *#ifndef* asks whether the preprocessor identifier *_PI_* is defined. If this is the first occurrence of the header file in the program, *_PI_* will not be defined and the preprocessor will examine the next statements. The preprocessor passes the *const* statement to the compiler, and the *#define* directive then defines the identifier *_PI_*. For subsequent occurrences of the *PI.h* header file, *#ifndef* will determine that *_PI_* is already defined and will ignore the subsequent statements in the file, avoiding a duplicate definition for *PI*.

A.12 A Comparison to Java

The following examples will enable you to compare a construct in Java with the equivalent construct in C++.

```// Java comment on a single line```
```/* Java comment```
```that crosses more than one line */```
```/** Javadoc style comments */```
	```// C++ comment on a single line```
	```/* C++ comment```
	```that crosses more than one line */```

```// Java uses packages to group related``` ```// classes together```	```// C++ uses libraries to group related``` ```// functions and classes together```

``java
// Java class
// Each member has an access modifier
// (public, private, protected, or none
// for package access)
class Person
{   public String name;
    public int age;
    public double gpa;
}   // end class
// Usually members of a class are declared
// private, but this example is
// essentially the equivalent of a C++
// struct. Note that there is no semicolon
// after the closing brace.
``
	``cpp
	// C++ class - by default, all members are
	// private unless labeled
	class Person
	{
	    public:
	    string name;
	    int age;
	    double gpa;
	}; // end class
	// C++ structure - by default, all members
	// are public unless labeled
	struct Person
	{ string name;
	    int age;
	    double gpa;
	}; // end struct
	``

``java
// Java supports single inheritance of
// classes. Interfaces can be used to
// specify additional behavior
``
	``cpp
	// C++ supports multiple inheritance
	``

``java
// Java does not support templates but
// does have a single inheritance
// hierarchy built upon the class Object
class Stack
{
  public void push(Object newItem) {
    ...
  }
  ...
} // end Stack
``
	``cpp
	// C++ supports templates as a
	// parameterized type
	
	template <class T>
	void stack<T>::push(T newItem)
	{
	...
	}
	``

``java
// Java does not rely on a preprocessor;
// functionality is provided by the Java
// language itself
``
	``cpp
	// C++ uses a preprocessor for compiler
	// directives such as file inclusion
	#include <iostream>
	#include "myClass.h"
	``

``java
// Java methods must appear as part of a
// class
``
	``cpp
	// C++ can have stand-alone functions
	``

``java
// Java constant
// Must be declared within a class or a
// method
final int SIZE = 50;
``
	``cpp
	// C++ constant
	// Can be declared globally or within a
	// class or a function
	const int SIZE = 50;
	``

```
// Java valued method
public bool isLeapYear(int year)
// Returns true if year is a leap year;
// otherwise returns false.
{
   bool leap = false;
   bool yearEndsIn00 = (year % 100 == 0);
   if (yearEndsIn00 && (year % 400 == 0))
      leap = true;
   else if (!yearEndsIn00 &&
                        (year % 4 == 0))
      leap = true;
   return leap;
} // end IsLeapYear
```

```
// C++ valued function
bool isLeapYear(int year)
// Returns true if year is a leap year;
// otherwise returns false.
{
   bool leap = false;
   bool yearEndsIn00 = (year % 100 == 0);
   if ( yearEndsIn00 && (year % 400 == 0)
   )
        leap = true;
   else if (!yearEndsIn00 &&
                        (year % 4 == 0))
        leap = true;
   return leap;
} // end isLeapYear
```

```
// Java variable declarations
// Variables must be declared within a
// class or a method
int     day, month, year;
double  power, x;
char    response;
bool    done;
// Simple reference declaration; no object
// is instantiated until a new operator
// is used. Java supports only dynamic
// allocation of objects:
Sphere ball;
// Creating an object using a default
// constructor:
Sphere ball = new Sphere();
// Using constructor with parameters:
Sphere ball = new Sphere(1.0);
```

```
// C++ variable declarations
// Variables can be declared globally
// as well as within classes and methods
int     day, month, year;
double  power, x;
char    response;
bool    done;
// Objects can be declared statically
// using the default constructor:
Sphere ball();
// Also by using a constructor with
// parameters:
Sphere ball(1.0);
// Dynamic allocation is supported using
// pointers and the new operator:
Sphere *ball = new Sphere();
```

```
// Equality in Java
// == and != check for shallow equality.
// For object equality, must override
// equals method from class Object
```

```
// Equality in C++
// == and != check for shallow equality.
// For object equality, must provide an
// operator function, such as == or !=
```

```
// Java array, primitive types        // C++ array
double[] r = new double[SIZE];        typedef double arrayType[SIZE];
double[] s = new double[SIZE];        arrayType r;
                                      double    s[SIZE];
for (int i = 0; i < SIZE; i++)
  r[i] = 0.0;                         for (int i = 0; i < SIZE; ++i)
                                          r[i] = 0.0;
// Java array, using references
Sphere marbles = new Sphere [SIZE];
for (int i=0; i<SIZE; i++)
  marbles[i] = new Sphere(0.3);
```

```
// Java Standard Output               // C++ Standard Output
System.out.println("Enter month and " + cout << "Enter month and "
    "day for year " + year +               << "day for year " << year
    " as integers: ");                     << " as integers: ";
```

```
// Java Standard Input                // C++ Standard Input
BufferedReader stdin = new BufferedReader( cin >> x >> y;
        new InputStreamReader(System.in));
String nextLine = stdin.readLine();
StringTokenizer input = new
                StringTokenizer(nextLine);
x = Integer.parseInt(input.nextToken());
y = Integer.parseInt(input.nextToken());
```

Summary

1. Each comment line in C++ begins with two slashes // and continues until the end of the line.

2. A C++ identifier is a sequence of letters, digits, and underscores that must begin with either a letter or an underscore.

3. You can use a *typedef* statement to declare new names for data types. These names are simply synonyms for the data types; they are not new data types.

4. You define named constants by using a statement of the form

   const *type* *identifier = value;*

5. Enumeration provides another way to name integer constants, as in

   enum {SUN, MON, TUE, WED, THU, FRI, SAT};

or to define an integral data type, as in

```
enum Day {SUN, MON, TUE, WED, THU, FRI, SAT};
```

6. C++ uses short-circuit evaluation for expressions that contain the logical operators `&&` (and) and `||` (or). That is, evaluation proceeds from left to right and stops as soon as the value of the entire expression is apparent.

7. The output operator `<<` places a value into an output stream, and the input operator `>>` extracts a value from an input stream. You can imagine that these operators point in the direction of data flow. Thus, in `cout << myVar`, the operator points away from the variable *myVar*—data flows from *myVar* to the stream—whereas in `cin >> myVar`, the operator points to the variable *myVar*—data flows from the stream into *myVar*.

8. The general form of a function definition is

    type name(formal argument declaration list)
    {
        body
    }

    A valued function returns a value by using the `return` statement. Although a `void` function can use `return` to exit, it can use only arguments to return values.

9. When invoking a function, the actual arguments must correspond to the formal arguments in number, order, and type.

10. A function makes local copies of the values of any actual arguments that are passed by value. Thus, the actual arguments remain unchanged by the function. Such arguments are, therefore, input arguments.

    A function does not copy actual arguments that are passed by reference. Rather it references the actual argument locations whenever the formal arguments appear in the function's definition. In this way, a function can change the values of the actual arguments, thus implementing output arguments.

    A function does not copy and cannot change a constant reference argument. If copying an input argument would be expensive, make it a constant reference argument instead of a value argument.

11. The general form of the `if` statement is

    ```
    if (expression)
        statement₁
    else
        statement₂
    ```

If *expression* is true, *statement₁* executes; otherwise *statement₂* executes.

12. The general form of the `switch` statement is

```
switch (expression)
{   case constant₁:
        statement₁
        break;
    . . .
    case constantₙ:
        statementₙ
        break;
    default:
        statement
}
```

The appropriate *statement* executes according to the value of *expression*. Typically, `break` (or sometimes `return`) follows the statement or statements after each `case`. Omitting `break` causes execution to continue to the statement(s) of the `case` that follows.

13. The general form of the `while` statement is

```
while (expression)
    statement
```

As long as *expression* is true, *statement* executes. Thus, it is possible that *statement* never executes.

14. The general form of the `for` statement is

```
for (initialize; test; update)
    statement
```

where *initialize*, *test*, and *update* are expressions. Typically, *initialize* is an assignment expression that occurs only once. Then if *test*, which is usually a logical expression, is true, *statement* executes. The expression *update* executes next, usually incrementing or decrementing the counter. This sequence of events repeats, beginning with the evaluation of *test*, until *test* is false.

15. The general form of the `do` statement is

```
do
    statement
while (expression);
```

Here, *statement* executes until the value of *expression* is false. Note that *statement* always executes at least once.

16. An array is a collection of elements that have the same data type. You can refer to the elements of an array by using an index that begins with zero. Arrays are always passed to functions as reference arguments.

17. A string is a sequence of characters. You can manipulate the entire string, a substring, or the individual characters.

18. A structure is a group of related items called data members, which can have different data types and can be structures or arrays.

19. If you detect an error during execution, you can *throw* an exception. The code that deals with the exception is said to *catch* or handle it.

20. A file is a sequence of components of the same data type. A program can write data to a file that exists after the program terminates execution. Such a file provides a way to keep a permanent record of a program's output as well as a way for one program to use another program's output as its input. A file that is not saved when program execution ends is useful when you need to store data temporarily but cannot retain it all conveniently in memory.

21. A text file is a file of characters that contains end-of-line symbols that you can read just as you read any other character in the file.

22. Although text files are files of characters, you can write integer or floating-point values to them. For example, if *x* contains the integer value 234, writing *x* to a text file places the character sequence *2, 3, 4* in the file. The system performs the conversion from the internal representation of the integer to the representation of the corresponding character sequence. Similarly, you can read characters, which represent numeric values, from a text file into an appropriate integer or floating-point variable.

23. A binary file stores its components by using the computer's internal representation. The components in a binary file must all be of the same data type.

24. A typical C++ program uses header files that you incorporate by using the *include* directive. A header file contains function declarations, constant definitions, *typedef* statements, enumerations, structure declarations, and other *include* statements. The program might also require an implementation file of function definitions that have been compiled previously and placed into a library. The operating system locates the required implementation file and combines it with the program in ways that are system dependent.

Cautions

1. Remember that = is the assignment operator; == is the equality operator.

2. Do not begin a decimal integer constant with zero. A constant that begins with zero is either an octal constant or a hexadecimal constant.

3. An expression with any nonzero value is true; one having a value of zero is false.

4. Without a *break* statement, execution of a case within a *switch* statement will continue into the next case.

5. You must be careful that an array index does not exceed the size of the array. C++ does not check the range of array indexes. Similar comments apply to strings.

6. When referencing an element of a multidimensional array, do not use comma-separated indexes, as you would do in a language such as Java. For example, *myArray[3,6]* does not reference the array element *myArray[3][6]*. The expression *3,6* is a comma expression whose value is that of the last item listed, namely 6. Thus, although *myArray[3,6]* is legal, its meaning is *myArray[6]*, which references the element *myArray[0][6]*.

7. Be careful when you reference the members of a structure. You must write both the structure variable and the member identifier. Be particularly careful when several structures contain some of the same member identifiers.

8. An exception that is not handled by using a *try-catch* block may cause abnormal program termination.

9. Opening an existing file for output erases the data in the file, unless you specify append mode.

10. Even though you can think of the standard input stream *cin* and the standard output stream *cout* as text files, there are exceptions:

    - Do not declare *cin* or *cout*.

    - Do not use the *open* or *close* functions with these files; *cin* is always open for reading and *cout* is always open for writing.

11. You must pass a stream variable to a function as a reference argument.

Self-Test Exercises

1. What values are assigned to the variables in the following sequence of C++ statements?

```
int a = 5;
a += 2;
int b = a++;
int c = (2*a + 3) % b;
int d = (b != c) && (a + b == 3*c);
int e = a <= b ? a : c;
```

2. Suppose that the *int* variables *a* and *b* have values 5 and 6, respectively. What output does the following statement produce?

```
cout << a << b << endl;
```

3. If *title* is a character string, what do the following statements display?

```
string title = "Walls and Mirrors";
cout << """ << title << ""\n";
```

4. What output, if any, does the following sequence of C++ statements produce?

```
int j = 13;
int k = 10;
while (j >= k)
{   if ( (k + 1 < 10) || (k > 12) )
        cout << "k is out of range.\n";
    else
        switch (k + 1)
        {   case 11:
                cout << "j = " << j << endl;
                break;
            case 12: case 13:
                j += 2;
                if (j < 15)
                    cout << "j = " << j << endl;
                else
                    cout << "k = " << k << endl;
        }   // end switch
    --j;
    ++k;
}   // end while
```

5. Write *if* statements that assign a letter grade of A, B, C, D, or F to the variable *grade* according to the value of *score*, as follows:

90 to 100 is A, 80 to 89 is B, 70 to 79 is C, 60 to 69 is D, and below 60 is F.

6. Can you write a *switch* statement to solve Self-Test Exercise 5? If so, will you have a better solution?

7. Write a function that returns the sum of the first *n* integers in an array of integers.

8. Consider the array that the following statements define:

```
const int DAYS_PER_WEEK = 7;
const int WEEKS_PER_YEAR = 52;
typedef double ArrayType[DAYS_PER_WEEK][WEEKS_PER_YEAR];
ArrayType minTemps;
```

Suppose, as you saw earlier in this appendix, that each column of the array represents the minimum temperatures for the seven days in a particular week. Write the C++ statements that perform the following:

a. Write the minimum temperature for each day of the first week.

b. Write the minimum temperature for the first day of each of the first five weeks.

c. Write all of the minimum temperatures so that the temperatures for each week appear on a separate line.

9. Consider the structure *student*, which was defined in the section of this appendix entitled "Structures Within Structures." Write the C++ references for the following items in *student*:

a. The state

b. The first digit in the zip code

c. The GPA

d. The first letter in the name

10. Consider the function *copyTextFile*, which makes a copy of a text file and was discussed in this appendix in the section "Text Files." Trace the execution of this function when *originalFile* looks like

a b <eoln> c d <eoln> <eof>

where <eoln> represents the end-of-line symbol and <eof> represents the end-of-file symbol. Indicate the contents of *ch* and *copyFile* and the positions of the file windows as you trace through the function.

Exercises

1. Given the sides of a triangle, write a function that returns the character *E* if the triangle is equilateral, *I* if it is isosceles, or *S* if it is scalene. Recall that a triangle is equilateral if all of its sides are equal, isosceles if two of its sides are equal, or scalene if none of its sides are equal.

2. Write a function that returns the quality-point value of a given letter grade according to the following scheme: A is 4, B is 3, C is 2, D is 1, F is 0, and I is 0. Use a *switch* statement.

3. Write a loop that reads letter grades, determines their validity, and computes a quality-point average. Assume that each course is three credits. Also, assume that the user will type Q to end the input. Call the function that you wrote in Exercise 2.

4. The following statements behave unexpectedly when you type *YES*. Describe this behavior and explain why it happens.

```
char response;
do
{  . . . (a sequence of statements)
   cout << "Do it again?";
   cin >> response;
} while ( (response == 'Y') || (response == 'y') );
```

5. Assume the array *minTemps* that Self-Test Exercise 8 describes. Consider the one-dimensional array *mt* of 364 (7 * 52) real numbers.

   a. Suppose that the first seven elements of *mt* represent the days in the first week, the second seven elements of *mt* represent the days in the second week, and so on. Which element of *mt* represents the 5th day in the 12th week? (That is, which element of *mt* corresponds to *minTemps[4][11]*?)

   b. Suppose that the first 52 elements of *mt* correspond to the first row of *minTemps*, the second 52 elements of *mt* correspond to the second row of *minTemps*, and so on. Which element of *mt* corresponds to *minTemps[4][11]*?

6. Consider the array *temps* that the following statements define:

```
typedef double    WeekType[DAYS_PER_WEEK];
typedef WeekType YearType[WEEKS_PER_YEAR];
YearType temps;
```

temps[12] is a one-dimensional array of seven real numbers. Suppose that you want to compute the average of these seven numbers by calling a function *average*. Write the function *average* so that *average(temps[12])* returns the desired average.

7. Write a function that creates a string from two given strings. The two strings are a person's first and last names. The resulting string is the person's entire name.

8. Consider the variable *csc212* as defined in the section of this appendix entitled "Arrays of Structures."

   a. Repeat Self-Test Exercise 9, but use *csc212[3]* instead of *student*.

   b. Write statements that read names into the *name* members of *csc212*.

9. Change the definition of the *name* member within the structure type *Person*, which appears in the section "Structures Within Structures," so that *Name* is a *struct* with three data members: *first*, *middle*, and *last*.

10. Consider the function *searchFileSequentially*, which appears in the section "Text Files." Modify the function to take advantage of a file whose names appear alphabetically. That is, the function should not always have to search the entire file to determine that a name does not appear within the file.

11. Consider two text files of integers sorted into ascending order. You can merge the two files into a third file that is the sorted combination of the two original files. For example, if the first file contains the integers 1, 4, and 8, and the second file contains the integers 2 and 4, the third file will contain 1, 2, 4, 4, and 8.

    Write a function that merges two sorted text files of integers into a third sorted text file of integers. Assume that each line of the files contains one integer.

12. Write a function

    ```
    void advanceTo(ifstream& myFile, char target)
    ```

    that will position the file window of the file associated with *myFile* directly over the first occurrence of the character that *target* specifies. If *target* is a blank, the function should position the window over the first blank in the file and *not* over an end-of-line symbol. If *target* does not appear in the file, the function should write a message to that effect.

13. a. Consider a text file of integers. Write a function that appends to this file the 20 integers that you read from the standard input stream. Use append mode.

    b. Consider a text file of nonnumeric data. Write a function that appends to this file the 20 characters that you read from the standard input stream. Use a temporary text file instead of append mode.

Programming Problems

1. Write a program that converts a linear measurement given in yards, feet, and inches to one that is in meters and centimeters. Assume that the input is integral and free of error. The output should also be integral and expressed in lowest terms. That is, a measurement of 3 meters and 105 centimeters should be expressed as 4 meters and 5 centimeters.

2. Write a program that determines whether any given N-by-N matrix of integers is a magic square. In a magic square, each row, column, and diagonal contain integers that have the same sum.

    For example, the following matrix is a magic square because the integers in each row, each column, and each diagonal have a sum of 15:

6	1	8
7	5	3
2	9	4

3. Write a program that will read English prose and list in alphabetical order all the words that occur in the prose, along with a count of the number of times each word occurs.

    The heart of this program will be a function that reads in a word. If you agree to treat any character other than the letters A through Z as a delimiter, you can define a word to be any string of up to eight characters that is surrounded by delimiters. If a string between delimiters is more than eight characters, read the entire string, but truncate it to eight characters when you record it.

    You can assume that the text will contain at most 100 distinct words.

4. Write a function that simulates binary addition with n-bit quantities. Number the bits from 0 to $n - 1$. Use an array `bitArray` to represent an n-bit quantity: The value of `bitArray[i]` is 1 if and only if the ith bit of the n-bit quantity is 1.

ASCII Character Codes

Dec	Char		Dec	Char		Dec	Char		Dec	Char
0	NUL		32	(blank)		64	@		96	` (reverse quote)
1	SOH		33	!		65	A		97	a
2	STX		34	"		66	B		98	b
3	ETX		35	#		67	C		99	c
4	EOT		36	$		68	D		100	d
5	ENQ		37	%		69	E		101	e
6	ACK		38	&		70	F		102	f
7	BEL		39	' (apostrophe)		71	G		103	g
8	BS		40	(		72	H		104	h
9	HT		41	)		73	I		105	i
10	LF		42	*		74	J		106	j
11	VT		43	+		75	K		107	k
12	FF		44	, (comma)		76	L		108	l
13	CR		45	–		77	M		109	m
14	SO		46	.		78	N		110	n
15	SI		47	/		79	O		111	o
16	DLE		48	0		80	P		112	p
17	DC1		49	1		81	Q		113	q
18	DC2		50	2		82	R		114	r
19	DC3		51	3		83	S		115	s
20	DC4		52	4		84	T		116	t
21	NAK		53	5		85	U		117	u
22	SYN		54	6		86	V		118	v
23	ETB		55	7		87	W		119	w
24	CAN		56	8		88	X		120	x
25	EM		57	9		89	Y		121	y
26	SUB		58	:		90	Z		122	z
27	ESC		59	;		91	[		123	{
28	FS		60	<		92	\		124		
29	GS		61	=		93	]		125	}
30	RS		62	>		94	^		126	~
31	US		63	?		95	_ (underscore)		127	DEL

Note: The codes 0–31 and 127 are for control characters that do not print.

C++ Header Files and Standard Functions

Here is a list of commonly used C++ headers. If an older version of the header exists, its name is shown in parentheses.

cassert *(assert.h)*

This library contains only the function *assert*. You use

     assert(*assertion*);

to test the validity of an assertion. If *assertion* is *false*, *assert* writes an error message and terminates program execution. You can disable all occurrences of *assert* in your program by placing the directive *#define NDEBUG* before the *include* directive.

cctype *(ctype.h)*

Most functions in this library classify a given ASCII character as a letter, a digit, and so on. Two other functions convert letters between uppercase and lowercase.

    The classification functions return a *true* value if *ch* belongs to the specified group; otherwise they return *false*.

isalnum(ch)	Returns *true* if *ch* is either a letter or a decimal digit
isalpha(ch)	Returns *true* if *ch* is a letter
iscntrl(ch)	Returns *true* if *ch* is a control character (ASCII 127 or 0 to 31)
isdigit(ch)	Returns *true* if *ch* is a decimal digit
isgraph(ch)	Returns *true* if *ch* is printable and nonblank
islower(ch)	Returns *true* if *ch* is a lowercase letter

`isprint(ch)`	Returns *true* if *ch* is printable (including blank)
`ispunct(ch)`	Returns *true* if *ch* is a punctuation character
`isspace(ch)`	Returns *true* if *ch* is a whitespace character: space, tab, carriage return, new line, or form feed
`isupper(ch)`	Returns *true* if *ch* is an uppercase letter
`isxdigit(ch)`	Returns *true* if *ch* is a hexadecimal digit
`toascii(ch)`	Returns ASCII code for *ch*
`tolower(ch)`	Returns the lowercase version of *ch* if *ch* is an uppercase letter; otherwise returns *ch*
`toupper(ch)`	Returns the uppercase version of *ch* if *ch* is a lowercase letter; otherwise returns *ch*

cfloat `(float.h)`

Defines named constants that specify the range of floating-point values.

climits `(limits.h)`

Defines named constants that specify the range of integer values.

cmath `(math.h)`

The C++ functions in this library compute certain standard mathematical functions. These functions are overloaded to accomodate *float*, *double*, and *long double*. Unless otherwise indicated, each function has one argument, with the return type being the same as the argument type (either *float*, *double*, or *long double*).

`acos`	Returns the arc cosine
`asin`	Returns the arc sine
`atan`	Returns the arc tangent
`atan2`	Returns the arc tangent x/y for arguments x and y
`ceil`	Rounds up

`cos`	Returns the cosine
`cosh`	Returns the hyperbolic cosine
`exp`	Returns e^x
`fabs`	Returns the absolute value
`floor`	Rounds down
`fmod`	Returns x modulo y for arguments x and y
`frexp`	For arguments x and *eptr*, where $x = m * 2^e$, returns m and sets *eptr* to point to e
`ldexp`	Returns $x * 2^e$, for arguments x and e
`log`	Returns the natural log
`log10`	Returns the log base 10
`modf`	For arguments x and *iptr*, returns the fractional part of x and sets *iptr* to point to the integer part of x
`pow`	Returns x^y, for arguments x and y
`sin`	Returns the sine
`sinh`	Returns the hyperbolic sine
`sqrt`	Returns the square root
`tan`	Returns the tangent
`tanh`	Returns the hyperbolic tangent

cstdlib *(stdlib.h)*

abort	Terminates program execution abnormally
abs	Returns the absolute value of an integer
atof	Converts a string argument to floating point
atoi	Converts a string argument to an integer
exit	Terminates program execution
rand	Returns a pseudorandom integer
srand	Initializes the pseudorandom number generator to either the argument or, if no argument is present, 1

cstring *(string.h)*

This library enables you to manipulate C strings that end in \0. Unless noted otherwise, these functions return a pointer to the resulting string in addition to modifying an appropriate argument. The argument *ch* is a character, *n* is an integer, and the other arguments are strings.

strcat(toS, fromS)	Copies *fromS* to the end of *toS*
strncat(toS, fromS, n)	Copies at most *n* characters of *fromS* to the end of *toS* and appends \0
strcmp(str1, str2)	Returns an integer that is negative if *str1* < *str2*, zero if *str1* == *str2*, and positive if *str1* > *str2*
stricmp(str1, str2)	Behaves like *strcmp*, but ignores case
strncmp(str1, str2, n)	Behaves like *strcmp*, but compares the first *n* characters of each string
strcpy(toS, fromS)	Copies *fromS* to *toS*
strncpy(toS, fromS, n)	Copies *n* characters of *fromS* to *toS*, truncating or padding with \0 as necessary
strspn(str1, str2)	Returns the number of initial consecutive characters of *str1* that are not in *str2*

strcspn(str1, str2)	Returns the number of initial consecutive characters of *str1* that are in *str2*
strlen(str)	Returns the length of *str*, excluding \0
strlwr(str)	Converts any uppercase letters in *str* to lowercase without altering other characters
strupr(str)	Converts any lowercase letters in *str* to uppercase without altering other characters
strchr(str, ch)	Returns a pointer to the first occurrence of *ch* in *str*; otherwise returns *NULL*
strrchr(str, ch)	Returns a pointer to the last occurrence of *ch* in *str*; otherwise returns *NULL*
strpbrk(str1, str2)	Returns a pointer to the first character in *str1* that also appears in *str2*; otherwise returns *NULL*
strstr(str1, str2)	Returns a pointer to the first occurrence of *str2* in *str1*; otherwise returns *NULL*
strtok(str1, str2)	Finds the next token in *str1* that is followed by *str2*, returns a pointer to the token, and writes *NULL* immediately after the token in *str1*

exception

Defines classes, types, and functions that relate to exception handling. A portion of the class exception is shown below.

```
class exception
{
public:
   exception() throw();
   virtual ~exception() throw();
   exception &operator=(const exception %exc) throw();
   virtual const char *what() const throw();
}
```

fstream (fstream.h)

Declares the C++ classes that support file I/O.

iomanip (iomanip.h)

The manipulators in this library affect the format of stream operations. Note that *iostream* contains additional manipulators.

`setbase(b)`	Sets number base to $b = 8$, 10, or 16
`setfill(f)`	Sets fill character to f
`setprecision(n)`	Sets floating-point precision to integer n
`setw(n)`	Sets field width to integer n

iostream (iostream.h)

The manipulators in this library affect the format of stream operations. Note that *iomanip* contains additional manipulators.

`dec`	Tells subsequent operation to use decimal representation
`endl`	Inserts new-line character \n and flushes output stream
`ends`	Inserts null character \0 in an output stream
`flush`	Flushes an output stream
`hex`	Tells subsequent I/O operation to use hexadecimal representation
`oct`	Tells subsequent I/O operation to use octal representation
`ws`	Extracts whitespace characters on input stream

string

This library enables you to manipulate C++ strings. Described here is a selection of the functions that this library provides. In addition, you can use the following operators with C++ strings: =, +, ==, !=, <, <=, >, >=, <<, and >>. Note that positions within a string begin at 0.

`erase()`	Makes the string empty
`erase(pos, len)`	Removes the substring that begins at position *pos* and contains *len* characters
`find(subString)`	Returns the position of a substring within the string
`length()`	Returns the number of characters in the string (same as *size*)
`replace(pos, len, str)`	Replaces the substring that begins at position *pos* and contains *len* characters with the string *str*
`size()`	Returns the number of characters in the string (same as *length*)
`substr(pos, len)`	Returns the substring that begins at position *pos* and contains *len* characters

Mathematical Induction

Many proofs of theorems or invariants in computer science use a technique called mathematical induction, or simply **induction**. Induction is a principle of mathematics that is like a row of dominoes standing on end. If you push the first domino, all the dominoes will fall one after another. What is it about the dominoes that allows us to draw this conclusion? If you know that when one domino falls the next domino will fall, then pushing the first domino will cause them all to fall in succession. More formally, you can show that all the dominoes will fall if you can show that the following two facts are true:

- The first domino falls.

- For any $k \geq 1$, if the kth domino falls, the $(k + 1)^{\text{th}}$ domino will fall.

The principle of mathematical induction is an axiom that is stated as follows:

AXIOM D-1. The principle of mathematical induction. A property $P(n)$ that involves an integer n is true for all $n \geq 0$ if the following are true:

   1. $P(0)$ is true.

   2. If $P(k)$ is true for any $k \geq 0$, then $P(k + 1)$ is true.

A **proof by induction on n** is one that uses the principle of mathematical induction. Such a proof consists of the two steps given in Axiom D-1. The first step is called the basis, or base case. The second step is the inductive step. We usually break the inductive step into two parts: the **inductive hypothesis** ("if $P(k)$ is true for any $k \geq 0$") and the **inductive conclusion** ("then $P(k + 1)$ is true").

Example 1

The following recursive function, which is given here in pseudocode, computes x^n:

```
pow2(in x:integer, in n:integer)

    if (n == 0)
        return 1
    else
        return  x * pow2(x, n-1)
```

You can prove that *pow2* returns x^n for all $n \geq 0$ by using the following proof by induction on n.

Basis. *Show that the property is true when n = 0.* That is, you must show that `pow2(x, 0)` returns x^0, which is 1. However, as you can see from the definition of *pow2*, `pow2(x, 0)` is 1.

Now you must establish the inductive step. By assuming that the property is true when $n = k$ (the inductive hypothesis), you must show that the property is true when $n = k + 1$ (the inductive conclusion).

Inductive hypothesis. *Assume that the property is true when n = k.* That is, assume that

$$\text{pow2(x, k)} = x^k$$

Inductive conclusion. *Show that the property is true when n = k + 1.* That is, you must show that `pow2(x, k + 1)` returns the value $x^{k + 1}$. By definition of the function *pow2*,

$$\text{pow2(x, k + 1)} = x * \text{pow2(x, k)}$$

By the inductive hypothesis, `pow2(x, k)` returns the value x^k, so

$$\text{pow2(x, k + 1)} = x * x^k$$
$$= x^{k + 1}$$

which is what you needed to show to establish the inductive step.

The inductive proof is thus complete. We demonstrated that the two steps in Axiom D-1 are true, so the principle of mathematical induction guarantees that *pow2* returns x^n for all $n \geq 0$. (**End of proof.**)

Example 2

Prove that

$$1 + 2 + \cdots + n = \frac{n(n+1)}{2} \text{ when } n \geq 1$$

It will be helpful to let S_n represent the sum $1 + 2 + \cdots + n$.

Basis. Sometimes the property to be proven is trivial when $n = 0$, as is the case here. You can use $n = 1$ as the basis instead. (Actually, you can use any value of $n \geq 0$ as the basis, but a value of 0 or 1 is typical.)

You need to show that the sum S_1, which is simply 1, is equal to $1(1 + 1)/2$. This fact is obvious.

Inductive hypothesis. Assume that the formula is true when $n = k$; that is, assume that $S_k = k(k + 1)/2$.

Inductive conclusion. Show that the formula is true when $n = k + 1$. To do so, you can proceed as follows:

$$
\begin{aligned}
S_{k+1} &= (1 + 2 + \cdots + k) + (k + 1) && \text{(definition of } S_{k+1}) \\
&= S_k + (k + 1) && \text{(definition of } S_k) \\
&= k(k + 1)/2 + (k + 1) && \text{(inductive hypothesis)} \\
&= (k(k + 1) + 2(k + 1))/2 && \text{(common denominator)} \\
&= (k + 1)(k + 2)/2 && \text{(factorization)}
\end{aligned}
$$

The last expression is $n(n + 1)/2$ when n is $k + 1$. Thus, if the formula for S_k is true, the formula for S_{k+1} is true. Therefore, by the principle of mathematical induction, the formula is true when $n \geq 1$. (**End of proof.**)

Example 3

Prove that $2^n > n^2$ when $n \geq 5$.

Basis. Here is an example where the base case is not $n = 0$ or 1, but instead is $n = 5$. It is obvious that the relationship is true when $n = 5$ because

$$2^5 = 32 > 5^2 = 25$$

Inductive hypothesis. Assume that the relationship is true when $n = k \geq 5$; that is, assume that $2^k > k^2$ when $k \geq 5$.

Inductive conclusion. Show that the relationship is true when $n = k + 1$; that is, show that $2^{k+1} > (k+1)^2$ when $k \geq 5$. To do so, you can proceed as follows:

$$(k + 1)^2 = k^2 + (2k + 1) \qquad \text{(square } k + 1\text{)}$$
$$< k^2 + k^2 \text{ when } k \geq 5 \qquad (2k + 1 < k^2; \text{ see Exercise 3)}$$
$$< 2^k + 2^k \text{ when } k \geq 5 \qquad \text{(inductive hypothesis)}$$
$$= 2^{k+1}$$

Therefore, by the principle of mathematical induction, $2^n > n^2$ when $n \geq 5$. (**End of proof.**)

Sometimes, the inductive hypothesis in Axiom D-1 is not sufficient. That is, you may need to assume more than $P(k)$. The following axiom is a stronger form of the principle of mathematical induction:

AXIOM D-2. The principle of mathematical induction (strong form). A property $P(n)$ that involves an integer n is true for all $n \geq 0$ if the following are true:

1. $P(0)$ is true.

2. If $P(0), P(1), \cdots, P(k)$ are true for any $k \geq 0$, then $P(k + 1)$ is true.

Notice that the inductive hypothesis of Axiom D-2 ("If $P(0), P(1), \cdots, P(k)$ are true for any $k \geq 0$") includes the inductive hypothesis of Axiom D-1 ("If $P(k)$ is true for any $k \geq 0$").

Example 4

Prove that every integer greater than 1 can be written as a product of prime integers.

Recall that a prime number is one that is divisible only by 1 and itself. The inductive proof is as follows:

Basis. The statement that you must prove involves integers greater than 1. Thus, the base case is $n = 2$. However, 2 is a prime number and, therefore, it trivially is a product of prime numbers.

Inductive hypothesis. Assume that the property is true for each of the integers $2, 3, \cdots, k$, where $k \geq 2$.

Inductive conclusion. Show that the property is true when $n = k + 1$; that is, show that $k + 1$ can be written as a product of prime numbers.

If $k + 1$ is a prime number, then there is nothing more to show. However, if $k + 1$ is not a prime number, it must be divisible by an integer x such that $1 < x < k + 1$. Thus,

$$k + 1 = x \star y$$

where $1 < y < k + 1$. Notice that x and y are each less than or equal to k, so the inductive hypothesis applies. That is, x and y can each be written as a product of prime numbers. Clearly $x * y$, which is equal to $k + 1$, must be a product of prime numbers. Because the formula holds for $n = k + 1$, it holds for all $n \geq 2$ by the principle of mathematical induction. (**End of proof.**)

Example 5

Chapter 2 discusses the following recursive definition:

$$rabbit(1) = 1$$
$$rabbit(2) = 1$$
$$rabbit(n) = rabbit(n - 1) + rabbit(n - 2) \text{ when } n > 2$$

Prove that

$$rabbit(n) = (a^n - b^n)/\sqrt{5}$$

where $a = (1 + \sqrt{5})/2$ and $b = (1 - \sqrt{5})/2 = 1 - a$.

Basis. $rabbit(0)$ is undefined, so begin at $n = 1$. Some algebra shows that $rabbit(1) = (a^1 - b^1)/\sqrt{5} = 1$. However, notice that $rabbit(2)$ is also a special case. That is, you cannot compute $rabbit(2)$ from $rabbit(1)$ by using the recurrence relationship given here. Therefore, the basis in this inductive proof must include $n = 2$.

When $n = 2$, some more algebra will show that $rabbit(2) = (a^2 - b^2)/\sqrt{5} = 1$. Thus, the formula is true when n is either 1 or 2.

Inductive hypothesis. Assume that the formula is true for all n such that $1 \leq n \leq k$, where k is at least 2.

Inductive conclusion. Show that the formula is true for $n = k + 1$. To do so, you can proceed as follows:

$$rabbit(k + 1) = rabbit(k) + rabbit(k - 1) \qquad \text{(recurrence relation)}$$
$$= [(a^k - b^k) + (a^{k-1} - b^{k-1})]/\sqrt{5} \qquad \text{(inductive hypothesis)}$$
$$= [a^{k-1}(a + 1) - b^{k-1}(b + 1)]/\sqrt{5} \qquad \text{(factorization)}$$
$$= [a^{k-1}(a^2) - b^{k-1}(b^2)]/\sqrt{5} \qquad (a + 1 = a^2; b + 1 = b^2)$$
$$= (a^{k+1} - b^{k+1})/\sqrt{5}$$

Because the formula holds for $n = k + 1$, it holds for all $n > 2$ by the principle of mathematical induction. (**End of proof.**)

Note that the previous proof requires that you show that $a + 1 = a^2$ and $b + 1 = b^2$. Although simple algebra will demonstrate the validity of these equalities, exactly how did we discover them after the factorization step? Some experience with inductive proofs will give you the confidence to determine and verify the auxiliary relationships—such as

$a + 1 = a^2$—that are necessary in a proof. Here, after we introduced the factors $(a + 1)$ and $(b + 1)$, we observed that if these factors were equal to a^2 and b^2, respectively, we could finish the proof. Thus, we tried to show that $a + 1 = a^2$ and $b + 1 = b^2$; indeed, we were successful. Inductive proofs often require adventurous algebraic manipulations!

Self-Test Exercises

1. Prove that $1 + 2^1 + 2^2 + \cdots + 2^m = 2^{m+1} - 1$ for all $m \geq 0$.

2. Prove that the sum of the first n odd positive integers is n^2.

3. Prove that $rabbit(n) \geq a^{n-2}$ when $n \geq 2$ and $a = (1 + \sqrt{5})/2$.

Exercises

1. Prove that the sum of the first n even positive integers is $n(n + 1)$.

2. Prove that $1^2 + 2^2 + \cdots + n^2 = n(n + 1)(2n + 1)/6$ for all $n \geq 1$.

3. Prove that $2n + 1 < n^2$ for all $n \geq 3$.

4. Prove that $n^3 - n$ is divisible by 6 for all $n \geq 0$.

5. Prove that $2^n > n^3$ when $n \geq 10$.

6. Prove that $n! > n^3$ when n is large enough.

7. Recall the following recursive definition from Chapter 2:

   $c(n, 0) = 1$
   $c(n, n) = 1$
   $c(n, k) = c(n - 1, k - 1) + c(n - 1, k)$ when $0 < k < n$
   $c(n, k) = 0$ when $k > n$

   a. Prove that $c(n, 0) + c(n, 1) + \cdots + c(n, n) = 2^n$.
      Hint: Use $c(n + 1, 0) = c(n, 0)$ and $c(n + 1, n) = c(n, n)$.

   b. Prove that $(x + y)^n = \displaystyle\sum_{k=0}^{n} c(n, k)\, x^k y^{n-k}$

8. Prove that $rabbit(n) \leq a^{n-1}$ when $n \geq 1$ and $a = (1 + \sqrt{5})/2$.

9. Suppose that the rabbit population doubles every year. If you start with two rabbits, find and prove a formula that predicts the rabbit population after n years.

Standard Template Library

Class *list*

The STL class *list* is a container class that has two data-type parameters. The first is the data type for the items in the container. The second is an allocator. Allocators manage memory allocation for a container. The default allocator is an object of class *allocator*, and is usually sufficient for most uses. Here is a partial listing of the member functions found in the STL class *list*:

```cpp
template <class T, class A = allocator<T> >
class list
{
public:
    list();
    // Default constructor; initializes an empty list.

    list(size_type num, const T& val = T());
    // Constructor; initializes list to have num elements
    // with the value val.

    list(const list<T> & anotherList);
    // Constructor; initializes list to have the same
    // elements as list anotherList.

    bool empty() const;
    // Determines whether the list is empty.

    size_type size() const;
    // Returns the number of items that are currently in the
    // list. size_type is an integral type.

    size_type max_size();
    // Determines the maximum number of items the list can
    // hold.

    iterator insert(iterator i, const T& val = T());
    // Inserts an item val into the list immediately before
```

```
// the element specified by the iterator i. An iterator
// to the newly inserted item is returned.

void remove(const T& val);
// Removes all items with value val from the list.

iterator erase(iterator i);
// Removes the item in the list pointed to by iterator i.
// Returns an iterator to the item following the removed
// item. If the item removed is the last item in the
// list, the iterator value will be the same as returned
// by end().

iterator begin();
// Returns an iterator to the first item in the list.
// If the list is empty, the iterator value will be the
// same as returned by end().

iterator end();
// Returns an iterator value that can be used to test
// whether the end of the list has been reached.

}   // end STL class list
```

Class *map*

The STL class *map* is an associative container class that stores sorted (key, value) pairs based on unique keys. The class *pair* that *map* uses to store the key and value is defined in *<utility>*. The class *map* has four data-type parameters. The first is the data type for the search key. The second is the data type for the items in the container. The third is an optional comparison function object for the elements of the map. The default comparison operator is <. The fourth parameter is an optional allocator. The STL class *multimap* is identical to *map*, except that it allows duplicate keys. A partial specification for the *map* class follows:

```
template <class Key, class T, class Compare = less<Key>
          class A = allocator<pair<const Key, T> > >
class map
{
public:
  explicit map(const Compare& cmp = Compare());
  // Default constructor; initializes an empty map
  // and comparison object

    template <class InputIter>
    map(InputIter first, InputIter last,
```

```
    const Compare& comp = Compare());
// Constructor: map is initialized with length last — first
// and filled with all values from the dereferenced
// input iterators on the range [first, last].

bool empty() const;
// Determines whether the map is empty.

size_type size() const;
// Determines the size of the map.
// The return type size_type is an integral type.

size_type max_size() const;
// Determines the maximum number of elements
// the map can hold.

Iter (const value_type& e)
Iter insert(Iter i, const value_type& e);
// Inserts element pair e into the map if a value_type
// with the same key is not already present in the map.
// Takes an optional iterator parameter as a hint as to where
// to insert.

Iter erase(Iter i);
// Removes the map element pointed to by iterator i

void erase(Iter first, Iter last);
// Removes all map elements in the range (first, last).

Iter find(const key_value& e) const;
// Returns an iterator that points to the element
// equal to e.
// Precondition: None.
// Postcondition: If element e was in the map, an iterator
// that points to e was returned; otherwise, the value
// returned by end() was returned.

size_type count(const key_type& k);
// Returns number of elements equal to k

Iter lower_bound(const key_type& k) const;
// Returns an iterator that points to the first key
// that is equal to or greater than k.

Iter upper_bound(const key_type& k) const;
// Returns an iterator that points to the first key
// that is greater than e
```

```
    void swap(map<Key, T, Compare>& m);
     // Exchanges maps.

    Iter begin();
    // Returns an iterator to the first element in the
    // map.

    Iter end();
    // Returns an iterator to test for the end of the
    // map.
}   // end STL map
```

Class *priority_queue*

The STL class *priority_queue* is an adapter container that has three data-type parameters. The first is the data type for the items in the container. The second is the container used in the implementation of the priority queue. The default container is an object of class *vector*. The third parameter is an optional comparison function object for the elements of the map. The default comparison operator is <. Here is a partial listing of the member functions found in the STL class *priority_queue*:

```
template <class T, class Container = vector<T>,
          class Compare = less<typename Container::value_type> >
class priority_queue

public:
    explicit priority_queue(const Compare& = Compare(),
                            const Container& = Container()) ;
    // Default constructor; initializes an empty priority queue.
    // The default comparison operator is <.
    // A comparison function object may be supplied.

    bool empty() const;
    // Determines whether the priority queue is empty.

    size_type size() const;
    // Determines the size of the priority queue.
    // The return type size_type is an integral type.

    const value_type& top() const;
    // Returns a reference to the highest priority element in the
    // priority queue.
```

```
    void pop();
    // Removes the highest priority element in the
    // priority queue.

    void push(const value_type& e);
    // Adds the item e to the priority queue.

}   // end STL priority_queue
```

Class *queue*

The STL class *queue* is another adapter class that has two data-type parameters. The first is the data type for the items in the container, and the second is the container used in the implementation of the queue. The default container is an object of class *deque*. Here is a partial listing of the member functions found in the STL class *queue*:

```
template <class T, class Container = deque <T> >
class queue
{
public:
    explicit queue(const& cnt = Container());
    // Default constructor; initializes an empty queue.

    bool empty() const;
    // Determines whether the queue is empty.

    size_type size() const;
    // Returns the number of items that are currently in the
    // queue. size_type is an integral type.

    T &front();
    // Returns a reference to the first item in the queue.

    T &back();
    // Returns a reference to the last item in the queue.

    void pop();
    // Removes the first item in the queue.

    void push(const T& x);
    // Inserts an item at the end of the queue.

} // end STL class queue
```

Class *set*

The STL class *set* is an associative container, but unlike *map*, it stores only one object, which represents both the key and the value. Also, the *set* class does not provide subscripting. Otherwise, the *set* member functions are comparable to the *map* member functions in the section above. The similar interfaces are possible through the definition of their container elements as a *value_type*. The *value_type* of a *set* is defined by its key type, whereas the *value_type* of a *map* is defined as a *pair*. The STL class *multiset* is identical to *set*, except that it allows duplicate keys. The class header and key type definition of the STL class *set* are listed below:

```
template <class Key, class Compare = less<Key>
          class A = allocator<Key, T> >
class set
{
public:

  // Like map, except that there is no subscript operator
  // and the value_type definition is as follows:
  typedef Key value_type;  // in a set, the Key is the value

}
```

Standard set algorithms such as union, intersection, difference, and subset are provided in *<algorithm>*. Here is a partial listing of the STL set functions:

```
OutputIter set_union(InputIter1 first, InputIter1 last,
                     InputIter2 first2, InputIter2 last2,
                     OutputIter result);
// Returns a set that is a union of two sets.

OutputIter set_difference(InputIter1 first, InputIter1 last,
                          InputIter2 first2, InputIter2 last2,
                          OutputIter result);
// Returns a set that has elements that belong to the
// first set, but not the second.

OutputIter set_intersection(InputIter1 first, InputIter1 last,
                            InputIter2 first2, InputIter2 last2,
                            OutputIter result);
// Returns a set that has elements that belong to both
// input sets.

bool includes(InputIter1 first, InputIter1 last,
              InputIter2 first2, InputIter2 last2);
// Tests whether set2 is a subset of set1.
```

Class *stack*

The STL class *stack* is an adapter class that has two data-type parameters. The first is the data type for the items in the container. The second is the container used in the implementation of the stack. The default container is an object of class *deque*. Here is a partial listing of the member functions found in the STL class *stack*:

```
template <class T, class Container = deque <T> >
class stack
{
public:
   explicit stack(const& cnt = Container());
   // Default constructor; initializes an empty stack.

   bool empty() const;
   // Determines whether the stack is empty.

   size_type size() const;
   // Returns the number of items that are currently in the
   // stack. size_type is an integral type.

   T &top();
   // Returns a reference to the top of the stack.

   void pop();
   // Removes the top item in the stack.

   void push(const T& x);
   // Adds an item to the top of the stack.

}  // end STL class stack
```

Class *vector*

The STL class *vector* is a container that has one data-type parameter, which is the data type for the items in the container. Indexing is provided with the subscript operator or with the *at* function, which provides range checking as well. Here is a partial listing of the member functions found in the STL class *vector*:

```
template <class T> class vector
{
public:
   vector();
   // Default constructor.

   vector(size_type n);
   // Creates a vector with n elements.
```

```
T &at(size_type n);
// Returns a reference to the item at index n.

bool empty() const;
// Determines whether the vector is empty.

size_type size() const;
// Determines the length of the vector.
// The return type size_type is an integral type.

void push_back(const T&);
// Inserts a new element at the end of the vector.

void pop_back();
// Removes the last element of the vector.

iterator insert(iterator i, const T& val);
// Inserts an item val into the vector.
// before the element specified by the iterator i.

iterator erase(iterator i);
// Removes element at i.


void clear();
// Erases all the elements in the vector.

iterator begin();
// Returns an iterator to the first element in the
// vector.

iterator end();
// Returns an iterator to test for the end of the
// vector.

}   // end STL vector
```

Heap Operations

The STL provides heap operations for containers in the `<algorithm>`. The heap functions require random-access iterators and are overloaded to allow a comparison function object to override the default < operator. The function specifications are listed below:

```
void push_heap(RandomIter first, RandomIter last);
void push_heap(RandomIter first, RandomIter last, Compare cmp);
// Push an item onto the heap.
```

```
// The value pushed is *(last-1).
// A comparison function object may be supplied.

void pop_heap(RandomIter first, RandomIter last);
void pop_heap(RandomIter first, RandomIter last, Compare cmp);
// Push an item onto the heap.
// Swaps first element with *(last-1) and makes [first, last-1]
// into a heap.
// A comparison function object may be supplied.

void make_heap(RandomIter first, RandomIter last);
void make_heap(RandomIter first, RandomIter last, Compare cmp);
// Turns an existing container into a heap.
// A comparison function object may be supplied.

void sort_heap(RandomIter first, RandomIter last);
void sort_heap(RandomIter first, RandomIter last, Compare cmp);
// Turns the heap back into the original container.
// A comparison function object may be supplied.
```

Sorting Algorithms

The STL provides several sort functions for containers in `<algorithm>`. These include full sorts, partial sorts, and partitioning. The functions are overloaded to allow a comparison function object to override the default operator <. Note that the STL class list should use its own sort function. Here is a listing of the STL sort functions:

```
void sort(RandomIter first, RandomIter last);
void sort(RandomIter first, RandomIter last, Compare cmp);
// Sorts first to last into ascending order by default.
// A comparison function object may be supplied.

void stable_sort(RandomIter first, RandomIter last);
void stable_sort(RandomIter first, RandomIter last, Compare cmp);
// Sorts first to last into ascending order by default.
// A comparison function object may be supplied.
// Preserves original ordering of equivalent elements.

void partial_sort(RandomIter first, RandomIter middle,
                  RandomIter last);
void partial_sort(RandomIter first, RandomIter middle,
                  RandomIter last, Compare cmp);
// Sorts the number of elements from first to last
// and places them in the range from first to middle.
// Elements from middle to last are not ordered.
```

```
// Default sort is in ascending order.
// A comparison function object may be supplied.

RandomIter partial_sort_copy(InputIter first, InputIter last,
                             RandomIter first2, RandomIter last2);
RandomIter partial_sort_copy(InputIter first, InputIter last,
                             RandomIter first2, RandomIter last2,
                             Compare cmp);
// Sorts the number of elements from first to last
// and copies them into a container in the range
// from first2 to last2.
// Default sort is in ascending order.
// A comparison function object may be supplied.

void nth_element(RandomIter first, RandomIter nth,
                 RandomIter, last);
void nth_element(RandomIter first, RandomIter nth,
                 RandomIter last, Compare cmp);
// The nth element becomes a dividing point for the container.
// The ranges from first to nth and nth to last are not sorted.
// All elements from first to nth are less than or equal to nth.
// All elements from nth to last are greater than nth.
// A comparison function object may be supplied.

BiIter partition(BiIter first, BiIter last,
                 Predicate p);
// The container is partitioned to place all elements that
// satisfy a particular predicate p before every element that
// does not satisfy the predicate p.
// The two ranges are not sorted.
// The return iterator points to either the first element that
// does not satisfy the predicate p or the end.
// Relative order of equivalent elements is not maintained.

BiIter stable_partition(BiIter first, BiIter last,
                        Predicate p);
// The container is partitioned to place all elements that
// satisfy a particular predicate p before every element that
// does not satisfy the predicate p.
// The two ranges are not sorted.
// The return iterator points to either the first element that
// does not satisfy the predicate p or the end.
// Relative order of equivalent elements is maintained.

OutputIter merge(InputIter first, InputIter last,
                 InputIter2 first2, InputIter2 last2,
                 OutIter res);
```

```
OutputIter merge(InputIter first, InputIter last,
                 InputIter2 first2, InputIter2 last2,
                 OutputIter res, Compare cmp);
// Takes two sorted ranges and
// merges them into another sorted container.
// A comparison function object may be supplied.
// For equivalent elements, elements from the first range will
// precede elements from the second.

void inplace_merge(BiIter  first, BiIter middle, BiIter last);
void inplace_merge(BiIter  first, BiIter middle, BiIter last,
                   Compare cmp);
// Takes two parts of a sorted container
// and merges them in place.
// The two ranges are first to middle and middle to last.
// A comparison function object may be supplied.
// For equivalent elements, elements from the first range will
// precede elements from the second.
```

Search Algorithms for Sorted Ranges

The STL provides a group of operations to find elements in a container within sorted ranges. The search functions are overloaded to allow a comparison function object to override the default < operator. Note that the same comparison object must be used for finding the elements as was used for sorting the elements. Here is a list of STL search functions for sorted ranges:

```
bool binary_search(ForIter first, ForIter last, const T& value);
bool binary_search(ForIter first, ForIter last, const T& value,
                   Compare cmp);
// Returns true if value appears in the sorted range
// from first to last.
// Returns false if value is not found.
// A comparison function object may be supplied.

ForIter lower_bound(ForIter first, ForIter last, const T& value);
ForIter lower_bound(ForIter first, ForIter last, const T& value,
                    Compare cmp);
// Returns an iterator pointing to the first occurrence of value
// in the sorted range from first to last.
// Returns last if value is not found.
// A comparison function object may be supplied.

ForIter upper_bound(ForIter first, ForIter last, const T& value);
ForIter upper_bound(ForIter first, ForIter last, const T& value,
                    Compare cmp);
```

```
// Returns an iterator pointing to one past the last occurrence
// of value in the sorted range from first to last.
// Returns last if value is not found.
// A comparison function object may be supplied.

pair<ForIter, ForIter> equal_range(ForIter first, ForIter last,
                                   const T& value);
pair<ForIter, ForIter> equal_range(ForIter first, ForIter last,
                                   const T& value, Compare cmp);
// Combines lower_bound() and upper_bound() to return a pair
// of iterators to the first and one past the last occurrences
// of value.
// Both iterators point to last if value is not found.
// A comparison function object may be supplied.
```

GLOSSARY

abstract base class   A class without instances that forms the basis of other classes that descend from it. An abstract base class must contain at least one pure virtual function.

abstract data type (ADT)   A collection of data values together with a set of well-specified operations on that data.

abstraction   See *data abstraction* and *functional abstraction*.

access time   The time required to access a particular item in a data structure such as an array, a linked list, or a file.

accessor   A member function of a class that returns the value of a data member. See also *mutator*.

activation record   A record that contains a function's local environment at the time of and as a result of the call to the function.

actual argument   A variable or expression that is passed to a function. An actual argument appears in a call to a function and corresponds to a formal argument in the function's declaration. See also *formal argument, reference argument*, and *value argument*.

adapter container   A container class that provides a restricted interface to another container used in its implementation.

address   A number that labels a location in a computer's memory.

adjacency list   The *n* linked lists that implement a graph of *n* vertices numbered 0, 1, . . . , $n - 1$ such that there is a node in the ith linked list for vertex *j* if and only if there is an edge from vertex *i* to vertex *j*.

adjacency matrix   An *n*-by-*n* array `matrix` that implements a graph of *n* vertices numbered 0, 1, . . . , $n - 1$ such that `graph[i][j]` is 1 if and only if there is an edge from vertex *i* to vertex *j*.

adjacent vertices   Two vertices of a graph that are joined by an edge. In a directed graph, vertex *y* is adjacent to vertex *x* if there is a directed edge from vertex *x* to vertex *y*.

ADT   See *abstract data type*.

aggregate data type   A data type composed of multiple elements. Some examples of aggregate data types are arrays, structures, and files.

algorithm   A step-by-step specification of a method to solve a problem within a finite amount of time.

allocate   See *dynamic allocation* and *static allocation*.

allocator   An object that manages the memory allocation for a container.

analysis of algorithms   A branch of computer science that measures the efficiency of algorithms.

ancestor class   See *base class*.

ancestor of a node n   A node on the path from the root of a tree to *n*.

argument   See *actual argument* and *formal argument*.

array   A data structure that contains a fixed maximum number of elements of the same data type that are referenced directly by means of an index, or subscript.

array-based implementation   An implementation of an ADT that uses an array to store the data values.

as-a   A relationship between classes whereby one class is implemented in terms of another through the use of private inheritance. See also *has-a* and *is-a*.

assertion   A statement that describes the state of an algorithm or program at a certain point in its execution.

associative container   A variable-sized container that supports efficient retrieval of elements (values) based on keys.

attribute   See *data member*.

average-case analysis   A determination of the average amount of time that a given algorithm requires to solve problems of size *n*. See also *worst-case analysis*.

AVL tree   A balanced binary search tree in which rotations restore the tree's balance after each insertion or deletion of a node.

axiom   A mathematical rule or relationship. Axioms can be used to specify the behavior of an ADT operation.

back of a queue   The end of a queue at which items are inserted.

backtracking   A problem-solving strategy that, when it reaches an impasse, retraces its steps in reverse order before trying a new sequence of steps.

balanced binary tree   A binary tree in which the left and right subtrees of any node have heights that differ by at most 1. Also called a *height-balanced tree*.

base case   The known case in either a recursive definition or an inductive proof. Also called the basis or degenerate case.

base class   A class from which another class is derived. The derived class inherits the base class's members. Also called the ancestor class or superclass. See also *derived class* and *inheritance*.

basis   See *base case*.

BFS   See *breadth-first search*.

BFS spanning tree   A spanning tree formed by using a breadth-first search to traverse a graph's vertices.

bidirectional iterator   An iterator that can move either ahead or back from the current item in a container.

Big O notation   A notation that uses the capital letter O to specify an algorithm's order. For example, "$O(f(n))$" means "order $f(n)$." See also *order of an algorithm*.

binary file   A file whose elements are in the computer's internal representation. A binary file is not organized into lines. Also called a general file or nontext file.

binary operator   An operator that requires two operands, for example, the + in 2 + 3. See also *unary operator*.

binary search An algorithm that searches a sorted collection for a particular item by repeatedly halving the collection and determining which half could contain the item.

binary search tree A binary tree where the search key in any node n is greater than the search key in any node in n's left subtree, but less than the search key in any node in n's right subtree.

binary tree A set of zero or more nodes, partitioned into a root node and two possibly empty sets that are binary trees. Thus, each node in a binary tree has at most two children, the left child and the right child.

binding The association of a variable with a memory address and the type of data the variable holds. See also *early binding* and *late binding*.

block A group of data records in a file.

block access Reading or writing a block of data associated with a file.

box method A systematic way to trace the actions of a recursive function.

breadth-first search (BFS) A graph-traversal strategy that visits every vertex adjacent to a vertex v that it can before it visits any other vertex. Thus, the traversal will not embark from any of the vertices adjacent to v until it has visited all possible vertices adjacent to v. See also *depth-first search*.

B-tree A balanced search tree whose leaves are at the same level and whose nodes each contain between $m - 1$ and $[m/2]$ records. Each nonleaf has one more child than it has records. The root of the tree can contain as few as one record and can have as few as two children. Typically, a B-tree is stored in an external file.

bubble sort A sorting algorithm that compares adjacent elements and exchanges them if they are out of order. Comparing the first two elements, the second and third elements, and so on, will move the largest element to the end of the array. Repeating this process will eventually sort the array into ascending order.

bucket A structure associated with a hash address that can accommodate more than one item. An array of buckets can be used as a hash table to resolve collisions.

buffer A location that temporarily stores data as it makes its way from one process or location to another. A buffer enables data to leave one process or location at a different rate than the rate at which it enters another process or location, thus compensating for the difference in these rates.

cardinality The number of elements in a set.

catch To handle, or deal with, an exception.

ceiling of x Denoted by $\lceil x \rceil$, the value of x rounded up. For example, $\lceil 6.1 \rceil = 7$.

chain A linked list used within separate chaining, which is a collision-resolution scheme associated with hashing.

chaining See *separate chaining*.

child of a node n A node directly below node n in a tree.

circuit A special cycle that passes through every vertex (or edge) in a graph exactly once.

circular doubly linked list A doubly linked list whose first node contains a *precede* pointer to the list's last node and whose last node contains a *next* pointer to the list's first node.

circular linked list   A linked list whose last node points to the first node in the list.

class   A C++ construct that enables you to define a new data type.

class diagram   A diagram in the Unified Modeling Language that you use to design a class. It specifies the name of the class, the data members of the class, and the operations.

class template   A specification of a class in terms of a data-type parameter.

client   The program, module, or ADT that uses a class.

closed-form formula   A nonrecursive algebraic expression.

clustering   The tendency of items to map into groups of locations in a hash table, rather than randomly scattered locations. This difficulty, typical of the linear-probing, collision-resolution scheme in hashing, can cause lengthy search times.

code   Statements in a programming language.

coding   Implementing an algorithm in a programming language.

cohesion   The degree to which the portions of a module are related.

collision   A condition that occurs when a hash function maps two or more distinct search keys into the same location.

collision-resolution scheme   The part of hashing that assigns locations in the hash table to items with different search keys when the items are involved in a collision. See also *bucket, chain, clustering, double hashing, folding, linear probing, open addressing, probe sequence, quadratic probing*, and *separate chaining*.

compiler   A program that translates a program written in a high-level language, such as C++, into machine language.

compile time   The time during which a compiler translates a program from source form into machine language. See also *runtime*.

complete binary tree   A binary tree of height h that is full to level $h - 1$ and has level h filled from left to right.

complete graph   A graph that has an edge between every pair of distinct vertices.

completely balanced binary tree   A binary tree in which the left and right subtrees of any node have the same height.

connected component   For a graph that is not connected, a subset of the graph's vertices that a traversal visits beginning at a given vertex.

connected graph   A graph that has a path between every pair of distinct vertices.

constructor   A method that initializes new instances of a class. See also *default constructor*.

container class   A class that holds a collection of objects.

containment   See *has-a*.

cost of a path   The sum of the weights of the edges of a path in a weighted graph. Also called the weight or length of a path.

cost of a program   Factors such as the computer resources (computing time and memory) that a program consumes, the difficulties encountered by those who use the program, and the consequences of a program that does not behave correctly.

cost of a spanning tree   The sum of the weights of the edges in a weighted graph's spanning tree.

coupling   The degree to which the functions in a program are interdependent.

cycle   A path in a graph that begins and ends at the same vertex. See also *circuit* and *simple cycle.*

data abstraction   A design principle that separates the operations that can be performed on a collection of data from the implementation of the operations. See also *functional abstraction.*

data field   See *data member.*

data flow   The flow of data between modules.

data member   A portion of a C++ structure or class that stores data of a particular type.

data record   An element in a file. A data record can be anything from a simple value, such as an integer, to a C++ structure, such as an employee record. See also *block* and *record.*

data structure   A construct that is defined within a programming language to store a collection of data.

deep copy   A copy that includes the data structures to which the object's data member(s) point. See also *shallow copy.*

default constructor   A constructor that has no arguments.

degenerate case   See *base case.*

depth-first search (DFS)   A graph-traversal strategy that proceeds along a path from a given vertex as deeply into the graph as possible before backtracking. That is, after visiting a vertex, a DFS visits, if possible, an unvisited adjacent vertex. If the traversal reaches a vertex that has no unvisited adjacent vertices, it backs up and then visits, if possible, an unvisited adjacent vertex. See also *breadth-first search.*

deque   A double-ended queue. This ADT can have items added to or deleted from either end.

derived class   A class that inherits the members of another class called the base class. Also called descendant class or subclass. See also *base class, inheritance,* and *multiple inheritance.*

descendant class   See *derived class.*

descendant of a node *n*   A node on a path from *n* to a leaf of a tree.

destructor   A method that performs all tasks necessary to deallocate an object.

DFS   See *depth-first search.*

DFS spanning tree   A spanning tree formed by using a depth-first search to traverse a graph's vertices.

dictionary   See *table.*

digraph   See *directed graph.*

Dijkstra's shortest path algorithm   An algorithm that solves the problem of finding the shortest path from a point in a graph (the *source*) to a destination.

direct access   A process that provides access to any element in a data structure by position without the need to first access other elements in the structure. Also called random access. See also *sequential access*.

direct access file   A file whose elements are accessible by position without first accessing preceding elements within the file.

directed edge   An edge in a directed graph; that is, an edge that has a direction.

directed graph   A graph whose edges indicate a direction. Also called a digraph. See also *undirected graph*.

directed path   A sequence of directed edges that begins at one vertex and ends at another vertex in a directed graph. See also *path* and *simple path*.

disconnected graph   A graph that is not connected; that is, a graph that has at least one pair of vertices without a path between them.

divide and conquer   A problem-solving strategy that divides a problem into smaller problems, each of which is solved separately.

double hashing   A collision-resolution scheme that uses two hash functions. The hash table is searched for an unoccupied location, starting from the location that one hash function determines and considering every n^{th} location, where n is determined from a second hash function.

doubly linked list   A linked list whose nodes each contain two pointers, one to the next node and one to the previous node.

dummy head node   In a linked list, a first node that is not used for data but is always present. The item at the first position of the list is thus actually in the second node.

dynamic allocation   The assignment of memory to a variable during program execution, as opposed to during compilation. See also *static allocation*.

dynamic binding   See *late binding*.

dynamic object   A dynamically allocated object. An object whose memory is allocated at execution time and remains allocated only as long as you want. See also *static object*.

early binding   The association of a variable with its type at compilation time. Also called static binding. See also *late binding*, *static method*, and *virtual function*.

edge   The connection between two nodes of a graph.

empty string   A string of length zero.

empty tree   A tree with no nodes.

encapsulation   An information-hiding technique that combines data and operations to form an object.

Euler circuit   An Euler circuit begins at a vertex v, passes through every edge exactly once, and terminates at v.

event   An occurrence, such as an arrival or a departure, in an event-driven simulation. See also *external event* and *internal event*.

event-driven simulation   A simulation that uses events generated by a mathematical model that is based on statistics and probability. The times of events are either read as input or computed from other event times. Because only those times at which the events occur are of interest and because no action is required at times between the occurrence of events, the simulation can advance from the time of one event directly to the time of the next. See also *time-driven simulation.*

event list An ADT within an event-driven simulation that keeps track of arrival and departure events that will occur but have not occurred yet.

exception An unusual or exceptional event that occurs during the execution of a program.

exception handler C++ code that executes to deal with an exception when one occurs.

exhaustive search A search strategy that must examine every item in a collection of items before it can determine that the item sought does not exist.

extensible class A class that enables you to add capabilities to its descendants without having access to the base class's implementation. Extensible classes should define virtual functions.

external event An event that is determined from the input data to an event-driven simulation. See also *internal event.*

external methods Algorithms that require external files because the data will not fit entirely into the computer's main memory.

external sort A sorting algorithm that is used when the collection of data will not fit in the computer's main memory all at once but must reside on secondary storage such as a disk. See also *internal sort.*

fail-safe programming A technique whereby a programmer includes checks within a program for anticipated errors.

Fibonacci sequence The sequence of integers 1, 1, 2, 3, 5, . . . defined by the recurrence relationship

$$a_1 = 1, a_2 = 1, a_n = a_{n-1} + a_{n-2} \text{ for } n > 2$$

field A component of a record.

FIFO See *first in, first out.*

file A data structure that contains a sequence of components of the same data type. See also *binary file, index file,* and *text file.*

file component An indivisible piece of data in a file.

file variable A C++ identifier that names a file.

file window A marker of the current position in the file.

first in, first out (FIFO) A property of a queue whereby the removal and retrieval operations access the item that was inserted first (earliest). See also *last in, first out.*

fixed size A characteristic of a data structure whose memory allocation is determined at compilation time and cannot change during program execution. See also *static allocation.*

folding A hashing technique that breaks a search key into parts and combines some or all of those parts, by using an operation such as addition, to form a hash address.

formal argument An identifier that appears in the declaration of a function and represents the actual argument that the calling program will pass to the function. See also *actual argument, reference argument,* and *value argument.*

4-node   A tree node that contains three data items and has four children. See also *3-node* and *2-node*.

free list   A list of available nodes used in an array-based implementation of an ADT or a data structure.

friend of a class   A class or nonmember function that can access the private and protected members of a given class.

front of a queue   The end of a queue at which items are removed and retrieved.

full binary tree   A binary tree of height *h* with no missing nodes. All leaves are at level *h*, and all other nodes each have two children.

functional abstraction   A design principle that separates the purpose and use of a module from its implementation. Also called procedural abstraction. See also *data abstraction*.

function member   See *member function*.

function object   Any object that can be called as if it is a function. An ordinary function is a function object, and so is a function pointer.

general file   See *binary file*.

general tree   A set of one or more nodes, partitioned into a root node and subsets that are general subtrees of the root.

global namespace   A collection of identifiers declared outside of a namespace. The identifiers in the global namespace are known everywhere in a program.

global variable   A variable declared in the main function of a program; that is, a variable whose scope is the entire program. See also *local variable*.

grammar   The rules that define a language.

graph   A set *V* of vertices, or nodes, and a set *E* of edges that connect the vertices.

graph traversal   A process that starts at vertex *v* and visits all vertices *w* for which there is a path between *v* and *w*. A graph traversal visits every vertex in a graph if and only if the graph is connected, regardless of where the traversal starts.

growth-rate function   A function of the size of a problem, used to specify an algorithm's order.

has-a   A relationship between classes whereby one class contains an instance of another class. Also called containment. See also *as-a* and *is-a*.

hash function   A function that maps the search key of a table item into a location that will contain the item.

hashing   A method that enables access to table items in time that is relatively constant and independent of the items by using a hash function and a scheme for resolving collisions.

hash table   An array that contains the table items, as assigned by a hash function.

head   See *head pointer*.

header   A mechanism that provides information about the contents of a library, including the declarations of functions, data types, and constants. In current versions of C++, the header is simply an abstraction that the compiler may map to a filename, or handle in a different manner. For older versions of C++ and user defined libraries, the header is usually a file. Also called a header file or specification file. See also *implementation file*.

header file   See *header*.

head pointer   A pointer to the first node in a linked list. Also called a head.

heap   A complete binary tree whose nodes each contain a priority value that is greater than or equal to the priority values in the node's children. See also *maxheap* and *minheap*.

heapsort   A sorting algorithm that first transforms an array into a heap, then removes the heap's root (the largest element) by exchanging it with the heap's last element, and finally transforms the resulting semiheap back into a heap.

height-balanced tree   See *balanced binary tree*.

height of a tree   The number of nodes on the longest path from the root of the tree to a leaf.

hierarchical relationship   The "parent-child" relationship between the nodes in a tree.

highly cohesive module   A module that performs one well-defined task. See also *cohesion*.

implement   (1) To create a program for an algorithm. (2) To use a data structure to realize an ADT.

implementation file   A file that contains function definitions for each function declared in a corresponding header.

index   (1) An integral value that references the elements of an array. Also called a subscript. (2) Another name for an index file.

index file   A data structure whose entries—called index records—are used to locate items in an external file. Also called the index.

index record   An entry in an index file that points to a record in the corresponding external data file. This entry contains a search key and a pointer.

induction   See *mathematical induction*.

inductive conclusion   See *inductive step*.

inductive hypothesis   See *inductive step*.

inductive proof   A proof that uses the principle of mathematical induction.

inductive step   The step in an inductive proof that begins with an inductive hypothesis ("if $P(k)$ is true for any $k \geq 0$") and demonstrates the inductive conclusion ("then $P(k + 1)$ is true").

infix expression   An algebraic expression in which every binary operator appears between its two operands. See also *postfix expression* and *prefix expression*.

information hiding   A process that hides certain implementation details within a module and makes them inaccessible from outside the module.

inheritance   A relationship among classes whereby a class derives properties from a previously defined class. See also *derived class* and *multiple inheritance*.

inorder successor of a node N The inorder successor of N's search key. The inorder successor is in the leftmost node of N's right subtree.

inorder successor of x The search key in a search tree that an inorder traversal visits immediately after x.

inorder traversal   A traversal of a binary tree that processes (visits) a node after it traverses the node's left subtree, but before it traverses the node's right subtree. See also *postorder traversal* and *preorder traversal*.

insertion sort   A sorting algorithm that considers items one at a time and inserts each item into its proper sorted position.

instance   An object that is the result of either declaring a variable of a particular class or calling *new* with a pointer to a class.

interface   The communication mechanisms between modules or systems.

internal event   An event that is determined by a computation within an event-driven simulation. See also *external event*.

internal node of a tree   A node that is not a leaf.

internal sort   A sorting algorithm that requires the collection of data to fit entirely in the computer's main memory. See also *external sort*.

invariant   An assertion that is always true at a particular point in an algorithm or program.

is-a   A relationship between classes whereby one class is a special case of another class. You implement an *is-a* relationship by using public inheritance. See also *as-a* and *has-a*.

iteration   (1) A process that is repetitive. (2) A single pass through a loop.

iterative solution   A solution that involves loops.

iterator   A class that interacts with another class representing a collection of objects to provide access to either the next or previous item within the collection. An iterator provides a way to cycle through the objects in the collection.

key   (1) The portion of an index record that corresponds to the search key in a record in an external data file. (2) Another name for search key.

language   A set of strings of symbols that adhere to the rules of a grammar.

last in, first out (LIFO)   A property of a stack whereby the deletion and retrieval operations access the most recently inserted item. See also *first in, first out*.

late binding   The association of a variable with its type during program execution. Also called dynamic binding. See also *early binding, static method*, and *virtual function*.

leaf   A tree node with no children.

left child of a node n A node directly below and to the left of node n in a tree.

left subtree of a node n The left child of node n plus its descendants in a tree.

length of a path   See *cost of a path*.

level of a node   The root of a tree is at level 1. If a node is not the root, then its level is 1 greater than the level of its parent.

LIFO   See *last in, first out*.

linear implementation   An array-based implementation or a pointer-based implementation.

linear linked list   A linked list that is not circular.

linear probing   A collision-resolution scheme that searches the hash table sequentially, starting from the original location specified by the hash function, for an unoccupied location.

linked list   A list of elements, or nodes, that are linked to one another such that each element points to the next element.

list   An ADT whose elements are referenced by their position. See also *sorted list*.

load factor   A measure of the relative fullness of a hash table, defined as the ratio of a table's current number of items to its maximum size.

local environment of a function   A function's local variables, a copy of the actual value arguments, a return address in the calling routine, and the value of the function itself.

local identifier   An identifier whose scope is the block that contains its declaration.

local variable   A variable declared within a function and available only within that function. See also *global variable*.

loop invariant   An assertion that is true before and after each execution of a loop within an algorithm or program.

loosely coupled modules   Two or more modules that are not dependent on one another. See also *coupling*.

machine language   A language composed of the fundamental instructions that a computer can execute directly.

mathematical induction   A method for proving properties that involve non-negative integers. Starting from a base case, you show that if a property is true for an arbitrary nonnegative integer k, then the property is true for the integer $k + 1$.

maxheap   Another name for a heap. See also *minheap*.

member   A component of a structure or class that is either data or a function. See also *data member* and *member function*.

member function   A function that is a member of a class. Also called a method.

memory leak   The failure to deallocate dynamically allocated memory that has no pointer to it.

mergesort   A sorting algorithm that divides an array into halves, sorts each half, and then merges the sorted halves into one sorted array. Mergesort can also be adapted for sorting an external file.

message   A request, in the form of a function call, that an object perform an operation.

method   See *member function*.

minheap   A complete binary tree whose nodes each contain a priority value that is less than or equal to the priority values in the node's children. See also *maxheap*.

minimum spanning tree   A graph's spanning tree for which the sum of its edge weights is minimal among all spanning trees for the graph.

modular program   A program that is divided into isolated components, or modules, that have clearly defined purposes and interactions.

module   An individual component of a program, such as a function, a group of functions, or other block of code.

multigraph   A graphlike structure that allows duplicate edges between its vertices.

multiple indexing   A process that uses more than one index file to an external data file.

multiple inheritance   A relationship among classes whereby a class derives properties from more than one previously defined class. See also *derived class*.

mutator   A member function of a class that changes the value of a data member. See also *accessor*.

namespace   A mechanism in C++ for logically grouping declarations and definitions into a common declarative region. Each identifier in the namespace has a unique meaning.

node   An element in a linked list, graph, or tree that usually contains both data and a pointer to the next element in the data structure.

nontext file   See *binary file*.

object   An instance of a class.

object-oriented programming (OOP)   A software engineering technique that views a program as a collection of components called objects that interact. OOP embodies three fundamental principles: encapsulation, inheritance, and polymorphism.

object type compatibility   A characteristic of objects that enables you to use an instance of a derived class instead of an instance of a base class, but not the converse. The object type of an actual argument in a call to a function can be a descendant of the corresponding formal argument's object type.

O($f(n)$)   Order $f(n)$. See *Big O notation* and *order of an algorithm*.

OOP   See *object-oriented programming*.

open   A process that prepares a file for either input or output and positions the file window. A state of readiness for I/O.

open addressing   A category of collision-resolution schemes in hashing that probe for an empty, or open, location in the hash table in which to place the item. See also *double hashing*, *linear probing*, and *quadratic probing*.

order of an algorithm   An algorithm's time requirement as a function of the problem size. An algorithm A is order $f(n)$ if constants K and n_0 exist such that A requires no more than $K * f(n)$ time units to solve a problem of size $n \geq n_0$. See also *Big O notation*.

order-of-magnitude analysis   An analysis of an algorithm's time requirement as a function of the problem size. See also *order of an algorithm*.

overloaded operator   An operator with multiple meanings, each of which is determined by the context in which the operator appears.

override   To redefine a virtual member function of a class within a derived class. See also *redefinition*.

palindrome   A character string that reads the same from left to right as it does from right to left, for example, "deed."

parameter   See *actual argument* and *formal argument*.

parent of a node *n*   The node directly above node *n* in a tree.

partition   To divide a data structure such as an array into segments.

path   A sequence of edges in a graph that begins at one vertex and ends at another vertex. Because a tree is a special graph, you can have a path through a tree. See also *directed path* and *simple path*.

perfect hash function   An ideal hash function that maps each search key into a unique location in the hash table. Perfect hash functions exist when all possible search keys are known.

pivot item   A central element in an algorithm. For example, the quicksort algorithm partitions an array about a particular item called the pivot.

planar graph   A graph that can be drawn in a plane in at least one way so that no two edges cross.

pointer   (1) A pointer variable in C++. (2) Generically, an element that references a memory cell. (3) Sometimes an indicator, such as an integer, to an element within a data structure. For example, an index record, which points to a data record in an external data file, contains such an indicator, namely, the number of the block that contains the data record.

pointer-based implementation   An implementation of an ADT or a data structure that uses pointers to organize its elements.

pointer variable   A C++ variable that references a memory cell. Also called a pointer.

polymorphism   The ability of a variable name to represent, during program execution, instances of different but related classes that descend from a common base class.

pop   To remove an item from a stack.

position–oriented ADT   An ADT whose operations involve the positions of its items. See also *value-oriented ADT*.

postcondition   A statement of the conditions that exist at the end of a module.

postfix expression   An algebraic expression in which every binary operator follows its two operands. See also *infix expression* and *prefix expression*.

postorder traversal   A traversal of a binary tree that processes (visits) a node after it traverses both of the node's subtrees. See also *inorder traversal* and *preorder traversal*.

precondition   A statement of the conditions that must exist at the beginning of a module in order for the module to work correctly.

predecessor   (1) In a linked list, the predecessor of node *x* is the node that points to *x*. (2) In a directed graph, vertex *x* is a predecessor of vertex *y* if there is a directed edge from *x* to *y*, that is, if *y* is adjacent to *x*. See also *successor*.

prefix expression   An algebraic expression in which every binary operator precedes its two operands. See also *infix expression* and *postfix expression*.

preorder traversal   A traversal of a binary tree that processes (visits) a node before it traverses both of the node's subtrees. See also *inorder traversal* and *postorder traversal*.

priority queue   An ADT that orders its items by a priority value. The first item removed is the one having the highest priority value.

priority value   A value assigned to the items in a priority queue to indicate the item's priority.

private inheritance   A form of inheritance whereby the public and protected members of a base class are private members of the derived class.

private section   The portion of a class that is accessible only by member functions and friends of the class.

probe sequence   The sequence of locations in the hash table that a collision-resolution scheme examines.

problem solving   The entire process of taking the statement of a problem and developing a computer program that solves that problem.

procedural abstraction   See *functional abstraction*.

protected inheritance   A form of inheritance whereby the public and protected members of a base class are protected members of the derived class.

protected section   The portion of a class that is accessible by member functions of both the class and a derived class.

public inheritance   A form of inheritance whereby the public and protected members of a base class remain, respectively, public and protected members of the derived class.

public section   The portion of a class that is accessible by any user of the class, including member functions of the class and any derived class.

pure virtual function   A virtual function with an undefined body, written as `virtual prototype = 0` within the class definition.

push   To add an item to a stack.

quadratic probing   A collision-resolution scheme that searches the hash table for an occupied location beginning with the original location that the hash function specifies and continuing at increments of $1^2, 2^2, 3^2$, and so on.

qualify   In C++, to relate an item `a` to an item `b` by writing `b.a`, in which case "`b` qualifies `a`" or "`a` is qualified by `b`."

queue   An ADT whose first (earliest) inserted item is the first item removed or retrieved. This property is called first in, first out, or simply FIFO. Items enter a queue at its back and leave at its front.

quicksort   A sorting algorithm that partitions an array's elements around a pivot p to generate two smaller sorting problems: Sort the array's left section, whose elements are less than p, and sort the array's right section, whose elements are greater than or equal to p.

radix sort   A sorting algorithm that treats each data element as a character string and repeatedly organizes the data into groups according to the ith character in each element.

random access   See *direct access*.

range query   An operation that retrieves all table items whose search keys fall into a given range of values.

rear of a queue   Another term for the back of a queue.

recognition algorithm   An algorithm, based on a language's grammar, that determines whether a given string is in the language.

record   A group of related items, called fields, that are not necessarily of the same data type. See also *data record*.

recurrence relation   A mathematical formula that generates the terms in a sequence from previous terms.

recursion   A process that solves a problem by solving smaller problems of exactly the same type as the original problem.

recursive call   A call within a function to the function itself.

red-black tree   A representation of a 2-3-4 tree as a binary tree whose nodes have red and black child pointers.

redefinition   A member function in a derived class that revises a nonvirtual member function in the base class and has the same declaration. See also *override*.

reference argument   A formal argument that represents an actual argument. Any change that the function makes to a reference argument changes the corresponding actual argument in the calling routine. You designate a reference argument in a function's declaration by following the argument's type with &. See also *value argument*.

right child of a node *n*   A node directly below and to the right of node *n* in a tree.

right subtree of a node *n*   The right child of node *n* plus its descendants in a tree.

rightward drift   (1) In an array-based implementation of a queue, the problem of the front of the queue moving toward the end of the array.   (2) In a C++ program, the problem of nested blocks bumping against the right-hand margin of the page.

root   The only node in a tree with no parent.

rotation   An operation used to maintain the balance of a red-black or AVL tree.

runtime   The execution phase of a program. The time during which a program's instructions execute. See also *compile time*.

scope of an identifier   The part of a program in which an identifier has meaning.

scope resolution operator   The C++ operator ::. When you implement any member function, you qualify its name with its class type followed by the scope resolution operator to distinguish it from other functions that might have the same name.

search   A process that locates a certain item in a collection of items.

search key   The part of a record that identifies it within a collection of records. A search algorithm uses a search key to locate a record within a collection of records. Also called a key.

search tree   A tree whose organization facilitates the retrieval of its items. See also *AVL tree, binary search tree, B-tree of degree m, red-black tree, 2-3 tree,* and *2-3-4 tree*.

selection sort   A sorting algorithm that selects the largest item and puts it in its correct place, then selects the next largest item and puts it in its correct place, and so on.

semiheap   A complete binary tree in which the root's left and right subtrees are both heaps.

separate chaining   A collision-resolution scheme that uses an array of linked lists as a hash table. The ith linked list, or chain, contains all items that map into location i.

sequential access   A process that stores or retrieves elements in a data structure one after another, starting at the beginning. See also *direct access*.

sequential access file   A file whose elements must be processed sequentially. That is, to process the data stored at a given position, you must advance the file window beyond all the data that precedes it.

sequential search   An algorithm that locates an item in a collection by examining items in order, one at a time, beginning with the first item.

shallow copy   A copy that does not include any data structures to which the object's data members might point. See also *deep copy of an object*.

shortest path   Between two given vertices in a weighted graph, the path that has the smallest sum of its edge weights.

siblings   Tree nodes that have a common parent.

side effect   (1) A change to a variable that exists outside of a function and that is not passed as an argument. (2) An occurrence that is not specified by a module.

simple cycle   A cycle in a graph that does not pass through a vertex more than once.

simple data type   A data type that is not aggregate, such as `int` or `double`.

simple path   A path in a graph that does not pass through a vertex more than once. See also *directed path*.

simulation   A technique for modeling the behavior of both natural and artificial systems. Generally, its goal is to generate statistics that summarize the performance of an existing system or to predict the performance of a proposed system. A simulation reflects long-term average behavior of a system rather than predicting occurrences of specific events.

software engineering   A branch of computer science that provides techniques to facilitate the development of computer programs.

software life cycle   The phases of software development: specification, design, risk analysis, verification, coding, testing, refining, production, and maintenance.

solution   Algorithms and ways to store data that solves a problem.

sorted list   An ADT that maintains its elements in sorted order and retrieves them by their position number within the list. See also *list*.

sorted order   The order of a collection of data that is in either ascending or descending order.

sorted run   Sorted data that is part of an external sort.

sorting   A process that organizes a collection of data into either ascending or descending order. See also *external sort* and *internal sort*.

sort key   The part of a record that determines the order of entire records within a collection of records. A sorting algorithm uses a sort key to order records within a collection of records.

source-inclusion facility   A facility that automatically places the contents of a file at a specified point in a program before the program is compiled. The `#include` statement provides this facility in C++.

source program   A program written in a programming language that needs to be compiled. For example, a C++ program. Also called source code.

spanning tree   A subgraph of a connected, undirected graph G that contains all of G's vertices and enough of its edges to form a tree. See also *BFS spanning tree* and *DFS spanning tree*.

specification file   See *header*.

stack   An ADT whose most recently inserted item is the first item removed or retrieved. This property is called last in, first out, or simply LIFO. Items enter and leave a stack at its top.

Standard Template Library (STL)   A library containing template classes for many commonly used ADTs, including lists, stacks, and queues. It also contains template functions for common algorithms such as sorting.

static allocation   The assignment of memory to a variable during compilation, as opposed to during program execution. See also *dynamic allocation*.

static binding   See *early binding*.

static method   A method whose body is determined (bound to the object) at compilation time. See also *early binding*, *late binding*, and *virtual function*.

static object   A statically allocated object. An object whose memory is allocated at compilation time and remains allocated for the duration of the program's execution. See also *dynamic object*.

string   A sequence of characters. A C++ string is an object of type `string`. A C string is an array that terminates with the character `/0`.

structure chart   An illustration of the hierarchy of modules that solve a problem.

subclass   See *derived class*.

subgraph   A subset of a graph's vertices and edges.

subscript   An integer that references the elements of an array. Also called an index.

subtree   Any node in a tree, together with all of the node's descendants.

subtree of a node n   A tree that consists of a child of n and the child's descendants.

successor   (1) In a linked list, the successor of node x is the node to which x points. (2) In a directed graph, vertex y is a successor of vertex x if there is a directed edge from x to y, that is, if y is adjacent to x. See also *predecessor*.

superclass   See *base class*.

symmetric matrix   An n-by-n matrix A whose elements satisfy the relationship $A_{ij} = A_{ji}$.

table   An ADT whose data items are stored and retrieved according to their search-key values. Also called a dictionary.

tail pointer   A pointer to the last node in a linked list. Also called a tail.

tail recursion   A type of recursion in which the recursive call is the last action taken.

template   See *class template*.

text file   A file of characters that are organized into lines.

3-node   A tree node that contains two data items and has three children. See also *4-node* and *2-node*.

throw   To indicate an exception.

time-driven simulation   A simulation in which the time of an event, such as an arrival or departure, is determined randomly and compared with a simulated clock. See also *event-driven simulation*.

top-down design   A process that addresses a task at successively lower levels of detail, producing independent modules.

top of a stack   The end of a stack at which items are inserted, retrieved, and deleted.

topological order   A list of vertices in a directed graph without cycles such that vertex x precedes vertex y if there is a directed edge from x to y in the graph. A topological order is not unique, in general.

topological sorting   In a directed graph without cycles, the process of arranging the vertices into a topological order.

traversal   An operation that visits (accesses) each element in an ADT or data structure.

tree   A connected, undirected graph without cycles. See also *binary tree* and *general tree*.

`try-catch` block   C++ code that deals with an exception when one occurs. A specific example of an exception handler.

2-node   A tree node that contains one data item and has two children. See also *4-node* and *3-node*.

2-3 tree   A tree such that each internal node (nonleaf) has either two or three children, and all leaves are at the same level. A node can have a left subtree, a middle subtree, and a right subtree.

   If a node has two children and contains one data item, the value of the search key in the node must be greater than the value of the search key in the left child and smaller than the value of the search key in the right child. If a node has three children and contains two data items, the value of the smaller search key in the node must be greater than the value of the search key in the left child and smaller than the value of the search key in the middle child; the value of the larger search key in the node must be greater than the value of the search key in the middle child and smaller than the value of the search key in the right child.

2-3-4 tree   A tree such that each internal node (nonleaf) has either two, three, or four children, and all leaves are at the same level. A node can have a left subtree, a middle-left subtree, a middle-right subtree, and a right subtree.

   If a node has two or three children, it adheres to the specifications of a 2-3 tree. If a node has four children and three data items, the value of the smaller search key in the node must be greater than the value of the search key in the left child and smaller than the value of the search key in the middle-left child; the value of the middle search key in the node must be greater than the value of the search key in the middle-left child and smaller than the value of the search key in the middle-right child; the value of the larger search key in the node must be greater than the value of the search key in the middle-right child and smaller than the value of the search key in the right child.

type compatible   See *object type compatible*.

unary operator   An operator that requires only one operand, for example, the − in −5. See also *binary operator*.

undirected graph   A graph that has at most one edge between any two vertices and whose edges do not indicate a direction. See also *directed graph*.

Unified Modeling Language (UML)   A modeling language used to express object-oriented designs. The UML provides notation for both diagrams and text-based descriptions. See also *class diagram*.

user   The person who uses a program.

user interface   The portion of a program that provides for user input or control.

value argument   A formal argument whose value is initially the value of the corresponding actual argument. Any change that the function makes to a value argument is not reflected in the corresponding actual argument in the calling routine. The default when you do not follow the argument's type with `&`. See also *reference argument*.

valued function   A function that returns a value. See also `void` *function*.

value-oriented ADT   An ADT whose operations involve the values of its data items. See also *position-oriented ADT*.

vertex   A node in a graph.

virtual function   A member function of a class that a derived class can override, that is, redefine. The body of a virtual function is determined at execution time. See also *early binding*, *late binding*, *static method*, and *virtual method table*.

virtual method   See *virtual function*.

virtual method table (VMT)   The table that exists for an object type that defines a virtual function. For every virtual function in the object, the object's VMT contains a pointer to the actual instructions that implement the function. This pointer is established by the constructor during program execution.

visit   The act of processing an item during a traversal of an ADT or a data structure.

VMT   See *virtual method table*.

`void` function   A function that does not return a value. See also *valued function*.

weighted graph   A graph whose edges are labeled with numeric values.

weight of an edge   The numeric label on an edge in a weighted graph.

weight of a path   See *cost of a path*.

worst-case analysis   A determination of the maximum amount of time that a given algorithm requires to solve problems of size *n*. See also *average-case analysis*.

Answers to Self-Test Exercises

1. $0 \leq index \leq n$ and $sum = item[0] + \cdots + item[index]$.

2. The specifications include type definitions, arguments, and pre- and postconditions.

```
sum(in anArray:arrayType, in n:integer):elementType
// Computes the sum of the first 5 positive elements
// in an array anArray.
// Precondition: The array anArray has n elements, n >= 5,
// at least 5 elements in anArray are positive.
// Postcondition: Returns the sum of the first 5 positive
// elements in anArray; anArray and n are unchanged.
```

Another solution:

```
computeSum(in anArray:arrayType, in n:integer,
           out sum:elementType, out success:boolean)
// Computes the sum of the first 5 positive elements in array
// anArray.
// Precondition: The array anArray has n elements.
// Postcondition: If anArray contains at least 5
// positive elements, then sum is sum of the first
// 5 positive elements and success is true.
// Otherwise, sum is 0 and success is false;
// anArray and n are unchanged.
```

Chapter 2

1. The product of n numbers is defined in terms of the product of $n - 1$ numbers, which is a smaller problem of the same type. When n is 1, the product is *anArray[0]*; this occurrence is the base case. Because $n \geq 1$ initially and n decreases by 1 at each recursive call, the base case will be reached.

2. ```
void computeProduct(const double anArray[], int n, double &product)
{
   if (n == 1)
      product = anArray[0];

   else
   { computeProduct(anArray, n-1, product);
      product = anArray[n-1] * product;
   } // end if
} // end computeProduct
```

3. ```
void countDown(int n)
// Precondition: n > 0.
// Postcondition: Writes n, n - 1, ... , 1.
{
   if (n > 0)
   {  cout << n << endl;
      countDown(n-1);
   }  // end if
}  // end countDown
```

4. ```
double product(const double anArray[], int first, int last)
// Precondition: anArray[first..last] is an array of real numbers, where
// first <= last.
// Postcondition: Returns the product of the numbers in
// anArray[first..last].
{
   if (first == last)
      return anArray[first];
   else
      return anArray[last] * product(anArray, first, last-1);
} // end product
```

5. *writeBackward*, *binarySearch*, *kSmall*, and the function *countDown* in Self-Test Exercise 3.

6. *c(4, 2) = 6*

7. The three recursive calls result in the following moves: Move a disk from *A* to *C*, from *A* to *B*, and then from *C* to *B*.

# Chapter 3

1. A wall is a visualization of abstraction and modularity. Modules should be as independent as possible: Walls prevent other parts of the program from seeing the details of modules. A contract is a
```

specification of what the module, which is behind the wall, is to do. The contract governs the slit in the wall; it specifies what is to be passed to the module and what will be passed out. The contract does not specify how to implement the module.

These concepts help during the problem-solving process by encouraging you to divide the problem into small parts and to focus first on what you want done rather than on how to do it.

2. `swap(inout aList:List, in i:integer, in j:integer)`
   `// Swaps the i`th` and j`th` items in the list aList.`

   ```
   // copy ith and jth items
   aList.retrieve(i, ithItem, success)
   aList.retrieve(j, jthItem, success)

   // replace ith item with jth
   aList.remove(i, success)
   aList.insert(i, jthItem, success)

   // replace jth item with ith
   aList.remove(j, success)
   aList.insert(j, ithItem, success)
   ```

   Notice that the order of operations is important because when you delete an item, *remove* renumbers the remaining items. If you did not assume that the items at positions *i* and *j* existed, you would have to check *success* after every operation.

3. milk, eggs, butter

4. Specify `createList`, `destroyList`, `isEmpty`, and `getLength` as you would for the ADT list.

   ```
   +insert(in newItem:ListItemType, out success:boolean)
   // Inserts newItem at the end of a list. The flag success
   // indicates whether the insertion was successful.

   +remove(out success:boolean)
   // Deletes the item at the end of a list. The flag success
   // indicates whether the deletion was successful.

   +retrieve(out dataItem:ListItemType, out success:boolean)
   // Sets dataItem to the item at the end of a list.
   // The list is left unchanged by this operation. The flag
   // indicates whether the retrieval was successful.
   ```

5. `+createSortedList()`
   `// `**`Precondition:`**` None.`
   `// `**`Postcondition:`**` An empty sorted list is created.`

```
+destroySortedList()
// Precondition: None.
// Postcondition: The list no longer exists.

+sortedIsEmpty():boolean {query}
// Precondition: None.
// Postcondition: Returns true if the list is empty;
// otherwise returns false.

+sortedGetLength():integer {query}
// Precondition: None.
// Postcondition: Returns the number of items that are in a sorted list.

+sortedInsert(in newItem:ListItemType, out success:boolean)
// Precondition: newItem is the item to be inserted.
// Postcondition: newItem is inserted into its proper sorted position in
// the sorted list and success is true. If the insertion was not
// successful, success is false and the list is unchanged.

+sortedRemove(in anItem:ListItemType, out success:boolean)
// Precondition: anItem is the item to be deleted.
// Postcondition: If anItem was in the list, it is deleted and success is
// true. Otherwise, success is false.

+sortedRetrieve(in index:integer, out dataItem:ListItemType,
                out success:boolean) {query}
// Precondition: index is the number of the desired item in the list.
// Postcondition: If 1 <= index <= sortedGetLength(), dataItem is the
// item in the list whose position number is index and success
// is true. Otherwise, success is false.

+locatePosition(in anItem:ListItemType, out position:integer,
                out isPresent:boolean)
// Precondition: anItem is the item to be located.
// Postcondition: If anItem is in the list, position is its position
// and isPresent is true. Otherwise, if anItem is not in the list,
// position indicates where it belongs in the list and isPresent is
// false. anItem and the list are unchanged.
```

6. `sortList(in aList:List, out aSortedList:SortedList)`
   ```
   // Creates a sorted list aSortedList from the items in the list aList.

   aSortedList.createSortedList()
   for (i = 1 to aList.getLength())
   {  aList.retrieve(i, item, success)
      aSortedList.sortedInsert(item, success)
   }
   ```

7. Duplicate values in an ADT list are permissible and do not affect its specifications, because its operations are by position. For a sorted list, however, you need to revise the specifications to accommodate duplicates. You could either prevent the insertion of duplicate items or allow duplicates. If you do allow the insertion of duplicates, you need to decide where to insert them, whether to delete all occurrences of an item or only the first instance, and which of several duplicate items to retrieve.

Chapter 4

1. Values of pointers displayed are indicated by *xxxx* in the following trace:

xxxx xxxx

7 11 11

7 18 18

7 4 18

2. **a.** No. If *cur* points to the last node and *prev* points to the next-to-last node, *prev->next = cur->next* sets the *next* pointer of the next-to-last node to *NULL*.

   b. This case is the same as deletion of the first node.

   c. Locating the last node requires a traversal of the list and so takes more effort than locating the first node. Once located, however, deleting the last node is easier than deleting the first node because you do not change *head*.

3. **a.**
```
head = new node;
head->item = 'J';
head->next = NULL;
p = new node;
p->item = 'E';
p->next = head;
head = p;
p = new node;
p->item = 'B';
p->next = head;
head = p;
```

   b.
```
head = new node;
head->item = 'B';
p = new node;
p->item = 'E';
```

```
    head->next = p;
    q = new node;
    q->item = 'J';
    q->next = NULL;
    p->next = q;
```

4. **a.** `prev->next = cur->next;`
   `cur->next = NULL;`
   delete `cur;`
   `cur = NULL;`

   b. `head = cur->next;`
   `cur->next = NULL;`
   delete `cur;`
   `cur = NULL;`

   c. `p = new node;`
   `p->item = 'A';`
   `p->next = head;`
   `head = P;`

   d. The pointer *head* points to a node that contains `'A'`; this node points to a node that contains `'J'`. The *next* portion of the last node is *NULL*.

5. **void** `displayNodeI(Node *head, int i)`
```
   {
      Node *cur = head;
      for (int count = 1; count < i; ++count)
         cur = cur->next;
      cout << cur->item << endl;
   }  // end displayNodeI
```

6. *i*, ignoring the assignments to *count* in the *for* statement.

7. **int** `ithItem(Node *head, int i)`
```
   {  if (i == 1)
         return head->item;
      else
         return ithItem(head->next, i-1);
   }  // end ithItem
```

8. *writeBackward2(pointer to 'B') // original call*
   writeBackward2(pointer to 'E')
   writeBackward2(pointer to 'J')
   writeBackward2(NULL)
   write J
   write E
   write B

9. **a.** After each deletion, the items are renumbered so that the original second item is now the first item. Thus, you can repeatedly delete the first item.

b. Yes.

c. The replacement works because deleting the last item in the list does not renumber the items.

d. The loop

```
for (int position = 1; position <= getLength(); ++position)
    remove(1);
```

does not work because the value of *getLength()* changes as items are deleted from the list. If you replaced *remove(1)* with *remove(position)*, the loop would still not work, because, in addition to the change in *getLength()* just mentioned, the items would be renumbered after the first deletion, so the new first item would not be deleted.

10. ```
List::~List()
{
    int len = getLength();

    // repeatedly delete the linked list's first node
    for (int position = 1; position <= len; ++position)
    {   Node *cur = head;
        head = head->next;
        cur->next = NULL;
        delete cur;
    } // end for
} // end destructor
```

# Chapter 5

1. The positions of the queens are given as *(row, column)* pairs.

Solution 1: $(2, 1), (4, 2), (1, 3), (3, 4)$

Solution 2: $(3, 1), (1, 2), (4, 3), (2, 4)$

2. $- * / a\,b\,c * + d\,e\,f$

3. $a\,b * c - d / e\,f - +$

4. $(a - b / (c + d * e)) - f$

5. No.

6. $<T> = \$ \mid cc<T>d$
```

Chapter 6

1. D, C, B, A.

2. `stack1`: 1 4 5;   `stack2`: 3 6   (elements listed bottom to top).

3. Use an array-based implementation if you know the maximum string length in advance and you know that the average string length is not much shorter than the maximum length. Clearly, you would use a pointer-based implementation if you could not predict the maximum string length. In addition, if the maximum string length is 300, for example, but the average string length is 30, a pointer-based implementation would use less storage on average than an array-based implementation.

4. Assuming that the specifications of the stack operations for both implementations are identical, the program itself should require no change. Both versions of the stack operations should perform identically on the client's side of the "wall." You must, of course, replace the array-based class definition for the stack with the pointer-based one.

5. **a.** The stack is empty when the last close brace is encountered. When the loop ends, `balanced-SoFar` is `false`.

    b. When the loop ends, the stack contains one open brace and `balancedSoFar` is `true`.

    c. When the loop ends, the stack is empty and `balancedSoFar` is `true`.

6. 2

7. *a b / c* ⋆

8. The precedence tests control association. The ≥ test enables left-to-right association when operators have the same precedence.

9. **a.** Stack contains A, then A B.

    b. Stack contains A, then A B, then A B D.

    c. Stack contains C, then C D, then C D H, then C D H G.

Chapter 7

1. A, B, C, D

2. `queue1`: 2 3 5;   `queue2`: 4 6   (elements listed front to back)

3. **a.** When the `for` loop ends, the stack and queue are as follows:

      Stack: a b c d a ← top

      Queue: a b c d a ← back

The *a* at the top of the stack matches the *a* at the front of the queue. After deleting the *a* from both ADTs, the *d* at the top of the stack does not match the *b* at the front of the queue, so the string is not a palindrome.

b. The letters that you delete from the stack and the queue are the same, so the string is a palindrome.

4. a. 1; **b.** 3; **c.** 3; **d.** 2; **e.** 3; **f.** 1 **g.** 2; **h.** 2; **i.** 1;

   j. 1; **k.** 1; **l.** 2

5. You cannot generate a departure event for a given arrival event independently of other events. So to read the file of arrival events and generate departure events, you would need to perform the same computations that the simulation performs.

6.

Time	Action	*bankQueue* (front to back)	*anEventList* (front to back)
29	Update *anEventList* and *bankQueue*: Customer 2 enters bank	23 2	A 30 3
	Customer 3 begins transaction, create departure event	23 2	A 30 3 D 31
30	Update *anEventList* and *bankQueue*: Customer 4 enters bank	23 2 30 3	D 31
31	Update *anEventList* and *bankQueue*: Customer 3 departs	30 3	*empty*
	Costumer 4 begins transaction, create departure event	30 3	D 34
34	Update *anEventList* and *bankQueue*: Customer 4 departs	*empty*	*empty*

Chapter 8

1. a. `Sphere mySphere(2.0);`

   b. `Ball myBall(6.0, "Beach ball");`

   c. `cout  <<  mySphere.getDiameter()  <<  "  "  <<`
      `myBall.getDiameter();`

2. `class` `Planet: public Ball`
   `{`
   `public:`
      `double getDistanceFromSun();`
      `void setDistanceFromSun(double newDistance);`

```
private:
    double distance;
};
```

3. **a.** *resetBall* cannot access *theRadius* directly. *theRadius* is private within *Sphere*, so a derived class cannot access it.

   b. *resetBall* can access *theRadius* directly. Instead of writing *setRadius(r)* in the implementation of *resetBall*, you can write *theRadius = r*. This change is unnecessary, however.

4. The function *play*, because CDP and DVDP must override it.

5. *aList* should be an instance of *SortedList*. An alphabetical list is identical to a sorted list of names with *ListItemType* defined to be a string. If you need new methods for *aList*, you could derive a new class from *SortedList*.

6. Yes. Because *aList* is an instance of the derived class, the derived class cannot be abstract. If the derived class failed to implement *displayList*, it would be an abstract base class with no instances possible.

7. A derived class cannot access and therefore cannot override a private method in its base class.

8.
```
NewClass<char> MyClass;
MyClass.setData('c');
cout << MyCLass.getData() << endl;
```

Chapter 9

1. $(n - 1) + (n - 2) + \ldots + 1 = n * (n - 1)/2$

2. $n + (n - 1) + \ldots + 2 = n * (n + 1)/2 - 1$

3. **a.** $O(n^3)$;   **b.** $O(\log n)$;   **c.** $O(n)$

4. **a.** You can stop searching as soon as *searchValue* is less than a data item, because you will have passed the point where *searchValue* would have occurred if it was in the data collection.

   b. Sorted data, using the scheme just described in the answer to Part a: best case: $O(1)$; average case: $O(n)$; worst case: $O(n)$.

   Unsorted data: $O(n)$ in all cases.

   c. Regardless of whether the data is sorted, the best case is $O(1)$ (you find the item after one comparison) and both the average and worst cases are $O(n)$ (you find the item after $n/2$ or n comparisons, respectively).

5. At each pass, the selected element is underlined.

20	<u>80</u>	40	25	60	30
20	30	40	25	<u>60</u>	**80**
20	30	<u>40</u>	25	**60**	**80**
20	<u>30</u>	25	**40**	**60**	**80**
20	<u>25</u>	**30**	**40**	**60**	**80**
20	25	**30**	**40**	**60**	**80**

6. Find the smallest instead of the largest element at each pass.

<u>20</u>	80	40	25	60	30
30	80	40	<u>25</u>	60	**20**
<u>30</u>	80	40	60	**25**	**20**
60	80	<u>40</u>	30	**25**	**20**
<u>60</u>	80	**40**	**30**	**25**	**20**
80	**60**	**40**	**30**	**25**	**20**

7.

Pass 1

<u>25</u>	<u>30</u>	20	80	40	60
25	<u>30</u>	<u>20</u>	80	40	60
25	20	<u>30</u>	<u>80</u>	40	60
25	20	30	<u>80</u>	<u>40</u>	60
25	20	30	40	<u>80</u>	<u>60</u>
25	20	30	40	60	**80**

Pass 2

<u>25</u>	<u>20</u>	30	40	60	**80**
20	<u>25</u>	<u>30</u>	40	60	**80**
20	25	<u>30</u>	<u>40</u>	60	**80**
20	25	30	<u>40</u>	<u>60</u>	**80**
20	25	30	40	**60**	**80**

There are no exchanges during Pass 3, so the algorithm will terminate.

8.

25	<u>30</u>	20	80	40	60
25	**30**	<u>20</u>	80	40	60
20	**25**	**30**	<u>80</u>	40	60
20	**25**	**30**	**80**	<u>40</u>	60
20	**25**	**30**	**40**	**80**	<u>60</u>
20	**25**	**30**	**40**	**60**	**80**

9. ▪ `mergesort` sorts an array by using a mergesort to sort each half of the array.

▪ Sorting half of an array is a smaller problem than sorting the entire array.

▪ An array of one element is the base case.

▪ By halving an array and repeatedly halving the halves, you must reach array segments of one element each—that is, the base case.

10. Vertical bars separate the array into regions, as the partition develops. The pivot is 38.

38 | <u>16</u> 40 39 12 27	pivot | unknown	Swap 16 with itself to move it to S_1.
38 | 16 | <u>40</u> 39 12 27	pivot | S_1 | unknown	
38 | 16 | 40 | <u>39</u> 12 27	pivot | S_1 | S_2 | unknown	
38 | 16 | 40 39 | <u>12</u> 27	pivot | S_1 | S_2 | unknown	Swap 12 and 40.
38 | 16 12 | 39 40 | <u>27</u>	pivot | S_1 | S_2 | unknown	Swap 27 and 39.
38 | 16 12 27 | 40 39	pivot | S_1 | S_2 | unknown	Swap 38 and 27 to position pivot.
27 16 12 | 38 | 40 39	S_1 | pivot | S_2	

11. a. A binary search is $O(\log n)$, so is faster than a mergesort, which is $O(n \log n)$.

   b. A binary search is $O(\log n)$, so is faster than displaying the array, which is $O(n)$.

Chapter 10

1. a. 60; **b.** 60, 20, 40; **c.** 20, 70; 10, 40; 30, 50;

   d. 20 and 70, 10 and 40, 30 and 50;

   e. 40, 20, 60; **f.** 10, 40, 30, 50; **g.** 70, 10, 30, 50

2. a. 1: A; 2: B, C; 3: D, E; 4: F; 5: G

   b. 1: A; 2: B; 3: C; 4: D; 5: E; 6: F; 7: G

3. 4

4. Complete: b, c, d, e; Full: e; Balanced: b, c, d, e.

5. Preorder: A, B, D, E, C, F, G; Inorder: D, B, E, A, F, C, G; Postorder: D, E, B, F, G, C, A.

6.

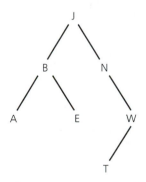

7. 60, 20, 10, 40, 30, 50, 70 is one of several possible orders. (This order results from a preorder traversal of the tree.)

8. The array is 30 20 50 10 25 40 60.

9.

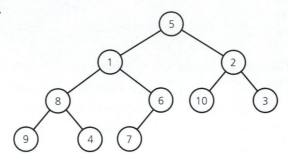

10. No. H should be in G's right subtree. U and V should be in T's right subtree.

11. The algorithm compares each given search key with the keys in the following nodes:

   a. 60, 20, 40, 30;   **b.** 60, 20, 10

12. Inserting the array elements into a binary search tree produces

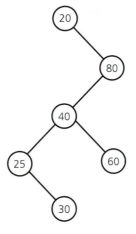

An inorder traversal of this tree results in the sorted array.

13. a.

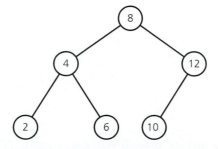

   b. The tree has minimum height and is complete but not full.

Chapter 11

1. `tableReplace(in t:Table, in x:KeyType,`
`            in replacementItem:TableItemType) throw TableException`

`t.tableDelete(x)`
`t.tableInsert(replacementItem)`

2. No.

3. It is neither a semiheap nor a heap.

4. After inserting 12:   After removing 12:

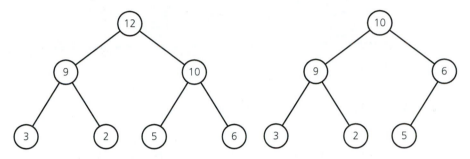

5. The array that represents the heap is 6 4 5 1 2 3.

6. The array that represents the heap is 7 5 6 4 3 2.

7. The array is 10 9 5 8 7 2 3 1 4 6.

Chapter 12

1.

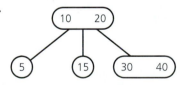

2. a.   **b.**

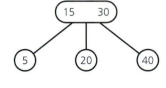

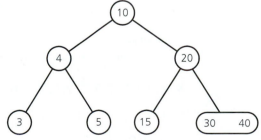

3. a. See the answer to Self-Test Exercise 1.

b.

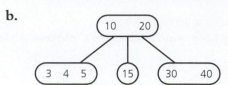

4.

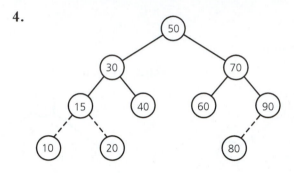

5. A balanced binary search tree.

6. Each node in a red-black tree requires memory for two pointers and two pointer colors. These pointers and pointer colors require no more memory than the four pointers in a node in a 2-3-4 tree. In addition, a node in a red-black tree requires memory for only one data item, whereas a node in a 2-3-4 tree requires memory for three data items.

7. `+tableDelete(in searchKey: KeyType) throw TableException`

```
i = h(searchKey)
while ( (table[i] is occupied and table[i].getKey() != searchKey)
        or (table[i] is deleted) )
   ++i

if (table[i] is not empty)
{  // table[i].getKey() == searchKey
   Mark table[i] deleted
}
else
   Throw a TableException
```

8. 8, 10, 1, 3, 5, 7, 9, 0, 2, 4, 6.

9. `table[1]` → 15 → 8

`table[2]` is *NULL*

`table[3]` → 17→ 24 → 10

`table[4]` → 32

Chapter 13

1. a. Directed, connected;   **b.** Undirected, connected

2. DFS: 0, 1, 2, 4, 3; BFS: 0, 1, 2, 3, 4.

3.

	0	1	2	3	4
0	0	1	0	0	0
1	0	0	1	1	0
2	0	0	0	0	1
3	0	1	0	0	0
4	1	0	0	0	0

4. a g d b e c f

 g a d b e c f

 a g d b e f c

 g a d b e f c

5. No. See Observation 2 on page 750.

6.

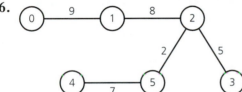

7.

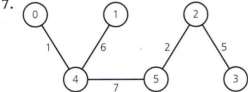

8. Path 0, 4, 2, 1 has weight 7.

 Path 0, 4, 2 has weight 5.

 Path 0, 4, 2, 3 has weight 8.

 Path 0, 4 has weight 4.

Chapter 14

1. Sequential access: Copy the original file *file1* into the file *file2*. Write a new block containing the desired record and 99 blank records. Copy *file2* to the original file *file1*.

Direct access: Create a new block containing the desired record and 99 blank records. Write the new block to the file as the 17th block.

2.
```
externalMergesort(in unsortedFileName:string, in
                   sortedFileName:string)
   Associate unsortedFileName with the file variable inFile
     and sortedFileName with the file variable outFile

   blocksort(inFile, tempFile1, numBlocks)
   // records in each block are now sorted; numBlocks == 16
   mergeFile(tempFile1, tempFile2, 1, 16)
      mergeRuns(tempFile1, tempFile2, 1, 1)
      mergeRuns(tempFile1, tempFile2, 3, 1)
      mergeRuns(tempFile1, tempFile2, 5, 1)
      mergeRuns(tempFile1, tempFile2, 7, 1)
      mergeRuns(tempFile1, tempFile2, 9, 1)
      mergeRuns(tempFile1, tempFile2, 11, 1)
      mergeRuns(tempFile1, tempFile2, 13, 1)
      mergeRuns(tempFile1, tempFile2, 15, 1)
   mergeFile(tempFile2, tempFile1, 2, 16)
      mergeRuns(tempFile2, tempFile1, 1, 2)
      mergeRuns(tempFile2, tempFile1, 5, 2)
      mergeRuns(tempFile2, tempFile1, 9, 2)
      mergeRuns(tempFile2, tempFile1, 13, 2)
   mergeFile(tempFile1, tempFile2, 4, 16)
      mergeRuns(tempFile1, tempFile2, 1, 4)
      mergeRuns(tempFile1, tempFile2, 9, 4)
   mergeFile(tempFile2, tempFile1, 8, 16)
      mergeRuns(tempFile2, tempFile1, 1, 8)
   copyFile(tempFile1, outFile)
```

3.
```
tableRetrieve(tIndex[1..20], tData, searchKey, tableItem)
  buf.readBlock(tIndex[1..20], 10)
  tableRetrieve(tIndex[1..9], tData, searchKey, tableItem)
     buf.readBlock(tIndex[1..9], 5)
     tableRetrieve(tIndex[1..4], tData, searchKey, tableItem)
        buf.readBlock(tIndex[1..4], 2)
        tableRetrieve(tIndex[1..1], tData, searchKey, tableItem)
           buf.readBlock(tIndex[1..1], 1)
           return false
```

4.
```
tableRetrieve(tIndex[1..20], tData, searchKey, tableItem)
  buf.readBlock(tIndex[1..20], 10)
  tableRetrieve(tIndex[11..20], tData, searchKey, tableItem)
     buf.readBlock(tIndex[11..20], 15)
     tableRetrieve(tIndex[11..14], tData, searchKey, tableItem)
        buf.readBlock(tIndex[11..14], 12)
```

```
j = 26
blockNum = 98
data.readBlock(tData, 98)
Find record data.getRecord(k) whose search key equals
tableItem = data.getRecord(k)
return true
```

Appendix A

1. *a* is 5, then 7, then 8; *b* is 7; *c* is 5; *d* is 1; *e* is 5.

2. 56

3. `<< Title <<`

4. `j = 13`

`j = 14`

`k = 12`

`k is out of range`

5.
```
if ((score >= 90) && (score <= 100))
    grade = 'A';
else if ((score >= 80) && (score < 90))
    grade = 'B';
else if ((score >= 70) && (score < 80))
    grade = 'C';
else if ((score >= 60) && (score < 70))
    grade = 'D';
else
    grade = 'F';
```

6. A `switch` statement is possible, but you need a `case` for each value of *score* between 0 and 100.

7.
```
int sum(int anArray[], int n)
{
    int s, i;
    for (s = 0, i = 0; i < n; s += anArray[i], ++i);
    return s;
} // end sum
```

8. a.
```
for (int day = 1; day <= DAYS_PER_WEEK; ++day)
    cout << minTemps[day-1][0] << " ";
```

b.
```
for (int week = 1; week <= 5; ++week)
    cout << minTemps[0][week-1] << " ";
```

c.
```
for (week = 1; week <= WEEKS_PER_YEAR; ++week)
{   for (day = 1; day <= DAYS_PER_WEEK; ++day)
```

```
            cout << minTemps[day-1][week-1] << " ";
        cout << endl;
    }    // end for
```

9. a. `student.address.state;` **b.** `student.address.zip[0];`

   c. `student.gpa;` **d.** `student.name[0]`

10. Underscores mark the position of the file window.

originalFile	ch	copyFile
<u>a</u> b *<eoln>* c d *<eoln>* *<eof>*	?	_
a <u>b</u> *<eoln>* c d *<eoln>* *<eof>*	a	a _
a b <u>*<eoln>*</u> c d *<eoln>* *<eof>*	b	a b_
a b *<eoln>* <u>c</u> d *<eoln>* *<eof>*	*<eoln>*	a b *<eoln>* _
a b *<eoln>* c <u>d</u> *<eoln>* *<eof>*	c	a b *<eoln>* c _
a b *<eoln>* c d <u>*<eoln>*</u> *<eof>*	d	a b *<eoln>* c d _
a b *<eoln>* c d *<eoln>* <u>*<eof>*</u>	*<eoln>*	a b *<eoln>* c d *<eoln>* _
		a b *<eoln>* c d *<eoln>* *<eof>*

Appendix D

1. Proof by induction on m. When $m = 0$, $2^0 = 2^1 - 1$. Now assume that the statement is true for $m = k$; that is, assume that $1 + 2^1 + 2^2 + \cdots + 2^k = 2^{k+1} - 1$. Show that the statement is true for $m = k + 1$, as follows:

$$(1 + 2^1 + 2^2 + \cdots + 2^k) + 2^{k+1} = (2^{k+1} - 1) + 2^{k+1}$$
$$= 2^{k+2} - 1$$

2. Proof by induction on n. When $n = 1$, the first odd integer is 1 and the sum is trivially 1, which is equal to 1^2. Now assume that the statement is true for $n = k$; that is, assume that $1 + 3 + \cdots + (2k - 1) = k^2$. Show that the statement is true for $n = k + 1$, as follows:

$$[1 + 3 + \cdots + (2k - 1)] + (2k + 1) = k^2 + (2k + 1)$$
$$= (k + 1)^2$$

3. Proof by induction on n. When $n = 2$, $rabbit\ (2) = 1 = a^0$. Now assume that the statement is true for all $n \leq k$; that is, assume that $rabbit\ (n) \geq a^{n-2}$ for all $n \leq k$. Show that the statement is true for $n = k + 1$, as follows:

$$
\begin{aligned}
rabbit\ (k + 1) &= rabbit\ (k) + rabbit\ (k - 1) \\
&\geq a^{k-2} + a^{k-3} \\
&= a^{k-3}\ (a + 1) \\
&= a^{k-3}\ (a^2) \\
&= a^{k-1}
\end{aligned}
$$

Index

C++ Operators

Operators within the same box have the same precedence, which is higher than operators in lower boxes.

Operator	Meaning	Associativity	Usage
`::`	global	right	`::` *name*
`::`	scope resolution	left	*class_name*`::`*member_name*
`->`	member selection	left	*pointer*`->`*member*
`.`	member selection	left	*object.member*
`[]`	array index	left	*array_name*`[`*expr*`]`
`()`	function call	left	*function_name*`(`*expr_list*`)`
`()`	type construction	left	`type` `(`*expr_list*`)`
`++`	post-increment	right	*lvalue*`++`
`--`	post-decrement	right	*lvalue*`--`
`typeid`	type identification	right	`typeid (`*type*`)` `typeid (`*expr*`)`
`dynamic_cast`	checked conversion	right	`dynamic_cast<`*type*`>(`*expr*`)`
`static_cast`	checked conversion	right	`static_cast<`*type*`>(`*expr*`)`
`reinterpret_cast`	unchecked conversion	right	`reinterpret_cast<`*type*`>(`*expr*`)`
`const_cast`	const conversion	right	`const_cast<`*type*`>(`*expr*`)`
`sizeof`	size of type	right	`sizeof (`*type*`)`
`sizeof`	size of object	right	`sizeof` *expr*
`++`	pre-increment	right	`++`*lvalue*
`--`	pre-decrement	right	`--`*lvalue*
`~`	bitwise complement	right	`~`*expr*
`!`	logical NOT	right	`!`*expr*
`+`	unary plus	right	`+`*expr*
`-`	unary minus	right	`-`*expr*
`*`	dereference	right	`*`*expr*
`&`	address of	right	`&`*lvalue*
`()`	cast	right	`(`*type*`)` *expr*

`new`	allocate	right	`new` *type*
			`new` *type* `(`*expr_list*`)`
			`new (`*expr_list*`)` *type*
			`new (`*expr_list*`)` *type* `(`*expr_list*`)`

`delete`	deallocate	right	`delete` *pointer* `delete[]` *pointer*
`->*`	member selection	left	*pointer*`->*`*pointer_to_member*
`.*`	member selection	left	*object*`.*`*pointer_to_member*